Land and
Post-Conflict Peacebuilding

Edited by Jon Unruh and Rhodri C. Williams

First published 2013
by Earthscan
2 Park Square, Milton Park, Abingdon, Oxon OX14 4RN

Simultaneously published in the USA and Canada
by Earthscan
711 Third Avenue, New York, NY 10017

Earthscan is an imprint of the Taylor & Francis Group, an informa business

Earthscan publishes in association with the International Institute for Environment and Development

© 2013 Environmental Law Institute and United Nations Environment Programme

The right of the editors to be identified as the authors of the editorial material, and of the authors for their individual chapters, has been asserted in accordance with sections 77 and 78 of the Copyright, Designs and Patents Act 1988.

All rights reserved. No part of this book may be reprinted or reproduced or utilised in any form or by any electronic, mechanical, or other means, now known or hereafter invented, including photocopying and recording, or in any information storage or retrieval system, without permission in writing from the copyright holders.

Trademark notice: Product or corporate names may be trademarks or registered trademarks, and are used only for identification and explanation without intent to infringe.

British Library Cataloguing-in-Publication Data
A catalogue record for this book is available from the British Library

Library of Congress Cataloging-in-Publication Data
Land and post-conflict peacebuilding/edited by Jon Unruh and Rhodri C. Williams.
    p. cm. – (Peacebuilding and natural resources; 2) Includes bibliographical references and index.
    ISBN 978-1-84971-231-6 (pbk : alk. paper) – ISBN 978-1-84977-579-3 (ebk) 1. Peace-building. 2. Land tenure–Political aspects.
3. Natural resources–Political aspects. I. Unruh, Jon Darrel.
II. Williams, Rhodri, 1959–
JZ5538.L36 2013
327.1'72–dc23

2011034079

Typeset in Times and Helvetica
by Graphicraft Limited, Hong Kong

Printed and bound by CPI Group (UK) Ltd, Croydon, CR0 4YY

Table of contents

List of figures and tables	vii
Preface	ix
Foreword	xiii
Acknowledgments	xvii

Land: A foundation for peacebuilding *Jon Unruh and Rhodri C. Williams*	1

Part 1: Peace negotiations — 21

Introduction

The Abyei territorial dispute between North and South Sudan: Why has its resolution proven difficult? *Salman M. A. Salman*	25
Land tenure and peace negotiations in Mindanao, Philippines *Yuri Oki*	69

Part 2: Response to displacement and dispossession — 93

Introduction

The role of restitution in post-conflict situations *Barbara McCallin*	99
Land issues in post-conflict return and recovery *Samir Elhawary and Sara Pantuliano*	115
Return of land in post-conflict Rwanda: International standards, improvisation, and the role of international humanitarian organizations *John W. Bruce*	121
Post-conflict land tenure issues in Bosnia: Privatization and the politics of reintegrating the displaced *Rhodri C. Williams*	145
Angola: Land resources and conflict *Allan Cain*	177

iv   Land and post-conflict peacebuilding

Refugees and legal reform in Iraq: The Iraqi Civil Code, international
standards for the treatment of displaced persons, and the art of attainable
solutions   205
Dan E. Stigall

Part 3: Land management   239
Introduction

Snow leopards and cadastres: Rare sightings in post-conflict Afghanistan   245
Douglas E. Batson

Community documentation of land tenure and its contribution to
state building in Afghanistan   265
J. D. Stanfield, Jennifer Brick Murtazashvili, M. Y. Safar, and
Akram Salam

Title wave: Land tenure and peacebuilding in Aceh   293
Arthur Green

Beyond land redistribution: Lessons learned from El Salvador's
unfulfilled agrarian revolution   321
Alexandre Corriveau-Bourque

Institutional aspects of resolving land disputes in post-conflict societies 345
Peter Van der Auweraert

Rebuilding peace: Land and water management in the Kurdistan Region
of northern Iraq   363
Nesreen Barwari

Transboundary resource management strategies in the Pamir mountain
region of Tajikistan   387
Ian D. Hannam

Part 4: Laws and policies   405
Introduction

Title through possession or position? Respect for housing, land, and
property rights in Cambodia   411
Rhodri C. Williams

Land conflicts and land registration in Cambodia   437
Manami Sekiguchi and Naomi Hatsukano

Legal frameworks and land issues in Muslim Mindanao   451
Paula Defensor Knack

Table of contents v

Unexplored dimensions: Islamic land systems in Afghanistan, Indonesia, Iraq, and Somalia   475
Siraj Sait

Customary law and community-based natural resource management in post-conflict Timor-Leste   511
Naori Miyazawa

Part 5: Lessons learned   533

Lessons learned in land tenure and natural resource management in post-conflict societies   535
Jon Unruh and Rhodri C. Williams

Appendices

List of abbreviations   577

Author biographies   581

Table of contents for *Post-Conflict Peacebuilding and Natural Resource Management*   589

Index   605

List of figures and tables

FIGURES

Sudan with the 1956 boundary between Northern and Southern Sudan (Map)	31
The borders of Abyei area as proposed by the government of Sudan (Map)	32
Map of the Abyei area as delimited by Abyei Boundaries Commission experts (Map)	37
The Permanent Court of Arbitration final award map of the Abyei area (Map)	43
Comparison of the Permanent Court of Arbitration award map with that of the Abyei Boundaries Commission experts map (Map)	44
Pre-conflict distributions of Bosnia's ethnic groups (Map)	147
Elevation and predominant land uses in Bosnia (Map)	150
Post-conflict distribution of Bosnia's ethnic groups (Map)	158
Urban population growth in war and peace in Angola, 1940–2009	190
Means of access to urban land in Luanda	191
Means of rural land acquisition by excombatants in Huambo Province	195
Quantity of rural land, in hectares, occupied according to distance from urban centers in Huambo Province	197
Property documents in the Kabul Provincial Court Archives, 2003	272
Sample land record from the village of Naw Abad in Kunduz Province	283
Information flows for parcel forms and maps relating to private land	288
Institutional linkages with the Iraq Property Claims Commission	359
Ethnic and religious groups in Iraq (Map)	366
Iraqi political boundaries (Map)	367
Nickel and limestone deposits in Mindanao (Map)	470

viii   Land and post-conflict peacebuilding

Roles of three societal stakeholders in a balanced state 514

Shift in balance of stakeholders' relationship in a post-conflict society (Timor-Leste) 514

Depleted forest on hillsides around Dili, Timor-Leste's capital city 516

Tara Bandu inception ceremony in Dili 520

Conceptual relationships between administrative and customary leadership 522

Tara Bandu ceremony in Dili with the president and prime minister of Timor-Leste in attendance 523

Order in which land disputes are taken to forums in Timor-Leste 525

Community perceptions of courts and traditional (customary) conflict resolution systems 525

Conceptual graph illustrating the relative roles of governmental administration and customary law governing natural resources in developing countries and in post-conflict Timor-Leste 528

TABLES

Means of legal recovery for displaced Iraqis 226

Land transfers in El Salvador, 1932–1998 326

Authorities to which land disputes cases were referred in 2008 445

Pre- and post-conflict forest cover in Timor-Leste 515

Preface

Decades of civil wars, international wars, and wars of secession demonstrate the strong relationship between natural resources and armed conflict. Disputes over natural resources and their associated revenues can be among the reasons that people go to war. Diamonds, timber, oil, and even bananas and charcoal can provide sources of financing to sustain conflict. Forests, agricultural crops, and wells are often targeted during conflict. Efforts to negotiate an end to conflict increasingly include natural resources. And conflicts associated with natural resources are both more likely to relapse than non-resource-related conflicts, and to relapse twice as fast.

Immediately after the end of a conflict, a window of opportunity opens for a conflict-affected country and the international community to establish security, rebuild, and consolidate peace—or risk conflict relapse. This window also presents the opportunity to reform the management of natural resources and their revenues in ways that would otherwise be politically difficult to achieve. Capitalizing on this opportunity is particularly critical if natural resources contributed to the onset or financing of conflict—and, if this opportunity is lost, it may never reappear. Moreover, poorly informed policy decisions may become entrenched, locking in a trajectory that serves the interests of a limited few.

Since the end of the Cold War, and particularly since 2000, substantial progress has been made in establishing institutional and policy frameworks to consolidate peacebuilding efforts. In 2005, the United Nations established the Peacebuilding Commission to identify best practices for peacebuilding. The commission is the first body to bring together the UN's humanitarian, security, and development sectors so that they can learn from peacebuilding experiences.

The Peacebuilding Commission has started to recognize the importance of natural resources in post-conflict peacebuilding. In 2009, along with the United Nations Environment Programme, the commission published a pioneering report— *From Conflict to Peacebuilding: The Role of Natural Resources and the Environment*—that framed the basic ways in which natural resources contribute to conflict and can be managed to support peacebuilding. Building on this report, the commission is starting to consider how natural resources can be included

x   Land and post-conflict peacebuilding

within post-conflict planning and programming in Sierra Leone, the Central African Republic, Guinea, and other countries.

Since the establishment of the Peacebuilding Commission, the policies governing post-conflict peacebuilding have evolved rapidly. In his 2009 *Report of the Secretary-General on Peacebuilding in the Immediate Aftermath of Conflict*, UN Secretary-General Ban Ki-moon articulated five priorities for post-conflict peacebuilding, all of which have natural resource dimensions. In his 2010 update to that report, Ban Ki-moon noted the pressing need to improve post-conflict natural resource management to reduce the risk of conflict relapse, and urged "Member States and the United Nations system to make questions of natural resource allocation, ownership and access an integral part of peacebuilding strategies." The Secretary-General's 2012 report on the topic highlighted progress over the previous two years and called on UN entities to more effectively share knowledge and leverage expertise on post-conflict natural resource management. And a 2011 UN report, *Civilian Capacity in the Aftermath of Conflict*, highlighted approaches for mobilizing civil society to support peacebuilding in many realms, including natural resources.

The World Bank has also begun focusing on natural resources: the Bank's 2011 *World Development Report*, for example, placed the prevention of fragility, conflict, and violence at the core of the Bank's development mandate. Drawing on the Bank's experiences around the world, the report focuses on jobs, justice, and security, and highlights the contribution of natural resources to these goals.

Despite growing recognition of the importance of post-conflict natural resource management, there has been no comprehensive examination of how natural resources can support post-conflict peacebuilding. Nor has there been careful consideration of the risks to long-term peace caused by the failure to effectively address natural resources. Practitioners, researchers, and UN bodies have researched specific resources, conflict dynamics, and countries, but have yet to share their findings with each other at a meaningful scale, and limited connections have been drawn between the various strands of inquiry. As a result, the peacebuilding community does not know what works in what circumstances, what does not, or why.

Given the complexity of peacebuilding, practitioners and researchers alike are struggling to articulate good practice. It is increasingly clear that natural resources must be included as a foundational issue; many questions remain, however, regarding opportunities, options, and trade-offs.

Against this backdrop, the Environmental Law Institute, the UN Environment Programme, the University of Tokyo, and McGill University launched a research program designed to examine experiences in post-conflict peacebuilding and natural resource management; to identify lessons from these experiences; and to raise awareness of those lessons among practitioners and scholars. The program has benefited from broad support, with the government of Finland—one of the few donor governments to explicitly recognize the role of natural resources in both conflict and peacebuilding efforts—playing a catalytic role by providing core financing.

Preface xi

The research program has been guided by the collective experiences of the four members of the Steering Committee: as the coordinators of the program and the series editors, we have drawn on our work in more than thirty post-conflict countries. Our experiences—which include leading environmental assessments in Afghanistan, developing forest law in Liberia, supporting land reform in Mozambique, and fostering cooperation around water in Iraq—have led to a shared understanding that natural resource issues rarely receive the political attention they merit. Through this research program and partnership, we hope to catalyze a comprehensive global effort to demonstrate that peacebuilding substantially depends on the transformation of natural assets into peacebuilding benefits—a change that must occur without mortgaging the future or creating new conflict.

Since its inception in 2007, the program has grown dramatically in response to strong interest from practitioners, researchers, and policy makers. Participants in an initial scoping meeting suggested a single edited book consisting of twenty case studies and crosscutting analyses. It soon became clear, however, that the undertaking should reflect a much broader range of experiences, perspectives, and dimensions.

The research program yielded 150 peer-reviewed case studies and analyses written by 225 scholars, practitioners, and decision makers from fifty countries. The case studies and analyses have been assembled into a set of six edited books, each focusing on a specific set of natural resources or an aspect of peacebuilding: high-value natural resources; land; water; resources for livelihoods; assessment and restoration of natural resources; and governance. Examining a broad range of resources, including oil, minerals, land, water, wildlife, livestock, fisheries, forests, and agricultural products, the books document and analyze post-conflict natural resource management successes, failures, and ongoing efforts in sixty conflict-affected countries and territories. In their diversity and number, the books represent the most significant collection to date of experiences, analyses, and lessons in managing natural resources to support post-conflict peacebuilding.

In addition to the six edited books, the partnership has created an overarching book, *Post-Conflict Peacebuilding and Natural Resources: The Promise and the Peril*, which will be published by Cambridge University Press. This book draws on the six edited books to explore the role of natural resources in various peacebuilding activities across the humanitarian, security, and development sectors.

These seven books will be of interest to practitioners, researchers, and policy makers in the security, development, peacebuilding, political, and natural resource communities. They are designed to provide a conceptual framework, assess approaches, distill lessons, and identify specific options and trade-offs for more effectively managing natural resources to support post-conflict peacebuilding.

Natural resources present both opportunities and risks, and postponing their consideration in the peacebuilding process can imperil long-term peace and undermine sustainable development. Experiences from the past sixty years provide many lessons and broad guidance, as well as insight into which approaches are promising and which are problematic.

xii Land and post-conflict peacebuilding

A number of questions, however, still lack definitive answers. We do not always understand precisely why certain approaches fail or succeed in specific instances, or which of a dozen contextual factors are the most important in determining the success of a peacebuilding effort. Nevertheless, numerous discrete measures related to natural resources can be adopted now to improve the likelihood of long-term peace. By learning from peacebuilding experiences to date, we can avoid repeating the mistakes of the past and break the cycle of conflict that has come to characterize so many countries. We also hope that this undertaking represents a new way to understand and approach peacebuilding.

Carl Bruch
Environmental Law Institute

David Jensen
United Nations Environment Programme

Mikiyasu Nakayama
University of Tokyo

Jon Unruh
McGill University

Foreword

Jeffrey D. Sachs
Director of the Earth Institute, Columbia University
Special Advisor to UN Secretary-General Ban Ki-moon
on the Millennium Development Goals

There are few social issues as complex and vexing as land rights. From the dawn of humanity, land has been a matter of individual survival, community well-being, cultural inheritance, political power, religious doctrine, and economic prospect. Disputes over land are among both the key causes and consequences of violent conflicts. Peacebuilding, as this superb book makes clear, involves difficult choices in building a post-conflict land settlement, the success of which will affect the quality and durability of the peace itself.

Even in peacetime, land requires an economic category of its own. Land is never simply just another interchangeable commodity bought and sold in a competitive market. Each land parcel is unique, defined by its specific location; its place in natural ecosystems; its relation to specific communities, infrastructure, cultural artifacts and traditions; and of course to neighboring land.

Even in a well-defined and functioning legal system, a landowner therefore has limited and complex rights to the land. The owner will generally have tightly circumscribed rights regarding how the land can be used: for example, what kinds of limits are placed on the height of buildings, their design, and their commercial use; whether surface water or groundwater can be taken for agricultural purposes; whether fences and other barriers can be built; whether outsiders have rights to use the land, such as for grazing animals or crossing the land; which animal and plant species must be protected; how dangerous chemicals must be avoided; and how the fruits of the land must be shared with others in the community.

The Western freehold model of land rights, in which land is individually owned and used according to a single owner's prerogatives, is therefore a purely theoretical case that rarely applies in practice. Land rights and claims must be regulated to balance household, community, national, and ecosystem needs in an efficient and equitable manner. Zoning, eminent domain, environmental regulation, public use of private land, and other doctrines are reflections in Western law of the inherent complexities of land use.

Of course no society gets these issues right all of the time, or perhaps even most of the time. Land rights are heavily contested and subject to rampant failures and conflicts. Private landowners (or nonowners as the case may be) frequently

xiv   Land and post-conflict peacebuilding

overhunt, overfish, or overharvest their lands, or intrude on common lands of the community. And of course politically powerful individuals, enterprises, and governments may mobilize force to dispossess weaker communities of their valued lands, as colonial powers have done throughout the ages.

Land pressures and conflicts are escalating in many parts of the world as a result of growing populations, the depletion of natural resources, increasing land degradation, encroaching water scarcity, and the onset of human-induced climate change. Communities therefore fight for access to natural resources—such as forests, pasturelands, and water supplies—and the ecosystem services they provide, and these fights often spill over into open conflict. In several parts of the world, populations hard-hit by scarcity or violence are forced to migrate, and thereby come into conflict when they impinge on the traditional lands of other communities.

This book picks up these complex themes at the next stage: after full-fledged conflict has engulfed a region and the fragile shoots of peace have begun to appear. Peace may bring the cessation of violent conflict, but also the continuation or even initiation of new cultural, ethnic, and economic conflicts. And land is likely to feature centrally in those new disputes. The preceding war will have displaced thousands, possibly even millions, of people. These internally displaced persons (IDPs) will want to return to their original homes in order to grow food and begin a new crop season. Yet when the IDPs return home, squatters or other IDP communities may now occupy their lands. Or the lands may have been damaged or irreparably destroyed by war, neglect, or plunder.

This fascinating set of case studies and powerful syntheses return again and again to the one overarching truth about land and peacebuilding: complexity. There are no off-the-shelf answers to questions of property restitution, redistribution of claims, individual versus community needs, evidence and titling, legal versus social norms, or competing legal systems that might apply. Since even a well-functioning legal system can barely cope with the various dimensions of efficient and equitable land use, it is hardly surprising that a post-conflict environment characterized by humanitarian urgency, competing political claims, destroyed land records, displaced populations, and multiple political forces (including outside powers and donor agencies) should have a very hard time coping with land disputes.

These detailed and insightful analyses will inform the work of every aid worker and peacebuilder, providing an invaluable set of experiences and options for managing land rights and disputes. Yet there are as many case studies of failure as of success, and even the successes are only provisional successes: cases of "so far, so good" in preserving a fragile peace and enabling a local economy to get back on its feet. The failures seem often to involve international donors who try to apply simplistic ideas about land rights to highly complex and contested circumstances. Americans, for example, tend to favor land titling for individual households, and tend to overlook community land rights and needs. European donors have tended to favor the restitution of land to former owners

Foreword **xv**

over other ethical and practical claims. Western legal systems have tended to neglect or shun other legal systems that may be operating in the region, such as land-law systems based on Islamic principles.

If there is one common truth in this highly varied experience it is that being open to complexity is vital for success, especially on the part of external actors (such as international donors and nongovernmental organizations) who will typically not appreciate all of the complex challenges facing local communities and national governments. Community participation also reveals itself to be vital in case after case. Participatory approaches may indeed be time consuming, but the societal payoffs are great in that community participation builds long-term legitimacy and a lasting sense of fairness.

The editors Jon Unruh and Rhodri C. Williams have assembled an outstanding group of contributors who tell their complicated stories with clarity and deep insight. This book will have an important positive impact on peacebuilding efforts. As local and international actors address the roiling challenges in places as diverse as Haiti, the Horn of Africa, and Central Asia, and as new tensions inevitably build in regions beset by demographic pressures and environmental shocks, development practitioners and policy makers will be empowered by this book to help keep the peace and contribute to the rebuilding of fair and resilient communities.

Acknowledgments

This book is the culmination of a five-year research project. It would not have been possible without the efforts and contributions of many individuals and institutions.

The volume editors are grateful to our managing editor, Peter Whitten; our manuscript editors, Amanda Morgan and Meg Cox, for their peerless editorial assistance; and assistant managing editor, Akiva Fishman. Nick Bellorini, of Earthscan, provided guidance through the early publishing process; Matt Pritchard, Elan Spitzberg, and Arthur Green created the maps; Joelle Stallone proofread the manuscript; Tessa Gellerson and Katarina Petursson coordinated the production process; and Valentina Savioli provided drafting assistance.

Research and publication assistance was provided by numerous research associates, interns, law clerks, law fellows, and visiting attorneys at the Environmental Law Institute, including Elliott August, Jessica Boesl, Susan Bokermann, Marion Boulicault, Gwen Brown, Brandee Cooklin, Caitlin Fogarty, Sara Gersen, Mara Goldberg, Adam Harris, Farah Hegazi, Katelyn Henmueller, Jennifer Jones, Zachary Jylkka, Rachel Kenigsberg, Shea Kinser, Tim Kovach, Erin Mayfield, Shanna McClain, Phoenix McLaughlin, Mark McCormick-Goodhart, KJ Meyer, Kate Powers, Rachel Roberts, Nick Sanders, Sarah Stellberg, Sameera Syed, Shuchi Talati, and Aaron Terr.

Peer reviewers were essential to ensuring the rigor of this volume. The editors would like to acknowledge the many professionals and scholars who contributed anonymous peer reviews.

A few chapters in this volume have been adapted with permission from earlier published versions. The editors wish to thank Practical Action Publishing for permission to print "International Standards, Improvisation and the Role of International Humanitarian Organizations in the Return of Land in Post-conflict Rwanda," by John W. Bruce; Rutgers Law Journal for permission to print "Refugees and Legal Reform in Iraq: The Iraqi Civil Code, International Standards for the Treatment of Displaced Persons, and the Art of Attainable Solutions," by Dan E. Stigall; and the Center on Housing Rights and Evictions for permission to print "Title through Possession or Position? Respect for Rights to Housing,

xviii   Land and post-conflict peacebuilding

Land and Property in the Wake of Cambodia's Transition," by Rhodri C. Williams. In addition, some of the material in "Snow Leopards and Cadastres: Rare Sightings in Post-Conflict Afghanistan," by Douglas E. Batson, is adapted from an earlier publication with the permission of the Military Geography Specialty Group of the Association of American Geographers.

Financial support for the project was provided by the United Nations Environment Programme, the government of Finland, the U.S. Agency for International Development, the European Union, the University of Tokyo Graduate School of Frontier Sciences and Alliance for Global Sustainability, the John D. and Catherine T. MacArthur Foundation, the Canadian Social Science and Humanities Research Council, the Philanthropic Collaborative, the Center for Global Partnership of the Japan Foundation, the Ploughshares Fund, the Compton Foundation, Zonta Club of Tokyo I, the International Union for Conservation of Nature's Commission on Environmental Law, the Nelson Talbott Foundation, the Jacob L. and Lillian Holtzmann Foundation, and an anonymous donor. In-kind support for the project was provided by the Earth Institute of Columbia University, the Environmental Change and Security Project of the Woodrow Wilson International Center for Scholars, the Environmental Law Institute, the Global Infrastructure fund Research Foundation Japan, the Japan Institute of International Affairs, McGill University, the Peace Research Institute Oslo, the United Nations Environment Programme, and the University of Tokyo.

The cover was designed by Nikki Meith. Cover photography is by Luke Powell, courtesy of the United Nations Environment Programme's Post-Conflict Disaster Management Branch.

Except as otherwise specifically noted, the maps in this publication use public domain data originating from Natural Earth (2009, www.naturalearthdata.com). The designations employed and the presentations do not imply the expressions of any opinion whatsoever on the part of UNEP or contributory organizations concerning the legal status of any country, territory, city or area or its authority, or concerning the delimitation of its frontiers or boundaries.

When available, URLs are provided for sources that can be accessed electronically. URLs contained in this book were current at the time of publication.

Land: A foundation for peacebuilding

Jon Unruh and Rhodri C. Williams

Managing land tenure is one of the most persistently troublesome issues in peacebuilding processes. At the same time, land and property rights offer valuable opportunities to deliver peace dividends to war-weary populations, as well as long-term improvements in livelihoods, governance, and the economy. For example, in post-conflict countries, where agriculture is often not only a subsistence activity but also the source of a substantial portion of gross domestic product, exports, and government revenues, there are often strong incentives for the development of large-scale agricultural plantations (De Schutter 2011). When the large-scale land acquisitions necessary for such activities compete with subsistence farming for the use of arable lands, inequities arise that can be addressed by the development of a credible and coherent system of land management. Paying attention to land issues can also help mitigate volatile ethnic, tribal, and religious claims on and attachments to lands (Bruch et al. 2009).

Although addressing post-conflict land disputes is rarely easy, doing so is often essential. In the worst case, failure to address tensions over land can create or perpetuate potentially destabilizing grievances. Successful approaches to land issues, however, can both consolidate progress toward sustainable peace and help to sustain peace over the longer term. In order to identify effective approaches for managing land and other natural resources in the course of peace processes, it is crucial to understand the nature of land tenure and underlying social relations during and after armed conflict.

Where countries emerging from conflict have addressed land issues effectively, doing so has laid the foundation for a durable peace. In Mozambique, for example, both the government and civil society understood that a progressive land policy was necessary to deal with post–civil war tensions over land. The 1997 Land Law takes into account the customary occupation of land, while also

---

Jon Unruh is an associate professor of geography at McGill University. Rhodri C. Williams is a human rights lawyer who specializes in land and forced-migration issues.

2 Land and post-conflict peacebuilding

including mechanisms to promote investment.[1] The law also supports local empowerment: because members of local communities are aware of their rights under the Land Law, they can use the law to gain access to capital, either for their own initiatives or by negotiating with investors and the state for agreements regarding access to land by outsiders (Tanner 2010). Similarly, Liberia and Sierra Leone have engaged in extended dialogues to build broad support for structural reforms of land management, and Bosnia, Rwanda, and Timor-Leste have made incremental gains under highly challenging circumstances.[2] Taken together, such experiences highlight both the opportunities that are inherent in making land a peacebuilding priority and the challenges associated with such efforts.

This book examines the diverse experiences of seventeen post-conflict countries in managing land tenure and related issues during the transition to peace. This chapter establishes the foundation for the more detailed treatments to follow. It begins with an overview of the importance of land management and governance to post-conflict peacebuilding. The chapter then provides a discussion of seven key challenges associated with land issues in post-conflict situations, and notes preliminary considerations of the ways in which these challenges can be approached. These challenges include: tenure security, prospects of renewed conflict, changes in land tenure, emergence of alternative tenure approaches, land law reform, urban areas, and interactions between efforts to resolve tenure issues and other peacebuilding activities. The chapter concludes with a guide to the contents of the book.

LAND MANAGEMENT AND PEACEBUILDING

Land is crucial to meeting some of the most basic human needs—from identity to shelter and sustenance. It is also central to livelihoods and food security: in post-conflict countries, 60 to 80 percent of livelihoods typically depend on agriculture and natural resources (Bruch et al. 2009; USAID 2009). United Nations studies on the relationship between natural resources and disarmament, demobilization, and reintegration have found that 50 percent of former combatants

---

[1] Land Law, Act No. 19/97, October, 1997. Most land rights practitioners and academics distinguish between traditional, indigenous, and customary land rights, all of which are frequently described as "informal," in distinction to the formal, typically legislative rules adopted by official state organs. When traditional land rights are under discussion, the focus is primarily on historical arrangements, even if these arrangements are still in effect. Referring to land rights as "traditional" implies that land rights do not change over time. Indigenous land rights are attached to specific indigenous groups. Such rights may be (or have elements of) traditional or customary rights, but they are linked to particular indigenous groups and, by definition, do not apply to others. Customary land rights are arrangements that are currently in effect and are generally nonstatutory. Of the three terms, "customary" is the broadest and most useful because it acknowledges that informal tenure arrangements change; that they can take on aspects of traditional, statutory, and indigenous systems; and that they can evolve to meet current needs that may not be answered by the structures of traditional or indigenous land rights. In short, customary systems are hybridized and take on new forms as needed.

[2] See, for example, Cotula, Toulmin, and Hesse (2004).

Land: A foundation for peacebuilding 3

participating in reintegration programs chose agriculture (in some cases, the proportion was as high as 80 percent) (UNDP and UNEP 2012), but that access to land can be a limiting factor for such programs (UNEP 2012).

In the wake of armed conflict, especially prolonged civil conflict, a significant proportion of affected populations will seek access to new land or restitution of abandoned property; both actions can present profound challenges to countries and governments recovering from conflict, particularly in light of the weakening or disintegration of both formal and customary institutions that are crucial to the administration of land-based resources.[3] After the ceasefire that ended the 1992–1995 conflict in Bosnia and Herzegovina, for example, well over 200,000 claims to property were asserted (Williams 2013a*).[4] The Mozambican civil war (1975–1991) dislocated 6 million people—approximately half the national population (USCR 1993). Conflicts in Iraq (since 2006) and Sudan (intermittent over the course of five decades) have led to similarly high levels of displacement; estimates indicate that 1.6 million people were displaced in Iraq, and 2.3 million in Sudan (IDMC 2012). Land issues are further complicated when widespread grievances over land access and distribution contributed to the conflict, as in El Salvador (Corriveau-Bourque 2013*) and Darfur (Flint and de Waal 2008; Tubiana 2007).

The search for new land, for restitution, and for redress of historical grievances can drive land and property rights issues to the fore over large areas, including urban centers, in a short period of time and for considerable numbers of people. And the post-conflict reestablishment of ownership, use, and access rights is likely to be as complicated as the histories of the lands in question. Nevertheless, depending on the size of the displaced population and the political sensitivity of land conflicts, addressing land issues can be one of the most important aspects of post-conflict stabilization.

Despite the importance of land to many aspects of peacebuilding—including livelihoods, macroeconomic recovery, governance, and reintegration of former combatants, in particular—it has been addressed unevenly in peacebuilding processes. However, after two decades of concerted efforts to support post-conflict peacebuilding efforts—often on an ad hoc basis—the international community is starting to conceive of peacebuilding more coherently and strategically. High-profile reports from the United Nations Secretary-General, the United Nations Environment Programme, the UN Civilian Capacity Senior Advisory Group, the World Bank, and fragile states (UNSG 2009, 2010, 2012; UNEP 2009; UN 2011; World Bank 2011; International Dialogue on Peacebuilding and Statebuilding 2011), along with ongoing work in academia, have given rise to a growing body

---

[3] *Affected population* refers to people who are seeking access to land at a given time; it includes refugees and internally displaced persons attempting to return to their lands of origin, dislocatees who cannot or do not wish to return to their areas of origin, and those who were displaced well before a conflict and who view the post-conflict period as an opportunity to regain long-lost lands. In addition to affected populations, other actors—including excombatants, opportunists, state actors, and individuals or entities with claims dating back to previous regimes—may also be pursuing access to new lands.

[4] Citations marked with an asterisk refer to chapters within this book.

4 Land and post-conflict peacebuilding

Post-conflict peacebuilding and natural resources: Key terms and concepts

Following conflict, peacebuilding actors leverage a country's available assets (including natural resources) to transition from conflict to peace and sustainable development. Peacebuilding actors work at the international, national, and subnational levels and include national and subnational government bodies; United Nations agencies and other international organizations; international and domestic nongovernmental organizations; the private sector; and the media. Each group of peacebuilding actors deploys its own tools, and there are a growing number of tools to integrate the peacebuilding efforts of different types of actors.

A post-conflict period typically begins after a peace agreement or military victory. Because a post-conflict period is often characterized by intermittent violence and instability, it can be difficult to pinpoint when the post-conflict period ends. For the purposes of this book, the post-conflict period may be said to end when political, security, and economic discourse and actions no longer revolve around armed conflict or the impacts of conflict, but focus instead on standard development objectives. Within the post-conflict period, the first two years are referred to as the *immediate aftermath of conflict* (UNSG 2009), which is followed by a period known as *peace consolidation*.

According to the United Nations, "Peacebuilding involves a range of measures targeted to reduce the risk of lapsing or relapsing into conflict by strengthening national capacities at all levels for conflict management, and to lay the foundations for sustainable peace and development" (UNSG's Policy Committee 2007). In many instances, this means addressing the root causes of the conflict.

There are many challenges to peacebuilding: insecurity, ethnic and political polarization (as well as marginalization), corruption, lack of governmental legitimacy, extensive displacement, and loss of property. To address these and other challenges, peacebuilding actors undertake diverse activities that advance four broad peacebuilding objectives:*

- *Establishing security*, which encompasses basic safety and civilian protection; security sector reform; disarmament, demobilization, and reintegration; and demining.
- *Delivering basic services*, including water, sanitation, waste management, and energy, as well as health care and primary education.
- *Restoring the economy and livelihoods*, which includes repairing and constructing infrastructure and public works.
- *Rebuilding governance and inclusive political processes*, which encompasses dialogue and reconciliation processes, rule of law, dispute resolution, core government functions, transitional justice, and electoral processes.

Although they are sometimes regarded as distinct from peacebuilding, both peacemaking (the negotiation and conclusion of peace agreements) and humanitarian assistance are relevant to peacebuilding, as they can profoundly influence the options for post-conflict programming. Peacemaking and humanitarian assistance are also relevant to this book, in that they often have substantial natural resource dimensions.

Successful peacebuilding is a transformative process in which a fragile country and the international community seek to address grievances and proactively lay the foundation for a lasting peace. As part of this process, peacebuilding actors seek to manage the country's assets— as well as whatever international assistance may be available—to ensure security, provide basic services, rebuild the economy and livelihoods, and restore governance. The assets of a post-conflict country include natural resources; infrastructure; and human, social, and financial capital. Natural resources comprise land, water, and other renewable resources, as well as extractive resources such as oil, gas, and minerals. The rest of the book explores the many ways in which land and other natural resources affect peacebuilding.

---

* This framework draws substantially from the *Report of the Secretary-General on Peacebuilding in the Immediate Aftermath of Conflict* (UNSG 2009), but the activities have been regrouped and supplemented by activities articulated in USIP and U.S. Army PKSOI (2009), Sphere Project (2004, 2011), UN (2011), UNSG (2010, 2012), and International Dialogue on Peacebuilding and Statebuilding (2011).

of knowledge (see sidebar), which offers better hope of understanding and addressing land issues following conflict.

Although land and property issues may be at the center of many civil conflicts or may emerge during conflict, they are most often addressed somewhat generally in peace accords, or through subsequent national legislative reforms. In other words, an understanding of how land and property rights issues play out at the individual, household, and community levels is rarely a standard component of the peace-process "packages" developed with the assistance of the international community. Thus, one of the primary goals of this book is to provide such understanding, which can then be integrated into such packages.

A peace accord or a military victory may broadly resolve an armed conflict, but the implementation of peace accords (or the creation of new structures associated with victory) raises new issues related to land and property rights. As noted earlier, the stresses of armed conflict often deprive civil institutions of both legitimacy and the ability to function effectively. This is especially the case where land or property rights played a significant role in causing or perpetuating conflict.[5] A de facto institutional vacuum may lead, in turn, to uncertainty in property relations that can not only significantly undermine agricultural recovery, economic opportunities, and food security, but can also intensify identity-driven disputes over areas gained or lost during the conflict by particular ethnic, religious, or otherwise defined groups. Although a peace process can attempt to reconstitute statutory and customary property administration institutions, ensuring that these institutions (1) are viewed as legitimate and (2) have the capacity to identify and resolve land and property rights issues may be elusive goals.

But the problem is yet more complicated. A peace process that attempts to address only pre-conflict land and property issues risks sidestepping the volatile problems that can develop *during* armed conflict. Such problems, which often become most significant at the close of conflict, can drive the post-conflict situation in new and unexpected directions, and thereby undermine the peace process. Examples include the emergence of black markets in land, animosity sparked by the perceived unfairness of restitution or redistribution, and intensified ethnic, religious, or other identity-related tensions over land. Even conflicts that did not initially have a land or property component can be complicated by the spatial nature of land- or property-related actions that occur in the course of conflict; examples include ethnic cleansing, the use of land rights as tools of belligerence,

---

[5] Although the terms *land rights* and *property rights* can be used interchangeably in legal parlance (Black 1990), the meanings are distinct as used in this book: *land rights* and *land tenure* refer to social relations regarding rural lands, whereas *property rights* refers to rights that are associated with immovable property, usually in urban or peri-urban areas. Generally speaking, the term *territory* can refer either to an official jurisdiction that has not yet become a state or a province of a country, or to a land area that has been historically linked to certain groups (for example, ethnic or religious groups). In this book, however, *territory* is used to refer to a subnational portion of a country that is politically or culturally distinct from the rest of the country.

6 Land and post-conflict peacebuilding

and the exploitation of land-based resources (such as diamonds or timber) to fund conflict.

TENURE SECURITY

Security of tenure is one of the most important objectives of land administration, not only in post-conflict situations, but also in the context of ordinary development. The development or restoration of a coherent system of land management can revitalize the credibility of government institutions and promote the rule of law: moreover, authoritative guarantees of tenure security have proved to be particularly important in ensuring investment in and productive use of land resources (World Bank 2003). The achievement of tenure security for internally displaced persons and refugees has also been identified as a key means of addressing conflict-related displacement (Williams 2011b).

At its most fundamental, tenure security concerns the predictability of property rights. While it is often assumed that such security implies ownership of private property, homes and lands can be occupied or used in a variety of ways that are deemed "secure"—through rent, leasehold, freehold, conditional freehold, transient rights, and a number of other collective and communal arrangements. While private property ownership is the form of tenure security that is most familiar and widespread in the developed world, it is only one of many forms of tenure that are capable of providing security.

Legal security of tenure—and its attendant positive economic and social benefits—is derived from (1) a set of rules that are clear, known to those who are affected by them, and justiciable, and (2) a legitimate administrative framework, which may be traditional, statutory, or customary (UN-HABITAT 2001). In essence, households and communities enjoy tenure security when they are protected from involuntary removal unless exceptional conditions apply, and then may be removed only through known, objective, nondiscriminatory proceedings that meet procedural requirements and are reviewed by an independent body (UN-HABITAT 2001).[6] The precise form that tenure takes is less important than the degree of security conferred through the clarity and effectiveness of the applicable rules.

In post-conflict environments, however, tenure security can be both highly complex and highly uncertain. In post-conflict Rwanda, for example, policies that forced several parties who claimed the same property to share the land violated constitutional protections but were implemented nonetheless, out of sheer expediency (Bruce 2013*). In other cases, including post-conflict Liberia, both statutory and customary rules and institutions intended to provide tenure security have been discredited, giving rise to conditions of radical insecurity, in which neither legitimate replacement norms nor institutions exist (Corriveau-Bourque 2011).

---

[6] The cross-cultural applicability of the concept of tenure security is evidenced by the breadth of support for its inclusion in the UN-HABITAT Agenda (UNGA 2001, 2002a, 2002b).

THE PROSPECT OF RENEWED CONFLICT

As noted earlier, after the end of armed conflict—especially prolonged civil conflict—affected populations quickly begin to seek access to land and land-based resources. Given the number of people often involved in conflicting claims, access to land and resources can quickly become a predominant concern. In El Salvador, for example, the vagueness of the 1992 peace accords with regard to local land tenure contributed to conflicting expectations; ultimately, land became a sticking point in the peace process, delaying demobilization and impeding the implementation of the land-related measures envisioned by the accords (Corriveau-Bourque 2013*). After the end of Mozambique's civil war, confusion about the resolution of land tenure disputes undermined the peace process (Unruh 2002). And in Iraq, since the 2003 invasion of the Allied Coalition, the unresolved property claims of displaced persons have fueled ongoing insurgency movements (Stigall 2013*), in a scenario similar to that seen in a number of other conflict-affected countries.

In countries subject to recurrent conflict, land tenure can play a significant role in the nature of conflict. In Somalia, for example, sections of the 1973 Unified Civil Code that abolished traditional clan and lineage rights to the use of and access to land and water resources led to significant grievances and ultimately contributed to the civil war (Hooglund 1999; Sait 2013*). In Liberia, land management continues to be contested and problematic: mismanagement of the dualistic system that regulated statutory and customary approaches to tenure led to widespread land grabbing and to the transfer of land to foreign companies through concessions, fueling the social tensions that had preceded the conflict (GRC 2007). And by 1990, when civil conflict broke out, the legal mechanisms for acquiring land deeds, especially in areas under customary regulation of tenure, had become controversial (Corriveau-Bourque 2011). In Afghanistan, tensions over the control of land administration reflect the ongoing reluctance of local communities to submit to central government control (Stanfield et al. 2013*). In Iraq, the issue of whether property claims can be adjudicated under domestic law has called into question the legitimacy and capacity of the judicial system as a whole (Stigall 2013*). Finally, in Latin America, rectifying the inequitable pre-conflict distribution of land was often fundamental to revolutionary goals (Bailliet 2003; Barquero 2004).

ARMED CONFLICT AND CHANGES IN LAND TENURE

Armed civil conflict profoundly changes relationships among people—and, because land and property rights are a system of rights and obligations governing human relationships, tenure arrangements can change rapidly during conflict. Violence, displacement, the destruction of property, battlefield victory and loss, and food insecurity, as well as the breakdown of property-related institutions and norms, significantly alter land use, settlement patterns, and production systems.

8 Land and post-conflict peacebuilding

In essence, armed conflict reconfigures the network of social relations upon which all land and property rights systems depend, often yielding deeply problematic social relations regarding land. One of the most acute examples of such difficulties is in the Middle East, where Palestinians who sell land to Jewish individuals or interests are potentially subject to a death sentence (Unruh 2002).

The conflict-related reconfiguration of social relations is virtually inevitable after civil war and other internal armed conflicts. Physical displacement may be the first and most dramatic step toward the transformation of land and property rights. Displacement changes, ends, or suspends existing rights and obligations regarding land and property, especially where the basis of a claim depends on physical occupation or social position. In Afghanistan, for example, attempts to restore tenure security after rights and obligations had been put on hold or disrupted by dislocation face significant difficulties (Alden Wily 2003). In many areas of the world, social position depends on location. Thus, in Liberia and Sierra Leone, for example, displacement weakened established social hierarchies, undermining the authority of traditional leaders and creating opportunities for rivals to take their place. Displaced chiefs and other local leaders not only ceased being leaders in their new locations but found upon their return that their positions were no longer recognized or had been occupied by others.

As displaced people attempt to access or use land and property in new locations, competing claims can lead to tensions and other problematic outcomes. In post-conflict Mozambique, for example, migrants, largeholders (those who hold large areas of land), and local customary groups clustered in agronomically valuable areas, where substantial incompatibilities in the groups' approaches to claims, land use, and land access created obstacles to the peace process (Hanlon 1991; Minter 1994). In Somalia, as civil conflict intensified in the early 1990s, certain areas of the country were claimed by nomadic pastoralists under clan-based, transient-access rights arrangements; by small-scale agriculturalists relying on customary rights of occupation; by large-scale land interests accessing land under the aegis of state-sanctioned statutory instruments; and by armed groups seeking access and control through force (Unruh 1995).

Displaced persons often develop greater political awareness while away from their home areas—which may lead them, on their return, to challenge post-conflict authority structures and sources of legitimacy. Such challenges have the potential to broadly reshape social relations and increase political tensions. Roman Krznaric has observed, for example, that Guatemalan refugees exiled in Mexico developed greater political awareness than those who stayed behind (Krznaric 1997). While in Mexico, the refugees had the opportunity to advance certain interests—such as those of women, and of members of lower socioeconomic strata—that had been suppressed in Guatemala.[7] In addition, some sectors of the returning Guatemalan refugee community developed organizational capacity and

---

[7] It is worth noting that the increased political awareness affected different groups of refugees in different ways (Krznaric 1997).

appropriated and used a transnational language of rights (including both human rights and refugee rights) (Krznaric 1997).

In addition to changing land-related social relations, violent civil conflict reduces the power and penetration of state law in affected regions. Early in a conflict, general insecurity, the illegitimate diversion of resources by armed actors or opportunistic parties, the occupation of territory by opposition groups or by populations that are sympathetic to them, and the destruction of land records may cripple or render inoperable the state's land and property administration institutions in certain areas; at the same time, statutory rules may become unenforceable or readily subject to corrupt use.

Perceived injustices in the state's pre-conflict administration of land rights can also undermine the legitimacy of the state, both before and during conflict. In the run-up to the conflicts in Liberia and Sierra Leone, corruption and discriminatory land policies and practices that targeted specific groups had produced deep distrust among large segments of the population, who saw the state as having little legitimacy with regard to land rights (Richards 2005). Such views can range from simple disappointment in the state, to distrust of the state, to outright hostility toward the state. Such hostility can be especially powerful where a state has engaged in mass evictions, land alienation, corruption, or intervention in agricultural production. Such actions are particularly likely to cause grievances when they (1) discriminate against members of particular ethnic or religious groups and (2) lead to displacement. A sense of injustice regarding land and property can become especially problematic if it combines with other grievances that are not necessarily related to land, further decreasing the state's influence and legitimacy. As described at length by Stathis N. Kalyvas, the merging of land-related and non-land-related issues can lead to both acute and long-lasting conflicts (Kalyvas 2006).

When the social fluidity associated with conflict creates opportunity for aggrieved segments of the population to act, the land and property arrangements that result may be very different from those that preceded conflict. In Darfur, for example, Arab pastoralists were encouraged to take over the land of neighboring groups; moreover, they viewed such actions as legitimate, in light of their sense that they had historically been discriminated against with respect to the distribution of both land and political power (O'Fahey 2008).

For many in conflict-affected settings, identity can be (or can become) powerfully and intricately bound up in perceived rights to specific lands. Ethnic identity, in particular, may be linked to conceptions of land, homeland, or territory (Green 2013). When armed conflict is under way, some groups—particularly ethnic, religious, or linguistic groups that have been historically dislocated from their original lands, and that may have immigrated to urban areas—will seize the opportunity to advance the goal of self-determination, which can eventually become a prominent feature in the conflict and in the subsequent peace process. In such a scenario, the parties to a conflict will often assert entirely contradictory claims to land. In Darfur, for example, various parties to the conflict had differing

10 Land and post-conflict peacebuilding

definitions, concepts, and views regarding land, intensifying the intractability of the conflict and rendering land issues even more difficult to address in the course of negotiating the two peace accords that have been signed to date (Unruh 2012a).

THE EMERGENCE OF ALTERNATIVE TENURE APPROACHES

Civil conflict is fueled, in part, by perceptions of legitimacy and illegitimacy. When perceptions of legitimate authority change, the emergence of new social arrangements is almost inevitable. Such developments are particularly relevant to land because claims to territory and associated resources are based primarily on notions of legitimacy and authority. For example, some land claims may be asserted on the basis of historical occupation and supported by oral histories that are derived, in turn, from myths about how various peoples came to exist in the world and to predominate in a particular region (Comaroff and Roberts 1977). Such claims can gain renewed strength during conflict, when the notion of returning to territory from which a given group departed or was expelled, recently or long ago, can gain prominence. In some cases, conflict is viewed as a unique opportunity to regain ancestral lands before peace is consolidated. The return of the Turkmen (who had been relocated under Saddam Hussein), to Kirkuk, Iraq, during the 2003 war, is an illustrative case (HRW 2004).

With wartime ideologies and aspirations still fresh in the minds of many, disappointment in a newly reconstructed post-conflict state can manifest itself in the development of alternative local regimes for land and property. Jocelyn Alexander has noted, for example, that after the war of liberation in Zimbabwe, a grassroots reaction against the state emerged with regard to land and property (Alexander 1996). Local distrust of the state continued even after the insurgency won independence in 1980, because local chiefs who had been allied with the previous Rhodesian administration were deliberately excluded not only from the reconstituted state but also from its efforts to establish land policies.

Where there is ongoing conflict with no accord or clear victor, the substantial reduction (and sometimes complete loss) of state power can lead to a search for alternative sources of order. Such was the case in Somalia, with the emergence of sharia courts—and, arguably, in Afghanistan, with the emergence of the Taliban. Both the sharia courts and the Taliban implemented their own enforcement mechanisms, including those that applied to land and property rights (Unruh 2002; Sait 2013*).

Finally, in the wake of conflict, important features of land and property rights systems may be abandoned, either because conflict has rendered dispute resolution mechanisms unworkable, or because local inhabitants believe there is little point in adhering to rules that others are not following. In Liberia, for example, in the absence of fair land administration and viable, legitimate customary and statutory institutional arrangements for land dispute resolution, tenure systems suffered marked degradation, and wartime approaches—in which tenure was supported by rule of the gun—emerged (Richards 2005).

LAND LAW REFORM

Land-related legislative changes mandated in a peace process and encouraged by the international community are intended to capitalize on a window of opportunity by (1) addressing grievances related to land administration, (2) promoting social change, and (3) aiding in post-conflict recovery and reconstruction. In both Liberia and Sierra Leone, where the inability to gain access to land had led many young men to join insurgent militias, post-conflict legislative changes were specifically designed to address the authority wielded by chiefs and elders, who had traditionally maintained their power—in part—by preventing young men from gaining access to land (Richards 2005).

Legislative changes can be profoundly out of step, however, with the emerging realities of land and property in post-conflict situations. New or modified legislation is typically superimposed on customary rights and obligations that can be stronger or more binding than the new or revised laws, given (1) the questionable legitimacy of a government that may have been associated with only one side of the conflict, (2) the general weakness of post-conflict governments, and (3) the lack of governmental capacity to implement and enforce the new or modified laws. In addition, relationships created and maintained during conflict to regulate property, land, and territory may be significantly stronger than any new norms that emerge in the context of a fragile peace and a war-weakened state. The relative strength of customary norms in comparison to new statutory law can be particularly pronounced among semiliterate, war-weary populations, and where mechanisms for disseminating and enforcing new laws are weak or nonexistent (Unruh 2002).

Nevertheless, the disconnect between legislative changes and reality is usually temporary and can subside as the state strengthens its capacity to effectively and legitimately assert itself. Moreover, a state that engages with or absorbs preexisting or conflict-derived arrangements regarding land, property, and territory is more likely to succeed in gaining legitimacy and authority. If the state attempts to outlaw such arrangements, the effort to use legislation to change social relations may fail or have unexpected outcomes—such as the creation of a black market in land—that can undermine peacebuilding.

In post-conflict Angola, the rapidity with which the government moved forward with recovery led to problematic reforms of the land law. As Allan Cain describes in this book, the haste with which Angola's post-conflict land law was formulated may explain its subsequent failure: in what was perhaps the quickest production of new land legislation in any post-conflict country, a draft of the new legislation was released in July 2002, just a few months after the official end of the conflict (Cain 2013*).

In light of the short time that had been allotted to revise the law, the Portuguese lawyers who guided the drafting process had simply imported numerous components of Portuguese land law; as a result, the new law failed to address the realities, needs, and problems of the post-conflict Angolan population (Cain 2013*). Although the government did invite public consultation on the 2002

12 Land and post-conflict peacebuilding

draft, it was unrealistic to expect meaningful input: in addition to the fact that the population was suffering from ongoing food insecurity and impoverishment (and therefore unlikely to be able to focus on public policy issues such as land legislation), the consultation also occurred before the return of displaced persons, and therefore failed to obtain adequate information on the intersection of the new law and the land problems that emerged during and after the return of the displaced.

Liberia, in contrast, has spent years attempting to develop a process that will yield a viable land law. Although there may be some value in passing or amending land laws sooner rather than later, Liberia does appear to be better off than Angola: not only is the process that Liberia has undertaken much more inclusive, giving voice to different sectors of society, but the Liberian government is also making a genuine effort to address serious land problems.

In sum, it is not necessarily better to create a post-conflict land law quickly, and doing so is arguably worse if the law fails to address post-conflict problems —which is extremely difficult to do within a short time frame. The lack of a land law years after the end of a conflict can be managed, as long as the populace sees that an inclusive process is under way, and careful use is made of other legal instruments, including decrees and legal rulings, to deal with large problems or categories of problems.

URBAN AREAS

Post-conflict property issues in urban and peri-urban areas deserve particular mention. Conflict-affected people whose homes have been destroyed, who are fleeing fighting in rural areas, or who are simply seeking food and services that are no longer available or reliable in their region of origin often occupy land plots, homes, and commercial properties on the fringes of urban areas, fueling the growth of squatter communities. Following conflict and before the identification or preparation of areas for resettlement, attempts to bring order to urban areas often involve evictions. When the users of such property make claims to remain there on the basis of current occupation, the threat of significant unrest arises. After the conflict in Liberia, for example, properties in and around Monrovia were occupied by squatters. The government's inability or unwillingness to evict the squatters led the original landowners to threaten eviction (Williams 2011a; Unruh 2009).

INTERACTIONS BETWEEN EFFORTS TO RESOLVE TENURE ISSUES AND OTHER PEACEBUILDING ACTIVITIES

In post-conflict situations, the potential for adverse interactions between the resolution of tenure issues and other components of peacebuilding underscores the importance of dealing effectively with land and property rights. In Afghanistan, for example, the interaction of land rights and road reconstruction has led to land grabbing and increased violence, both of which threaten peacebuilding gains.

The land grabbing has its origins in large-scale dislocation, the increasing value of land close to roads (and the failure by planners to properly understand the impacts of road reconstruction in land value), and a governance environment in which both corruption and violent conflict (including the widespread use of improvised explosive devices) are pervasive (Unruh and Shalaby 2012).

So far, neither the Afghan government nor the international community has been able to manage the problem of widespread land seizures. All nine provinces where the percentages of government-seized agricultural land are highest lie along the largest road rebuilding project, known as the Ring Road. In three of these provinces, between 80 and 90 percent of the land area has been subject to land grabbing (Helmand, 90 percent; Nangarhar, 80 percent; and Nimroz, 80 percent); in three other provinces, more than 100 percent of the land has been grabbed (Baghlan, 110 percent; Kandahar, 111 percent; and Logar, 190 percent)—indicating that the land has been grabbed repeatedly (Reydon 2006).

A broad trend toward large-scale acquisition of agricultural land also has important implications for post-conflict situations, as the growth of commercial investment (frequently encouraged as part of peacebuilding) intersects with land issues. Countries such as Cambodia have provided early indications of the risks attendant upon development schemes that promote foreign investment through long-term land leases and concessions established without consultation, compensation, or even adequate notice for local residents (Williams 2013b*). Concerns about such actions have led to an ongoing policy debate that has questioned the potential benefits of such investments (including jobs, revenues, and the transfer of skills and technology) and revealed the associated risks (such as corruption, the expulsion of subsistence farmers from their lands, and the exhaustion of the soil) (Cotula et al. 2009; von Braun and Meinzen-Dick 2009; Zagema 2011; Deininger and Byerlee 2011). Human rights advocates, such as Olivier De Schutter, have long expressed concerns about this trend (De Schutter 2011); and recently, many development practitioners have questioned its risks as well, particularly with respect to post-conflict or otherwise fragile countries. But the phenomenon shows no signs of slowing down in the near term—as is indicated, for example, by reports that nearly one-tenth of the land in South Sudan had already been promised to investors before the country's independence (Deng 2011).

Angola serves as an example of the problematic intersection of land rights recovery and landmine clearance, two peacebuilding priorities that occur on the same lands, at the same time, and for the benefit of the same people, but are undertaken separately. In Angola, this intersection led to land grabbing, lack of access to areas adjacent to mined and demined areas, corruption in land administration and markets,[8] and obstacles to the return of refugees and internally displaced persons (IDPs) (Unruh 2012b).

---

[8] Corruption in land administration usually relates to fraudulent claims (altered or false deeds and titles), whereas corruption in land markets has to do with transactions involving deception, coercion, or bad faith (including selling the same parcel of land multiple times).

14   Land and post-conflict peacebuilding

Post-conflict Sierra Leone exemplifies the sometimes negative interactions between the post-conflict priorities of reconstituting land rights and ensuring food security. In this case, landholding lineages retained their rights to land within chiefdoms but were worried that renting out land for agricultural purposes to IDPs, excombatants, and migrants who were willing to farm it might lead the renters to make permanent claims on the land. The fear was so great that many lineages did not allow renters on their land at all—leaving a significant portion of the population lacking secure rental access to land and creating large-scale unemployment in rural areas. The enforced idleness of a great deal of arable and previously cultivated land also led to extreme food and livelihood insecurity in both urban and rural areas (Unruh 2008).

The interaction between multiple land tenure regimes, each of which may be unproblematic on its own, can exacerbate tensions in post-conflict situations. In particular, tensions over land rights between pastoralists and agriculturalists in a number of conflicted-affected countries—including Afghanistan, Somalia, and Sudan—highlight the need to manage such interactions better and more deliberately after conflict (Alden Wily 2013; Stanfield et al. 2013*; Flint and de Waal 2008; Markakis 1993).

ADDRESSING THE CHALLENGES

The twenty-one chapters in this book examine the critical role of land and property in post-conflict peacebuilding, describing experiences in seventeen countries (see figure 1) and drawing on the experiences of many more. The twenty-five authors of these chapters include practitioners, field researchers, policy makers, and scholars with firsthand experience in the countries and regions they write about. Some chapters examine specific countries, including Afghanistan, Angola, Bosnia and Herzegovina, Burundi, Cambodia, El Salvador, Indonesia (Aceh), Iraq, the Philippines, Rwanda, Sudan and South Sudan, Tajikistan, and Timor-Leste. Others take a more thematic view, examining issues such as titling, legal and institutional reform, laws and policies, land registration systems, Islamic and customary law, land and property restitution, land conflicts and conflict resolution, peace negotiations, post-conflict displacement and reintegration, and international standards and the role of the international community.

The book is divided into five parts. Part 1 consists of two chapters on peace negotiations. The first examines Sudan and South Sudan, and the second the Philippines and Mindanao. These two chapters describe the challenges and opportunities presented by various approaches that have been used to address land issues through peace negotiations; they also highlight the complexity of including land issues in peace negotiations and the difficulties involved in implementing negotiated resolutions.

The six chapters in part 2 explore various aspects of managing the return of refugees and displaced persons, who often number in the hundreds of thousands or even millions. Two chapters examine frameworks that have been used to address

Land: A foundation for peacebuilding   15

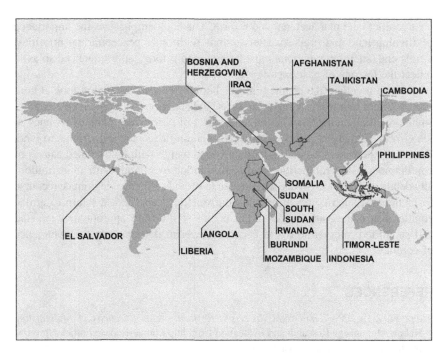

Figure 1. Post-conflict and conflict-affected countries from which lessons have been drawn in this book, either through case studies or broader thematic analyses

displacement and dispossession of land and property, and four chapters examine specific experiences from Angola, Bosnia and Herzegovina, Iraq, and Rwanda.

Part 3, which consists of seven chapters on land management, explores measures that can provide consistent leverage in resolving conflicts and managing the problematic and often volatile land-related issues that emerge in post-conflict situations. Among the tools and techniques examined in part 3 are those that have been used to strengthen capacity for protecting housing, land, and property rights; resolving land disputes; building cooperation; and engaging in fair and sustainable land relations in post-conflict situations.

Although tools and techniques for managing land in post-conflict situations are essential, they must be backed up and given legitimacy by legal means. The five chapters in part 4 focus on laws and policies, emphasizing the importance of revising land and property laws after armed conflict in order to ensure a durable peace. The chapters explore land disputes; legal pluralism, including customary and Islamic law; and approaches to developing, revising, and implementing land-related policies and legislation capable of addressing housing, land, and property rights.

Part 5, a concluding chapter for the entire book, distills the lessons of the previous chapters, placing them within the broader context of the literature on

16 Land and post-conflict peacebuilding

post-conflict land management and reform. The book emphasizes the importance of aligning land and property interventions with other peacebuilding priorities; to this end, such interventions must be assigned priority and sequenced so as to reflect the lessons of past experiences.

Taken together, the chapters in this book offer a wide-ranging look at both successes and failures in efforts to address land and property rights in post-conflict situations. As the chapters illustrate, the onset of peace may add new urgency to the efforts of many rural resource users to claim or reclaim their rights to land. Wartime experiences involving land may also merge with land-related causes of conflict, increasing competition and confrontation over land. With an institutionally debilitated and war-weary state unable to provide effective, legitimate recourse for claimants, such competition and confrontation can spark a return to armed conflict. But as the contributions to this book also illustrate, appropriately targeted and supported interventions can become powerful deterrents to the resurgence of conflict.

REFERENCES

Alden Wily, L. 2003: *Land rights in crisis: Restoring tenure security in Afghanistan.* Kabul: Afghanistan Research and Evaluation Unit. http://unpan1.un.org/intradoc/groups/public/documents/apcity/unpan016656.pdf.

———. 2013. Resolving natural resource conflicts to help prevent war: A case from Afghanistan. In *Livelihoods, natural resources, and post-conflict peacebuilding*, ed. H. Young and L. Goldman. London: Earthscan.

Alexander, J. 1996. Things fall apart, the centre can hold: Processes of post-war political change in Zimbabwe's rural areas. In *Society in Zimbabwe's Liberation War*, ed. N. Bhebe and T. O. Ranger. London: Villiers Publications.

Bailliet, C. 2003. Property restitution in Guatemala: A transitional dilemma. In *Returning home: Housing and property restitution rights of refugees and displaced persons*, ed. S. Leckie. Ardsley, NY: Transnational Publishers.

Barquero, R. 2004. *Access to land in post-conflict situations: A case study in Nicaragua.* Rome: Food and Agriculture Organization of the United Nations.

Black, H. C. 1990. *Black's law dictionary.* 6th ed. St. Paul, MN: West Publishing.

Bruce, J. W. 2013. Return of land in post-conflict Rwanda: International standards, improvisation, and the role of international humanitarian organizations. In *Land and post-conflict peacebuilding*, ed. J. Unruh and R. C. Williams. London: Earthscan.

Bruch, C., D. Jensen, M. Nakayama, J. Unruh, R. Gruby, and R. Wolfarth. 2009. Post-conflict peacebuilding and natural resources. *Yearbook of International Environmental Law* 19:58–96.

Cain, A. 2013. Angola: Land resources and conflict. In *Land and post-conflict peacebuilding*, ed. J. Unruh and R. C. Williams. London: Earthscan.

Comaroff, J., and S. Roberts. 1977. The invocation of norms in dispute settlement. In *Social anthropology and law*, ed. I. Hamnet. London: Academic Press.

Corriveau-Bourque, A. 2011. This land is not for you: Post-war land tenure systems in crisis in central and northwestern Liberia. Master's thesis, Department of Geography, McGill University.

———. 2013. Beyond land redistribution: Lessons learned from El Salvador's unfulfilled agrarian revolution. In *Land and post-conflict peacebuilding*, ed. J. Unruh and R. C. Williams. London: Earthscan.

Cotula, L., C. Toulmin, and C. Hesse. 2004. *Land tenure and administration in Africa: Lessons of experience and emerging issues*. London: International Institute for Environment and Development. http://pubs.iied.org/pdfs/9305IIED.pdf.

Cotula, L., S. Vermeulen, R. Leonard, and J. Keeley. 2009. *Land grab or development opportunity? Agricultural investment and international land deals in Africa*. London: International Institute for Environment and Development; Rome: Food and Agriculture Organization of the United Nations and International Fund for Agricultural Development. www.ifad.org/pub/land/land_grab.pdf.

Deininger, K., and D. Byerlee. 2011. *Rising global interest in farmland: Can it yield sustainable and equitable benefits?* With the assistance of J. Lindsay, A. Norton, H. Selod, and M. Stickler. Washington, D.C.: World Bank. http://siteresources.worldbank.org/INTARD/Resources/ESW_Sept7_final_final.pdf.

Deng, D. K. 2011. *The new frontier: A baseline survey of large-scale land-based investment in Southern Sudan*. Researched by Generation Agency for Development and Transformation–Pentagon and the South Sudan Law Society. Report 1/11 (March). Oslo: Norwegian People's Aid. www.npaid.org/filestore/NPA_New_Frontier.pdf.

De Schutter, O. 2011. The green rush: The global race for farmland and the rights of land users. *Harvard International Law Journal* 52 (2): 503–559.

Flint, J., and A. de Waal. 2008. *Darfur: A new history of a long war*. London: Zed Books.

GRC (Governance Reform Commission, Republic of Liberia). 2007. The way forward: Land and property right issues in the Republic of Liberia. Monrovia.

Green, A. 2013. Social identity, natural resources, and peacebuilding. In *Livelihoods, natural resources, and post-conflict peacebuilding*, ed. H. Young and L. Goldman. London: Earthscan.

Hanlon, J. 1991. *Mozambique: Who calls the shots?* Bloomington: Indiana University Press.

Hooglund, E. 1999. Government and politics. In *Somalia: A country study*, ed. H. C. Metz. 4th ed. Washington, D.C.: Library of Congress, Federal Research Division.

HRW (Human Rights Watch). 2004. *Claims in conflict: Reversing ethnic cleansing in northern Iraq*. Report No. 16 (4E). www.hrw.org/sites/default/files/reports/iraq0804.pdf.

IDMC (Internal Displacement Monitoring Centre). 2012. *Global overview 2011: People internally displaced by conflict and violence*. Geneva, Switzerland. www.internal-displacement.org/publications/global-overview-2011.

International Dialogue on Peacebuilding and Statebuilding. 2011. A new deal for engagement in fragile states. www.oecd.org/dataoecd/35/50/49151944.pdf.

Kalyvas, S. N. 2006. *The logic of violence in civil war*. Cambridge, UK: Cambridge University Press.

Krznaric, R. 1997. Guatemalan returnees and the dilemma of political mobilization. *Journal of Refugee Studies* 10 (1): 61–78.

Markakis, J. 1993. Introduction. In *Conflict and the decline of pastoralism in the Horn of Africa*, ed. J. Markakis. London: Macmillan Press.

Minter, W. 1994. *Apartheid's contras: An inquiry into the roots of war in Angola and Mozambique*. London: Zed Books.

O'Fahey, R. S. 2008. *The Darfur sultanate: A history*. New York: Columbia University Press.

18 Land and post-conflict peacebuilding

Reydon, B. P. 2006. Social embeddedness, institutions for rural land management and land grabbing: The cases of Afghanistan and Brazil. Land Tenure Centre / Terra Institute. www.terrainstitute.org/pdf/Social%20Embeddedness.pdf.

Richards, P. 2005. To fight or to farm? Agrarian dimensions of the Mano River conflicts (Liberia and Sierra Leone). *African Affairs* 105:571–590.

Sait, S. 2013. Unexplored dimensions: Islamic land systems in Afghanistan, Indonesia, Iraq, and Somalia. In *Land and post-conflict peacebuilding*, ed. J. Unruh and R. C. Williams. London: Earthscan.

Sphere Project. 2004. *Humanitarian charter and minimum standards in disaster response.* Geneva, Switzerland. http://ocw.jhsph.edu/courses/refugeehealthcare/PDFs/SphereProject Handbook.pdf.

———. 2011. *Humanitarian charter and minimum standards in humanitarian response.* Geneva, Switzerland. www.sphereproject.org/resources/download-publications/?search =1&keywords=&language=English&category=22.

Stanfield, J. D., J. Brick Murtazashvili, M. Y. Safar, and A. Salam. 2013. Community documentation of land tenure and its contribution to state building in Afghanistan. In *Land and post-conflict peacebuilding*, ed. J. Unruh and R. C. Williams. London: Earthscan.

Stigall, D. E. 2013. Refugees and legal reform in Iraq: The Iraqi Civil Code, international standards for the treatment of displaced persons, and the art of attainable solutions. In *Land and post-conflict peacebuilding*, ed. J. Unruh and R. C. Williams. London: Earthscan.

Tanner, C. 2010. Land rights and enclosures: Implementing the Mozambican Land Law in practice. In *The struggle over land in Africa: Conflicts, politics and change*, ed. W. Anseeuw and C. Alden. Cape Town, South Africa: HSRC Press.

Tubiana, J. 2007. Darfur: A war of land? In *War in Darfur and the search for peace*, ed. A. de Waal. Cambridge, MA: Harvard University Press.

UN (United Nations). 2011. Civilian capacity in the aftermath of conflict: Independent report of the Senior Advisory Group. New York. www.civcapreview.org/LinkClick .aspx?fileticket=K5tZZE99vzs%3d&tabid=3188&language=en-US.

UNDP (United Nations Development Programme) and UNEP (United Nations Environment Programme). 2012. *Maintaining peace and security: The role of natural resources in DDR programmes.* Geneva, Switzerland.

UNEP (United Nations Environment Programme). 2009. *From conflict to peacebuilding: The role of natural resources and the environment.* Nairobi, Kenya. http://postconflict .unep.ch/publications/pcdmb_policy_01.pdf.

———. 2012. *Greening the blue helmets: Environment, natural resources and UN peace-keeping operations.* Nairobi, Kenya. http://postconflict.unep.ch/publications/UNEP_greening _blue_helmets.pdf.

UNGA (United Nations General Assembly). 2001. Reports of the Second Committee. A/56/PV.90. December 21.

———. 2002a. Resolution 205. A/RES/56/205 (2002). February 26.

———. 2002b. Resolution 206. A/RES/56/206 (2002). February 26.

UN-HABITAT (United Nations Agency for Human Settlements). 2001. The global campaign for secure tenure: Implementing the HABITAT Agenda. Nairobi, Kenya. http://vasilievaa.narod.ru/mu/unhabitatmoscow/tenure.asp.htm.

Unruh, J. D. 1995. Post-conflict recovery of African agriculture: The role of "critical resource" tenure. *Ambio* 24:343–350.

Land: A foundation for peacebuilding **19**

———. 2002. Local land tenure in the peace process. *Peace Review* 14:337–342.

———. 2008. Land policy reform, customary rule of law and the peace process in Sierra Leone. *African Journal of Legal Studies* 2:94–117.

———. 2009. Land rights in postwar Liberia: The volatile part of the peace process. *Land Use Policy* 26:425–433.

———. 2012a. Land and legality in the Darfur conflict. *African Security* 5:105–128.

———. 2012b. The interaction between landmine clearance and land rights in Angola: A volatile outcome of non-integrated peacebuilding. *Habitat International* 36:117–125.

Unruh, J., and M. Shalaby. 2012. Road infrastructure reconstruction as a peacebuilding priority in Afghanistan: Negative implications for land rights. *In Assessing and restoring natural resources in post-conflict peacebuilding*, ed. D. Jensen and S. Lonergan. London: Earthscan.

UNSG (United Nations Secretary-General). 2009. *Report of the Secretary-General on peacebuilding in the immediate aftermath of conflict.* A/63/881-S/2009/304. June 11. New York. www.unrol.org/files/pbf_090611_sg.pdf.

———. 2010. *Progress report of the Secretary-General on peacebuilding in the immediate aftermath of conflict.* A/64/866-S/2010/386. July 16 (reissued on August 19 for technical reasons). New York. www.un.org/ga/search/view_doc.asp?symbol=A/64/866.

———. 2012. *Report of the Secretary-General on peacebuilding in the aftermath of conflict.* September. New York.

UNSG's (United Nations Secretary-General's) Policy Committee. 2007. Conceptual basis for peacebuilding for the UN system. May. New York.

USAID (United States Agency for International Development). 2009. *A guide to economic growth in post-conflict countries.* January. Washington, D.C. http://pdf.usaid.gov/pdf _docs/PNADO408.pdf.

USCR (United States Committee for Refugees). 1993. *World refugee survey.* Washington, D.C.

USIP (United States Institute of Peace) and U.S. Army PKSOI (United States Army Peacekeeping and Stability Operations Institute). 2009. *Guiding principles for stabilization and reconstruction.* Washington, D.C.: Endowment of the United States Institute of Peace.

von Braun, J., and R. Meinzen-Dick. 2009. "Land grabbing" by foreign investors in developing countries: Risks and opportunities. Policy Brief No. 13. Washington, D.C.: International Food Policy Research Institute. www.presentationsistersunion.org/_uploads/ fcknw/Land_Grabbing.doc.

Williams, R. C. 2011a. *Beyond squatters' rights: Durable solutions and development-induced displacement in Monrovia, Liberia.* Norwegian Refugee Council Thematic Report. Oslo: Norwegian Refugee Council. www.nrc.no/arch/_img/9568756.pdf.

———. 2011b. *From shelter to housing: Security of tenure and integration in protracted displacement settings.* Norwegian Refugee Council Thematic Report. Oslo: Norwegian Refugee Council. http://reliefweb.int/sites/reliefweb.int/files/resources/9642928.pdf.

———. 2013a. Post-conflict land tenure issues in Bosnia: Privatization and the politics of reintegrating the displaced. In *Land and post-conflict peacebuilding*, ed. J. Unruh and R. C. Williams. London: Earthscan.

———. 2013b. Title through possession or position? Respect for housing, land, and property rights in Cambodia. In *Land and post-conflict peacebuilding*, ed. J. Unruh and R. C. Williams. London: Earthscan.

20   Land and post-conflict peacebuilding

World Bank. 2003. Land policies for growth and poverty reduction. World Bank Policy
   Research Report. Washington, D.C.: World Bank; Oxford, UK: Oxford University Press.
   http://siteresources.worldbank.org/EXTARD/Resources/336681-1295878311276/26384
   .pdf.
————. 2011. *World development report 2011*. Washington, D.C. http://siteresources
   .worldbank.org/INTWDRS/Resources/WDR2011_Full_Text.pdf.
Zagema, B. 2011. Land and power: The growing scandal surrounding the new wave of
   investments in land. Oxfam Briefing Paper No. 151. Oxford, UK: Oxfam.

PART 1

Peace negotiations

Introduction

In countries from El Salvador to Sudan, and Nepal to the Philippines, grievances over the ownership, distribution, and use of land have contributed to the onset of conflict or have emerged in the course of hostilities and displacement, and they have exacerbated the effects of conflict on vulnerable populations. Land is also important for the reintegration of former combatants and the creation of favorable conditions for livelihoods, food security, and economic growth. Moreover, the negotiation of contested rights to land and property is crucial to providing durable solutions for displaced civilian populations. For these reasons, land is one of the most important and contentious natural resource issues addressed in many peace negotiations.

The two chapters in this part highlight the complexity of negotiating resolutions to disputes over land and territory, as well as the challenges to implementing such resolutions.

Salman M. A. Salman traces the long and complex process for negotiating a resolution to a persistent territorial dispute in "The Abyei Territorial Dispute between North and South Sudan: Why Has Its Resolution Proven Difficult?" The Abyei area is on the border between Sudan and what has become the new state of South Sudan. Because of the multiplicity of claims, actors, and interests involved, numerous agreements regarding the disputed territory have been reached and then broken. Various international interlocutors—including the Abyei Boundaries Commission, the Permanent Court of Arbitration, the United Nations, the African Union, and the United States—have sought to facilitate resolution of the conflict, with varying degrees of effectiveness. Although an agreement was signed as recently as June 2011 by the government of Sudan and the Sudan People's Liberation Movement/Sudan People's Liberation Army (representing South Sudan), Salman argues that a durable resolution to the Abyei territorial dispute is attainable only by the traditional leaders of the Misseriya and Ngok Dinka tribes themselves. The two tribes lived in peace for a long time, and differences between members of the two communities were resolved by their leaders on the basis of the traditions and customs of the two tribes. In other words, although international mediation is potentially a valuable tool, it must be accessible and legitimate to local constituencies in order to succeed. Salman concludes by considering how the failure to resolve this dispute has continued to destabilize relations between Sudan and the new state of South Sudan.

In Mindanao, Philippines, local conflicts have made the implementation of peace agreements more difficult. In "Land Tenure and Peace Negotiations in Mindanao, Philippines," Yuri Oki analyzes the phenomenon of *rido:* feuding between families and clans often caused by disputes over ancestral land domains and characterized by violent retaliations. Oki argues that the roots of the civil war—and of enduring poverty—in Mindanao lie not in the clash between Muslims

24 Land and post-conflict peacebuilding

and Christians, but rather in the control and management of land and related natural resources. Competition over land has been a continuous source of conflict because land provides subsistence to local populations and power to clans. The potential to extract copper, gold, nickel, and other minerals exacerbates these conflicts. Although rido is a traditional practice and widely accepted, its recent exercise has exploited ambiguities in national law, caused corruption to become more entrenched, solidified vested interests' control over land, and disrupted a long-lasting peace between the rebels and the government of the Philippines. Nevertheless, Oki notes, the inhabitants of Mindanao have actively supported a peacebuilding process through civil society peace initiatives, NGOs' provision of humanitarian assistance to displaced people, and coordination with international donors that can act as intermediaries with the government.

Many other chapters of this volume touch on land-related challenges to the conclusion and implementation of peace agreements. Many of the challenges are practical, such as responding to displacement and dispossession (addressed in part 2). Other challenges are legal and political. For example, Paula Defensor Knack's chapter, "Legal Frameworks and Land Issues in Muslim Mindanao," in part 4, highlights constitutional challenges to a law meant to implement the peace agreement between the government of the Philippines and rebels in Mindanao. Peace agreements are an important first step in the peacebuilding process, even though it is challenging to negotiate and implement their provisions related to land and territory. When peace agreements are negotiated and implemented in a manner that respects both international standards and local context, they have the potential to permanently end hostilities, establish a framework for post-conflict reconciliation and rebuilding, and guide international assistance in many sectors—not least in the area of land tenure.

The Abyei territorial dispute between North and South Sudan: Why has its resolution proven difficult?

Salman M. A. Salman

Abyei is an area on the border between Northern and Southern Sudan that has been the focus of a dispute between the two parts of the country since independence of Sudan in 1956. This dispute has a number of unique aspects. First, it concerns not only the question of to which of the disputing parties the territory belongs, but also the boundaries and limits of the territory itself. The issue of the boundaries needed to be resolved first, to be followed by a referendum in which the residents of Abyei would decide which part of the country, the North or the South, the area would become part of. In the interim, the area would be placed under special administrative arrangements. The second unique aspect is the large number of agreements that have been concluded by the disputing parties—not to resolve the dispute itself but to put forth arrangements and mechanisms for resolving it. Third is the significant contribution of the international community to the dispute resolution process. This has involved a major role by the United States; the Abyei Boundaries Commission (ABC), composed of independent experts; and the Permanent Court of Arbitration (PCA) in The Hague, as well as the United Nations and the African Union. Indeed, there is no precedent for resolution by the PCA, or any other international tribunal, of a country's internal territorial dispute. Fourth, in addition to the government of Sudan (GOS) and the Sudan People's Liberation Movement/Sudan People's Liberation Army (SPLM/A) (and now the government of South Sudan), the dispute involves the Ngok Dinka, a Southern tribe, and the Misseriya, a Northern tribe, each claiming the area, and both deeply enmeshed in the dispute. Indeed, the crux of the dispute gradually shifted since 2009 from the limits and boundaries of the Abyei area to whether the Misseriya are entitled to participate in the referendum.

This chapter reviews the recent history of the Abyei dispute and the agreements that have been reached to resolve it, and analyzes the decisions of the ABC and the PCA. It examines the reasons for not undertaking the referendum

---

Salman M. A. Salman is an academic researcher and consultant on water law and policy. He previously served as lead counsel and water law adviser with the Legal Vice Presidency of the World Bank.

26   Land and post-conflict peacebuilding

on the future of the area, as scheduled, and the aftermath, including the takeover of the area by GOS forces in May 2011. The chapter also discusses the implications of the dispute and the failure thus far to resolve it for the Abyei area, and for the future relations between Sudan and the new state of South Sudan.[1]

RECENT HISTORY OF THE ABYEI DISPUTE

The recent history of the Abyei dispute dates back to the beginning of the twentieth century.[2] After the Anglo-Egyptian forces conquered Sudan in 1898, they confirmed existing provincial boundaries, including the borders between Northern and Southern Sudan. However, in 1905 authority over nine chiefdoms of the Ngok Dinka was transferred from the Southern province of Bahr el Ghazal to the Northern province of Kordofan, and the border between Northern and Southern Sudan was adjusted accordingly. No movement of people was involved, only the map was redrawn to reflect this redistricting. The territory in question is known as the Abyei area.

The main reason for the transfer of the area to the North was the contentious relationship between the Misseriya and Ngok Dinka tribes. The Misseriya lived and moved in the southern part of Kordofan Province, near the border with Bahr el Ghazal Province. The Ngok Dinka lived in the northern part of Bahr el Ghazal Province, adjacent to where the Misseriya lived. The two tribes share parts of the Abyei area and have conflicting claims on it. In 1905, the British colonial administration

> concluded that it made sense to put the two contending groups under the same administration. For one thing it was much more difficult to reach the area from the British headquarters in Bahr el Ghazal than it was from Kordofan. In addition, it would be more effective to adjudicate the dispute if the two parties were under the same provincial administration. . . . As a result, the anomaly of a southern Sudanese group administered as part of northern Sudan was created (Petterson 2008, 22–23).

The relationship between the Ngok Dinka and the Misseriya, from the time of the transfer through the remainder of the colonial era, was by and large peaceful, despite their basic differences. The Ngok Dinka are part of the larger Dinka tribe, which is a Nilotic African tribe. It is the largest, wealthiest, and politically

---

[1] This chapter uses the terms *Southern Sudan* and *Northern Sudan* to refer to the two parts of the country before the independence of South Sudan. On February 13, 2011, one week after the Southern Sudan referendum results were officially announced, showing that the overwhelming majority of Southern Sudanese voted for secession (see note 19), the government of Southern Sudan decided to call their new country the Republic of South Sudan. Accordingly, the chapter uses the term *South Sudan* when referring to the new state.

[2] See "Milestones in the Abyei Territorial Dispute between North and South Sudan," at the end of this chapter.

The Abyei territorial dispute 27

Notes: A – The Hala'ib Triangle is claimed by Sudan and de facto administered by Egypt.
B – The Ilemi Triangle is claimed by Ethiopia, South Sudan, and Kenya and de facto controlled by Kenya.

strongest group in the South. Many of the influential Southern politicians and academicians are from the Dinka tribe. Its members practice indigenous religions, although many of the political leaders have embraced Christianity, and some members of the tribe have converted to Islam. The Misseriya, on the other hand, are Arabs and Muslims. A wealthy tribe with huge numbers of livestock, its members move across Southern Kordofan and the Abyei area in search of fodder and water for their livestock. A number of their tribal leaders are prominent members of political parties in the North.

Problems between the two tribes emerged following the outbreak of civil war between the North and the South in August 1955, a few months before Sudan became independent on January 1, 1956. Naturally, the Ngok Dinka sided with the Southern movement, while the Misseriya sided with the Northern government in Khartoum. The first round of civil war ended with the conclusion of the Addis

28   Land and post-conflict peacebuilding

Ababa Agreement on the Problem of South Sudan (Addis Ababa Agreement) on March 12, 1972, between the Government of the Democratic Republic of the Sudan and the Southern Sudan Liberation Movement.[3]

The Addis Ababa Agreement, in article 3(c), defined the Southern provinces of Sudan to include "the Provinces of Bahr El Ghazal, Equatoria and Upper Nile in accordance with their boundaries as they stood January 1, 1956, and other areas that were culturally and geographically a part of the Southern Complex as may be decided by a referendum." Although the agreement did not refer explicitly to Abyei, it was understood and agreed that the second part of the definition referred to Abyei because of the geographical and cultural aspects of the area and its residents. However, the agreement did not specify the boundaries of the area, or establish a process for defining and delimiting them. It called for a referendum on whether the area would be part of the Southern or the Northern Sudan, but did not go into any detail, or specify a schedule for the referendum. Nothing substantive with regard to Abyei took place following the conclusion of the Addis Ababa Agreement; no special administrative arrangements were put in place,[4] and no referendum was held.

The Addis Ababa Agreement granted Southern Sudan self-government and established a People's Regional Assembly and a High Executive Council as the legislative and executive organs there. It excluded certain matters from their authority, conferring them instead on the national government in Khartoum, and included detailed provisions on the relationship between the two parts of the country. However, the agreement faced a number of difficulties as well as successive major breaches by the GOS that led eventually to its collapse in 1983 (Alier 1990). In that year, the SPLM and the SPLA were established, and they led the renewed civil war that broke out in 1983. The old alliances of the Khartoum government and the Misseriya tribe on the one hand, and the SPLM/A and the Ngok Dinka tribe on the other hand, were revived and grew stronger during the civil war, and each tribe fought on the side of its respective ally. As a consequence, the relationship between the two tribes worsened, and occasionally they fought each other. As with the larger North-South conflict, the ethnic and religious differences between the Misseriya and the Ngok Dinka no doubt exacerbated the conflict between them.

Negotiations between the GOS and the SPLM/A, which started in 2002 in Kenya, led to the conclusion of a series of agreements and protocols which were later consolidated and signed as the Comprehensive Peace Agreement (CPA) on January 9, 2005.[5] Those agreements and protocols started with the Machakos Protocol that was concluded on July 20, 2002. That protocol granted Southern Sudan the right of self-determination, to be exercised through a referendum to

---

[3] For the complete text of the Addis Ababa Agreement, see www.goss-online.org/magnoliaPublic/en/about/politicalsituation/mainColumnParagraphs/00/content_files/file3/Addis%20Ababa%20Agreement.pdf.

[4] A presidential decree was issued in 1974 placing the Abyei area administratively under the presidency, but nothing was done to implement that decree.

[5] For the complete text of the CPA, see www.sd.undp.org/doc/CPA.pdf.

be held on January 9, 2011, six months before the end of a six-year interim period on July 8, 2011. On that date, according to paragraph 2.5 of the Machakos Protocol, "there shall be an internationally-monitored referendum, organized jointly by the government of Sudan and the SPLM/A, for the people of the South Sudan to confirm: the unity of the Sudan . . . or to vote for secession." The six-year interim period was intended to give the Southern Sudanese the opportunity to make an informed decision on the choice between unity and secession.

The Machakos Protocol was followed on September 25, 2003, with the Agreement on Security Arrangements. This agreement confirmed the existence of two separate armed forces during the interim period: the Sudanese Armed Forces (SAF) and the SPLA, with both forces treated equally as part of Sudan's National Armed Forces. It also established Joint/Integrated Units from the two armed forces. The Agreement on Wealth Sharing was concluded on January 7, 2004, and dealt mainly with the sharing of natural resources, particularly oil, between the North and the South. Three more agreements were concluded on May 26, 2004. The first was on power sharing and included detailed governance provisions. The second dealt with the states of Southern Kordofan and Blue Nile, which are geographically part of Northern Sudan but identify culturally with Southern Sudan. This agreement devolved more powers to those states and called for popular consultations on implementation of the agreement at the end of the interim period. The third agreement, known as the Abyei Protocol but formally titled "The Resolution of the Abyei Conflict,"[6] is discussed in more detail below.

Thus, six agreements were concluded between 2002 and 2004. On December 31, 2004, two annexures were concluded spelling out detailed implementation arrangements for these agreements, including the Abyei Protocol. This brought to a successful conclusion an arduous negotiation process that had spanned almost three years.

As indicated above, these documents made up the CPA, which was signed on January 9, 2005.[7] The CPA was signed by the then – first vice president of the Republic of the Sudan and the chairman of the SPLM/A. It was witnessed by envoys of thirteen countries and organizations: the presidents of Kenya and Uganda and representatives of Egypt, Italy, the Netherlands, Norway, the United Kingdom, the United States, the African Union, the European Union, the Intergovernmental Authority on Development (IGAD),[8] the Arab League, and the United Nations.

---

[6] The title of the protocol was changed on December 31, 2004, to the Protocol between the Government of the Sudan and the Sudan People's Liberation Movement/Army on the Resolution of the Abyei Conflict. It is noteworthy that the protocol used the term *Abyei conflict* and not *Abyei dispute*. For the complete text of the Abyei Protocol, see www.gossmission.org/goss/images/agreements/Abyei_protocol.pdf.

[7] The CPA is also known as the Naivasha Agreement, after the town in Kenya where most of the agreements of the CPA were concluded.

[8] IGAD is a regional organization of East African countries dedicated to achieving peace, prosperity, and regional intergration. Negotiations on the CPA were conducted under the auspices of IGAD. At that time, its members were Djibouti, Eritrea, Ethiopia, Kenya, Somalia, Sudan, and Uganda. (Following independence, South Sudan became a member.)

30 Land and post-conflict peacebuilding

The Interim National Constitution of the Republic of the Sudan was issued on July 6, 2005,[9] six months after the conclusion of the CPA.[10] It incorporated the basic undertakings of the CPA, including those relating to Abyei.[11]

THE ABYEI PROTOCOL AND OTHER AGREEMENTS ON THE ABYEI DISPUTE

During the negotiations for the CPA, the issue of Abyei turned out to be more difficult and complex than was thought by the two parties. There was no agreement on the boundaries or the size of the Abyei area. The GOS took the stand at the beginning of the negotiations that the borders between the North and the South were to be as they stood on independence day, January 1, 1956 (see figure 1), and were not subject to negotiations or change.

The SPLM argued that Abyei was an exception to the issue of Sudan's January 1, 1956, borders, as it was addressed in the 1972 Addis Ababa Agreement, and insisted that it be addressed during the CPA negotiations. The GOS later agreed to discuss Abyei but insisted that the area south of the Bahr el Arab River (also known as the Kiir River) was the only area transferred to the North in 1905, and thus the only area that should be considered as the Abyei area. Under this scenario, the Bahr el Arab River would become the natural boundary between the North and the South in that area, as indicated in figure 2, in case the area becomes part of the South. Abyei Town, the main city in the area, falls north of the Bahr el Arab River, and thus would not be included in the area proposed by the government.[12] The SPLM insisted that the area was far larger than that, extending well into Kordofan, running south of Lake Keilak to the area immediately south of Muglad Town. Negotiations on this matter became deadlocked. Thus, the crux of the Abyei dispute at that time was that a certain area was transferred from Southern Sudan to Northern Sudan, but there was no agreement on its boundaries or size.

The United States, which was actively involved in the Sudan peace negotiations, attempted to break the deadlock over Abyei. On March 19, 2004, the then – U.S. special envoy to Sudan, Senator John Danforth, presented proposals to the two parties, including a definition of the area and a process for delimiting

---

9   See www.mpil.de/shared/data/pdf/inc_official_electronic_version.pdf for the complete text of the interim constitution.

10 The first six months after the CPA was signed were primarily devoted to adopting the interim constitution. Article 226 set an interim period to start on July 9, 2005, and to last until July 8, 2011, six months after the referendum on the status of Southern Sudan on January 9, 2011. The first six months (January 9 to July 8, 2005) are referred to as the pre-interim period.

11 Article 183 of the interim constitution incorporated the main provisions of the Abyei Protocol.

12 The GOS and the Misseriya claim that Abyei Town was actually established some years after the transfer of the area to the North. See Zainelabideen (2009).

The Abyei territorial dispute 31

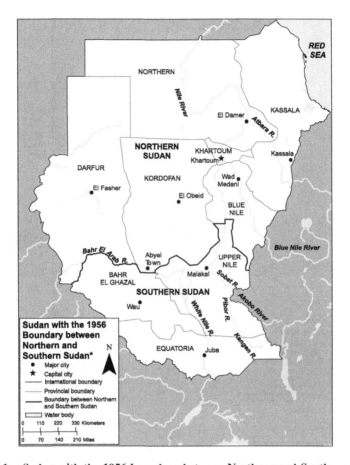

Figure 1. Sudan with the 1956 boundary between Northern and Southern Sudan

it and resolving the dispute.[13] Those proposals were accepted by both parties and became the basis for the Abyei Protocol, which was concluded on May 26, 2004, and formed part of the CPA.[14] The Abyei Protocol did not attempt to resolve the conflict; it simply established arrangements and mechanisms for resolving it.

---

[13] In the context of this chapter, in line with boundaries' terminology, *define* means to generally describe the limits of an area; *delimit* means to mark its boundaries on a map; and *demarcate* means to mark its boundaries on the ground.

[14] The footnote to the Abyei Protocol states: "This is the full text of the proposal entitled 'Principles of Agreement on Abyei,' presented by US Special Envoy Senator John Danforth to H.E. First Vice President Ali Osman Mohamed Taha and SPLM/A Chairman Dr. John Garang on the 19th of March 2004. The parties hereby declare to adopt these Principles as the basis for the resolution of Abyei Conflict."

32 Land and post-conflict peacebuilding

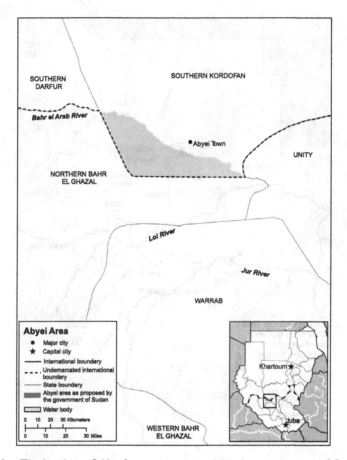

Figure 2. The borders of Abyei area as proposed by the government of Sudan
Source: PCA (2009), reprinted with permission from Terralink.

In line with the U.S. proposals, Abyei was defined under paragraph 1.13 of the Abyei Protocol "as the area of the nine Ngok Dinka chiefdoms transferred to Kordofan in 1905."[15] The protocol placed Abyei under the presidency (consisting of the president of the Republic of the Sudan and the two vice presidents)

---

[15] It should be added in this context that academics and politicians from the Misseriya tribe do not agree with this definition, and claim that the Abyei area belonged historically to the Misseriya who migrated there in the eighteenth century, and that they were the ones who welcomed the Ngok Dinka in the Abyei area many years later (Zainelabideen 2009). On the other hand, Dinka academics and politicians hold exactly the opposite view, namely that the Ngok Dinka lived in the Abyei area long before the Misseriya, and they were the ones who welcomed the Misseriya to the area (Deng 1986). This chapter does not attempt to address those claims and is focused primarily on the dispute resolution process and the challenges facing it.

The Abyei territorial dispute   **33**

and stated that it would be administered by an executive council elected by the residents of Abyei. Pending that election, the council's initial members would be appointed by the presidency. The protocol stated that the residents of Abyei comprised the members of the Ngok Dinka community and other Sudanese residing in the area, and that such residents would be citizens of both Kordofan and Bahr el Ghazal.[16] It also included detailed provisions on the sharing of the revenue from the oil produced in the Abyei area during the interim period.[17]

More importantly, the protocol set forth arrangements for delimiting the boundaries of Abyei, as well as for a referendum on its status.[18] This referendum was scheduled to take place on January 9, 2011, simultaneously with the Southern Sudan referendum, offering Abyei residents the choice of retaining their special administrative status in Northern Sudan or becoming part of Bahr el Ghazal in Southern Sudan. However, as discussed later, this referendum did not take place on January 9, 2011, as stipulated under the Abyei Protocol, although the Southern Sudan referendum did take place. On that date, and for the next six days (ending on January 15, 2011), the people of Southern Sudan voted overwhelmingly to secede from Sudan.[19]

As mentioned earlier, the dispute over Abyei also involves the Southern tribe of the Ngok Dinka and the Northern tribe of the Misseriya. The leadership of the national government and the SPLM/A includes prominent members of

---

[16]   The two states with which Abyei has been associated, Kordofan and Bahr el Ghazal, were divided in 2005—Kordofan into Northern and Southern Kordofan, and Bahr el Ghazal into Northern Bahr el Ghazal, Western Bahr el Ghazal, Warrab, and Lakes states. The issues of Abyei concern the current states of Southern Kordofan and Northern Bahr el Ghazal.

[17]   The Abyei Protocol set the following percentages for sharing Abyei net oil revenues: 50 percent for the national government, 42 percent for the government of Southern Sudan, and 2 percent each for Bahr el Ghazal State, Kordofan State, the Ngok Dinka, and the Misseriya. For an analysis of sharing of oil revenues from the region, see Wennmann (2012).

[18]   The fact that the Abyei Protocol called for the status of the Abyei area (after its boundaries are demarcated) to be determined by referendum rather than for its outright return to Southern Sudan, from where it was transferred in 1905, may have been based on the precedent of the Addis Ababa Agreement, which also called for a referendum on the status of the area. The referendum was seen in both instances as conferring legality and legitimacy to any changes of the boundaries between the North and the South as they stood on January 1, 1956. It is also worth noting that placing the Abyei area under the presidency, as stipulated by the Abyei Protocol, is perhaps based on the similar arrangement pronounced by the 1974 presidential decree, which was issued as a result of the Addis Ababa Agreement (see note 4).

[19]   The results of the referendum were officially announced on February 7, 2011, and indicated that close to 99 percent of the Southern Sudanese voters opted for secession (Southern Sudan Referendum Commission 2011). Consequently, and as per the CPA, the state of South Sudan formally came into existence on July 9, 2011, following the end of the interim period on July 8, 2011.

34 Land and post-conflict peacebuilding

the Misseriya and Ngok Dinka, respectively, some of whom played key roles in the Abyei negotiations. The Misseriya claim that they are residents of the Abyei area, and as such they are entitled to participate in the Abyei referendum. This demand is categorically rejected by the SPLM and the Ngok Dinka who argue that the Misseriya have only grazing rights in the Abyei area, and as such are not residents of the area. This issue has now become the crux of the dispute, and its resolution has thus far eluded the two parties. The discovery of oil in and around Abyei has been another complicating factor, because whichever way Abyei goes, the oil resources within the area will go with it.

Both sides agreed under the Abyei Protocol that Abyei is the area of the nine Ngok Dinka chiefdoms transferred to Kordofan in 1905. The dispute has been, however, over the boundaries of that area. The GOS and the Misseriya argued that the area in question was a triangle of land south of the Bahr el Arab River, and that the Ngok Dinka expanded north of the river, including to Abyei Town itself, only after 1905. The SPLM and the Ngok Dinka, on the other hand, claimed that the area extended far north of the Bahr el Arab River and well into Kordofan, close to the town of Muglad, the heart of the Misseriya tribe. To determine the boundaries of Abyei, the GOS and the SPLM agreed, under paragraph 5.1 of the Abyei Protocol, to establish the Abyei Boundaries Commission (ABC), which was to include independent experts and representatives of the local communities and the local administration, and was to complete its work within the first two years of the interim period.

Because the Abyei Protocol dealt mainly with the basic elements for resolving the dispute, more detailed arrangements needed to be worked out and agreed upon. Thus, on December 17, 2004, seven months after the Abyei Protocol was signed, the two parties concluded the Understandings on the Abyei Boundaries Commission, referred to as the Abyei Annex or Abyei Appendix to the Abyei Protocol. This document specified that the ABC would consist of fifteen members: five appointed by the GOS, representing the government, the Misseriya, and the administrators of Abyei; five appointed by the SPLM, representing the SPLM, the Ngok Dinka, and the administrators of Abyei; and five impartial experts, to be appointed by the United States, United Kingdom, and IGAD. The ABC would be chaired by one of the experts. It was to hear testimony from representatives of the people of Abyei and its neighbors and the two conflicting parties, and to consult the British archives and other relevant sources on Sudan. It was required under the Abyei Annex to submit its report to the presidency by July 2005, and not two years after the interim period began, as had been stipulated in the Abyei Protocol. Its report would be considered final and binding.

On December 31, 2004, the two parties concluded the Implementation Modalities of the Protocol on the Resolution of the Abyei Conflict, which addressed the timing, executing body, funding sources, composition, and procedures for a number of elements of the Abyei Protocol. This document also established mechanisms for selecting the members of the ABC. It became part of annexure II of the CPA.

The Abyei territorial dispute   35

As indicated earlier, the CPA was signed on January 9, 2005. It consisted of a chapeau,[20] six separate protocols and agreements, and two annexures, as described above. As mentioned above, one of the protocols and one of the annexures dealt specifically with the Abyei dispute.

The next step toward resolving the Abyei dispute was conclusion of the March 12, 2005, agreement on the Text of the Terms of Reference for the Abyei Boundaries Commission. This agreement reiterated the mandate and structure of the ABC. It listed the five appointees from each of the two parties and set out the ABC's work program, schedule, and funding. It established Nairobi as the seat of the ABC. By that time, the United States, United Kingdom, and IGAD had selected the commission's five experts.[21] By mid-March 2005, the fifteen-member ABC was in place.

On April 11, 2005, the delegations of the GOS and the SPLM agreed, in Nairobi, on the Rules of Procedure for the Abyei Boundaries Commission. This document described in detail the ABC's work program, including field visits, hearing of presentations by representatives of both sides, and, after completion of this process, evaluation of the evidence and preparation of a final report. The ABC was to endeavor to reach a decision by consensus, but if this was not possible, the experts would have the final say.[22] However, the other ten members of the ABC would continue to be part of the process of hearings, field visits, and deliberations. The report would become a public document after its formal presentation to the presidency.

Thus, a wide range of legal instruments were concluded by the two parties with the hope that they would pave the way for a just, peaceful, and sustainable resolution of the Abyei dispute. Unfortunately, that did not turn out to be the case, as discussed in the next parts of this chapter.

THE ABYEI BOUNDARIES COMMISSION REPORT

Following agreement on the Rules of Procedure, the GOS and the SPLM submitted their preliminary presentations to the experts on April 12, 2005, through their

---

[20] The chapeau is the umbrella agreement that was signed by the two parties and the thirteen witnesses on January 9, 2005, and which listed and attached the other agreements and protocols constituting the CPA.

[21] The five experts were Ambassador Donald Petterson (former U.S. ambassador to Sudan), the U.S. appointee; Douglas Johnson (scholar and expert on Southern Sudan), the UK appointee; and three IGAD appointees: Godfrey Muriuki (University of Nairobi), Kassahun Berhanu (University of Addis Ababa), and Shadrack Gutto (a South African lawyer). Ambassador Petterson was selected as the chair of the ABC in accordance with the wishes of the GOS and the SPLM.

[22] Donald Petterson raised the question as to why the two sides would delegate to five outsiders the power to make the decision on the boundaries of Abyei. He answered the question: "For one, they knew they couldn't do it themselves. And it's possible that one or both sides figured it would be better that blame for an adverse decision would fall on the outsiders, not on themselves. Beyond that is the fact that each side believed its case was ironclad" (Petterson 2008, 24).

36   Land and post-conflict peacebuilding

members in the ABC. Subsequently, the ABC visited Abyei for six days, collecting testimony from members of both tribes.

In addition to receiving oral and written testimony, and after the visit to the Abyei area in April, the experts examined historic documents at the National Records Office in Khartoum, as well as in the United Kingdom. Final presentations were heard in June, after which the report was completed by the experts and presented to the presidency on July 14, 2005 (ABC 2005). This was just a few days after the interim constitution was adopted on July 6, 2005. Subsequent to the adoption of the constitution, the SPLM joined the ruling National Congress Party (NCP) as a junior partner in the government, and John Garang, the leader of the SPLM/A, returned to Khartoum, where he was sworn in as the first vice president.[23]

The ABC report found that "no map exists showing the area inhabited by the Ngok Dinka in 1905. Nor is there sufficient documentation produced in that year by Anglo-Egyptian Condominium authorities that adequately spell out the administrative situation that existed in that area at that time" (ABC 2005, 4). The report stated further that "in 1905 there was no clearly demarcated boundary of the area transferred from Bahr el-Ghazal to Kordofan" (ABC 2005, 20). The report rejected both: (i) the claim of the GOS that the area transferred in 1905 lay entirely south of the Bahr el Arab River, and (ii) the claim of the Ngok Dinka that their boundary with the Misseriya should run from Lake Keilak to Muglad Town (ABC 2005).

The report classified land rights in three categories: dominant (full rights evidenced by permanent settlements), secondary (involving seasonal use of land), and shared secondary (exercised by two or more communities). It presented the following conclusions:

- The Ngok Dinka "have a legitimate dominant claim to the territory from the Kordofan–Bahr el Ghazal boundary north to latitude 10°10′ N," extending from the boundary with Darfur Province in the west to Upper Nile Province in the east, as these boundaries stood at independence in 1956 (ABC 2005, 21).
- From latitude 10°10′ N and up to latitude 10°35′ N, "the Ngok and the Misseriya share isolated occupation and use rights" (ABC 2005, 21). Thus, this area should be divided between them, and the northern boundary should be located at latitude 10°22′30″ N.
- "The western boundary shall be the Kordofan-Darfur boundary as it was defined on 1 January 1956. The southern boundary shall be the Kordofan-Bahr el-Ghazal-Upper Nile boundary as it was defined on 1 January 1956. The eastern boundary shall extend the line of the Kordofan-Upper Nile boundary

---

[23]   John Garang was killed in a plane crash on July 30, 2005 (three weeks after he was sworn as first vice president), as he flew from Uganda to Southern Sudan. He was succeeded by his deputy, Salva Kiir Mayardit.

The Abyei territorial dispute 37

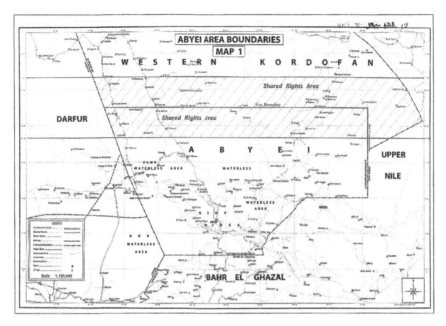

Figure 3. Map of the Abyei area as delimited by Abyei Boundaries Commission experts
Source: PCA (2009), reprinted with permission from Terralink.

at approximately longitude 29°32'15" E northwards until it meets latitude 10°22'30" N" (ABC 2005, 22).
- "The Ngok Dinka and the Misseriya should retain their established secondary rights to the use of land north and south of this boundary" (ABC 2005, 22).[24]

Figure 3 shows the Abyei area as delimited in the ABC report.

The ABC report accommodated a large part of the SPLM's claims by extending the Abyei area well into Kordofan, and rejecting the government's claim that Abyei was limited to the land south of the Bahr el Arab River. The SPLM and the Ngok Dinka immediately accepted the report and asserted that, according to the agreements signed by the two parties, it was final and binding. The government and the Misseriya rejected the report, claiming that the ABC

---

[24] The ABC report called for the demarcation of the northern and eastern boundaries by a survey team comprising three professional surveyors, one nominated by the GOS, one by the government of Southern Sudan, and the third by IGAD, to be assisted by four representatives, one from the Ngok Dinka, one from the Misseriya, and two from the presidency. The ABC report also asked the presidency to send the nominations for this team to IGAD for final approval by the international experts. Thus, the experts extended their authority beyond issuance of the report.

38 Land and post-conflict peacebuilding

had exceeded its mandate by taking into consideration developments in the area after it was transferred to the North in 1905.

Thus the arduous work of the ABC did not attain the expected results. A stalemate developed that would last for three years before the next attempt to resolve the dispute.

STALEMATE, SETBACKS, AND THE DECISION TO SEEK ARBITRATION

The rejection by the government and the Misseriya of the ABC report was the first major setback in the implementation of the CPA; as it took place less than a week after the NCP and SPLM government was constituted. The rejection of the report resulted in a complete stalemate on the Abyei dispute. The boundaries of the Abyei area remained without agreement, and its status uncertain. Without a clear demarcation of the Abyei area, it would not be possible to meaningfully implement the provisions of the Abyei Protocol regarding the administrative arrangements for the area during the interim period leading to the referendum. Henceforth, Abyei has remained the thorniest issue in the North-South peace process and relations.

In October 2007, the SPLM withdrew from the national government over a number of issues, including the refusal of the NCP to accept the ABC report. The SPLM ministers eventually returned to their ministries, but the Abyei dispute remained unresolved. Diplomatic efforts by the IGAD and the U.S. special envoy to Sudan continued but did not lead to a breakthrough.

In May 2008, fighting broke out between the Sudanese army and the SPLA in Abyei Town, and the city was devastated. The fighting had erupted over a personal argument between government and SPLA soldiers (*Sudan Tribune* 2008). United Nations officials estimated that one hundred people might have been killed, and that 30,000 residents of Abyei Town and 20,000 from neighboring villages fled at the height of the fighting. That incident underscored the fragility of the situation in Abyei, and indicated the threat to the larger North-South peace process posed by the failure to resolve the Abyei dispute.

The fighting and devastation of Abyei Town prompted the two parties to rethink their strategies and return to the negotiating table over the Abyei dispute. Consequently, on June 8, 2008, two weeks after the outbreak of the fighting, they signed the Road Map for Return of IDPs [internally displaced persons] and Implementation of the Abyei Protocol. The agreement dealt in detail with security arrangements, deploying in Abyei a new integrated battalion with troops from the SAF and the SPLA, as well as a police unit and a force from the United Nations Mission in Sudan (UNMIS). The agreement also required the government to provide the necessary resources for the return of civilians to their homes. It established interim arrangements for administering the Abyei area, based on the Abyei Protocol. These arrangements included interim boundaries for the area as well as the appointment by the presidency of a chief administrator from the SPLM and a deputy administrator from the NCP, both residents of the Abyei area.

The agreement reconfirmed the oil revenue shares agreed upon earlier (see note 17), and established a fund to develop the areas along the North-South border and to finance joint projects there. The GOS would contribute 50 percent and the government of Southern Sudan 25 percent of their Abyei oil revenues, respectively, to this fund.

In a major breakthrough, the agreement also stated that the parties would submit the dispute over the findings of the ABC to binding arbitration. This became possible when the SPLM dropped its demand that the ABC report be considered final and binding. The two parties agreed to work out the terms of reference for the arbitration, including the process for selecting arbitrators, issues to be referred for arbitration, procedures, the decision-making process, and enforcement. The agreement called for the entire arbitration process to be completed within six months from the date of establishment of the tribunal. More importantly, it stated that if the two parties failed to reach agreement within one month on the arbitration tribunal, the secretary-general of the PCA would establish one within fifteen days, and would finalize procedures and terms of reference in accordance with PCA rules and international practices. Those provisions on arbitration were confirmed in a Memorandum of Understanding on the Abyei Arbitration signed by the two parties on June 21, 2008.[25]

On July 7, 2008, both parties signed the Arbitration Agreement between the Government of Sudan and the Sudan People's Liberation Movement/Army on Delimiting Abyei Area.[26] That decision was another major attempt to resolve the Abyei dispute, and is also another significant step in the internationalization of the dispute, as discussed below.

THE PERMANENT COURT OF ARBITRATION: PROCESS AND AWARD

Under the Arbitration Agreement, the parties agreed to refer their dispute for final and binding arbitration to the PCA, governed by the PCA's Optional Rules

---

[25] In article 3.2, the Arbitration Agreement consolidated the Memorandum of Understanding on the Abyei Arbitration and the Road Map for Return of IDPs and Implementation of Abyei Protocol. For the complete text of the Arbitration Agreement, see www.pca-cpa.org/upload/files/Abyei%20Arbitration%20Agreement.pdf.

[26] One other unique aspect of the Abyei dispute is that the arbitration before the PCA was between the GOS and the SPLM. The SPLM was, at that time, a junior, albeit an important, partner in the GOS, as established by the CPA and the interim constitution, and held important portfolios, including the first vice president, as well as the minister of foreign affairs. However, the SPLM was an adversarial party against the GOS before the PCA. In fact, the minister of foreign affairs was also a member of the SPLM delegation to the arbitration hearings before the PCA in The Hague. This dilemma was also faced earlier when the Road Map for Return of IDPs and Implementation of the Abyei Protocol was concluded, but that agreement was eventually signed by representatives of the NCP and the SPLM. However, in the PCA process, only one of the parties had to be a state, because the dispute was adjudicated, under the PCA's Optional Rules for Arbitrating Disputes between Two Parties of Which Only One is a State (PCA 1993).

40   Land and post-conflict peacebuilding

for Arbitrating Disputes between Two Parties of Which Only One is a State. The PCA arbitral tribunal was to determine whether the ABC had exceeded its mandate—to delimit the area of the nine Ngok Dinka chiefdoms that had been transferred to Kordofan in 1905.[27] If it determined that the ABC did not exceed its mandate, the tribunal should make a determination to that effect and issue an award for the full and immediate implementation of the ABC report. If it determined that the ABC did exceed its mandate, the tribunal should make a declaration to that effect, and should proceed to delimit the area of the nine Ngok Dinka chiefdoms transferred to the North in 1905. The tribunal was to work in accordance with the provisions of the CPA, particularly the Abyei Protocol and Appendix, and the interim constitution—and with other relevant principles of law and practice as the tribunal may determine to be relevant.

The tribunal consisted of five arbitrators.[28] Each party appointed two arbitrators, and these four arbitrators were tasked with appointing a presiding arbitrator. However, none of the five candidates they identified was accepted by both parties, and the PCA secretary-general appointed the presiding arbitrator.[29] The tribunal adhered to a very tight schedule. Memorials were filed on December 18, 2008, and counter-memorials on February 13, 2009, with the rejoinder filed on February 28. Oral hearings took place at The Hague from April 18 to 23, and the tribunal issued its award on July 22, 2009.

The award is a fairly detailed one, spanning more than 270 pages (Salman 2010). It started with a discussion of the geography of Sudan, the history of the Abyei dispute, the peace process, and the instruments it had produced. It suggested three motivations for the original transfer of the nine Ngok Dinka chiefdoms to the North: (1) to pacify the area and end attacks by the Humr (a subgroup of the Misseriya) on the Ngok Dinka, (2) to demonstrate an authoritative presence to the inhabitants of the area, and (3) to bring the feuding tribes under a single administration (PCA 2009).[30]

The parties' arguments were summarized at length, particularly on the question of whether the ABC had exceeded its mandate either procedurally or substantively. The tribunal also discussed the question of whether Abyei was defined

---

[27] That mandate was stated in the Abyei Protocol and reiterated in the Abyei Appendix and the ABC Terms of Reference and Rules of Procedure.

[28] Unlike the International Court of Justice (which is also at The Hague, and is usually referred to as the ICJ), the PCA does not have its own regularly presiding judges. Instead, each party to a case appoints an equal number of arbitrators. Once appointed, those arbitrators together recommend a presiding arbitrator to the two parties.

[29] The GOS appointed Awn Al-Khasawneh and Gerhard Hafner. The SPLM appointed Michael Reisman and Stephen Schwebel. The secretary-general of the PCA appointed Pierre-Marie Dupuy as the presiding arbitrator, because the nominees of the four arbitrators for this position were all rejected by either of the two parties, or by both of them.

[30] The ABC report stated that the reason for the transfer of the nine Ngok Dinka chiefdoms to the North was the Ngok Dinka complaint about the Humr raids (ABC 2005).

The Abyei territorial dispute **41**

in 1905 in a tribal sense or a territorial sense. This was particularly relevant with regard to the ABC inquiry into the Ngok Dinka settlements and grazing rights. The tribunal also discussed the basis on which it should review the ABC analysis and conclusions, distinguishing between the criteria of reasonableness and correctness, and noted that it had to defer to the ABC's interpretation of its mandate as long as that interpretation was reasonable (PCA 2009).[31]

The tribunal basically accepted the ABC's classification of land rights into dominant (permanent), secondary (seasonal), and shared secondary rights. Based on its reading and interpretation of the evidence presented by the two parties, the tribunal reached the following conclusions:

- Northern boundary: The ABC experts did not exceed their mandate in ruling that "the Ngok have a legitimate dominant claim to the territory from the Kordofan–Bahr el Ghazal boundary north to latitude 10°10′ N" (PCA 2009, para. 131.1). However, they did exceed their mandate with regard to the shared secondary rights area between latitudes 10°10′ N and 10°35′ N. The northern boundary of the area of the nine Ngok Dinka chiefdoms transferred to Kordofan in 1905 runs along latitude 10°10′00″ N, from longitude 27°50′00″ E to 29°00′00″ E.
- Southern boundary: The ABC experts did not exceed their mandate in ruling that "the southern boundary shall be the Kordofan–Bahr el Ghazal–Upper Nile boundary as it was defined on 1 January 1956" (PCA 2009, para. 131.3); and the boundaries as established by the ABC were confirmed.[32]
- Eastern boundary: The ABC experts exceeded their mandate in ruling that "the eastern boundary shall extend the line of the Kordofan–Upper Nile boundary at approximately longitude 29°32′15″ E northwards until it meets latitude 10°22′30″ N" (PCA 2009, para. 131.3). The eastern boundary of the area runs in a straight line along longitude 29°00′00″ E, from latitude 10°10′00″ N south to the Kordofan–Upper Nile boundary as it was defined on January 1, 1956.
- Western boundary: The ABC experts exceeded their mandate in ruling that "the western boundary shall be the Kordofan-Darfur boundary as it was defined on 1 January 1956" (PCA 2009, para 131.3). The western boundary runs in a straight line along longitude 27°50′00″ E, from latitude 10°10′00″ N south to the Kordofan-Darfur boundary as it was defined on January 1, 1956, and continuing on the Kordofan-Darfur boundary until it meets the southern boundary.
- Grazing and other traditional rights: The ABC experts did not exceed their mandate in ruling that "the Ngok and Misseriya shall retain their established

---

[31] For further analysis of this issue, see Crook (2009).
[32] There has been no dispute with regard to the southern boundary, since the GOS has taken the position that the triangle falling south of the Bahr el Arab River was the area transferred to Kordofan in 1905.

42 Land and post-conflict peacebuilding

secondary rights to the use of land north and south of this boundary" (PCA 2009, para. 131.5). Furthermore, the arbitral tribunal ruled that "The exercise of established traditional rights within or in the vicinity of the Abyei Area, particularly the right (guaranteed by Section 1.1.3 of the Abyei Protocol) of the Misseriya and other nomadic peoples to graze cattle and move across the Abyei Area (as defined in this Award) remains unaffected" (PCA 2009, para. 770.e.2).

The map of Abyei as defined by the arbitral tribunal is shown in figure 4.

The size of the Abyei area, as delimited by the tribunal award, is about 10,460 square kilometers. This is a considerable reduction from the area set by the ABC report, which was 18,559 square kilometers for the area below 10°22′30″ N, or 25,293 square kilometers for the area below 10°35′ N. This substantial reduction made it easier for the GOS to accept the decision of the tribunal, and indeed to present it as a victory, even though the area was still larger than what the government initially presented. Figure 5 compares the PCA tribunal award map with that of the ABC report.

As a result of the reduction of the Abyei area in the eastern part, some major oil fields, including Heglig and Bamboo, reverted to Northern Sudan, with Defra oil field falling within the Abyei area.[33] On the other hand, the Bahr el Arab River, which is the main river in the area, together with other rivers and tributaries of the Bahr el Arab River, such as Ragaba ez Zarga (or Ngol River), Ragaba umm Biero, and Ragaba el Shaib, all fell largely within the Abyei area as delimited by the tribunal award. The established secondary rights of the Ngok Dinka and Misseriya to the use of land north and south of Abyei were confirmed by the tribunal award. The award also confirmed the exercise of established traditional rights within or in the vicinity of the Abyei area, particularly the right of the Misseriya and other nomadic peoples to graze cattle and move across the Abyei area.[34] Thus, according to the tribunal award, the Ngok Dinka and the

---

[33] The GOS indicated, immediately after the PCA tribunal award was issued, that the government of Southern Sudan would no longer receive any of the revenue from the oil in those fields, now that they were no longer in the Abyei area. The government of Southern Sudan responded that it would still claim those oil fields as part of Southern Sudan when the process of delimiting the complete borders between the North and the South commenced (*Sudan Tribune* 2009c). Oil has not been a concern to either the Misseriya or the Ngok Dinka, as the claims of both of them emphasized land and water. Neither tribe has received any benefits from the Abyei oil, despite the entitlement of each, under the CPA, to 2 percent of its revenues (see note 17).

[34] The tribunal addressed the grazing rights of the Misseriya in case Abyei becomes part of an independent South Sudan. The tribunal stated in this connection that "the jurisprudence of international courts and tribunals as well as international treaty practice lend additional support to the principle that, in the absence of an explicit prohibition to the contrary, the transfer of sovereignty in the context of boundary delimitation should not be construed to extinguish traditional rights to the use of land" (PCA 2009, para. 753).

The Abyei territorial dispute 43

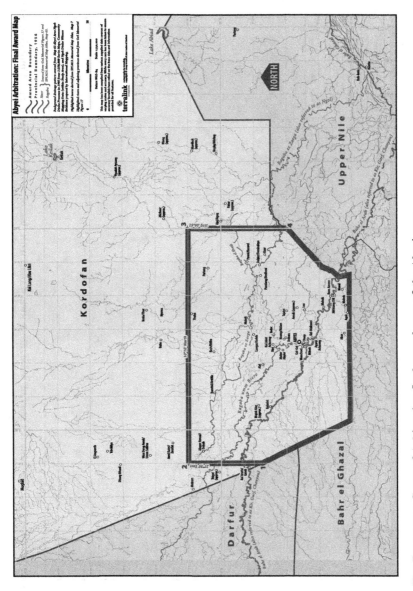

Figure 4. The Permanent Court of Arbitration final award map of the Abyei area
Source: PCA (2009), reprinted with permission from Terralink.

44 Land and post-conflict peacebuilding

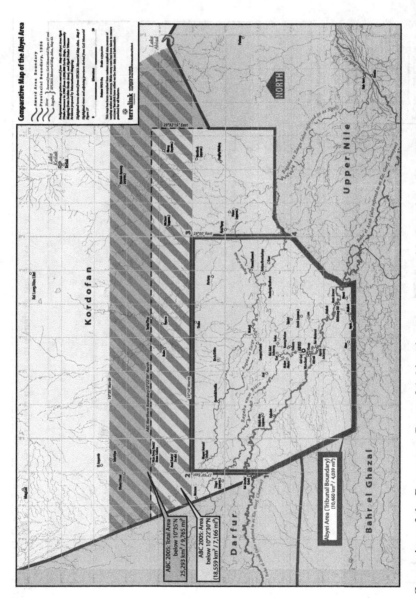

Figure 5. Comparison of the Permanent Court of Arbitration award map with that of the Abyei Boundaries Commission experts map
Source: PCA (2009), reprinted with permission from Terralink.

The Abyei territorial dispute   45

SPLM/A got land and water, the GOS got most of the oil fields in the area,[35] and the Misseriya's grazing rights within and around the Abyei area were confirmed.

In a dissenting opinion, Awn Al-Khasawneh (one of the tribunal members appointed by the GOS) called his colleagues' opinions unpersuasive and self-contradicting, and disagreed with the test of reasonableness. He accused the majority of exceeding its own mandate, and asked who "gave the Experts or the Tribunal the right to reduce the Misseriya to second class citizens in their own land and to create conditions which may deny them access to water" (PCA 2009, Dissenting Opinion, para. 203).

Both the GOS and the SPLM accepted the PCA tribunal award.[36] The United Nations, European Union, United States, and IGAD also welcomed the decision and saw it as a major step toward resolving the Abyei dispute. On the other hand, the leaders of the Misseriya tribe rejected the decision. They claimed that the territory delimited by the PCA tribunal award as the Abyei area gave too much of their own land and villages to the Ngok Dinka, and restricted their rights over the area to grazing rights.[37] They saw the dissenting opinion as reflecting and vindicating their position. The rejection by the Misseriya of the tribunal award presented a major setback to the attempts to resolve the Abyei dispute, and threw the whole process into uncertainty. The rejection took the parties back to July 2005 when the GOS and the Misseriya rejected the ABC report.

THE ABYEI AREA REFERENDUM: WHY IT WAS NOT UNDERTAKEN

Demarcation of the Abyei area was supposed to be the next step following issuance of the PCA tribunal award. However, that did not take place because of the rejection by the Misseriya of the award and their opposition to any demarcation of the area based on that award. A second stalemate developed and lasted until negotiations between the GOS and the SPLM on the Abyei referendum commenced in late 2009. On December 30, 2009, five months after the PCA tribunal award was issued, the National Assembly passed both the Southern Sudan Referendum Act and the Abyei Area Referendum Act.[38]

The Southern Sudan Referendum Act listed a number of issues that need to be resolved by the two parties. These issues include nationality; currency; public service; position of Joint/Integrated Units (JIUs); international agreements and

---

[35]   For discussion of oil in the Abyei area and its quantity and likely depletion dates, see ICG (2007).

[36]   The Ngok Dinka were initially disappointed that the Abyei area was reduced considerably from that delimited by the ABC, but they did not oppose the tribunal award. Indeed, later on they embraced the award and demanded its full and immediate implementation.

[37]   For the views of those leaders, see *Sudan Tribune* (2009a).

[38]   For the major points raised during the discussion of the Abyei Area Referendum Act, and the Misseriya protest against the act, see *Sudan Tribune* (2009b).

46 Land and post-conflict peacebuilding

treaties; debts and assets; oil fields, production, and transport; oil contracts; water resources; and property.[39] These issues are in addition to disputes on a number of border areas between Northern and Southern Sudan. These borders extend for more than 2,000 kilometers, and a joint committee had started working on their demarcation for some time before the Southern Sudan Referendum Act was adopted. However, as with Abyei dispute and the post-referendum issues, not much progress took place on any of the borders issues.[40] Henceforth, the pending issues between the North and the South could be clustered into three separate groups: the issues listed under the Southern Sudan Referendum Act, the border issues, and the Abyei dispute.

The Abyei Area Referendum Act confirmed the boundaries of the Abyei area (as determined and delimited by the PCA tribunal award), notwithstanding the Misseriya rejection of the award. The act also confirmed the date for the Abyei referendum (January 9, 2011, as determined by the Abyei Protocol of the CPA and the interim constitution). It called for an Abyei Area Referendum Commission to be established as a legally and financially independent entity with its head office in Abyei Town, and branch offices where the commission deemed necessary. The act gave the commission wide powers with regard to the conduct of the referendum, including preparing registration forms and determining the number and location of the polling stations and the polling schedule. The commission was to conduct the referendum in collaboration with the Abyei administration, the national government, and the government of Southern Sudan, under international supervision. The act invited the thirteen countries and organizations that had witnessed the signing of the CPA, as well as international, regional, and local nongovernmental organizations, to supervise the Abyei referendum.

The Abyei Area Referendum Act was silent on who are considered as residents of the Abyei area, and thus would be eligible to participate in the referendum. As mentioned earlier, the Abyei Protocol (paragraph 6.1) defined the residents of Abyei as "the Members of the Ngok Dinka community and other Sudanese residing in the area" and stated that the criteria for residence should be worked out by the Abyei Area Referendum Commission, which is yet to be established.

---

[39] See article 67 of the act. In addition to those issues, the article added "any other issues to be agreed upon by the two parties."

[40] On June 21–22, 2010, representatives of the ruling NCP and the SPLM met in Mekelle, Ethiopia, to discuss the post-referendum issues. On June 23 they signed the Mekelle Memorandum of Understanding between the NCP and SPLM on Post-Referendum Issues and Arrangements (Mekelle MOU). The Mekelle MOU stated that negotiations on post-referendum issues would be conducted by a joint negotiating team consisting of six members from each party, to be assisted by a joint technical secretariat. The Mekelle MOU clustered the issues to be negotiated into four categories: (i) citizenship; (ii) security; (iii) financial, economic, and natural resources; and (iv) international treaties and legal issues. However, the pending issues on the Abyei dispute were not discussed or referred to in the MOU. For the complete text of the Mekelle MOU, see www.cmi.no/sudan/doc/?id=1283.

The act did not reiterate the definition of residency, as it did with other provisions of the Abyei Protocol and other parts of the CPA. Perhaps the reason for this was the demand of the Misseriya tribe that they also be mentioned by name in the act as residents of the Abyei area, which was vehemently rejected by the SPLM and the Ngok Dinka. It seems that the compromise reached by the framers of the act was neither to reiterate the Abyei Protocol's definition (which specified the Ngok Dinka) nor to mention the Misseriya by name, but to leave the issue to the Abyei Referendum Commission. This approach must also be seen as a way of allaying the disappointment of the Misseriya over the incorporation by the act of the boundaries of the Abyei area as established and delimited by the tribunal award.

However, the adoption of the Abyei Area Referendum Act did not pave the way for holding the referendum in Abyei on January 9, 2011, as envisaged under the Abyei Protocol. The Misseriya, with support from the GOS, insisted that they are residents of the Abyei area, and that they have lived there long before the Ngok Dinka moved to the area. They contended that they are covered by the Abyei Protocol under "other Sudanese residing in the area." Thus, they believe, they have the right to participate in the referendum. They also raised the point that they are entitled under the Abyei Protocol to 2 percent of the net oil revenue from the Abyei area, on par with the Ngok Dinka (see note 17). This, in their view, is a clear recognition of their equal rights with the Ngok Dinka over the Abyei area, and that such equality should extend to participating in the referendum on equal footing with the Ngok Dinka.

The SPLM and the Ngok Dinka rejected this demand. They contend that the Misseriya are not specifically mentioned, like the Ngok Dinka, as residents of the area under the Abyei Protocol, and accordingly are not eligible to participate in the referendum. Moreover, they claim that the definition of the Abyei area under the Abyei Protocol makes it clear that the area is exclusively a Ngok Dinka area. They also interpret the PCA tribunal award which confirmed the Misseriya's grazing rights as an indication that the Misseriya are not residents of the Abyei area but are only rights holders.

This issue has turned out to be the crux of the Abyei dispute, overshadowing the original issue of the size and borders of the Abyei area. The extension of the Abyei area by both the ABC report, and later by the tribunal award, beyond the triangle south of the Bahr el Arab River (as claimed by the GOS and agreed to by the Misseriya) must have prompted the claim of the Misseriya that they are residents of the expanded Abyei area. As indicated earlier, the Misseriya claimed, and complained, that the tribunal award gave too much of their own land and villages to the Ngok Dinka. Furthermore, because of this basic difference, the Abyei Referendum Commission has not been established. Differences persisted on who should head the commission, as each party insisted on its chairmanship.[41]

---

[41] The SPLM insisted that since the Southern Sudan Referendum Commission was headed by a Northerner (Southern Referendum Commission 2011), then the Abyei Area Referendum Commission should be headed by a Southerner.

48   Land and post-conflict peacebuilding

Moreover, the boundaries of the Abyei area have not yet been demarcated because of the rejection by the Misseriya of the PCA tribunal award.

Various attempts to reach a compromise on the residency issue took place in 2010. Those attempts included interventions by the U.S special envoy,[42] as well as the African Union.[43] However, as 2010 was coming to a close, it became clear that the Abyei referendum would not take place as scheduled, because the issues in dispute were far from being resolved. As indicated earlier, on January 9, 2011, and as envisaged under the Machakos Protocol of the CPA, the Southern Sudan referendum took place, and the people of Southern Sudan voted overwhelmingly to secede from Sudan, complicating further the process for resolving the Abyei dispute. The Abyei referendum that was supposed to take place simultaneously with the Southern Sudan referendum, as stipulated under the CPA, simply slipped away.[44]

AFTERMATH OF THE FAILURE TO UNDERTAKE THE ABYEI AREA REFERENDUM

As the people of Southern Sudan started voting on January 9, 2011,[45] a series of clashes took place in the Abyei area between the Misseriya and the Ngok Dinka. It was reported that a number of people from the two tribes, as well as a number of soldiers, were killed during the three days of clashes. Ironically, the clashes

---

[42] Representatives of the two parties, with mediation by the U.S. special envoy to the Sudan, Scott Gration, met in Addis Ababa in October 2010 to discuss pending issues on the peace process, including Abyei. On October 12, after nine days of intensive discussion, the parties announced that they had not been able to agree on the eligibility criteria for the voters in the Abyei referendum (*Sudan Tribune* 2010). Although the parties agreed to meet again in Addis Ababa in late October, that meeting was postponed to give the mediators more time to try to reach a compromise.

[43] The African Union established a special committee named the African Union High-Level Implementation Panel on Sudan (AUHIP), headed by Thabo Mbeki, the former president of South Africa. The AUHIP is mediating the pending issues between the North and the South, including the Abyei dispute (AUHIP 2010).

[44] Questions were raised as to why the SPLM did not insist on the Abyei referendum taking place simultaneously with the Southern Sudan referendum as stipulated under the CPA and the interim constitution. The main reason for this, in the author's view, was that the SPLM was concentrating on the Southern Sudan referendum and did not want anything to jeopardize or detract from the carrying out of that referendum on January 9, 2011, as planned.

[45] The residents of the Abyei area did not participate in the Southern Sudan referendum because Abyei was placed under the presidency, and as such was not part of Southern Sudan. Two questions arose in this connection: (i) Under the Abyei Protocol, the residents of Abyei area would be citizens of both Kordofan and Bahr el Ghazal (see note 16). If they are citizens of the southern state of Bahr el Ghazal (now Northern Bahr el Ghazal), would they not be entitled to vote? (ii) Would the Ngok Dinka of the Abyei area, being Southerners, not be entitled to vote in the referendum on par with the other Southerners residing in Northern Sudan? Those questions were not raised, and it seemed the issue was sidelined by the other developments in the Abyei area.

led the leaders of the two tribes to conclude an agreement on January 13, 2011, independently of the GOS and the SPLM. The agreement dealt with compensation payments to the families of those killed during the three days of clashes. It also dealt with allowing the Misseriya to move in the Abyei area with their cattle to get access to water and grazing (*Sudan Tribune* 2011a). This agreement was endorsed by the GOS and the SPLM through another agreement concluded on January 17, 2011. The two parties also agreed to assign to the JIUs the responsibility for law and order in the Abyei area. The two agreements were concluded at the town of Kadugli, capital of the state of Southern Kordofan, and referred to as the Kadugli agreements. The Kadugli agreements did not, however, go beyond these issues, and unfortunately they did not last for long. Clashes erupted again a few days later and continued intermittently during February and March, resulting in a number of deaths and forcing the United Nations to beef up its presence in the Abyei area in an attempt to keep peace there (*Sudan Tribune* 2011b). Each side blamed the other for the collapse of the Kadugli agreements.

The deterioration of the situation in Abyei prompted the President of the United Nations Security Council (UNSC) to issue a statement on March 3, 2011, on the situation in Abyei. The statement expressed UNSC's deep concern over the fighting, condemned the use of violence, and "underlined the urgent need for a political agreement on the status of Abyei in the framework of ongoing discussions between the CPA parties" (UN 2011a). This statement was, no doubt, another milestone in the internationalization of the Abyei dispute.

The steady deterioration of the situation in Abyei and the continuation of the clashes and deaths on both sides, following the collapse of the Kadugli agreements, and perhaps the statement by the President of the UNSC, prompted the GOS and the SPLM to sign, on March 4, 2011, another agreement to contain the situation (Abyei Agreement).[46] The agreement called for the full and immediate implementation of the Kadugli agreements, and established a mechanism consisting of an equal number of representatives from each party for overseeing implementation of the agreements. It instructed an immediate withdrawal of the forces of the two parties from the Abyei area, and their replacement by soldiers from the JIUs. The agreement gave the United Nations unhindered access to all of the Abyei area within the PCA boundaries, "consistent with the CPA," and requested the United Nations to facilitate implementation of the two earlier Kadugli agreements. This agreement resembled in a number of aspects the Road Map for Return of IDPs and Implementation of the Abyei Protocol, which was concluded on June 8, 2008, after the outbreak of fighting in the Abyei area early that month. The history of the Abyei dispute resolution process keeps repeating

---

[46] The agreement was signed by two high level politicians—the presidential adviser for security affairs signed on behalf of the GOS, while the minister of the armed forces of the government of Southern Sudan signed for the SPLM. For the agreement, see http://unmis.unmissions.org/Portals/UNMIS/2011Docs/Abyei%20Agreement%204%20 March%202011_En.pdf.

50 Land and post-conflict peacebuilding

itself, albeit without achieving its intended objective. This agreement was considered a continuation of the earlier two Kadugli agreements (of January 13 and 17, 2011), and the three agreements were henceforth referred to collectively as the Kadugli agreements.

Subsequent to the failure of the two parties to undertake the referendum in the Abyei area, some ideas for resolution of the Abyei dispute started being discussed publicly. One of those ideas was giving the Misseriya who reside in the Abyei area for more than six months a year the right to participate in the referendum. Another idea was to establish Abyei as an integration area with special ties to both states of Sudan and South Sudan. A third proposal floated was to divide the Abyei area, as delimited by the PCA tribunal award, between the Misseriya and the Ngok Dinka (and hence between Sudan and the new state of South Sudan). Another idea raised was referring the dispute over whether the Misseriya are entitled to vote for international adjudication or arbitration, or to have the dispute referred to and decided by the traditional leaders of the two tribes. The possibility of formally extending the period for resolving the pending issues between the North and the South, including the Abyei dispute, by six to twelve months beyond the interim period (which would end on July 8, 2011), was also raised. However, no agreement was reached on any of these proposals, as none of them was acceptable to both parties. Each party stuck firmly to its position as each continued to believe that its case is ironclad.[47]

However, the brief calm that followed the Kadugli agreements did not last long. The cycle of ups and downs continued in the Abyei area. On March 11, 2011, one week after the Abyei Agreement was concluded, the government of Southern Sudan issued a strongly worded statement accusing the GOS of trying to overthrow the government of Southern Sudan by arming and supplying militias opposed to it, accusations that were denied by the GOS. The government of Southern Sudan indicated that it would complain to the UNSC and suspended talks and contacts with the GOS on all the pending issues, including Abyei (*Sudan Tribune* 2011c).[48] It should be added in this connection that the security situation in a number of areas in Southern Sudan had been steadily deteriorating in the latter years of the interim period. Military clashes with armed militias, intertribal fights, and food shortages have been regularly reported since early 2009 (UNHCR 2009; Schomerus and Allen 2010). Suspension of talks on all pending issues between the two parties was indeed a major reversal of the attempts and hopes to find a resolution to those issues, particularly the Abyei dispute. Nonetheless, the

---

[47] The SPLM asked that the Abyei area be transferred to Southern Sudan through a presidential decree since the referendum did not take place. This was of course rejected by the GOS and the Misseriya.

[48] The UNSC invited both the secretary general of the SPLM as well as the representative of the GOS to its 6499th meeting held on March 21, 2011 to discuss the "Reports of the Secretary-General on the Sudan." However, no decisions were made on the complaint of the SPLM (UNSC 2011a).

mediation efforts of the African Union High-Level Implementation Panel on Sudan (AUHIP) and the United States continued,[49] and the presidency held a few meetings. As per the instructions of the presidency, the Joint Defense Council ceased to exist as of April 10, 2011, and the mandate of the JIUs established under the Agreement on Security Arrangements of September 23, 2003, also ended on that date. However, a battalion of the JIUs was kept at Abyei, as well as in the oil fields (*Sudan Vision* 2011), but it did not seem effective in keeping peace and order.[50]

By mid-April 2011, there was a general resignation among all the parties and the mediators that the Abyei dispute, and perhaps most other pending issues between the North and the South, would most likely remain without resolution by the end of the interim period and the emergence of South Sudan as an independent state on July 9, 2011. Indeed, the United Nations itself seemed to think that this would be the likely situation on that date. Briefing the UNSC on April 20, 2011, the Assistant Secretary-General for Peacekeeping Operations of the UN voiced his concern over the slow progress on several outstanding issues from the 2005 CPA, including the Abyei dispute. He stated that: "Due to . . . disagreements, there is a possibility that the residual CPA issues will not be solved and/ or that the post-referendum negotiations will not be concluded by 9 July [the expected date when Southern Sudan becomes independent]" (UN 2011a).

However, one other major complication took place toward the end of April. On April 22, 2011, the government of Southern Sudan issued a draft of the Transitional Constitution of the Republic of South Sudan.[51] Article 1(2) of the draft defined the territory of the Republic of South Sudan to comprise "all lands and air space that constituted the three former Southern Provinces of Bahr el Ghazal, Equatoria and Upper Nile in their boundaries as they stood on January 1, 1956, and the Abyei Area, the territory of the nine Ngok Dinka chiefdoms transferred from Bahr el Ghazal Province to Kordofan Province in 1905 as defined by the Abyei Arbitration Tribunal Award of July 2009." The president of Sudan responded by claiming that the Abyei area belongs to North Sudan, and warned that the North would revoke its recognition of South Sudan's independence if the latter claimed ownership of Abyei in its constitution (*Sudan Tribune* 2011d).

---

[49] On March 31, 2011, the United States announced the appointment of Ambassador Princeton Lyman as its new special envoy, replacing Scott Gration. Ambassador Lyman and Thabo Mbeki both visited Sudan in early April.

[50] Article 4 of the Agreement on Security Arrangements, which is set out in chapter VI of the CPA, states that "there shall be formed Joint/Integrated Units consisting of equal number from the Sudanese Armed Forces (SAF) and the Sudan People's Liberation Army (SPLA) during the Interim Period. The Joint/Integrated Units shall constitute a nucleus of a post referendum army of Sudan, should the result of the referendum confirm unity, otherwise they would be dissolved and component parts integrated into their respective forces." The decision of the presidency to keep a battalion at Abyei after dissolution of the JIUs is a clear amendment of the agreement.

[51] For the complete text of the Transitional Constitution of the Republic of Southern Sudan, see www.sudantribune.com/IMG/pdf/The_Draft_Transitional_Constitution_of _the_ROSS2-2.pdf.

52   Land and post-conflict peacebuilding

Those developments showed a clear hardening of the positions of the parties over Abyei, and a further deterioration of the relationship between them.

On May 2, 2011, elections were held in the state of Southern Kordofan, one year after the general elections in Sudan, because of disputes over voter registration in the state. As indicated earlier, the Southern Kordofan and Blue Nile states are geographically part of Northern Sudan but identify culturally more with Southern Sudan, and there is a separate protocol calling for popular consultations in these two states. Moreover, the Abyei Protocol stated that the residents of Abyei area would be citizens of both Kordofan and Bahr el Ghazal. The SPLM and the NCP, in addition to other political parties, filed candidates for gubernatorial and legislative elections. However, the elections process was marred by disputes between the NCP and SPLM, with the latter claiming major irregularities in the voting process, and declaring in advance their rejection of the results. On May 15, 2011, the Elections Commission announced the NCP candidate as the winner of the gubernatorial elections, and the SPLM asserted its nonrecognition of the results.[52] This situation added more complications to the already tense situation in Abyei, and the overall relations between the North and the South.

Just as the aftermath of the elections was being debated, the GOS announced that on May 20, 2011, forces of the SPLA ambushed and killed twenty-two soldiers of the SAF, who were part of the JIUs, as they were moving out of Abyei Town. The government also stated that many other soldiers were wounded and scores were missing. The government claimed that the assailed troops were moving out of the Abyei area in implementation of the Kadugli agreements and were being escorted by the UN peacekeeping force (UNMIS) in the area. At the beginning, the SPLA/M denied that they carried out the attack and asked for an investigation; UNMIS said that the attack was carried out by unknown assailants. However, the government of Southern Sudan later apologized to the UN for the attack. The GOS criticized the UN for failure to assign blame to Southern Sudan for the attack. The following day the SAF launched heavy ground and air assaults on the positions of the SPLA in the Abyei area, and on May 21, it announced that it had taken over Abyei Town and the surrounding areas. Subsequently, and on that same day, the president of Sudan issued two decrees dissolving the Abyei Administrative Council and dismissing its head (a Southerner) and his deputy (a Northerner), as well as the directors of the five departments that administered the area. (This was the GOS/SPLM joint body established by the presidency under the Abyei Protocol.) The government of Southern Sudan denounced the takeover of the area and the dissolution of the administration of Abyei, and stated that this was done without consultations with them and was a gross violation of the CPA.

The takeover of Abyei and the declaration by the GOS that Abyei is a Northern territory meant that the GOS had decided to impose its earlier claim that the area that was transferred to the North from the South was only the triangle

---

[52]   The Elections Commission also announced that the NCP won twenty-two seats in the parliamentary elections, while the SPLM won only ten seats.

The Abyei territorial dispute 53

south of the Bahr el Arab River (see figure 2). The GOS also reasserted its claim that this line is the 1956 North-South border, which is sacrosanct. As a result of the fighting and widespread looting in Abyei Town and the surrounding area, a large number of Ngok Dinka refugees crossed the Bahr el Arab River southward. The UN estimated their numbers as being in the tens of thousands (UN 2011b).

Meanwhile, the fifteen members of the UNSC began a visit to Sudan. On May 20, 2011, on their way to Sudan, they met in Addis Ababa with the African Union Peace and Security Council. The members of the UNSC had planned to travel thereafter to Khartoum, Juba, and Abyei, but an announcement was issued cancelling the visit to Abyei following its takeover by the government forces. The members of the UNSC arrived in Khartoum on May 21, 2011, and issued a statement on May 22, 2011. The statement indicated that the takeover of Abyei by the GOS constituted a serious violation of the CPA and threatened to undermine the mutual commitment of the parties to avoid a return to conflict and resolve all remaining CPA and post-CPA issues peacefully. The statement called on the Sudanese government to withdraw its forces from Abyei and to halt its military operations there. It also denounced the attack by the SPLA on the SAF units that triggered the retaliation by the Northern government, and the attack against the UNMIS forces escorting the SAF soldiers on May 19, 2011. The statement deplored the unilateral decision by the president of Sudan to dissolve the Abyei Administrative Council and called for its reinstatement. It urged both parties to restore calm, uphold the CPA, and recommit to a negotiated political settlement of the future status of Abyei, including under the auspices of the African Union High-Level Implementation Panel (AUHIP). In parallel to the statement of the UNSC, the UN Secretary-General Ban Ki-moon strongly condemned the continuing violence in the Abyei area (UN 2011c). While in Khartoum, the UNSC members were not met by the vice president of Sudan or the minister of foreign affairs, as was planned. The members visited Juba thereafter, and travelled to the border areas near Abyei to assess the situation and needs of the Ngok Dinka who fled Abyei.

Similarly, the governments of the United States, United Kingdom, and France denounced the killing of the Northern Sudanese soldiers and the takeover of Abyei by the SAF, called the takeover disproportionate, and demanded an immediate withdrawal of the Sudanese government forces from Abyei and reinstatement of the Abyei administration.

On May 26, 2011, one week after the takeover of Abyei, the Sudanese army declared the end to military operations in Abyei, and called on the Ngok Dinka, Misseriya, and other tribes to return to Abyei Town. The Misseriya welcomed the takeover of Abyei, and it was reported that they had indeed started moving into the area. The GOS announced the appointment of an army officer to be in charge of Abyei. It also announced that the mandate of the UNMIS would end on July 8, 2011, as originally scheduled, and that it would not be renewed, and asked for the withdrawal of all military and civilian personnel of UNMIS from Northern Sudan by that date. Meanwhile, the government of Southern Sudan indicated that a new and revamped role for the UN military and civilian personnel of

54   Land and post-conflict peacebuilding

UNMIS would be worked out and agreed upon with the United Nations for the new state of South Sudan.

On May 28, 2011, the vice president of the government of Southern Sudan, Riek Machar, arrived in Khartoum and held a meeting on May 30 with the vice president of Sudan, Ali Osman Taha. The meeting concentrated on the recent developments in Abyei, but also dealt with the other pending issues. However, the meeting did not result in an agreement on how to deal with the situation; instead a decision was made to set up a joint committee that would look into ways to defuse the crisis (*Sudan Tribune* 2011e).[53]

The government of Southern Sudan wanted to contain the situation so that it would secede on July 9, 2011, without the threat of conflict with the North overshadowing the festivities of independence. However, it became clear, as of the end of May 2011, that the Abyei dispute as well as all the pending issues would await the birth of the new state of South Sudan on July 9, 2011, and would have to be dealt with by two sovereign states. This would no doubt make the negotiations more complex and intricate, as negotiations between two states are usually more difficult than negotiations between geographical units within one state.

No doubt, the ambush and killing of SAF soldiers by the SPLA and the takeover of the Abyei area by the GOS troops marked a major reversal to the attempts to resolve the Abyei dispute peacefully. Those developments showed clearly the repercussions and impact of the Abyei dispute on the overall relationship between the North and the South, and between the Misseriya and the Ngok Dinka, as well as on the attempts to resolve the other pending issues. Indeed, the Abyei dispute is now the thorniest issue between the two parties and will clearly be the maker or breaker of the whole peace process. It is quite ironic, and indeed very sad, that the ambush and killing of the Northern Sudanese soldiers and the takeover of Abyei by the Sudanese government took place almost exactly seven years after the Abyei Protocol was concluded by the GOS and the SPLM/A on May 26, 2004, aiming to resolve the Abyei dispute.

CONCLUSION

The unique nature and complexity of the Abyei dispute are quite evident. It is a dispute about both the boundaries and size of the area as well as to whom it

---

[53] The *Sudan Tribune* also reported that "Western officials have revealed to the *New York Times* that there are behind the scenes efforts to bring in Ethiopian peacekeepers into Abyei to act as buffer between the North and South. 'We need something quick for Abyei, and the Ethiopians are it,' a Western diplomat said Monday. Under the proposal, the northern army would withdraw from the Abyei area in the next few weeks, and in their place would come thousands of Ethiopian soldiers until a permanent solution could be reached" (*Sudan Tribune* 2011e). However, no mention of this proposal was made by either party. Ethiopia indicated that it would be willing to send troops and play a role in resolution of the Abyei dispute, but only if asked explicitly by both parties.

belongs. Because of the duality of the issues involved, the parties agreed on a two-stage resolution process, namely a quasi-judicial process for determining the boundaries and size of the area, to be followed by a political process, the referendum, which would decide which part of the country the area would belong. However, the first stage of the process agreed upon for delimiting and demarcating the area (the ABC report) turned into a source of dispute and resulted in adjudication before the PCA. The decision of the PCA tribunal was supposed to bring to an end the first stage of the dispute: the Abyei area had been delimited and was awaiting demarcation. That did not happen because of substantial opposition by the Misseriya. The second stage was supposed to be the referendum, scheduled for January 9, 2011, in which the residents of the Abyei area were to decide which part of the country—the North or the South—the area would become part of. That did not happen either because of disagreement over who the residents are of the Abyei area. Accordingly, seven years after the Abyei Protocol was signed, the Abyei dispute has eluded all attempts and hopes for its resolution.

Completion of the first stage took more than five years, beginning with the signing of the Abyei Protocol in May 2004. It required the conclusion of a large number of agreements to clarify and elaborate on the provisions of the Abyei Protocol, including the more wide-ranging CPA, signed in January 2005; the Understandings on the Abyei Boundaries Commission (the Abyei Annex or Appendix) of December 2004; and the Implementation Modalities of the Protocol on the Resolution of the Abyei Conflict, signed in December 2004. Following the signing of the CPA on January 9, 2005, a number of other agreements were also concluded to clarify and elaborate the process for resolving the dispute, including the Text of the Terms of Reference for the Abyei Boundaries Commission (March 2005) and the Rules of Procedure for the Abyei Boundaries Commission (April 2005). All those agreements did not lead to resolution of the dispute. More agreements were needed to move the process forward, including the Road Map for Return of IDPs and Implementation of the Abyei Protocol (June 2008), which was concluded after the fighting that led to the devastation of Abyei Town; the Memorandum of Understanding on the Abyei Arbitration (June 2008); and the Arbitration Agreement on Delimiting the Abyei Area (July 2008). The Abyei Area Referendum Act adopted on December 30, 2009, should also be considered an agreement as it was only adopted by the National Assembly after an agreement on its details was reached by the NCP and SPLM.[54] Mention should also be made of the Kadugli agreements of January 13 and 17, 2011, as well as the

---

[54] The speaker of the National Assembly of Sudan declared the membership of those elected from constituencies within Southern Sudan for the National Assembly as having lapsed on March 31, 2011, as a result of the decision of Southern Sudan to secede from Sudan. The members of the assembly from Southern Sudan argued that their membership would only lapse at the end of the interim period on July 8, 2011. However, they reluctantly agreed to leave the assembly. This had no doubt added to the acrimonious atmosphere between the two parties.

56 Land and post-conflict peacebuilding

Abyei Agreement of March 4, 2011. As a result, the Abyei dispute, no doubt, has one of the largest number of agreements aimed at its resolution.

The resolution process agreed by the two parties was itself unusual and required substantial international intervention at three levels. The U.S. special envoy to Sudan broke the deadlock over the definition of the Abyei area, and basically drafted the Abyei Protocol, which the two parties adopted in May 2004. The ABC experts were appointed by the United States, United Kingdom, and IGAD, and included an American, a Briton, and three Africans. Rejection of the ABC report by the GOS and the Misseriya in 2005 led to adjudication before the PCA in 2009. Indeed, the Abyei dispute is the first internal territorial dispute to be adjudicated before, and decided on by, an international tribunal. Mention should also be made of the mediation efforts of the U.S special envoys to Sudan as well as the AUHIP. Although the ABC report was rejected by the GOS, that report made it easier for the government to accept the PCA tribunal award, and even to portray it as a victory, because it decreased the Abyei area delimited by the ABC by almost half. However, the Misseriya rejection of the tribunal award, because of their claim that the award took away large areas of their territory and added it to the Abyei area, threw the whole process into uncertainty. As a result, demarcation of the area has not yet taken place.

Consequently, the second stage of the dispute resolution process, the referendum, did not take place as envisaged, as the process continued to be fraught with disagreements. Although the Abyei Area Referendum Act was adopted by the National Assembly in December 2009, the issue of who has the right to participate in the referendum was left unresolved, with the Misseriya demanding the right to participate, a demand the Ngok Dinka and SPLM vehemently reject. Indeed, the question of whether the members of the Misseriya tribe are residents of the Abyei area, and thus are entitled to vote in the Abyei referendum, has become the crux of the dispute, and has overshadowed the original main issue of the dispute of defining, delimiting, and demarcating the Abyei area. Henceforth, the dispute has become more about who has the right to participate in the referendum than about the size and boundaries of the Abyei area.

The complexity of the Abyei dispute stems from the multiplicity of the parties, claims, and issues. As stated throughout this chapter, the dispute involved not only the GOS and the SPLM, but also the Misseriya and the Ngok Dinka tribes. The claims extend beyond land to include oil and water resources. Oil remained the main contentious issue between the North and the South,[55] while water and grazing rights are the focal points of the dispute for the Misseriya. Indeed, the Abyei dispute shows clearly the centrality of water resources in post-conflict

---

[55] It is estimated that 75 percent of the proven oil resources in Sudan would fall within South Sudan following its decision to secede. On the other hand, the entire oil infrastructure of pipelines, refineries, ports, port facilities, and human resources are in the North. Thus, it is argued that this situation may provide incentives for the two parties to look for solutions to the pending issues and existing disputes, including Abyei.

The Abyei territorial dispute 57

situations (Salman 2011, 2013). The issues have gradually changed during the last six years from delimiting and demarcating the Abyei area to who is entitled to participate in the referendum. Because of these complexities, the interim period during which the Abyei dispute was supposed to have been resolved witnessed, instead, a widening gap in and the hardening of positions. The decision of the Southern Sudanese to secede from Sudan has exacerbated the already existing complications, because negotiations between two states are likely to be more difficult than negotiations between units within one state. Moreover, and as discussed earlier, the Southern Sudan Referendum Act of 2009 listed ten issues that need to be discussed and resolved by the two parties. All of those issues remained without a resolution when Southern Sudan voted overwhelmingly for secession, more than a year after the act was adopted; and all remained unresolved by the end of May 2011. Those issues are in addition to some serious border issues which remain disputed by the two parties. Thus, by the end of May 2011, the two parties had three clusters of complex issues that await resolution: the Abyei dispute, the borders, and the issues listed in the Southern Sudan Referendum Act.

Of all the ideas put forth to resolve the Abyei dispute, as discussed in the previous section of this chapter, the proposal to take the dispute back to the traditional leaders of both tribes seems, in the author's view, to be the one with the best chance of providing a resolution to the dispute. The Misseriya and the Ngok Dinka lived in peace for a long time prior to the eruption of the civil war in 1955. Differences between members of the two communities were resolved by their leaders on the basis of the traditions and customs of the two tribes. Those leaders know better than anyone else (the GOS and the government of South Sudan included) the boundaries and rights of each community, and the timing and manner in which such rights are exercised. Indeed, the dispute should have been placed, from the very beginning of the process, in the hands of the traditional leaders and should not have been dealt with by the politicians and international experts and entities. A resolution of the dispute by the leaders of the two tribes is more likely to be acceptable to the members of the two tribes, and accordingly should be more implementable and sustainable than a resolution by the two governments or by a third party.

It may be argued that it may be too late to refer the dispute to the leaders of the two communities because the events in Abyei since 2005 have resulted in an acrimonious environment and have widened the gap between the members of the two tribes. It may also be argued that the decisions of the ABC and PCA, and the takeover of the area by the GOS on May 20, 2011, may harden the position of the SPLM and the Ngok Dinka. This all may be true. Yet, resorting to the leaders of the two communities remains, in this author's view, the only viable, or perhaps even possible, option. The Kadugli agreements, despite their collapse, indicate the willingness of the parties to discuss the dispute, and their ability to reach agreements on some of its aspects.

The seeds of the Abyei dispute were sown by an act intended to achieve administrative convenience and expediency—bringing two feuding tribes under

58   Land and post-conflict peacebuilding

one jurisdiction by transferring a Southern Sudan area to the North where it could be more easily governed by the Anglo-Egyptian colonial administration. That 1905 decision by mid-level provincial administrators mushroomed, a century later, into a national dispute, posing a major and serious threat to the entire relations between Northern and Southern Sudan, as well as between the Misseriya and the Ngok Dinka, and prompting major international interventions which had limitations. Now the Abyei dispute poses a major threat to the relations between Sudan and the new state of South Sudan, particularly after the developments since May 19, 2011. Clearly, some of the worst problems can result from some of the best intentions.

The opening paragraph of the Abyei Protocol stated that "Abyei is a bridge between the north and the south, linking the people of Sudan." The Road Map for Return of IDPs and Implementation of the Abyei Protocol called on the presidency to "work at making Abyei a model for national reconciliation and peace building" (Road Map of Abyei Protocol 2008, para. 3.8). No doubt, these were lofty aspirations when the CPA was being negotiated and finalized, and during the early years of the interim period. Regrettably, Abyei is currently the thorniest issue between Sudan and the new state of South Sudan. It is now quite apparent that the relations between the two states will depend heavily on a resolution of the Abyei dispute in a manner that is acceptable not only to the GOS and the government of South Sudan, but also to the Misseriya and the Ngok Dinka tribes. Whether that is still achievable seems as remote as ever.

EPILOGUE

The developments discussed and analyzed in this chapter were current through May 31, 2011. From that time through July 10, 2011, three major developments took place in the Sudan North-South relations that will affect the Abyei dispute.

The first and most important development was, as expected, the formal secession of South Sudan and its emergence as an independent state on July 9, 2011. On that date South Sudan became the 193rd member of the global family of nations, and the 54th African state. As a result, all the pending issues between North and South Sudan, including any negotiations and agreements on Abyei, would henceforth be between two sovereign nations.

The second development was the rapid deterioration of the situation in the state of Southern Kordofan following the announcement of the results of the May 2011 elections. As indicated earlier, the NCP gubernatorial candidate was declared the winner over the SPLM candidate. On June 5, 2011, fighting erupted and escalated in the following weeks between GOS forces and the SPLA. The fighting forced thousands to flee the state capital Kadugli and surrounding areas, and sparked an international concern over the humanitarian situation there and the overall North-South relations. The UN suspended its operations and evacuated most of its staff from the state. As indicated earlier, a separate protocol of the CPA dealt with the states of Southern Kordofan and Blue Nile, calling for popular consultations there. Moreover, the Abyei area was administered as part

The Abyei territorial dispute 59

of Kordofan before the CPA was concluded, and Abyei residents were considered citizens of both Kordofan and Bahr el Ghazal states.

The third major development took place on June 20, 2011, while the fighting was going on in the state of Southern Kordofan. On that day, the GOS and the SPLM signed in Addis Ababa, Ethiopia, an agreement on Temporary Arrangements for the Administration and Security of the Abyei Area (Abyei Addis Ababa Agreement).[56] The agreement, which was brokered by the AUHIP and other international mediators, was also signed by Thabo Mbeki, for the AUHIP, as a witness. The preamble of the agreement (referred to as the introduction) confirmed (1) the boundaries of the Abyei area as defined by the PCA tribunal award, and (2) the provisions of the Abyei Protocol as modified by the agreement. It also confirmed the 1956 borders between the North and the South, unless changed as a result of the outcome of the referendum foreseen in the Abyei Protocol, or other decision of the parties on the final status of Abyei.

The agreement mandated the redeployment of both the SAF and the SPLA from the Abyei area, immediately "consequent on" the deployment of an Interim Security Force for Abyei (ISFA) which shall consist of one armored brigade of Ethiopian troops. Hence, with the exception of the ISFA, the agreement declared the Abyei area as demilitarized. The mandate of the ISFA included monitoring and verification; protection of monitoring teams; security within the Abyei area; and protection of the borders of the Abyei area from incursions by unauthorized elements. The mandate also included support and capacity building to the Abyei police service; facilitation and protection of humanitarian assistance; and protection of civilians under imminent threat. A committee consisting of the GOS, SPLM, and the UN was assigned the task of drafting the detailed mandate of the ISFA which would be submitted to the UNSC. The GOS and the SPLM would request the UNSC to approve the deployment, mandate, and the financing of the ISFA, with the understanding that the mandate shall not be changed without the agreement of the GOS, the SPLM, and the Government of Ethiopia. The force commander of the ISFA shall report to the UN. The annex to the agreement established a timetable for the deployment of the ISFA, with the day of the authorization by the UNSC as the D-day, and with the deployment of the main body of the ISFA by the ninth day thereafter, and the handover of responsibilities between the tenth and thirteenth day from the D-day.

A Joint Military Observer Committee (JMOC) consisting of an equal number of observers from both parties, to be stationed at Abyei, is also established under the agreement. The force commander of the ISFA shall chair the JMOC which shall liaise with the ISFA in carrying out its functions. The JMOC shall submit its reports to the Abyei Joint Oversight Committee (AJOC) discussed below.

---

[56] The full name of the agreement is the Agreement between the Government of the Republic of Sudan and the Sudan People's Liberation Movement on Temporary Arrangements for the Administration and Security of the Abyei Area. For the text of the agreement, see www.sudantribune.com/IMG/pdf/Abyei_Agreement_20110620.pdf.

60   Land and post-conflict peacebuilding

The agreement established the Abyei Area Administration, which consists of a chief administrator, his deputy, and five heads of department (the executive council). The chief administrator shall be a nominee of the SPLM agreed by the GOS, while his deputy shall be a nominee of the GOS agreed by the SPLM. Of the five heads of department, three shall be nominees of the SPLM, and two of the GOS. The decision of the executive council shall be taken by consensus. The local council (a legislative body) shall continue to consist of twenty members as indicated in the Abyei Protocol, with the chairmanship resting with the GOS. This was, more or less, the same administrative structure that existed before the GOS forces overtook Abyei on May 21, 2011, and dissolved the executive council and the local council.

In addition, the agreement established the AJOC, which consists of four members, with each party appointing two members. The AJOC would be chaired jointly by two members, one from each party. The African Union Commission chairperson shall appoint a nonvoting member, while the ISFA commander shall attend the AJOC meetings as a nonvoting member when security matters are discussed. On behalf of the president of Sudan and the president of South Sudan, the AJOC shall exercise political and administrative oversight over the executive council, and shall deal with any matter in case of a deadlock in the executive council. The budget of the Abyei area is prepared by the executive council and approved by the local council, and shall be financed jointly by the GOS and government of South Sudan (GOSS).

The agreement called for the return of the former residents of Abyei to their former places of residence. It also required the parties to ensure that humanitarian assistance reaches those in need, and to facilitate the work of the UN and other humanitarian agencies. The parties shall make a joint appeal for assistance for the return and rehabilitation of those displaced or affected by the conflict. Under the subtitle "Pastoralist Migration," the agreement confirmed the right of the pastoral nomads to enjoy rights of migration and access to pasture and water in accordance with traditional migration routes in the Abyei area, and consistent with the Abyei Protocol. The Abyei Police Service (APS) shall be established, with the AJOC determining its size and composition. A special unit of the APS shall deal with the issues arising from the nomadic migration, including accompanying nomads within the Abyei area on their annual migration.

With regard to the process for resolution of the final status of Abyei, the agreement indicated the commitment of the parties to a peaceful resolution, and stated that they shall consider in good faith proposals that the AUHIP shall make to resolve the matter. As mentioned above, the preamble to the agreement stated that borders between the North and the South will be inviolate unless changed as a result of the outcome of the referendum foreseen in the Abyei Protocol. However, no new date or procedures for the referendum are included in the agreement, nor does the agreement address who would be eligible to vote, although this has been the main reason for the impasse.

The agreement requested the African Union and the UN to support the agreement and its implementation, and the UNSC to approve the deployment,

The Abyei territorial dispute **61**

mandate, and the financing of the ISFA. On June 27, 2011, the UNSC unanimously adopted Resolution 1990 (UNSC 2011b). The resolution established and renamed the force as the United Nations Interim Security Force for Abyei (UNISFA), consisting of a maximum of 4,200 military personnel, fifty police personnel, and appropriate civilian support. The resolution elaborated the mandate of UNISFA to include, inter alia, monitoring and verification of the redeployment of any SAF and SPLA from the Abyei area as defined by the PCA, and declared the Abyei area as demilitarized from any forces except UNISFA and the APS. The mandate also included demining assistance and technical advice, strengthening the capacity of the APS, assisting in providing security for the oil infrastructure in the Abyei area, and facilitating the delivery of humanitarian aid and the free movement of the humanitarian personnel. Acting under chapter VII of the Charter of the United Nations,[57] the resolution authorized UNISFA to take actions to protect UNISFA and UN personnel, facilities, installations, and equipment; ensure the security and freedom of movement of UN personnel; protect civilians in the Abyei area under imminent threat of physical violence; protect the Abyei area from incursions by unauthorized elements; and ensure security in the Abyei area.

The resolution urged the GOS and GOSS to fulfill their commitment under the CPA to peacefully resolve the final status of Abyei, and to consider in good faith proposals that the AUHIP shall make to resolve the matter. The resolution requested the UN Secretary-General to keep the UNSC regularly informed of the progress in implementing the agreement and to report no later than thirty days after the adoption of the resolution, and every sixty days thereafter. It also requested the Secretary-General to ensure that effective human rights monitoring is carried out in the Abyei area, and the results included in the Secretary-General's report to the UNSC. UNISFA's role in the implementation of the agreement would be reviewed by the UNSC not later than three months after adoption of the resolution. The conclusion of the agreement and the adoption of the resolution are the most remarkable developments in the internationalization of the Abyei dispute, coinciding with the emergence of South Sudan as an independent nation.

The failure to undertake the Abyei referendum on January 9, 2011, and the end of the interim period and the emergence of South Sudan as an independent nation on July 9, 2011, have rendered the Abyei Protocol largely obsolete. New arrangements were urgently needed for the Abyei area, which are now reflected in the Abyei Addis Ababa Agreement, and elaborated on and strengthened by the UNSC resolution. Although called temporary, those arrangements are likely to last for a long time, because the main issue of who has the right to vote in the referendum has proven difficult to resolve. If and when peace and security

---

[57] Chapter VII of the UN Charter authorizes the UNSC to take such action by air, sea, or land forces as may be necessary to maintain or restore international peace and security, should other measures—such as complete or partial interruption of economic relations and of rail, sea, air, postal, telegraphic, radio, and other means of communication, and the severance of diplomatic relations—be considered inadequate.

62 Land and post-conflict peacebuilding

return to the Abyei area, it would be timely and appropriate to take the dispute back to the traditional leaders of the Ngok Dinka and Misseriya, as recommended in this chapter. After the failure of the GOS, SPLM, the UN, the AUHIP, other mediators, international commissions, and tribunals, the traditional leaders are the only remaining viable alternative for resolving the Abyei dispute.

Milestones in the Abyei territorial dispute between North and South Sudan

- 1905   Transfer of nine Ngok Dinka chiefdoms from Southern to Northern Sudan.
- August 1955   Outbreak of civil war between Northern and Southern Sudan.
- January 1, 1956   Independence of Sudan from the Anglo-Egyptian condominium rule.
- March 12, 1972   Conclusion of the Addis Ababa Agreement on the Problem of Southern Sudan, ending the conflict between the North and the South.
- May 1983   Outbreak of renewed civil war between the South (led by the SPLM/A), and the North, following collapse of the Addis Ababa Agreement.
- July 20, 2002   Signature of the Machakos Protocol between the GOS and the SPLM/A, granting Southern Sudan the right of self determination.
- September 25, 2003   Signature of the Agreement on Security Arrangements between GOS and the SPLM/A.
- January 7, 2004   Signature of the Agreement on Wealth Sharing between GOS and the SPLM/A.
- March 19, 2004   Senator John Danforth, U.S. special envoy to Sudan, presented his proposals for resolution of the Abyei conflict to the two parties, which accepted them.
- May 26, 2004   Signature of the Resolution of the Abyei Conflict between GOS and SPLM/A (the Abyei Protocol), reflecting Senator Danforth's proposals.
- May 26, 2004   Signature of the Agreement on the Resolution of the Conflict in Southern Kordofan and Blue Nile States between GOS and SPLM/A.
- May 26, 2004   Signature of the Agreement on Power Sharing between GOS and SPLM/A.
- December 17, 2004   Signature of the Understandings on the Abyei Boundaries Commission (also known as the Abyei Annex, or Appendix).
- December 31, 2004   Signature of the Implementation Modalities of the Protocol on the Resolution of the Abyei Conflict.

The Abyei territorial dispute   63

- January 9, 2005   Signature of the Comprehensive Peace Agreement (the CPA) (which included the agreements and protocols between the GOS and the SPLM/A referred to above).
- March 12, 2005   Signature of the Text of the Terms of Reference for the Abyei Boundaries Commission (ABC).
- March 15, 2005   Completion of the selection of the members of the ABC.
- April 11, 2005   Signature of the Rules of Procedure for the ABC.
- April 2005   Members of the ABC visited the Abyei area and Khartoum.
- June 2005   Members of the ABC completed their report.
- July 6, 2005   Issuance of the Interim National Constitution of the Republic of the Sudan.
- July 14, 2005   Presentation of the ABC report to GOS and SPLM/A; the report was rejected by GOS.
- October 2007   SPLM withdrew from the national government, protesting a number of issues, including failure to implement the ABC report.
- May 2008   Outbreak of fighting between GOS forces and SPLA in Abyei Town.
- June 8, 2008   Signature of the Road Map for Return of IDPs (internally displaced persons) and Implementation of the Abyei Protocol. The agreement confirmed a role in the peacekeeping process in Abyei for UNMIS.
- June 21, 2008   Signature of the Memorandum of Understanding on the Abyei Arbitration.
- July 7, 2008   Signature of the Arbitration Agreement between GOS and SPLM/A on Delimiting Abyei Area, referring the Abyei dispute to the Permanent Court of Arbitration (PCA).
- October 2008   PCA tribunal for the Abyei dispute was constituted.
- April 18, 2009   Oral hearings by the two parties before the PCA tribunal.
- July 22, 2009   Issuance of the award of the PCA tribunal on the Abyei dispute.
- July 22, 2009   GOS and SPLM/A accepted award; the Misseriya rejected it.
- December 30, 2009   Adoption of the Southern Sudan Referendum Act and the Abyei Area Referendum Act.
- June 2010   Establishment of the Southern Sudan Referendum Commission.
- June 2010   Conclusion of the Mekelle Memorandum of Understanding between the NCP and SPLM on Post-Referendum Issues and Arrangements; no mention of Abyei pending issues.

64   Land and post-conflict peacebuilding

- October 2010

  Addis Ababa meeting of the two parties failed to resolve, among other things, the pending issues on the Abyei dispute.

- January 9, 2011

  Planned date for the Southern Sudan and Abyei referendums; the latter did not take place.

- January 9, 2011

  Clashes took place between the Misseriya and the Ngok Dinka in the Abyei area, lasting for three days.

- January 13 and 17, 2011

  Conclusion of the Kadugli agreements between the leaders of the Misseriya and the Ngok Dinka for ending the clashes which erupted that week. The agreements collapsed a few weeks later.

- February 7, 2011

  Results of Southern Sudan referendum announced, showing that close to 99 percent of the voters opted for secession; GOS officially accepted the results.

- February 2011

  Clashes continued between the Misseriya and the Ngok Dinka in the Abyei area.

- March 3, 2011

  The President of the UNSC issued a statement expressing concern over the situation in Abyei.

- March 4, 2011

  Conclusion of the Abyei March 4 Agreement between the GOS and the SPLM, attempting to contain the situation in Abyei.

- March 11, 2011

  Government of Southern Sudan claimed plot by Khartoum to overthrow the government in Southern Sudan and announced suspension of talks and contacts with the GOS on all pending issues, including Abyei, as well as plans to lodge a formal complaint to the UNSC.

- March 21, 2011

  The UNSC considered the "Reports of the Secretary-General on the Sudan," but no further action was taken.

- April 9, 2011

  Presidency decided to end mandate of the Joint/ Integrated Units, but a battalion was kept at Abyei and oil fields.

- April 20, 2011

  The Assistant Secretary-General for Peacekeeping Operations of the UN briefed the UNSC over the slow progress on several outstanding issues from the 2005 CPA, including the Abyei dispute.

- April 22, 2011

  Draft constitution of the Republic of South Sudan issued; it includes the Abyei area as part of South Sudan.

- April 27, 2011

  President of Sudan rejected inclusion of Abyei as part of the state of South Sudan, and threatened to revoke recognition of South Sudan's independence if the latter claimed ownership of Abyei in its constitution.

The Abyei territorial dispute   65

- May 15, 2011   Results of gubernatorial and legislative elections in Southern Kordofan state announced, with the NCP candidate as the winner for the gubernatorial elections. SPLM asserted its nonrecognition of the results.
- May 20, 2011   GOS announced the ambush and killing by SPLA forces of twenty-two of its soldiers. The SPLM denied involvement in the attack.
- May 21, 2011   GOS took over the Abyei area and announced dissolution of the Abyei Administrative Council.
- May 22, 2011   Members of the UNSC started a visit to Khartoum, and cancelled their planned visit to Abyei.
- May 22, 2011   The UNSC issued a statement from Khartoum deploring the killing of the GOS soldiers and the occupation by the GOS forces of the Abyei area, and called for withdrawal of those troops.
- May 23, 2011   Members of the UNSC visited Juba.
- May 29–30, 2011   Vice president of the government of Southern Sudan visited Khartoum and met with the vice president of Sudan on Abyei. However, no agreement was reached on how to deal with Abyei's takeover by the GOS forces, and the aftermath.
- June 5, 2011   Fighting erupted in the state of Southern Kordofan following the announcement of the May election results, which were rejected by the SPLM.
- June 20, 2011   Conclusion in Addis Ababa of the agreement on Temporary Arrangements for the Administration and Security of the Abyei Area, between the GOS and the SPLM.
- June 27, 2011   UNSC issued Resolution 1990, incorporating and elaborating the agreement on Temporary Arrangements for the Administration and Security of the Abyei Area.
- July 9, 2011   South Sudan formally seceded from Sudan and emerged as an independent nation.

REFERENCES

ABC (Abyei Boundaries Commission). 2005. *Abyei Boundaries Commission report.* July 14. Djibouti: Intergovernmental Authority on Development. www.sudantribune.com/IMG/pdf/Abey_boundary_com_report-1.pdf.

Alier, A. 1990. *Southern Sudan: Too many agreements dishonored.* Exeter, UK: Ithaca Press.

AUHIP (African Union High-Level Implementation Panel on Sudan). 2010. Statement of the AUHIP report on negotiations on the Sudan framework agreement. Khartoum, Sudan. www.africa-union.org/root/ar/index/AUHIP_Statement1.pdf.

Crook, J. R. 2009. Abyei arbitration—Final award. *American Society of International Law Insights* 13 (15). www.asil.org/insights090916.cfm.

66 Land and post-conflict peacebuilding

Deng, F. 1986. *The man called Deng Majok—Biography of power, polygyny, and change.* New Haven, CT, and London: Yale University Press.

ICG (International Crisis Group). 2007. *Breaking the Abyei deadlock.* Africa Briefing No. 47. October 12. www.crisisgroup.org/en/regions/africa/horn-of-africa/sudan/B047-sudan-breaking-the-abyei-deadlock.aspx.

PCA (Permanent Court of Arbitration). 1993. Permanent Court of Arbitration optional rules for arbitrating disputes between two parties of which only one is a state. www.pca-cpa.org/showfile.asp?fil_id=194.

———. 2009. In the matter of an arbitration before a tribunal constituted in accordance with article 5 of the arbitration agreement between the government of Sudan and the Sudan People's Liberation Movement/Army on delimiting Abyei area and the Permanent Court of Arbitration optional rules for arbitrating disputes between two parties of which only one is a state, between the government of Sudan and the Sudan People's Liberation Movement/Army, final award. www.pca-cpa.org/showfile.asp?fil_id=1240.

Petterson, D. 2008. Abyei unresolved: A threat to the North-South agreement. In *Implementing Sudan's comprehensive peace agreement: Prospects and challenges.* Washington, D.C.: Woodrow Wilson International Center for Scholars Africa Program.

Road Map of Abyei Protocol (Road Map for Return of IDPs and Implementation of Abyei Protocol). 2008. http://unmis.unmissions.org/Portals/UNMIS/2008Docs/Abyei%20Roadmap.pdf.

Salman. S. M. A. 2010. The Abyei territorial dispute between Northern and Southern Sudan and the decision of the Permanent Court of Arbitration. *Nature of Law Newsletter,* September. The World Bank Legal Vice Presidency. http://web.worldbank.org/WBSITE/EXTERNAL/TOPICS/EXTLAWJUSTICE/0,,contentMDK:22607203~pagePK:148956~piPK:149081~theSitePK:445634,00.html.

———. 2011. The new state of South Sudan and the hydro-politics of the Nile Basin. *Water International* 36 (2): 154–166.

———. 2013. Water resources in the Sudan north-south peace process and the ramifications of the secession of South Sudan. In *Water and post-conflict peacebuilding,* ed. E. Weinthal, J. Troell, and M. Nakayama. London: Earthscan.

Schomerus, M., and T. Allen. 2010. *Southern Sudan at odds with itself—Dynamics of conflict and predicaments of peace.* London: Development Studies Institute, London School of Economic. www.humansecuritygateway.com/documents/LSE_SouthernSudanAt OddsWithItself_DynamicsOfConflictAndPredicamentsOfPeace.pdf.

Southern Sudan Referendum Commission. 2011. Results for the referendum of Southern Sudan. http://southernsudan2011.com.

Sudan Tribune. 2008. Sudan's Abyei is devastated after heavy fighting. May 24. www.sudantribune.com/spip.php?article27276.

———. 2009a. Sudan Misseriya community refuse to implement Abyei ruling. October 5. www.sudantribune.com/spip.php?article32687.

———. 2009b. Sudan parliament adopts Abyei referendum law amid Messeriya protest. December 30. www.sudantribune.com/spip.php?article33635.

———. 2009c. Sudan's SPLM says Abyei oil fields still up for grabs. July 22. www.sudantribune.com/spip.php?article31902.

———. 2010. North-South talks over Abyei referendum fail, new round scheduled. October 12. www.sudantribune.com/spip.php?article36576.

———. 2011a. Rival Abyei tribes ink framework agreement, independently, to end clashes. January 13. www.sudantribune.com/Rival-Abyei-tribes-ink-framework,37612.

The Abyei territorial dispute 67

———. 2011b. Sudan's CPA parties set up joint committee to address security in Abyei. March 4. www.sudantribune.com/Sudan-s-CPA-parties-set-up-joint,38180.

———. 2011c. SPLM accuses Sudanese president of seeking to overthrow the South's government. March 12. www.sudantribune.com/SPLM-accuses-Sudanese-president-of,38269.

———. 2011d. Sudan President Al-Bashir threatens to wage war in South Kordofan, says Abyei will "remain northern." April 27. www.sudantribune.com/Sudan-President-Al-Bashir,38717.

———. 2011e. North & South Sudan agree to form joint committee on Abyei. May30. www.sudantribune.com/North-South-Sudan-agree-to-form,39061.

Sudan Vision. 2011. JIU withdraw, keep units in Abyei and oil fields. April 10. www.sudanvisiondaily.com/modules.php?name=News&file=article&sid=72682.

UN (United Nations). 2011a. Sudan: UN official warns of threats ahead of formal separation of south. April 20. www.un.org/apps/news/story.asp?NewsID=38160&Cr=unmis&Cr1=&Kw1=sudan&Kw2=&Kw3.

———. 2011b. Food and water most urgent needs for civilians displaced by Abyei clashes— UN. May 26. www.un.org/apps/news/story.asp?NewsID=38516&Cr=abyei&Cr1.

———. 2011c. Sudan: UN demands halt to fighting and immediate troop withdrawal from Abyei. May 22. www.un.org/apps/news/story.asp?NewsID=38467&Cr=Sudan&Cr1=.

UNHCR (United Nations High Commissioner for Refugees). 2009. Deteriorating security in parts of South Sudan hampers refugee returns. March 24. www.unhcr.org/49c908c92.html.

UNSC (United Nations Security Council). 2011a. Official communiqué of the 6499th (closed) meeting of the Security Council. www.securitycouncilreport.org/atf/cf/%7B65BFCF9B-6D27-4E9C-8CD3-CF6E4FF96FF9%7D/Sudan%20SPV%206499.pdf.

———. 2011b. Resolution 1990. S/RES/1990 (2011). June 27. www.un.org/News/Press/docs//2011/sc10298.doc.htm.

Wennmann, A. 2012. Sharing natural resource wealth during war-to-peace transitions. In *High-value natural resources and post-conflict peacebuilding*, ed. P. Lujala and S. A. Rustad. London: Earthscan.

Xinhua News. 2011. UN Security Council expresses deep concern over fighting in Abyei. March 3. http://news.xinhuanet.com/english2010/world/2011-03/04/c_13760069.htm.

Zainelabideen, A. 2009. *The Abyei crisis between international law and the matter of arbitration.* [In Arabic.] Beltsville, MD: International Graphics.

Land tenure and peace negotiations in Mindanao, Philippines

Yuri Oki

Mindanao, an island in the southern Philippines, was called a promised land during the American colonial period because of its rich resources and pleasant climate. Mindanao has experienced insurgency since the 1970s, which was long believed to be rooted in ethnic conflict between Christians and Muslims. However, recent quantitative and qualitative studies (Lingga 2007; Matuan 2007) have found another important aspect of the conflict: *rido*, or feuding between clans, families, and kinship groups, which is characterized by a series of violent retaliatory acts (Torres 2007), usually arising out of land disputes.

This chapter focuses on land disputes as an important cause of rido and how land and other resources may be managed to make and sustain peace. It is based on a combination of documentary resources and interviews conducted by the author in the Philippines and Japan.[1] The chapter begins by outlining the historical context of conflict in Mindanao and then examines the causes and dynamics of the conflict, the role that minerals and other natural resources play with respect to ancestral domain, and the factors associated with successful peacebuilding. The chapter concludes by identifying lessons learned, focusing on principal attributes of the Mindanao conflict that relate to land tenure.

HISTORICAL BACKGROUND

To understand the conflict in Mindanao, it is important to understand the history of Muslims in the region and the steps that have been taken in the ongoing peace process.

Yuri Oki holds a master's degree in international studies from the University of Tokyo and is currently pursuing her studies at the Graduate Institute of International and Development Studies, Geneva.

[1] The names of interviewees have been withheld to protect their privacy.

70 Land and post-conflict peacebuilding

Muslims in Mindanao

The early inhabitants of Mindanao were animists who lived in small communities comprised of extended families. By the thirteenth century, Mindanao had a predominantly Muslim population and was ruled by Islamic sultans and *datus* (chiefs). Muslims in Mindanao resisted Catholic conversion by Spanish colonists who arrived in the sixteenth century—unlike the populations of neighboring Luzon and Visayas, who converted to Catholicism. Mindanao remained a frontier, preserving its indigenous culture until the end of the Spanish period in 1898.

American colonization followed the Spanish era and lasted until Philippine independence in 1946. Immigrants appointed by the American colonial government often resettled on farmlands previously owned by the Muslims in the area. Immigrants raised subsistence crops, and areas containing high-value resources such as copper and nickel were controlled by the American colonial government, even when the land was owned by Muslims and indigenous groups. Indigenous Muslims' rights to the land were jeopardized, and they were unable to enjoy the profits from the extractive resources of Mindanao. Exploitation of Mindanaoan resources continued after Philippine independence; in the 1960s, the government accelerated the resettlement of Filipinos from north to south. Over the years, new settlers have gained power and have established claims to land in Mindanao, while indigenous Muslims have been relocated to the rural areas of the island.

The Muslims in Mindanao are often referred to as Moros, a name given by the Spanish to Islamic inhabitants of the southern Philippines. The name, which originally had negative connotations, was eventually embraced by Muslim groups discontented with exploitation of the resources within their homeland. Use of the term *Moro* has a long history (Majul 1964). Not all Muslims are Moros. The definition of this term has changed over time, and it now refers to Muslims who are radically discontented with the central government of the Philippines and who are involved with the insurgency. *Muslim Moros* is the term used to differentiate Muslims from the radical Moros. These people also long for emancipation from the resource exploitation of the central government and believe that Moros are entitled to autonomy within the boundaries of the Republic of the Philippines.

While many scholars argue that ethnicity and religion are two separate concepts, the mainstream argument in defining ethnicity and religion is that they are often interwoven to complement one other (Gordon 1964). Ethnicity and religion are not considered a single concept in Mindanao. Muslim ethnicity does not necessarily entail the religious meaning of Islam; ethnicity in Mindanao involves the daily practices and beliefs of people with Muslim ancestors, who have been discriminated against since the colonial era. Hence the ethnic concept of "Moro" adds the locality of Mindanao to the conventional understanding of "Muslim." Ethnic attributes such as customs and spoken languages, including tribal dialects, serve as core variables in defining who people are and where they

Land tenure and peace negotiations in Mindanao 71

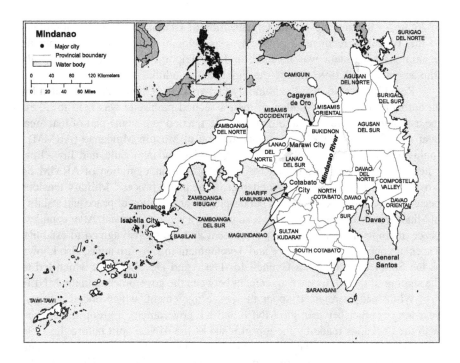

come from, more strongly than whether they are Christian, Muslim, or from another group. The Muslim community has not shared in profits gained by more recent settlers through exporting agricultural commodities such as bananas, pineapples, and coconuts.

The resettlement policy marginalized the Muslims economically by exploiting natural resources within the boundaries of their homeland. Muslim inhabitants were not included in the resettlement policy, and only immigrants received the privilege of living in the land blessed in resources. The Muslims faced not only economic deprivation but also political disenfranchisement and displacement from their homelands. Land has been and remains the central cause of the conflict in Mindanao. In the mid-1970s, a group of Muslim youth formed the Moro National Liberation Front (MNLF) in response to grievances and frustrations that had accumulated from the time of American colonization and were now directed at the government of the Philippines.

The peace process

The government and armed forces of the Philippines have been confronting the MNLF since the 1970s. In response to the Muslims' demand for autonomy in Mindanao, the Philippine government developed a general autonomy framework, known as the Tripoli Agreement, which both parties signed on December 23,

72 Land and post-conflict peacebuilding

1976, under the auspices of the Organization of Islamic Countries.[2] Subsequent to the Tripoli Agreement, a plebiscite was held in thirteen provinces, but no unanimous agreement was reached, and the Tripoli Agreement was not fully implemented until 1996, during the Fidel Ramos administration.

Republic Act No. 6734, commonly known as the Organic Act, provided for an autonomous area in Mindanao; then a second plebiscite was held to assess the aspirations of Muslims living in areas designated to become part of that area, later to be known as the Autonomous Region in Muslim Mindanao (ARMM).[3] In this second plebiscite, only Lanao del Sur, Maguindanao, Sulu, and Tawi-Tawi voted in favor of joining the ARMM. The official inauguration of ARMM on November 6, 1990, began a new chapter in the peace process. Military tensions began to lessen in the early 1990s; but despite the anticipation of peace and stability in Mindanao, there was no concrete road map for a peace agreement. After countless peace attempts and failures, the government and the MNLF agreed to establish a special zone focusing on peace and development in war-torn areas, also known as the Southern Philippines Council for Peace and Development, which led to the signing of the 1996 peace agreement between the government and the MNLF.

While people rejoiced about the peace agreement, which ended a thirty-year-long conflict between the MNLF and the government, a group dissatisfied with the decisions made by the top officials of the MNLF split before the 1996 peace agreement to form the Moro Islamic Liberation Front (MILF), which sought the complete independence of Mindanao from the Philippines. Generally, the MILF is thought to be more radical than the MNLF.

The Gloria Macapagal-Arroyo administration began a new policy aimed at ending the conflict with the MILF in 2001. Also in 2001, Republic Act No. 9054 was passed to incorporate Marawi City and Basilan in the ARMM. From 2001 to 2002, the government and the MILF resumed high-level peace talks and signed a general framework for further peace talks building up to a final peace agreement. Yet in 2003, government forces attacked a major MILF camp, and military tensions escalated until both parties called for a ceasefire. From 2003 to 2005, unofficial peace talks were held, and observers from Malaysia facilitated peace negotiations. In 2006 talks resumed in Malaysia, and rough agreement on the issue of ancestral domain was reached. August 4, 2008, would have been a historic day, as it was the day set for the signing of a memorandum of agreement on ancestral domain (MOA-AD).[4] However, the Supreme Court issued a temporary

---

[2] For the complete text of the Tripoli Agreement, see www.usip.org/files/file/resources/collections/peace_agreements/tripoli_12231976.pdf.

[3] The plebiscite was held in the following provinces: Basilan, North Cotabato, Davao del Sur, Lanao del Norte, Lanao del Sur, Maguindanao, Palawan, South Cotabato, Sultan Kudarat, Sulu, Tawi-Tawi, Zamboanga del Norte, and Zamboanga del Sur.

[4] The full name of the agreement is the Memorandum of Agreement on the Ancestral Domain Aspect of the GRP-MILF Tripoli Agreement on Peace of 2001. For its complete text, see www.archive.org/stream/MOA-AD-2008-GRP-MLF/MOA-AD-GRP-MILF-2008#page/n1/mode/2up.

CAUSES AND DYNAMICS OF THE CONFLICT

The conflict in Mindanao is rooted in and influenced by complex and interrelated social and economic factors.

Ancestral domain

The term *ancestral domain* refers to land that was owned, before the colonial era, by the indigenous people from whom today's Muslim Moros—as well as the non-Muslim indigenous people of Mindanao, known as the *Lumads*—are descended.

The Spanish colonial government sent Christian missionaries to attempt to convert and control the Islamic sultans. The American colonial administration took a different approach, adopting a migration policy that strongly encouraged Christian Filipinos to migrate and to bring Christian values to Mindanao.

In the 1980s, the Ferdinand Marcos and Corazon Aquino regimes continued this resettlement policy. Once the government adopted the resettlement policy and agricultural reform nationwide, Mindanao became a center of commodity exports and became home to more settlers from Visayas and Luzon.

Mindanao was and is known for the wealth of its natural resources—including both agricultural products such as coconuts, bananas, and mangos, and high-value resources such as coal, natural gas, copper, and gold. Bananas are the major crop, and Mindanao is a hub for distribution to Asian markets such as Japan and Korea.[5] Local inhabitants have claimed rights over both agricultural land and high-value natural resources found in Mindanao, whether in the ARMM or elsewhere.

The question of which areas of Mindanao constitute ancestral domain is extremely controversial and still under negotiation. Potential domain lands are scattered within Mindanao and are not always contiguous; resolution of their status requires stakeholder consensus. Resolving this issue has the potential to trigger new confrontations between the government and the remaining insurgent groups. There is also a lingering misconception that ancestral domain only involves land claimed by the Muslims; in fact, it also involves land claimed by the indigenous Lumads. Just as the Mindanao conflict has multiple root causes, the issue of ancestral domain has multiple dimensions.

---

[5] Bananas constitute 25 percent of the Philippines's commodity exports; more than 50 percent are produced in the giant banana plantations in Mindanao. Dole, Del Monte, Chiquita, and Sumisho Fruits are the dominant plantation owners. Japan has been a major market for bananas and pineapples; 84 percent of the imported bananas and 91 percent of imported pineapples in Japan are from Mindanao (Japanese Chamber of Commerce and Industry of Mindanao 2009).

74 Land and post-conflict peacebuilding

In 1997, the Indigenous Peoples Rights Act (Republic Act No. 8371) was passed. It defined rights over ancestral domain and recognized the indigenous cultural community, indigenous people, and their cultural and customary practices.[6] Under this act, the term *indigenous people* was defined as "inhabitants currently residing within the ancestral land" and "former inhabitants who are descendents at the time of conquest or colonization, that are now displaced or resettled." Under this definition, the Lumads, descendants of Muslims from the Sultanate era, and Christian descendants of people who settled in Mindanao before the colonial era fall into the category of indigenous people.

Preceding the 1996 peace agreement, the Philippine government and the MNLF had agreed on the establishment of autonomy within the republic for the southern Philippines, as discussed in the 1976 Tripoli Agreement and again in the Organic Act (Republic Act No. 6734), which was signed in 1989. However, in its efforts to implement the Tripoli Agreement, the government proposed a list of provinces to be included in the new autonomous region that was shorter than the list called for by the MNLF. This led to lingering discontent. The ARMM, established partly in response to the 1996 agreement, was intended to address that concern.

The Tripoli Agreement focused on three long-standing issues: the division of natural resources, administrative systems, and public administration. The 1996 peace agreement and the following plebiscite in 2001 established the building blocks for an autonomous region in the southern Philippines comprising five Muslim-oriented provinces and one city. It also empowered the legislative and

---

[6] The act specified that the term *ancestral domain* refers to

> all areas generally belonging to ICCs/IPs [indigenous cultural communities and indigenous people] comprising lands, inland waters, coastal areas, and natural resources therein, held under a claim of ownership, occupied or possessed by ICCs/IPs, themselves or through their ancestors, communally or individually since time immemorial, continuously to the present except when interrupted by war, *force majeure* or displacement by force, deceit, stealth or as a consequence of government projects or any other voluntary dealings entered into by government and private individuals/corporations, and which are necessary to ensure their economic, social and cultural welfare. It shall include ancestral lands, forests, pasture, residential, agricultural, and other lands individually owned whether alienable and disposable or otherwise, hunting grounds, burial grounds, worship areas, bodies of water, mineral and other natural resources, and lands which may no longer be exclusively occupied by ICCs/IPs but from which they traditionally had access to for their subsistence and traditional activities, particularly the home ranges of ICCs/ IPs who are still nomadic and/or shifting cultivators (Republic Act No. 8371, ch. II, sec. 3(a)).

It identified *ancestral lands* as

> land occupied, possessed and utilized by individuals, families and clans who are members of the ICCs/IPs since time immemorial, by themselves or through their predecessors-in-interest, under claims of individual or traditional group ownership, continuously, to the present except when interrupted by war, *force majeure* or displacement by force, deceit, stealth, or as a consequence of government projects and other voluntary dealings entered into by government and private individuals/corporations including, but not limited to, residential lots, rice terraces or paddies, private forests, swidden farms and tree lots (Republic Act No. 8371, ch. II, sec. 3(b)).

administrative branches of the autonomous government to oversee mining and natural resources in the region.

During negotiations, the MNLF demanded the following: the establishment of sharia (Islamic law) courts in the Philippines; allowing Muslim judges and lawyers in all courts, including the Supreme Court; the establishment of a directly elected legislative assembly in the ARMM; and the right to send representatives to the national legislature representing the ARMM and the Muslims in Mindanao. Most of the demands have been met on paper, but Muslims are still fighting to see them implemented. Only one Muslim judge has sat in the Supreme Court, and this only occurred because he was appointed directly by then-President Aquino. Although the Tripoli Agreement was a significant milestone in the peace process, negotiation of many important details was postponed, and the agreement frequently included language such as "to be determined later."

The 1976 Tripoli Agreement called for the autonomous region to have its own economic system—including an Islamic bank and financial system— independent of the central financial system of the Philippines, and it clearly indicated that Mindanao's natural resource management should be under the jurisdiction of the national government:

> Mines and mineral resources fall within the competence of the Central Government, and a reasonable percentage deriving from the revenues of the mines and minerals be fixed for the benefit of the areas of the autonomy.[7]

The ambiguity of the term "reasonable percentage" was a factor in negotiations for the August 2008 peace agreement; Muslims insisted on specifying the percentage in the agreement. At the signing of the Tripoli Agreement in 1976, it was clear that both the MNLF and the Philippine government sought control over resource-rich provinces such as Sultan Kudarat, the area between south-central Mindanao and Maguindanao Province, including parts of the Liguasan Marshland,[8] which has rich natural gas reserves.

Ancestral domain and insurgency groups

The Moro uprising, with goals ranging from self-identification to reclaiming ancestral homeland to independence from the Philippines, began with the MNLF in the early 1970s. After several negotiation attempts, the Tripoli Agreement was signed in 1976. Despite hopes that this agreement would end the Mindanao conflict, differences arose in the understanding of its terms.

After the agreement was signed, the government proposed a thirteen-province Muslim autonomous region. Although it was not clearly stipulated in the

---

[7] Sec. 3, item 10.

[8] The Liguasan Marshland is forty kilometers long and thirty kilometers wide and is located along the Pulangi River. It runs through three provinces: Davao del Sur, Maguindanao, and North Cotabato.

76 Land and post-conflict peacebuilding

agreement, the government insisted that the arrangement be subject to a plebiscite. In the first plebiscite, held in 1989, only four provinces joined; in the second plebiscite, in 2001, one province and one city joined. After the first plebiscite, a compromise plan was adopted, and two separate regional governments were established. In 1996, these became one autonomous region, the ARMM.

At the time of the Marcos administration, the central government recruited ex-MNLF commanders as officials in the autonomous government, giving them economic incentives such as market licenses, timber concessions, and export-import licenses. The recruitment continued until the end of the Marcos administration in 1986. Subsequently, the Aquino administration took a robust approach to peace negotiations with the MNLF, aimed at ending the armed conflict and establishing more substantive regional autonomy.

Fighting between the government and rebel forces continued despite the 1996 peace agreement, as the more radical and religious MILF, which split off from the MNLF, continued to confront the Philippines armed forces. Although the World Bank has assessed the MILF as less of a threat than other Islamic fundamentalist organizations in East Asia, it is reported to have ties with the militant groups Abu Sayyaf and Jamaat al-Islamiyah (Schiavo-Campo and Judd 2005).[9]

The MILF has gone further than the MNLF in demanding complete independence for the western part of Mindanao. It is frequently asserted, both by local inhabitants and by foreign aid agencies, that the MILF's intention in demanding Moro independence was not simply to reclaim their ancestral land and pass it on to their heirs but also to gain legal control of the land and its natural resources under both sharia and Philippine law (Schiavo-Campo and Judd 2005; Doyle, Wicks, and Nally 2007).

Ancestral domain and clan conflict

Rido, or clan disputes, can range from small-scale quarrels to false accusations, looting, and even killings. As one of the many root causes of the Mindanao conflict, rido often leads to associations between clan members and fighting between separatist groups.

Protagonists in the Mindanao conflict are members not only of a separatist group but also of a clan. Some clans and clan chiefs have political power over villages or *barangays* (the smallest municipal units in the Philippines) and are capable of carrying out local public administration on behalf of the ARMM government.

---

[9] Abu Sayyaf is active in Mindanao and in the Sulu archipelago on the islands of Basilan and Jolo. Jamaat al-Islamiyah, based in Indonesia, has been accused of the 2002 and 2005 terrorist bombings in Bali (U.S. DOS 2007). Both groups are included on the UN Security Council's list of terrorist organizations linked to al Qaeda or the Taliban (UNSC 2010).

Land tenure and peace negotiations in Mindanao 77

Often, MILF members disguise themselves as farmers in the daytime and turn into combatants at night. Combat in Mindanao usually takes the form of ambushes that occur at night or in the early morning. Whether a person is associated with the MILF is not easy to determine, even by local residents, as MILF members generally do not wear uniforms. When in fear for themselves or their families, they may pull out weapons hidden underneath their clothes, instantly becoming combatants.

Mindanaoans, both combatants and noncombatants, have a strong sense of attachment to and respect for their clans, and separatist rebels are often drawn into rido disputes. Surprisingly, rido seems to occur more frequently among rich and educated clans (Makinano and Lubang 2001).

Clan and ethnic groupings differ in different areas of Mindanao. Clans are often ethnically diverse—for example, a Christian woman who married a Muslim man would become a member of his (Muslim-oriented) clan. The high chief of a clan may or may not condone cross-clan marriage. Two clans could be rivals even though they are both Muslim or could trade with each other even if one is Christian and the other Muslim. In addition to Christian- and Muslim-oriented clans, there are also Lumad clans. It is not necessarily the bloodline that defines individuals in Mindanao, but their ethnic affiliation, language, and daily customs.

Mapping the ethnic affiliations of each clan can help donor agencies understand grassroots politics and unravel the complexities of rido. This in turn can lead to understanding of the large-scale conflict between the Philippines armed forces and the MILF. Filipino scholars argue that one of the major causes of rido is competition for access to and control of resource-rich land.

A recent field study (Canuday 2007) described a typical case that involved both large-scale (between the Philippines armed forces and the MILF) and small-scale (rido) conflict. It took place in the barangay of Linantangan—in Mamasapano town in Maguindanao Province, which is part of the ARMM. Linantangan has suffered from feuds between community leaders and the barangay chair,[10] Chair Bangadan. He was forced to leave the barangay as tension over a land dispute escalated into bloody conflict.

As the dispute intensified, both government and rebel groups got involved, broadening the conflict. The Philippines armed forces deployed two battalions to the vicinity of the barangay and began recruiting volunteers to assist in controlling the area around the house of Chair Bangadan.[11] Meanwhile, several

---

[10] A barangay chair is different from a mayor of a city, or high chief, who is usually the most respected person in the barangay. He may hold the title of datu or another word for Muslim tribal chief, which is equivalent to a Western duke.

[11] Volunteers are recruited through two organizations: CAFGUs (civilian armed forces geographical units), which are primarily civilian reservist groups affiliated with the armed forces, and CVOs (civil volunteer organizations), which perform a similar function in support of both the armed forces and the police.

78   Land and post-conflict peacebuilding

armed groups, including MILF and ex-MNLF combatants, joined forces to strengthen their power over the barangay. Concerned that the Philippines armed forces might gain control and remove Chair Bangadan, MILF members distributed firearms and ammunition to supporters in the community.

In 2005, intense fighting broke out between the MILF and government forces when MILF guerrillas assaulted the patrol base of a Philippines military battalion located in a coconut grove along the main road, resulting in seven armed forces casualties. In response, the Philippines armed forces started a massive ground and air attack. The MILF released a public statement that the assault had not been sanctioned by the central committee and that the decision leading to the attack was made by a few rogue guerrillas outside of the MILF. Such episodes occur frequently.

This is just one example of a smaller conflict escalating into a much larger clash. The Philippines armed forces had stationed a patrol base as a protective measure to guard the families of the barangay chair. However, the MILF saw this as a conspiracy between the barangay chair and the armed forces, and feared that the government could be covertly controlling the barangay.

MINING IN MINDANAO

Ancestral domain involves not only land but also the natural resources it contains. High-value resources include copper, nickel, gold, rubber, timber, natural gas, coal, and crude oil. There is also the potential for hydropower and geothermal power. This section focuses on mining.

In the 1970s, small-scale mines began operating in parts of Mindanao, and many of these operations grew significantly. Such companies include Manila Mining Corporation, operating in Surigao del Norte Province extracting gold, copper, and silver, and TVI Pacific, a Canadian-affiliated mining company operating in Zamboanga del Norte Province extracting copper, gold, and silver. Global mining companies such as the Swiss Xstrata and the Australian BHP Billiton have affiliated operations in Mindanao.

The Philippines ranks in the world's top ten in the mine production of gold and nickel, and is a major producer of copper (Brown et al. 2011). Mining is one of the Philippines' major export industries and revenue sources. Mining policy in the Philippines focuses on exporting low-quality product for further refinement elsewhere. Despite its low-grade mineral ores, the mining sector contributes more than 2 percent of the country's gross domestic product, generating US$3 billion annually (USGS 2011).

The Philippines is ranked second, after Indonesia, in the Asia-Pacific region in terms of mineral prospectivity (the potential for finding minerals) (Pacheco-Sabando 2009). Notwithstanding its potential for natural resource development, which could benefit the local communities, investment in Mindanao remains low because of its political uncertainty and security concerns. In the past, mining sites have been the target of sabotage by indigenous communities and the MILF.

Land tenure and peace negotiations in Mindanao   79

Insurgent groups sometimes generate revenue by charging a fee for guarding a mining company's facilities and workers.

The Mining Act of 1995 (Republic Act No. 7942) specifies two avenues through which foreign companies can operate concessions in the Philippines: the exploration permit (which also addresses mineral production sharing, coproduction, or joint venture) and the financial or technical assistance agreement (FTAA) for large-scale exploration, development, and utilization of mineral resources. Exploration permits can be for up to eight years, while FTAAs are twenty-five-year contracts and require a minimum investment of US$50 million for mine development. Under the Mining Act, the contractor can convert an exploration permit totally or partially into a mineral agreement with the government following the submission and approval of a declaration of project feasibility and a work program. The mineral agreements differ from FTAAs in that they involve mineral production-sharing, coproduction, or joint-venture agreements. The mineral agreements are limited to a Filipino citizen or organizations (corporations, partnerships, associations, and cooperatives) with at least 60 percent Filipino capital ownership. Additionally, the government can offer incentives for foreign investment such as tax holidays and waivers of value-added tax or capital duty.

Copper and gold mines in South Cotabato Province had been previously owned by WMC Philippines—an affiliate of an Australian mining company, holding one of only three FTAAs registered in the country in 2000. The copper mine popularly known as the Tampakan mine, containing deposits of an estimated 12.8 million metric tons of copper and 15.2 million ounces of gold, is on the border between the ancestral domain areas of South Cotabato Province, Columbio in Sultan Kudarat Province, and Kibalawan in Davao del Sur Province. In 2005, Xstrata tried to acquire shares in WMC Philippines but failed. Instead, WMC accepted an offer from BHP Billiton Australia.

The nickel mining company Rio Tuba Corporation is a dominant nickel producer in the ancestral domain area of Palawan Island. Although 60 percent of its shares are owned by Filipino interests, 40 percent are owned by interests from Japan, and all production was sold to Japan's Pacific Metals Company in 2000. The mine holds a joint venture agreement with Sumitomo Metal Mining Company, Japan's largest nickel producer. Because of its limited domestic resources, Japan has been the primary market for the Philippines mining industry; a majority of nickel and copper concentrates are exported to Japan through affiliates of major trading companies such as Sumitomo, Mitsui, and Mitsubishi.

Coalbed methane is another resource for which foreign investors see Mindanao as a potential development frontier. Natural gas found in the coalbeds can be utilized for a variety of purposes with lower drilling costs than open-pit coal mines. Most coal mined in the Philippines is subbituminous, a type of coal that is not cost-efficient because of its relatively low density and high water content, but it can be combined with imported coal to generate enough electricity to supply the country. Of nineteen coal districts in the Philippines, seven are located in Mindanao,

80　Land and post-conflict peacebuilding

partially in ancestral domain areas (DOE 2007), with an estimated 900 million tons of coal reserve potential.[12]

The Mining Act's encouragement of the opening up of the Philippine mining industry to foreign investment became one of the main motivations for the Muslim Moros, along with Christians and Lumads, to demand rights to their ancestors' land and its natural resources.

Natural resources and the peace process

There can be no peace in Mindanao without resolving the issue of ancestral domain land and its resources. Real progress on this issue has been made in the past—for example, the 1996 peace agreement between the MNLF and the government gave Muslims authority over specific areas of ancestral domain. Yet sporadic armed conflicts between the Philippines military and the MILF continued after the signing of this agreement, despite a ceasefire agreed to in 2003. The peace process has been stagnant since then, and the 2008 MOA-AD has remained unsigned due to legal challenges.

Limited data make it difficult to quantify the socioeconomic costs of the conflict in Mindanao. According to Salvatore Schiavo-Campo and Mary Judd, the direct costs of the conflict appear low compared to those of other civil conflicts (Schiavo-Campo and Judd 2005). These seemingly low costs have served as justification for the international community to abandon the Mindanao conflict, and no UN mandate has ever been assigned to Mindanao. The socioeconomic costs have been underestimated as researchers have difficulty assessing the wide variety of impacts the conflict has on people's daily lives.

Schiavo-Campo and Judd estimated losses from the fighting between 1970 and 2000 at US$2 billion to US$3 billion (Schiavo-Camp and Judd 2005). Filipino media reports vary in the number of casualties, making it challenging for researchers to analyze the direct impacts of the conflict.

Complicating the situation, the communist New People's Army (NPA) also targets foreign companies attempting to exploit natural resources in the Philippines. It was accused of setting fire to buildings owned by Sagittarius Mines and firing shots at buildings in the company compound in 2008 (MAC 2008). The controversial Sagittarius Mines, a subsidiary of the Swiss Xstrata, is preparing to open its largest copper and gold mine in Southeast Asia, which is expected to begin operating in 2016. The project is currently undergoing a feasibility study; the mine, located in South Cotabato Province, is estimated to contain 13.5 million tons of copper and 15.8 million ounces of gold (Reuters 2009).

In 2000, President Arroyo produced a presidential manifesto on ending the conflict between the government and the MILF, bringing peace and development to the islands of Mindanao, and eradicating the NPA by the end of her term of

---

[12] An ongoing study is attempting to estimate the potential more precisely (NEDO 2009).

office in 2010.[13] The Coordinating Committee on the Cessation of Hostilities, jointly chaired by the Philippines military, the MILF, and the International Monitoring Team,[14] was convened in 2003, subsequent to the establishment of the Office of the Presidential Adviser on the Peace Process. Peace negotiations between the Philippine government and the MILF continued behind the scenes although the Philippines military continued to fight both the MILF and the NPA.

After five years of negotiations, the MOA-AD was finalized and ready to be signed by the president and Ebrahim Murad, the leader of the MILF, in August 2008 in Kuala Lumpur, Malaysia. However, as mentioned earlier, a day before the scheduled signing, the Philippine Supreme Court issued a ruling preventing signing until a consensus of all stakeholders was achieved. A former member of the International Monitoring Team described the events like this:

> We . . . flew to Kuala Lumpur the morning of the scheduled signing of MOA-AD. Representatives from MILF were there as well, waiting for the signing ceremony to begin. Soon we found out that representatives from the GRP [government] side were not on the plane. We waited until our cell phones began to ring and found out [about] the restraining order of the Supreme Court and its acceptance by the GRP.[15]

In October 2008, the court declared MOA-AD unconstitutional.[16]

---

[13] Vice President Arroyo assumed the office of the presidency on June 30, 2010, upon the impeachment of then-president Estrada. President Arroyo was reelected for a full six-year term in 2004.

[14] The International Monitoring Team was originally composed of sixty members from Malaysia, Brunei, and Libya. With headquarters in Cotabato City, it monitored the ceasefire and the peace process between the government and the MILF. Japan joined the team in October 2006 and dispatched development experts to facilitate the peace negotiations and the socioeconomic development of Mindanao.

[15] Interview, Tokyo, October 5, 2008.

[16] A report on the Supreme Court's decision stated:

> The MOA-AD with MILF would set up the Bangsamoro Homeland with the Bangsamoro Judicial Entity (BJE) as its governing body in parts of Mindanao. Under the agreement, the BJE would have the power to set up its own security, trade, education, elections, and the right to explore and develop natural resources in the said territory. . . . The Court held that respondents' failure to consult the local government units or communities constitutes a departure by respondents from their mandate under EO [Executive Order] No. 3. Moreover, respondents exceeded their authority by the mere act of guaranteeing amendments to the Constitution. EO No. 3 defines the authority of the GRP [Philippines government] Negotiating panel. The contents of the MOA-AD are matters of paramount public concern involving public interest in the highest order. . . . The Court stressed that the MOA-AD cannot be reconciled with the present Constitution and laws. Not only its specific provisions but the very concept underlying them, namely, the associative relationship envisioned between the GRP and the BJE, are unconstitutional, for the concept presupposes that the associated entity is a state and implies that the same is on its way to independence (Rempillo 2008).

For more analysis on the Supreme Court's decision, see Paula Defensor Knack, "Legal Frameworks and Land Issues in Muslim Mindanao," in this book.

82 Land and post-conflict peacebuilding

Prior to the Supreme Court order, thousands of local residents, accompanied by local officials and Catholic priests, had demonstrated in the streets of the city of Zamboanga, which was listed as part of the ancestral domain in the MOA-AD. They opposed the MOA-AD provisions for the establishment of independent legal, banking, education, civil service, security, and trade systems by the Moros. Other protests erupted just before and after the Supreme Court order was issued. A petition requesting a halt to the signing of the MOA-AD was submitted to the Supreme Court by the vice governor of North Cotabato, a mayor from Zamboanga del Norte, the mayor of Iligan City, and Ernesto Maceda, a long-time politician and former senate president, who formed a group to oppose the MOA-AD. Opposition to the MOA-AD was based not only on its implications for agricultural land rights but also on the potentially high value of the mineral resources.

The MOA-AD contained lists of barangays and municipalities to be classified as ancestral domain. Among the lands listed was a rubber plantation belonging to the vice governor of North Cotabato. It has been said that the governor used his political power to convince other mayors that their private land would also be subject to dispossession under the agreement. Then he and his allies submitted a petition that the Supreme Court took into account in issuing its restraining order.[17]

Rubber is considered the easiest natural resource to extract and most cost-efficient in Mindanao; owners of rubber plantations are zealous about their land rights. Mindanao's fertile soil produces high-quality rubber. Rubber plantations exist throughout the ARMM, including barangays in Zamboanga del Norte Province, which contributes 48 percent of the national rubber production. Zamboanga Sibugay, another province with some barangays potentially on the ancestral domain list, contains a substantial proportion of the rubber plantation area in the Philippines: 19,576 hectares out of 81,925 hectares for the country as a whole. North Cotabato Province has an even larger rubber plantation area, about 23,432 hectares (Philippine Information Agency 2008; *Mindanao Examiner* 2008), and is a frequent site of battles between the Philippines military and the MILF. Another area with rubber planations is the island of Basilan, site of a key MILF military base and of frequent battles between the Philippines military and the MILF as well as Abu Sayyaf.

Natural resources and insurgency groups

Foreign companies carrying out resource development in the Mindanao conflict zone have had to take intensive security precautions. The mining companies locate their compounds close to the mining site and employ private security guards, ranging from routine gate guards to heavily armed forces ready to protect the compound from attack. In some cases, companies have admitted to paying protection money to insurgent groups; for example, the King King Mine paid

---

[17] Member of an international donor agency interviewed by the author, December 2008, Tokyo.

roughly US$2 million to insurgent groups during the lifespan of the project (Doyle, Wicks, and Nally 2007). This practice is illegal, but for mining companies, it can be the cost of doing business in Mindanao.

Political corruption also contributes to the complexity of the Mindanao conflict. The law requires prior informed consent to the development plan by indigenous stakeholders. However, companies often provide information only to the clans with which they are familiar, while disregarding other stakeholding clans (Doyle, Wicks, and Nally 2007). Mining giants such as Xstrata and BHP Billiton have established affiliated companies to extract minerals at a low cost in the conflict zone where ancestral domain tenure has been disputed. By paying protection money to rebel groups, mining giants can operate safely in the conflict-torn areas.

At times, foreign mining companies negotiate with clan chiefs on payments in return for permits to extract minerals.[18] The Philippines has relatively strict laws protecting the environment and indigenous communities, but in many localities these laws are viewed merely as guidelines and are often disregarded (Doyle, Wicks, and Nally 2007).

Judging from interviews conducted from December 2006 to February 2009 in Mindanao and in Japan, such arrangements are almost never exposed, because an informant could be easily identified as rumors travel quickly through small communities. Informants who disclose information that could harm their clans risk violent retaliation against themselves and their families. Betrayal of the clan is considered the most despicable act an individual can perform. As a result, illegal dealings between companies and clans are almost never disclosed.

FACTORS THAT AFFECT SUCCESS IN PEACEBUILDING

Since the beginning of the conflict in the 1970s, civil society organizations have become powerful advocates for peace throughout the island, uniting people of different religions. Moros, Lumads, and Christians have worked together, and at times separately, for peace and stability in Mindanao. The 1996 peace accord fulfilled the MNLF's demand for a Muslim autonomous area but only partially. For example, the current ARMM includes five provinces and one city rather than the initially requested thirteen. The remaining eight provinces contain copper and gold resources, which the central government and foreign investors have long exploited. Additionally, although a general framework for further peace talks has been signed by the government and the MILF, a peace agreement has yet to be finalized.

Support from the Islamic community

The Organization of the Islamic Conference helped to mediate the peace process in the buildup to the 1996 agreement. As a neighboring country, and a

---

[18] Representatives from nongovernmental organizations interviewed by the author, Davao City, Philippines, February 12, 2007.

84   Land and post-conflict peacebuilding

Muslim-oriented country valuing the Koranic principle of mediation, Malaysia has been a core member of the International Monitoring Team, facilitating multiple peace negotiations both before and after the ceasefire agreement of 2003. International organizations and bilateral donors have helped to promote peace and development in Mindanao.[19] But much of the recent mediation effort has been carried out by the International Monitoring Team. Without its presence, the process building up to the August 2008 MOA-AD could not have taken place. Although the failure of this agreement to take effect is discouraging,[20] mediation and ceasefire monitoring have helped to alleviate tensions between the Philippine government and army and the MILF.

Stakeholder consensus

The terms of the MOA-AD seem to provide concrete strategies for managing and allocating ancestral domain lands. Annexes list provinces that could be included in a possible expansion of the current ARMM boundaries, known as the Bangsamoro Juridical Entity.[21] The agreement appears to give absolute autonomy over ancestral domain to the indigenous people. But there are complications.

The areas proposed for the Bangsamoro Juridical Entity fall in two categories. Those in category A are subject to a plebiscite within twelve months of the signing of the MOA-AD, and those in category B are subject to a plebiscite not earlier than twenty-five years after the signing. Category B includes several mining sites that are already in operation, such as the well-known copper mining site in the municipality of Tampakan, being developed by Xstrata. The MOA-AD could possibly secure twenty-five years for foreign investors to operate in the region while the central government continues to receive their royalty payments.

As discussed earlier, the vice governor of North Cotabato, out of anxiety that his rubber plantation would be included in category B of the Bangsamoro Juridical Entity, signed a petition along with several allies asking the Supreme

---

[19] International organizations with projects in Mindanao include the World Bank, Asian Development Bank, Islamic Development Bank, United Nations Development Programme, and European Union. Bilateral donors include the U.S. Agency for International Development, Australian Agency for International Development, Canadian International Development Agency, and Japan International Cooperation Agency.

[20] Mindanao peace negotiators now face the decision of whether to continue to base talks on the MOA-AD or to disregard that document and start from scratch under newly elected President Benigno Aquino III.

[21] Paragraph 5 under MOA-AD's Concepts and Principles section states: "Both Parties agree that the Bangsamoro Juridical Entity (BJE) shall have the authority and jurisdiction over the Ancestral Domain and Ancestral lands, including both alienable and non-alienable lands encompassed within their homeland and ancestral territory, as well as the delineation of ancestral domain/lands of the Bangsamoro people located therein." It establishes a ratio for distribution of profits, royalties, bonuses, and taxes derived from natural resources extracted from the area: 75 percent to the BJE and 25 percent to the central government.

Court to postpone the signing of the MOA-AD. This petition became a justification for the Supreme Court to issue its restraining order suspending the signing of the MOA-AD pending consent from stakeholders.

Reintegration

Several successful events followed the 1996 peace agreement, most notably the reintegration program, which saw about 6,000 former MNLF combatants join the national army. But many excombatants also joined the MILF, often saying that they cannot ally themselves with an army that used to be their enemy simply because a peace accord was signed. Thus the lingering effects of prolonged civil war threaten achievement of a stable peace. The success of the disarmament, demobilization, and reintegration process following the 1996 agreement was believed to be a milestone in the Mindanao peacebuilding process. An official disarmament ceremony was held for ex-MNLF soldiers who were to join the ARMM government. However, hope for peace vanished after excombatants dropped out of the reintegration program, though there are no data to explain the reason for their departure.

Negotiations continued after the failure of the MOA-AD in 2008. President Arroyo made the disarmament of MILF soldiers a condition of resuming the peace negotiations (Abangan 2008). The MILF refused to disarm before the peace accord was signed, as this would allow the Philippines military to gain strategic superiority. This disagreement widened the rift between the Philippine government and the MILF.

LESSONS LEARNED

In the complex Mindanao conflict, small- and large-scale conflicts are intricately interwoven; all these conflicts share the common issue of ancestral domain. Competition over land tenure has been the major source of conflict—for example, the MILF's demand for complete autonomy over mineral-rich areas owned by indigenous Muslims in Mindanao.

Four salient attributes of the Mindanao conflict directly pertain to land tenure:

1. Local conflict (rido) and larger-scale military conflict can affect and aggravate each other in complex ways.
2. Ambiguities in the law have exacerbated the conflict. Issues include an unusual mixture of Islamic and secular law, and discrepancies between the Mining Act and the Indigenous Peoples Rights Act.
3. The mining industry in Mindanao, in which foreign investors are heavily involved, has a complex influence on the conflict and on chances for peace.
4. Widespread corruption has created patron-client relationships that sometimes link ostensible enemies in covert cooperation.

86 Land and post-conflict peacebuilding

Rido and the insurgency

Ethnic affiliations and clan traditions are key to understanding the conflict in Mindanao and to solving the underlying issue of rido. Researchers have argued that land tenure is the root of the conflict (Lingaa 2007). Seemingly petty disputes over land intensify as perpetrators of rido involve other members of the clan, usually members of their extended families.

A local inhabitant has a greater chance of being the victim of a rido incident than of being the victim of large-scale fighting between the Philippines military and the MILF. But when rido and large-scale conflict intermingle, the result can be complex. For example, a MILF member whose clan is engaged in rido may provide weapons to members of his clan. The MILF can thus use rido to expand its presence and power in the region.

As ancestral domain is land that once belonged or now belongs to the indigenous people, regardless of their ethnic affiliation, it has deep implications as one of the many causes of rido. Ancestral domain provides land for farming and fulfilling basic human needs. At the same time, it is a potential resource extraction site that can be bargained over with the government and foreign investors, a heritable fixed asset for future generations, and a sign of the wealth of the land-owning clan.

As observed in other conflict-torn regions, the complexity of the Mindanao conflict suggests that the transition from conflict to reconciliation is challenging. Peace negotiations are not necessarily concluded in an official manner, such as in the form of an official peace agreement, before entering into a final consolidation phase. For instance, the 1996 peace agreement between the government and the MNLF was concluded while conflict was ongoing. Mindanao experienced both a consolidation phase and a conflict phase even after the 1996 agreement.

Any country suffering from conflict, like Mindanao, struggles to find a way out. Mindanao may be unique in the diversity of the factors that caused the conflict. Rido, the confrontation between the government and Muslim insurgency groups, and the high incidence of poverty in parts of Mindanao are the main root causes. When several variables must be dealt with, conflict analysis becomes a harder task. The analysis can be further complicated when parties do not share the same goals, such as concluding a peace agreement and progressing to the next stage of the peacebuilding process.

Legal issues

The legislature and the judiciary have also played a role in exacerbating the conflict. For instance, in Mindanao, sharia (Islamic) courts function as district courts, and trials in the sharia district courts cannot be appealed to the Supreme Court unless on questions of law or for abuse of discretion committed by the judge of the district court.

The Mining Act, which encourages foreign investment, conflicts with the Indigenous Peoples Rights Act. There can be tension between the goals of achieving economic growth and protecting the rights of indigenous people and their entitlement to ancestral domain. In 2000, the Department of Environment and Natural Resources asked the Supreme Court to clarify legal and constitutional challenges to the Mining Act and the Indigenous Peoples Rights Act, arguing that the contradictions between the two laws were hampering foreign investment. The Supreme Court reaffirmed the Indigenous Peoples Rights Act, allowing indigenous people control over resources within the limits set by the act. However, the act does not provide for indigenous control over high-value resources such as copper and gold, and the Supreme Court ruled in favor of the government's full control over these (Lyday 2000).

Mining

The mining industry in the Philippines is heavily dependent on exporting ore, both to developed countries such as Japan and the United States and to emerging markets such as China. The mining sector also includes a number of transnational mining companies, with home countries in Australia, Canada, Japan, the United Kingdom, and the United States. According to a report by a fact-finding team from the United Kingdom, "in efforts to encourage such foreign direct investment, the Philippines government appears willing to circumvent its own laws protecting the environment and human rights and reduce standards below acceptable international practice. . . . The emphasis on export-driven mining based on foreign investment may diminish rather than improve the possibility of a balanced, long-term, sustainable development strategy" (Doyle, Wicks, and Nally 2007, iii).

It could be argued that the government of the Philippines is exploiting the conflict in Mindanao to gain time for foreign investors to extract the resources, resulting in royalty payments to the government. The benefits of large-scale foreign mining almost never trickle down to the most needy. Mining rarely creates jobs for local residents. Open-pit mining, the most common process in Mindanao, uses sophisticated technologies that are mainly operated by mining specialists and not local trainees.

Nickel strip mining causes severe ecological damage, such as the flattening of mountaintops and the creation of craters with massive amounts of tailings, and can cause serious health issues. Mining involves the use of hazardous chemicals such as cyanide to extract gold from the ore. These chemicals can also cause numerous health issues for nearby inhabitants.

Cathal Doyle, Clive Wicks, and Frank Nally expressed their concern in their fact-finding report that protection money had been paid to terrorist groups (Doyle, Wicks, and Nally 2007), a practice about which former foreign mining company employees had testified at the hearing in the Canadian parliament. Given this testimony, chances are that corruption and the illegal flow of cash will only

88 Land and post-conflict peacebuilding

increase the risk of a rent-seeking economy, further marginalizing indigenous people. Moreover, protection money paid by foreign mining giants may produce steady income for landowners, local militias, and police. The situation will consequently strengthen ties between patrons and clients, and in the worst cases will create client-followers (people who do favors for clients in exchange for pay and thus rely on the benefits that clients receive from their patrons).

Minerals found in Mindanao, such as copper, gold, and nickel, may not appear as intriguing as the diamonds that are so often the focus of conflict, but play a crucial role in the conflict. In Mindanao, natural resources contribute to the transition to peace and at the same time, paradoxical as it may seem, exacerbate the conflict. The main concern of stakeholders—such as the government of the Philippines, local bureaucrats, insurgency groups, and indigenous communities—is the income derived either directly from resource development and extraction on ancestral land or as a commission for facilitating an agreement between landowners and mining companies.

Corruption

As seen in the failed 2008 peace agreement, stakeholders sometimes face a choice between securing their vested interests, for example in a rubber plantation or mine, or supporting peace. To protect vested interests, stakeholders may become, caught in patron-client relationships and become part of a rent-seeking economy, hoping to continuously reap benefits from the client, who may be in association with the MILF. Stakeholders caught in the turmoil of the patron-client model must play a two-faced role, publicly denouncing the MILF's insurgent activities while privately dealing with MILF members in order to protect their vested interests. In this respect, breaking the chain between patron and client is a priority.

While conducting interviews about land tenure and Mindanao's resource sector, including the mining industry, it became apparent to this author that qualitative data collection is an extremely delicate matter. Interviewees are cautious about how and to what extent they answer questions, especially when they involve sensitive issues such as patron-client relationships and their specific terms. Contacting informants in public was done carefully, as rumors spread easily in small communities. Interviewees often expressed apprehension that they might be seen by people who could inform others, resulting in harassment, blackmail, and threats against family members. Corruption is a sensitive topic to research due to the security needs of the informants, but it should be publicly addressed by researchers from donor agencies and academia.

CONCLUSION

Mindanao is a case study of the complexity of natural resource management in post-conflict societies. The conflict in Mindanao is more than an outcome of

Land tenure and peace negotiations in Mindanao   89

economic disparity due to a clash between Muslims and Christians. It is not based only on insurgency groups' desire for self-determination, but is also a conflict over the control and management of natural resources, deeply enmeshed with rido or local clan conflict. Poverty in Mindanao is characterized by recurring rido and by heavy reliance on primary commodities.

Peace between the MILF and the government of the Philippines has been a long-standing aspiration of the people in Mindanao. The vested interests of different parties to the conflict have been woven into complex layers for more than three decades. Conflicts of interest occur regularly between local and international insurgency groups, local politicians and bureaucrats, religious leaders, black market businessmen, and other civilians. The challenge is to find a solution in which all parties concerned can benefit.

This chapter has focused mainly on the negative aspects of land and resource management in the Mindanao peacebuilding process. However, it is also true that the quest for peace is uniting the diverse inhabitants of Mindanao. Grassroots groups, nongovernmental and nonprofit organizations, academics, and religious groups have been organizing peace walks, regional gatherings, and symposia to promote the peace process and provide basic necessities to people displaced by the conflict.

Civil society peace initiatives have helped protect human security and defeat fears of violence and deprivation. International donors are actively participating not only as project implementers but as facilitators, bridging the gap between the government (both of the Philippines and of the ARMM) and civil groups. In this regard, encouraging both bottom-up and top-down approaches may lead to effective steps forward in the peace process. In Mindanao, human security is at risk, and fear of violence is widespread, both because of the conflict between the government and the insurgency and because of smaller-scale rido. Mindanaoans have not only been deprived of basic necessities due to the destruction of social capital caused by the intensification of civil war, but they also fear losing their land tenure and cash incomes. Fear of violence and deprivation reinforce each other, making it harder to address agenda items one at a time. Land tenure is merely one component of the conflict in Mindanao.

REFERENCES

Abangan, J. D. 2008. House reps want updates on peace talks. Quezon City, Philippines: Philippines Information Agency. www.pia.gov.ph/?m=12&fi=p080917htm&date=09/17/2008.

Brown, T. J., T. Bide, A. S. Walters, N. E. Idoine, R. A. Shaw, S. D. Hannis, P. A. J. Lusty, and R. Kendall. 2011. *World mineral production: 2005–2009*. Nottingham, UK: British Geological Society. www.bgs.ac.uk/downloads/start.cfm?id=1987.

Canuday, J. J. 2007. Big war, small wars: The interplay of large-scale and community armed conflicts in five central Mindanao communities. In *Rido: Clan feuding and conflict management in Mindanao*, ed. W. M. Torres III. Manila, Philippines: Asia Foundation.

DOE (Department of Energy, Republic of the Philippines). 2007. DOE, USGS sign MOU to maximize RP'S coal potential. Media release. Manila. www.doe.gov.ph/news/2007-03-07-doe%20signs%20mou.html.

90   Land and post-conflict peacebuilding

Doyle, C., C. Wicks, and F. Nally. 2007. *Mining in the Philippines: Concerns and conflicts.* West Midlands, UK: Society of St. Columban. www.eccr.org.uk/module-Downloads -prep_hand_out-lid-15.html.

Gordon, M. 1964. *Assimilation in American life.* New York: Oxford University Press.

Hayase, S. 1988. The establishment of Maguindanao/Islam nation—an exploratory consideration of Islamic history in the Philippines. [In Japanese.] Report No. 35. Kagoshima, Japan: Division of History, Kagoshima University.

Japanese Chamber of Commerce and Industry of Mindanao. 2009. *Survey on Mindanao: Agriculture.* [In Japanese.] Davao City, Philippines. http://jccm.jp/index.php/2009-05 -29-06-43-06/2009-05-29-06-53-45.

Lingga, A. S. M. 2007. Dynamics and management of rido in the province of Maguindanao. In *Rido: Clan feuding and conflict management in Mindanao,* ed. W. M. Torres III. Manila, Philippines: Asia Foundation.

Lyday, T. Q. 2000. The mineral industry of the Philippines. In *U.S. Geological Survey minerals yearbook 2000.* http://minerals.usgs.gov/minerals/pubs/country/2000/9326000.pdf.

MAC (Mines and Communities). 2008. Xstrata under attack in the Philippines. April 1. www.minesandcommunities.org/article.php?a=8366.

Majul, C. A. 1964. Theories of the introduction and expansion of Islam in Southeast Asia. *Silliman Journal* 11 (4): 335–398.

Makinano, M. M., and A. Lubang. 2001. *Disarmament, demobilization and reintegration: The Mindanao experience.* Ottawa, Canada: Foreign Affairs and International Trade Canada. www.international.gc.ca/arms-armes/isrop-prisi/research-recherche/intl_security -securite_int/makinano_lubang2001/section01.aspx.

Matuan, M. I. 2007. Inventory of existing rido in Lanao del Sur (1994–2004). In *Rido: Clan feuding and conflict management in Mindanao,* ed. W. M. Torres III. Manila, Philippines: Asia Foundation.

Mindanao Examiner. 2006. More rubber plantations in Mindanao by 2010. September 28.

NEDO (New Energy and Industrial Technology Development Organization). 2009. *Fossil fuels country database, Philippines.* [In Japanese.] Kanagawa, Japan. www.nedo.go.jp/ sekitan/database/country/c0017.htm.

Pacheco-Sabando, L. 2009. Environmental baseline study for water and soil quality of mineral exploration areas of San Jose, Palo, Leyte and Palanog, Tacloban City. Pacific Metals Canada Philippines. www.philippinemetals.com/i/pdf/TechReports/01 -ENVIRONMENTAL-SAMPLING-FOR-PMCPI-pacheco.pdf.

Philippine Information Agency. 2008. President visits North Cotabato to look into needs of rubber industry. July 21. http://archives.pia.gov.ph/?m=12&sec=reader&rp=1 &fi=p080721.htm&no=6&date=07/21/2008.

Rempillo, J. B. 2008. SC declares MOA-AD unconstitutional. Manila: Supreme Court of the Philippines. http://sc.judiciary.gov.ph/publications/benchmark/2008/10/100811.php.

Reuters. 2009. Xstrata ups Tampakan mineral resource estimate 9 pct. October 20. www.reuters.com/article/idUSMAN48683120091020.

Schiavo-Campo, S., and M. Judd. 2005. *The Mindanao conflict in the Philippines: Roots, costs, and potential peace dividend.* Washington, D.C.: World Bank, Conflict Prevention and Reconstruction Unit.

Sen, A. 2006. *Identity and violence.* New York: W. W. Norton.

Torres, W. M., III., ed. 2007. *Rido: Clan feuding and conflict management in Mindanao.* Manila, Philippines: Asia Foundation.

UNSC (United Nations Security Council). 2010. The consolidated list established and maintained by the 1267 Committee with respect to Al-Qaida, Usama bin Laden, and the Taliban and other individuals, groups, undertakings and entities associated with them. www.scribd.com/doc/35037022/Taliban-Alquaida-List-29-03-2010-Consolidated -List.

USGS (United States Geological Survey). 2011. *2009 minerals yearbook: Philippines.* Advanced release. May. http://minerals.usgs.gov/minerals/pubs/country/2009/myb3-2009- -rp.pdf.

U.S. DOS (United States Department of State). 2007. Terrorist organizations. In *Country report on terrorism 2006.* Washington, D.C.

PART 2

Response to displacement and dispossession

PART 2.

Introduction

One of the most pressing issues facing countries immediately after conflict is managing the reintegration of refugees and displaced persons. The numbers of persons uprooted from their homes and lands may range from the hundreds of thousands to the millions, as in Afghanistan, Bosnia and Herzegovina, and Iraq. Peace agreements set out mechanisms for addressing the land and property claims of displaced persons, and practice in this area has also been guided by a number of key standards that reflect basic international legal obligations accepted by most countries. One of the most important nonbinding but influential "soft law" standards is the 1998 Guiding Principles on Internal Displacement, which clarify states' responsibility to address displacement of people within their own borders, in contrast to international refugee law, which protects persons who have fled their country of habitual residence. More recently, the 2005 Principles on Housing and Property Restitution for Refugees and Displaced Persons (also known as the Pinheiro Principles) have asserted a right to post-conflict restoration of property to displaced persons on the basis of international best practice.

Regional efforts to address displacement and property dispossession have also taken on an increasingly important role. This is particularly true in Africa, where the 2006 Pact on Security, Stability, and Development in the Great Lakes Region includes protocols on property issues and internal displacement, and the African Union adopted the first regional convention on internal displacement in 2009.

The first two chapters in this part examine the normative frameworks relevant to displacement and dispossession. The remaining four chapters discuss practical experiences of displacement and dispossession in Rwanda, Bosnia and Herzegovina, Angola, and Iraq.

Barbara McCallin reviews the history of the Pinheiro Principles from adoption to application in "The Role of Restitution in Post-Conflict Situations." Rather than portraying the principles as a universal model for addressing all post-conflict housing, land, and property issues, she analyzes the challenges and limitations of restitution-based approaches in countries with informal land tenure systems and limited state capacity. She argues that the Pinheiro Principles, which mainly provide restorative justice for displaced people and refugees, should be integrated with long-term reforms to address the structural causes of land disputes. Ideally humanitarian actors and land experts will be engaged in the development of land policies that account for the complexity of land tenure issues in post-conflict situations.

Samir Elhawary and Sara Pantuliano take a more critical view of the Pinheiro Principles in "Land Issues in Post-Conflict Return and Recovery." They note that return and restitution may be irrelevant to the real challenges of reintegrating displaced persons in some post-conflict situations—for example, where displacement

96   Land and post-conflict peacebuilding

has exacerbated preexisting and potentially irreversible demographic trends, such as urbanization, and where land and property relations were economically unsustainable prior to displacement. Elhawary and Pantuliano argue in favor of a much broader and more integrated approach to land issues, in which restitution as promoted by the Pinheiro Principles may or may not play a role. The authors conclude with recommendations for return and recovery strategies that can enhance the durability of peace.

Turning to lessons from field experience, John W. Bruce argues for a context-sensitive approach to issues such as restitution in "Return of Land in Post-Conflict Rwanda: International Standards, Improvisation, and the Role of International Humanitarian Organizations." In reviewing responses to displacement following the unsuccessful 1993 Arusha Peace Accords and the subsequent genocide in Rwanda, Bruce highlights opportunities and challenges in post-conflict situations where international standards can provide important guidance but where their application may reignite ethnic tensions that are still capable of destabilizing the country. Bruce cautions against the strict implementation of standards such as the Pinheiro Principles, arguing that such standards should be considered only a broad framework for international and national practice, and that they should be construed in a manner compatible with the political reality and historical land relations prevailing in specific post-conflict situations.

International attempts to control land administration in order to facilitate return and resettlement can be problematic, particularly where local support is lacking. Challenges related to this approach are the focus of the chapter "Post-Conflict Land Tenure Issues in Bosnia: Privatization and the Politics of Reintegrating the Displaced," by Rhodri C. Williams. Williams describes the ethnic conflict in Bosnia and Herzegovina that ended with the signing of the 1995 Dayton Accords and the simultaneous economic transition that involved privatization and transformation of the country's land administration system. He then analyzes post-conflict land tenure issues and the risk of overreach in inter-national efforts to steer complex return processes. Noting the relationship between reintegration of displaced persons and broader land administration policies, Williams contends that understanding the role of land as a political and economic asset is central to the long-term effectiveness of post-conflict reintegration efforts that have land and property dimensions.

After conflict, land can be central to social reconstruction, and resolution of land issues is often at the core of peacebuilding. In "Angola: Land Resources and Conflict," Allan Cain examines land management after decades of conflict in Angola, from 1975 to 2002. The chapter reviews the central role of land and land disputes in Angola's history, from land appropriation in the colonial period, through widespread abandonment of land during the civil war due to massive internal displacement of people, to post-conflict land disputes. Cain discusses how to allocate land titles more equitably, especially to poor communities, and how to protect poor communities' land rights and prevent arbitrary evictions. He suggests adapting the legal framework for land tenure and management to post-conflict realities and implementing the principle of public consultation introduced in Angola's 2004 Land Law. Cain concludes that devolution of decision-making authority to municipalities and incorporation of international good-practice norms into Angola's national legislation are expected to improve land management, strengthen land tenure rights, and ultimately help maintain peace in the country.

Dan E. Stigall takes up the relationship between international norms and national legislation for addressing displacement in "Refugees and Legal Reform in Iraq: The Iraqi Civil Code, International Standards for the Treatment of Displaced Persons, and the Art of Attainable Solutions." Iraqi civil law is frequently applicable to the situation of displaced persons, and Stigall analyzes the extent to which it comports with international standards such as the Guiding Principles on Internal Displacement and the Pinheiro Principles. He argues that the Iraqi Civil Code provides adequate protection and means for displaced persons to reclaim their property and obtain restitution in most situations. However, he concludes, limited legislative modifications accompanied by an increase in the institutional capacity of Iraqi civil courts could help leaders to effectively deal with Iraq's post-conflict displacement crisis, thereby affirming the rule of law and supporting Iraq's economic recovery.

A common thread in these chapters is the need to adapt international standards regarding displacement and dispossession to local contexts in order to ensure that their application is undertaken in a manner that is legitimate and effective, and that avoids unintended negative consequences. The chapters also highlight a range of approaches that may be used to promote durable solutions to displacement and remedies for dispossession. These approaches include the identification of contextually appropriate mechanisms; support to institutions for land dispute resolution; development of pragmatic and broad approaches to structural problems and to protection of housing, land, and property rights; consideration of the rights and concerns of displacement-affected populations as well as of people who have actually been displaced; and planning and coordination to ensure that immediate-term humanitarian programming complements long-term peace objectives. All of these require a deep understanding of local political, institutional, and social realities.

The role of restitution in post-conflict situations

Barbara McCallin

Land and property disputes are a frequent cause of conflict and an unavoidable consequence of it. People displaced by conflict leave behind their land and property, which may be occupied or destroyed in their absence. In the post-conflict period, this situation is an obstacle to return and other durable solutions. As disputes between pre-conflict owners or users and current occupants can endanger the fragile post-conflict environment, there has been a growing recognition within the international community that housing, land, and property (HLP) issues should be addressed more systematically in post-conflict national and international responses.

While land issues have so far been mainly addressed through development programs, humanitarian organizations, typically dealing with emergency relief and early recovery, have shown increased interest in addressing HLP issues by supporting a restitution approach. In places such as the Balkans, Timor-Leste, and Iraq, UN agencies and peacekeeping missions have supported property dispute resolution efforts. By returning property to its original owner or user, property restitution provides a remedy for earlier violations and displacement and attempts to consolidate the peacebuilding process. Humanitarian activities include relief but also protection, advocacy, and support for livelihood projects. The aim of humanitarian efforts is not to engage in long-term reform but rather to intervene in the short term, during conflicts or in the first few years of peace, to help the most vulnerable populations. This may explain why the involvement of humanitarian organizations in HLP issues has focused mainly on return, displaced people, and restitution of land and property.

Several land specialists, more familiar with the complexity of the social, economic, political, and legal relations that constitute land tenure relations, have underlined the limitations of the current humanitarian approach. A 2009 publication, *Uncharted Territory: Land, Conflict and Humanitarian Action*, with contributions from land experts, academics, and practitioners, reviews key criticisms and

---

Barbara McCallin is a housing, land, and property adviser at the Geneva-based Internal Displacement Monitoring Centre of the Norwegian Refugee Council.

100 Land and post-conflict peacebuilding

suggests improvements (Pantuliano 2009). The book argues that by limiting interventions to restitution, humanitarian efforts fail to address the structural causes affecting land tenure, which are often the origin of conflict in agrarian societies. When this is the case, a return through restitution to the status quo ante is unlikely to be sufficient to build a sustainable peace. For that, phenomena such as unequal distribution of land; large-scale land acquisitions (often referred to as *land grabbing*) by governments, elites, and private investors; and insecure land access require forward-looking structural reform more than restorative justice, according to this critique.

While it is clear that restitution cannot address all HLP issues resulting from a conflict, this does not mean that its value should be denied in all circumstances, and advocating for a broader approach to land problems should not result in eliminating the restitution option where it proves appropriate.

Criticisms of the humanitarian approach have recently focused on the UN's 2005 Principles on Housing and Property Restitution for Refugees and Displaced Persons (also called the Pinheiro Principles, after the rapporteur Paulo Sérgio Pinheiro)—an important summary of legal and best-practice documents on displaced populations and restitution—arguing that the principles ignore the root causes of conflict over land and are difficult to apply in situations in which landownership and registration do not follow Western norms. These critiques often focus on what the Pinheiro Principles are not (a guide to all post-conflict HLP issues) rather than what they are (a guide to restitution).

This chapter describes the Pinheiro Principles, the context in which they were created, and examples of situations in which they have been applied. Examples draw on the experience of the Norwegian Refugee Council, which has significant experience in providing legal assistance and mediation on HLP issues. It highlights some shortcomings as well as creative ways to adapt the Pinheiro Principles to situations in which informal and unregistered property predominates. The first section describes how the right to restitution has been recognized by international law and in UN resolutions. The second section reviews the Pinheiro Principles. Next, the chapter assesses the principles' impact at the global, regional, and national levels by analyzing treaties and other documents and nongovernmental organization (NGO) field practices. The fourth section examines the challenges faced by restitution in informal land tenure systems. Lastly, the chapter discusses the limitations of the restitution approach and the need for humanitarians to coordinate with land experts to develop a broader approach to HLP issues.

The criticism of the humanitarian approach to HLP issues helped many humanitarian organizations realize that addressing HLP sustainably requires envisaging other types of intervention besides restitution. This does not invalidate the Pinheiro Principles but situates them as one of the tools available. An adequate response requires that humanitarians, development specialists, and land experts coordinate their efforts from the beginning of the post-conflict phase to combine the best of both approaches—a human-rights-based approach providing restorative justice for violations resulting from the conflict, and a reformative approach promoting changes required to the land tenure system to address the structural causes of land disputes.

THE EMERGENCE OF A RIGHT TO PROPERTY RESTITUTION

Addressing HLP issues in post-conflict situations has increasingly been recognized as essential to achieving sustainable peace and durable solutions for displaced people. Until now, the international community has addressed these issues mainly through property restitution. This focus is the result of two parallel evolutions, one political and the other legal.

After the end of the Cold War, the ideological incentive to provide asylum quickly faded. Support grew for solutions facilitating return (Williams 2007; Leckie 2003) and the protection of displaced people within their own countries. Access to and repossession of housing and property were key to sustainable return, and thus the international community's interest in HLP issues increased. The Office of the United Nations High Commissioner for Refugees (UNHCR), as a result of its role in repatriation of refugees, particularly emphasized the link between return and property repossession.[1] This has been reflected in voluntary repatriation agreements between the UNHCR and refugees' countries of origin, in which the recovery of homes has often been mentioned as one of the elements creating the conditions for return in safety and dignity (Leckie 2003). Similarly, numerous recent peace agreements have explicitly referred to the right of displaced people to return to their homes and have their property returned to them.[2]

The increased interest in return and HLP issues has corresponded with the progress of the notion of restorative justice, which aims to restore victims to the situation they were in before their rights were violated (Williams 2007). For displaced people whose housing rights have been violated, restitution of property can undo and physically reverse the consequences of past violations. Restitution also contributes to the return of the rule of law after a conflict. Redressing past violations helps deter future violations; restoring justice removes a potential source of tension, therefore contributing to a sustainable peace. Of course, this can only be effective if the political, social, and security conditions exist that allow returnees to continue to have control over their repossessed property.

The human rights instruments that appeared after World War II upheld the need for reparations and restitution not only between states but also between a state and its nationals (Williams 2007). This approach has since been reaffirmed repeatedly, establishing a strong basis for restitution. The UN's approach to this issue, expressed in its Basic Principles and Guidelines on the Right to a Remedy and Reparation for Victims of Gross Violations of International Human Rights

---

[1] In a 2001 internal memorandum, UNHCR underlined the importance of HLP issues: "Experience has shown that voluntary repatriation operations are unlikely to be fully successful or sustainable in the longer term if housing and property issues—being an integral part of return in safety and dignity—are left unattended."

[2] Parties to such agreements have included Bosnia and Herzegovina, Cambodia, El Salvador, Eritrea, Ethiopia, Guatemala, Kosovo, Liberia, Mozambique, Rwanda, Sierra Leone, Sudan, and Tajikistan. For the details on HLP provisions in such peace agreements, see Leckie (2007).

102 Land and post-conflict peacebuilding

Law and Serious Violations of International Humanitarian Law (UNGA 2005), confirms restitution as one form of reparation for human rights violations—along with compensation, rehabilitation, and guarantees of nonrepetition. International humanitarian law, which prohibits arbitrary displacement and destruction of property, also envisages restitution as a key remedy as specified in the Rome Statute of the International Criminal Court.[3] Decisions from human rights treaty bodies on adequate housing, rights of indigenous people, and the right to respect of privacy and the home also affirm the right to restitution. Numerous UN resolutions (addressing either specific country situations or themes such as eviction, freedom of movement, and displaced people's rights) also affirm the right of displaced people to repossess their land and property (Leckie 2007). As mentioned earlier, these rights are also upheld in a number of peace agreements.

Restitution rights are therefore firmly established in a variety of international documents. But at the national level, restitution programs and attention to HLP issues have had varying degrees of success (Leckie 2007), depending on the political and security situation but also the attention given to the matter by the international community. Bosnia and Herzegovina's restitution process can be considered a success, since 93 percent of the 200,000 people who submitted a restitution claim repossessed their property; but this was the result of close monitoring by the international community combined with sanctions, which overcame national resistance. In contrast, in Cambodia, the United Nations Transitional Authority did not systematically address HLP issues (UNSC 2007).

THE PINHEIRO PRINCIPLES

It was against this background that the Pinheiro Principles were adopted by the United Nations in 2005 after a consultation process involving NGOs, governments, specialized agencies such as UNHCR and the Office of the High Commissioner for Human Rights, and property experts. The Pinheiro Principles (UN 2005) build on international human rights and humanitarian standards. They reaffirm displaced people's right to voluntary return to their homes as well as the notion that housing and property restitution contributes to the establishment of the rule of law and consolidation of peace, therefore preventing future displacement. They consolidate in one document various legal standards supporting HLP restitution for returnees and displaced people.

The objective of the Pinheiro Principles is to help national and international actors address legal and technical issues related to HLP restitution where displacement has led people to be arbitrarily deprived of their homes, land, and properties— regardless of the cause of displacement (conflict or natural disaster). The Pinheiro

---

[3] Article 75, paragraph 2 of that statute says: "The Court may make an order directly against a convicted person specifying appropriate reparations to, or in respect of, victims, including restitution, compensation and rehabilitation." (For complete text of the Rome Statute of the International Criminal Court, see http://untreaty.un.org/cod/icc/statute/romefra.htm.)

Restitution in post-conflict situations **103**

Principles also recognize compensation as a potential solution (principle 21), but emphasize restitution as the preferred remedy and limit compensation to cases in which restitution is impossible (principles 2.1, 2.2, and 21.2) or the injured party voluntarily accepts compensation in lieu of restitution (principle 21).

There are three durable solutions to displacement—return, local integration, and resettlement. Restitution is considered a better remedy than compensation because it restores victims to the situation that existed before they were displaced and allows them to choose between these three options, while compensation is less favorable to the return option. To prevent pressure on the choice between these solutions, the Pinheiro Principles state that return should not be a precondition of restitution, which exists as a distinct right (principle 10.3). Another purpose of this provision is to ensure that the remedies offered are not guided by political interests but remain the choice of the victims. Countries wanting to limit the return of displaced people would rather provide compensation than restitution. Compensation can be seen as a way to consolidate ethnic cleansing—for example, in Bosnia and Herzegovina, where the compensation fund envisaged in the Dayton Peace Agreement never received funds from the international community for fear that it would compromise victims' ability and desire to return home by too quickly offering an easy alternative. In contrast, Bosnian and Herzegovina politicians opposed to multiethnicity pushed for the compensation option to facilitate local integration of the displaced in areas where they would belong to a majority group.

The Pinheiro Principles do not create new legal standards, and are not binding in themselves, but they restate rights expressed in a variety of binding international instruments (Pinheiro 2005). They cover a wide range of rights related to displacement and HLP such as nondiscrimination, freedom of movement, and protection from arbitrary displacement. Under the latter category, they prohibit forced evictions and destruction of houses and crops and arbitrary confiscation or expropriation of land. Individuals' rights to privacy, respect for the home, and peaceful enjoyment of possession limit states' interference with homes and possessions to situations in which the interest of society is at stake. Principle 4, which addresses gender equality, mentions aspects that can be particularly problematic for women and girls, who often do not enjoy secure tenure because, in many cases, they access land through their male relatives. Widows may also become landless or homeless if no equal access to inheritance exists. Principle 4 recommends that restitution programs and policies recognize joint ownership rights of both male and female heads of household and do not disadvantage women and girls.

In addition to reaffirming legal standards, the Pinheiro Principles provide guidance on practical, legal, procedural, and institutional aspects of restitution based on lessons learned, notably in the Balkans but also in Iraq and South Africa. The intention is to facilitate an approach to HLP restitution that is consistent and in line with international standards. In terms of process, the Pinheiro Principles recommend that restitution mechanisms should be accessible and sensitive to age and gender (principle 13), and should ensure consultation and participation of affected individuals and groups (principle 14). To address the absence or loss of

104   Land and post-conflict peacebuilding

ownership documents, principle 15 provides that authorities should replace such documents at minimum cost and that HLP records should be protected or formalized if necessary to ensure security of tenure. This last provision recognizes that formalization may not always be the best way to ensure secure tenure.

The Pinheiro Principles call for restitution programs to recognize not only owners but also tenants and other legitimate users of land and houses (principle 16). Existing occupants of housing or land subject to restitution are another category of people who may be in need of protection when restitution takes place, as some might themselves become displaced and homeless. While their rights should not prejudice those of legitimate owners, they should be protected from forced eviction and provided with alternative accommodation if they have nowhere else to go. If they invested in good faith in the property, their right to compensation should be examined (principle 17).

To be efficient, restitution mechanisms also need to provide for enforcement. Measures should also be taken to discourage looting of vacated HLP through information campaigns and prosecution when necessary (principle 20), as looting renders homes uninhabitable and is a serious obstacle to return. Finally, the Pinheiro Principles underline the responsibility of the international community to promote and protect the right to HLP restitution and to voluntary return. The international community can also be instrumental in promoting the inclusion of HLP restitution provisions in peace agreements and voluntary repatriation agreements, cooperate with national governments to ensure compatibility of HLP restitution policies with international standards, and monitor implementation (principle 22).

THE IMPACT OF THE PINHEIRO PRINCIPLES

The Pinheiro Principles helped put HLP issues on the humanitarian agenda. In 2005, the year they were adopted, the United Nations carried out a review of the humanitarian response capacity of UN agencies, NGOs, the Red Cross/Red Crescent, and other key humanitarian organizations. The resulting report recommended dividing the humanitarian response into sectors or clusters and assigning to each a lead agency responsible for the coordination of assistance (United Nations Emergency Relief Coordinator and Under-Secretary for Humanitarian Affairs 2005). It also recommended steps to improve leadership and coordination in humanitarian emergencies as well as humanitarian financing. Eleven clusters were identified, including protection,[4] and were established at the global level and in some cases at the country level.

The review identified shelter, land, and property as areas with a significant response gap. As a result, HLP became one of five areas of responsibility in the protection cluster, and an HLP subcluster was created in 2007, chaired by the

---

[4]   The other clusters were agriculture, camp coordination and management, early recovery, education, emergency shelter, emergency telecommunication, health, logistics, nutrition, and water, sanitation, and hygiene.

United Nations Human Settlements Programme (UN-HABITAT). Its main objectives are to develop and disseminate HLP standards, tools, and guidelines; promote a rights-based approach to HLP issues; and educate humanitarians, authorities, and affected populations on HLP rights.

In 2007, a group of agencies published the *Handbook on Housing and Property Restitution for Refugees and Displaced Persons* to facilitate the implementation of the Pinheiro Principles.[5] Since the handbook's publication, however, there have been few initiatives promoting the Pinheiro Principles, even among these agencies. This may be the result of early criticism that the handbook, the Pinheiro Principles, and restitution in general were not adapted to countries without land and property registries—the large majority of countries affected by displacement. As a result, dissemination of and training on the Pinheiro Principles has been limited, and there has been no systematic effort to document their use in post-conflict situations.

There have, however, been a few significant direct and indirect references to the Pinheiro Principles. In 2007, a UN report on the protection of civilians (UNSC 2007) identified the need to address post-conflict HLP issues as a major challenge for the protection of civilians. This significantly raised the profile of HLP issues in the humanitarian sphere. The report listed HLP issues in conflict and post-conflict situations, such as forced evictions, destruction of property, and loss of ownership documentation, and made suggestions to address them. While it did not refer specifically to the Pinheiro Principles, its recommendations were clearly informed by them. It recommended that the United Nations systematically address HLP issues through preventive action and that references to HLP issues be included in future peace agreements and Security Council resolutions as part of the terms of reference for peacekeeping missions. The report also underlined the need to facilitate registration of land and property and issue ownership documents.

In 2010, the Parliamentary Assembly of the Council of Europe adopted recommendations on property issues faced by refugees and displaced people (PACE 2010). These built on the European Convention on Human Rights and the European Court's jurisprudence as well as the Guiding Principles on Internal Displacement (UNCHR 1998) and the Pinheiro Principles. They called for member states trying to resolve post-conflict HLP issues of refugees and internally displaced persons to take into account the Pinheiro Principles as well as other relevant Council of Europe instruments. The Pinheiro Principles could indeed be relevant for several members of the Council of Europe facing property restitution issues, including Croatia, Cyprus, Georgia, Kosovo, and Turkey.

---

[5] Participants included several UN agencies—the Office for the Coordination of Humanitarian Affairs' Inter-agency Internal Displacement Division; Office of the High Commissioner for Refugees; Food and Agriculture Organization; and Office of the High Commissioner for Human Rights—and the Norwegian Refugee Council's Internal Displacement Monitoring Centre. For the handbook, see www.unhcr.org/refworld/docid/4693432c2.html.

106 Land and post-conflict peacebuilding

In Africa, the Pact on Security, Stability and Development in the Great Lakes Region (Great Lakes Pact), which entered into force in June 2008, adopted (in article 13) the Protocol on the Property Rights of Returning Persons.[6] The protocol, adopted in November 2006, represents an interesting adaptation of the Pinheiro Principles to the African context, and it refers to the Pinheiro Principles as a reference to consider when addressing illegal appropriation, occupation, or use of property.[7]

This protocol is the first binding multilateral instrument affirming the property restitution rights of displaced people. Its main objectives are to protect the HLP of displaced people, facilitate their restitution, and create a framework for addressing HLP disputes. Compensation is also envisaged for land and property lost or destroyed in the context of development-induced displacement (article 8). While based on preexisting international and regional standards, the protocol is also designed to address the specific needs of the region. Since it applies to countries with limited state institutions at the local level and almost no rural land and property registration, it recognizes the role of alternative and informal community-based mechanisms and recommends that formal judicial procedures adopt simplified requirements for proof of ownership, such as testimonies (article 4.3). It calls for specific protections for women and children (articles 3, 5, and 6), who are often disadvantaged by customary and traditional rules. It also calls for protection of the rights of pastoralists and other groups "whose mode of livelihood depends on special attachment to their lands" (article 7) and requires that they be allowed to return to their land or, if that is not possible, that they be provided alternative land of equal value, failing which compensation should be given. The protocol also calls for land registration schemes to recognize statutory and customary land tenure systems (article 4).

Many of the provisions included in the protocol are very similar to those of the Pinheiro Principles, notably in relation to the protection of women, children, and people with special attachment to land and the recognition of various forms of ownership and possessory rights as subject to restitution.

The African Union Convention for the Protection and Assistance of Internally Displaced Persons in Africa (also called the Kampala Convention), adopted in

---

[6] The Great Lakes Pact was ratified by eleven states: Angola, Burundi, Central African Republic, Democratic Republic of the Congo, Republic of Congo, Kenya, Rwanda, Sudan, Tanzania, Uganda, and Zambia. For its complete text, see https://icglr.org/IMG/pdf/Pact_on_Security_Stability_and_Development_in_the_Great_Lakes_Region_14_15_December_2006.pdf.

[7] Article 3, paragraph 3, of the Protocol on the Rights of Returning Persons states, "Member states shall ensure that the property of internally displaced persons and refugees shall be protected in all possible circumstances against arbitrary and illegal appropriation, occupation or use, taking into account the United Nations Principles on Housing and Property Restitution." For the complete text of the protocol, see www.internal-displacement.org/8025708F004BE3B1/%28httpInfoFiles%29/84E06BF26DBB560BC12572FB002C02D6/$file/Final%20protocol.PropertyRights%20-En%20r.pdf.

October 2009, is less specific with regard to property and does not mention the Pinheiro Principles.[8] Nevertheless, in article 11.4, it calls for simplified procedures where necessary to address disputes related to the land and property of internally displaced persons. Article 11.5 requires restitution to be provided, on their return, to communities with special dependency and attachment to their land, which refers to indigenous people and other groups such as pastoralists. This last provision actually contradicts Pinheiro principle 10.3, which states that restitution should exist independently from return. This contradiction reflects one of the difficulties in implementing the Pinheiro Principles in informal land tenure settings where land rights may be based on use more than ownership. In such cases, it is difficult to envisage restitution of land if return does not take place.

At the national level, Colombia's Constitutional Court recommended using the Pinheiro Principles to shape national restitution policy. A 2007 decision emphasized the obligation of the government to protect internally displaced people's right to reparation and restitution of HLP.[9] It based this approach partly on the Pinheiro Principles, which it said were part of Colombia's constitutional framework and should therefore form the basis of any restitution policy.

Some NGOs—such as the Centre on Housing Rights and Evictions, Displacement Solutions, and the Norwegian Refugee Council (NRC)—have used the Pinheiro Principles for training purposes or legal assistance. The Norwegian Refugee Council's Information, Counselling and Legal Assistance (ICLA) program, which addresses HLP disputes, is an example of the need to better disseminate information on the Pinheiro Principles. This author consulted ten NRC country offices with an ICLA program and found that only two (in Colombia and Southern Sudan) actively use the principles in their practice, training, and advocacy.[10] In Colombia, NRC's partners have organized workshops for public servants throughout the country using the Pinheiro Principles as a basis for discussion. The workshops were part of a consultation process on the drafting of the National Land Restitution Plan.

In other countries with ICLA programs, NRC's experience has been that the Pinheiro Principles are seldom or never mentioned as a reference or for advocacy purposes by NGOs, government officials, or even international organizations. NRC offices that do not incorporate the Pinheiro Principles in their work mention the lack of awareness of them (Liberia, Côte d'Ivoire) or the fact that they are not adapted to the complexities of customary land tenure and traditional dispute resolution (Afghanistan and Uganda). There is very little monitoring of how civil

---

[8] For the convention, see www.africa-union.org/root/AR/index/Convention%20on%20 IDPs%20_Eng_%20-%20Final.pdf.

[9] Constitutional Court of the Republic of Colombia, Ref. T-1.642.563, Sentencia T-821, October 5, 2007, para. 60.

[10] The ten countries were Afghanistan, Azerbaijan, Burundi, Colombia, Côte d'Ivoire, Georgia, Lebanon, Liberia, Sudan (particularly then Southern Sudan, now South Sudan), and Uganda.

108   Land and post-conflict peacebuilding

society organizations, authorities, or international organizations such as UNHCR have used the Pinheiro Principles for program, policy, or advocacy purposes, so it is difficult to assess whether NRC's experience is representative of the overall picture. However, it provides information on how they could be used and on some of the difficulties in implementing them.

IMPLEMENTATION IN INFORMAL LAND TENURE SYSTEMS

The Pinheiro Principles were a significant achievement: a reference tool gathering relevant legal standards and best practices and promoting a more systematic and consistent approach to the HLP rights of refugees and displaced people. This achievement was, however, soon challenged by two main criticisms of the Pinheiro Principles and of restitution in general: (1) they are not adapted to informal land tenure systems, and (2) they may address individual claims effectively but fail to address the structural causes of land disputes.

Restitution faces several practical and conceptual challenges in countries with informal land tenure systems and legal pluralism—the coexistence of different sources of authority (traditional and statutory) that regulate similar matters. Jon Unruh has defined legal pluralism with regard to land tenure as "the different sets of rights and obligations concerning land and property, within multiple social fields" (Unruh 2009, 53–54). In many countries affected by displacement in Africa and Asia, rural lands are held and transferred mainly according to traditional or customary rules, which are not necessarily recognized and endorsed by the formal legal system. Restitution attempts in such contexts are particularly difficult in the absence of cadastral records or documents proving ownership or possessory rights.[11] The Pinheiro Principles do lack guidance in that regard. In Africa, the Great Lakes Protocol on Property Rights of Returning Persons elaborates on the Pinheiro Principles by suggesting the use of traditional dispute resolution mechanisms and alternative forms of evidence. The latter can include geographical boundary markers, community mapping, and the use of witnesses to determine rights to restitution.

Conflict and displacement add another layer of complexity to land disputes, as they disrupt the usual ways of regulating land relations by dispersing communities and undermining the capacity of authorities to carry out their land-related functions. New practices and actors emerge during the conflict, which may create problems in the post-conflict phase when displaced people and returnees are confronted with competing land tenure systems.

Côte d'Ivoire illustrates the diversity of overlapping bodies addressing HLP disputes in the aftermath of a conflict. In addition to the mechanism specified by the statutory system—the village land management committee (Comité

---

[11] *Possessory rights* are the rights that accrue from physically occupying a land parcel. Legal recognition of possessory rights can vary; in some cases, possession can give rise to ownership claims through adverse possession or occupation.

Restitution in post-conflict situations 109

Villageois de Gestion Foncière Rurale, set up to implement the 1998 rural land law), which is hardly functional—certain traditional chiefs also address land disputes; and some ministries have encouraged NGOs to create peace committees whose role includes the resolution of land disputes. Many of these committees were set up before the return of the displaced, so their authority is often contested by returnees and traditional authorities. Certain regions have also seen the development of ad hoc committees set up by special-interest groups, such as the youth, who contest the authority of the chiefs and promote their own solutions to land disputes (IDMC 2009). This creates a situation of legal uncertainty in which any decision by one body can be contested by another.

Legal pluralism represents a practical obstacle to restitution programs, as it poses the question of which institution should be in charge of their implementation. Customary and traditional authorities are used by far the most frequently to address land and property disputes, mostly as a result of their proximity and accessibility. Their decisions are usually respected as a result of their own social acceptance. In contrast, state institutions are frequently absent at the local level or may have been weakened by the conflict, depriving them of effective means of implementing restitution. The Pinheiro Principles attempt to address this situation by recommending that HLP restitution programs integrate alternative or informal dispute resolution mechanisms as long as they comply with international standards.[12] However, it is unclear which institution or mechanism would ensure conformity of traditional authorities' decisions to such standards if the state lacks capacity to do so—which is usually the reason it had to rely on traditional institutions in the first place.

Another frequent but ill-informed criticism of the Pinheiro Principles (and of property restitution more generally) is that they can only be adapted to Western-style individual ownership and not to other types of tenure. It is admittedly difficult to implement restitution in informal land tenure systems. But the Pinheiro Principles were intended to protect not only property rights but also other possessory rights. The expression "housing, land, and property," used throughout the Pinheiro Principles, aims precisely at ensuring that restitution benefits owners of property and nonowners equally through implementation of housing rights (Leckie 2003),[13] and protects all types of tenure related to housing and land, including informal types. Principle 15.3 provides that registration systems should record or recognize the possessory rights of traditional and indigenous communities to collective land, and principle 16 addresses the rights of tenants and nonowners "to return

---

[12] According to principle 12.4 of the Pinheiro Principles, "States may integrate alternative or informal dispute resolution mechanisms into these [restitution] processes, insofar as all such mechanisms act in accordance with international human rights, refugee and humanitarian law and related standards, including the right to be protected from discrimination" (UN 2005, 9).

[13] See also Pinheiro (2005), paragraphs 34–36, for legal references to the right to adequate housing.

110 Land and post-conflict peacebuilding

and repossess and use their housing, land and property in a similar manner to those possessing formal ownership rights" (UN 2005, 12).[14]

If the Pinheiro Principles do apply to informal HLP rights, restitution of such rights may be more problematic than that of formal rights in situations where several rights coexist on the same piece of land (for example, grazing rights, the right to plant trees, and the right of access or easements) or where rights are held collectively. This situation is not covered in the Pinheiro Principles. Moreover, the provision for registering repossessed properties in order to increase security of tenure brings with it the risk of losing the recognition of some of these rights in the course of the formalization process.[15] Many formalization processes tend to concentrate all land rights in an individual title deed. This is the case, for instance, in Côte d'Ivoire, where the rural land law provides for recognition of customary rights and their transformation into individual title deeds. In such a process, secondary access rights to the land such as those mentioned above disappear, dispossessing several types of users. This is typically a topic on which the Pinheiro Principles would need to be supplemented by guidance from land experts on ways to preserve multiple land rights with or without registration.

The Pinheiro Principles also provide for recognition and registration of collective land belonging to traditional and indigenous communities, and for filing of collective restitution claims.[16] However, neither the Pinheiro Principles nor the *Handbook on Property Restitution for Refugees and Displaced Persons* provide guidance on how this could be done. In practice, it is widely admitted that humanitarian organizations trying to implement restitution programs in informal land tenure situations lack expertise on collective land titling, which could protect customary interests in post-conflict situations.[17] Without such expertise, it is difficult to design adequate responses to the problem.

Restitution may also prove difficult where land tenure rights are strictly linked to the use of the land. In such cases, displacement, even if forced by conflict,

---

[14] Paragraph 62 of Pinheiro (2005) states: "Tenants and other non-owners do have rights of possession, including security of tenure, which protect them from forced eviction and displacement."

[15] According to principle 15.2 of the Pinheiro Principles, "States should ensure that any judicial, quasi-judicial, administrative or customary pronouncement regarding the rightful ownership of, or rights to, housing, land and/or property is accompanied by measures to ensure registration or demarcation of that housing, land and/or property as is necessary to ensure legal security of tenure" (UN 2005).

[16] According to principle 13.6 of the Pinheiro Principles, "States should ensure that users of housing, land and/or property, including tenants, have the right to participate in the restitution claims process, including through the filing of collective restitution claims" (UN 2005).

[17] As one writer has put it, "a common shortfall is the sector's overempha[s]is on the ownership of individual assets to the exclusion of the more expansive, valuable and threatened properties that are logically held collectively. . . . [There] is a lack of familiarity with the dynamics of a regime that is first and foremost a community-based system of property relations, with complex patterns of ownership and access" (Alden Wily 2009, 37).

Restitution in post-conflict situations **111**

may affect the persistence of land rights, especially if displacement lasted for a long time and if more recent occupants have invested in the land and acquired possessory rights to it. Principle 17 protects secondary occupants from arbitrary or unlawful forced eviction but gives precedence to legitimate owners, tenants, and other rights holders. In such cases, a strict application of the principle may not be understood or could be considered unfair by long-term occupants, in particular where customary and traditional justice tend to privilege reconciliation and compromise rather than restorative justice, which identifies a winner and a loser.

The experience of NRC's legal assistance program illustrates both the difficulties of applying the Pinheiro Principles in informal settings and their utility. As mentioned previously, very few NRC ICLA teams have been using the Pinheiro Principles. Several (in Afghanistan, Burundi, and Uganda) consider the principles difficult to adapt to traditional dispute resolution mechanisms. In Burundi, for instance, traditional mechanisms focus on conflict resolution and compromise, which often involve sharing between the parties rather than restitution. Systematic restitution in Burundi appears materially impossible as a result of the very long period of displacement, the lack of accurate land and property registries and documentation, and the risk of overlapping claims. The lack of state capacity, in particular at the local level, the ineffective judiciary, and the lack of resources combined with the high number of claims on a very small and densely populated territory are other challenges to restitution and compensation in Burundi. As a result, most claims presented before the Commission Nationale des Terres et Autres Biens (land commission), or in traditional dispute resolution mechanisms, result in sharing of the contested land in order to accommodate as many returnees as possible and defuse return-related land conflicts.

Several of the ICLA offices that are not using the Pinheiro Principles and consider their implementation difficult in customary contexts have nonetheless expressed interest in being trained on them. Their objective is to increase their knowledge of the Pinheiro Principles to explore possibilities to adapt them to their specific context (in Afghanistan, Côte d'Ivoire, and Liberia). This apparent contradiction reflects the dual nature of the Pinheiro Principles: a compilation of existing binding legal standards (nondiscrimination, gender equality, the right to protection from displacement), which should apply in all situations, and best practices, which may be more difficult to adapt universally, in particular with regard to some procedural and institutional requirements.

The way NRC ICLA teams in South Sudan are using the Pinheiro Principles illustrates how they can be applied in informal land tenure situations. The Land Act for Southern Sudan includes a section on land restitution and compensation, which grants power to traditional authorities to address such matters. NRC ICLA teams in South Sudan are using the Pinheiro Principles and the *Handbook on Property Restitution for Refugees and Displaced Persons* to guide their interactions with traditional authorities, notably to underline principles, such as nondiscrimination and accessibility, called for in international human rights standards. For NRC's ICLA program in South Sudan, the Pinheiro Principles represent the only available guidance on the matter so far.

112 Land and post-conflict peacebuilding

BEYOND RESTITUTION

The focus on restitution promoted by the Pinheiro Principles has been criticized by some land specialists, who argue that restitution fails to address the structural issues that are often a cause of land conflict in agrarian societies. Such issues include unequal distribution of land and the resulting landlessness, as well as the pressure over land resulting from economic or political interests, which can endanger the security of tenure of certain groups and lead to land grabbing and displacement, as has happened in Colombia. Because of these issues, some land experts have questioned whether restoring the status quo ante is practicable or even desirable if it results in return to an unjust situation that may have caused the conflict in the first place and that could continue to endanger peacebuilding efforts (Alden Wily 2009). The focus on restitution linked to conflict-related dispossession, they argue, also detracts attention from other HLP violations that often occur in post-conflict situations, such as land grabbing by governments, elites, and private investors (Alden Wily 2009). The breakdown of law and order associated with the conflict may even increase after peace is proclaimed, as some take advantage of the relative security to take land before displaced people return.

Addressing these issues in a way that supports sustainable peace requires forward-looking structural reform more than restorative justice. The resolution of certain land access problems also may be better addressed through development and urbanization rather than property restitution. In such cases, reparation in the form of grants for urban housing or business capital might be preferable to restitution (Alden Wily 2008). An increasing number of HLP and land specialists are calling for a broader approach to land that would address land and properties not only through restitution and compensation but also through a restructuring of land relations to address pre-conflict problems as well as those that arose during and after the conflict.

However, such reforms are often outside the ambit and expertise of humanitarians and their donors, who consider involvement with such issues too complex, politically sensitive, and development oriented. The challenge is therefore to bridge the knowledge and programmatic gap between humanitarians and land specialists in post-conflict situations, in order to improve mutual understanding and ensure that short-term humanitarian efforts do not hinder long-term efforts to address the structural causes of tensions over land. This broader approach to land issues should be integrated within the overall humanitarian and recovery response (Pantuliano and Elhawary 2009).

CONCLUSION

The Pinheiro Principles represent the culmination of long-standing efforts to assert the rights of refugees and displaced people to restitution. The utility of HLP restitution has been demonstrated on numerous occasions, notably in Bosnia and Herzegovina, where the process allowed for restitution of 200,000 homes (Williams

Restitution in post-conflict situations **113**

2007). The difficulties in implementing it in certain situations should not discredit its utility in helping to remedy the human rights violations suffered by refugees and displaced people. A recent ruling by the African Commission on Human and Peoples' Rights shows how HLP restitution can also benefit forcibly evicted people without formal land titles. The ruling condemned Kenya for the expulsion of the Endorois indigenous communities from their land and upheld their right to both restoration of their land and compensation. This decision was the first to define in detail indigenous people's rights to land in Africa (HRW 2010).

The Pinheiro Principles helped keep HLP restitution issues on the humanitarian agenda. Where their implementation proved difficult as a result of informal land tenure and limited state capacity, the Pinheiro Principles paved the way for locally adapted instruments such as Africa's Great Lakes Protocol on Property Rights of Returning Persons. Further practical guidance is needed, notably on ways to engage with traditional dispute resolution mechanisms where states lack capacity. This involves monitoring their decisions, ensuring conformity to international standards, and balancing restorative justice (which emphasizes restitution) with conflict resolution and community reconciliation (which emphasize compromise and sharing).

Since the Pinheiro Principles were adopted, thinking among human rights activists and humanitarians on HLP issues has evolved significantly, notably as a result of the criticisms made by land experts of their exclusive focus on restitution. Following the initial enthusiasm, many realized that what worked in the Balkans could be more difficult to achieve in most countries affected by displacement. The next step was to try to make restitution work by adapting the Pinheiro Principles to field reality. At the same time, recognition grew that, while restitution remains a valid approach, it does not suffice to address the land tensions at the origin of many conflicts and should be combined with broader land policies. The problem is therefore not the Pinheiro Principles themselves, which should not be blamed for what they are not, but the lack of guidance on ways other than restitution to address land issues in post-conflict situations.[18] This need for an integrated and coordinated approach to land issues is increasingly recognized; such an approach should be at the heart of humanitarian and early recovery efforts, notably through the work of the HLP subcluster.

REFERENCES

Alden Wily, L. 2008. Land in emergency to development transitions: Who does what? Or is there something we are missing here? Session presented at the conference "Uncharted Territory: Land, Conflict and Humanitarian Action," sponsored by the Humanitarian Policy Group, Overseas Development Institute, London.

---

[18] UN-HABITAT is currently developing a document providing guidance on land issues in post-conflict situations, which should contribute to filling the gap.

114   Land and post-conflict peacebuilding

————. 2009. Tackling land tenure in the emergency to development transition in post-conflict states: From restitution to reform. In *Uncharted territory: Land, conflict and humanitarian action*, ed. S. Pantuliano. Rugby, Warwickshire, UK: Practical Action Publishing.

HRW (Human Rights Watch). 2010. Kenya: Landmark ruling on indigenous land rights. New York. www.hrw.org/en/news/2010/02/04/kenya-landmark-ruling-indigenous-land-rights, Switzerland.

IDMC (Internal Displacement Monitoring Centre). 2009. *Whose land is this? Land disputes and forced displacement in the western forest area of Côte d'Ivoire.* Geneva, Switzerland.

Leckie, S., ed. 2003. *Returning home: Housing and property restitution rights of refugees and displaced persons.* Ardsley, NY: Transnational Publishers.

————. 2007. *Housing, land and property restitution rights of refugees and displaced persons: Laws, cases, and materials.* New York: Cambridge University Press.

PACE (Parliamentary Assembly of the Council of Europe). 2010. Solving property issues of refugees and displaced persons. Resolution 1708 and Recommendation 1901 of the Parliamentary Assembly of the Council of Europe. http://assembly.coe.int/Main.asp?link= /Documents/AdoptedText/ta10/ERES1708.htm.

Pantuliano, S., ed. 2009. *Uncharted territory: Land, conflict and humanitarian action.* Rugby, Warwickshire, UK: Practical Action Publishing.

Pantuliano, S., and S. Elhawary. 2009. Uncharted territory: Land, conflict and humanitarian action. Humanitarian Policy Group Policy Brief 39. London: Overseas Development Institute.

Pinheiro, P. S. 2005. Explanatory notes on the principles on housing and property restitution for refugees and displaced persons. New York: United Nations Commission on Human Rights, Sub-commission on the Promotion and Protection of Human Rights. www1.umn.edu/humanrts/instree/housing-finalreport2006.html.

UN (United Nations). 2005. United Nations principles on housing and property restitution for refugees and displaced persons [Pinheiro Principles]. E/CN.4/Sub.2/2005/17. June 28. New York: United Nations Commission on Human Rights, Sub-commission on the Promotion and Protection of Human Rights. www.unhcr.org/refworld/docid/41640c874.html.

UNCHR (United Nations Commission on Human Rights). 1998. *Report of the Representative of the Secretary-General, Mr. Francis M. Deng, submitted pursuant to commission resolution 1997/39. Addendum: Guiding principles on internal displacement.* E/CN.4/ 1998/53/Add.2. February 11. www.unhcr.org/refworld/docid/3d4f95e11.html.

UNGA (United Nations General Assembly). 2005. Basic principles and guidelines on the right to a remedy and reparation for victims of gross violations of international human rights law and serious violations of international humanitarian law. Resolution 60/147 of 16 December 2005. www2.ohchr.org/english/law/remedy.htm.

United Nations Emergency Relief Coordinator and Under-Secretary for Humanitarian Affairs. 2005. *Humanitarian response review.* www.unicef.org/emerg/files/ocha_hrr.pdf.

UNSC (United Nations Security Council). 2007. *Report of the Secretary-General on the protection of civilians in armed conflicts.* S/2007/643. October 28. www.un.org/Docs/sc/ sgrep07.htm.

Unruh, J. 2009. Humanitarian approaches to conflict and post-conflict legal pluralism in land tenure. In *Uncharted territory: Land, conflict and humanitarian action*, ed. S. Pantuliano. Rugby, Warwickshire, UK: Practical Action Publishing.

Williams, R. C. 2007. The contemporary right to property restitution in the context of transitional justice. ICTJ Occasional Paper Series. New York: International Center for Transitional Justice. http://ictj.org/sites/default/files/ICTJ-Global-Right-Restitution-2007 -English.pdf.

Land issues in post-conflict return and recovery

Samir Elhawary and Sara Pantuliano

Violent conflict has many causes that often interact and change over both time and space. This is particularly the case in what have become known as protracted crises or complex emergencies. In these contexts, there is increasing recognition that land issues are often central to the dynamics of conflict and post-conflict situations (Pantuliano 2009). Grievances over landownership and access are often a source of conflict, such as in Rwanda (Musahara and Huggins 2005), Colombia (Elhawary 2009), and Timor-Leste (Fitzpatrick 2002). Belligerents and others who exploit conflict also often seek to own or control land, or resources that lie beneath it, either for profit or as part of military strategy. This has been the case, for example, in the Darfur region of Sudan (Pantuliano and O'Callaghan 2006), Colombia (Elhawary 2009), and the Democratic Republic of the Congo (Vlassenroot 2008).

Forced displacement and subsequent land appropriation in these contexts is often a means to reward allies, acquire or secure access to resources, manipulate elections, or create ethnically homogenous areas (de Waal 2009). Even when land relations are not a central driver of conflict, they are usually affected by conflict, particularly if there is protracted displacement and land is occupied opportunistically. This results, in many cases, in overlapping or competing land rights and claims, an increase in the legal pluralism of land governance,[1] lost or destroyed documents, lack of adequate housing stock, and increased land pressure, often in the absence of an institutional framework that can effectively resolve these conflicts (Huggins 2009). These land issues affect both the choice to return and the prospects for recovery in post-conflict situations.

This chapter discusses the importance of access to and recovery of land in supporting transitions from conflict to peace. While emphasizing the importance of returning internally displaced persons (IDPs) and refugees to their former areas, the authors warn that restitution and return must be considered in the context of

---

Samir Elhawary is a research fellow at the Overseas Development Institute. Sara Pantuliano heads the Humanitarian Policy Group at the Overseas Development Institute.

[1] *Legal pluralism* refers to the existence of multiple systems of authority over land, based on statutory, customary, or religious norms (Unruh 2009).

116 Land and post-conflict peacebuilding

broader land and property rights issues so as to avoid engendering further conflict. The chapter outlines legal, institutional, and customary aspects of land management that must be considered in post-conflict situations. The chapter concludes with potential solutions, outlining necessary steps for humanitarian and aid actors in addressing land issues and facilitating the peacebuilding process.

FACTORS COMPLICATING RETURN AND RECOVERY

Efforts by international organizations to end conflict and the associated social, economic, and political upheaval involve support for three transitions: a social transition from violence to the end of hostilities, a political transition from wartime government or no government to post-war government, and an economic transition from wartime accumulation and distribution to equitable, transparent, and sustainable post-war development (Paris and Sisk 2009). Central components and indicators of these transitions include the return of displaced populations to their countries or areas of origin and their recovery and reintegration into society.

As a result, peacebuilding efforts tend to focus on recovery, rehabilitation, reintegration, resettlement, and reconstruction activities aimed at a return to what is perceived as normal pre-war conditions (Keen 2008). These are based on the assumption that there is a clear dichotomy between war and peace. Post-conflict situations are thus usually conceptualized as blank slates from which to initiate recovery and the broader transition to peace (Cramer 2006). Yet violent conflict not only destroys political, economic, and social structures but also allows alternate systems to emerge in their place (Duffield 2001; Cramer 2006).

This transformation is part of an "accelerated transition" that accentuates processes of social and economic change that in most cases are already irreversibly under way (de Waal 2009). After protracted conflicts, a return to past structures and processes is usually unfeasible and may be undesirable, as they may fail to resolve grievances that led to the conflict in the first instance or that emerged during the conflict. The challenge for a conflict or post-conflict response is to evaluate whether those structures and processes enhance or threaten the effort to strengthen governance and support livelihoods—and to untangle, build upon, and reshape them accordingly (Cramer 2009).

Unfortunately, such considerations seldom guide international efforts to support the return of IDPs and refugees. Once a conflict is deemed to have ended, displaced people are encouraged to return to their areas of origin without an adequate understanding of the role that land issues have played in the dynamics of the conflict. This is evident in a strict adherence to the United Nations Principles on Housing and Property Restitution for Refugees and Displaced Persons (COHRE 2005). Also known as the Pinheiro Principles, they provide guidance on managing the technical and legal issues associated with housing and property restitution. The principles are grounded in the idea that people have the right to return not only to their areas of origin but also to the property they left behind.

Land issues in post-conflict return and recovery **117**

Restitution rights are, of course, critically important to millions of uprooted people throughout the world, but restitution is only one of myriad land and property issues that arise in conflict and post-conflict countries (Leckie 2009). Return is a much more complex business than it appears, and it is dangerous to limit engagement on land and property issues to a mechanical application of the Pinheiro Principles (Alden Wily 2009). Refugees and IDPs may never have had property in the first instance, may not be able to access their property, may have settled on land they know belongs to others but have nowhere else to go, or may be in direct competition with others, including the state and its foreign or local business partners. In all these cases, the focus on land issues must be much broader and integrated within the overall humanitarian and recovery response (Pantuliano 2009). Failure to do so will lead to responses that at best miss important opportunities and at worst feed tensions or create conflict between different groups seeking access to land.

Developments in Afghanistan provide an example of this issue. Within two years after the 2001 military intervention by coalition forces, it was estimated that more than 3.5 million refugees and 700,000 IDPs returned to their homes (Amnesty International 2003). This return was largely encouraged for political reasons. The international community was keen to show improvements that would justify the intervention; Iran and Pakistan saw it as an opportunity to alleviate the pressure of accommodating large numbers of refugees in their countries; the Afghan government used the process as legitimation of its state building process; and the Office of the United Nations High Commissioner for Refugees sought to demonstrate its relevance to the international community (Turton and Marsden 2002).

This massive return increased land tenure insecurity and aggravated conflicts over land. It has been estimated that between 2002 and 2003, 60 percent of returnees were landless, while 60 percent of those going back to rural areas between March 2002 and May 2004 appeared to be relying on land as a means of survival (Ozerdem and Sofizada 2006). Despite this level of landlessness, refugees and IDPs were encouraged to return without the legal and procedural safeguards necessary to address land-related issues, hindering the sustainability of their return and recovery (Alden Wily 2009).

This is not to say that the Pinheiro Principles do not have value in contexts such as Afghanistan. Return is not a precondition for restitution or compensation, and attention should be paid to the rights and needs of displaced people (and other vulnerable groups) irrespective of their chosen location. Humanitarian organizations have successfully used the principles to help many refugees and IDPs to regain access to or receive compensation for their land and property, including in contexts in which land tenure is mainly governed by informal or customary mechanisms (see Barbara McCallin "The Role of Restitution in Post-Conflict Situations," in this book). However, restitution alone is not sufficient, and in cases in which land and property are disputed or governed by legal pluralism, it must be accompanied by efforts to reform land policy.

118   Land and post-conflict peacebuilding

POTENTIAL SOLUTIONS

Land and property issues are complex and politically sensitive. But humanitarian and peacebuilding actors can play a significant role in addressing these issues and achieving a more effective and sustainable transition to peace if they are guided by the following recommendations:

- As discussed above, engagement needs to go beyond a sole focus on restitution and compensation—which, although important, can overlook wider structural issues such as competition over land, demographic pressure, corrupt and dysfunctional land registration, and inadequate land laws.
- Effectively supporting return and recovery processes requires addressing land issues at an early stage. Humanitarian organizations can help national and international actors to develop more appropriate responses by investing in more thorough analyses of land and property issues and by monitoring and documenting abuses. To be successful, any attempt to promote effective return and recovery processes must be based on an understanding of the relationship between land and conflict, and the structures and processes that characterize the post-conflict period.
- Legal support and capacity building for vulnerable communities can help resolve disputes and strengthen their ability to engage in land policy reform. These efforts should emphasize the rights of women and other vulnerable groups.
- Rehabilitating land management and administration systems after conflict is a crucial endeavor that requires significant expertise. Conventional cadastral systems are often inappropriate in volatile post-conflict situations as they fail to take into account legal pluralism and communal land governance.
- Efforts to address land issues in post-conflict situations must go beyond displaced populations to take into account the rights and concerns of resident populations. Return and recovery strategies need to address land access and the security of property rights more broadly, especially given the institutional vacuum that often characterizes post-conflict transitions. Addressing these issues in peace negotiations is crucial to prevent continued instability and to sustain reintegration, including reengagement in traditional land uses that sustain the agricultural production, food security, and trade on which recovery depends.
- Land and property issues need to be included in peace negotiations and reflected in peace agreements and UN Security Council resolutions. Agreements should seek to recognize and protect customary and long-term occupancy until mechanisms to deal with disputes are operational. Humanitarian and peacebuilding actors should include land and property issues in advocacy messages while peace negotiations are ongoing.
- Effectively addressing these issues will require adequate expertise, leadership, and coordination. The first phase of post-conflict interventions often has too few land tenure experts, and many actors claim that these issues lie outside their remit or are too politically sensitive to tackle. Land and property issues

Land issues in post-conflict return and recovery 119

should be approached systematically within UN peacekeeping missions and large-scale humanitarian responses to reflect their important role in displacement, return, and reintegration. Agreement must be sought within the United Nations on the most suitable institutional arrangement to provide leadership and coordination for the development of a framework for dealing with land and property matters on which the aid community can agree.

- Lastly, a better informed and coordinated approach can help ensure that land issues are addressed more adequately during return and recovery processes, thereby supporting wider efforts to promote peace and stability. These efforts need to be harmonized and based on partnerships with national actors in order to ensure that responses are on a firm footing locally and do not come to an abrupt end when international actors leave.

Tackling these issues will always pose substantial challenges to those engaged in post-conflict recovery, but the failure to take them into account and develop effective strategies is likely to create problems that will pose even greater challenges.

REFERENCES

Alden Wily, L. 2009. Tackling land tenure in the emergency to development transition in post-conflict states: From restitution to reform. In *Uncharted territory: Land, conflict and humanitarian action*, ed. S. Pantuliano. Rugby, Warwickshire, UK: Practical Action Publishing.

Amnesty International. 2003. *Out of sight, out of mind: The fate of the Afghan refugees.* London: Amnesty International.

COHRE (Centre on Housing Rights and Evictions). 2005. *The Pinheiro Principles: United Nations principles on housing and property restitution for refugees and displaced persons.* Geneva, Switzerland.

Cramer, C. 2006. *Civil war is not a stupid thing: Accounting for violence in developing countries.* London: Hurst and Company.

———. 2009. Trajectories of accumulation through war and peace. In *The dilemmas of statebuilding: Confronting the contradictions of post-war peace operations*, ed. R. Paris and T. Sisk. London: Routledge.

de Waal, A. 2009. Why humanitarian organizations need to tackle land issues. In *Uncharted territory: Land, conflict and humanitarian action*, ed. S. Pantuliano. Rugby, Warwickshire, UK: Practical Action Publishing.

Duffield, M. 2001. *Global governance and the new wars: The merging of development and security.* London: Zed Books.

Elhawary, S. 2009. Between war and peace: Land, conflict and humanitarian action in Colombia. In *Uncharted territory: Land, conflict and humanitarian action*, ed. S. Pantuliano. Rugby, Warwickshire, UK: Practical Action Publishing.

Fitzpatrick, D. 2002. Land policy in post-conflict circumstances: Some lessons from East Timor. New Issues in Refugee Research Working Paper 58. Geneva, Switzerland: Office of the United Nations High Commissioner for Refugees. www.unhcr.org/cgi-bin/texis/vtx/home/opendocPDFViewer.html?docid=3c8399e14&query="New issues in Refugee Research".

120   Land and post-conflict peacebuilding

Huggins, C. 2009. Land in return, reintegration and recovery processes: Some lessons from the Great Lakes region of Africa. In *Uncharted territory: Land, conflict and humanitarian action*, ed. S. Pantuliano. Rugby, Warwickshire, UK: Practical Action Publishing.

Keen, D. 2008. *Complex emergencies*. Cambridge, UK: Polity Press.

Leckie, S. 2009. Leader of the pack: Who will take the lead on post-conflict HLP issues? In *Uncharted territory: Land, conflict and humanitarian action*, ed. S. Pantuliano. Rugby, Warwickshire, UK: Practical Action Publishing.

Musahara, H., and C. Huggins. 2005. Land reform, land scarcity and post-conflict reconstruction: A case study of Rwanda. In *From the ground up: Land rights, conflict and peace in sub-Saharan Africa*, ed. C. Huggins and J. Clover. Nairobi, Kenya: African Centre for Technology Studies; Pretoria and Cape Town, South Africa: Institute for Security Studies.

Ozerdem, A., and A. H. Sofizada. 2006. Sustainable reintegration to returning refugees in post-Taliban Afghanistan: Land-related challenges. *Conflict, Security and Development* 6 (1): 75–100.

Pantuliano, S., ed. 2009. *Uncharted territory: Land, conflict and humanitarian action*. Rugby, Warwickshire, UK: Practical Action Publishing.

Pantuliano, S., and S. O'Callaghan. 2006. *The protection crisis: A review of field-based strategies for humanitarian protection in Darfur*. Humanitarian Policy Group Discussion Paper. London: Overseas Development Institute.

Paris, R., and T. Sisk, eds. 2009. *The dilemmas of statebuilding: Confronting the contradictions of postwar peace operations*. London: Routledge.

Turton, D., and P. Marsden. 2002. *Taking refugees for a ride? The politics of refugee return to Afghanistan*. Kabul: Afghanistan Research and Evaluation Unit.

Unruh, J. 2009. Humanitarian approaches to conflict and post-conflict legal pluralism in land tenure. In *Uncharted territory: Land, conflict and humanitarian action*, ed. S. Pantuliano. Rugby, Warwickshire, UK: Practical Action Publishing.

Vlassenroot, K. 2008. Land tenure, conflict and household strategies in the DRC. In *Beyond relief: Food security in protracted crisis*, ed. L. Alinovi, G. Hemrich, and L. Russo. Rugby, Warwickshire, UK: Practical Action Publishing.

Return of land in post-conflict Rwanda: International standards, improvisation, and the role of international humanitarian organizations

John W. Bruce

Rwanda has had to deal with successive waves of refugees returning to the country following civil war and genocide. The returns, beginning in 1994, involved unprecedented portions of the country's population, in a nation already plagued by one of the highest person-to-land ratios in Africa. The returns confronted both the international community and the new government with urgent and difficult choices in an environment of continuing ethnic tension. This chapter explores the process of return and land restitution, the challenges and decisions made to meet them, and the role played by international humanitarian agencies in the return and restitution process.

Refugee return and land access in Rwanda have been extraordinarily complex matters, with some refugees leaving just in time for those returning to take up their homes and lands. In Rwanda—as in Sudan, Burundi, South Africa, and Mozambique—the peace negotiations addressed such land issues in order to end the violent contention for political dominance between factions with strong ethnic identifications. In Rwanda, the Hutu and Tutsi were the ethnic factions involved in the conflict and subsequent displacements. Tensions can emerge between international standards protecting the rights of refugees and displaced persons to return to their land and the compromises that needed to be struck and honored to obtain (and maintain) peace. This chapter examines those tensions and their implications and assesses the response of international humanitarian organizations and nongovernmental organizations (NGOs) involved in reconstruction. It seeks to draw from that experience some lessons that may be valuable in future refugee returns.

John W. Bruce has worked on land policy and law in developing countries for forty years, primarily in Africa. He is a former director of the Land Tenure Center, University of Wisconsin–Madison, and from 1996 to 2006 he served as senior counsel (land law) at the World Bank. This chapter has been adapted and updated, with permission, from a chapter in *Uncharted Territory: Land, Conflict and Humanitarian Action*, ed. S. Pantuliano. (Rugby, Warwickshire, UK: Practical Action Publishing, 2009).

122 Land and post-conflict peacebuilding

COMPETITION FOR LAND AS A CAUSE OF THE CONFLICT

Rwanda is the most densely populated country in Africa and has one of the highest ratios of people to arable land. It has a population growth rate of 3.1 percent, and population density has increased from 101 people per square kilometer in the early 1960s to 303 people per square kilometer today.[1] In the last fifty years, the Rwandan population has almost tripled. Most rural Rwandans have held their land under systems of customary land tenure. As the population has grown, land has been subdivided among heirs, and the decades-old practice of selling land held under customary tenure has continued. The average size of a family farm holding (a household's parcels of farmland) fell from 2 hectares in 1960 to 1.2 hectares in 1984 and to just 0.7 hectares in the early 1990s. In 2001 almost 60 percent of households had less than 0.5 hectares to cultivate. The Food and Agriculture Organization of the United Nations (FAO) recommended 0.9 hectares as a minimum size for an economically viable cultivation plot in Rwanda (Baig et al. 2007). Land has historically been distributed unequally, and growing land markets may be increasing the concentration of landownership. In 1984 an estimated 16 percent of the population owned 43 percent of the land, whereas the poorest 43 percent of the population owned just 15 percent. Estimates of landlessness range from 10 to 20 percent. While 47.5 percent of the population was categorized as poor in 1990, this figure had risen to 64.1 percent by 2000 (Musahara and Huggins 2005; Huggins n.d.), although recent data from the Rwandan government shows a decline in the percentage of households categorized as poor or at risk (UNFPA/Rwanda 2007).

Scholars largely agree that land scarcity and consequent poverty and desperation have played a role in persistent social and civil conflict in Rwanda. However, different authors see the connection between land and conflict in different ways.[2] Some emphasize roles played by population growth and land scarcity (Andre and Platteau 1998), "environmental scarcity" (Percival and Homer-Dixon 1995), the social construction of ethnicity, elite capture of land and power, poor land governance, and emerging class tensions due to inequality and poverty (Gasana 2002). Past conflict and the potential for conflict over land in Rwanda involve a convergence of these factors, and it is not the purpose of this chapter to try to assign relative weights to them. The government recognizes the role of competition for land both in its policy documents and in the priority it has given land as a policy issue, and few would dispute that effective management of competition for land will be critical to the maintenance of peace.[3]

The story of the civil conflict and the return of successive waves of refugees to Rwanda will only be very briefly summarized here. The Tutsi (14 percent of

---

[1] Many estimates are higher—often up to 320 people per square kilometer.
[2] Kathrin Wyss provides a good short summary of the literature on land as a cause of conflict in Rwanda (Wyss 2006).
[3] Much of the recent literature has pointed out that the conflict was neither a simple conflict between Tutsi and Hutu nor exclusively over land. Herman Musahara and Chris Huggins provide a nuanced discussion (Musahara and Huggins 2005).

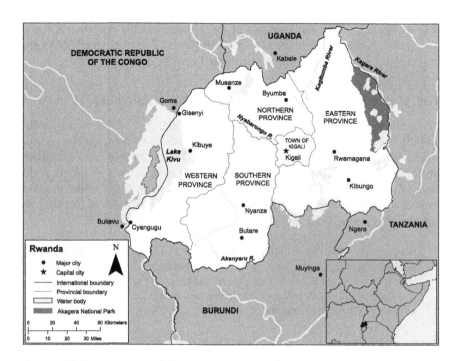

the population) had ruled Rwanda at the advent of colonialism, dominating the Hutu majority. The Belgian colonialists had given preference to the Tutsi in matters of governance, exacerbating ethnic distinctions and tensions, but in the run-up to independence, they embraced majority rule, shifting power to the Hutu. Pogroms against the Tutsi began in 1959, and by the end of the 1980s an estimated 700,000 Tutsis—perhaps a third of the Tutsi population—were in neighboring countries, primarily Burundi, Zaire (present-day Democratic Republic of the Congo), Tanzania, and Uganda. Those who remained—both Hutu and Tutsi—moved onto the land the refugees had left behind. Extensive Tutsi royal pastures were converted to farming and occupied by predominantly Hutu cultivators.

From time to time, the Hutu-dominated government invited exiled Tutsi populations to return. In 1966 the government issued legislation on the reintegration of refugees (Presidential Decree on the Reintegration of Refugees, No. 25/10, 26 February 1966), but this severely limited the freedom of choice of residence and the freedom of movement. It provided that in no circumstances could returnees reclaim the lands they had been using where the lands had been occupied by others or designated for some other purpose by the authorities. The government was determined to protect ethnic land gains; one president of the period compared Rwanda to a full glass that would only overflow again if refugees returned (Prunier 1997; Semujanga 2002). In 1990 the Rwandan Patriotic Front (RPF)—recruited from the Tutsi diaspora—launched an armed struggle against the government. More killings and displacements followed. The insurrection was

124　Land and post-conflict peacebuilding

waged primarily in the northern part of the country, and the government found it increasingly difficult to contend with the Rwandan Patriotic Army (RPA), the military arm of the RPF. Peace negotiations began in Arusha, Tanzania.

THE 1993 ARUSHA PEACE ACCORDS AND THEIR SEQUEL

In August 1993 the Arusha Peace Accords were signed. The provisions of the accords have had a decisive influence on land access for returnees. The accords consist of a general agreement and six protocols. The Protocol on the Repatriation of Refugees and the Resettlement of Displaced Persons affirms, in article 1, the right of return. Per article 2, all people are free to "settle down in any place of their choice"; however, they only enjoy this freedom to the extent that they do not "encroach upon the rights of other people." Article 3 states:

> For purposes of settling returnees, the Rwandese Government shall make lands available, upon their identification by the "Commission for Repatriation" so long as they are not currently occupied by individuals. The Commission shall be at liberty to explore and choose, without any restriction, resettlement sites throughout the national territory.

In article 28, the protocol further specifies that housing schemes in settlement sites should be "modelled on the 'village' grouped type of settlement to encourage the establishment of development centres in the rural area and break with the traditional scattered housing." The protocol did not provide for how land would be given to the returnees for agriculture or cattle (Jones 2003). A joint RPF/government team traveled throughout the country in the months following the signing of the protocols to identify potential settlement sites.

However, most striking is article 4 of the protocol, which states that each person has a right to reclaim his or her property upon his or her return, but then goes on to "recommend . . . that in order to promote social harmony and national reconciliation, refugees who left the country more than 10 years ago should not reclaim their properties, which might have been occupied by other people."[4] They were instead to be provided with land elsewhere. This was a major concession from the RPF. An RPF stalwart from that period explained: "We had been told that 'the glass was full.' How could we come back? Rwanda is small, but it can accommodate us all if the land is better managed. We made this decision because we did not want to create new refugees. It would not have been intelligent."[5] Lisa Jones concludes:

---

[4] It was suggested to the author that article 4 had some legal basis in a prescription rule, but most dismissed this as a post hoc rationalization.

[5] This chapter, in some parts, quotes from communication to the author in Rwanda in November and December 2006. Those who spoke with the author wished, for varying reasons, not to be identified by name, which the author respected. In most cases the author is able to identify them by their role.

Return of land in post-conflict Rwanda **125**

The "ten-year rule" was painfully negotiated primarily as a pragmatic (and political) solution for achieving peaceful return. Given the ethnic tensions that existed and the history of past and recent conflict, it seems highly likely that if complete restitution of properties had been allowed immediately, there would have been considerable social upheaval and further outbreaks of violence—particularly as there had been a concerted redistribution of properties (Jones 2003, 203).

The ten-year rule was and is often presented as "a reconciliation measure" and is so described in a National Unity and Reconciliation Commission survey on land, property, and reconciliation (NURC 2005). It should be noted that this provision did not affect refugees who had left the country in the ten years before the signing of the protocol nor those displaced internally; the protocol did not affect their right to reclaim their land.

Despite the concessions on land made by the RPF in the negotiations, Hutu extremists in government and the armed forces saw the accords as a betrayal by their government. In April 1994 they responded to the peace accords and the prospect of Tutsi return by launching a rampage of killing by Hutu militia. Over 800,000 Tutsi and moderate Hutus throughout the country died in the ensuing communal violence. The genocide came to an end with the disintegration of the government and the national army and the occupation of Kigali in July 1994 by the RPA.

In the wake of the RPF victory, around 700,000 refugees returned to Rwanda, primarily Tutsi returning from Uganda, Burundi, Zaire, and Tanzania. They are referred to in Rwanda as the "old caseload," the "old case returnees," or the "1959 refugees" (referring to the year when many of them fled the country). At the same time, between 2 million and 3 million Hutu fled Rwanda for Zaire and Tanzania—some fearing retribution for the genocide; others were forced to flee with retreating militia and remnants of the former army.

THE OLD CASELOAD RETURNS

The genocide and the collapse of the Hutu government and army led to a more rapid advance by the RPA than anticipated, and the RPF suddenly found itself in the government. A minister in the first post-genocide government remembers:

> The government was set up after the genocide. The NGOs and international organizations had a more powerful presence than our government. We just had guns to provide security. I belonged to the first government. We negotiated with the International Red Cross. We had no salaries, nothing. We needed beans and maize for six months to survive. We got major assistance, and it was really appreciated. But there were so many NGOs operating. We didn't know how many, we didn't know where they were or what they were doing, but we met and met and finally reached understandings.

Asked about the handling of land issues, he continued:

126 Land and post-conflict peacebuilding

The international community did not seem to understand the land issue. The claims were social and political. The international community was preoccupied with the size of the return and how many would have to be accommodated. After the genocide, there was a total loss of focus on land. There had been plans for land to be identified beforehand, for the refugees and cattle to wait at the border, to be provided with goods and funds, their animals vaccinated. None of this happened.

Another minister in the first post-genocide government remembered: "RPF when gaining territory said that it would gather returnees into camps, but after 1994 many people just went home." The refugee return was for all practical purposes uncontrolled. Refugees flowed into the country in the wake of the RPF as it occupied territory in its advance toward Kigali. International agencies had fled the country during the genocide and in its immediate aftermath. They returned within months, but there was a hiatus. And the government took time to organize. A veteran RPF politician recounts the difficulty of the early days in government and of getting a handle on the resettlement: "We had just arrived. There were only a few of us who were politicians. We were running here and there. The returnees cut down much of Gishwati Forest before we even knew about it."

One consequence of the massive outflow of Hutu from the country after the genocide was that many returning Tutsi found that their lands—even if they had been occupied by Hutu for many years—were now available for reoccupation. Jones notes that there were some cases in which some Tutsi returnees simply took houses and land from Hutus but that the majority of the returnees did not resort to violence and did not seek to occupy their old homes (Jones 2003).[6] Tutsi refugees who had left the country after 1983 (ten years before the accords) could reclaim their lands, as could those who had been internally displaced or had simply lost land.[7]

Under the Protocol on Repatriation and Resettlement, the government was to compensate those who could not reclaim their old land by "putting land at their disposal and helping them to resettle" (article 4). The new RPF government was responsible for providing unoccupied lands as resettlement sites. In fact, there was little in the way of unoccupied land. Another veteran RPF official remembers:

Akagera Park was one-seventh of the country, too much compared to parks in other nations. So we reduced it. In other areas, we assumed that if land was free, people could recover it. If the land was taken by government or the church, it would need to be returned or compensation provided.

---

[6] Jones observed that there were some violent property takeovers by Tutsi returnees and that a few did challenge the ten-year rule but were rarely successfully (Jones 2003).

[7] In comments on a draft of this chapter, Sorcha O'Callaghan, head of Humanitarian Policy for the British Red Cross, noted that there were many new households among the returnees created by marriages in exile, which had never had their own landholdings in Rwanda, although they would have had claims to parental land.

Return of land in post-conflict Rwanda 127

The Minister of State of Lands described the process as follows:

> As they returned, some of the former 1959 refugees briefly occupied land and property that had been abandoned by the refugees in 1994. Other former refugees were granted public state land, and vacant land on which they could resettle and produce. They received to this effect: the Mutara Game Reserve, two thirds of the Akagera National Park, and the Gishwati Mountain Forest; as well as land belonging to certain state-owned projects that were partitioned and distributed to the 1959 refugees. Communal land, woody areas on fertile land, pastures, and areas near the shallow sections of marshlands were allocated to the 1959 refugees (Hajabakiga 2004).

Some of these areas of spontaneous resettlement have required continuing government attention. For example, the United Nations High Commissioner for Refugees (UNHCR)/Rwanda estimated that 8,000 displaced families who settled within Gishwati Forest in northwest Rwanda had to be expelled later for environmental reasons and, after substantial delays, were resettled in Gitarama (UNHCR/Rwanda 2000). The same report describes these refugees of 1994–1996:

> These returnees had no land and property to go back to and installed themselves in houses deserted in towns, commercial centres, and in rural areas. Mostly, they did not believe that Rwandans who had fled in 1994 would return and made little effort to take up the often marginal land allocated to them by the government (UNHCR/Rwanda 2000, 24).

But in other areas, with the help of international humanitarian agencies, returnees settled in villages (*imidugudu*), as envisaged in the Arusha Peace Accords. They formed the nuclei of new resettlement villages. Sites were identified in a hasty process by government teams, based in part on visits made by teams during the period between the Arusha Peace Accords and the genocide.

UNHCR and other humanitarian organizations launched a major shelter program that involved the building or renovation of over 100,000 houses, most of them in the imidugudu.[8] The owners of land acquired for the imidugudu were never compensated. Because land was considered to be state-owned, in theory, even those displaced had claims only to compensation for houses and crops. An NGO worker involved in providing food and shelter to the new imidugudu remembers: "At that time, no one even asked, 'Whose land is this being allocated?'" Another NGO worker involved recalls:

> We were assisting them. Many things had been destroyed, we were starting from zero. At first it was pure relief, providing pots, jerry cans, blankets, cups.

---

[8] UNHCR/Rwanda indicates that a little over one quarter of these units are in the imidugudu (UNHCR/Rwanda 2000), but other sources suggest that most—and possibly a large majority—were in the imidugudu (HRW 2001).

128   Land and post-conflict peacebuilding

Then the shelter programme, and houses built to government specs. The '94 returnees first had to stay with family, but wanted housing in the imidugudu. Some '94s also occupied houses and others had to stay outside. You still see these lines of houses with no services. The NGOs backed off because of lack of services. Government was very unhappy; it was very contentious.

During this period, it is remarkable that the RPF government remained fully committed to the provisions of the Arusha Peace Accords, including the ten-year rule and provisions on resettlement villages. After all, the government with which the RPF had negotiated the accords had collapsed. Assumptions that the parties had shared at Arusha were no longer valid; no one had anticipated the genocide and the dramatic outflow of Hutu refugees. Jones observed that "despite the conditional wording, the [ten-year] provision has largely been treated as mandatory in its implementation" (Jones 2003, 206–207). A former minister from this period explained: "Arusha was well negotiated. It offered the promise of political stability. It was our Bible." When the new constitution was drafted, many of the provisions of the accords were incorporated verbatim.[9] The continuing commitment of the government to the principles of the accords appears to have stemmed from the RPF's consciousness of a need to build trust among the Hutu population, given the narrowness of its core ethnic Tutsi constituency.

THE NEW CASELOAD RETURNS

The second major wave of returnees—called the "new caseload"—consisted of the Hutu who fled the country in 1994 and then returned, largely in 1994–1997. This return came in a number of stages—the first being a sudden and unanticipated mass return from Goma, Zaire, in July and August 1994, following attacks by the army on the refugee camps and the insurgents and a cholera outbreak in the camps in North Kivu. There were further huge returns in November and December 1996 following an illegal *refoulement* (forced return of refugees) by the Tanzanian government, continuing through 1997.

Most of the Hutu who had fled to Zaire came from central and northern Rwanda, and few Tutsi returnees had resettled in that part of the country. The Hutu returning to those areas were able to reintegrate without too much difficulty. But in other areas of the country, Hutu returned to find land occupied by recent Tutsi returnees. Especially in late 1996 and 1997, the two waves of returnees overlapped to some extent. In September 1996, the Ministry of Agriculture issued an instruction that established communal commissions to find abandoned land for returning refugees, giving priority to Tutsi returnees, and allocating it to them on a temporary basis until the return of the owners. However, when Hutu began

---

[9] It is not clear whether the government continues to consider the accords operational or whether they have effectively been replaced by the new constitutional provisions, which vary from the accords in some respects. A number of officials consulted were of the latter opinion.

to return, fears of retribution for the genocide meant that, at first, few Hutu returnees were brave enough to press their claims. But by the end of 1997, a presidential address threatening action by the army against Tutsi who refused to vacate formerly Hutu-held properties upon the return of the rightful owners resulted in more claims and evictions of temporary allottees (Hajabakiga 2004).

Those Tutsi moved into the early imidugudu, as did some Hutu who had failed to find accommodations elsewhere. But in some areas, an expedient referred to as "land sharing" was initiated. This was done initially on local initiative. Kibungo Prefecture in eastern Rwanda had received large numbers of Tutsi returnees in 1994, and in 1996, there began a major influx of Hutu refugees, who found their former lands occupied. A veteran politician reported: "We tried to implement the accords, but in some areas like Kibungo we needed to do land sharing. We had to adapt. Even now we have to adapt." The local *préfet* (governor of the province) launched a series of community meetings to encourage the earlier Tutsi returnees to share their land with the returning Hutu. Patricia Hajabakiga writes: "The government policy of plots sharing has been encouraged to allow old case refugees of 1959 to get a piece of land in order to earn a living" (Hajabakiga 2004, 7). One former official remarked: "Those '94 returnees who had occupied land and houses in Kibungo knew that it was temporary. They knew the houses and crops did not belong to them. We managed to convince them to share. It was very satisfactory." This approach was adopted sporadically elsewhere in the country, including in Kigali Rural and Umutara.

Compliance with land sharing was in theory voluntary, but pressure from officials is said to have been intense. A UNHCR staffer familiar with the process explained:

> Regarding land access, local officials tried to negotiate access to land for returnees. But some parties were threatened by occupants or neighbours. Authorities got involved, and these situations were resolved not legally but by negotiations. People had no choice. It's all about access to services. If you didn't do it, you would have a problem. You go along to get along.

It is not possible to determine the extent of land sharing. It was done on local initiative, and this makes it difficult to quantify the process. What is clear is that those who lost land in the land-sharing process did not receive compensation. As Jones indicates, this was a violation not only of Rwanda's obligations under international agreements but also of the new constitution's property guarantees (Jones 2003). Nonetheless, the government clearly considers land sharing an acceptable expedient and still resorts to it in special cases—without compensation. Some such cases are noted later in this chapter.

IMIDUGUDU AND THE HABITAT POLICY

Article 28 of the Arusha Peace Accords' Protocol on Repatriation and Resettlement states that settlement sites should be "modelled on the 'village' grouped type of

130   Land and post-conflict peacebuilding

settlement to encourage the establishment of development centres in the rural areas and break with the traditional scattered housing." This reflected a policy dating back to the colonial period, when the Belgians had sought to group peasants in *paysannat* (resettlement schemes to consolidate scattered rural homesteads into villages).[10] In 1996, the new government adopted a National Habitat Policy that stated that dispersed patterns of homesteads in the countryside were an inefficient use of land and called for the regrouping of all inhabitants into villages. This converted a program of refugee resettlement into a major social engineering initiative. The policy was adopted by the cabinet in 1996 but was never debated or endorsed in parliament or in public, and implementation proceeded without a solid legal basis.

From the beginning, there were problems with sites and services. An NGO worker who provided services to the program remembers: "Mistakes were made. Houses were put in with no services. You need water, you need a market, and a health centre nearby. People were promised electricity but never got it." And while it was said that compulsion would not be used, the Ministry of Interior and Communal Development issued an instruction prohibiting people from constructing homes on their own land if these were outside imidugudu. Refugees who returned after January 1997 to find their homes destroyed could not simply rebuild on their former land but were required to construct new homes in imidugudu. Some households moved voluntarily, but in other cases, forced removals to imidugudu occurred. While the villagization program was supposed to allow for more efficient land use in rural areas, those who were forced into villages usually never gave up their old land and just had to go further to farm it. And while the National Habitat Policy recognized that expropriations of land were involved in villagization and stated that compensation would be paid, this happened only in a small minority of cases. If compensation was received, it was in the form of compensatory plots in the imidugudu.

One of the first signs of unease with imidugudu in the international humanitarian community came in 1998. In April, the Association for Cooperative Operations Research and Development (ACORD)—one of the international NGOs working in the country—published a study that raised serious questions about the wisdom of the villagization program (ACORD 1998). The study was initiated in response to early drafts of a land law that contained articles that would have legitimated some of the abuses associated with the creation of imidugudu. The report raised numerous concerns about the implementation of imidugudu, including poor choice of sites; sites lacking economic opportunities or raising environmental issues; failure to involve the concerned populations in the choice of sites; negative effect of distance from homes in the villages to productive resources; failure to

---

[10]   One of the objectives of the paysannat was to establish minimum holding sizes, creating farms deemed large enough to be commercially viable by colonial authorities. The program has been criticized and has proven impossible to sustain (Blarel et al. 1992). The holdings in the former paysannats were gradually subdivided and are indistinguishable from other holdings.

Return of land in post-conflict Rwanda 131

systematically address issues of landholding; weak policy development, resulting in inconsistencies and disorder in implementation; and the creation of some settlements consisting entirely of widowed women. It also noted the failure of the government to address more fundamental land reform issues, such as the holdings of the Roman Catholic Church and political and economic elites.

Forced relocation became a much more serious issue when, in the northwest, villagization became a counterinsurgency strategy during the 1997–1998 insurgent incursions from Zaire. Jones probably reflects the opinion of most of the international humanitarian community when she describes the imidugudu process as a reasonable expedient but says that this changed when the army began large-scale forcible relocations in the northwest (Jones 2003). In May 2001, Human Rights Watch issued a report claiming that tens of thousands of people had been resettled against their will and that many of them had had to destroy their homes as part of the government's efforts to control the population (HRW 2001). It urged the international community to press for a reexamination of the program. The Rwanda Initiative for Sustainable Development and Oxfam also raised concerns about resettlement. In the end, donor assistance for the program dried up.

What was the extent of implementation of the program? It varied widely from province to province. Nelson Alusala notes that 90 percent of the population in Kibungo and Umutara prefectures live in grouped villages, reflecting the large number of Tutsi who fled to Uganda and who, when they returned, were accommodated in the villages (Alusala 2005). Ruhengeri (in the Northern Province) is third, with more than 50 percent, and Gisenyi (in the Western Province) is fourth, with 13 percent. Only a very limited number of people live under this program in other areas.

Despite the decline in support for the imidugudu policy and shift away from aggressive implementation, villagization remains a central component of the government's 2005 Organic Land Law and strategy for transforming the rural system. Land holdings in rural areas can no longer be demolished in order to construct new houses, and the government continues to inform rural households they will need to eventually resettle to villages. This is especially prevalent in the northern and western regions of the country, where scattered households located on the hillsides have been told they will need to move to a collective settlement located on the top of the hill or in the valley bottom.

THE ROLE OF INTERNATIONAL HUMANITARIAN ORGANIZATIONS

What influence has the international humanitarian community had over these events? UNHCR was mandated by the Dar es Salaam Summit of February 1991 to be a lead agency for organizing the repatriation of refugees over a six-month period and to provide shelter and related social infrastructure in new villages. This mandate was reiterated in the Arusha Protocol on Repatriation and Resettlement. In collaboration with the UN Research Institute for Social Development, UNHCR was mandated to prepare a socioeconomic profile of the

132 Land and post-conflict peacebuilding

refugees and a study of the country's absorption capacity in order to facilitate reintegration and plan international development assistance.

A major UNHCR/Rwanda retrospective on its role in Rwanda stresses the size of the task: an old caseload consisting of 608,000 returnees in 1994; 146,476 in 1995; and another 40,000 in 1996–1999, for a total just under 800,000; and a new caseload of 600,000 returnees in 1994; 79,302 in 1995; 1,271,936 in 1996; and over 200,000 in 1997, for a total of more than 2 million (UNHCR/Rwanda 2000). The total number of returnees was just under 3 million. Over six years, UNHCR spent US$183 million on projects to help reinstall the 3 million returnees and reconstruct the country (UNHCR/Rwanda 2000).

The UN Assistance Mission for Rwanda—established to assist with the implementation of the Arusha Peace Accords—was withdrawn at the commencement of the genocide but returned in July 1994. By the end of 1994, UNHCR had begun organizing repatriations, and at the end of December, through Operation Retour, UNHCR—with the International Organization for Migration and British Direct Aid—began to coordinate transport for internally displaced persons back to their communes of origin. In September 1994 the UN Human Rights Field Operation in Rwanda was established and was in place through July 1998. Its work focused on gross human rights violations and did not extend to land issues.

In November 1995, UNHCR embarked on a rural shelter program. It supported the construction or rehabilitation of around 100,000 houses over a five-year period between 1995 and 1999, providing shelter for half a million Rwandans. The 2000 report indicates that of those, 27 percent were in resettlement sites, while 73 percent were in scattered or clustered locations throughout the country (UNHCR/Rwanda 2000). UNHCR helped with site identification and planning as well as technical and supervisory support during construction.[11] That shelter program drew the UNHCR into land matters.

The UNHCR/Rwanda retrospective in 2000 touches on land sharing. It remarks that following the mass return of the refugees in 1996, there were conflicting claims and the government adopted different policies in different localities. While in some cases people were moved onto recently opened public land, in others, "land had to be shared by mutual consent." It concludes: "The latter worked fairly well in Kibungo Prefecture, for instance. After verifying that land was being shared by consent of the rightful owners, the UNHCR quickly proceeded to distribute shelter materials and helped returnees to build houses" (UNHRC/Rwanda 2000, 26).

UNHCR and other UN agencies strongly supported the imidugudu program. In 1997 the program was endorsed—with some qualifications—in a report commissioned by FAO's Land Tenure Service (Barriere 1997). A 1999 report by

---

[11] Human Rights Watch suggests that the 27 percent figure may refer to houses actually constructed by UNHCR, with the remainder being houses constructed by local people from building materials distributed by UNHCR through local authorities, and that some—perhaps most—of those building materials were provided in connection with imidugudu (HRW 2001).

Return of land in post-conflict Rwanda **133**

a UNHCR-funded shelter evaluation team argued that there were no viable alternatives and that "rather than discussing the policy, the international community should ensure provision of the technical backstopping and training to allow the policy not to become a failure" (UNHCR/Rwanda 2000, 42).

The UNHCR/Rwanda report acknowledged that "the perceived involuntary nature" of some resettlement activities had caused several governments to withhold support but argues that by 1999 the Rwandan government was paying more attention to the need to respect individual rights (UNHCR/Rwanda 2000, 42). It suggests that UNHCR made an effort to distinguish between cases of voluntary and coerced villagization schemes and in effect supported imidugudu when it appeared to be voluntary and with the consent and knowledge of the beneficiaries. The report states that local authorities were encouraged to ensure that farm plots were allocated for each family near the villages, noting that "UNHCR facilitated the provision of farm plots to residents, but it was and continues to be the government responsibility to carry out the distribution process" (UNHCR/Rwanda 2000, 46). The report admits that some beneficiaries had to walk up to several kilometers to their farm plots and that this was "indeed an inconvenience and an issue to be addressed."

In the end, UNHCR remained a supporter of imidugudu. In 2000 the Thematic Consultation on Resettlement was launched as a means of continuing the dialogue and reaching a consensus among the development partners. The framework adopted in February 2000 contained a number of cautionary points but reaffirmed the UN commitment to support the program. In 2000 the UN community adopted the Framework for Assistance in the Context of the Imidugudu Policy, which encourages the government to continue a dialogue on the issue, to adopt a more participatory rights-based approach, and to resolve legal issues related to landownership and use. The 2000 UNHCR/Rwanda retrospective concludes that the imidugudu contributed to the peaceful resolution of a number of land disputes between old caseload refugees, new caseload refugees, and survivors of the genocide. It asks: "Was the shelter program in Rwanda a success? So far, property-related conflict has been avoided, unlike in the former Yugoslavia" (UNHCR/Rwanda 2000, 49). This seems spurious. The absence of overt conflict in response to the imidugudu program probably had less to do with the virtues of the program than with the general atmosphere of fear and exhaustion.

UNHCR is no longer a major player in land policy in Rwanda. Other donors—such as the U.S. Agency for International Development, the UK Department for International Development (DFID), and the European Commission— stepped into its shoes as relief and reconstruction gave way to development programming and have been far more wary of imidugudu. Opposition to the program has also developed within the government. In 2006 a draft Law on Habitat was proposed by the Ministry of Infrastructure that might have revitalized the program, but it contained substantial provisions that weakened property rights and was strongly opposed by the Ministry of Land, Environment, Forestry, Water and Mines. It was withdrawn from parliamentary consideration in December 2006.

134   Land and post-conflict peacebuilding

A thorough examination of the imidugudu experience by Human Rights Watch concluded:

> In an ironic twist, the program which donors supported in the hopes of ending homelessness covered another which caused tens of thousands of Rwandans to lose their homes. Praise for the generosity and promptness with which donors responded to the housing program must be tempered by criticism of their readiness to ignore the human rights abuses occasioned by the rural reorganization program that operated under its cover (HRW 2001, sec. XV, para. 1).

The facts seem clear enough, and it is important to better understand why the mistakes were made—not in the interest of assigning blame but in the interest of avoiding them in the future.

UNHCR's concern with the immediate needs of returnees for shelter appears to have overridden any qualms it may have had regarding the potential land problems of a resettlement program. Recall the comment by a minister in the first government quoted earlier: "The international community did not seem to understand the land issue. The claims were social and political. The international community was preoccupied with the size of the return and how many would have to be accommodated." This preoccupation is understandable, given the chaotic conditions in which it was initiated. Faced with the huge challenge of delivering shelter—which UNHCR documents repeatedly emphasize as its priority—the delivery of that housing is obviously far easier if it can be done in concentrations rather than in scattered hamlets. The simple logistical advantages of the approach the government proposed must have been very seductive to UNHCR.

When it became a major social engineering exercise—and in one part of the country became central to an anti-insurgency strategy—why did the international humanitarian community not more critically examine its role? The 2001 Human Rights Watch report concludes that, ultimately, human rights seem not to have been a priority of donors, who failed to mount a serious critique of the policy. A number of factors may account for this failure. One is guilt over the international community's failure to mount an effective response to the events leading to the genocide. The new government had moral authority as the representative of those who had been brutalized and a clear sense of what it wanted to do. That combination would not have been easy to resist, and with early information from the field being patchy and inconsistent, it would have been easy to set aside misgivings. In addition, the same Human Rights Watch report cites competition in resettlement—between the UN Development Programme and UNHCR in particular.

In the end, UNHCR seems to have provided little by way of a moderating influence. It was instead the NGOs working in rural development and human rights as well as academic researchers who raised concerns about its implementation and provided critical intelligence. The Lutheran World Federation had by 1997 issued instructions to staff that they could assist in resettlement only where movement into the new villages was voluntary, where those who moved into the

Return of land in post-conflict Rwanda 135

villages were not required to destroy their existing housing, and where there was a reasonable level of service provision (HRW 2001). In April 1998, ACORD published its critique of the viability and technical soundness of the program. A 1999 study from the Rural Development Sociology Group at Wageningen University (Hillhorst and van Leeuwen 1999) also raised concerns. It is difficult to tell how aware most donors were of the issue, but a 1999 retrospective study by the Organisation for Economic Co-Operation and Development (Baaré, Shearer, and Uvin 1999)—examining the ability of donors to influence policy in the pre- and post-conflict situations—makes virtually no mention of the land issue. The first full documentation of the human rights abuses associated with the program emerged in 2001 in the Human Rights Watch report.

A further contribution by the NGO community in this area deserves attention. Rwanda has some multipurpose membership organizations that have made important contributions to the debate on land—such as the national farmers' organization, the Union of Agriculturalists and Stockholders of Rwanda—but the post-conflict period saw the emergence of the first specialized land NGO: LandNet Rwanda. LandNet Rwanda was created in 1999 in connection with DFID-initiated work to establish an Africa-wide network of national chapters of LandNet Africa. Its specialization in land has made it a valuable player in policy discussions. It is itself a network of local and international NGOs dealing with land policy issues in Rwanda and has strong DFID and Oxfam connections. In Rwanda, CARE International provided early support, detailing a staff member to work on setting up the organization, providing initial office space and services and modest initial funding.

While selected NGOs have provided alerts and important information on land issues, they have not created significant programs in this area. CARE has supported LandNet Rwanda, and in the context of its other programs, it is to a limited extent addressing land dispute resolution. The International Rescue Committee cosponsored, with DFID and the Swedish International Development Cooperation Agency, a 2005 opinion survey titled "Land, Property and Reconciliation" (NURC 2005). Oxfam has engaged primarily through support of LandNet Rwanda. The Norwegian Relief Association is providing funding to support studies by Africa Rights at several sites in Rwanda on the land access issues facing women— widows in particular—as well as monitoring by the Community of Indigenous People of Rwanda (Communauté des Autochtones Rwandais, or CAURWA) of Batwa land access.[12] The Norwegian Refugee Council and Swisspeace have published studies seeking to draw attention to continuing land-related human rights violations (NRC 2005; Wyss 2006). The limited operational engagement of these organizations with land issues is not surprising, given the sensitivity of the issue and the uncertain policy environment of the past decade.

---

[12] Rwanda's indigenous forest dwellers—the Batwa—have suffered land loss as a consequence of refugee return. Disadvantaged for many decades with respect to land access, they found their forest habitats seriously reduced by the resettlement of returnees in parks and forest reserves.

136 Land and post-conflict peacebuilding

There are local civil society organizations (CSOs) through whom such international NGOs could work, but they are weak and reluctant to assert themselves. Herman Musahara and Chris Huggins note that even when CSOs have had opportunities to put forward their views on land in contexts such as the IMF/World Bank Poverty Reduction Strategy Paper process leading to the 2002 Poverty Reduction Strategy, they have hung back (Musahara and Huggins 2004). The authors attribute this to damaged social structures from the genocide, links between government and most CSOs, and the centuries-old tradition of centralized, exclusivist governance.

THE CONTINUING RETURN: THE "NEW" NEW CASELOAD

Most of the publications on refugee return and land tenure in Rwanda seem to assume that returns are substantially over. While most refugees have returned, quite large numbers continue to do so, and this has important implications for land tenure security. In June 2006, Tanzania expelled 500 speakers of Rwandan (Rwandaphones) by force. In July 2006 a convention was signed between Tanzania and Rwanda, and in September 2006, 6,000 Rwandaphones were expelled from Tanzania. They came from the Karagwe District of Tanzania, bordering Rwanda, and were part of a predominant Tutsi pastoralist community with origins in the colonial period—a community that had quietly absorbed large numbers of other Rwandans leaving the country more recently. Those who returned included a large number of women, children, and the elderly. While there have been migrants from Rwanda in this area of Tanzania for a generation, 80 percent of those returned were recent migrants, who had move to Tanzania between 1995 and 2005. UNHCR estimates that some 40,000 may be returned to Rwanda. Tanzania says that it considers them illegal immigrants. UNHCR staff note an urgent need to identify parcels to cultivate and to provide incomers with cultivation kits. UNHCR was told by the Rwandan government that over 24 billion Rwanda francs (US$40 million) had been budgeted for the resettlement of more than 60,000 Rwandans and 80,000 head of cattle that may be repatriated from Tanzania (UNHCR/Rwanda 2006b). Staff at UNHCR's Kigali office in December 2006 wondered: "Shall we call these the 'new, new caseload'?"

Considerable numbers of Rwandans remain outside the country. UNHCR's "Rwanda at a Glance" summary for November 2006 notes that some 48,435 refugees and 4,721 asylum seekers from Rwanda were in other African countries (UNHCR/Rwanda 2006a). Of these, the largest numbers and those most likely to return home live in the Democratic Republic of the Congo (formerly Zaire), Uganda, and Burundi. (These include recent and continuing flows from Rwanda to the countries of those concerned that they would be implicated by the 1,545 gacaca courts discussing and now bringing indictments against those involved in the genocide.) UNHCR is tracking current returns. The same summary document indicates that during 2005, 9,600 refugees returned, and 5,620 have returned home since January 2006. In October 2006 alone, over 3,000 refugees and asylum seekers returned, and late 2006 saw the voluntary return of 13,200 asylum seekers

Return of land in post-conflict Rwanda **137**

from Burundi. The Tanzanian case mentioned previously is instructive in that very few of those expelled from Tanzania appear in the UNHCR statistics, as they are not officially refugees and did not request asylum. UNHCR thus understates the scale of the problem significantly, although the actual extent is not clear.

The Ministry of Land, Environment, Forestry, Water and Mines (MINITERE) indicated that an interministerial commission, including MINITERE and the Ministry of Agriculture, is trying to identify land for these returnees and is looking into land held by the army, research farms, and possibly land sharing of allocations received by earlier returnees in portions of Akagera National Park. Some of those expelled from Tanzania are being settled in Akagera under the land-sharing principle. Informants reported many small huts in the park as well as many cattle going into the park. The refugees have brought substantial numbers of cattle with them, although theirs are certainly not the only cattle going into the park; there are regular rumors of large herds in the area belonging to military commanders. Bugesera, near the border with Burundi, is another area to which these returnees are said to be going in significant numbers. While land is available there, the area is drought-prone and the soil is poor.

Land sharing is also still being carried out in the densely populated Musanze District in Northern Province, where old caseload refugees are now pressing land claims. Local officials explained that these old caseload refugees had been back in the country since 1994 in most cases but had come to this area in 2001. Due to insurgency in the area, they had not been able to obtain land. When things were calmer, they asked for land and needed to be accommodated. A farmers' union worker explained: "When an old case refugee comes and claims land, and the occupants refuse, and say 'I don't know you,' then you go to the authorities for mediation. They rely on local elders." One official noted that local residents had complained that "these are people whose families came to this area as feudal officials; how can we be asked to share land with them?" But, he said, they must share, and the sharing has begun. The process had begun in two sectors, and there are four where it will be carried out. Another official explained: "No one likes giving up land, but people have a good will and it is going smoothly. It will be finished in a year. Of course the land plots are very small, no one can get as much as a hectare."

DRAWING A LINE UNDER CRISIS: NO EASY TASK

MINITERE understood the urgent need to reestablish stability in landholding, to affirm property rights, and to create security of tenure, and the 2005 Land Law provides for the systematic demarcation of holdings, the issuance of long-term leaseholds, and their registration. The Ministry of Environment and Lands is now the agency responsible for implementing the law and is moving to achieve these objectives. Pilot work under the new law began with substantial support from DFID. The program detailed by MINITERE and Johan Pottier provides a thorough

138   Land and post-conflict peacebuilding

critique of the new law in terms of the practical problems that could arise in its implementation in Rwanda (MINITERE 2006, 2007; Pottier 2006).[13]

At the same time, however, proposals for land use master planning, villagization, and land consolidation threaten new dislocations. Ordinary Rwandans hear about these proposals in an atmosphere of uncertainty and mistrust. One informant spoke of Rwanda as "a culture of rumors." Programs that interfere with landholdings will be viewed with suspicion, and planners will find ethnic motivations attributed to them.

Unfinished business from the conflict also continues to create insecurity. The government has launched the gacaca process to prosecute those guilty of genocide, and the National Service of Gacaca Jurisdictions estimates that some 761,000 people will be indicted during this process.[14] It is possible that the gacaca will order remedies that return land, creating further uncertainties. A number of local situations contain seeds of conflict. In the north, in former Ruhengeri, resettlement abuses during the Hutu insurgency have never been satisfactorily resolved (NRC 2005). In the east, a traditional expansion area with substantial pastures, there are said to have been large-scale land acquisitions (often referred to as *land grabbing*) by elites and the military after 1994 (Musahara and Huggins 2004). At the same time, refugee return continues, increasing the pressure on land.

Ethnic tensions persist, and NGO reports castigate the government for ethnic favoritism in land matters. The NRC report on resettlement complains generally of "the blatant protection of the interests of returning Tutsi refugees to the detriment of the Hutu—their preferential treatment in allocation and distribution of assistance, in land sharing and resettlement" (NRC 2005, 12). Similarly, a Swisspeace report asks, in an accusatory tone, whether the government's land reform program represents "the restoration of feudal order or genuine transformation" (Wyss 2006, 1). These statements are neither constructive nor accurate. While the RPF government has certainly been most concerned with finding land for the 1959 refugees, it has done so with restraint and with some attempt at even-handedness—to an extent remarkable in the wake of the genocide.

Although overt conflict over land is no longer taking place, very real competition for land and many disputes over land still exist—colored by past events. One hears widely differing assessments of the potential for a return to conflict. One informant spoke of continuing tensions over land—tensions being passed down generations: "A father walks his son past a house he had owned, or land the family had owned. He points them out to his son, and says, 'This was ours, and then they took it.' The boy will remember." Another informant, an NGO worker with long experience in rural communities, reports: "The mentality has changed. Post-genocide work has helped so much, because victims were supported. When you go to the hills, you feel no identity differences." Another

---

[13] The discussion in this section of current land policy initiatives exists in a more extended version in Bruce (2007).

[14] For more on the gacaca process, see Wolters (2005).

Return of land in post-conflict Rwanda 139

informant acknowledges continuing tensions and insecurity over land and argues: "Land registration is our last chance."

THE PINHEIRO PRINCIPLES: RULES, IMPROVISATION, AND INTERNATIONAL HUMANITARIAN AGENCIES

What can international humanitarian agencies involved in conflict and post-conflict situations learn from the Rwanda experience?

First, for people on the ground there is no clear-cut distinction between conflict and the post-conflict period; these states do not exist on a spectrum but overlap. Countries that have been in serious conflict may suddenly find peace, but peace is not the absence of competition or even limited conflict—just the absence of war. Competition over land, expressed through disputes, continues after peace and may threaten to regress into conflict. Land claims and grievances must be addressed promptly but with restraint and balance.

Second, inputs from the international community on best practices in land tenure and lessons for post-conflict situations should begin—at least in countries where land has played a significant role in conflict—during the peacemaking process. In the case of Rwanda, it is clear that the international community did not provide the expertise that would have helped the parties at Arusha arrive at more adequate formulations and solutions.

Third, the focus on the shelter needs of returnees must be supplemented by a well thought through strategy for access to productive land resources for returnees—a strategy sensitive to the rights of existing land occupants. In Rwanda it seems that a narrow focus on shelter led humanitarian agencies in an unfortunate direction. Shelter was most easily provided in the village context, and this may have delayed recognition by UNHCR and others of the shortcomings of villagization.

Fourth, where land issues are likely to surface, it would be prudent to involve some NGOs with substantial experience in land tenure issues. In Rwanda, the input of such NGOs was critical in eventually identifying the serious shortcomings of well-intentioned programs. In the case of resettlement, the alert provided by such players was effective in causing a withdrawal of donor funding. Subsequently, human rights organizations have taken a lead role in critically assessing policy and legal proposals in the land sector.

Fifth, NGOs with an interest in these land tenure issues should seek to develop sustainable and informed input from civil society. In the case of Rwanda, international NGOs contributed to the creation of a national land NGO: LandNet Rwanda. Such NGOs and CSOs may be more constrained by political pressures than their international counterparts, but they can play a critical role in informing government action.

Donors and international humanitarian organizations can do several things to be more effective—both during the run-up to peace and after the conflict comes to an end:

140 Land and post-conflict peacebuilding

- Raise awareness of international standards during peace negotiations. Parties should work with these standards in mind.
- Inform participants of current trends in land policy and land law reform, and provide them with opportunities to discuss these with knowledgeable individuals in relation to their country.
- Involve NGOs and others with strong competence in development and land policy—in particular, in the planning for return and its implementation.
- Remind negotiators of the needs of those who may not be at the bargaining table, such as female-headed households and forest dwellers.
- Approach proposals to fund resettlement programs cautiously, watching out for compulsion and the appropriation of land from existing users. Restitution of prior landholdings is the preferable solution and is required by international standards where possible.
- In the post-conflict period, support programs that reestablish security of land tenure and discourage programs that undermine security.
- Support the development of local CSOs with expertise in land and with constituencies who rely on the land for their livelihoods, and encourage public consultation on changes in land policy and law.
- To the extent possible, ease pressure on land by supporting non-land-based solutions for returnees—for example, training and microfunding—and skills that are often in demand in post-conflict situations, such as the building trades, simple machinery repair (bicycles, tires, fishing equipment), and provision of mobile phone access.

A final issue deserves highlighting here—a cautionary tale relating to international standards and political reality. In Rwanda, the government has tried to adhere to the land provisions of the Arusha Peace Accords even where these provisions, such as the ten-year rule, have been labeled a violation of human rights. When officials in the first RPF government were asked why they had persisted in attempts to see that the provisions of the accords on land were honored—when conditions had changed so completely—they emphasized that the new government considered that its political legitimacy in the eyes of many Rwandans hinged upon its compliance with the accords.

Critical analyses of post-conflict programming in Rwanda tend to highlight noncompliance with international standards. These standards tend to be stated unconditionally. Most recently, the Pinheiro Principles (the UN Principles on Housing and Property Restitution for Refugees and Displaced Persons)[15] provide, in part, that:

---

[15] The principles are named after Paulo Sérgio Pinheiro of Brazil and were approved by the UN Sub-commission on the Promotion and Protection of Human Rights (a subcommittee of the Committee on the Elimination of Racial Discrimination) in August 2005.

Return of land in post-conflict Rwanda 141

10.1 All refugees and displaced persons have the right to return voluntarily to their former homes, land or places of habitual residence, in safety and dignity. . . .

10.2 States shall allow refugees and displaced persons who wish to return voluntarily to their former homes, lands or places of habitual residence to do so. This right cannot be abridged under conditions of state succession, nor can it be subject to arbitrary and unlawful time limitations. . . .

18.3 States should ensure that national legislation related to housing, land and property restitution is internally consistent, as well as compatible with pre-existing relevant agreements, such as peace agreements and voluntary repatriation agreements, so long as those agreements are themselves compatible with international human rights, refugee and humanitarian law and related standards. . . .

21.1 All refugees and displaced persons have the right to full and effective compensation as an integral component of the restitution process. Compensation may be monetary or in kind. States shall, in order to comply with the principle of restorative justice, ensure that the remedy of compensation is only used when the remedy of restitution is not factually possible, or when the injured party knowingly and voluntarily accepts compensation in lieu of restitution, or when the terms of a negotiated peace settlement provide for a combination of restitution and compensation (UN 2005).

Note the tension between the terms of the Arusha Peace Accords and international standards such as those enunciated in the Pinheiro Principles. Section 10 makes unconditional statements about the right to return to residences and lands, and 18.3 suggests that peace agreements must be honored in national legislation only where they do not contravene international standards reflecting those rights. But in 21.1, the possibility of compensation in case of failure of restitution is admitted, and one of the narrow cases in which it is said to be allowable is "when the terms of a negotiated peace settlement provide for a combination of restitution and compensation."

In this context, it is important to recognize that in situations such as Rwanda, people who occupy the land of those who have fled do not necessarily do so without legal sanction. Their occupation may be entirely legal under the law at the time it occurs. In other cases, occupation may not have had legal sanction initially but may be viewed under national law as having acquired legitimacy by the passage of time. One is thus often faced with the need to balance two inconsistent sets of rights—both valid under national law and whose justice is deeply felt by claimants. It will not be possible to fully satisfy both claims, and negotiation is required.

The Pinheiro Principles are quite right to insist upon restitution as the preferred solution. But those principles must be understood as principles rather than strict rules requiring compliance. How should one look at a provision such as the ten-year rule in relation to these principles? It is certainly an arbitrary limitation on the right of restitution. It was politically necessary at the time of the peace

142   Land and post-conflict peacebuilding

negotiations, and the government sought to honor it, suggesting that it retained some political importance in the post-conflict period. Political bargains in peace negotiations may contravene international standards and yet may be needed to find and maintain peace. As Jones notes, some of the solutions brought forth by the Rwandan government have raised valid concerns, but critics have not always been able to propose convincing alternative solutions to the country's land and economic crisis (Jones 2003).

Finally, it is important to recognize that there is a discrepancy between the international standards relating to the right to property of returnees and displaced persons on the one hand and those standards applicable to citizens who have remained in place on the other. Standards applying to the former group—the returnees—are more highly developed, presumably because the returnees are more vulnerable and have more often been abused. In contrast, international law provides little effective protection to the property rights of ordinary citizens (Seidl-Hohenveldern 1999). While the Universal Declaration of Human Rights in article 17 provides that citizens should not be "arbitrarily deprived" of their property rights, there is no clear standard for arbitrariness and no universally accepted requirement of or standard for appropriate compensation for the compulsory taking of land by the state. Returnees and displaced persons may enjoy a legal and sometimes a practical advantage here because international humanitarian organizations are on the ground to take their part. While protecting returnee rights is entirely appropriate, care must be taken to balance this with respect for the land rights of those who have remained behind. The rights of both groups must be balanced, and as a result, it may not be feasible to fully honor the claims of either.

It is important that the international community approach future situations of refugee return with a strong commitment to international standards but also with a thorough understanding of the history of land claims and a realistic appreciation of what is politically possible.

REFERENCES

Alusala, N. 2005. Disarmament and reconciliation: Rwanda's concerns. ISS Occasional Paper No. 108. Washington, D.C.: Institute for Security Studies. http://www.iss.co.za/pubs/papers/108/Paper108.pdf.

Andre, C., and J. P. Platteau. 1998. Land relations under unbearable stress: Rwanda caught in the Malthusian trap. *Journal of Economic Behavior and Organization* 34 (1): 1–47.

ACORD (Association for Cooperative Operations Research and Development). 1998. *Situation socio-economique du village* (imidugudu)*: La villagization est-elle la solution au probleme foncier au Rwanda?* Kigali.

Baaré, A., D. Shearer, and P. Uvin. 1999. The limits and scope for the use of development assistance incentives and disincentives for influencing conflict stituations – Case study: Rwanda. Paris: Organisation for Economic Co-operation and Development. www.peacedividendtrust.org/EIPdata/Library/Political%20Economy%20of%20Conflict/OECD_ODAincentives_Rwanda.pdf.

Baig, A., P. Farran, S. Haba, I. Ibambe, A. M. Jose, S. Kozak, B. Larielle, et al. 2007. *Turning Vision 2020 into reality: From recovery to sustainable human development; National human development report Rwanda 2007*. United Nations Development Programme Rwanda. http://hdr.undp.org/en/reports/national/africa/rwanda/RWANDA_2007_en.pdf.

Barriere, O. 1997. *Cadre juridique de la reforme fonciere au Rwanda: Analyses et propositions preliminaries* (Legal framework of land reform in Rwanda: Preliminary analyses and proposals). Rome: Food and Agriculture Organization of the United Nations.

Blarel, B., P. Hazell, F. Place, and J. Quiggin. 1992. The economics of farm fragmentation: Evidence from Ghana and Rwanda. *World Bank Economic Review* 6 (2): 233–254.

Bruce, J. W. 2007. Drawing a line under crisis: Reconciling returnee land access and security of tenure in post-conflict Rwanda. HPG Background Paper. London: Overseas Development Institute.

Gasana, J. K. 2002. Natural resource scarcity and violence. In *Conserving the peace: Resources, livelihoods and security*, ed. R. Matthew, M. Halle, and J. Switzer. Winnipeg, Canada: International Institute for Sustainable Development / International Union for Conservation of Nature.

Hajabakiga, P. 2004. Addressing land issues in post-conflict settings: The case of Rwanda. Paper for the "Land in Africa: Market Asset or Secure Livelihood?" conference, London, November 8–9.

Hillhorst, D., and M. van Leeuwen. 1999. Villagization in Rwanda. Wageningen Disaster Studies No. 2. Wageningen, Netherlands: Wageningen University Rural Development Sociology Group.

HRW (Human Rights Watch). 2001. *Uprooting the rural poor in Rwanda*. New York; Washington, D.C.; London; Brussels. www.hrw.org/reports/2001/rwanda/rwnvilg-15.htm#P1191 _191065.

Huggins, C. n.d. The challenges of land scarcity and protracted social conflict in Rwanda. Draft discussion paper. Nairobi, Kenya: African Centre for Technology Studies.

Jones, L. 2003. Giving and taking away: The difference between theory and practice regarding property in Rwanda. In *Returning home: Housing and property restitution rights for refugees and displaced persons*, ed. S. Leckie. New York: Transnational Publishers.

MINITERE (Ministry of Lands, Environment, Forestry, Water and Mines, Republic of Rwanda). 2006. The Organic Land Law: Bringing the law into effect. Kigali.

———. 2007. Summary of proposed trials work: From strategy to 10-year plan. Kigali.

Musahara, H., and C. Huggins. 2004. Land reform, land scarcity and post-conflict reconstruction: A case study of Rwanda. Policy brief. Nairobi, Kenya: African Centre for Technology Studies.

———. 2005. Land reform, land scarcity, and post-conflict reconstruction: A case study of Rwanda. In *From the ground up: Land rights, conflict and peace in Sub-Saharan Africa*, ed. C. Huggins and J. Clover. Nairobi, Kenya: African Centre for Technology Studies; Pretoria and Cape Town, South Africa: Institute for Security Studies.

NRC (Norwegian Refugee Council). 2005. *Ensuring durable solutions for Rwanda's displaced people: A chapter closed too early*. Geneva, Switzerland.

NURC (National Unity and Reconciliation Commission, Republic of Rwanda). 2005. Opinion survey: Land, property and reconciliation. Kigali: UK Department for International Development / Swedish International Development Cooperation Agency / International Rescue Committee.

144   Land and post-conflict peacebuilding

Percival, V., and T. Homer-Dixon. 1995. Environmental scarcity and violent conflict: The case of Rwanda. Project on Environment, Population and Security. Occasional paper. Washington, D.C.: American Association for the Advancement of Science and University of Toronto.

Pottier, J. 2006. Land reform for peace? Rwanda's 2005 land law in context. *Journal of Agrarian Change* 6 (4): 509–537.

Prunier, G. 1997. *The Rwanda crisis, 1959–1994.* London: Hurst.

Seidl-Hohenveldern, I. 1999. *International economic law.* 3rd ed. Alphen aan den Rijn, Netherlands: Kluwer Law International.

Semujanga, J. 2002. *The origins of the Rwandan genocide.* Amherst, NY: Humanity Books.

UN (United Nations). 2005. United Nations principles on housing and property restitution for refugees and displaced persons [Pinheiro Principles]. E/CN.4/Sub.2/2005/17. June 28. New York: United Nations Commission on Human Rights, Sub-commission on the Promotion and Protection of Human Rights. www.unhcr.org/refworld/docid/41640c874.html.

UNFPA/Rwanda (United Nations Population Fund/Rwanda). 2007. *Rwanda 2007 country office annual report.* Kigali.

UNHCR/Rwanda (United Nations High Commissioner for Refugees/Rwanda). 2000. *Rwanda recovery: UNHCR's repatriation and reintegration activities in Rwanda from 1994–1999.* Johannesburg, South Africa: HRP Printers.

———. 2006a. Rwanda at a glance. Kigali.

———. 2006b. *Situation report on expelled Rwandaphones of Tanzania.* Kigali.

Wolters, S. 2005. The gacaca process: Eradicating the culture of impunity in Rwanda. ISS Situation Report. Washington, D.C.: Institute for Security Studies.

Wyss, K. 2006. A thousand hills for 9 million people: Land reform in Rwanda; Restoration of feudal order or genuine transformation? Swisspeace Working Paper No. 1/2006. Geneva, Switzerland: Swisspeace.

Post-conflict land tenure issues in Bosnia: Privatization and the politics of reintegrating the displaced

Rhodri C. Williams

Land tenure issues in post-conflict Bosnia and Herzegovina[1] have been influenced by the fact that land in Bosnia, while a scarce and sought-after resource, is not capable of providing quick returns. The collapse of Yugoslav socialism left behind a landscape of small, neglected agricultural plots, failed industrial complexes, and unplanned, inadequately serviced peri-urban settlements. Significant governance reform and private investment remain necessary before the economic potential of Bosnia's land can be fully realized.

While not a high-value economic asset in post-conflict Bosnia, land became a high-value political asset. Faced with international pressure to allow property restitution and the return of displaced people, nationalist leaders in Bosnia allocated public land to displaced people of their own ethnicity in a bid not only to provide for their immediate humanitarian needs as they vacated claimed property but also to permanently integrate them in order to secure local ethnic constituencies. International attempts to encourage the restoration of a multiethnic Bosnia by restricting land allocations were overly broad and economically destabilizing and were abandoned in 2002.

Ultimately, neither international ambitions to reintegrate Bosnia through widespread return of displaced people nor domestic nationalist agendas to perpetuate ethnic separation through resettlement were entirely successful. Return and resettlement patterns varied widely, and the economic and spatial legacy of socialism often had a crucial influence both on individuals' choices regarding durable solutions and on the success of international and domestic programs meant to influence such choices. Thus, although the post-conflict land tenure debates focused on humanitarian and human rights issues associated with the immediate post-conflict phase, many of the outcomes were determined by governance and economic reform factors typically associated with longer-term development. Although post-conflict tensions over land resources tend to be primarily economic in nature, understanding the significance of land as a political asset is crucial to peacebuilding efforts, particularly in the wake of ethnic conflict and displacement.

Rhodri C. Williams is a human rights lawyer who specializes in land and forced-migration issues.

[1] In this chapter, the term *Bosnia* is used to refer to Bosnia and Herzegovina.

146 Land and post-conflict peacebuilding

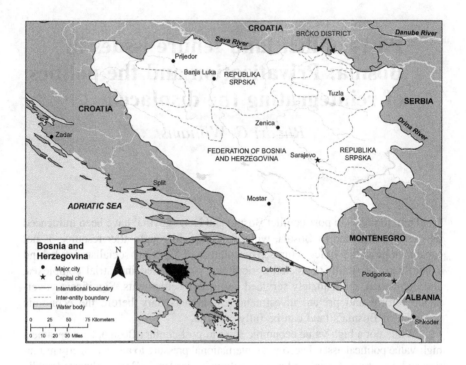

BACKGROUND

The 1992–1995 conflict in Bosnia took place in the broader context of the collapse of the Socialist Federal Republic of Yugoslavia (SFRY). The unraveling of this multinational socialist state resulted from the confluence of a vacuum of political authority, economic collapse, and the long-standing failure of the Yugoslav authorities either to address ethnic grievances or to provide sufficiently durable institutions to contain them. In a series of crises from 1990 to the present, all six of the constituent republics of the SFRY (Bosnia, Croatia, the former Yugoslav Republic of Macedonia, Montenegro, Serbia, and Slovenia) eventually achieved statehood, and one autonomous province, Kosovo, controversially declared independence.

Prior to the conflict, Bosnia's history was marked by a delicate but sustained pattern of accommodation among three dominant sectarian groups: Muslim Bosniaks who descended from Slavic converts to Islam during Ottoman rule (1463–1878), Catholic Bosnians who came to identify themselves with the Croats of neighboring Croatia, and Orthodox Bosnians who looked to coreligionists in Serbia to the East. Although Bosnian Muslims, Croats, and Serbs are united by ethnicity and language, their religious and cultural differences led them to consider themselves to be separate ethnic groups (see figure 1).

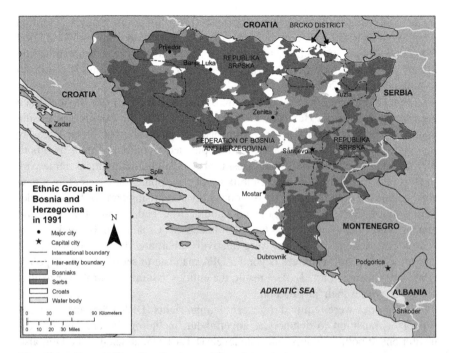

Figure 1. Pre-conflict distributions of Bosnia's ethnic groups
Source: Ceha (2008).

The 1992–1995 conflict in Bosnia and the Dayton Peace Agreement

Attempts to contain competition between the SFRY's various ethnic groups through a complex system of constitutional decentralization broke down as severe economic pressures at the end of the Cold War laid bare the fragility of the SFRY's institutions (Woodward 1995). In the conflict that raged after Bosnia's declaration of independence in 1992, the Bosniaks fought largely to uphold the integrity of the country, while nationalist Bosnian Croat and Serb contingents sought to create ethnically pure enclaves with a view to possible secession. In this context, control of strategically important territory was central to the conflict aims of all parties. Such control was typically achieved through the ethnic cleansing of opposing ethnic groups and the prevention of their return through the destruction of their property or its allocation within local ethnic patronage networks (Cox and Garlick 2003).

By 1995, ethnic cleansing and conflict had killed over 100,000 people and displaced half the population, with 1 million Bosnians seeking shelter abroad and a further 1 million internally displaced. The homes and lands of those uprooted were neglected, destroyed, or occupied by others. The economy essentially ground to a halt, with agricultural, commercial, and industrial activities crippled

148   Land and post-conflict peacebuilding

by the double legacy of conflict and socialism (FAO 1999a). As many as 2 million people countrywide were receiving some form of food ration from the World Food Program (Watson and Filipovitch 1998). Even today, landmine contamination affects nearly 1 million people, primarily in rural areas where land is central to livelihoods (ICBL 2008).

In recognition of the regional nature of the conflict, the 1995 Dayton Peace Agreement on Bosnia-Herzegovina (DPA) that ended the conflict in Bosnia applied not only to the domestic actors but also to the neighboring former Yugoslav republics of Croatia and Serbia, which had pursued a conflict of their own both directly and through proxies within Bosnia. The post-conflict political framework in Bosnia confirmed the de facto unmixing of the population by creating a new state composed of two federal units—one entity comprising parts of Bosnia under Serb control (Republika Srpska), and another (the Federation of Bosnia and Herzegovina) composed of cantons dominated by Croats and Bosniaks. New central government institutions were relatively weak and did not enjoy explicit control over natural resources beyond a DPA mandate to set foreign trade policy (DPA 1995, annex 4, art. 3). As a result, the entities assumed control over natural resources within their jurisdiction.

All parties were required to respect human rights (DPA 1995, annex 6) and support a transition to democratic government, including the creation of new institutions at both the entity and state levels (DPA 1995, annex 4). The DPA also mandated a large peacekeeping force led by the North Atlantic Treaty Organization (NATO) and a powerful civilian administration, led by the Office of the High Representative (OHR), with powers to pass laws and dismiss public officials where necessary to implement the peace (DPA 1995, annexes 1A and 10). In addition to such coercive means, the international community offered positive incentives for reform in the form of economic assistance and the prospect of Bosnian integration into European and Atlantic institutions.

The conflict in Bosnia involved both systematic destruction and massive redistribution of wealth. But it was not fought over natural resources, and natural resources were not used to sustain the conflict, as has been the case in many other conflicts (UNEP 2009). As a result, the DPA did not address natural resources as such. The post-conflict period has seen significant unregulated extraction of high-value natural resources, particularly timber (ESI 2004). However, such activities arguably represent a means rather than an end; for the nationalist power structures that diverted power from Bosnia's formal institutions and resisted implementation of the DPA, resource extraction has been part of a broader pattern of illicit income streams that have supported the pursuit of essentially political goals.

Given that the conflict was fought over political control of territory and populations, the DPA firmly specified the parties' obligations to take specific steps, including restitution of property, to facilitate the return of displaced people to their homes (DPA 1995, annex 7). In the post-conflict period, land has been important for meeting residential, subsistence, and commercial needs, but has not been associated with quick profits or even longer-term speculation. Instead, control of land has primarily been associated with humanitarian aims (reintegration of displaced people) and political goals (engineering of Bosnia's post-conflict demographic structure).

For domestic parties, allocation of land to resettle displaced people represented a means of addressing humanitarian needs while achieving pragmatic goals related to the consolidation of political constituencies and patronage networks. International actors, by contrast, were driven by the conviction that Bosnia's displacement crisis should be resolved through the return of displaced people to their original homes rather than by their resettlement elsewhere. Land allocation to displaced people also raised complicated issues related to economic transition, privatization, governance reform, and European integration.

History of land tenure and administration in Bosnia

Bosnia lies at the heart of the western Balkans and is characterized by a variegated topography and climate. Most of the land in Bosnia is hilly or mountainous, and both urban settlements and agricultural activities tend to be concentrated in lowlands and river valleys. The northernmost part of Bosnia, which borders on the Sava River, is a relatively flat and fertile extension of the Pannonian plain. This region, comprising 40 percent of Bosnia's territory, was home to over half its population and 70 percent of its cultivated land before the 1992–1995 conflict (JLZ 1983). Aside from agriculture, other primary activities such as animal husbandry, forestry, and mining have traditionally played an important role in the area's economy (see figure 2).

After several centuries as an independent principality, Bosnia was incorporated into the Ottoman Empire in the early sixteenth century. Given its location, it became a bridgehead for further conquests to the north and a military frontier zone when these territories fell to the Austro-Hungarian Empire in the late seventeenth century. Over time, the essentially feudal Ottoman timar land administration system gave way to a landed hereditary aristocracy (JLZ 1983; Malcolm 1996). As the Ottoman Empire receded, the Austro-Hungarian Empire took over the administration of Bosnia from 1878 until the empire's breakup in 1918. The Austrians made only incremental changes to the Ottoman system, introducing a two-book system with separate land registries and cadastres, promoting optional redemption of serfs, and imposing only light regulation on the system of *vakufs* (Muslim charitable trusts) that had come to hold one-third of all usable land in Bosnia (Malcolm 1996). Moves to promote agricultural development and establish foreign agrarian colonies on newly available land along the former frontier came in the context of broader investment in primary industries and transport infrastructure (Malcolm 1996).

In 1918, Bosnia was incorporated into the newly independent Kingdom of Serbs, Croats, and Slovenes (the first Yugoslavia). The mandatory abolition of serfdom followed in 1919, accompanied by land reform that broke up Bosnia's largest estates, transferring title to the families that had worked them as serfs

150 Land and post-conflict peacebuilding

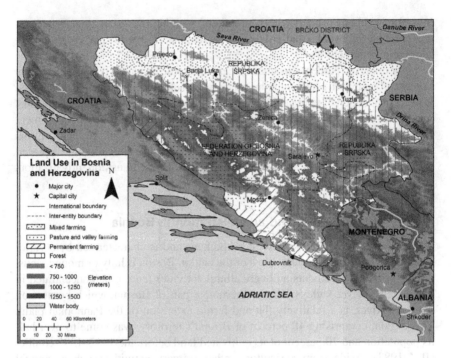

Figure 2. Elevation and predominant land uses in Bosnia
Source: University of Texas Libraries (1992).

(Malcolm 1996). The worldwide economic crisis of the 1930s was felt severely in underdeveloped Bosnia, and an already large agrarian population increased to comprise nearly 85 percent of the region's households by the early 1930s (JLZ 1983). Bosnia was devastated during World War II but emerged as one of the constituent republics of the SFRY (the second Yugoslavia), created in 1945 and ruled by the Partisan leader Josip Broz Tito.

The early years of Tito's Yugoslavia were characterized by Stalinist centralized control. However, even the most radical post-conflict rounds of nationalization did not do away with private property rights altogether but simply limited their scope. Residential property was limited to two large or three small apartments, while rural households were limited to ten hectares of high-grade agricultural land (UN-HABITAT 2005). All housing and land in excess of these limits was nationalized, along with all business enterprises and urban land. While nationalization affected both the urban and rural holdings of vakufs and other religious foundations, much forest land was already state property in Bosnia and simply remained so. Commercial use of private property was strictly regulated, with private rent levels set by local governments and agriculturalists subjected to forced delivery quotas at fixed prices (Palairet 2000).

After Tito's break with Stalin in 1948, centralization was reversed, and successive constitutional reforms led to significant devolution of powers, both in a political sense (from the central government to the republics) and in economic activity. The "self-management" system adopted by the SFRY in the 1970s replaced central planning with "an intricate system of negotiations and voluntary agreements among countless autonomous actors" (ESI 2004, 13). Such actors included both commercial enterprises and non-economic institutions, comprising "all other subjects that were socially useful but not productive in economic terms" such as administrative bodies, municipal governments, public housing enterprises, universities, and hospitals (UN-HABITAT 2005, 18). An important component of self-management was the institution of socially owned property, which effectively diffused responsibility for previously state-owned property, attributing it to the Yugoslav people collectively. A long-term legacy of this system has been the erosion of any form of accountability in Bosnia, with self-management itself a poor substitute for democratic interest politics, and social ownership a means of externalizing the costs of failure to invest in public assets onto society as a whole (ESI 2004).

Surprisingly, the overwhelming majority of rural landholdings in Bosnia (about 90 percent) remained in private hands by the time of the 1992–1995 conflict. Early attempts at forced collectivization were abandoned in the face of rural unrest and hunger, and nationalization of private land beyond the ten hectare agrarian maximum yielded little due to the effects of prior land reform and natural fragmentation under Bosnian inheritance law. What land did fall to the state eventually became socially owned and was made available to large agricultural combines, which monopolized virtually all government agricultural programs and subsidies (ESI 2004). Official Yugoslav ideology favored industrialization and a phasing out of rural smallholder farming, but little assistance was provided to peasants in achieving this transition. Meanwhile, poor transport and low official prices for agricultural produce led peasants to avoid placing their crops on the market (Palairet 2000). Instead, working-age men endured lengthy commutes to factory jobs, while the rest of the family grew crops for household subsistence or simply held onto unused land as a hedge against future insecurity. This resulted in the creation of a large peasant-worker class in Bosnia that was impoverished by the post-conflict collapse in industry but no longer able to fall back on commercial agricultural production.

In cities and towns throughout the former Yugoslavia, post-conflict industrialization reinforced trends toward urbanization, placing new pressures on housing markets and infrastructure. During the 1950s, employees were required to pay into a general housing fund that subsidized construction, and tenants were granted stronger rights to state-allocated apartments (UN-HABITAT 2005). With the introduction of self-management, most urban land and much of the apartment stock became socially owned property. Apartments were allocated by the enterprises or institutions that had built them according to official criteria and waiting lists. Recipients acquired occupancy rights to socially owned apartments, allowing them and their households to remain permanently as long as they did not leave the apartment for more than six months without justification. Although need was meant to be a key criterion in allocation, apartments were often used

152 Land and post-conflict peacebuilding

by employers "to lure scarce skilled labor and management to their enterprises," creating a situation in which all paid into housing funds but the most privileged received the highest benefits (Le Normand 2008, 6).

With socially owned apartments largely reserved to the management class, urban socially owned land came under pressure from peasant-workers seeking to establish a residential foothold near their workplace. In Yugoslavia, municipal governments were responsible for allocating the right to use urban land plots to individuals or enterprises against a fee meant to cover extension of utilities and services. This right could not be privately exchanged as such, but did automatically transfer to buyers of private property built on lawfully allocated construction land. In the 1960s, a wave of illegal construction broke over the outskirts of Yugoslavia's towns, with private individuals staking out available construction land to build homes (Palairet 2000). Although such informal settlements could legally have been destroyed, squatters tended to be tolerated and eventually issued user rights to their plots (Ó Tuathail and Dahlman 2006). However, plans to upgrade informal settlements foundered on the fact that neither self-builders nor municipalities had the means to pay for the extension of utilities to unplanned lots scattered at the urban periphery (Le Normand 2008). Even in city centers, mismanagement resulted in extensive deterioration of infrastructure and depreciation of public assets (ESI 2004).

In short, the situation immediately prior to the 1992–1995 hostilities was already characterized by the effects of chronic mismanagement of land resources. Fragmentation of rural land plots combined with policies discouraging commercial agriculture had led to both the loss of farming skills and degradation of land and rural infrastructure through a long-term lack of investment. The same factors had also contributed to a spontaneous and unregulated migration to peri-urban settlements, where patterns of squatting and illegal construction on socially owned land were tolerated but not made sustainable through the extension of infrastructure and utilities.

ANALYSIS

This case study focuses on the interplay between land tenure issues and international efforts to promote the return of displaced people during the first decade of implementation of the Dayton Accords in Bosnia, from 1996 to 2006. It includes the stabilization phase immediately after the conflict, but focuses on the tensions that arose as the transition phase slowly and fitfully gave way to consolidation and early recovery. In Bosnia, transitional priorities such as demobilization and refugee return were often described as Dayton tasks, reflecting the fact that both the national obligations to undertake them and the international role in their oversight clearly derived from the peace agreement. By contrast, the consolidation and early recovery phase tends to be associated with Europe, as European institutions and European Union (EU) integration were meant to replace the post-conflict DPA framework, providing positive incentives for the national authorities to push on with governance and economic reforms beyond those envisioned in the peace agreement.

Post-conflict land tenure issues in Bosnia 153

The struggle to shift the footing of the international intervention in Bosnia fully "from Dayton to Europe" continues to this day, with ongoing debate about when to completely phase out the OHR, relinquishing its intrusive mandate in favor of the soft power wielded by the EU Special Representative, an office that was merged with OHR in 2002 (ICG 2009). In many respects, Bosnia's progress toward normalcy has been extremely rapid, with the insertion of peacekeeping forces and demobilization accomplished shortly after the conflcit, regular local and national elections being held since 1996, completion of property restitution by 2003, and the return of over 1 million people, or nearly half of those displaced. Most of Bosnia's remaining problems fall within the Europe docket, but are of such severity that they continue to threaten the post-conflict gains made in the Dayton era. These include weak, divided political leadership and endemic obstacles to economic growth (ESI 2004).

Demands on land in Bosnia have been made on the basis of both humanitarian need and the need to achieve broader economic reform. Humanitarian measures related to land include both the restitution of abandoned land and homes to people displaced from them during the conflict and the allocation of socially owned land to groups made vulnerable during the conflict—including displaced people. These measures have been intensely political, with international efforts to re-create multicultural constituencies by returning displaced people to their homes competing directly with the efforts of nationalist parties to perpetuate ethnic separation by permanently resettling displaced coreligionists.

In theory, the conflict-related humanitarian issues related to restitution and allocation of land should have been dealt with during the transitional (Dayton) phase, allowing an orderly shift of attention and resources to the reform-related economic issues meant to be addressed during the consolidation (European) phase. In practice, it proved no easier to draw a neat line between these phases at the micro-level of land tenure issues than at the macro-level of national politics. Instead, the persistent legacy of communist laws and practices frustrated the agendas of both international and domestic parties, whose efforts to promote their favored humanitarian outcomes may, in turn, have complicated the prospects of longer-term land tenure reform.

International return policies

The early peacebuilding priorities of the international community in Bosnia involved establishing basic security and setting the political foundations for a viable state. The return of displaced people was understood from the beginning to be the key to restoring political stability, and was promoted as a central aim—even when it threatened to undermine security conditions. The extraordinary emphasis placed on return was rooted in the fact that it was seen as an antidote to the strength of the nationalist parties that had sought to partition Bosnia, which were granted broad autonomy and recognition elsewhere in the DPA. International state building efforts aspired to "override such divisions . . . from above" through support to Bosnia's nascent state institutions, but also crucially "from below" through return

154 Land and post-conflict peacebuilding

(Cousens and Cater 2001, 45). In this context, return came to dominate the civilian peacebuilding agenda to the virtual exclusion of topics such as urbanization and agricultural reform, which at first "seemed irrelevant and were largely ignored" (Rose, Thomas, and Tumler 2000, 8).

The fact that early peacebuilding did not explicitly address land administration issues did not reflect satisfaction with Bosnia's post-conflict land tenure system, but rather the sense that such issues were best addressed through political and development processes outside the immediate scope of the post-conflict settlement. However, the DPA did provide key parameters for such processes. First, it demarcated the internal boundaries between Bosnia's entities and guaranteed its external borders and sovereignty. Second, it obligated the authorities throughout Bosnia to restore displaced people's property and create viable conditions for their return. These provisions promised to restore basic order and legal certainty to post-conflict land relations, fulfilling an important precondition for their longer-term reform.

The key development questions surrounding land in post-conflict Bosnia had more to do with unlocking long-suppressed potential than with resolving burning disputes. For land tenure reform in Bosnia, "the fact that the country is in transition from socialism to capitalism is just as important as the fact that there was a war" (Rose, Thomas, and Tumler 2000, vii). After the conflict, rural land remained locked in a network of small and fractured subsistence plots that were often hoarded and left fallow, rather than put to productive use through active sales and lease markets. Meanwhile, urban areas displayed the effects of decades of unplanned growth and neglect of public services and utilities.

Land administration problems were essentially political, and the fundamental nature of the reforms needed to address them—privatization, markets, and better governance—had been a matter of consensus, at least in principle, since well before the conflict. On the other hand, however pressing these goals may have been, they were not, in and of themselves, central Dayton tasks and required local knowledge, development expertise, resources, political judgment, and democratic legitimacy beyond what the international community could offer. To give just one example, possible means of privatizing socially owned agricultural land included transfer to local government authorities, sale to the highest bidder, preferential sale to buyers in a position to consolidate the land with adjoining privately held parcels, and restitution to pre-nationalization owners. Given the bewildering array of policy options, technical issues, and budgetary implications inherent in land tenure questions, international actors involved in peacebuilding tended to leave such issues largely to those working on development.

In practice, however, it proved impossible to completely separate the process of land tenure reform from the priority goal of return. By 1998, restitution of the property of displaced people had clearly emerged as the main policy supported by international actors to promote return. However, from the earliest days of the return process, it was clear that simply restoring rights to and possession of land would not automatically foster sustainable return. For rural returnees, the effects of the conflict posed significant sustainability issues, particularly when agricultural land they depended on for subsistence was contaminated by landmines (Keith 1999). However, longer-term transitional issues weighed heavily as well. The collapse of Bosnian industry precluded a return to the pre-conflict peasant-worker lifestyle with its minimum benefits of social security access and wage supplements to agricultural income. As a result, less developed parts of Bosnia saw a forced retreat into the wholesale reliance on subsistence farming that had been abandoned by previous generations, leaving the preferred option for many "to emigrate or, in the case of the displaced, never to return" (ESI 2004, 29).

Indeed, although post-conflict Bosnia has seen significant returns to rural areas, the conflict almost undoubtedly accelerated a process of urbanization that had gathered pace before the conflict as peasant-workers moved from remote farms to informal peri-urban settlements (OHR 1998a). Urbanization has been supported by significant post-conflict returns to cities and towns, such as those of Muslims to Doboj and Prijedor (both in northern Bosnia) and Serbs to Drvar (in western Bosnia). An equally or more significant factor in urbanization has been the re-settlement of displaced people who did not wish to return to their pre-conflict homes. Their resettlement was often supported by grants of socially owned land by local nationalist authorities, in an effort to offset the effects of return by members of other ethnic groups or even directly discourage it. These resettlement measures were perceived as a direct challenge to international efforts to support political reintegration, and resulted in a dramatic expansion of international return activities, with measures in support of restitution supplemented by a new arrogation of temporary control over transactions in socially owned land throughout Bosnia.

Property restitution, return, and the rule of law

International efforts to support return got off to a slow and confused start in Bosnia, with ad hoc efforts to negotiate return quotas with local authorities, uncoordinated reconstruction projects, and projects conditioning economic assistance on support for returns producing few results in the field (ESI 1999). Those returns that did occur early on were primarily majority movements—of displaced people back to areas under the control of their coreligionists—rather than the minority returns to ethnically cleansed areas promoted by the international community in order to support reintegration.

In 1997, the OHR joined its political power to the United Nations High Commissioner for Refugees' mandate to coordinate returns under annex 7 of the DPA, creating a new Reconstruction and Return Task Force (RRTF) to coordinate the process. Conditions for progress improved with the use of donor-funded reconstruction to induce return to destroyed rural villages, as well as introduction of greater freedom of movement through the introduction of uniform license plates in both entities and increased willingness by peacekeeping forces to arrest indicted war criminals and provide security in return areas. However, there were clear signs that low-level ethnic cleansing and reallocation of abandoned housing was continuing. As a result, a number of Dayton-mandated agencies began to

156   Land and post-conflict peacebuilding

focus return efforts on ending property reallocation and restoring abandoned homes to their displaced owners. Through this process, the RRTF established the Property Law Implementation Plan, an interagency effort to coordinate restitution policy and monitoring throughout the country (Philpott 2005).

This effort restored some 200,000 homes throughout Bosnia to their former residents, setting an international precedent and laying the groundwork for significant minority return and political stabilization. Under heavy international pressure, both Bosnian entities passed legislation in 1998 annulling wartime rules allowing abandoned property to be reallocated, canceling all legal rights to use abandoned property, and setting out a procedure for displaced people to claim their former homes and lands from local administrative bodies (OHR 1998b, 1998c). During 1999, OHR used its powers to amend the post-conflict restitution laws, harmonizing and tightening their provisions in response to obstructive practices noted by field monitors (Williams 2005).

Notably, the restitution laws provided for the return of private property of any kind, whether it was held in fully registered ownership or merely lawfully possessed by its pre-conflict resident. However, the only category of socially owned property liable to restitution consisted of apartments to which pre-conflict occupancy rights pertained. Socially owned agricultural land and business properties were not subject to restitution, except that user rights to land on which private houses had been built were implicitly restored along with the houses. While the inclusion of socially owned apartments was necessary if restitution was to have any effect on urban return, the modalities of restoring these conditional quasi-ownership rights exacerbated return-related tensions that had been inherent in the DPA from the beginning.

The contingent nature of rights to socially owned property had originally been exploited by the warring parties, who cynically used socialist rules penalizing absence from an apartment to cancel the occupancy rights of displaced victims of ethnic cleansing. Although the international community stopped this practice, the restitution laws imposed new penalties on pre-conflict occupancy right holders who failed to return to their apartments. Unlike private property, which was subject to virtually unconditional restitution, the restoration of occupancy rights was subject to conditions meant to encourage return. Under the laws, pre-conflict occupancy right holders faced legal deadlines to reclaim their apartments. These conditions were clearly analogous to the old use requirements, in that unjustified failure to return could again result in the cancellation of displaced people's rights (Williams 2005).

Following an extended debate, OHR removed these conditions, noting their exploitation by local actors to thwart return, and instead equated occupancy rights in socially owned apartments with private property. A key motivation for this change was the concern that compelling the displaced to return in order to exercise their rights was putting the cart before the horse. From the beginning of the restitution process, international actors had been aware that if they focused exclusively on return, they risked being drawn into a highly politicized debate among national actors. "Achieving returns was, above all, a political process, rather than technical or humanitarian" in nature (ESI 1999, 3). In analyzing the motivations of the different parties, many observers found that, while none had a direct political interest in promoting return, all had an interest in meeting the criteria for future European integration—including the requirement "that laws ... be implemented transparently and fairly" (ICG 1999, 22). This clearly militated in favor of OHR "shifting the focus of its pressure away from the inter-ethnic element (reversing ethnic cleansing) towards the rule of law element (eliminating misuse of housing)" (ESI 1999, 15).

The elimination of legal conditions for restoring abandoned socially owned apartments was a crucial first step in rearticulating restitution as a vehicle of rights rather than of return. As this shift became an increasingly explicit article of international policy in Bosnia, it exposed differences over return among international actors contested on similar terms to some of the domestic parties' disputes (Philpott 2005). By explicitly accepting that the beneficiaries of restitution were free either to return to their properties or to treat them as assets to assist in resettling elsewhere, OHR broke down resistance to the process among hard-line nationalists who no longer faced the specter of the full rollback of their wartime gains (Cox and Garlick 2003). However, as the restitution process accelerated countrywide, another set of problems became increasingly obvious, highlighting the fact that even if the relationship between restitution and return was now settled, that between restitution and resettlement of those who did not wish to return was not.

Resettlement and land allocation

Acceptance of property restitution on the basis of individual rights represented a compromise between international interests in mass return and domestic nationalist interests in mass resettlement. Although it was seen as a retreat from the assertion in the DPA that "early return of refugees and displaced persons is an important objective of the settlement of the conflict in Bosnia" (DPA 1995, annex 7, art. 1.1), it was arguably necessary in light of another DPA principle: the obligation to respect the voluntary and informed choice of destination of all displaced people and refugees within Bosnia (art. 1.4). While it was now clear that return could not be a precondition for restitution, completion of the restitution process remained necessary in order to allow all claimants to make fully voluntary choices between return and resettlement. However, full implementation of the restitution process clearly implied a great deal of secondary displacement of current occupants, and serious questions remained about how to provide both short-term shelter and long-term housing assistance to such people.

With donor reconstruction-driven return to destroyed property firmly established by 1999, the shift in focus to restitution-driven return to occupied urban homes underscored these questions (ESI 1999). At that point, nearly 100,000 occupied urban apartments were in contention nationwide; where would those

158 Land and post-conflict peacebuilding

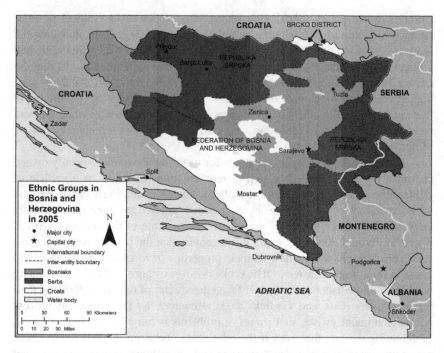

Figure 3. Post-conflict distribution of Bosnia's ethnic groups
Source: Zec and Hamzic (2006).

families go? Many occupants were themselves displaced people who had claims to homes elsewhere. When such occupants faced eviction while their own claims were still pending, or when they had no such claim, the restitution laws obligated local authorities to provide temporary accommodation on a humanitarian basis. However, when displaced occupants did not wish to return to their pre-conflict property, and would not be able to cover their own resettlement costs by selling it, some type of resettlement assistance was necessary. Proposals by entity-level and local authorities in Bosnia to provide such assistance—often on the basis of grants of socially owned construction land—were initially accepted, albeit with skepticism, by international officials.

International actors in Bosnia tended to see local resettlement initiatives as one of a number of stratagems to maintain the effective partition of the country brought about by ethnic cleansing (see figure 3). Most observers accepted that nationalists on all sides of the conflict stood to gain by maintaining ethnic separation and preventing the watering down of their political constituencies. The Bosniaks, as a plurality of the population, had less to lose in this regard than the Serbs and Croats, but Muslim nationalist leaders took few concrete actions to back up their rhetorical support for return (ICG 1999). Meanwhile, Serb and Croat nationalists staunchly opposed return, claiming that none of the displaced people they represented wanted to go back to their pre-conflict homes. Stratagems

Post-conflict land tenure issues in Bosnia   159

for discouraging return had taken a number of forms in Bosnia, all of which had been defended on more-or-less credible humanitarian grounds while serving more-or-less obvious segregationist designs.

The most obviously obstructive practices—property confiscations—were adopted during the conflict and countered through the restitution laws. These practices built on the failure to protect fleeing minorities and the destruction of their property or its reallocation to coreligionists displaced from other parts of the country. In any given area, reallocation not only physically blocked return of the original owners but also discouraged the return of current occupants to their original homes by giving them an incentive to remain. The humanitarian grounds given for adopting such policies were often a pretext, with the best-appointed abandoned homes serving as patronage rewards for the loyalty of local military, judicial, or police officials (Cox and Garlick 2003). The seriousness of efforts to maintain ethnically pure constituencies was demonstrated immediately after the conflict by instances of self-cleansing—in which nationalist paramilitaries forced their coreligionists out of homes on territory slated to be transferred to the control of other groups under the DPA and into homes abandoned by ethnic minorities elsewhere (OSCE 1996).

This practice—permanently resettling members of one group in homes from which members of another group had been displaced—was not the only practice involving openly hostile resettlement of displaced people. Displaced people were also moved to locations where, even if they did not occupy property belonging to people of another ethnic group, their physical presence was intended to discourage the other group's return (UNCHR 1998). The most notable example involved free allocation of construction land in the south of the country to displaced Croats, who were helped—initially with resources provided by the government of neighboring Croatia—to construct homes in strategic areas where the return of other groups to ethnically cleansed villages could threaten the consolidation of a Greater Croatia (ESI 2004). Similar practices included occupying properties, such as grazing land or religious facilities, that could not be claimed by individuals under the restitution laws but that were central to the livelihoods or cultural practices of returning communities. Some practices, such as destroying abandoned apartment buildings and issuing user rights to new structures, were more clearly extensions of wartime property reallocation.

A third and less obviously objectionable practice involved the ostensibly humanitarian resettlement of people displaced when the housing they occupied was claimed by its original owners. After the adoption of the restitution laws, proposals proliferated to allocate land for this purpose. In Sarajevo, construction land was earmarked for ambitious plans to build new settlements for Muslims evicted from claimed properties (ICG 1999). Meanwhile Republika Srpska (RS) began, with tacit international consent, an entity-wide program of allocating socially owned land plots to displaced Serbs (Ó Tuathail and Dahlman 2006). Initially, the RS government promised to provide homes on allocated lands; but in practice, insufficient resources existed to do more than waive the fee normally

160   Land and post-conflict peacebuilding

collected by local municipalities for such allocations and to sporadically provide construction materials (ESI 2004).

While takeovers of private homes and property clearly violated the letter of the DPA and were cut short by the restitution laws, the allocation of socially owned land to promote resettlement potentially violated the DPA's spirit. Hostile resettlement practices involved violations of the authorities' obligations to support return that were obvious enough to lead the OHR to issue a temporary decision meant to ban this practice in May 1999, soon after the restitution process began (OHR 1999b). The decision voided, retroactively to the outbreak of the conflict, all allocation decisions related to socially owned land previously "used for residential, religious or cultural purposes, or for private agricultural or business activities" (OHR 1999a). This decision left a great deal of undeveloped land at the edges of cities and towns and on the premises of socially owned agricultural combines available for legal allocation and resettlement.

Faced with increasingly widespread land allocation that supported ostensibly voluntary resettlement without directly threatening existing return movements, the international community had difficulty articulating a skepticism that nevertheless remained deep-seated. Suspicions related to land allocation were rooted in the conviction that local nationalists, having failed to block incoming returns by members of rival groups, were now seeking to clandestinely shore up their political base by minimizing outgoing returns by their coreligionists to other areas. Such practices would be consistent with a practice of maintaining "captive" ethnic constituencies, as in Mostar, where hardline Croat authorities not only resisted minority return but sought to "prevent the departure of Croats living as displaced people . . . by threatening to withdraw their rights to pension, education and social services" (ICG 1999, 13).

Nationalist parties, particularly on the Serb and Croat sides, had also actively discouraged their displaced constituents from casting their votes at their places of origin during Bosnia's periodic elections (ICG 2002). Such pressure on displaced people to vote where they were displaced was thought to be one of the major factors behind the triumph of nationalist parties throughout Bosnia in the first post-conflict elections, held in September 1996 (Cousens and Cater 2001). This was one of two credible (and not mutually exclusive) views of the agendas driving local land allocation policies that emerged as immediate post-conflict concerns gave way to peacebuilding priorities: "the first as part of a top-down designer strategy to consolidate ethnic cleansing and secure nationalist homelands, the second as a bottom-up ad hoc adaptation to the desperate circumstances newly evicted displaced people found themselves in after 1998" (Ó Tuathail and Dahlman 2006, 306).

As land allocation became more widespread and visible in returnee areas in the RS, OHR came under increasing political pressure, particularly from Bosniaks, to go beyond the earlier decision protecting community and cultural property and ban the practice altogether. These developments coincided with the August 1999 appointment of a new high representative, the Austrian Wolfgang

Post-conflict land tenure issues in Bosnia 161

Petritsch, who would quickly adopt a more assertive use of the OHR's powers in support of his conviction that return constituted "the single most important issue for the reconstruction of Bosnia" (OHR 2000a).

In December 1999, OHR extended its earlier decision limiting land allocation by a further six months, appending an unusual explanatory note that described both the perils in any eventual expansion of the ban and methods for taking such a step (OHR 1999c). The note effectively conceded that the earlier decision had been violated with impunity, that OHR did not have the capacity or a mechanism for enforcing it, that some local authorities had complained that it had blocked legitimate investment projects, and that OHR itself had not yet decided what legislative amendments would be adequate to justify removal of the ban. On the other hand, the note asserted that extension of the ban would strengthen local RRTF officers' ability to monitor it, pointed out that the domestic authorities had taken no steps to reform the relevant law themselves, and noted that exceptions could be allowed for legitimate investment projects.

These observations foreshadowed a radically expanded decision in April 2000, which shifted the burden of proof, assuming that all allocations of socially owned land were discriminatory unless proven otherwise. All allocations of socially owned land since the outbreak of the conflict were deemed null and void, except when OHR issued a waiver based on "a clear showing by the competent authorities . . . that a proposed transfer . . . is non-discriminatory and in the best interests of the public" (OHR 2000b). In this decision, OHR added to its already considerable peacebuilding responsibilities the role of "the central planning authority for all of Bosnia . . . for which it had little personnel capacity, no in-house expertise and an already acknowledged enforcement problem" (Ó Tuathail and Dahlman 2006, 313).

Noncompliance with the decision remained widespread, and even the few waiver requests that came in quickly outstripped the capacities of the single human rights officer initially put in charge of reviewing them from an office in Sarajevo. Through its description of socially owned land as "the patrimony of all the citizens of the municipality, [including] . . . displaced persons who were formerly domiciled in the municipality," the OHR had also equated land allocation with wartime property confiscations, encouraging inflated expectations of what it could do to tackle the problem (OHR 2000c).

For many Muslims and international observers, land allocation was little more than a bid to consolidate ethnic cleansing by other means:

> As the international community has become increasingly determined to uphold the right of refugees to repossess their property, the nationalist regimes have fought back by focusing on creating incentives for their own displaced persons to settle permanently where it will benefit their respective national agendas. . . . Land allocation policy in the RS seems, in fact, to be specifically targeted at diluting the demographic and political effects of . . . return, since land grants occur most frequently in those areas of return that had non-Serb majorities before the war (ICG 2002, 11–12).

162 Land and post-conflict peacebuilding

Whatever the intentions of local authorities, however, there is evidence that land allocation programs not only speeded property restitution but may have even facilitated minority return. Gearóid Ó Tuathail and Carl Dahlman cite the European Stability Initiative (ESI), a research organization hired by OHR, which found no measurable effect on minority return (Ó Tuathail and Dahlman 2006). In fact, despite the failure of the OHR decision to control allocations, ESI found that less than 5 percent of the displaced in Bosnia had received an allocation and only a small minority of these had the resources to actually begin building a house on their plots. For local authorities, who had committed to implementing property restitution but were reluctant to house those vacating claimed properties in rudimentary temporary accommodations, the allocation of free land was a face-saving alternative. It served both those local authorities still tacitly interested in permanent resettlement of their coreligionists and others merely eager to be seen as having the wherewithal to provide evictees with the prospect of permanent housing. Grants of land may also have blunted any resentment felt by the evicted toward returning minorities, decreasing resistance to return (ESI 2007).

Whatever the psychological effect of land allocations on the return process, the wholesale distribution of such plots to members of the local ethnic majority continued to be seen by international observers as both discriminatory and negligent. Local authorities were bound under the DPA to create the conditions for return and yet were devoting much of the scarce public resource they presided over to resettlement projects. The international community initially refused to accept land plots as a form of alternative accommodation, in part because the latter was meant to be means-tested and temporary rather than distributed indiscriminately to occupants of claimed properties (OHR 2000f). However, later amendments sought to link entitlement to alternative accommodation to the question of whether land plot beneficiaries had sought OHR waivers (Philpott 2006). Ultimately, the fact that most beneficiaries were too poor to build on such plots disqualified the plots as either alternative accommodation or a basis for permanent resettlement.

In its report to OHR, ESI advocated dropping the ban and focusing instead on encouraging sustainable and democratically legitimate approaches to land use planning that would identify and address the real housing and livelihood needs of Bosnia's citizens (Ó Tuathail and Dahlman 2006). The approach suggested by ESI reflected two realities: (1) the OHR ban had merely made land transfers illegal without stopping them, fostering legal insecurity and inhibiting legitimate investment; and (2) land allocation policies had failed to either block return or support sustainable resettlement for those who did not wish to return. As Ó Tuathail and Dahlman note, neither the "top-down" goal of consolidating ethnic cleansing nor the "bottom-up" goal of sustainably housing evictees had been achieved (Ó Tuathail and Dahlman 2006, 306). As it became clear that the Dayton concerns regarding return that had justified the ban were not salient, attention turned to the Europe issues raised by the persistence of the underlying construct of socially owned land.

Moving toward Europe

Although the land allocation ban remained unenforceable, it was extended twice under High Representative Petritsch, essentially for lack of a better idea. In both cases, the decision noted that "the conditions in which the authorities . . . are able to dispose or otherwise allocate state-owned real property, including former socially owned property, in a manner that is non-discriminatory and in the best interest of the public do not now exist throughout Bosnia" (OHR 2000g, 2001a). The second extension decision also sought to mitigate the impact on investment by exempting leases of certain nonprivatized business premises. In August 2001, OHR facilitated the convening of a domestic working group to seek a legislative solution to the problem (OHR 2001b). The conclusions of the working group reflected increasing awareness of the economic aspect of land allocation, with greater reference to promoting transparent land development policies and accommodating privatization and denationalization. The conclusions included the first hint of a retreat from the presumption that all allocations were discriminatory, with a call for realistic approaches to past transactions that took into account "the interests of those individuals who, in good faith, personally invested their time, money and effort in an attempt to build a new life" (OHR 2002a).

During the same month, May 2002, Lord Paddy Ashdown of the United Kingdom took over as high representative and quickly established that the priorities of his tenure would be anti-corruption efforts, judicial reform, and economic development: "first justice, then jobs, through reform" (OHR 2002b, 2002d). However appropriate this shift from Dayton issues to European concerns may have been in light of the impending completion of the restitution process, the OHR would nevertheless have to find a solution to the land allocation problem. In short order, Lord Ashdown found himself accepting the resignation of an RS mayor for failing to act on a previous OHR decision revoking a waiver (OHR 2002c), extending the allocation ban for a third time with further investment-friendly categories exempted (OHR 2002e), and using his powers to remove the resigned mayor's successor on the same grounds (OHR 2002f).

However, even as the new high representative dutifully hewed to his predecessor's line on the return aspect of land allocations, development-related issues related to housing and land were piling up. The post-conflict property restitution process was on course for completion during 2003, with a number of municipalities having already processed their entire caseload by late 2002 (OHR 2002h). As this process concluded, the emphasis began to shift to provision of services that would both make return sustainable and provide a safety net to the most vulnerable people affected by the process. Accordingly, "full implementation of Annex VII [of the DPA]" was defined as allowing safe return to restituted homes "with equal expectations of employment, education and social services" (OHR 2003a). For those with "no prospect of being able to provide for their own needs" after the restitution process, the Property Law Implementation Plan agencies

164　Land and post-conflict peacebuilding

urged the competent ministers to "begin instituting measures that would ensure a seamless transition from provision of alternative accommodation under the property repossession laws to effective long-term social policies" (OHR 2003b).

Outside of the return discussion, the impact of Bosnia's neglected land tenure system on the economic development prioritized by the new high representative was increasingly clear. One of the original planks of Lord Ashdown's employment strategy involved "reforms on property and landownership law, so that people can invest and plan with confidence" (OHR 2002b). This led to the inclusion of entity-level laws on land registry, drafted with international assistance, on the list of twelve laws "crucial for the creation of the 'Single Economic Space' and the normal functioning of the [Bosnian] economy" (OHR 2000d, 2002d). In the event, OHR imposed many of these laws in October 2002, controversially exercising its Dayton powers to forward essentially post-Dayton, consolidation-phase goals (OHR 2002g).

Claims to nationalized property constituted another persistent land issue, with the need to move rapidly (so as not to deter investment) conflicting with the overambitious denationalization proposals put forward by entity authorities without the resources to implement them (OHR 2000e). As a result, the socialist construct of socially owned property remained in place by default, undercutting both transparency and legal certainty in transactions related to urban construction land and the rural holdings of former agricultural combines.

This situation became increasingly untenable after a February 2000 Constitutional Court ruling that asserted "a constitutional duty to transform all socially owned property into other forms of ownership, and in particular privately owned property."[2] With both the futility of the land allocation ban and the necessity of land tenure reform well established, the scene was set for a shift in international policy. This was foreshadowed in the final OHR decision extending the ban in April 2003, which explicitly gave entity-level authorities one month to adopt legislation, "in particular the consolidated and harmonized Law on Construction Land" regulating the nondiscriminatory allocation and management of socially owned property (OHR 2003c).

On May 16, 2003, the OHR imposed harmonized Laws on Construction Land in both entities (OHR 2003d, 2003e). Tellingly, although the news release announcing the imposition referred to the return rationale for the original decision, it gave equal weight to the 2000 Constitutional Court ruling and claimed to "clarify the issue of landownership, removing a major obstacle to economic growth" (OHR 2003f). The imposed laws fulfilled the Constitutional Court's criteria by dividing socially owned construction land into state-owned and private property, largely on the basis of whether it had already been developed by a private actor. However, in doing so, the new laws dropped OHR's previous insistence that all prior allocations be scrutinized to ensure their nondiscriminatory nature. Instead, allocations

---

[2] Partial decision U5/98-II of 18 and 19 February 2000, Constitutional Court of Bosnia and Herzegovina.

Post-conflict land tenure issues in Bosnia   165

undertaken during the period covered by the ban were again effectively presumed nondiscriminatory, with the onus on aggrieved parties to bring specific allegations (of wrongfully cancelled pre-conflict use rights) under a special review procedure. A two-year deadline was set for such claims, after which people who had been allocated land plots for resettlement were free to seek their transformation into private property.

In recent years, there have been a number of attempts to take stock of the effects of international reconstruction and return efforts (Kirkengen 2006; Bagić and Dedić 2005), including surveys of social and political attitudes in Bosnia that incorporate questions about the effect of returns (Oxford Research International 2007). However, little attention has been paid to the specific outcomes of post-conflict land allocations and broader resettlement efforts. Many settlements on allocated land plots may have been abandoned due to viability or safety concerns. A survey of resettlement plots in two RS municipalities (Ó Tuathail and Dahlman 2006) noted significant problems with the sites chosen, including dangerous locations (floodplains and steep slopes), little available arable land, and long distances to urban markets and jobs. Predictably enough in light of the difficulties in upgrading pre-conflict peri-urban settlements, very few plots had been provided with electrical, water, and sewage connections; access roads remained poor and sometimes impassable; and residents enjoyed little access to medical care, schools, refuse collection, and other social services.

From this perspective, anecdotal findings related to Doboj, an RS municipality (ESI 2007), are likely to be borne out more generally. There, it appears that the land allocation provided an important psychological boost to property restitution and broader reconciliation by allowing occupants of claimed homes to move out with a sense that their long-term housing needs would be met (ESI 2007). In practice, however, the policy failed to provide solutions to more than a fraction of this population; of 26,000 Serbs displaced to Doboj at the end of the conflict, only about 2,000 remained on allocated plots by 2007 (ESI 2007).

OHR's May 2003 abandonment of its attempt to control land allocations came at a time when property restitution was nearing completion; a formal handover of all remaining return issues to domestic authorities was planned for the end of the year (OHR 2003g). By this time, it was clear that return would be a significant factor, and that a degree of Bosnia's pre-conflict multiethnicity would be restored. Although the nationalist political parties that had prosecuted the conflict continued to pursue ethnic engineering goals, they were quick to accommodate to a new reality in which minority returnee communities demanded services, and more traditionally ideological—if still tacitly ethnically aligned— opposition parties presented real alternatives to voters. Some unresolved issues remained regarding restitution and return, but the attention of all actors was shifting. In effect, the struggle between international integrative forces and domestic partitionist forces had been fought to a draw.

In fact, the international community had always drawn a rhetorical link between resolution of displacement issues and development questions such

166   Land and post-conflict peacebuilding

as land tenure reform. For instance, the first OHR decision suspending land allocations was justified with reference both to return and to the assertion that "reallocation and . . . unlawful sale of socially-owned land also threatens to undermine the processes of [post-nationalization] restitution and privatization" (OHR 1999a). Likewise, a number of early land tenure reform efforts by development actors consciously sought to support durable solutions to displacement. In 2000, for instance, a study on the Bosnian real-estate market commissioned by OHR noted the importance of effective legal institutions to allowing displaced people to freely exercise the rights restored to them through the restitution process:

> [A] functioning property market can have profound and positive effects on the success of policies dealing with the war displaced. These effects include: giving prospective returnees and displaced persons more information on the value of affected property rights and therefore a basis for making decisions on whether to return or to invest in their properties, and providing additional options for economic use of properties, such as the opportunity to sell or exchange homes to which they do not wish to return (Rabenhorst 2000, 4).

Given the international community's continued commitment to promoting return in 2000, such arguments might have been premature, whatever their merit. In fact, the Dayton implementation agenda tended to accord land tenure issues relatively low priority until late in the restitution process, at times to its own detriment. For instance, early warnings by the Food and Agriculture Organization of the United Nations (FAO) that landmine contamination of agricultural land could hinder rural return and perpetuate dependence on humanitarian aid went largely unheeded as international mine clearance agencies set their priorities (Keith 1999). In the process of drawing up agricultural policies jointly with the entities, FAO emphasized the responsibility of the agricultural sector to support postconflict recovery and relied on lessons learned by the RRTF in proposing specific measures that would support reintegration of displaced people (FAO 1999a). Nevertheless, the resulting policies were not given high priority by the international community and were shelved by entity-level authorities after elections in 2000 (ESI 2004). As late as the end of 2010, Bosnia's legal framework for agriculture and rural development remained incomplete (Commission of the European Communities 2010).

With time, remaining displacement issues have come to be viewed as a legacy of the conflict and discussed primarily in terms of integration of internally displaced persons into residual reconstruction programs and improved social protection systems, as well as regional cooperation to resolve outstanding refugee issues (Commission of the European Communities 2008). Meanwhile, the trend since the final OHR decision returning authority over land allocations to domestic actors has been for land tenure reform to be cast predominantly as an economic transition issue associated with the European integration process (Commission of the European Communities 2008; FAO 2006).

Ultimately, the land allocation process in Bosnia did not meet the expectations of any of the parties involved. The international community found itself unable to enforce the transfer ban it had declared and ultimately dropped it. In cases where land allocations were clearly meant to discourage return, they failed, and even where they genuinely sought only to cushion the humanitarian impact of the return process for those evicted from claimed properties, the failure to back up allocation with construction assistance and service connections led to widespread abandonment of plots. Both partitionist and integrative attempts to engineer demographic developments by restoring or allocating land—and even the provision of land as humanitarian assistance—failed without the type of investment and security that only longer-term reform could bring.

FACTORS AND CONSTRAINTS AFFECTING OUTCOMES

Before considering general factors affecting land tenure policies related to the reintegration of displaced people, it is important to examine the relevance of the Bosnian case as a model for peacebuilding practice. A number of factors made Bosnia unusually susceptible to international efforts to promote reconstruction and reconciliation.

- *Tradition of tolerance.* Although it is possible to overstate the extent to which the Bosnian ethnic groups lived in harmony before the conflict, there is a genuine tradition of tolerance that has contributed to public acceptance of the legitimacy of post-conflict institutions and laws. The most striking examples involve evidence that many minority returnees have come to accept and trust local officials and even police in areas from which they were brutally expelled only a little over a decade ago (ESI 2007). The contrast with Kosovo, where the ethnic Albanian experience of decades of official discrimination has effectively delegitimized many public bodies, is instructive (Katz and Philpott 2006).
- *Massive international investment.* Per capita spending on the Bosnian reconstruction has dwarfed that in other emergency settings, and the international civilian and military presence has been large and sustained.
- *Strong international mandate.* The international community's influence in Bosnia has been immeasurably strengthened by the OHR's mandate to take measures such as imposing laws and dismissing public officials where necessary to ensure implementation of the DPA. The fact that Bosnian politicians did not challenge the legitimacy of these powers until recently provided international actors with leverage to force domestic actors to agree to necessary but politically unpopular steps such as property restitution. However, the practical limits of these powers were demonstrated by the widespread flouting of the land allocation ban, and their legitimacy has come into increasing question as Bosnia moves from post-conflict reconstruction to European integration (ICG 2009).

168 Land and post-conflict peacebuilding

- *Positive incentives.* Bosnia's geographical position at the edge of Europe has made it a credible candidate for integration into regional and trans-Atlantic organizations such as the Organization for Security and Co-operation in Europe, the Council of Europe, NATO, and the EU. This has allowed peacebuilding actors to act as gatekeepers to these bodies, holding out the prestige and recognition conferred by admission in exchange for adoption of the reforms necessary to join.
- *Nature of the resolution of the conflict.* None of Bosnia's three ethnic groups was decisively militarily defeated or expelled, and thus all three have been required to engage with each other. This is in strong contrast to, for example, Croatia and Kosovo, where large Serb minorities fled nearly en masse and have experienced difficulty reestablishing themselves as either a demographic or a political presence. In the area of property restitution, for instance, the similar situations of the three parties in Bosnia gave each not only something to lose but also something to gain from supporting the process. Likewise, land allocation in support of resettlement was employed in various manners and to various extents by all sides in Bosnia.
- *Unitary legal tradition.* Arguably, an enduring effect of Ottoman rule was the widespread acceptance of uniform legal rules and institutions for land administration, resulting from the pressure on productive land to support nearly constant military campaigns. The result has conformed to the widespread observation that rising land values encourage formal property rights frameworks (Deininger 2003). Bosnia's tradition of centralized land administration has meant that parallel systems for land administration there, although developed by conflicting parties, were largely compatible because they were all based on shared legal and institutional premises. Thus, while post-conflict Bosnia is characterized by a degree of institutional multiplicity typical of federal systems, domestic legal pluralism has not been an issue. On the other hand, during the early period of implementation of the DPA, internationally imposed requirements for restitution were in clear conflict with domestic administrative practices favoring permanent resettlement of displaced populations (Waters 1999).

Keeping the above in mind, the Bosnian case can nevertheless contribute a good deal to understanding of the use of land to support post-conflict reintegration of displaced people. One key similarity between Bosnia and other post-conflict situations is the extent to which demographic and socioeconomic trends that preceded the conflict have shaped the parameters for peacebuilding. In Bosnia, a process of informal urbanization had been underway since the 1960s, with rural workers establishing footholds at the edges of cities by constructing housing on undeveloped land. These settlements were tolerated and formalized, but often remained unconnected to services and utilities because of their unplanned and scattered locations. The conflict in Bosnia accelerated urbanization, with thousands of people who were ethnically cleansed from the countryside resettling in cities such as Sarajevo and Tuzla. Even when displaced people return to their original homes, they often leave younger family members behind in urban areas where they tend to have better educational and employment opportunities.

LESSONS LEARNED

The central lesson to be drawn from post-conflict land administration in Bosnia is the need to fully understand the agenda and motives of local actors in relation to land and property resources, as well as to realistically assess the capacity of international actors to intervene in these issues in a sustained and constructive manner. On the national side, it is particularly important to recognize that established patterns of land use and administration are likely to be mobilized to serve particular post-conflict ends. In the case of Bosnia, Yugoslav-era practices of unplanned urbanization provided a blueprint for resettlement policies that served both the legitimate objective of housing people displaced by the post-conflict restitution process and more problematic goal of ethnic engineering.

In other settings, both local land administration traditions and the aims of the parties to the conflict may differ significantly. However, land will almost inevitably be an issue, due to its combined symbolic, economic, and strategic importance. Moreover, local authorities will inevitably have better knowledge of local land issues and greater capacity to administer land and property than international actors. In Bosnia, this was reflected by the fact that the international community was late to awaken to the potentially discriminatory aspects of land allocation, failed to appreciate the reasons that allocation programs would be unlikely to be sustainable, and overreached in attempting to assume authority over past and future allocations.

This is not to say that the international community should be passive in the face of arbitrary and discriminatory land administration practices. Rather, experience in Bosnia underscores the advantage of timely, achievable measures to preempt or mitigate efforts to manipulate land assets over sweeping attempts to ban or retroactively undo them. In this sense, the original OHR decision of May 1999 banning land allocations that were manifestly intended to discourage return appears to have been both clearly warranted and precisely targeted. By contrast, later decisions retroactively extending the ban to all allocations simply forced most such transactions into informal channels, discouraged legitimate investments, and damaged OHR's credibility.

While these conclusions might appear to be relatively straightforward, they come at a time of ongoing debate over the appropriate role of international actors in engaging in post-conflict housing, land, and property (HLP) issues. For instance, the United Nations Human Settlements Programme (UN-HABITAT), the agency that currently chairs the main international humanitarian working group on HLP matters, has in the past recommended an unusually robust approach. In its 2007 *Post-Conflict Land Administration and Peacebuilding Handbook*, it proposed that peacekeeping missions should enjoy a remit to temporarily substitute themselves

170   Land and post-conflict peacebuilding

for national land administration bodies, with powers to secure and protect land records, ban unlawful land transfers, facilitate dispute resolution, issue building permits, inventory abandoned property and allocate it for use, and, after one year, facilitate root-and-branch reform of the national land administration and management function (UN-HABITAT 2007).

Subsequent statements of international policy on post-conflict HLP matters have been less ambitious in scope. For instance, UN-HABITAT and others have encouraged humanitarian actors working in the field in post-conflict situations to take a do-no-harm approach and to refrain from interposing themselves in HLP disputes wherever possible (GLTN, CWGER, and UN-HABITAT 2009). Similarly, a checklist on HLP issues for UN humanitarian coordinators framed its recommendations primarily in terms of assessment, monitoring, capacity-building, and advocacy with national actors, rather than assumption of an executive role (PCWG 2009).

In the context of this ongoing effort to identify the appropriate role of international actors in post-conflict land management, a number of specific lessons drawn from the experience in Bosnia may be helpful:

- *Participatory processes and voluntariness.* It is now increasingly well established in international law and humanitarian policy that choice of destination for internally displaced persons should be voluntary, and that domestic authorities have the primary duty to create the conditions for the exercise of free and informed choice between return and resettlement elsewhere in the country. As such, even indirect pressure to stay (such as the allocation of land without fees or means-testing) or to return (such as the closure of camps and exclusive availability of humanitarian aid at return sites) is suspect.

  In this context, experience in Bosnia shows that economic support measures— including those that can be achieved through land tenure reform and participatory land use planning—are more likely to achieve meaningful integration than attempts to restore or provide land as an incentive to return or resettle. Indeed, voluntary choices on ending displacement can be facilitated by ensuring that aid and reintegration support follows displaced people, not the other way around. For instance, in the case of Bosnia, FAO has recommended demand-driven forms of agricultural assistance to displaced people with rural backgrounds, such as extension services and micro-lending (FAO 1999b).

- *Assessing available land.* A key lesson from Bosnia is that significant support to current occupants of claimed properties may be necessary to lay the ground for restitution. However, one of the most important parameters in any provision of land to displaced people, whether for immediate humanitarian shelter or longer-term resettlement, is the need to ensure that the selected sites are both physically appropriate and legally unencumbered. Settling displaced people on land that is exposed to natural hazards, owned or claimed by others, or lacking in services and transportation infrastructure is unsustainable and may be politically destabilizing.

Post-conflict land tenure issues in Bosnia   171

For instance, the relatively widespread abandonment of allocated land plots in Bosnia was largely due to poor physical features, services, and location. Unresolved land tenure and privatization issues, along with the destabilizing effect of the OHR decisions banning allocations, tended to undermine the legal certainty of such allocations as well (Ó Tuathail and Dahlman 2006). Given Bosnia's pre-conflict history of expanding informal settlements, the interest of displaced people in urban resettlement should have been anticipated—along with the limitations of indiscriminate land plot allocation as a device for sustainably achieving this end.

- *Nondiscrimination and means-testing.* Land allocation policies would clearly be discriminatory if eligibility were defined solely on the basis of ethnicity. In Bosnia, land was made available to an ostensibly ethnicity-neutral group— people vacating claimed property—in a situation in which this status clearly correlated with ethnicity at the local level. Measures that could be taken to avoid the possibility of discrimination in such situations might also constitute the basis of sound social welfare policy.

In particular, the Bosnian experience speaks for the development of criteria for land and housing allocation that focus on objective need, including means-testing, and planned and flexible forms of assistance that correspond to beneficiaries' objective situations. In many parts of Bosnia, separate, parallel programs have been set up under various laws to provide social protection in a manner that fails to distinguish between vulnerable groups (such as indigent returnees or people seeking resettlement) and politically favored groups such as war veterans. Such failure to coherently prioritize the aims of social welfare programming renders it unlikely that any of the objectives for such programming will be achieved.

Ultimately, the Bosnian example underscores the legal and practical limitations of attempts to secure sustainable post-conflict demographic outcomes by restoring or allocating land to displaced people. In cases such as Bosnia, where basic elements of land administration—such as participatory planning, agricultural policy, taxation, registration, infrastructure, and utilities and service provision—are near collapse, attempts to promote either return or resettlement are unlikely to be viable without broader reform. Equally important, but more elusive in practice, durable solutions should be driven by the choices of the displaced and supported by the efforts of domestic and international authorities, not the other way around.

REFERENCES

Bagić, D., and D. Dedić. 2005. The impact of aid for reconstruction of homes in Bosnia and Herzegovina. UTV Working Paper 2005:1. Stockholm: Swedish International Development Cooperation Agency. www.sida.se/Documents/Import/pdf/20051-The -Impact-of-Aid-for-Reconstruction-of-Homes-in-Bosnia-Herzegovina.pdf.

172 Land and post-conflict peacebuilding

Ceha. 2008. Simplified ethnic map of Bosnia and Herzegovina in 1991 superposed on 2008 municipal borders. http://commons.wikimedia.org/wiki/File:BiHSimplifiedEthnic1991.gif.

Commission of the European Communities. 2008. *Bosnia and Herzegovina 2008 progress report*. Brussels. http://ec.europa.eu/enlargement/pdf/press_corner/key-documents/reports _nov_2008/bosnia_herzegovina_progress_report_en.pdf.

————. 2010. *Bosnia and Herzegovina 2010 progress report*. Brussels. http://ec.europa .eu/enlargement/pdf/key_documents/2010/package/ba_rapport_2010_en.pdf.

Cousens, E., and C. Cater. 2001. *Toward peace in Bosnia: Implementing the Dayton Accords*. International Peace Academy Occasional Paper Series. Boulder, CO: Lynne Rienner.

Cox, M., and M. Garlick. 2003. Musical chairs: Property repossession and return strategies in Bosnia and Herzegovina. In *Returning home: Housing and property restitution rights of refugees and displaced persons*, ed. S. Leckie. Ardsley, NY: Transnational Publishers.

Deininger, K. 2003. *Land policies for growth and poverty reduction*. A World Bank policy research report. Oxford, UK: World Bank / Oxford University Press.

DPA (Dayton Peace Agreement on Bosnia-Herzegovina). 1995. *The general framework agreement for peace in Bosnia and Herzegovina*. www.ohr.int/dpa/default.asp?content _id=380.

ESI (European Stability Initiative). 1999. *Interim evaluation of the Reconstruction and Return Task Force (RRTF): Minority return programmes in 1999*. Berlin.

————. 2004. *Governance and democracy in Bosnia and Herzegovina: Post-industrial society and the authoritarian temptation*. Berlin.

————. 2007. *A Bosnian fortress: Return, energy and the future of Bosnia*. Berlin.

FAO (Food and Agriculture Organization of the United Nations). 1999a. *A medium-term agriculture sector strategy for the Federation of Bosnia and Herzegovina*. Rome.

————. 1999b. *A medium-term agriculture sector strategy for Republika Srpska*. Rome.

————. 2006. *European Union accession and land tenure data in Central and Eastern Europe*. FAO Land Tenure Policy Series No. 1. Rome.

GLTN (Global Land Tool Network), CWGER (Cluster Working Group on Early Recovery), and UN-HABITAT (United Nations Human Settlements Programme). 2009. *Land and conflict: A handbook for humanitarians*. Draft. September. http://postconflict.unep.ch/ humanitarianaction/documents/02_03-04_03-08.pdf.

ICBL (International Campaign to Ban Landmines). 2008. *Landmine monitor country report: Bosnia and Herzegovina*. www.icbl.org/lm/2008/countries/bih.php.

ICG (International Crisis Group). 1999. Preventing minority return in Bosnia and Herzegovina: The anatomy of hate and fear. ICG Report No. 73. Brussels.

————. 2002. The continuing challenge of refugee return in Bosnia and Herzegovina. Balkans Report No. 137. Brussels.

————. 2009. Bosnia's incomplete transition: Between Dayton and Europe. Europe Report No. 198. Brussels.

JLZ (Jugoslavenski Leksikografski Zavod). 1983. *The Socialist Republic of Bosnia and Herzegovina—An offprint of the Enciklopedija Jugoslavije*. Zagreb.

Katz, D., and C. Philpott. 2006. Returning to basics: Property rights in South-East Europe. In *Realizing property rights*, ed. H. de Soto and F. Cheneval. Zurich, Switzerland: Rüffer and Rub.

Keith, S. 1999. Land use and land tenure. Annex 3 in *A medium-term agriculture sector strategy for the Federation of Bosnia and Herzegovina and Republika Srpska*. FAO Technical Cooperation Programme.

Post-conflict land tenure issues in Bosnia 173

Kirkengen, K. L. 2006. *Norwegian housing and return projects in Bosnia and Herzegovina.* Norwegian Resource Bank for Democracy and Human Rights Report 18/2006. www.jus.uio.no/smr/english/about/programmes/nordem/publications/nordem-report/2006/1806.pdf.

Le Normand, B. 2008. The house that market socialism built: Reform, consumption and inequality in socialist Yugoslavia. Max Weber Programme Working Paper 2008/33. San Domenico di Fiesole, Italy: European University Institute. http://cadmus.eui.eu/dspace/bitstream/1814/9289/1/MWP_2008_33.pdf.

Malcolm, N. 1996. *Bosnia: A short history.* 2nd ed. London: Papermac.

OHR (Office of the High Representative). 1998a. *Reconstruction and Return Task Force Report.* March.

———. 1998b. Extension of deadline for reclaiming socially owned apartments. News release. September 17.

———. 1998c. Decisions by the high representative on property laws. News release. November 6.

———. 1999a. Decision suspending the power of local authorities in the Federation and the RS to re-allocate socially-owned land in cases where the land was used on 6 April 1992 for residential, religious, cultural, private agricultural or private business activities. May 26.

———. 1999b. Decision on socially owned land. News release. May 27.

———. 1999c. Decision extending until 30 June 2000 the decision on certain types of socially-owned land of 26 May 1999. December 30.

———. 2000a. High representative meets displaced persons and refugee associations. News release. January 26.

———. 2000b. Decision on re-allocation of socially owned land, superseding the 26 May 1999 and 30 December 1999 decisions. April 27.

———. 2000c. High representative's decision on state-owned real property. News release. April 27.

———. 2000d. Resolving the issue of land ownership in BiH. News release. June 15.

———. 2000e. The high representative annuls RS restitution laws. News release. August 31.

———. 2000f. Continued progress/obstacles in property law implementation. News release. November 23.

———. 2000g. Decision extending by three months—until 30 Marhc [*sic*] 2001—the validity of the 27 April 2000 decision on the re-allocation of socially owned land. December 20.

———. 2001a. Decision extending the validity of the 27 April 2000 decision on the re-allocation of socially owned re-allocation of socially owned [*sic*] land until the authorities pass appropriate legislation or latest until 31 July 2002. March 30.

———. 2001b. OHR and council of ministers meet on land allocation. News release. August 9.

———. 2002a. OHR supports commission's recommendations on land allocation. News release. May 17.

———. 2002b. High representative proposes 10-point plan to fight corruption and create jobs. News release. May 27.

———. 2002c. OHR comments on resignation of Doboj mayor. News release. June 18.

———. 2002d. OHR calls on government leaders to end damaging legislative delays. News release. June 27.

———. 2002e. Decision on further extending the decision on land allocation of 27 April 2000 until the 31 March 2003. July 31.

174 Land and post-conflict peacebuilding

———. 2002f. High representative removes acting mayor of Doboj municipality. News release. September 3.

———. 2002g. High representative enacts key economic legislation. News release. October 21.

———. 2002h. All property claims solved in Lopare, Sekovici, Kresevo and Srbac. News release. October 22.

———. 2003a. Property law implementation is just one element of annex VII. News release. February 27.

———. 2003b. OHR, OSCE and UNHCR remind local authorities of the need to plan for social welfare housing. News release. March 27.

———. 2003c. High representative extends ban on the allocation of state-owned land. News release. April 1.

———. 2003d. Decision enacting the law on construction land of the federation of Bosnia and Herzegovina. May 16.

———. 2003e. Decision enacting the law on construction land of Republika Srpska. May 16.

———. 2003f. High representative imposed decisions to accelerate resolution of property disputes. News release. May 16.

———. 2003g. BiH institutions assume responsibility for return process. News release. December 30.

OSCE (Organization for Security and Co-operation in Europe). 1996. *Special report: Musical chairs—property problems in Bosnia and Herzegovina.* Vienna.

Ó Tuathail, G., and C. Dahlman. 2006. The "West Bank of the Drina": Land allocation and ethnic engineering in Republika Srpska. *Transactions of the Institute of British Geographers* 31 (3): 304.

Oxford Research International. 2007. The silent majority speaks: Snapshots of today and visions of the future in Bosnia and Herzegovina. www.undp.ba/index.aspx?PID=7&RID=413.

Palairet, M. 2000. The mismanagement of the Yugoslav rural economy, 1945–1990. www.esiweb.org/pdf/bridges/bosnia/Palairet_YugoslavRural.pdf.

PCWG (Protection Cluster Working Group Sub-Working Group on Housing, Land and Property). 2009. Humanitarian coordinator and resident coordinator checklist of housing, land and property rights and broader land issues throughout the displacement timeline from emergency to recovery. www.internal-displacement.org/8025708F004BE3B1/(httpInfoFiles)/430298C3C285133DC12576E7005D360D/$file/HC%20Checklist%20on%20HLP%20and%20Land%20Issues_Final2.pdf.

Philpott, C. 2005. Though the dog is dead, the pig must be killed: Finishing with property restitution to Bosnia-Herzegovina's IDPs and refugees. *Journal of Refugee Studies* 18 (1): 1–24.

———. 2006. From the right to return to the return of rights: Completing post-war property restitution in Bosnia Herzegovina. *International Journal of Refugee Law* 18 (1): 30–80.

Rabenhorst, C. 2000. *The real estate market in Bosnia-Herzegovina: Current status and recommendations for reform.* www.urban.org/publications/411101.html.

Rose, R., J. Thomas, and J. Tumler. 2000. *Land tenure issues in post-conflict countries: The case of Bosnia and Herzegovina.* Bonn: Deutsche Gesellschaft für Technische Zusammenarbeit.

Post-conflict land tenure issues in Bosnia 175

UNCHR (United Nations Commission on Human Rights). 1998. Situation of human rights in the territory of the former Yugoslavia: Final report of Ms. Elisabeth Rehn, Special Rapporteur of the Commission on Human Rights on the situation of human rights in Bosnia and Herzegovina, the Republic of Croatia and the Federal Republic of Yugoslavia. E/CN.4/1998/63. January 14. New York: United Nations.

UNEP (United Nations Environment Programme). 2009. *From conflict to peacebuilding: The role of natural resources and the environment.* Nairobi, Kenya. http://postconflict .unep.ch/publications/pcdmb_policy_01.pdf.

UN-HABITAT (United Nations Human Settlements Programme). 2005. *Housing and property rights: Bosnia and Herzegovina, Croatia, and Serbia and Montenegro.* Nairobi, Kenya.

———. 2007. *A post-conflict land administration and peacebuilding handbook.* Volume 1, *Countries with land records.* www.unhabitat.org/pmss/listItemDetails.aspx?publication ID=2443. Nairobi, Kenya.

University of Texas Libraries. 1992. Bosnia land use map from the former Yugoslavia. Perry Castañeda Library Map Collection. www.lib.utexas.edu/maps/bosnia/bosnia_landuse.jpg.

Watson, F., and A. Filipovitch. 1998. Reconstruction in Bosnia: Implications for food security and the future of food aid. *Field Exchange*, January. http://fex.ennonline.net/3/ bosnia.aspx.

Waters, T. W. 1999. The naked land: The Dayton Accords, property disputes, and Bosnia's real constitution. *Harvard International Law Journal* 40 (2): 517–593.

Williams, R. C. 2005. Post-conflict property restitution and refugee return in Bosnia and Herzegovina: Implications for international standard-setting and practice. *New York University Journal of International Law and Politics* 37 (3): 441–553.

Woodward, S. 1995. *Balkan tragedy: Chaos and dissolution after the Cold War.* Washington, D.C.: Brookings Institution.

Zec and N. Hamzic. 2006. Ethnic composition of Bosnia & Herzegovina in 2005. http:// commons.wikimedia.org/wiki/File:Ethnic_Composition_of_BiH_in_2005.GIF.

Angola: Land resources and conflict

Allan Cain

Angola is often cited as a classic case of natural resources sustaining a conflict (Hodges 2001). Angola's protracted civil war (1975–2002) was mainly financed through the wholesale extraction of oil and diamonds. The armed struggle for liberation from Portuguese rule started in 1961, but resistance had begun earlier due to the wide-scale expropriation by the colonial regime of another key resource, land. As in other southern Africa countries, the demand for land rights became a pillar of the independence movement. The four decades of armed conflict were characterized by land expropriation, forced removals, resettlement, and the massive internal displacement of rural and urban populations.

As a colony, Angola enjoyed only about twenty years without conflict: from the last colonial military campaigns in 1941 to the beginning of the liberation war in 1961 (Sogge 2009). As in other countries in southern Africa, the struggle for land rights became synonymous with the independence movement. During the civil war after independence in 1975, warring parties used forced removals of populations from their lands as tools of war. Opposition forces attacked rural settlements and forced families and entire villages and towns to flee to provincial cities, where they became dependent on government and donor aid. Whole provinces became depopulated as internally displaced persons (IDPs) abandoned their lands and migrated to the coast and eventually to the region around the capital city of Luanda. However, in the post-conflict situation, populations began to return to their areas of origin, according to a study commissioned by the Ministry of Urbanism, resulting in a significant deconcentration of urban IDPs in some provincial cities (DWA 2002).

Since the end of the armed conflict in 2002, Angola's recovery and remarkable economic growth have been fuelled by the extractive industries of petroleum and diamonds. The consolidation of peace, however—the reintegration of politically divided populations and excombatants—is much more linked to access to land. Land is not the only resource important to peacebuilding in post-conflict Angola, but it is a primary factor in social reconstruction.

Allan Cain is the executive director of Development Workshop Angola.

178 Land and post-conflict peacebuilding

The issue, which is little understood and often neglected in discussions of the causes and resolution of the Angolan conflict, is the focus of this chapter. The chapter begins by discussing precolonial collective land tenure and the later effects of the appropriation of land by the colonial power, which sowed the seeds of conflict, and Angolan resistance. The chapter then examines land management during and after the conflict, and considers the risks that resulted from avoiding land rights issues at the end of the conflict, which contributed to the residual land disputes that remained dormant throughout the southern African region only to reemerge decades later. The last sections of the chapter identify factors for successful peacebuilding and recommendations for legal and governance frameworks, and address the importance of involving communities and civil society in land-related decisions.

BACKGROUND

The following section details land management practices of precolonial communities that inhabited the area that is now Angola. Increasing levels of settlement induced physical changes to the land that forced communities to adapt. The next section examines the Portuguese colonial expansion, the resulting land appropriation, and the economic, political, and social effects of Portuguese colonialism on the Angolans and on land management.

Precolonial context and the seeds of conflict

Traditional land management practices were strongly influenced by the nature of the land and the environmental conditions in the different ecological regions of what is now Angola. As settlement and land use practices affected the environment, cultural and management traditions adapted to the changes (Avillez 1974). Pre-Bantu hunters and gatherers lived in small, decentralized communities, and land and other natural resources were exploited without strong traditions of tenure or ownership. Conflict has always been a key factor in environmental change and in determining who gets access to, or benefits from, the resource base. By the fifteenth century, the Bantu expansion southward from the Congo River basin had forcibly expelled the previous occupants. There was a new need to sustain larger sedentary groups of people, which in turn led to the development of agriculture and the introduction of the concept of permanent possession of land. Land became the collective property of the clan. The ethnic groups who had previously occupied much of the territory were pushed into the drier semidesert regions of the south and east, where hunting and gathering came to be supplemented by seminomadic pastoralism. Land use changes resulted in negative ecological impacts since much of the previously forested area was cleared for agriculture and transformed into savanna.

The transformation of land use and the introduction of the concept of collective land tenure required the transformation of landownership and the creation or adaptation of a mythology to justify it. The memory that the same land had

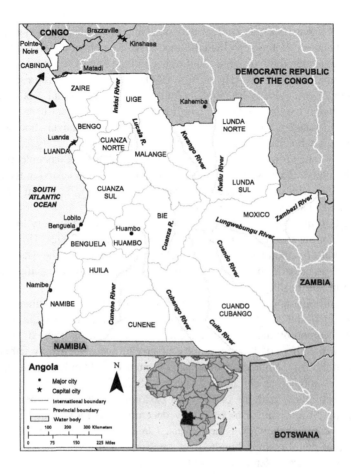

been occupied by others under a different ownership regime had to be erased. This new metaphysical vision was built on the concept that the earth does not belong exclusively to the living, but also to the ancestors and to the yet unborn people of the future. Land management was entrusted to the tribal chiefs, who were considered descendants of the original occupants and held the land for the clan members, who were the collective owners. Collective ownership was based on kinship, which was defined in different ethnic groups on the basis of various matrilineal or patrilineal relationships. In all cases, kinship ties were decisive in defining access to land and other socioeconomic relations (Henderson 1990).

The Kongo of northern Angola, for instance, were a matrilineal people. Membership in a clan or lineage, as well as all authority, derived from a mythical ancestor, strongly linked with place and associated with symbolically important features in the environment. Myths gave value to the land, making it the patrimony of the different groups, which could not be taken away from individual members because it could never become the property of one person (Margarido 1972).

180 Land and post-conflict peacebuilding

Matriarchal lineage not only conferred membership in the clan but also guaranteed access to the clan territory, of which the ancestors, founders of the first settlements, were still considered the owners. Land rights and the line of descent passed from maternal uncle to nephew (Henderson 1990). The clan was represented and administered by an elder who regulated most social relations and was the arbiter of questions on the distribution of land for family or individual use.

The Umbundu of the central highlands region were a relatively homogeneous ethnic group who had developed a settled, village-based society. Settlements traditionally ranged from ten to fifty households and up to 1,000 people, normally related by blood. Ownership of the village and its lands was vested in the current elder (*sekulu*), who was usually a descendant of the founder, for whom the village was normally named (Henderson 1990).

The traditional agricultural methods were characterized by very long fallow periods allowing the soil to recover its fertility (Pacheco 2002). However, the densification of settlements and intensification of land use by the establishment of fixed permanent farming sites in a region of high seasonal rainfall led to a decrease in soil fertility.

In traditional communal systems practiced in the central highlands region, any member of the community had the right to cultivate one or more parcels of the land occupied by the community. This right, after being granted, was never lost by the members of the community or group, even when they temporarily abandoned the land. Nonmembers of the community could only acquire this right if they were adopted as children by clan members (Pacheco 2002).

The settlement patterns of the agro-pastoral peoples of southern Angola, such as the Ambo, tended to be highly decentralized. Individual family units normally occupied their own farmsteads. Clans laid claim to loosely defined districts that could contain hundreds of families, each occupying between five and twenty hectares (Henderson 1990).

Colonial appropriation of land and Angolan resistance

The first Portuguese contact with Angola occurred when Diogo Cao, a Portuguese explorer, reached the mouth of the Congo River in 1482 (Russell-Wood 1998). A European military presence was not established until the mid-sixteenth century, when an alliance was formed with the Kongo Kingdom against Jagas invaders from the east. Portuguese permanent settlement of parts of the coastal region began with the founding of Luanda in 1592, which comprised a fort, mission, and administrative center, near the site of a local coastal fishing village (Oyebade 1997).

The arrival of the Portuguese disrupted all aspects of the traditional society. The slave trade and its later manifestation, the contract labor system, undermined family- and clan-based social cohesion and existing economic, religious, and political institutions. The forced expropriation of lands held under customary land tenure was a major shock to traditional social structures in that the clans,

Land resources and conflict in Angola 181

which were formed around common ancestry, were forced to abandon the lands by which they were bound to their ancestors (Neto 2000).

Portuguese colonial expansion was fuelled by the slave trade. More than one a million slaves were exported to Brazil by the end of the seventeenth century, severely depopulating much of what is now Angola. Angola has never recovered from the effects of this depopulation or from regional economic distortions caused by the slave trade, which planted the seeds for future conflict. While Portuguese slave and trade routes penetrated the territory of what is now Angola, the forcible occupation of territory beyond the coastal region only began with the nineteenth-century scramble for Africa by European colonial powers. Aside from profit from the slave, ivory, and (later) rubber trades, Portugal sought to extract tribute from Angola by taxing subjected peoples and exploiting their manual labor.

Laws enacted in 1838 and 1865 governing land concessions to Europeans allowed unoccupied land to be appropriated for white settlement. *Unoccupied land* was interpreted as land not being farmed at the moment but did not include lands lying fallow as part of traditional shifting agriculture (de Santa Rita 1940). These colonial laws ignored traditional customary law, which defined land as belonging to the community and not to individuals (Bender 1978).

The eventual borders of Angola were mapped out between 1880 and 1920 based on military conquest and consolidation of Portuguese power, with varying degrees of resistance by the African clans and chiefdoms within it. This was accompanied by politico-administrative measures directed at the submission of Angolans to Portuguese sovereignty and their integration into the monetary economy and the colonial market. Conflicts between indigenous communities and the Portuguese administration emerged from that period on, due to abusive occupation of lands by merchants and colonial enterprises, principally in the area between Malange and Luanda (Neto 2000). Resistance to the Portuguese occupation continued into the early twentieth century through sporadic ethnic-based movements that grew in reaction to colonial occupation and fiscal demands.

After 1900, Portuguese settlement policies turned African-European contact into a largely employee-employer relationship, exploiting the colonial institution of contract labor (Caetano 1946). African agriculture suffered serious setbacks. The combination of low prices paid for agricultural produce, soil depletion through excessive cultivation of cash crops, and increased European confiscation of choice lands reduced Africans' annual incomes, and obliged many men to abandon their lands and look for wage work in order to sustain their families. A large number of African men from the populous central highlands were forced by these economic circumstances, or under the contract labor laws, to work in coffee plantations in northern Angola. Strict vagrancy laws held that any African not under contract be considered a vagrant and available for forced or cheap labor. This proletarianization of the African countryside proved beneficial to European planters by providing them with an increased number of cheap laborers (Bender 1978).

182　Land and post-conflict peacebuilding

Portuguese domination inevitably obliged African families to abandon their lineage-based economies and to accept a market economy, producing cash crops or entering into labor contracts in order to pay taxes (Margarido 1972). As taxes were levied per household, there were increasing pressures for the nuclear family to enter the cash economy and assume effective permanent ownership of the parcels of land that they used or kept fallow for future use (Pacheco 2002).

The decree of November 28, 1907 that set aside native reserves for the exclusive use of Africans was never implemented. But this law provided Europeans with a legal vehicle for taking over choice areas in Angola's rural central highlands, arguing that Africans should be moved to the humid zones where "whites showed little desire or capacity to settle" (Ferreira 1954, 48). Forced removals of Africans to make way for white settlers accelerated throughout this period.

In 1919 an ambiguous new law recognized the principle of setting aside lands for exclusive use by indigenous people (Pacheco 2002), but did not grant them property rights, either individual or collective. This law marked the beginning of the period of large-scale alienation of lands by Portuguese and other foreign entrepreneurs. At this time, the Norton de Matos government's land reforms promised Africans five times the amount of land that they actually cultivated in a given year, in order to take into account traditional shifting cultivation.[1] In reality, however, interpretations of the designation "cultivated lands" were often in dispute, and the law was rarely respected. Consequently, many African lands that were ostensibly legally protected were granted as concessions to Europeans, contributing to a further decline in African agriculture. According to Gerald J. Bender, ex-*colonos* (those who left the established Portuguese settlement plan in Angola), along with other Europeans desiring these African-held lands, benefited from flagrant misinterpretations of the land laws (Bender 1978).

The period coincided with penetration into Angola of the world agricultural economy, spurred by price increases in the international markets for products such as coffee, sisal, tobacco, and cotton. Forcible occupation of land, paralleled with the coercive mobilization of Angolan contract labor, fueled more conflict. In the 1922 Revolt of Catete, indigenous communities contested the abusive expropriation of their land for the cultivation of cotton. In northeast Angola (in what are now the provinces of Uige, Zaire, Bengo, and Cuanza Norte), serious social and racial tensions existed due to the expropriation of lands by the Portuguese.

The major underlying objective of the white settlement policy, as outlined in Portugal's Colonial Act of 1933, was to secure Portuguese sovereignty in Angola (Bender 1978). Beginning in the 1940s, the resettlement programs for Africans (as opposed to Europeans) usually implied the grouping together of dispersed African peoples, but in reality segregated Africans from whites and reduced the quality and size of African-owned lands (Childs 1944). "Settlement" for Africans was nearly always synonymous with the loss of their best lands (Bender 1978).

---

[1] José Maria Mendes Ribeiro Norton de Matos was a reformist governor of Angola until 1926.

The occupation of Angola lands by Portuguese colonos gained momentum after the Second World War. During this period of large-scale Portuguese migration, the colonial regime also reinforced its military occupation of Angola, and for almost two decades, it quashed overt forms of African resistance. Also during this time, Portuguese authorities confiscated some of the best lands for distribution to colonos. For the first time, colonial settlement policies of appropriation of African lands began to put pressure on more densely populated regions such as the central highlands, with negative ecological impacts. With the increase in demographic pressure, the duration of the fallow period diminished, and families were obliged to return to cultivate the same land parcels year after year without allowing time for them to recover their fertility (Pacheco 2002). Contrary to popular belief, soils in the central highlands had always been fragile, and during this period they rapidly became depleted.

In the 1950s, the colonial government launched an ambitious program to encourage Portuguese immigration to Angola with generous land grants and financial support. Large settlement areas were expropriated from the original African residents in districts including Cela in Cuanza Sul Province (300,000 hectares) and Matala in Huila Province (420,000 hectares). Grants of farmland made to colono families ranged from 5 to 120 hectares, and tracts of formerly communal pasture of up to 1,000 hectares per family were granted for grazing cattle (Bender 1978). The estates of colonos were on the best lands, closest to markets and accessible to transport routes (Pacheco 2002). They were made available by the removal of thousands of Africans from their traditional lands. The displaced were often moved into areas already occupied by other Africans, thereby compounding the negative impact of the settlements by increasing occupation densities on ecologically overstressed lands. In an attempt to strengthen Portuguese cultural dominance, the settlement policy prohibited Africans from being farmers or workers in the white settlement areas (Ventura 1955). On the other hand, whenever the colonial settlers required access to abundant labor, the estates integrated entire African villages into "their" lands (Pacheco 2002).

Aside from the effects of colonial proletarianization and the transformation of a large proportion of rural Angolans into small-scale individual peasant land-holders, the economy generally did not benefit much from its transition from traditional to modern commercial agriculture. Most colonial immigrants were not experienced farmers and lacked financial or business capacity, which prevented them from reaching levels of productivity superior to those of the indigenous people (Pacheco 2002). Colonos often lacked the capacity to use the lands that had been allocated to them. Many European land concessions originally expropriated from Africans later reverted to the state as a result of the owner's failure to meet the minimum required percentage of cultivated area (Childs 1944).

By the first half of the twentieth century, Angolans in large areas of the country had given up their traditional communal forms of land management and had become peasant smallholders and agricultural laborers. This end result was not a stated objective of colonial land policies but rather the outcome of the

184 Land and post-conflict peacebuilding

implementation of a liberal and varied interpretation of such policies. The dominant economic unit became the nuclear family, although the clan and ethnic traditions remained important in the domain of cultural resistance. Too often, colonial settlers inadvertently exacerbated resentment by ignoring ancestral rights of possession and traditional systems of use, as well as the cultural values related to the plots of land on which Angolans' ancestors were buried (Pacheco 2002). The seeds of conflict were nurtured during the decades of enforced colonial peace before 1961.

LAND MANAGEMENT DURING AND AFTER CONFLICT

The next section probes the shifts in Angolan landownership in the lead-up to and after independence, discussing land policy developments prior to the liberation war and the European takeover of African agricultural lands during the conflict. This is followed by an examination of the abandonment of land caused by the subsequent civil war, the ensuing migration of displaced people to urban areas, and the resettlement process and land reform that have taken place since the conflict.

Forced removals and the struggle for independence

In 1961, the political situation in Angola had become critical, and the nationalist movements launched the liberation war. The unjust land tenure system was one of the main reasons that Angolans sympathized with nationalist ideas and armed struggle. The initial Portuguese reaction to uprisings both in the countryside and in Luanda was two-tracked: they reinforced their military occupation and at the same time attempted to appease the African population by granting them Portuguese citizenship. The legal reforms of September 1961 eliminated forced labor and did away with institutionalized racial discrimination. Official policy emphasized racial integration in the new *colonatos* (settlement schemes). An increased and stable European settler presence, however, remained fundamental to the colonial government's strategy, and settlement programs were the foundation of this strategy (Bender 1978).

Decree No. 43894 of September 6, 1961, protected African lands (in theory) by creating three classes of land: (1) urban areas, including the respective suburbs; (2) lands held communally by Africans; and (3) land that was not considered to fall into either of those categories. This third category of land was, therefore, available for European concessions. Furthermore, the decree "stipulated that second-class land [i.e., land in the second category] must encompass an area five times that occupied by a village (in order to take into account patterns of shifting cultivation) and, recognizing the Africans' 'inalienable' rights to this land, . . . prohibited their expulsion" (Bender 1978, 181).

In practice, however, the regulation was not publicized. Africans were not informed of the rights that the new decree conferred on them. The agencies of the colonial state, responsible for its enforcement, were ill prepared to implement this decree and often represented personal or commercial interests that the decree threatened. Often those responsible for demarcation of these lands failed to publicize the decree or interfered with its adequate implementation.

The delimitation of the second-class land was strongly opposed by white settlers in Angola. They understood that if the decree was rigorously implemented no concessions would be available in highly populated regions such as the central highlands. In practice, the African lands were never delimited; contrary to the intention of the decree. African lands were simply defined as tracts that were not urban land or European land. "Neither white settlers nor government officials, especially those responsible for land demarcation (Direccao dos Servicos Geograficos e Cadastrais [Directorate of Geographic and Cadastral Services]), understood, accepted, or respected African land rights" (Bender 1978, 182). It was easy for any colono wanting to acquire a parcel of land to convince African peasants, who were becoming increasingly impoverished, to apply for ownership of the parcel and then sell it to them at a low price.

The white settlers successfully lobbied to revise the 1961 land decree, and the government passed a new law protecting the interests of the white settler population but not those of the indigenous people. The new legislation recognized only two categories of land, urban and rural, making it easier for Portuguese individuals to acquire large tracts of land.

During the independence war (1961–1974), the amount of land conceded to Europeans increased each year, while the amount of land held by Africans decreased. Between 1968 and 1970, the amount of European-held land in the Huambo Province increased by 110 percent (from 249,039 to 526,270 hectares), while the area cultivated by Africans was reduced by 37 percent. In many cases, this displacement of Africans resulted in a drop in rural productivity (Bender 1978). From the mid-1960s until 1972, the average African family landholding was reduced from 4.1 to 2.0 hectares in the province of Malange (MIAA 1973). In the central highlands, the most densely populated region in the interior, agricultural activity was so intense that there were no vacant lands available for concession. The demarcations, however, followed illegal processes that ranged from ignoring community land limits to displacement of whole villages. As a result, the average landholding of African family units decreased from 8.9 to 5.6 hectares during this period (MIAA 1973; Carriço 1971).

As part of the Portuguese counterinsurgency effort during the war of independence, more than 1 million Africans were forced off their land and moved into large *aldeamentos* (protected strategic settlements). By the early 1970s, the resettlement program had uprooted almost one-quarter of Angola's rural population (Sogge 1992). Protected settlement areas were located along major roads in areas that could be easily controlled by Portuguese security forces. The relocation opened up a considerable amount of African land for distribution to white settlers and produced an increased supply of African labor for the plantation economy (Bender 1978).

On the eve of independence, 6,412 registered commercial farmers possessed almost 4.5 million hectares but used on average only 11 percent of their lands. In contrast, approximately 1 million traditional peasants occupied a little more

186 Land and post-conflict peacebuilding

than 4.3 million hectares, overstressing soils by cultivating almost 50 percent of the land at any given time. The national territory was divided in half by a virtual line passing north-south through Camacupa in Bié Province. Land to the west of this line had been mapped and parceled into concessions mainly for Portuguese commercial farmers. To the east of this meridian, communal systems of land and semisubsistence agriculture predominated. This eastern half of the territory was inhabited by around 10 percent of the population, and the presence of European farmers was rare. The southern margins of this region were still inhabited by pre-Bantu groups such as the Bushmen, who observed communal property and collective water rights and practiced pastoralism and transhumance (Pacheco 2002).

By the end of the colonial period, white settlers had claimed 41 percent of all surveyed farmlands, most of which they never used. With the establishment of forest and game reserves, more land was barred from use by African farmers and pastoralists. Demographic and political pressures meant that Angolan farmers used what limited lands they retained more intensively, with shorter fallow periods, further exhausting the soils (Sogge 1992).

Independence, civil war, and the abandonment of rural lands

Angola gained independence from Portugal in November 1975. Independence prompted a massive exodus of Portuguese settlers. Thousands of plantations were abandoned and effectively nationalized under the new constitution (Hodges 2001). Article 12 of the constitution stated that "all the existing natural resources in the soil and in the sub-soil . . . are property of the State, who will determine the conditions of their profit and use." The state as owner could transmit land use rights to others. The state became the owner of lands that were not definitively privately owned. Abandoned private land, according to article 12, could be appropriated "because of the unjustified absence of the proprietor for more than 45 days."

However, the legal procedures surrounding such appropriations were unclear, and in practice many people simply seized abandoned land and property for themselves. Sometimes those who claimed ownership were the original owners of the land, who had lost it to the Portuguese colonists, or their descendants. In other cases they were landless or homeless people displaced by the fighting. But often they were people connected to the dominant political and military group in the area, who took the lands as spoils of war (Foley 2007). Naturally, local farmers near those abandoned lands occupied them. Plantations were sometimes occupied by former workers of those estates. However, farms under the administrative control of the state, especially plantations, were not invaded.

In the course of time, areas actually farmed by state enterprises diminished, leaving the lands they held more or less vacant. The weakness of state enterprises meant that only about 10 percent of the lands previously occupied by commercial farmers were fully utilized. Reoccupation of these lands happened quietly, and state institutions at the local level paid little attention to managing or preventing it (Pacheco 2002).

There was a vacuum of state administration during this period. Traditional authorities were ignored but were left to function, albeit outside of any legal or institutional framework. Customary practices were neither attacked by the state nor incorporated into the law. Traditional practice was not officially recognized or applied consistently. Peasants were de facto excluded from political processes, particularly those related to land.

After independence in 1975, individuals were no longer able to buy private land but were instead granted occupation rights, which meant that they had the exclusive right to use the land, although it formally belonged to the state. This provision was included in Angola's Civil Code, inherited from colonial times, which remained the legal framework governing land rights even after independence. There was a widely held perception that the problem of land had disappeared with the departure of the Portuguese colonialists.

Angola descended into civil war almost immediately following independence. Power struggles between former liberation movements were bolstered by the Cold War as Angola became a hotspot in geopolitical struggles. While significant land conflicts prior to independence were indeed rare, land pressures were brought again to the fore by the civil war. The first land conflicts appeared with the increase in the numbers of IDPs, when peasants fled the conflict in the central highlands and resettled in pastoral and transhumance areas farther south. Other conflicts became critical as populations fled to the safety of urban and semi-urban zones, particularly on the Atlantic coast, where the influx of IDPs increased demographic pressures dramatically. These latter land issues do not necessarily stem from unjust implementation of the law but rather are an outcome of the civil conflict.

Because of the abandonment of rural lands in war zones, even subsistence cultivation was drastically reduced, and vacant land in inaccessible areas increased. The absence of individuals and families who publicly contested ownership of lands during this period created the illusion that land problems had ceased to exist. Consequently, the government did not feel the need to legislate on land issues, nor did it receive any public pressure to do so.

This situation began to change in the mid-1980s, due to the failure of the state collectivist experiments, and with the first signs of economic reform taking place with openings for the private sector. The ceasefire in 1991 and the prospect of communities returning to their original homes put land back on the agenda. While a land law commission had existed since 1986, a new land law was approved quickly, without public debate, by the Permanent Commission of the People's Assembly on August 21, 1992, before the old assembly dissolved itself. A month later, Angola's first multiparty elections tragically resulted in a return to civil war. The renewed conflict reached a level of violence previously unknown; it spread to cities across the country and produced a new wave of IDPs.

The 1992 Land Law was part of a body of legislation that attempted to transform Angola from a centralized economy to a market economy by defining land titles and use rights. The law introduced the concept of community rights

188   Land and post-conflict peacebuilding

to land. While it continued to recognize state ownership, it formalized the framework for concessions and also recognized the rights of titleholders from before independence whose properties had been nationalized. While it maintained the principle of concession of use rather than permanent ownership, it allowed these rights and titles to be inherited or transferred.

The law validated the pattern of distribution inherited from colonial-era legislation and in turn did not recognize the rights of possession by peasant farmers or communities. Again, these farmers and their communities did not have the opportunity to register their properties or gain restitution for their lands that had been expropriated during the colonial settlers' landgrab.

In the seven years after the law was enacted, the government distributed more than 2 million hectares of land (Pacheco 2002), equivalent to 50 percent of the land held by commercial farmers in colonial times. This was distributed to a small number of mainly absentee owners, who paid insignificant prices for secure tenure rights in order to eventually exploit these lands commercially. The insecurity during most of the decade following the publication of the 1992 law meant that most of these concessions remained unoccupied. As happened in colonial times, the modern commercial sector was allocated an excess of underused land, which was set aside by the new owners for possible future use or speculation. Local peasant farmers, on the other hand, were treated by the Angolan state much like they had been treated under the colonial regime (Pacheco 2002). They were left with small, often scattered parcels of land divided between tiny irrigated garden plots and less fertile, seasonally used *lavras* (plowed plots) for staple crops. The latter were located at a distance from village centers and were cultivated at great risk during the conflict and often pillaged by warring parties (Development Workshop Angola 2008).

The traditional land rights of peasants and smallholders were not dealt with under the 1992 Land Law, even though the rights of communities were supposed to be protected under this legislation. The law introduced a new concept of *povoaçao rural* (rural village) without defining its legal status. Communities could actually be prejudiced if the rights were conferred to the traditional leader himself rather than to a community that had no legal identity and thus no legal standing to protect its interests. There are no provisions under law for communities to sanction traditional leaders who abuse their fiduciary responsibility or do not exercise it appropriately.

No provision was made for existing or previous possession or occupants' rights (*usucapiao*) by which property rights may be acquired through continued use over time. The law also lacked provisions for cooperatives or farmer associations that occupied the lands of former colonial estates with encouragement from the post-independence People's Movement for the Liberation of Angola government. The law did not deal with conflicts between holders of different types of rights or claims, or with such issues as use of land for the public interest. It only imperfectly regulated rural land concessions, and it did not deal with urban land issues at all. In a rapidly urbanizing country, this was a major shortcoming.

Internal displacement and flight to the cities

During the civil war, both sides used forced displacement of civilians as a weapon of war. Early in the conflict, the National Union for the Total Independence of Angola (União Nacional para a Independência Total de Angola–UNITA) rebel forces destabilized the countryside, laying landmines, and using other forms of armed violence to push into towns, where they became a burden on the government. Towns became defensive islands where government forces needed to feed and protect large concentrations of IDPs, and medical and social services had to deal with the wounded and disabled. Later in the conflict, when government forces took the offensive, they cleared populations from large parts of the countryside to provide free-fire zones in order to deny the rebel forces opportunities for recruitment or access to local food supplies. Local civilian populations, particularly in the central highlands, became the chief victims of the conflict, sustaining much higher casualties than either of the warring sides.

Over the course of the civil war, millions of people fled the fighting in the countryside and headed for the relative safety of towns and cities in the affected provinces (see figure 1). Often the populations of whole villages were displaced when their settlements were overrun or threatened by the warring armies. In some of these cases homogeneous communities, often with their traditional leadership intact, sought temporary refuge in the outskirts of towns and cities. In these areas of peri-rural or peri-urban resettlement, the IDPs sought temporary access to lands that belonged to local communities. The resident community often saw the IDPs as adoptive members with a temporary right to use the land. Local-level understandings were often reached that, when the reasons for granting that right changed (for example, when the IDPs returned to their area of origin), the land would be returned to its original users. As there was a limited amount of such land available, the potential for conflict was great, but disputes were often resolved within customary frameworks when these mechanisms were recognized by both IDPs and members of the settled community. IDPs provided a cheap form of labor for those who managed to maintain agricultural production in some of the safer districts under government control.

As the conflict spread across the country and entered provincial capitals as well, populations fled once more, this time to the big cities on the coast and eventually to Luanda. There, they initially sought temporary shelter in the homes of relatives but eventually set up homes in *musseques* (shantytowns), building their basic dwellings on land obtained through a variety of informal mechanisms and investing what little money they had in home improvements. (Figure 2 summarizes the various ways people access land in Luanda.) But the informal land occupation or purchase documents that they obtained, albeit in good faith, were not legal titles even if witnessed by local authorities and were of little value when presented in a dispute over land with the state or a private company.

When the flight to the cities began at the beginning of the civil war, pressure on land was not substantial (Robson and Roque 2001). People often occupied sites that appeared to be empty and then informed the *bairro* (neighborhood) authorities,

190 Land and post-conflict peacebuilding

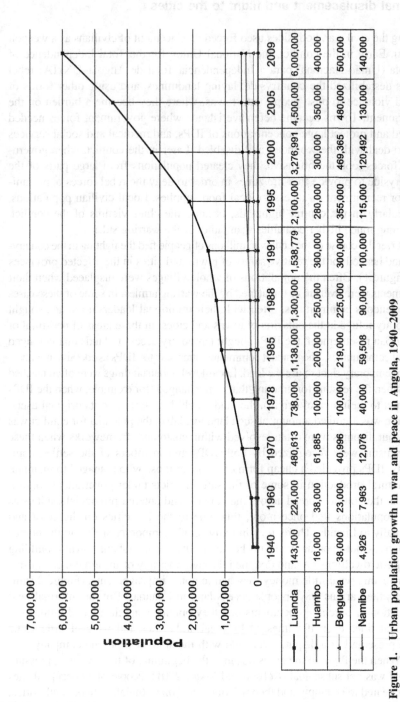

Figure 1. Urban population growth in war and peace in Angola, 1940–2009
Sources: Monteiro (1973, 58); post-1973 data developed from geographic information system (GIS) remote-sensing data collected by Development Workshop Angola.

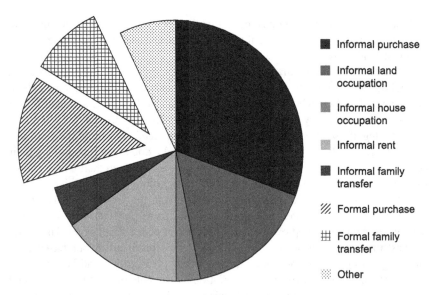

Figure 2. Means of access to urban land in Luanda
Source: Development Workshop Angola (2004).

the administration or the *soba* (neighborhood chief), depending on the location, and asked for recognition of occupancy.[2] The peri-urban bairros of provincial towns of the interior (such as Huambo) always had sobas, and they designated an area where a new arrival could build.[3] Having family already living in the bairro was important for this process. Relatives could present new arrivals to the bairro authorities, thus diminishing the problems associated with being strangers and legitimizing their desire to live in the area. As the conflict progressed, the situation changed—particularly in Luanda, where land pressures increased and social capital in the form of kinship networks weakened. Over the conflict years, the sobas' authority and control diminished. In Huambo, a city severely affected by the conflict, instability and the resulting frequent migrations meant that government control remained relatively weak even in the early post-conflict period. It became increasingly rare for a person to find an empty plot to occupy

---

[2] For example, in the final years of the colonial period, the peri-urban neighborhoods of Luanda consisted mostly of fields, farms, and areas set aside for future development. During the years immediately after independence there was no control of these areas, which were still unoccupied. Many people interviewed by Development Workshop Angola said that all they had to do was occupy it.

[3] There are few sobas in Luanda, although some, displaced from rural districts during the conflict, did appear in peri-urban zones with large numbers of IDPs. Witnesses for land transactions in Luanda therefore are normally figures appointed by the local administration as bairro coordinators. Usually they are long-standing members of the commission of local residents or are senior residents who are respected in the neighborhood.

192   Land and post-conflict peacebuilding

and then inform the local authorities so that they could recognize the acquisition. As pressures increased, land could only be acquired through purchase on the informal land market.

A false sense of security of land tenure became the norm in urban areas throughout the country for those who had occupied or purchased their lands in good faith.[4] Families who had purchased a plot of land and had a signed bill of sale, often witnessed by the soba or a local administration official or even notarized, felt legally secure in their occupation and proceeded to build their houses. Similarly, former land occupiers who had obtained a document recognizing their occupation from the local authorities felt that they had secured their tenure rights. In fact, only those who have gone through the arduous and expensive process of obtaining a formal title to occupation rights from the provincial government have any legal status. Under the current land law, these rights are only granted in the few areas where an approved urban development plan already exists. Therefore, the vast majority of those who feel that they have occupied or purchased their land in good faith, or started out with an informal occupation and later regularized it, are in fact still at risk of expropriation by the state or even by commercial developers who have secured clear legal concessions to tracts of urban land.[5]

Opportunities to obtain a legally titled building plot from the provincial government are very limited, even for long-term urban residents who placed their names on waiting lists years ago. When prospective owner-builders have identified a desired plot of land, they must submit an application to the local administration and then obtain approval from various bureaucracies, including the municipal administration and finally the provincial government. This can take many months, sometimes years, and may be expensive: as well as paying for the land, the applicant often has to pay bribes at each stage.[6] In Luanda in 2004, of the 600 formal requests that reached the provincial government each month through this referral system from municipal and *comuna* administrations,[7] only about thirty (5 percent) were actually processed (Development Workshop Angola and Centre for Environment and Human Settlements 2005). The few fortunate enough to

---

[4] The concept of *occupation in good faith* is used in this chapter to describe the sense of secure tenure that peri-urban settlers have from holding a witnessed land purchase contract or other document demonstrating the recognition of their occupation by a locally recognized authority, whether government appointed or customary. These forms of proof of occupation have no legal status under current Angolan legislation.

[5] Angolan cadastral and property title records have not been systematically updated since independence in 1975. There is no accurate estimate at the national level of the proportions of land that fall into public, private, communal, and informal domains. Development Workshop Angola's 2004 study of peri-urban Luanda found that over 80 percent of land is informally occupied.

[6] According to the World Bank's 2006 *Angola Country Economic Memorandum*, Angola is one of the most difficult countries in the world in which to transfer and register property titles, ranking 161st out of 175 countries.

[7] The *comuna* is the administrative district below the municipality level. Administrators for both levels are appointed by provincial governors.

receive approval through the official system often were only granted a provisional occupation permit (*direito precario*) that must be renewed every two years.

Development Workshop Angola, a nonprofit organization that has worked in Angola since 1981 to improve settlements and livelihoods of the poor, released a study in 2004 demonstrating that less that 20 percent of the urban population has what the state considers formal land tenure. The remainder may lose any residual rights that they may have held under recent land legislation. Neither occupation in good faith nor usucapiao provide any tenure protection under this new legislation, and as of mid-2010, informal land occupation could be considered illegal, leaving the vast majority of urban poor and those who migrated to the city during the conflict in this category.

Forced removals began in 2001 with Luanda's inner-city Boavista bairro. Two thousand houses were destroyed, and the families were transported forty kilometers to share tents and makeshift facilities at Zango on the city's periphery while they waited for the alternative housing that had been promised. As property values rose rapidly, other inner-city bairros were cleared of low-income residents to allow commercial or formal-sector land development. These populations were moved to dormitory townships like Panguila on the fringes of the city, two hours' travel from residents' previous places of employment and schools. While forced removals slowed in the months before the 2008 parliamentary elections, they started in earnest again in 2009, with displacements of thousands of families to make way for high-end commercial housing developments. Ambitious slum eradication proposals have been published that threaten displacement of tens of thousands of households in the near future and their replacement by multistory commercial buildings. New land legislation not only removes any vestige of occupants' tenure rights but also gives the state new powers to designate future land use in the name of the public good, making it eligible for expropriation for commercial or private development.

The accumulated assets of wartime migrants to Luanda and other cities have been invested in land they have purchased or been assigned to occupy by local authorities and the housing they have subsequently built there. A family's savings usually takes the form of cement blocks or roof sheets that, room by room, eventually become substantial housing. Forced removals alienate the poor from their savings and remove them from sources of employment and other livelihood opportunities. The rise in urban property values could benefit the poor who occupy most of the inner-city and peri-urban land, but ironically, it threatens to weaken the socioeconomic situation of the poor and urban migrants who had sought safe haven there.

Post-conflict resettlement and reintegration

Even before the end of the armed conflict, the Angolan government, with assistance from the United Nations Office for the Coordination of Humanitarian Affairs (OCHA), attempted to incorporate into law a set of principles protecting the rights

194   Land and post-conflict peacebuilding

of IDPs. As early as October 2000, while the conflict still raged in the central provinces, the Angolan Council of Ministers approved the Norms on the Resettlement of Displaced Populations.[8] This decree aimed to facilitate the return of IDPs to their areas of origin, guarantee them minimal standards of social infrastructure and basic land access, and ensure that the resettlement process was carried out in a participatory way, without coercion. This was a remarkable government order—the first in the world guaranteeing the rights of IDPs and incorporating international best practices. It was also one of the first Angolan legal instruments that introduced the concept of public participation in physical settlement planning. The minimum plot size of one hectare was considered by Angolan agronomists to be insufficient for subsistence farming, particularly in regions such as the central highlands where soils are poor, but the law stipulated that this land must be nonmarginal and the size should be increased depending on family size and need.

When mass return and resettlement of IDPs actually took place in late 2002 and 2003, the government had little capacity to assist the process or guarantee the minimum standards mapped out in the law described above. At the time of the ceasefire, the government effectively administered no more than 25 percent of the national territory. Therefore, reestablishing state administration took priority over creating conditions for resettlement. As a result, the return and resettlement of IDPs was done largely through their own resources, and assistance came mainly from the local communities. The main driving force for the rapid return of rural IDPs to their areas of origin was their need to reclaim family lands and the fear of finding it staked out by an intruder or usurper. OCHA estimated that by 2004 only about 30 percent of returnees were settled in conditions that met the minimal conditions prescribed by law.

The international community was unable to assist this resettlement process. The Angolan OCHA mission was rapidly downsized; it closed in 2004. At this time also, most of the international donors were rapidly redeploying to address new conflict challenges in Iraq and Afghanistan. The diminishing resources of the international community were invested in the return of refugees from neighboring countries and the demobilization of excombatants, which were considered a higher priority in securing the peace.

The aims of both the government's and the international community's strategies for disarmament, demobilization, and reintegration was to socially and economically reintegrate excombatants into their communities of origin.[9] However, demobilized excombatants from the UNITA rebel forces faced serious challenges of reintegration into communities that they may have previously terrorized or looted. The

---

[8] Decreto 1/01, Normas sobre o reassentamento das populações deslocadas, January 5, 2001.

[9] The disarmament, demobilization, and reintegration program is supported by the World Bank and the Ministry of Assistance and Social Reintegration (Ministério da Assistência e Reinserção Social) through the Institute for the Social Reintegration of Ex-Combatants.

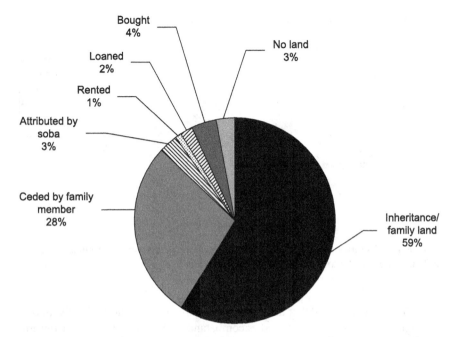

Figure 3. Means of rural land acquisition by excombatants in Huambo Province
Source: Development Workshop Angola (2004).

acquisition of sufficient land in these communities is fundamental to building sustainable livelihoods and in turn reducing risks that excombatants will return to arms, as they did in two previous failed peace processes in 1992 and 1998. There is also the risk of these excombatants reverting to banditry or joining the underemployed in the margins of the cities.

Development Workshop Angola carried out a study in Huambo Province of the problems of land acquisition for excombatants during the two years after demobilization (Development Workshop Angola 2004). This research indicated that access to a sufficient quantity and quality of land is problematic for many of the demobilized in Huambo. Excombatants often had left their family land more than thirty years ago, and upon returning found themselves excluded from or bypassed by the normal inheritance processes that are the most common means of acquiring land. Figure 3 summarizes the various ways excombatants acquire land in Huambo.

Excombatants often have received proportionally less land than their peers. At the time of the study most excombatants and other returnees could meet only about half of their livelihood needs from the land they had acquired. Most, therefore, had chosen to settle in the hinterlands, fifteen to thirty kilometers from provincial urban centers (see figure 4), where they were able to supplement their incomes by engaging in petty trading or laboring in the informal economic sector.

196 Land and post-conflict peacebuilding

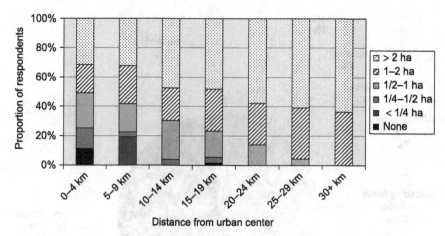

Figure 4. **Quantity of rural land, in hectares, occupied according to distance from urban centers in Huambo Province**
Source: Development Workshop Angola (2004).

The study indicated that in both rural and urban areas, alternative livelihood strategies were also required, and excombatants needed assistance in acquiring new skills and survival strategies. It is evident that the Angolan disarmament, demobilization, and reintegration program was not completely successful in resettling demobilized soldiers in their rural areas of origin. Programs to help excombatants, IDPs, and returning refugees to acquire adequate land to resettle have not been adequately implemented to date. However, the Institute for Social Reintegration of Ex-Combatants did adopt the recommendation to develop and provide training programs in alternative job skills. For instance, excombatants trained in the building trades have migrated to the cities and have found gainful employment, thanks to Angola's current building boom.

The Angolan demobilization and reintegration program limited its assistance to 100,000 UNITA soldiers; it excluded their wives and girls who had been abducted by them from guaranteed direct assistance such as educational and economic opportunities. In particular, girls under eighteen years of age who had been forcibly recruited (as cooks, porters, "wives," and other types of helpers) should have received special attention as child soldiers. To grant these women access to assistance exclusively through the partners they were forced to marry has encouraged them to stay in situations that many have expressed a desire to leave (Nielsen 2008).

Resettlement of IDPs, excombatants, and returning refugees produced innumerable local conflicts over land allocation, often resulting in clashing interests between the returnees and those who had stayed behind in their areas of origin. Those who stayed in their original communities are understandably unsympathetic, particularly toward excombatants, since they suffered repeatedly from the theft of their assets by warring parties who alternatively occupied their districts over the almost four decades of conflict. Conflict was further exacerbated by external humanitarian actors who, according to their particular mandates, provided relief goods to target groups (such as the demobilized and refugees) but not to others who were equally vulnerable (such as IDPs and local communities). The acquisition of land by returning groups depended on garnering the goodwill of existing landholders and avoiding local conflict whenever possible. The state had limited presence in areas of post-war resettlement, and the Angolan justice apparatus was one of the weakest of all state institutions. Municipal courts, which normally would have jurisdiction over land disputes, did not exist outside a few of the major cities.

The role of traditional authority in land management had been eroded through the years of colonial rule and civil war. However, the return and resettlement of almost 3 million people to their rural areas of origin provided a renewed role for traditional leaders in dealing with local land conflicts and providing testimony regarding families' historical land claims.

Reform and the new land law

It was widely agreed that the 1992 Land Law was outmoded, had been poorly applied, and ignored the urban context. The government released new draft land legislation in July 2002 and, for the first time in Angolan history, invited public consultation. The new legislation presented an opportunity to contribute to conflict resolution, reconstruction, and poverty reduction. The debate on this legislation was launched at a crucial time—a few months after the end of the civil war—that was opportune for the consolidation of peace, reconstruction, and future development of the country (Development Workshop Angola 2003). A group of civil society organizations launched the Rede de Terra (Land Network) to work in parallel with the government's Land Technical Commission to facilitate public discussion and debate. Development Workshop Angola was engaged by the Ministry of Urbanism to study the issue of informal land occupation around the principal urban centers, and conducted a media survey to track public awareness of the land issue through articles in the official and independent press. The participatory action research approach it adopted engaged local community leaders and civil society, linked with public consultation, and effectively increased public awareness of land issues in this period.

The new law, like the previous one, placed responsibility on the state to manage land access, but the state institutions that regulate land access were weak and lacked adequate capacity to implement the legislation and regulations in a transparent and accountable manner. State management of land remained disorganized and open to abuse. Until the end of the conflict, the rights to de facto occupation of land and occupation in good faith were tacitly acknowledged. However, the prevailing view of government at both central and provincial levels, as well as some elements within the private sector, was that informal occupation increases urban development costs and should be either limited or prevented. Civil society, on the other hand, argued that most of those who settled in peri-urban

198 Land and post-conflict peacebuilding

areas during the conflict had occupied the land in good faith after purchasing it or having had it allocated to them by local authorities. Very few people had actually squatted on land in a clandestine or illegal manner. Most families had documents of some kind that they felt gave them security of tenure. However, fewer than 20 percent of the families actually held a legal title.

International good practice, as mapped out in instruments such as the Habitat Agenda, called for governments to introduce policies that progressively recognize existing land occupations and to eventually transform them into secure tenure rights through processes of physical upgrading and consultative planning (UNCHS 1996). Angola formally endorsed these principles at the Istanbul City Summit in 1996 and was obliged to incorporate the principles into national legislation.

After two years of widespread debate, the new land law was finally passed by the parliament in 2004. It did not meet all of civil society's expectations and incorporated only a few of their recommendations. The principle of public consultation became part of the official preamble to the law. The concept of community land was incorporated in the recognition of customary tenure, but the law took a strong position on the elimination of usucapiao. Existing land occupiers were given three years to acquire formal title from municipal or provincial government authorities, after which time informal occupation would become illegal.

The government passed regulations in 2007 detailing the procedures for formalizing rural land tenure. The regulations for securing tenure in peri-urban areas, where the majority of the poor live, had not yet been published at the time of this writing. The minister of urbanism and housing requested Development Workshop Angola's assistance in drafting such regulations, drawing from the Habitat principles and similar legislation in Mozambique and Brazil. Development Workshop Angola proposed the recognition of occupation in good faith, the articulation of gender-equitable tenure rights, and mechanisms for recognizing development zones in peri-urban areas in which upgradeable collective tenure could be recognized. These mechanisms would facilitate the government's ambitious urban requalification programs and provide a framework to minimalize forced removals and evictions.

With rising land values, there is increasing pressure to eliminate informal inner-city settlements (musseques) and open up these areas for commercial development. Lacking a clear policy on urban land development, the government and private-sector partners have embarked on an increasingly aggressive program of slum clearance and the removal of the poor to the periphery of the city.

FACTORS THAT AFFECT SUCCESS IN PEACEBUILDING

When Development Workshop Angola first started studying the land question in the mid-1990s, Angola was still embroiled in civil war. Local disputes over land were often lost in the general preoccupation with macro-level hostilities; indeed, they had not been adequately addressed since the country's independence from Portugal in 1975. Development Workshop Angola realized early on that the

Land resources and conflict in Angola **199**

conditions were in place for land conflicts to spiral out of control, possibly even posing a threat to lasting peace in the country. That concern prompted it to engage in advocacy and research, together with partner institutions,[10] on actions and policies in defense of the land tenure rights of conflict-affected populations in Angola's urban centers.

Several issues relating to land stood out as needing to be addressed in order for effective peacebuilding processes to work. First, property rights needed to be clarified for returning IDPs, refugees, demobilized excombatants, and displaced residents from the countryside seeking refuge in the larger urban centers. As described above, those who fled the violence and settled in musseques invested what little money they had in their homes, but were unable to obtain legal title to their property that would hold up in court.

Landownership and occupation issues emerged in the countryside as well. Rural resettlement under areas without support services or where infrastructure has been destroyed is a major challenge. Landmines left over from the conflict pose an additional danger. Only 30 percent of the areas of return were considered fit for resettlement by United Nations standards.[11] Development Workshop Angola worked with local partners to campaign for a new land policy and law to formalize the poor's informal occupation rights and their access to land. Secure tenure would release poor people's capital so that they could improve their built environment and their living and working conditions, and promote a peaceful transition to development—that is, if market interests could be made compatible with the poor's.

The end of the conflict compounded these issues when a scramble for land between powerful commercial interests and peasants threatened evictions of families who had fled the conflict-ravaged countryside to make homes on land without sufficient legal title. Disagreements over land became more frequent as conflict gave way to peace. In rural communities, fertile agricultural ground with relatively easy access to urban markets was in high demand. These sites frequently became the focus of disputes between residents and returning IDPs, refugees, and demobilized excombatants as well as more powerful official interests. In urban areas the poor risked being uprooted from their homes because their sprawling musseques frequently occupied ideal locations for elite housing developments, offices, and roads.

RECOMMENDATIONS

Angola has inherited a varied and complex set of landholding and land use practices, the evolution of which has been influenced by ecological conditions, customary and cultural traditions, the colonial past, years of conflict and forced

---

[10] Development Workshop Angola's partner institutions included the Centre for Environment and Human Settlements, One World Action, and members of the Angolan Rede de Terra.

[11] The UN's Norms for Humanitarian Settlement and the Sphere Principles (Sphere Project 2000) became the basis for Angolan legislation on resettlement in 2001.

200 Land and post-conflict peacebuilding

migrations, massive urbanization, and the socioeconomic development of the nation. From colonial times until the recent end of the conflict, Angolan legislators have demonstrated a consistent tendency to contain or circumscribe the land rights of the country's rural and poor peri-urban populations and to direct land resources to the hands of a few, while at various times supporting the development of commercial farming and mineral extraction (Clover 2005).

In light of that heritage and current needs, the following recommendations are offered.

1. The legal framework for land tenure and management must be adapted to the Angolan post-conflict reality. A land cadastral system legitimizing the injustices of colonial appropriation in rural areas and a faith in urban master planning are the two principles upon which legal title is presently based. These are insufficient tools to meet Angola's complex post-conflict land and settlement challenges. A more appropriate tenure framework could be based on the principle of scalable or upgradeable rights that expand upon existing categories of tenure. The framework should include the following principles:
   a. Community or collective tenure.
   b. Recognition of occupation in good faith.[12]
   c. Temporary occupation rights that may be periodically renewed and eventually upgraded.
   d. Surface rights that are granted when land falls within a cadastre or urban plan.
   e. Titled concession (as specified under the 2007 regulations).
   f. Freehold tenure with rights to transfer title.
   Only the last three of these may allow the sale or other transfer of land titles.
2. The 2004 Land Law introduced the important principle of public consultation; regulations and procedures have not yet been put in place to ensure that those affected by plans and land management decisions have opportunities to be heard and see their interests protected. Vigilance, media attention, and consistent, coordinated efforts are needed to protect and promote the interests of the majority and of economically vulnerable communities.
3. Communities need to gain corporate rights to own and manage property within governance frameworks that identify and protect their collective interests and prevent misappropriation by designated leaders.
4. Angolan land laws have left families with scattered micro-scale holdings, without the possibility of expansion, and without reserves or fallow lands, which are indispensable to maintaining soil fertility. The right of tenure of these small parcels and the right to reserve land for fallow, wood lots, forests, grazing, or transhumance, and access to water resources must be clarified. Advances in agricultural technology also need to be harnessed to preserve and improve soil fertility and to increase yields from small landholdings.

---

[12] Under the Civil Code this is defined as *usucapiao* or adverse occupation.

Land resources and conflict in Angola **201**

5. Transparency within the municipal, provincial, and national government agencies responsible for allocating land titles will be a deterrent to misallocation of concessions and help level the playing field. This in turn will give local individuals and families the opportunity to compete for such concessions.

6. The implementation of current land laws present many opportunities for violations and potential conflicts while increasing the state's power to confiscate land for public use. Regulations need to be introduced to limit the government's power to expropriate land for eventual transfer to commercial or private interests, and to otherwise prevent or limit abuses and conflicts.

7. Regularizing the hundreds of thousands of existing land occupations, and transforming them step by step into titles, will be a massive task and could not be accomplished within the three-year window allocated by law. Coordinated representation and advocacy are needed to extend the three-year limit, modify the legislation, and introduce appropriate implementing regulations. The government's capacity to administer land needs to be greatly enhanced—particularly at the level of the municipalities, which, under a 2007 decentralization law, were given the responsibility of managing land units up to 1,000 square meters.

8. Information systems for land transaction records need to be set up in municipalities so that decisions can be made and conflicts adjudicated locally. A simple way to minimize corruption and abuse (and therefore avoid conflict) is to make land records public as they are in South Africa and Namibia. Municipal land information systems need to be kept current and should also be linked with the planned cadastral system, which is to be managed at the national level. The municipal system should post for public scrutiny all proposed transfers or changes of land use in order to allow affected people or communities sufficient time for consultation and, if need be, to register their objections through appropriate legal channels.

9. The guarantee of land rights for IDPs through legislative decree provided a set of benchmarks for future government planning and introduced the important concept of participation and consultation, which should be incorporated into future land and planning laws. These principles can be used to seek a level of restitution that will ensure minimal human settlement conditions for conflict-affected families. Communities and civil society should work to ensure that these resettlement principles gain greater acceptance and compliance from the government agencies responsible for social assistance.

10. Communities and civil society should continue to advocate that the Angolan government recognize the legitimacy of the right of occupation in good faith. A degree of legitimacy for temporary tenure should be recognized until a fully functional land registration system is in place.

11. The fact that informal settlements continue to grow rapidly in the post-war period means that slum prevention should be a priority for planners. Development Workshop Angola's research in 2004 indicated that in Luanda

202 Land and post-conflict peacebuilding

more than 70,000 new households are created every year (Development Workshop Angola and Centre for Environment and Human Settlements 2005). Slum upgrading, while essential, is extremely expensive and both socially and politically problematic; slum prevention, through increased offers of legal land, is much simpler. The government has adopted a strategy of setting aside municipal land reserves for low- to middle-income housing in new satellite neighborhoods to help meet existing housing needs. However, these reserves must be integrated into the existing urban centers to prevent them from intruding on peri-rural peasants' lands or, even worse, becoming ghettos far from urban centers, resembling South African apartheid-era townships.

CONCLUSION

The post-war period in Angola provides an opportunity to resolve long-standing problems that, if left untended, may result in renewed conflict in the future. Angola's legacy of conflict, which was partly fuelled by injustice related to land appropriation by the governing elites (both exogenous and indigenous), must still be addressed. Successive revisions of land legislation have not fundamentally addressed the underlying problems that originally led to conflict.

Conflicts are still occurring between former IDPs and long-term residents and between farmers and pastoralists. Information about conflicts between peasants and commercial farmers has begun to appear in the press, illustrating emerging tensions in the provinces of Cuanza Sul, Huambo, Huila, and Cunene. At the same time, rising urban land values and pressure from property developers have led to highly publicized conflicts in the cities of Luanda and Benguela. It is likely that these conflicts will become even more predominant in the future. New conflicts are likely to emerge as the government's plans for the building of 1 million houses and the creation of land reserves push city limits out into the peri-rural greenbelts presently occupied by peasant farmers. Acquisition of land by the state for the public interest needs to be done in a transparent way with good consultation, with the aim of building local community buy-in. At present, the state's underdeveloped land administration institutions will have technical difficulties (from the social, agricultural, and legal points of view) in arbitrating or managing related conflicts.

The incorporation of international norms of good practice into Angolan legislation can result in real improvements in procedures for managing land and protecting the tenure rights of vulnerable groups. The introduction of the concepts of public consultation and participatory planning in the 2001 Decree on IDP Resettlement may have influenced the inclusion of these concepts in the land and planning laws drafted the following year. Public consultation on the 2004 Land Law was permitted to extend beyond the original six months to a full two years. The challenge remains, however, to fully incorporate these principles into the application of rights-based legislation.

The land law and other centrally planned laws, such as the Mining Act, have provided the state with better tools to manage natural resources. While many officials feel that these tools are necessary to restore order to the uncontrolled economy left at the end of the conflict, these tendencies run against current international practice of strengthening citizens' rights by introducing elements of participatory democracy that engage affected communities in the local-level decisions that affect them. The government's decision to assign to municipalities the power of decision making on local-level domestic-scale land management, and the creation of new municipalities with fiscal authority, are positive reforms in this direction.

Through networks such as the Rede de Terra and the independent media, it is important that Angolan civil society continue its advocacy for the promotion of land tenure rights and the protection of the urban and rural poor against arbitrary and forced removals. Land has become, for the first time, a political issue debated regularly in the parliament and is influencing the platforms of political parties. Opportunities are increasing for civil society and community representatives to employ emerging local spaces such as municipal forums and consultative councils in order to bring the debate on land rights into the public arena. Land issues are likely to be high on the agenda of elected municipal councils when they are instituted within the next several years as part of Angola's promised democratic reforms.

REFERENCES

Avillez, F. 1974. *Introdução ao estudo da economia da agricultura dita tradicional, Lições de Economia Rural*. Curso Superior de Agronomia e Silvicultura, University of Luanda, Huambo.

Bender, G. J. 1978. *Angola under the Portuguese*. London: Heinemann.

Caetano, M. 1946. *Relacoes das colonias de Angola e Mocambique com os territorios estrangeiros visinhos*. Lisbon, Portugal: Imprensa Nacional.

Carriço, J. 1971. *Economia da pequena empresa no Central Highlands 1964–1972*. Luanda: University of Luanda.

Childs, G. M. 1944. Notes on civil administration in Angola: Civilizing words. Unpublished paper.

Clover, J. 2005. Land reform in Angola: Establishing the ground rules. In *From the ground up: Land rights, conflict and peace in sub-Saharan Africa*, ed. C. Huggins and J. Clover. Pretoria, South Africa: Institute for Security Studies.

Development Workshop Angola. 2002. *Study for a legal and institutional framework for improving land management in Angola—land management and land tenure in peri-urban areas*. Luanda: Ministry of Urbanism and Public Works and the Ad-hoc Technical Group for Habitat.

———. 2003. *Land access in peri-urban Angola: Its role in peace and reconstruction*. Luanda.

———. 2004. *Land and reintegration of ex-combatants in post-war Angola*. Luanda.

———. 2008. *Land tenure and rights in Mombolo, Huambo Province: Results of a pilot project for individual rural land demarcation*. Luanda.

204   Land and post-conflict peacebuilding

Development Workshop Angola and Centre for Environment and Human Settlements. 2005. Terra: Urban land reform in post-war Angola. Occasional Paper No. 5. Luanda: Development Workshop Angola.

Ferreira, V. 1954. Regioes de povoamento europeu nos planaltos de Angola. In *Estudos Ultramarinos*, vol. 3, part 2, *Angola e os seus problemas*. Lisbon, Portugal: Agencia Geral do Ultramar.

Foley, C. 2007. The law of the land. *Guardian*, March 30. http://commentisfree.guardian .co.uk/conor_foley/2007/03/angolan_land_rights.html.

Henderson, L. W. 1990. *A igreja em Angola: Um rio com varias correntes*. Lisbon, Portugal: Alem-Mar.

Hodges, A. 2001. *Angola: From Afro-Stalinism to petrodiamond capitalism*. Bloomington: James Curry / Indiana University Press.

Margarido, A. 1972. The Tokoist church and Portuguese colonialism in Angola. In *Protest and resistance in Angola and Brazil*, ed. R. Chilcote. Berkeley: University of California Press.

MIAA (Missao de Inqueritos Agricolas de Angola). 1973. *Estatisticas agricolas correntes (1971–1972)*, vols. 10 and 29, 1967/8. Luanda.

Monteiro, R. L. 1973. A *familia nos musseques*. Luanda: Fundo de Accao Social no Trabalho em Angola.

Neto, M. C. 2000. Angola no século XX (até 1974). In *O imperio Africano (séculos XIX e XX)*. Lisbon, Portugal: Edições Colibri.

Nielsen, R. 2008. *Women's land rights in post-conflict Angola*. Report 125. Seattle, WA: Rural Development Institute.

Oyebade, A. 1997. *Culture and customs of Angola*. Westport, CT: Greenwood Press.

Pacheco, F. 2002. *The issue of land and agriculture in Angola*. Rome: Food and Agriculture Organization of the United Nations.

Robson, P., and S. Roque. 2001. Here in the city. Occasional Paper No. 2. Luanda: Development Workshop Angola.

Russell-Wood, J. R. 1998. *The Portuguese empire 1415–1808*. Baltimore, MD: Johns Hopkins University Press.

de Santa Rita, J. G. 1940. O contacto das racas nas colonias, seus efeitos politicos e sociais. Legislacao Portuguesa. In *Congresso do mundo Portugues*, vol. 15, part 2. Lisbon, Portugal: Comissao Executiva dos Centenarios.

Sogge, D. 1992. *Sustainable peace: Angola's recovery*. Harare, Zimbabwe: Southern African Research and Documentation Centre.

———. 2009. Angola "failed" yet "successful." Working Paper No. 81. Madrid, Spain: Fundación para las Relaciones Internacionales y el Diálogo Exterior.

Sphere Project. 2000. *Humanitarian charter and minimum standards in disaster response*. Geneva, Switzerland. http://helid.digicollection.org/en/d/Jh0226e/3.2.2.html.

UNCHS (United Nations Conference on Human Settlements—Habitat II). 1996. Istanbul declaration on human settlements and the habitat agenda. www.un-documents.net/ ac165-14.htm.

Ventura, R. 1955. O caso de Cela e a colonização étnica de Angola. In *Congresso dos economistas Portugueses (Problems das economias ultramarinas); I Seccdo-colonizacao etnica (Comunicacoes e debates)*. Lisbon, Portugal: Instituto Nacional d'Estatistica.

World Bank. 2006. *Angola country economic memorandum: Oil, broad-based growth, and equity*. Africa Region Macroeconomics, Report 35362-AO. Washington, D.C.

Refugees and legal reform in Iraq: The Iraqi Civil Code, international standards for the treatment of displaced persons, and the art of attainable solutions

Dan E. Stigall

Although the U.S. military has withdrawn from Iraq, Iraq continues to face one of the most acute displacement crises in the world (IRC 2011). Over 5 million Iraqis have been displaced by violence, with 2.7 million of them internally displaced within Iraq (Younes and Rosen 2008). Such a situation creates not only a humanitarian crisis but also an opportunity for insurgents and militia groups to exploit the displacement crisis in order to legitimate themselves and achieve geopolitical goals. Consequently, the problem of displacement and the search for a solution to the current crisis— once salient issues for military commanders conducting counterinsurgency operations—will now be left to Iraqi authorities. The goals and challenges of a sovereign Iraq, however, will be largely the same as those faced by the military commanders who once toiled there. As the U.S. Army Field Manual 3-24, *Counterinsurgency*, states:

> Long-term success in [counterinsurgency] depends on the people taking charge of their own affairs and consenting to the government's rule. Achieving this condition requires the government to eliminate as many causes of the insurgency as feasible. . . . Over time, counterinsurgents aim to enable a country or regime to provide the security and rule of law that allow establishment of social services and growth of economic activity. [Counterinsurgency] thus involves the application of national power in the political, military, economic, social, information, and infrastructure fields and disciplines (U.S. Army 2006, 13).[1]

Dan E. Stigall is a trial attorney in the Office of International Affairs of the U.S. Department of Justice. Any opinion expressed is solely that of the author and not necessarily that of the Department of Justice. A version of this article was initially published in the *Rutgers Law Record* and is adapted here with the journal's express permission.

[1]   See also U.S. Army (2008b, para. 3-37): "Dislocated civilians are symptoms of broader issues such as conflict, insecurity, and disparities among the population. How displaced populations are treated can either foster trust and confidence—laying the foundation for stabilization and reconstruction among a traumatized population—or create resentment and further chaos. Local and international aid organizations are most often best equipped to deal with the needs of the local populace but require a secure environment in which to operate. Through close cooperation, military forces can enable the success of these organizations by providing critical assistance to the populace."

206 Land and post-conflict peacebuilding

Current reports indicate that large-scale displacement in Iraq is driving civilians to join militias (both the Mahdi Army and Sunni militias) because of the need for services and the desire to belong to "new communities" (Younes and Rosen 2008, 4). Displacement has become an engine of the insurgency. It is critical, therefore, to find adequate remedies for displaced persons as well as policies to effect property restitution and resettlement. The solutions must be effective, durable, and—most important—attainable.

The government of Iraq has already taken some minor steps to address the crisis. For instance, funds have been allotted to help resettle displaced persons through limited grants and assistance with rent.[2] Such positive initiatives will certainly assuage the suffering of the displaced and foster their return home. Even so, the return of displaced persons will require more than the mere provision of funds. It will require the return of property belonging to the displaced—property that, in many cases, is currently occupied by people who have no intention of giving it up (Younes and Rosen 2008). Such property disputes are typically the proper subject of civil courts and a nation's substantive civil law (Jwaideh 1953; Bell, Boyron, and Whittaker 1998).

Iraq differs in many ways from Afghanistan, the other major front of current U.S. military engagements in the Middle East. While Iraq was a rogue state under Saddam Hussein, it was not a failed state. Unlike Afghanistan, it has historically maintained a strong central government that was capable of extending its power throughout the majority of its realm. Iraq also has maintained some relatively effective governmental institutions. Among the more vibrant elements of Iraqi government are its judiciary and sophisticated legal culture. From the perspective of those seeking to effect reconstruction and to counter certain problems associated with war and insurgency, the existence of such functional institutions allows for options that might be unavailable elsewhere.

In evaluating the state of Iraq's substantive law and seeking solutions, it is important to find remedies and mechanisms for restitution that comport with international standards. Those standards are not the easiest to discern, as there is no comprehensive treaty setting forth all the rights and obligations owed by states vis-à-vis displaced persons. As a result, one must look to numerous other instruments such as the International Covenant on Civil and Political Rights (ICCPR), the International Covenant on Economic, Social and Cultural Rights (ICESCR), and the Geneva Conventions (Phuong 2004). Two nonbinding instruments, however, have been promulgated to assist international actors in identifying rights and duties regarding displaced persons: the Guiding Principles on Internal Displacement (Guiding Principles) and the Principles on Housing and Property Restitution for Refugees and Displaced Persons (Pinheiro Principles) (Paglione 2008).

The Guiding Principles, which were finalized in 1998 (UNCHR 1998; Brookings Institution 2000), are a set of guidelines developed in an attempt to enhance

---

[2] See, for example, Council of Ministers Decree, No. 262 of 2008 (on file with author).

Refugees, displaced persons, and legal reform in Iraq 207

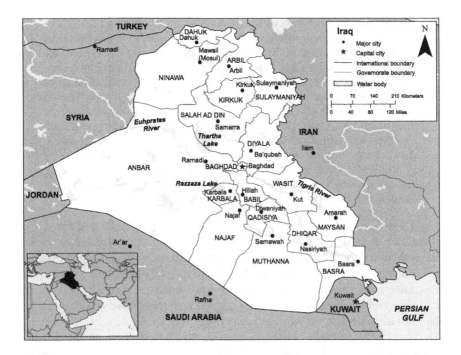

protection and assistance for persons forcibly displaced within their own countries by events such as violent conflicts, gross violations of human rights, and natural and manmade disasters (Kälin 2008). As Walter Kälin states:

> The Principles consolidate into one document the legal standards relevant to the internally displaced drawn from international human rights law, humanitarian law and refugee law by analogy. In addition to restating existing norms, they address gray areas and gaps identified in the law. As a result, there is now for the first time an authoritative statement of the rights of internally displaced persons and the obligations of governments and other controlling authorities toward these populations (Kälin 2008, xi).

The Pinheiro Principles—named for Paulo Sérgio Pinheiro—are a more recently formulated set of international standards, which were endorsed by the UN Sub-commission on the Promotion and Protection of Human Rights in 2005 (Leckie 2006). They were "designed to assist all relevant actors, national and international, in addressing the legal and technical issues surrounding housing, land and property restitution in situations where displacement has led to persons being arbitrarily or unlawfully deprived of their former homes, lands, properties or places of habitual residence" (UN 2005, sec. I, para. 1.1). A director of one nongovernmental organization describes their function as follows:

208 Land and post-conflict peacebuilding

They provide practical guidance to governments, UN agencies and the broader international community on how best to address the complex legal and technical issues surrounding housing, land and property restitution. They augment the international normative framework in the area of housing and property restitution rights, and are grounded firmly within existing international human rights and humanitarian law. They re-affirm existing human rights and apply them to the specific question of housing and property restitution. They elaborate what states should do in terms of developing national housing and property restitution procedures and institutions, and ensuring access to these by all displaced persons. They stress the importance of consultation and participation in decision making by displaced persons and outline approaches to technical issues of housing, land and property records, the rights of tenants and other non-owners and the question of secondary occupants (Leckie 2006, 16).

There is considerable overlap between the two instruments and few areas of contrast. Both delineate a number of rights to be afforded displaced persons, and both do so in a maximalist fashion that tends, at times, to go beyond existing law (Phuong 2004). There are, however, differing levels of detail vis-à-vis their interaction with substantive law. The Pinheiro Principles, for instance, contain a more detailed articulation of the procedural and substantive requirements of the restitution mechanism they envision (UN 2005). Differences in their respective levels of acceptance, however, suggest consideration of both instruments when evaluating a domestic legal regime's compliance with international standards. This is because the Guiding Principles, though lacking in detail, have attained a broad measure of international support and are therefore considered to be more authoritative (Kälin 2008).[3] The Pinheiro Principles, in contradistinction,

---

[3] Kälin summarizes the broad support for the Guiding Principles thus:

> The Heads of State and Government assembled in New York for the September 2005 World Summit unanimously recognized them as an "important international framework for the protection of internally displaced persons" (UN General Assembly GA Resolution A/60/L.1 para. 132), and the General Assembly has not only welcomed "the fact that an increasing number of States, United Nations agencies and regional and non-governmental organizations are applying them as a standard" but also encouraged "all relevant actors to make use of the Guiding Principles when dealing with situations of internal displacement" (A/RES/62/153, para. 10). At the regional level, the Organization of African Unity (now the African Union) formally acknowledged the principles; the Economic Community of West African States (ECOWAS) called on its member states to disseminated and apply them; and in the Horn of Africa, the Intergovernmental Authority on Development (IGAD), in a ministerial declaration, called the principles a "useful tool" in the development of national policies on internal displacement. In Europe, the Organization for Security and Co-operation in Europe (OSCE) recognized that the principles as "a useful framework for the work of the OSCE" in dealing with internal displacement, and the Parliamentary Assembly of the Council of Europe as well as its Council of Ministers urged its member states to incorporate the principles into their domestic laws. The number of states that have incorporated the Guiding Principles into their domestic laws and policies is growing (Kälin 2008, vii–viii).

Refugees, displaced persons, and legal reform in Iraq 209

have more detail but have not yet reached the level of international acceptance of the Guiding Principles.[4]

This chapter compares the substantive provisions of Iraqi civil law to both instruments—layering them together as an overlay above a map of Iraq's legal terrain. Doing so makes clear the points of intersection between the requirements of international law (as interpreted by these instruments) and a nation's substantive civil law. These intersections occur at three distinct points: the architecture of ownership, the mechanism of restitution, and the protection given to secondary occupants. This chapter then analyzes the demands of the international standards for the treatment of displaced persons on the substantive civil law of Iraq in order to determine if existing Iraqi civil law comports with such standards and, if not, to identify those areas where it is lacking. Such an analysis is useful for determining the extent to which Iraqi civil law, unadulterated by outside mechanisms and foreign interference, can serve as a fully compliant restitution scheme and the degree to which augmentation or legislative reform is required.

THE CURRENT LEGAL FRAMEWORK

While many Iraqis were displaced prior to 2003, the crisis continues as Iraqis flee to escape unceasing sectarian and ethnic violence. As noted by David Enders in 2011, "the 'Baghdad Belt,' the demographically mixed cities and villages that ring the capital . . . have seen some of the worst violence of the last eight years" (Enders 2011). And according to UNHCR estimates for 2006, approximately 500,000 Iraqis were internally displaced that year alone, with 40,000 to 50,000 fleeing each month (UNHCR 2007). The Commission for the Resolution of Real Property Disputes (CRRPD), the only such entity functioning in Iraq, addresses exclusively—as specified by its statute—those claims that arose between July 17, 1968, and April 9, 2003.[5] There is now no mechanism in place to assist with post-2003 property restitution claims or the ongoing displacement crisis. Iraqis displaced thereafter must find recourse through the ordinary court system. This, however, is not cause for grief. The Iraqi civil law system is a sophisticated, modern system, which—in spite of the need for some amendments—is more than capable of addressing the needs of displaced persons and those who have lost property (Stigall 2005).[6]

---

[4] For further discussion of the Pinheiro Principles, see Barbara McCallin, "The Role of Restitution in Post-Conflict Situations," and Samir Elhawary and Sara Pantuliano, "Land Issues in Post-Conflict Return and Recovery," both in this book.

[5] Statute of the Commission for the Resolution of Real Property Disputes, Order Number 2 of the Year 2006. Unofficial English translation by the Reparations Programmes Unit, International Organisation for Migration, Geneva. www.brookings.edu/projects/idp/Laws-and-Policies/~/media/Files/Projects/IDP/Laws%20and%20Policies/Iraq_2006_PropertyResolution.pdf.

[6] For a further discussion of areas of the Iraqi Civil Code in need of amendment, see Hamoudi (2008a).

210 Land and post-conflict peacebuilding

The Iraqi Civil Code can be aptly described as a member of the civilian (Continental civil law) family that is deeply informed by Islamic legal influences. The code was enacted in the twentieth century, when Iraq blended into its legal culture many elements of the Continental civil law tradition (Jwaideh 1953). The Iraqi Civil Code was principally authored by Abd al-Razzāq al-Sanhūrī, who was then the dean of the Iraqi Law College (Jwaideh 1953). Zuhair Jwaideh notes that as Iraq approached modernity, "the conditions under which [Ottoman law] had been enacted had completely changed and legislation for a new and unified civil code became a necessity" (Jwaideh 1953, 178). The substance of this new civil code was taken largely from Egyptian law (which mirrored the French Civil Code), then-existing Iraqi laws (such as those from the *Mejelle* and other Ottoman legislation), and from Islamic law (Jwaideh 1953). The code made "every effort to coordinate between its provisions which stem from two main sources: Islamic law and Western law, resulting in a synthesis in which the duality of sources and their variance is almost imperceptible" (Arabi 1995, 167).

The Iraqi Civil Code contains the principal legislation dealing with property (of every variety) and, thus, is the primary source of law governing property restitution and remedies associated with displacement (Jwaideh 1953). The question then arises as to how that system comports with the international standards set forth and the demands of those standards on a nation's substantive civil law.

A MEANS OF RESTITUTION

Catherine Phuong, a lecturer in law at the University of Newcastle, in England, notes that although there is no explicit provision in the main international human rights instruments (such as the ICCPR and the ICESCR) that guarantees the right of restitution of property, there is an emerging trend toward providing restitution and compensation for loss of property to displaced persons (Phuong 2004). Both the Guiding Principles and the Pinheiro Principles—consistent with their maximalist positions—affirmatively require states to supply some sort of restitution mechanism for this purpose. The Guiding Principles state:

> Competent authorities have the duty and responsibility to assist returned and/or resettled internally displaced persons to recover, to the extent possible, their property and possessions which they left behind or were dispossessed of upon their displacement. When recovery of such property and possessions is not possible, competent authorities shall provide or assist these persons in obtaining appropriate compensation or another form of just reparation (Kälin 2008, 133–134).

Those same authorities are also tasked with the duty of facilitating the safe, voluntary return of internally displaced persons to their homes or places of habitual residence, or facilitating their voluntary resettlement in another part of the country (Kälin 2008).

The Pinheiro Principles elaborate on that responsibility, noting that states should establish "procedures, institutions and mechanisms to assess and enforce housing, land and property restitution claims" (UN 2005, sec. V, para. 12.1), and that all refugees and displaced persons who were arbitrarily or unlawfully deprived of property have a right to have that property restored to them or, alternatively, to be compensated for such property in a judgment by an independent and impartial tribunal. Thus, both instruments impose an affirmative duty on the part of governments to facilitate the restitution of property to the displaced.

Neither the Guiding Principles nor the Pinheiro Principles, however, give a great deal of substantive detail on the nature of the restitution rights to be afforded. Nonetheless, it is possible to distill from these principles a responsibility on the part of governments to provide a mechanism whereby displaced persons can seek restitution.

As to the type of mechanism to be provided, both sets of principles provide that this can be done via new procedures and mechanisms or through the use of the existing legal infrastructure—so long as it is has adequate resources. The question of which mechanism is best for effecting property restitution has been given much attention in recent years. Scott Leckie has noted that "any attempt to deal adequately with housing and property issues must be entrenched within a legal framework" and that "practice has clearly shown that a consistent legal framework should ideally be in place prior to instigating the claims process. A clear and consistent legal framework is vital for restitution programs to succeed" (Leckie 2003, 399). Leckie also notes, however, that legal complexities and problematic regulatory frameworks have served to stall restitution efforts in the past. Such complexities have, unfortunately, resulted in a subtle bias against organic legal institutions and an unnecessary push to effect property restitution extrajudicially. Specifically regarding Iraq, a 2008 paper from the Brookings Institution notes:

> One of the lessons drawn from the CRRPD is that a judicial or quasi-judicial process is unlikely to be successful in dealing with large numbers of claims. The CRRPD which has been a quasi-judicial process has been bogged down with bureaucratic processes, including provision for valuation by multiple experts to assess the value of claims, extensive formal requirements for documentation and application of Iraqi civil and procedural law in some areas. Administrative processes are generally easier than judicial processes to implement and should be the predominant mechanism for future reparation mechanisms. Otherwise, the whole judicial system could be clogged up with property compensation/ reparation cases, with lengthy delays not just for those seeking recovery of their property but many other legal issues as well (Ferris 2008, 26–27).

The Brookings paper is full of important data and interesting insights. Further, its author—a notable human rights advocate and a scholar of considerable merit— should be lauded for her heroic efforts to draw greater attention to the issue of displacement. Nonetheless, the paper misses the mark when drawing its

212   Land and post-conflict peacebuilding

conclusions from the CRRPD. The CRRPD is not an Iraqi court and does not adjudicate its claims in accordance with the Iraqi Civil Code. It is a sui generis commission—akin to an administrative entity—with its own unique structure and procedure. Even if it were considered quasi-judicial, extrapolating from the experience of the CRRPD that "a judicial or quasi-judicial process is unlikely to be successful in dealing with large numbers of claims" (Ferris 2008, 26) is a bit like damning the entire concept of automotive transport because your car has a flat tire. The CRRPD is just one of many competing quasi-judicial models. Its success or failure will certainly have causes related to its unique circumstances rather than to some feature of the entire universe of possible judicial or quasi-judicial models. It is, therefore, improper to foreclose the possibility of a judicial or quasi-judicial role without greater analysis of the specific weaknesses in the existing model.

In addition, it is important that the analysis of the displacement mechanism not be trapped in structures of thought so rigid that the value of domestic legal institutions is completely disregarded. There are very basic reasons for preferring a judicial model, such as the need to resolve conflicting claims and the need to provide a forum in which grievances can be aired and adjudicated peacefully, thus reducing the appetite for revenge (Nagle 2000). As Richard Posner notes:

> [T]he passion for revenge may seem the antithesis of rational, instrumental thinking—may seem at once emotional, destructive, and useless. It flouts the economist's commandment to ignore sunk costs, to let bygones be bygones. When there is no possibility of legal redress to deter an aggressor, potential victims will be assiduous in self-protection (Posner 1998, 50).

For such reasons, the role of courts in resolving property disputes is vital. However, even if one were to discount the role of judges and courts as a conflict-resolving mechanism, there are two very practical reasons why the Iraqi judiciary and Iraqi law cannot be pushed aside in this matter: the immediacy of the crisis and the cultural importance of Iraqi civil law.

Acute crises require immediate responses

Some commentators have advocated abandoning Iraqi courts altogether and have even called for the creation of "new administrative procedures for resolving property disputes" because "Iraq's property laws are complex" and its courts are "not up to the job" (Ferris and O'Hanlon 2008).[7] As this chapter will demonstrate, Iraqi civil law does contain some weaknesses but is by no means unusually

---

[7]   For an interesting discussion of such assertions in international development discourse, see Beard (2007, 76), who notes: "Indeed, development theory today can be characterized not by an incapacity to accept Third World lack, but rather by its incapacity not to view Third World peoples as lacking."

complex. Moreover, the appropriate solution for the problems associated with a struggling Iraqi judicial system is to make the needed changes to Iraq's substantive law in a way that is consistent with the Iraqi legal tradition. In that regard, it is essential to focus energy and resources on correcting the Iraqi legal system's institutional weaknesses rather than on depriving its courts of their natural jurisdiction, diverting their authority to a nonexistent entity, and ignoring existing legal institutions in favor of a conceptual mechanism that does not yet exist and that will operate by a new law still to be enacted, let alone tested in practice.

Further, not every dispute will require lengthy adjudication. Some cases of obvious squatting do not necessitate lengthy legal battles, as there is no plausible claim on the part of the illegal occupant. Cases of outright and flagrant squatting are seldom the subject of a court proceeding but, instead, can be resolved simply by direct appeal to law enforcement personnel who can review the property records, evaluate the situation, allow the owner of the property to go back to his or her home, and have the squatter removed. In Iraq, many of these cases are currently being addressed through direct government action. For instance, Prime Minister Nouri al-Maliki issued a general eviction order that, beginning on August 1, 2008, gave all individuals occupying the houses of displaced persons one month to either vacate the property or face eviction. In order to enforce this order, the Iraq government undertook a large-scale eviction and property restitution campaign (IDP Working Group 2008). Local authorities ordered all squatters to leave public property, although some "local authorities are applying the Eviction Order only to certain areas or land" (IDP Working Group 2008, 14). The Iraqi Army was given a leading role in directly facilitating displaced persons' return, evicting squatters, and restoring property to its true owners. The U.S. military assisted in this restitution process (Garcia-Navarro 2008). Myriad cases of displacement will be resolved in this manner and, therefore, will not be a burden on the Iraqi court system.

Using the existing legal machinery is also appropriate because Iraq's displacement crisis is not a fait accompli but an ongoing event (Tavernise 2008). Depriving courts of jurisdiction over such matters would have meant removing a domestic institution from the critical role it was designed to play and creating a legal deprivation without end. Civil courts would have lost their authority to hear property disputes for the foreseeable future. Such long-term institutional starvation is inimical to a broader state building effort (Paris 2004).

The ongoing nature of the displacement crisis also demonstrates the need for immediate action, using existing laws and institutions to the maximum extent possible. As displaced persons rapidly exhaust their savings while living abroad, time is a critical factor. Any hypothetical "concept court" or new administrative procedure would take a great deal of time to create, as it would have to be formulated, debated, and then enacted in accordance with the Iraqi legislative process (Ardolino 2008). Opposing political forces would need to agree on its substance, the terms of its operation, the reach of its jurisdiction, its means

214   Land and post-conflict peacebuilding

of compensation, the method of its composition, its duration, and a host of other factors. Only after the completion of this lengthy legislative process could such a hypothetical entity and its new rules even begin to be tested in practice.

In contrast to the lengthy ordeal that would necessarily precede the formation of a new entity or the passage of a sweeping new law, domestic courts are present and functioning now—with a well-defined functional competence and a trained cadre of professional jurists. While reports indicate that there is currently a glaring lack of willingness on the part of some judicial entities in Iraq to enforce court orders and judgments, such unwillingness is not due to a defective judicial model but, quite the contrary, to a lack of political will on the part of those charged with administering the current model. Problems associated with a lack of political will are not solved through the imposition of new institutions but through the ascendance of new governments and new administrators—or through a change in the outlook of those currently in power. In other words, if a government simply does not prioritize the enforcement of court orders, no amount of institutional tinkering is going to improve the enforcement problem. The lack of governmental support becomes a barrier *erga omnes* (Latin for "in relation to everything"). This is because the problem lies not with the institution but with the attitude and philosophy of the government charged with administering it.

That said, there are some signs that issues of displacement are being taken increasingly seriously by the current regime. Further, there are indications of progress in strengthening the Iraqi judiciary, with the number of Iraqi judges more than doubling (from 500 to 1,200) between 2006 and 2008 (Leinwand 2008). If that trend continues, the decisions made by Iraqi courts should be implemented appropriately. As for the means by which such decisions are made and the laws guide them, however, the Iraqi Civil Code was enacted decades ago, has been tested in practice, is currently in force, and is engrained in the socio-juridical consciousness of the Iraqi polity (Hamoudi 2008b; Stigall 2006). Given those facts, the acute nature of the current crisis, and the realization that any solution must be one that can be implemented immediately, the solution to the current displacement crisis must involve improving the existing judicial apparatus and must be based on Iraqi law now in force.

Substantive law, cultural ties, and legitimacy

Apart from the immediacy of the crisis, cultural factors weigh in favor of utilizing existing legal institutions. Particular sensitivity should be given to a nation's substantive law, as it is often deeply engrained as a cultural identifier in the collective conscience of the population and can be a source of cultural or national pride (Malaurie 1997). Further, in the broader context of a state building effort, the nature of a nation's substantive law becomes particularly salient: the most successful programs to restore the rule of law in weakened or failed states have been those rooted in the traditions of the local citizenry (Coyle 2003). Preexisting

Refugees, displaced persons, and legal reform in Iraq   215

organic legal systems often have the advantage of being tested through years of legal practice. They are generally part of a political bargain that was struck long ago and that carries with it a certain sense of local ownership and acceptance. As a result, they are more likely to be perceived as legitimate. A legitimacy deficit can lead to rejection, which can quickly lead to failure. Ash Bali notes that a better model for a more robust nation-building project is the indigenous ownership of both institutional design and implementation, along with external logistical support. He posits that "for new state institutions to be stable and durable, they must be the product of local political bargains commanding sufficient consensus to bolster their perceived legitimacy" (Bali 2005, 438–439). This echoes the lessons of current counterinsurgency doctrine, which holds that "long-term success in [counterinsurgency] depends on the people taking charge of their own affairs and consenting to the government's rule" (U.S. Army 2006, para. 1-4).

Specifically regarding Iraqi substantive law, Haider Ala Hamoudi, an associate professor at the University of Pittsburgh School of Law and a notable scholar of Islamic and Iraqi law, has stated:

> I suppose if I had to analogize, within Iraq, reverence to the Civil Code is more or less like American reverence to the Constitution. In Iraq, constitutions come and go, they are politically motivated, they are hard to take as seriously, but the Civil Code is central to the legal theology. Sure a clause here or there might be amended, but as a general matter it has proved remarkably durable. Get lawyers in Iraq, from any place, including the Kurdish self rule areas that have not been under Arab control for nearly two decades, including the most religious and the most secular, the most Kurdish and the most Arab, the most Sunni and the most Shi'i and they all know the Civil Code and can quote its provisions, and the commentaries, thereto, very liberally. . . .
>
> Finally, Sanhuri's code took years to draft and years to pass. Consultations, discussions, meetings, arguments, within legislatures and the legal community as well as broader society seemed endless. When it was finally done, everyone knew what it was and what it was going to do. It grew fairly deep roots after that. The CPA [Coalition Provisional Authority] gave us on the Iraqi side a day to review their drafts [of legislation]. Nobody knew about them until they were enacted. Once enacted, few paid attention because they had not been discussed. No discussion, no understanding, and no understanding, no implementation (Hamoudi 2008b).

Professor Hamoudi's words resonate much like those of the French jurist Phillippe Malaurie, who noted—in the context of French law—that the French code has

> permeated deep into our national culture. The Civil Code is part of our national heritage, just like French-style gardens, the palace of Versailles, Philippe de Champaigne or General de Gaulle. At stake in codification is our culture and our identity. The Civil Code has been more that the symbol of national unity. . . . The Civil Code is at the same time the cause, the witness and the consequence of our cultural identity (Malaurie 1997).

216 Land and post-conflict peacebuilding

This process of enactment and continuous acceptance within the polity over successive generations imbues such legislation with cultural importance and with a legitimacy derived from what Richard Posner has described as "epistemic democracy" (Posner 1998, 14). The cultural importance of Iraqi legal institutions must, therefore, be taken into account when proposing long-term modifications to the Iraqi legal system and its substantive civil law. A review of that law reveals some blind spots and areas in need of improvement—but an overall formidable and fair legal regime which is well suited for the task of restitution.

THE ARCHITECTURE OF OWNERSHIP

Both the Guiding Principles and the Pinheiro Principles require that displaced persons be allowed to exercise full ownership of property without illegal interference or discrimination. The Guiding Principles provide that "no one shall be arbitrarily deprived of property and possessions" (Kälin 2008, 95). Further, "property . . . left behind by internally displaced persons should be protected against destruction . . . [or] appropriation" (Kälin 2008, 96). The Pinheiro Principles, in turn, state that "everyone has the right to the peaceful enjoyment of his or her possessions" (UN 2005, sec. III, para. 7.1) and that "everyone has the right to be protected against being arbitrarily displaced from his or her home, land or place of habitual residence" (UN 2005, sec. III, para. 5.1). The Pinheiro Principles also require "states [to] incorporate protections against displacement into [their] domestic legislation, consistent with international human rights and humanitarian law and related standards, and [to] extend these protections to everyone within their legal jurisdiction" (UN 2005, sec. III, para. 5.2). One may distill from these combined principles a general requirement for the full protection of ownership of private property, untainted by discrimination or governmental arbitrariness—a requirement that the Iraqi legal system fully satisfies.

The Iraqi Civil Code states that everything is subject to ownership except those things that, by their nature or by law, are excluded. Property is defined as everything that has a material value. The Iraqi Civil Code recognizes the right to complete private ownership of property. Under the code, the owner of the property is considered to be the owner of everything commonly considered to be an essential element of it. Perfect ownership of property vests the owner with the absolute right to dispose of his or her property through use, enjoyment, and exploitation of the thing owned, as well as its fruits, crops, and anything else that it produces. No exception is made for gender, class, religion, or sect, as this is a universally applied right. Further, as articulated in section IV of the code, Iraqi civil law protects the property owner from displacement through a system of legal protections and actions designed to oust usurpers and fend off adverse possessors. This legal construction of ownership comports with the international standards set forth in the Guiding Principles and Pinheiro Principles, as it makes no distinction based on gender or status and protects the owner's absolute right over the property owned.

REMEDIES FOR THE DISPOSSESSED

As noted, Iraqi law allows for the full protection of private ownership. To protect this right, the Iraqi Civil Code has in place a number of legal actions. That legislative scheme has been addressed in detail elsewhere (Stigall 2006, 2008), and only key points will be emphasized here. It is critical to note two characteristics of Iraqi law that have direct bearing on the plight of the displaced. First, one does not lose ownership through nonuse under Iraqi law. Second, adverse possession that is obtained by force, deceit, or in secret has no effect whatsoever on the property's ownership.[8] The Iraqi Civil Code's hostility toward possession that is tainted by coercion, secrecy, or ambiguity is critical to those who are displaced through violent or deceptive means. The fact that possession coupled with coercion is not recognized by the law means that a militia member who forcibly ousts a resident and then maintains possession of his or her home through the use or threat of force has no legal claim. The Iraqi Civil Code's refusal to recognize ambiguous or secret possession means that persons occupying homes must openly claim them as their own—bringing the fact of their adverse possession into the open and, thus, identifying themselves as displacers.

Displaced persons can regain possession via a possessory action. In this regard, there are aspects to possessory rights that are uniquely positive in the context of a post-conflict displacement scenario. Should records be lost and the ability to prove ultimate ownership thereby compromised, a displaced person can seek instead to prove that he or she had uninterrupted possession of an immovable property for one full year or more. If the displaced person can meet this standard (which does not require proof of title) then he or she may, within one year of the date of being displaced, commence legal proceedings to have his or her possession restored. It is also important to emphasize that possession may not be obtained by extrajudicial means—even if it is to retake previous and rightful possession. The only means of reinstating possession is through judicial process. This is consonant with the civil law tradition of reclaiming possession through a possessory action (Yiannopoulos 1991), as well as with the desired goal of regulating all disputes within a legal framework rather than allowing the displacement crisis to blossom into private, interneighborhood warfare (U.S. Army 2006).

Further, along with the possessory action imported from the Continental civil law tradition, the Iraqi Civil Code maintains remnants of the law of usurpation, which is derived from the Mejelle (Tyser, Demetriades, and Effendi 1967). Commentators note that Islamic jurisprudence is traditionally hostile to the wrongful taking of property. For instance, the eminent Khaled Abou El Fadl notes: "Hanafi jurist al-'Ayni (d. 855/1451) argues that the usurper of property, even if a government official [al-zalim], will not be forgiven for his sin, even if he repents

---

[8] Iraqi Civil Code. 1990. Reprinted in *Business Laws of Iraq*. Translated by N. H. Karam. London: Graham and Trotman.

218   Land and post-conflict peacebuilding

a thousand times, unless he returns the stolen property" (El Fadl 2003, 51). This is reflected in the modern Iraqi Civil Code's usurpation provisions. A 2002 case in the English House of Lords, when discussing the applicability of such law, noted:

> Articles 192 to 201 of the Iraqi Civil Code provide remedies for the civil wrong of usurpation, or misappropriation. The Code contains no definition of usurpation. Mance J held that under Iraqi law a usurper need not actually take the asset from the possession or control of its owner. Property can be usurped by keeping. Whether keeping amounts to usurpation depends on a combination of factors, including whether the alleged usurper has conducted himself in a manner showing that he was "keeping" the asset as his own.[9]

Under Iraqi law, both movable and immovable property that has been usurped by another must be returned to the rightful owner. The provisions in this regard label anyone who takes the property of another a usurper and impose on such an individual an intimidating set of obligations and liabilities. In the case of immovable property, article 197 of the Iraqi Civil Code provides that "the usurper is under an obligation to restitute it to the owner together with the comparable (true) rent; the usurper shall be liable if the immoveable has suffered damage or has depreciated even without encroachment on his part." Someone who usurps a usurper (a third possessor) has the same status as the original usurper and the same liability for damage—though the rightful owner has the option of collecting damage from either usurper or claiming part from each.

Regarding those who were forced not only to leave their property but also to convey it to another via a forced contract, the notion of the "vices of consent" reflected in article 115 of the Iraqi Civil Code also holds that contracts cannot be tainted by duress, fraud, or error. Duress, under the Iraqi Civil Code, refers to the illegal forcing of a person to do something against his or her will. It exists when there is a threat of death or bodily harm, a violent beating, or great damage to property, but not for lesser threats such as a threat of imprisonment or of a less severe beating. A threat to one's honor, however, may also constitute duress. This characteristic of Iraqi law is crucial to displaced persons, as it means that contracts that are forced or otherwise tainted will not be recognized. The nullification of contracts tainted by duress is a common feature of both Continental civil law and Islamic law. In his discussion of the Iraqi Civil Code, Oussama Arabi notes that "the most objective type of legally defective contract is that obtain[ed] under duress, where threats of death, bodily harm, or imprisonment render the contract null and void [bāṭil]. This category is the commonest kind of contract defect treated by Muslim jurists" (Arabi 1995, 156).

There are occasions, however, when the threat is not against the person conveying the property but against a third party with whom the property owner

---

[9] *Kuwait Airways Corp. v. Iraqi Airways Co.* 2002. A.C. 19 (H.L.) (U.K.).

shares a degree of affinity. In that regard, El Fadl notes that "most Muslim jurists also recognised threats of harm to third parties as duress. But they disagreed over who the third party may be. Some only recognised threats directed at parents or offsprings [sic], and a few recognised even threats directed at strangers" (El Fadl 1991, 129). The Iraqi Civil Code, like other civil codes in the French family, takes a middle ground on the issue of third parties, stating only that a threat to cause injury to one's parents, spouse, or an unmarried relative on the maternal side may rise to the level of duress. As addressed more fully below, the Iraqi law in this regard is unduly restrictive and in need of amendment.

It is worth mentioning another provision of the Iraqi Civil Code that is of great benefit to displaced persons. Article 435 notes that time limits barring the hearing of a case are suspended by an "impediment rendering it impossible for the plaintiff to claim his right." This rule is of obvious benefit to persons who are unable to reach their homes due to violence or who are trapped in Jordan, Syria, Egypt, or elsewhere, and who might otherwise see their legal rights extinguished by the passage of time. Together with the provisions protecting ownership, allowing actions to regain property, and allowing rescission of forced contracts, these laws provide a phalanx of protections for the displaced property owner.

DESTROYED PROPERTY

Aside from adverse possession, another cause of displacement is the destruction of property. In the ordinary case, involving non-Coalition actors,[10] the primary civil remedy for the destruction of property is an action in tort. The Iraqi Civil Code contains a general article, article 202, stating that "every act which is injurious to persons such as murder, wounding, assault, or any other kind of [infliction of] injury entails payment of damages by the perpetrator." In cases of murder or injuries resulting in death, the perpetrator is obligated to pay compensation to the dependents of the victim who were deprived of sustenance because of the wrongful act. Every assault that causes damage, other than damage expressly detailed in other articles, also requires compensation. This article has been incorrectly interpreted in the past as mandating strict liability for all damages (Amin 1990; Stigall 2008), but Iraqi jurisprudence has actually interpreted it as requiring some deviation from a normal standard of care (Al Hakim, Al Bakri, and Al Bashir 1980).

The Iraqi Civil Code allows only limited forms of *respondeat superior* (literally, "let the master answer," a legal doctrine referring to one person's liability for the actions of another), which are clearly delineated. These include the liability of owners of animals for damage by their animals; the liability of the father or grandfather of a minor who causes injury; and the liability of owners of buildings

---

[10] In this chapter, *Coalition* refers to the Multi-National Force-Iraq, an international coalition force composed of twenty-six nations, including the United States. It operated in Iraq under the unified command of the U.S. military officers, at the Iraqi government's request, and in accordance with United Nations Security Council resolutions.

220   Land and post-conflict peacebuilding

that collapse due to dilapidation. The most significant exception to the rule against vicarious liability, however, is that government municipalities and commercial entities are not liable for injuries caused by their employees during the course of their service.

There are, as one might expect, defenses to liability and exceptions to the general rule, such as in cases of force majeure. In addition, personal injuries are permissible when committed in order to ward off public injury. No claim for damages resulting from any unlawful act can be brought after three years from the day that the injured person became aware of the injury, nor can any claim be brought after fifteen years from the day of the occurrence. As noted above, however, such time limitations are subject to exceptions, such as when an impediment prevents the exercise of a right.

Thus, the Iraqi Civil Code contains a rich and detailed regime of law allowing for civil actions against those who cause damage to another—including the damaging or destruction of their property. Displaced persons, therefore, have a remedy not only for property taken from them but also for property that has been intentionally damaged or destroyed. They may both reclaim their property and assert a claim for any diminution in its value due to the action of a third party.

SECONDARY OCCUPANTS

The Guiding Principles do not specifically mention secondary occupants. The Pinheiro Principles, however, do address this issue. They provide that states should protect such persons from unlawful eviction but that, when such evictions are warranted, the secondary occupants should be afforded due process, an opportunity for consultation, reasonable notice, and appropriate legal remedies. Further, where property has been sold by secondary occupants to third parties acting in good faith, the Pinheiro Principles provide that "states may consider establishing mechanisms to provide compensation to injured third parties" (UN 2005, sec. V, para. 17.4). Where the circumstances indicate that the property being sold was illegally acquired, however, such compensation is not required. Iraqi law fully comports with these requirements.

Under article 1148 of the Iraqi Civil Code, persons who, in good faith, purchase property from secondary occupants are "good faith possessors." Such persons are allowed to appropriate the surpluses and benefits of the thing possessed during the time of their possession. They would also have an action against the secondary occupant who sold the land, through application of the general tort action in articles 202 and 204. Such persons would not, however, obtain ownership of the property unless they got the property through a normal means of conveyance or acquisition—such as a donation or sale by the true owner.

Regarding those who sign a lease to live in a place (renters), the Iraqi Civil Code has a highly regulated legal regime. The code defines a lease, in article 722, as "the alienation of a definite advantage in return for a defined

Refugees, displaced persons, and legal reform in Iraq 221

consideration for a certain specified period by which the lessor will be bound to enable the lessee to enjoy the leased [property]." This is a definition that comports with both Continental civil law and Ottoman law.[11]

Under Iraqi Civil Code, article 750(1), a lessor is "bound to repair and restore any defect in the leased property" that has resulted in interference with its intended use. If the lessor fails to do so, the lessee may either rescind the contract or, with a court's permission, carry out the repairs and restoration and claim the expenses from the lessor. If, for some reason not imputable to the lessee, the property becomes unfit for its intended use, or if such use is appreciably diminished, the lessor must restore the land to its original condition. If the lessor fails to do so, the lessee may demand a reduction in the rent or rescind the contract. If the leased property perishes in its entirety during the lease, the contract is considered rescinded.

The leased property is considered to be a trust in the hands of the lessee. Any use by the lessee of the property other than in accordance with ordinary use is considered to be an encroachment, and the lessee will be held liable for all damage resulting therefrom. Like other Iraqi contracts, a contract of lease may contain stipulations such as "an option to rescind the lease within a certain period of time," as per Iraqi Civil Code, article 726. If such an option was for both the lessor and the lessee, the lease will be rescinded if either party rescinds the contract within the stated time limit. There is an automatic option available to every lessee who has leased something without inspecting it, allowing him or her to accept or rescind the lease after inspection. This right does not extend to lessors.

A lease in Iraq may last for quite a long time. Normally, a lease that is perpetual—made for a period exceeding thirty years—may be terminated after the lapse of thirty years. If, however, the lease contract stipulates that the lease will continue in force as long as the lessee continues to pay rent, it is considered to be a contract for the lifetime of the lessee.

If leased property is usurped by a third party and the lessee is unable to reclaim the property from the usurper, the lessee may claim rescission of the contract or reduction of the rent. If the lessee has not reclaimed the property— but could have done so—the lessee shall not be exonerated from payment of the rent. The lessee may, however, commence proceedings against the usurper for damages.

If either party fails to perform any obligation in the lease contract (to pay rent, etc.), the other party may demand rescission of the contract and damages— but only after having first served notice, requiring the other party to perform his or her obligation. If the leased property is destroyed, the contract of lease is terminated.

Accordingly, one sees in the Iraqi Civil Code's provisions on leases that the lessee has a number of rights and protections against eviction. The lessor has a

---

[11] This legal concept has deep legal roots and is commonly accepted. See, for example, the Louisiana Civil Code of 1870.

222 Land and post-conflict peacebuilding

number of obligations to maintain the property and, if the property becomes unfit for habitation, the lessee can rescind his contract and is not bound to pay rent. There are, of course, limitations that are inherent in the concept of a lease. For instance, because the property belongs to the lessor, the lessee is primarily reliant on the lessor to take action to restore the property and remove impediments to its use. Further, the primary remedy of a lessee is always rescission and damages. If property is destroyed, there is no legal right to a new home—only rescission of the contract. Likewise, if the lessee is dispossessed and cannot reclaim possession, his or her only option is to rescind the contract and find housing elsewhere.

BLIND SPOTS: MILITARY DAMAGE AND INTERFERING LEGISLATION

The analysis above demonstrates that the Iraqi Civil Code provides a system of rules that is well suited for the task of regulating the claims of those displaced by conflict in Iraq. It provides a mechanism to protect ownership and other rights in property, allows owners a means of redress against adverse possessors, and—where appropriate—protects the rights of secondary occupants. Like any functional legal system, it enforces one property right against another and thus serves as an excellent means of effecting restitution in situations where persons have been dispossessed by others. As demonstrated, however, there are weaknesses in substantive Iraqi civil law that arise, in part, from legislation external to the Iraqi Civil Code—weaknesses that should be remedied so that Iraqi law can better comply with international standards and more effectively address the needs of Iraqi citizens. Those weaknesses are principally in the areas of military damage and the separate statutes that eclipse or otherwise weaken the protections provided by the Iraqi Civil Code.

Military damage

Aside from adverse possession of property, another means of causing displacement is through the destruction of property. As noted above, the Iraqi Civil Code offers a clear civil action against those who wrongfully destroy the property of another—though that option changes when the property is destroyed by military action undertaken by Coalition forces. The remedies for persons displaced in such a manner have historically been quite limited. This is because the ability to bring a claim for combat-related damage against Coalition forces or contractors working with the Coalition is practically nonexistent.

The first regulation of the Coalition Provisional Authority stated that the authority "shall exercise powers of government temporarily in order to provide for the effective administration of Iraq during the period of transitional administration," and that it "is vested with all executive, legislative and judicial authority necessary to achieve its objectives" (Murphy 2004, 602). Importantly, the regulation also provided that "'laws in force in Iraq as of April 16, 2003 shall continue to

Refugees, displaced persons, and legal reform in Iraq 223

apply' unless they would inhibit the CPA or conflict with its regulations or orders, and only until such time as they were suspended or replaced by the CPA or 'democratic institutions of Iraq'" (Murphy 2004, 602).

The most important CPA legislation in terms of tort liability was CPA Order Number 17, which stated that, "unless provided otherwise herein, the MNF [multinational forces], the CPA, Foreign Liaison Missions, their Personnel, property, funds and assets, and all International Consultants shall be immune from Iraqi legal process" (Bremer 2004, sec. 2, para. 1). That same order also stated that all "MNF, CPA and Foreign Liaison Mission Personnel, and International Consultants shall be subject to the exclusive jurisdiction of their Sending States. They shall be immune from any form of arrest or detention other than by persons acting on behalf of their Sending States" (Bremer 2004, sec. 2, para. 3). With regard to contractors, it expressly provided:

> Contractors shall be immune from Iraqi legal process with respect to acts performed by them pursuant to the terms and conditions of a Contract or any sub-contract thereto. Nothing in this provision shall prohibit MNF Personnel from preventing acts of serious misconduct by Contractors, or otherwise temporarily detaining any Contractors who pose a risk of injury to themselves or others, pending expeditious turnover to the appropriate authorities of the Sending State (Bremer 2004, sec. 4, para. 3).

As a result, most Coalition personnel working in Iraq were granted a rather generous shield of immunity, while ordinary Iraqi citizens (and others found within the jurisdiction of Iraq) were not. This did not mean, however, that Iraqi citizens were completely without recourse. A means of asserting claims against U.S. forces is allowable under two different statutory schemes: the International Agreements Claims Act (IACA)[12] and the Foreign Claims Act (FCA).[13]

The IACA allows settlement of meritorious claims against the United States pursuant to U.S. obligations under international law. A status of forces agreement (SOFA) is the most common form of agreement to trigger application of the IACA.[14] In such cases, the terms of the applicable SOFA generally provide the mechanisms for investigating and settling (or denying) claims against U.S. forces. Prior to the implementation of the SOFA with Iraq, however, the IACA did not apply; and, as discussed below, even with the current security agreement in force, its applicability is questionable. Thus, the FCA has been the principal device for Iraqi citizens seeking a remedy for damage occasioned by Coalition forces.

The FCA permits the settlement of claims arising outside the United States and submitted by foreign governments and inhabitants of foreign countries. Under the FCA, meritorious claims for property losses, personal injury, or death caused by military personnel or members of the civilian component of the U.S. forces

---

[12] 10 U.S.C., sec. 2734(a) (2005).
[13] 10 U.S.C., sec. 2734 (2005).
[14] See, for example, Bredemeyer (1997).

224   Land and post-conflict peacebuilding

may be settled in order "to promote and maintain friendly relations" with the country where U.S. forces are operating. The foreign claims commissioners apply local law and customs to determine liability and the amount of any award, and their decisions on claims are final.[15] Claims under the FCA are paid entirely with U.S. funds, but the claimants usually receive payment in the local currency (U.S. Army 2008a). The statute has been widely used to pay claims submitted by local nationals in Iraq, Afghanistan, Kosovo, and Bosnia and Herzegovina (Masterton 2005).

The FCA permits recovery for damages caused by "noncombat activities" and negligent or wrongful acts by U.S. military personnel and employees. Commentators note that there is no requirement that the negligent or wrongful acts occur within the scope of the perpetrator's employment (Masterton 2005). The FCA, therefore, is frequently used by foreign inhabitants to recover for damage caused by off-duty military personnel in traffic accidents and similar incidents.

The key exception to this payment scheme, however, is that it does not permit payment for combat-related damage. Army Regulation (AR) 27-20 notes that "a claim for death, personal injury, or loss of or damage to property may be allowed under this chapter if the alleged damage results from noncombat activity or a negligent or wrongful act or omission of Soldiers or civilian employees of the Armed Forces of the United States, . . . regardless of whether the act or omission was made within the scope of their employment."[16] The regulation defines "noncombat activities" as

> authorized activities essentially military in nature, having little parallel in civilian pursuits, which historically have been considered as furnishing a proper basis for payment of claims. Examples are practice firing of missiles and weapons, training, and field exercises, maneuvers that include the operation of aircraft and vehicles, use and occupancy of real estate in the absence of a contract or international agreement covering such use, and movement of combat or other vehicles designed especially for military use. Certain civil works activities such as inverse condemnation are also included. Activities excluded are those incident to combat, whether in time of war or not, and use of military personnel and civilian employees in connection with civil disturbances.[17]

While the regulation leaves open room for recovery for wrongful acts committed by soldiers, its exclusion of activities "incident to combat" swallows the activities most likely to destroy housing, such as bombing or extensive use of weapons.

In an effort to overcome this gap in the ability of Iraqi citizens to file a claim, military commanders used the flexibility of the Commander's Emergency Response Program (CERP), which allows them to expend funds in order to facilitate certain

---

[15]   U.S. Department of the Army, Regulation 27-20, Claims, paras. 10-5a and 10-6f(3) (8 Feb. 2008) [hereinafter AR 27-20].

[16]   AR 27-20, para. 10-3(a).

[17]   AR 27-20, Glossary, sec. II (Terms).

specified objectives (Davis 2004). In implementing CERP, the U.S. Congress authorized the Department of Defense to use funds "to respond to urgent humanitarian relief and reconstruction . . . by carrying out programs that will immediately assist the Iraqi people, and to establish and fund a similar program to assist the people of Afghanistan" (Davis 2004, 204). On July 27, 2005, the undersecretary of defense (comptroller) issued guidance that broadened the permissible uses for CERP to include the repair of damage resulting from U.S., Coalition, or supporting military operations and is not compensable under the FCA; condolence payments to individual civilians for death, injury, or property damage resulting from U.S., Coalition, or supporting military operations; and payments to individuals upon release from detention (Santiago 2006). Thus, the gap left by the FCA was bridged, to a degree, by military commanders through the use of CERP.

A key feature of CERP, however, is that it is a tool at the discretion of the military commander and does not in any way create a right for the person who has lost property or been displaced (GAO 2008). In other words, CERP is a matter of command grace rather than an Iraqi citizen's right (see table 1). The ability of the displaced Iraqi citizen to receive restitution for destroyed property through that legal mechanism is, therefore, somewhat limited. Where U.S. contractors or Coalition forces are concerned, this is a rather pronounced blind spot.

Recent developments have done little to bridge the gap. The 2008 security agreement between Iraq and the United States addresses compensation for military damage in article 21.[18] Pursuant to that provision, Iraq waived the right to claim compensation "for any damage, loss, or destruction of property, or compensation for injuries or deaths" inflicted upon "members of the force or civilian component." As for damage to ordinary civilians, however, article 21 provides that:

> United States Forces authorities shall pay just and reasonable compensation in settlement of meritorious third party claims arising out of acts, omissions, or negligence of members of the United States Forces and of the civilian component done in the performance of their official duties and incident to the non-combat activities of the United States Forces. United States Forces authorities may also settle meritorious claims not arising from the performance of official duties. All claims in this paragraph shall be settled expeditiously in accordance with the laws and regulations of the United States. In settling claims, United States Forces authorities shall take into account any report of investigation or opinion regarding liability or amount of damages issued by Iraqi authorities.

The language of the security agreement is striking in three regards: (1) it is mandatory in nature (seemingly obligating the United States to pay some claims); (2) it is vague in detail, deferring to U.S. law rather than establishing a claims

---

[18] Agreement between the United States of America and the Republic of Iraq on the Withdrawal of United States Forces from Iraq and the Organization of their Activities During their Temporary Presence in Iraq, signed in November 2008 and put into effect in January 2009. For its complete text, see http://graphics8.nytimes.com/packages/pdf/world/20081119_SOFA_FINAL_AGREED_TEXT.pdf.

Table 1.   Means of legal recovery for displaced Iraqis

Nature of dispossession	Available remedy	Comment	Provision	Limitation
Adverse possession of property	Possessory action	Restitution is possible, but time limits in ICC art. 435 could apply.	ICC arts. 1145–1152	Some evidence is required on the part of the claimant.
	Usurpation action	Possessory action is available where proof of ownership is lacking.	ICC arts. 192–201	
Property destroyed by insurgents/militia	Civil tort action	This allows compensation for destroyed property.	ICC arts. 202, 204–231	There is no guarantee that the defendant can pay damages that are awarded.
Property destroyed by military operation	Military claim or CERP	This falls into a jurisdictional and administrative blind spot, which military commanders can avoid through CERP.	SOFA art. 21 (Foreign Claims Act and CERP)	CERP is a tool to be used at the military commander's discretion, not a restitution mechanism.
Rented property destroyed	Action under ICC arts. 202, 204, and 755	Rent is no longer paid once the contract is rescinded.	ICC art. 751	Displaced renters are not necessarily entitled to new housing.
Forced contract	Rescission of contract under ICC art. 112	This is an indirect form of coercion that is sometimes used by militias and others seeking to oust particular residents from their homes.	ICC art. 112	This applies only in cases of threats to the person conveying property and his or her parents, spouse, or an unmarried relative on the maternal side.

Note: ICC: Iraqi Civil Code; CERP: Commander's Emergency Response Program; SOFA: status of forces agreement.

mechanism; and (3) it limits the sorts of payable claims to those "incident to the non-combat activities of the United States Forces." While the SOFA, therefore, seems to implement some form of official claims process, the language seems to keep in place the current statutory scheme by formally agreeing that such claims will not encompass combat-related damage and by stating that the claims will be governed according to "the laws and regulations of the United States." This would indicate that claims by Iraqi citizens will continue to be governed by the combination of the FCA and CERP discussed above.

However, even if this language is interpreted to implicate the IACA (as that legislative scheme applies to agreements between the United States and other nations, if the agreements provide for "settlement or adjudication and cost sharing of claims against the United States"),[19] payment under that legislative scheme is discretionary, stating that "when the United States is a party to an international agreement which provides for the settlement or adjudication and cost sharing of claims against the United States . . . the Secretary of Defense or the Secretary of Homeland Security or their designees *may* . . . reimburse the party to the agreement [or] . . . pay the party to the agreement the agreed pro rata share of any claim, including any authorized arbitration costs, for damage to property owned by it, in accordance with the agreement" (emphasis added). Nothing in the statutory language of the IACA actually requires payment. Further, both the security agreement and the statutory language of the IACA provide that combat-related damage is not payable.

Accordingly, in most cases, the current security agreement does not provide a restitution mechanism for Iraqis who are displaced due to military action. Therefore, the gap in the current restitution scheme in Iraq is still present. To remedy this deficiency, either the FCA should be amended or new legislation should be introduced to create a claims process whereby such claims could be "investigated, adjudicated, and settled" (Prescott 1998, 1). This could be effected through U.S. legislation modifying current restrictions, or through Iraqi legislation permitting such claims to be paid from Iraqi funds. While such a solution would not necessarily empower a domestic Iraqi entity, it must be remembered that domestic courts rarely have the ability to enforce judgments against other sovereign nations. Unlike a judgment against an Iraqi, when it comes to a judgment against another sovereign nation, a host of legal realities and jurisdictional limitations would necessarily render Iraqi judgments against the United States useless. Accordingly, any realistic solution must rely on modifications to U.S. law or an agreed-upon settlement mechanism in order to completely close the hole that was torn open in Iraqi civil law through post-invasion legislative modification. Although U.S. troops have withdrawn from Iraq, numerous claims related to military damage likely still linger, and those aggrieved Iraqis should not be left without recourse.

---

[19] 10 U.S.C., sec. 2734a(a) (2006).

228   Land and post-conflict peacebuilding

Interfering legislation

Not all weaknesses in Iraqi civil law governing the rights of displaced persons are due to external interference or foreign meddling. Procedural requirements, some of which are addressed in detail below, can serve to hinder displaced persons' return and resettlement by creating obstacles that they are in no position to surmount. Some areas of substantive law, likewise, are cause for concern. A comprehensive review of Iraqi legislation should be undertaken to identify all such legal hindrances. What follows in this chapter does not constitute a complete analysis of all aspects of Iraqi civil law in need of modification. While such a project (and the concomitant reforms it would surely bring) would be of great benefit to Iraq, the aims of this chapter are far more modest. The discussion below seeks to identify a few of the most obvious shortfalls of the legislation currently in force and some easy steps that could be taken to address some of Iraq's most pressing legal issues regarding land.

At a 2008 conference in Amman, Jordan, sponsored by the U.S. Institute for Peace, Iraqi jurists expressed concern over Iraq's Land Registration Law—a statute separate from the Iraqi Civil Code—which could possibly allow the transfer of property in situations where there has been coercion (Isser and Van der Auweraert 2009). This statute could overrule the protections granted by the Iraqi Civil Code that, as described above, would invalidate any transaction tainted by undue coercion. Allowing coerced transfers of property would inflict significant injustice on the victims of such violence and sow further discord among Iraqi citizens. Accordingly, Iraq's Land Registration Law should be amended so that the protections of the Iraqi Civil Code apply in all transfers.

Likewise, although the Iraqi Civil Code's provisions on leases are equitable in operation, Iraqi lease law becomes problematic with the provisions of a separate statute known as Lease Law No. 87 of 1979—a statute that supersedes the Iraqi Civil Code and prevents Iraqi citizens from availing themselves of its protections. For instance, article 17(1) of Lease Law No. 87 states that if a lessee does not pay the rent within seven days after its due date, the lessor shall warn him or her through a notary public that he or she has eight days from the date of notification to pay the rent. The lessee shall pay all the expenses incurred by the lessor in making this notification. The lessee may benefit from this eight-day window of protection once a year, starting from the date of the last warning. Thereafter, the lessor may evict the lessee at any time if the lessee does not pay the rent within fifteen days after its due date. Further, article 17(7) of the law states that if the leased property remains uninhabited for more than forty-five days without any excuse, the lessor may institute eviction proceedings.

Such a legal scheme creates numerous problems for displaced persons, as there is no exception in the law to extend the forty-five-day period for reasons associated with displacement. Thus, displaced persons who rent their homes may return to find themselves legally evicted. Once again, a statute separate from the

Iraqi Civil Code serves to undo the protections of the legal scheme. Commentators have noted the undesirability of such legislation in the context of displacement. Rhodri Williams, a consultant with the Brookings–Bern Project on Internal Displacement, has proposed several specific legal initiatives to augment the Iraqi government's ability to remedy the ills associated with its displacement crisis. For example, Williams notes: "The Iraqi authorities should clearly state that the long-standing provisions of the Iraqi Civil Code on property title remain in force. These rules specify that true title does not pass with property acquired unlawfully; that transfers of property made under duress are invalid; and that those wrongfully dispossessed are entitled to the return of their property as well as compensation for lost income streams such as rental agreements or crops" (Williams 2008, 4).

In order to do so, the government of Iraq must undertake a review of all civil legislation in force—including the Land Registration Law and Lease Law No. 87 of 1979—and ensure that none of them operate to eclipse or otherwise limit the protections expressly granted under the Iraqi Civil Code. In other words, the code's provisions invalidating transfers of property that are made under duress, fraudulently, or clandestinely should prevail in all circumstances, and no legislation should operate in a way that interferes with those protections. Any such legislation should be repealed or amended, so that the protections of the Iraqi Civil Code again occupy a place of preeminence in the legal order.

LEGISLATIVE ADJUSTMENTS TO MEET CONTEMPORARY CHALLENGES

As demonstrated above, the Iraqi Civil Code provides an adequate legal scheme for providing restitution to property owners who have been displaced or who have suffered a loss due to damaged property. Given its cultural importance, any adjustments made to Iraqi substantive law should be carefully considered and made within the context of Iraq's legal tradition—one which has strong ties to the French Civil Code as well as to the law of the Ottoman Empire (Jwaideh 1953). In that regard, an analysis of the Iraqi system of civil law reveals means by which Iraqi law could be adjusted in order to strengthen the ability of displaced persons to regain their property: providing exemptions from time limits, broadening the application of duress, and adopting the traditional civilian concepts of *lésion* (the substantive unfairness of a transaction due to the disproportionate nature of the contract) (Bell, Boyron, and Whittaker 1998) and *negotiorum gestio* (management of the affairs of another).

Revising statutes of limitations to protect claimants

As noted above, consistent with the civilian concept of *contra non valentum agere nulla currit praescriptio* (a Latin maxim meaning "prescription does not run against a party unable to act"), the Iraqi Civil Code contains provisions that

230   Land and post-conflict peacebuilding

lift time limits in cases where a person has not been capable of exercising his or her rights. Williams suggests that the Iraqi government "should clearly state that the current violence makes it presumptively impossible for displaced persons to invoke remedies under the Code, in order to ensure that their claims are preserved against the workings of statutes of limitations" (Williams 2008, 5). Additional legislation could, therefore, be enacted to reinforce the existing protections available under Iraqi law and state unequivocally that claims for lost or damaged property are not to be extinguished due to the passing of time, so long as the current conflict and violence continues.

Broadening the scope of duress

The Iraqi Civil Code's treatment of duress contains strong protections for those forced to sign contracts. These protections, however, have significant limitations in terms of scope, as duress is only actionable where the threat is to cause injury to one's parents, spouse, or an unmarried relative on the maternal side. This leaves a host of family members available as targets for duress—mainly those unmarried family members outside the party's immediate family and married family members on the maternal side. Given the current circumstances in Iraq and the innumerable ways of inflicting duress and cruelty, such limitations are clearly inappropriate.

In order to remedy this problem, article 112 of the Iraqi Civil Code should be amended to allow that duress can serve to vitiate a contract when threats are directed against third parties. Models for such legislative changes exist to guide Iraqi legislators in this amendment. In 1984, the scope of duress was broadened in Louisiana, another civil law jurisdiction, which adheres to the same basic precepts in the realm of contract defects. Writing on this legislative change, the renowned jurist Saul Litvinoff noted that French doctrine favored a broader application of duress so that duress against a wider spectrum of third parties could result in rescission of a contract (Litvinoff 1989). Of that change, Litvinoff writes:

> A new article makes duress effective as a vice of consent not only when directed against a spouse, an ascendant, or a descendant of a party to a contract, but also when directed against others, such as a person toward whom a party may feel strong friendship or with whom a party may have a close relationship either based on or productive of strong affection. In such a case the court is allowed the discretion necessary to find whether a particular relation between a party to a contract and a third person is of a nature such as to make that party vulnerable to duress exerted through the creation of a situation of danger to the third person. That solution, which is perfectly consistent with societal values, is recommended by French doctrine (Litvinoff 1989, 105–106).

By emulating this legislative change, article 112 of the Iraqi Civil Code could be changed to allow duress to be actionable against third parties if the court finds that the particular relation between a party to a contract and the third person is

Refugees, displaced persons, and legal reform in Iraq 231

of such a nature as to make that party vulnerable to duress. This would keep all contracts from being unreasonably undermined while allowing that—in appropriate circumstances—duress against others can result in undue coercion.

It must be noted that this is not merely a European notion. Citing Islamic jurists, Khaled Abou El Fadl notes that "Ibn Hazm, for example, after citing a *hadith* (*hadith* are sayings . . . by the Prophet often serving as the basis of legislation) stating that Muslims are brothers, argues that it follows that they should protect each other. Since Muslims are joined by mutual empathy, harm to a third party, even a stranger, will cause enough grief to constitute duress" (El Fadl 1991, 152n126). Broadening the scope of duress in Iraqi law would, therefore, be consistent with the practices of other civil law jurisdictions (such as France and Louisiana) as well as in keeping with Islamic law. It would also ensure that contracts involving threats against people who are not family members of the victim are not considered valid.

Protecting against forced transfers of property through lésion

Displacement of persons in Iraq has been perpetrated in numerous ways, including violence and the threat of violence.[20] While the sight of someone signing a contract at gunpoint might be an obvious indication of duress and would give rise to rescission based on the principles discussed above, not all forms of duress are so apparent or easy to prove. Someone who is forced to sell property due to threats made to a family member or some equally pernicious, though indirect, exercise of violence may not be able to prove his or her claim in a legal forum. In such circumstances, Iraqi legislators may provide some relief through the adoption of a variant of the traditional civilian concept of lésion.

The classic example of lésion as a reason to invalidate a contract is in the sale of an immovable property for less than seven-twelfths of its value. In 1830, Antoine Marie Demante explained this concept:

> Though, in general, lésion is not a cause of restitution in major transactions, the law, taking into account the position of the seller and that the need for money often forces a seller to sell property for less than the fair price, grants the seller an action in rescission; but to use that action it is necessary: 1) that the object sold be immovable property; 2) that the lésion is more than seven-twelfths. As for the rest, this action for rescission, founded on notions of equity, exists notwithstanding any clause or contrary stipulation because such clauses, which elsewhere have become the style, are infected with the same vice that plagues the underlying sale (Demante 1830, 174).[21]

The French legal tradition, therefore, automatically concludes that certain contracts are so disproportionate or contain certain indications of unfairness that give

---

[20] See, for example, Ridolfo (2006).
[21] Translation provided by Dan E. Stigall, author of this chapter.

232   Land and post-conflict peacebuilding

rise to an automatic right of rescission to the seller. Commentators note that the concept has expanded through time and that, through legislative augmentation, numerous types of contracts in contemporary France are now subject to rescission because of various indications of unfairness (Bell, Boyron, and Whittaker 1998).

The Iraqi Civil Code—a descendant of the French Civil Code—could be amended to incorporate this concept and tailor it to the specific context of Iraq. This could be done in an obvious manner, such as adjusting the proportion in the selling price of the immovable upward or downward. It could also be done in a more creative way, such as deeming all transfers of property conducted in a certain place during a certain time unfair due to the level of violence and history of displacement.[22] Displaced persons, therefore, would be granted an additional protection through their ability to rescind certain transfers of immovable property based on objective criteria.

Managing the affairs of another, or negotiorum gestio

Another traditional civilian concept that could be incorporated into the Iraqi Civil Code is that of negotiorum gestio, or *gestion d'affaires*. This concept, which is Roman in origin, is a defining feature of the French system of civil law (Bell, Boyron, and Whittaker 1998). Pursuant to this doctrine, a quasi-contract is formed where a person voluntarily and intentionally performs a useful act for the benefit of another or on another's behalf (Bell, Boyron, and Whittaker 1998). The classic example of such an act is boarding up a vacationing neighbor's windows as a hurricane approaches, or mending his roof prior to a storm.

> The justification for the obligations imposed on both parties by *gestion d'affaires* is said to lie in a policy of encouraging citizens to help each other by requiring some recompense when they attempt to do so: it fosters, therefore, a limited altruism. This lies behind the requirement of an intention to act on behalf of or for the benefit of (*'pour le compte'*) the *maître* [the owner of the property] and it distinguishes *gestion d'affaires* from *enrichissement sans cause* where no such requirement is made. As a result, in general it will not arise where a person acts in his own interest even though this benefits the would-be *maître* (Bell, Boyron, and Whittaker 1998, 403).

Once such an act has been performed, the owner must indemnify the helper for the useful and necessary expenses he or she incurred during the altruistic intervention (Bell, Boyron, and Whittaker 1998). Commentators note that this

---

[22] For a discussion of the application and challenges of such an approach in Bosnia and Herzegovina, see Rhodri C. Williams, "Post-Conflict Land Tenure Issues in Bosnia: Privatization and the Politics of Reintegrating the Displaced," in this book.

requirement that the helper's acts be useful allows courts to keep philanthropy from becoming "a screen for ill-timed, inappropriate or selfish interventions" (Bell, Boyron, and Whittaker 1998, 404; citations omitted).

The concept of negotiorum gestio serves "the uniquely civilian goal of providing an incentive to protect another's interests in the exceptional case in which a person is unable to manage his own affairs" (Martin 1994, 212). Amending the Iraqi Civil Code to incorporate a negotiorum gestio provision might well serve to encourage citizens to care for one another's property to a greater degree, take steps to ensure that others do not occupy it while the owner is absent, and deter others from damaging or taking it. Joseph Raz referred to such norms as "principles guiding behavior," which can shape the social order by providing motivation to induce individuals to behave in a certain manner (Raz 1980, 124–125). As other commentators have noted: "Laws may significantly reduce the incidence of certain acts, thereby preventing people from forming habits they might otherwise form; and second, laws may be part of the complex mixture of forces that contribute to the shaping of people's moral ideas" (Wolfe 2000, 68). Given the unique property issues that confront contemporary Iraq, such legislative encouragement is worth a try.

Summary

It must be reemphasized that the suggestions above do not constitute all the potential modifications that could be made in Iraqi civil law to facilitate the return and resettlement of refugees and displaced persons. Such a project would go far beyond the confines of a single chapter. Furthermore, none of the proposed modifications alone would cure all the ills associated with the current displacement crisis or reverse the processes giving rise to continued displacement. Nonetheless, the modifications would constitute definite improvements and would help Iraqi civil law to better address the problems confronting displaced persons. Duress could be broadened through minor legislative changes that would leave Iraqi law in line with both Continental civil law and Islamic legal tradition. Moreover, as the concepts of lésion and negotiorum gestio are firmly grounded in the Continental civil law tradition to which Iraq belongs, Iraqi judges could look to the jurisprudence of Continental civil law jurisdictions around the globe to help define and apply these new provisions. This would occur through application of article 1(3) of the Iraqi Civil Code, which states that judges shall be guided by the judgments of the "judiciary and jurisprudence in Iraq and then of the other countries the laws of which are proximate to the laws of Iraq."

While none of these amendments would be a panacea for all of Iraq's displacement woes, together with the constellation of protections currently available in the Iraqi Civil Code, they would buttress the legal armaments available to the displaced and facilitate the just resolution of property disputes in a forum that is fair, effective, and legitimate.

234 Land and post-conflict peacebuilding

CONCLUSION

The displacement crisis in Iraqi is real and ongoing. The large-scale displacement—which once served to drive civilians to join militias and, thereby, fuel an insurgency which plagued the U.S. military effort (Younes and Rosen 2008)—continues to plague Iraq after the U.S. military's departure. The International Rescue Committee notes, "As the U.S. government withdraws its troops from Iraq, it leaves behind a major crisis in the region—with three million Iraqis displaced and desperate and tens of thousands of others in danger because they worked for the U.S. military" (IRC 2011). Solutions to this crisis must, therefore, be quickly sought and immediately implemented. The solutions must comport with international standards but must also—given the nature of the crisis—be effective, immediate, and durable. These criteria mandate that a solution be found within the existing legal machinery in Iraq.

The Guiding Principles on Internal Displacement and the Pinheiro Principles articulate the rights and obligations relating to displaced persons under international law. Those instruments make certain demands on a nation's substantive civil law, primarily in the way the nation's legal architecture frames the nature of property ownership, the means of restitution, and the protection given to secondary occupants. Iraqi's civil law system, currently the only option for those displaced since 2003, is a modern, advanced system that recognizes and protects private ownership through its sophisticated regime of legal actions. It provides for actions by which displaced persons can reclaim their property and even allows for lesser property rights (such as possessory rights) that can be utilized by people whose records have been destroyed during the conflict. A series of legal provisions regulate the rights and duties of secondary occupants, giving them appropriate protections and a fair amount of due process.

Thus, the existing Iraqi civil law system is an adequate legal scheme for providing restitution to property owners who have been displaced or who have suffered a loss due to damaged property. Although it contains a major blind spot in its lack of remedies for those who lose property due to military action, such a blind spot is not due to any organic defect in the Iraqi legal system but, rather, to the imposition of legislation by the CPA. In addition, further legislative action could provide even greater protections to displaced persons by giving the protections of the Iraqi Civil Code a place of greater preeminence in the legal system, dispensing with unnecessary legal provisions that inhibit the protections contained in the Iraqi code, and ensuring that claims are not extinguished by the passage of time. Further, broadening the scope of duress and incorporating the concepts of lésion and negotiorum gestio would augment the existing legal system in a way that better serves the interests of the displaced and in a manner consistent with the Iraqi legal tradition.

With the current state of affairs in Iraq, time is of the essence. By devoting resources now to Iraq's civil courts, increasing their institutional capacity, making minor legislative modifications, and preparing for the claims to come, the

Refugees, displaced persons, and legal reform in Iraq   235

government of Iraq can effectively confront the challenge before it. Acting otherwise would only result in wasted time and prolonged suffering. It would also make Iraqi law—with all its history and cultural importance—one more victim of the displacement crisis. Policymakers would do very well, in that regard, to heed the words of Michel de Montaigne, who wrote: "It is very easy to accuse the government of imperfection, for all mortal things are full of it. It is very easy to engender in a people contempt for their ancient observances; never did a man undertake that without succeeding. But as for establishing a better state in place of the one they have ruined, many of those who have attempted it have achieved nothing for their pains" (Montaigne 1580/1958, 498).

REFERENCES

Al Hakim, A. M., A. B. Al Bakri, and M. T. Al Bashir. 1980. *The compendium on the theory of obligation in the Iraq Civil Code.* Translated by H. Hamoudi. Baghdad: al-Jumhūrīyah al-'Irāqīyah, Wizārat al-Ta'līm al-'Ālīwa-al-Bahth al-'Ilmī.

Amin, S. H. 1990. *Legal system of Iraq.* Glasgow, Scotland: Royston.

Arabi, O. 1995. Al-Sanhūrī's reconstruction of the Islamic law of contract defects. *Journal of Islamic Studies* 6 (2): 153–172.

Ardolino, B. 2008. Inside Iraqi politics – Part 3. Examining the legislative branch. *Long War Journal,* February 13. www.longwarjournal.org/archives/2008/02/inside_iraqi _politic_2.php.

Bali, A. U. 2005. Justice under the occupation: Rule of law and the ethics of nation-building in Iraq. *Yale Journal of International Law* 30:431–438.

Beard, J. 2007. *The political economy of desire: International law, development and the nation state.* New York: Routledge-Cavendish.

Bell, J., S. Boyron, and S. Whittaker. 1998. *Principles of French law.* Oxford, UK: Oxford University Press.

Bredemeyer, A. C. 1997. International agreements: A primer for the deploying judge advocate. *Air Force Law Review* 42:101–105.

Bremer, L. P. 2004. Coalition Provisional Authority Order Number 17 (revised): Status of the Coalition Provisional Authority, MNF–Iraq, certain missions and personnel in Iraq. www.unhcr.org/refworld/docid/49997ada3.html.

Brookings Institution. 2000. *International colloquy on the guiding principles of internal displacement.* Washington D.C. www.brookings.edu/~/media/Files/events/2000/0921 _guidingprinciples/20000921_Background.pdf.

Coyle, M. 2003. Toward an Iraqi legal system: A U.S.-sponsored plan in the works. *National Law Journal,* April 21.

Davis, B. 2004. Contract and fiscal law developments of 2003: The year in review. Appendix A—Department of Defense (DOD) legislation for fiscal year (FY) 2004. *Army Lawyer,* January, 199–221.

Demante, A. M. 1830. *Programme du cours de droit civil français.* Paris: Alex-Gobelet.

El Fadl, K. A. 1991. The common and Islamic law of duress. *Arab Law Quarterly* 6 (2): 121–159.

———. 2003. Islam and the challenge of democratic commitment. *Fordham International Law Journal* 27:4–51.

236   Land and post-conflict peacebuilding

Enders, D. 2011. Huge numbers of Iraqis still adrift within the country. Pulitzer Center on Crisis Reporting. December 11. http://pulitzercenter.org/reporting/iraq-mosul-displaced -sectarian-violence-kurds-arabs-sunni-shiite-muslims-government.

Ferris, E. G. 2008. The looming crisis: Displacement and security in Iraq. Policy Paper No. 5. Washington D.C.: Brookings Institution.

Ferris, E. G., and M. E. O'Hanlon. 2008. Iraq's displaced millions. *Washington Times*, August 21. www.brookings.edu/opinions/2008/0821_iraq_ferris.aspx.

GAO (United States Government Accountability Office). 2008. Military operations: Actions needed to better guide project selection for commander's emergency response program and improve oversight in Iraq. Memorandum to Congressional Committees. www.gao.gov/new.items/d08736r.pdf.

Garcia-Navarro, L. 2008. In Iraq, those displaced by violence return home. National Public Radio, October 9. www.npr.org/templates/story/story.php?storyId=95567785.

Hamoudi, H. A. 2008a. Baghdad booksellers, Basra carpet merchants, and the law of God and man: Legal pluralism and the contemporary Muslim experience. *Berkeley Journal of Middle Eastern and Islamic Law* 1 (1): 83–126.

———. 2008b. Legal change and Iraq. *Opinio Juris*, June 20. http://opiniojuris.org/2008/06/20/legal-change-and-iraq/.

IDP Working Group. 2008. Internally displaced persons in Iraq: Update September 2008. Amman, Jordan: Internal Displacement Monitoring Centre. www.internal-displacement .org/8025708F004CE90B/(httpDocuments)/D877BC914C6A92B3C125750D004BBF6B/$file/IDP+WG+Update+on+IDPs_returnees_Sep08.pdf.

IRC (International Rescue Committee). 2011. Major displacement crisis continues as U.S. troops leave Iraq: U.S. and coalition governments have responsibility to help the most vulnerable. December 14. www.rescue.org/press-releases/major-displacement-crisis -continues-us-troops-leave-iraq-12267.

Isser, D., and P. Van der Auweraert. 2009. Land, property, and the challenge of return for Iraq's displaced. Special Report No. 221. Washington D.C.: United States Institute of Peace. www.usip.org/files/resources/1.pdf.

Jwaideh, Z. E. 1953. The new civil code of Iraq. *George Washington Law Review* 22:176–185.

Kälin, W. 2008. Guiding principles on internal displacement: Annotations. Studies in Transnational Legal Policy, No. 38. Washington D.C.: American Society of International Law. www.asil.org/pdfs/stlp.pdf.

Leckie, S., ed. 2003. *Returning home: Housing and property restitution rights of refugees and displaced persons.* Ardsley, NY: Transnational Publishers.

———. 2006. New housing, land and property restitution rights. *Forced Migration Review*, no. 25 (May 3). www.reliefweb.int/rw/RWB.NSF/db900SID/KHII-6PG523? OpenDocument.

Leinwand, D. 2008. Wheels of justice slowly returning to Iraqi courts. *USA Today*, February 26. www.usatoday.com/printedition/news/20080227/a_iraqicourts27.art.htm.

Litvinoff, S. 1989. Vices of consent, error, fraud, duress, and an epilogue on lesion. *Louisiana Law Review* 50:6–116.

Malaurie, P. 1997. Les enjeux de la codification. *Actualité Juridique Droit Administratif* 9:642–646.

Martin, C. L. 1994. Louisiana State Law Institute proposes revision of negotiorum gestio and codification of unjust enrichment. *Tulane Law Review* 69:182–212.

Masterton, R. P. 2005. Managing a claims office. *Army Lawyer*, September, 29–53.

Refugees, displaced persons, and legal reform in Iraq 237

Montaigne, M. de. 1580/1958. *Complete essays of Montaigne*. Translated by D. M. Frame. Stanford, CA: Stanford University Press.

Murphy, S. D., ed. 2004. Contemporary practice of the United States relating to international law: Use of force and arms control; Coalition laws and transition arrangements during occupation of Iraq. *American Journal of International Law* 98 (July): 601–606.

Nagle, L. E. 2000. The Cinderella of government: Judicial reform in Latin America. *California Western International Law Journal* 30 (Spring): 345–370.

Paglione, G. 2008. Individual property restitution: From Deng to Pinheiro—And the challenges ahead. *International Journal of Refugee Law* 20 (3): 391–412.

Paris, R. 2004. *At war's end: Building peace after civil conflict*. Cambridge, UK: Cambridge University Press.

Phuong, C. 2004. *The international protection of internally displaced persons*. Cambridge, UK: Cambridge University Press.

Posner, R. A. 1998. *Law and literature*. Rev. and enl. ed. Cambridge, MA: Harvard University Press.

Prescott, J. M. 1998. Operational claims in Bosnia-Herzegovina and Croatia. *Army Lawyer*, June, 1–24.

Raz, J. 1980. *The concept of a legal system: An introduction to the theory of legal system*. 2nd. ed., reprinted 2003. Oxford, UK: Clarendon Press of Oxford University Press.

Ridolfo, K. 2006. Iraq: Displacement crisis worsened by violence. Radio Free Europe. www.globalsecurity.org/wmd/library/news/iraq/2006/04/iraq-060421-rferl01.htm.

Santiago, J. C. 2006. Contract and fiscal law developments of 2005—The year in review: Fiscal law—Operational funding. *Army Lawyer*, January, 163–166.

Stigall, D. E. 2005. Courts, confidence, and claims commissions: The case for remitting to Iraqi civil courts the tasks and jurisdiction of the Iraqi Property Claims Commission (IPCC). *Army Lawyer*, March, 28–41.

———. 2006. Iraqi civil law: Its sources, substance, and sundering. *Journal of Transnational Law and Policy* 16 (1): 1–73. www.law.fsu.edu/journals/transnational/vol16_1/Stigall.pdf.

———. 2008. A closer look at Iraqi property and tort law. *Louisiana Law Review* 68 (3): 765–822.

Tavernise, S. 2008. Fear keeps Iraqis out of their Baghdad homes. *New York Times*, August 23. www.nytimes.com/2008/08/24/world/middleeast/24baghdad.html.

Tyser, C. R., D. G. Demetriades, and I. H. Effendi, trans. 1967. *The Mejelle: Being an English translation of Majallah El-Ankam-I-Adliya and a complete code of Islamic civil law*. Lahore: All Pakistan Legal Decisions.

UN (United Nations). 2005. United Nations principles on housing and property restitution for refugees and displaced persons [Pinheiro Principles]. E/CN.4/Sub.2/2005/17. June 28. New York: United Nations Commission on Human Rights, Sub-commission on the Promotion and Protection of Human Rights. www.unhcr.org/refworld/docid/41640c874. html.

UNCHR (United Nations Commission on Human Rights). 1998. *Report of the Representative of the Secretary-General, Mr. Francis M. Deng, submitted pursuant to commission resolution 1997/39. Addendum: Guiding principles on internal displacement*. E/CN.4/ 1998/53/Add.2. February 11. www.unhcr.org/refworld/docid/3d4f95e11.html.

UNHCR (United Nations High Commissioner for Refugees). 2007. UNHCR launches new appeal for Iraq operations. Press release. January 8. www.unhcr.org/45a243a54.html.

U.S. Army (United States Department of the Army). 2006. *Counterinsurgency*. Field Manual 3-24. December 15. Washington, D.C. www.fas.org/irp/doddir/army/fm3-24.pdf.

238   Land and post-conflict peacebuilding

————. 2008a. Legal services: Claims procedures. Pamphlet 27-162. Washington, D.C.

————. 2008b. *Stability operations.* Field Manual 3-07. Washington, D.C. usacac.army. mil/cac2/repository/FM307/FM3-07.pdf.

Williams, R. C. 2008. Applying the lessons of Bosnia in Iraq: Whatever the solution, property rights should be secured. Brookings–Bern Project on Internal Displacement. www.brookings.edu/papers/2008/0108_iraq_williams.aspx.

Wolfe, C. 2000. Forum on morality: Public morality and the modern Supreme Court. *American Journal of Jurisprudence* 45:65–92.

Yiannopoulos, A. N. 1991. Possession. *Louisiana Law Review* 51:523–538.

Younes, K., and N. Rosen. 2008. Uprooted and unstable: Meeting urgent humanitarian needs in Iraq. Washington D.C.: Refugees International. www.refugeesinternational.org/ sites/default/files/UprootedandUnstable.pdf.

PART 3

Land management

Introduction

Even as international and national actors in post-conflict situations come to grips with immediate humanitarian priorities, there is a need to begin taking steps to address broader land tenure issues. Post-conflict land issues present tremendous technical and political challenges, and it remains unclear what types of measures can provide consistent leverage for resolving conflicts and managing the many, often volatile land-related problems. Drawing from experiences in a range of countries, the seven chapters in this part offer a variety of tools and techniques for strengthening capacity for land administration; protecting housing, land, and property rights; resolving disputes over land; and promoting equitable and sustainable land relations in post-conflict societies.

Although these tools and techniques have been applied by domestic and international actors in numerous peacebuilding settings, this part does not present all possible post-conflict land management tools. Nor do the authors advocate the adoption of such tools without prior consultation, analysis, and tailoring to ensure that they will be appropriate and effective in a particular peacebuilding context. Instead, the tools presented here constitute a representative sample of the broad variety of approaches that have allowed progress to be made in addressing post-conflict land issues.

The first two chapters—examining experiences in Afghanistan—highlight tools for addressing the reconstruction of land tenure and land administration after decades of conflict. In "Snow Leopards and Cadastres: Rare Sightings in Post-Conflict Afghanistan," Douglas E. Batson examines the importance of and the challenges associated with establishing a cadastre system (particularly, the Land Administration Domain Model, LADM) to record basic information such as boundaries, rights and interests, and uses of land. Batson notes that although cadastres are an indispensable tool for institutionalizing the rule of law and the proper management of natural resources, many peacebuilding programs fail to utilize or strengthen them. Batson concludes that as a repository of land information, the LADM has the potential to help people address not only land tenure insecurity but also environmental degradation and population displacement in Afghanistan.

Tools for coping with the absence of a centralized land tenure system in Afghanistan are examined in "Community Documentation of Land Tenure and Its Contribution to State Building in Afghanistan," by J. D. Stanfield, Jennifer Brick Murtazashvili, M. Y. Safar, and Akram Salam. This chapter emphasizes the benefits of working with local communities to encourage them to develop and administer their own property records. Drawing on the experiences of a rural

242   Land and post-conflict peacebuilding

land administration project based on the ADAMAP method,[1] the authors argue that the development of local administrative capacity to manage property records can contribute substantially to post-conflict rebuilding by creating transparent and effective institutions governing land. The authors observe that another important aspect of community-based land administration is the potential for strengthening state-community relations through collaboration between government agencies and local institutions in the maintenance of property documentation.

International assistance for addressing land administration after conflict frequently focuses on establishing private property rights, with an emphasis on issuing formal titles. There are many challenges to introducing such systems, particularly in regions where land is held and used according to customary laws. In such circumstances, international interventions have rarely lived up to expectations. In "Title Wave: Land Tenure and Peacebuilding in Aceh," Arthur Green explores property rights and land tenure security in a post-conflict context that was simultaneously a post-disaster context after the 2004 Indian Ocean tsunami. Green argues that the state-administered land registration program, known as the Reconstruction of Aceh Land Administration System (RALAS), failed to successfully address property issues in Aceh because it did not take into account the effects of the war on political, social, and economic relations concerning land. Green concludes that in order to better support peacebuilding in post-conflict situations such as Aceh, practitioners must pay attention to conflict dynamics in land tenure–security programs. Furthermore, alternative approaches to land titling should be explored—for example, the provision of communal titles.

In many conflict-affected countries where lack of access to land is a standing grievance—for example in El Salvador, Guatemala, and Nepal—there are often calls for redistributive land reform. Many obstacles prevent the realization of such reform. In "Beyond Land Redistribution: Lessons Learned from El Salvador's Unfulfilled Agrarian Revolution," Alexandre Corriveau-Bourque examines problematic approaches to contested agricultural land issues in the peacemaking and peacebuilding process in El Salvador. He reviews state-led land reforms in the 1980s and 1990s, noting the inability of peacebuilding programs to address rural poverty. Corriveau-Bourque argues that the 1992 peace agreement—the Chapultepec Peace Accords, signed between the government and the Farabundo Martí National Liberation Front (Frente Farabundo Martí de Liberacíon Nacional, or FMLN) under United Nations auspices—focused on the establishment of political stability to the detriment of the substantial agrarian reform needed to redress socioeconomic inequalities. By cementing structural land scarcity and protecting elite control of land, Corriveau-Bourque argues, the peace agreement failed to address land-related root causes of conflict, and many Salvadorans remained poor and landless.

---

[1] ADAMAP stands for: *A*sk for community cooperation; *D*elineate the boundaries of different types of lands; *A*greements are prepared; *M*eet, discuss, and approve the agreements and delineations; *A*rchive the agreements and delineations; and *P*repare for the continual updating and security of property records.

Rebuilding capacity to peacefully resolve land disputes is critical in both stabilization and longer-term development in post-conflict countries. In "Institutional Aspects of Resolving Land Disputes in Post-Conflict Societies," Peter Van der Auweraert discusses how and when the international community should intervene in the resolution of post-conflict land disputes. Regarding the design of post-conflict land programming, Van der Auweraert argues for the importance of assessing whether a land dispute poses a threat to peace, and of conducting practicability studies on the ability of specific institutions to properly and efficiently resolve land conflicts. Drawing from experiences in previous post-crisis land dispute programs, he analyzes institutional arrangements that can be employed in various situations. These include the establishment of an ad hoc land commission, recourse to the local judicial system, use of customary law–based dispute resolution mechanisms when they are available, and adoption of a multi-institutional approach. Van der Auweraert concludes that before the international community engages with land issues, a detailed analysis of the dispute-resolution process in light of country-specific factors is critical. Such an analysis will contribute to the achievement of stable and durable results.

Local ownership and leadership in peacebuilding processes is essential, and this extends to dispute resolution. In "Rebuilding Peace: Land and Water Management in the Kurdistan Region of Northern Iraq," Nesreen Barwari reviews the structure, achievements, and limitations of the Kurdistan reconstruction program as an example of a community-led reconstruction initiative. From 1991 to 2003 this program supported displaced persons in their choice to return to their lands or to relocate to safe and undisputed parts of the country. Combining active local involvement with financial and technical aid provided by donors and humanitarian nongovernmental organizations, the Kurdistan reconstruction program assisted with access to housing and water resources. Barwari's chapter also examines the uncommon practice of resolving disputes over land and water at the same time. In settings where there is insufficient water for rain-fed agriculture, such as northern Iraq, land reform is meaningless if it is not accompanied by guarantees of sufficient water to make the land productive. Barwari concludes by stressing the importance of expanding successful short-term measures into long-term projects for promoting full national reconstruction, economy recovery, and lasting peace.

The last chapter of this part—"Transboundary Resource Management Strategies in the Pamir Mountain Region of Tajikistan," by Ian D. Hannam— examines the Pamir Alai Mountain (PALM) project, which was developed by the Tajik government in collaboration with the Global Environment Facility and the United Nations Environment Programme as one of a number of projects implemented under foreign donor assistance to help improve the sustainable management of land following the country's civil war. The PALM project developed long-term strategies for domestic and transboundary natural resource management. Hannam highlights three approaches that influenced the positive outcome of the project: the involvement of local communities in the decision-making process,

244   Land and post-conflict peacebuilding

close collaboration with the Tajik government, and technical support from international agencies to implement conflict resolution programs and promote civil society initiatives.

Together, the seven chapters in this part present and analyze a broad selection of tools and approaches for addressing land issues that are central to peacebuilding. These methodologies may be used at different stages of the peacebuilding process, at different levels of governance, and by different actors. They range from development or improvement of cadastres and land information databases, to enhanced local land administration, land tenure reform, and the development of transboundary land management plans. These and other experiences show that involvement of civil society and traditional leaders should be integrated into almost any approach if that approach is to be effective. Many of the efforts discussed here have had mixed success, with some of the chapters describing mistakes best avoided in future—underlining both the opportunities and the challenges presented by land administration issues in post-conflict situations.

Snow leopards and cadastres: Rare sightings in post-conflict Afghanistan

Douglas E. Batson

Good land administration benefits individuals, government, businesses, and the environment, especially in post-conflict countries. The Working Party on Land Administration of the United Nations Economic Commission for Europe (UNECE) states that "the inter-relationship of people and land is fundamental to human existence" (UNECE 2005, 4). The same publication lists "support environment management" as one of thirteen benefits of effective land administration (UNECE 2005, 6). UNECE defines land administration as the formal systems "necessary to register land and property and hence to provide secure ownership in land, investments and other private and public rights in real estate. A system for recording landownership, land values, land use and other land-related data is an indispensable tool for a market economy to work properly, as well as for sustainable management of land resources" (UNECE 1996, 7). Of course, in peaceful and prosperous developed nations, land administration and environmental concerns rank high on the political, social, and legal agendas.

But can good land administration be achieved in post-conflict Afghanistan, where poverty, unemployment, and a demographic youth bulge overtax the fledgling, democratically elected government and fuel a narcotics-based economy and a tenacious insurgency? The protracted human conflict has degraded the natural environment to the point where, even if the current insurgency were quelled, Afghanistan faces "a future without water, forests, wildlife and clean air" (UNEP 2003, 5).

Given these circumstances, it comes as no surprise that the United Nations Environment Programme (UNEP) found that Afghanistan's long-term environmental degradation is caused, in part, by a complete collapse of regional and national forms of governance (UNEP 2003). Afghanistan expert Barnett R. Rubin foresees a decades-long transition from customary law to civil and state law. Keenly aware that a lack of basic law enforcement undermines the legitimacy

---

Douglas E. Batson is a political geography analyst at the National Geospatial-Intelligence Agency of the U.S. Department of Defense. Some of the material in this chapter appeared in the newsletter of the Military Geography Specialty Group of the Association of American Geographers; it appears here by permission.

246   Land and post-conflict peacebuilding

of any government, Rubin, from his 2006 travels in the country, recognizes the value of local governance:

> The only capacities for dispute resolution and law enforcement in much of the country consist of village or tribal councils and mullahs who administer a crude interpretation of sharia. During the years required for [judicial] reform, the only actual alternatives before Afghan society are enforcement of such customary or Islamic law or no law at all (Rubin 2006).

In 1962 the biologist Rachel Carson published *Silent Spring*, a book that raised environmental awareness and sparked the ecology conservation movement in the United States. The title was inspired by a John Keats poem, "La Belle Dame sans Merci," which describes a desolate place where "no birds sing." This chapter posits that lessons learned from land-related initiatives at the local level are the basis for an Afghanistan that will not become a silent spring.

The chapter argues further that a critical omission in reconstruction and development programs in Afghanistan has been in not recording the locally determined relationships between people and land, information typically registered in a cadastre. Indeed, cadastral survey parties have been all too rare in Afghanistan, almost as rare as a sighting of the legendary snow leopard, not reportedly seen in many years.

The chapter begins with an overview of the challenges faced in rebuilding Afghanistan, specifically the need for a cadastre system that records the relations between people and land. It then discusses the problems of refugee resettlement, the population explosion, and the environmental destruction from decades of conflict. The chapter then focuses on the importance of land tenure security and describes local initiatives that have contributed to security. It continues by discussing the importance of dispute resolution to tenure security and how environmental initiatives, while generally lower in priority on political, social, and legal agendas, can be embraced when local communities share a stake in the success of environmental protection. The chapter concludes by stressing the important role of the cadastre system, particularly the Land Administration Domain Model.

REBUILDING AFGHANISTAN

Reconstructing Afghanistan requires many forms of action, and one focus must be on land administration. A cadastral (land and property registry) system can reduce both conflict and environmental degradation by bringing land matters into the public forum. However, nine years into post-conflict reconstruction, little headway has been made toward untangling the successive impacts that tribalism, communism, Islamic theocracy, and now the lure of a free-market economy have had on land and property in Afghanistan. Aid workers in the country, exhausted by ever-urgent humanitarian needs, are loath to begin long-term development projects in the face of dwindling donor support and escalating violence.

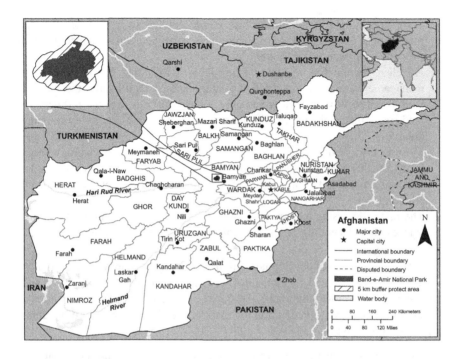

Conor Foley, a consultant to human rights and refugee organizations, speaks to land administration with his charge to the international community: "Good governance, respect for human rights and the rule of law are not 'optional extras' when it comes to rebuilding a country, but an intrinsic part of the process of reconstruction" (Foley 2006, 3). The UN Human Settlements Programme (UN-HABITAT) reminds planners that long after the media, emergency services personnel, and stability forces pull out of a country, post-conflict land management "is dependent on political will and a determination to build effective systems—including technical and governance—over long periods. As a rule of thumb, it takes about 25 years to build such a system" (UN-HABITAT 2007, 65).

The Geographic Research Branch of the UK Defence Geographic Centre summarized how decades of chaos has affected the relationship of people to land in Afghanistan and underscored why it will take a quarter century to institute a land administration system in Afghanistan (UK Defence Geographic Centre 2006). In brief:

- The present legislation on land tenure in Afghanistan is complex, uncertain, and incomplete. Land relations in Afghanistan have been governed by a number of legal frameworks, and these frameworks have been interpreted differently by successive administrations; therefore, identifying the current law is a challenge.

248 Land and post-conflict peacebuilding

- Stark inequalities in landownership, ethnic conflict over land access, and mismanaged land reforms by the state have generated and sustained conflict over the past twenty-five years.
- No clear regime for managing land rights exists, and, by default, many management functions have fallen to the courts, which handle the bulk of land disputes. With instability and coercion by warlords over the last decade, land rights management and dispute resolution have lost credibility in many areas.
- Most rural Afghans regulate their landownership relations by custom, without using officials or courts. Customary sector management offers a strong foundation, but it is rife with practices that favor wealthier elites, men, and dominant ethnic groups.
- The rules addressing who may own land in Afghanistan and in what circumstances vary depending on the type of land under consideration.

Reconstruction and development programs in Afghanistan will succeed only if the locally determined relationships between people and land are clear and consistent—and, most important, registered in a cadastre. The International Federation of Surveyors (Fédération International des Géomètres, or FIG) defines a cadastre this way:

> A Cadastre is normally a parcel based and up-to-date land information system containing a record of interests in land (e.g., rights, restrictions and responsibilities). It usually includes a geometric description of land parcels linked to other records describing the nature of the interests, and ownership or control of those interests, and often the value of the parcel and its improvements (FIG 1995).

Now, for the first time in history, the systematic recording of informal land rights and interests is feasible with the Land Administration Domain Model (LADM), a new approach to land administration. The LADM, with spatial and legal-administrative components, can locate, describe, and record customary social tenures, even claims with no apparent legal basis. The model is compelling because it makes explicit more than just ownership rights—for environmental conservation purposes, the LADM can record stewardship responsibilities and restrictions on harmful practices; for improving governance more broadly, it can harmonize local decisions with regional or national land policies as these essential services are reestablished.

REFUGEE RESETTLEMENT, THE POPULATION EXPLOSION, AND ENVIRONMENTAL DAMAGE

In Afghanistan the competition over land and other natural resources is exacerbated by three sources—returning refugees, a population explosion, and environmental degradation from decades of conflict. An estimated 4.6 million repatriated refugees have returned to Afghanistan from neighboring countries since 2002. A degraded environment makes their resettlement very difficult, as seen in the example of Kelagay.

From 1990 to 2006, Kelagay was an empty, dusty plain, the site of an old Soviet military base and an abandoned village, whose broken walls stood in the midst of untended fields. But since 2006, frantic construction has been going on in that part of Baghlan Province, as Afghan laborers have built high-walled compounds and flat-roofed houses from mud and straw. The building boom began when the entire population of a ruined village, called Naseri Chehl Kapa, came back that summer after twenty-six years as refugees in Pakistan. Because their numbers had increased with the arrival of a new generation, they occupied government land well beyond their original village and fields, up to and across the nearby road. Within a week of their arrival, the returned villagers began dividing up the land parcels and buildings. The *New York Times* quoted one villager: " 'This is our ancestral land; our forefathers lived here,' said Haji Abdul Jabar, who is building a large compound that will house his family and those of his seven brothers" (Gall 2006). But what did the Jabar brothers find when they attempted to return to their ancestral livelihoods of agriculture and animal husbandry?

The Jabar brothers probably found land that had become infertile and arid, and thus impossible to cultivate. As a result, their young male offspring, who knew nothing of agriculture and livestock as refugees in Pakistan, will likely flock to the cities to eke out an existence in the slums. There, with no home or means of support, they will be predisposed to recruitment by the purveyors of instability: crime bosses, drug traffickers, and the Taliban.

The Afghan population explosion, from 11 million in 1970 to over 30 million today, worsens the competition for land and other resources (World Bank 2009). The geographer Nigel Allan has stated that the land cannot support the current huge population—and will never be able to do so (Allan 2007). Allan was not taking the environmental degradation (recent drought, denuded forests, and erosion) into account in his warning about Afghanistan's high birth rate. The stark imbalance he noted between population and natural resources thwarts reconstruction efforts altogether and foreshadows renewed conflict in Afghanistan, this time over access to resources for survival as opposed to ideology.

A January 2003 UNEP assessment of the Afghan conflict's environmental damage warned that a return to 1970s-like peace on the pastures would be impossible. While "over 80 percent of Afghan people live in rural areas, they have seen many of their basic resources—water for irrigation, trees for food and fuel— lost in just a generation" (UNEP 2003). Decades of conflict, drought, and neglect have left unclear who is responsible for Afghanistan's natural environment. In 2007, Afghanistan's Ministry of Agriculture and Food predicted grave consequences if the government and international aid organizations continued to ignore the country's deteriorating environment. A summary of the UNEP report noted some stark facts:

250 Land and post-conflict peacebuilding

- Up to 50 percent of Afghan farmlands have not been cultivated for the past twenty years.
- Afghanistan's agricultural produce has decreased by 50 percent.
- Soil fertility is declining, salinization is on the increase, water tables have dramatically fallen, and devegetation is extensive.
- More than 80 percent of Afghan land is subject to wind and soil erosion.
- Over 70 percent of forests have been lost since 1985.
- Deforestation makes Afghanistan increasingly vulnerable to natural disasters, namely flooding and landslides.
- The eradication of Afghan forests has led to rapid expansion of deserts in the southern, eastern, and northern regions of the country (IRIN 2007).

Hazrat Hussain Khaurin, director of the Forests and Rangeland Department of the Ministry of Agriculture and Food, asserts that "neither the government nor impoverished Afghan farmers have the basic technology or required resources to resist widening desertification" (IRIN 2007). Similarly, Abdul Rahman Hotaky, chairman of the Afghan Organization of Human Rights and Environmental Protection, described the multiple social, environmental, and economic implications of desertification for the Jabar brothers, their extended families, and millions like them: "Desertification has exacerbated already widespread poverty among many Afghan farmers who seem hapless to tackle problems created by this natural crisis" (IRIN 2007).

LAND TENURE

Security of tenure is the most pressing post-conflict land issue in Afghanistan. Owning the land in the Western sense, recorded in deeds and titles, is not the primary concern. An explanation of the difference is warranted.

> In antiquity to effect a transaction the parties involved would meet at the city gates in the presence of the community elders, . . . or assemble somewhere else in public and there agree upon their terms. The transaction may or may not have been written, depending upon local custom. But whether recorded in parchment, books, or peoples' memory, the transaction was public, and therefore considered legitimate.
>
> This universal human practice is the basis for deeds, the written record of transfers of rights, ownership, or possession between parties. . . . After the industrial revolution Western countries found a need to record the ownership of land parcels in a way that would make transactions easier to track and more readily available to government and financial institutions. This led to a shift to an absolute individual land parcel record of who owns what and where. . . . This protected both the lender and the borrower. For the government, ownership was clear for taxation purposes. . . .
>
> Unlike a deed, which is a physical object, a title is conceptual. A title is a right a state gives to a certain person or persons recognizing the legitimate ownership

or possession of a given property. There may be a document that acknowledges this title, but the title itself is the right, not the piece of paper. Whereas a deed always involves two parties and records a transaction at a certain time, a title ... merely declares who has what rights to what property (Batson 2008, 87).

Guaranteeing that millions of Afghans can hold their lands securely is crucial for the country's long-term stability. Holding—not owning—the land implies a dependence upon state authority for protection from those who might try to seize the property. Thus the Afghans' most immediate worry is forced eviction, whether by the state or a third party. The layers of complexity and potential for conflict are compounded when, for example, the state suddenly claims ownership of land long held by people through custom and tradition. Officially, these people are landless, but nevertheless "the wealth of all of these poor people is tied up in their land and housing" (IRIN 2003). Unfortunately, the time and expense (including bribes to government officials to make sure they do their routine jobs) of acquiring and registering land titles often undermines the goal of secure tenure for the poor.

Leaders of post-conflict countries are often pressured by citizens who clamor for land reform. In many cases, hastily enacted national policies "confuse 'ownership' with 'security of tenure,' resulting only in ... delays in extending effective security of tenure" to those who direly need it (Cousins and Kingwill 2006, 1). Similarly, cadastres designed by external parties tend to serve the interests of national elites and outside groups rather than those of the local people, who are usually poor. If a cadastre does not reflect local arrangements, it is open to abuse, particularly in post-conflict countries.

LOCAL LAND INITIATIVES IN AFGHANISTAN

To succeed, land tenure policies must reflect local realities. There are local land initiatives in Afghanistan that have been, or could be, harmonized with regional or national land policies and land administration. These include community mapping and land titling activities.

Community mapping

Community-based creation and maintenance of land rights records is a bottom-up response to weak state institutions. Centralized land-governing institutions have not enjoyed public confidence among Afghans. In response to increasing insecurity of tenure on Afghan rangelands, a problem that has arisen in recent years, a Rural Land Administration Project (RLAP) team has created a community initiative to produce and record community agreements about who holds the legitimate rights to use which pasture lands for particular purposes during specific times of the year. David Stanfield, president of the Terra Institute, has declared that RLAP's participative, transparent, and observable processes—conducted under the rubric of land titling and community recording of locally derived agreements on the

252 Land and post-conflict peacebuilding

legitimate users of rangeland—has demonstrated the viability of community-based mapping in rural Afghanistan (Stanfield 2007).[1]

A valuable resource from Afghanistan's constitutional monarchy still exists to aid community mapping. Between 1965 and 1978, one-third of Afghan agricultural lands, or 12.9 million *jerib* (a traditional unit of land that equals a fifth of a hectare, 2,000 square meters, or 0.494 acre), were professionally surveyed by the Afghan Geodesy and Cartography Head Office (Safar 2007). This enormous undertaking, covering 25,800 square kilometers (nearly the size of Rwanda), was not used in a land registration system or to issue formal titles. Cadastral surveyors compiled the names of probable parcel owners to dispel any notion that they were also official government title adjudicators. Despite being decades old, these painstakingly assembled graphical and textual records survived the conflicts and could contribute to a future land administration system. The owners and occupants certainly have changed, but the parcel boundaries probably remain much the same, as there have been few subdivisions and consolidations, at least in villages such as Kelagay.

Land titling and economic restructuring

From 2004 to 2009, the Land Titling and Economic Restructuring in Afghanistan (LTERA) program initiated two projects in selected urban areas. Funded by the U.S. Agency for International Development (USAID) and implemented by the Emerging Markets Group, LTERA presented a five-pronged approach to land titling and economic restructuring: a land registration system, a mapping and land information system, tenure regularization, a policy and legal framework, and the release of public land to private ownership (Gebremedhin 2006).

LTERA has done important work in rehabilitating and reorganizing deeds in provincial court archives, although little progress has been made in simplifying land titling procedures, clarifying the legal framework for property rights, reducing the cost of transactions, or reorganizing land administration agencies. Two LTERA projects are worth special consideration: the upgrading of informal settlements in two districts of Kabul and the rehabilitation of court archives (*makhzan*).

Upgrading of informal settlements in Kabul

LTERA selected two community development councils that were established by UN-HABITAT in districts 7 and 13 of Kabul. These areas were chosen, in part, because the communities had already established representative bodies (*shuras*), and both residents and the municipality were willing to participate in the program. Although the shuras had been involved in previous upgrading projects,

---

[1] For more information, see J. D. Stanfield, Jennifer Brick Murtazashvili, M. Y. Safar, and Akram Salam, "Community Documentation of Land Tenure and Its Contribution to State Building in Afghanistan," in this book.

the issue of land tenure security had not been addressed prior to the LTERA project. In District 13, newly established land-clarification boards review property deeds presented by informal settlers. Ninety-five percent of these are informal, customary deeds. Disputes settled at the community level avoid the bureaucratic and uncertain procedures of the Kabul courts. Once community consensus is reached about who lives—or has the right to live—where, LTERA requests the municipality to issue a certificate of comfort. While not a property deed, it offers a valuable form of tenure security (USAID 2009a).

From this pilot program to formalize informal settlements, LTERA has developed preliminary proposals to create a legal basis for regularizing tenure in other settings. The team has developed a replicable and cost-effective methodology to upgrade basic services, regularize tenure, and integrate informal settlements into a municipality's urban planning process. The projects in Districts 7 and 13 tested an incremental, community-based method of upgrading and regularizing tenure. These neighborhoods were chosen partly because their problems were obvious. Informal settlers lived in fear of forced eviction and therefore had no incentive to improve their dwellings, start businesses, or upgrade their neighborhoods. According to Dr. Gregory Maassen, LTERA chief of party from 2006 to 2009:

> We estimate that in Districts 7 and 13, the implementation of the 1978 Kabul Master Plan would result in evicting 2,000 households (about 14,000 people). We are preparing a land use plan for the districts. The plan contains alternative land development options which better reflect current land patterns, provide residents access to basic services, and considerably minimize the number of evictions. Once approved by the municipality, it will halt forced evictions (Maassen 2007).

A 2006 preliminary study of the LTERA project in District 7 was conducted by the Cooperation for the Reconstruction of Afghanistan (CRA), an Afghan nongovernmental organization well versed in the techniques and philosophy of community action. CRA identified the benefits of improved tenure security as measured by increased business activity and housing construction, especially where improvement in security was accompanied by community organization and physical upgrading of the district's streets and drainage systems. Interviews with community leaders and residents also showed that people's perceptions of tenure security and general conditions have improved significantly since the implementation of the project. In summary, the work done by the community was due largely to the organizational and guiding efforts of CRA and financial support from USAID and the Emerging Markets Group (USAID 2009a). Several benefits accrued:

More construction occurred. Forty-six houses were either reconstructed or extended in the pilot area since the implementation of the project, which represents 9 percent of all houses in the area. All but one of these houses are

254 Land and post-conflict peacebuilding

constructed of brick and concrete, which requires a substantially greater investment than the usual mud construction.

More businesses opened. The number of business enterprises increased from 117 to 126, an increase of 7 percent from November 2005 to September 2006.

The price of vacant land increased. Although house prices appeared to have stabilized or, in some instances decreased, the price of vacant land increased by as much as 50 percent since the project was implemented. There were fewer houses on the market than before the project started. There were fewer properties available for rent, and rents increased by an average of 30 percent after September 2005.

Land tenure was more secure. Thirty residents of District 7 were interviewed about their knowledge of the LTERA upgrading effort. All but one felt more secure as a result of the project and believed that the area would eventually be formally incorporated into the city plan. Three respondents noted that the mere fact that roads and drains had been constructed had resulted in improved perceptions of secure tenure.

There was a positive impact on community development. The shura and community leaders involved with the property adjudication process reiterated their support for the project and confirmed that it had resulted in improved perceptions of tenure security and increased economic activity.

Lessening fear of forced eviction, resolving disputes, demarcating plots, providing funds to upgrade community infrastructure, fostering community development—each success, no matter how small, builds upon the others to provide security of tenure and upgrading of the settlement.

Restoration of legal documentation in registration courts

When land disputes occur in Afghanistan, taking matters to the courts often adds to the woes of returnees and others dispossessed of their land due to conflict or large-scale land acquisitions (often referred to as *land grabbing*). Plagued by corruption, inefficiency, delays, and a lack of enforcement, the justice system disappoints many Afghans, who resort to customary dispute resolution methods.

In Afghanistan the primary courts in both urban and rural districts prepare title deeds when people come to the judges to acquire them. The provincial appeals courts, located in the provincial capitals, maintain the archives of deeds documenting the transfer of title according to procedures established by the Supreme Court. These archives, which contain all primary and provincial court documents and are maintained by the judiciary, are called makhzan. But "maintained" may be too kind a word. During the Afghan civil war, the archives suffered neglect and destruction and were left in generally poor condition. Many legal documents, including title deeds, were stolen, destroyed, or falsified, and fraudulent new title deeds were created for dubious property transactions.

To restore confidence in the judicial system, it is essential to rehabilitate the legal archives and make them accessible to the public, especially for land and property disputes. The goal of LTERA's makhzan rehabilitation program is to build on efforts started by previous USAID-supported programs to improve land tenure security through the implementation of a cost-effective, transparent, accessible, and simple system for preparing, archiving, and consulting deeds. The reorganization of the archives concentrates on three objectives: classifying the original legal documents to make them more accessible to the public and the judiciary; maintaining the documents in the archives for future use in building a land information system; and digitizing the documents to make them more secure and more quickly accessible, especially for use in delivering duplicate titles.

By the end of its five years the LTERA project had digitized 616,498 deeds and "reorganized close to 7 million legal documents, including 1,077,000 title deeds, representing over 80 percent of the total number of title deeds registered with courts in Afghanistan" (USAID 2009a, 32). The computerization of the archives and the digitization of title deeds not only preserve the documents, which were often in very poor condition, but also make digital copies available, replacing hand-prepared duplicates. A transparent recording and archiving process and secure access to the legal information limits corruption by making it more difficult to falsify existing title deeds or introduce new falsified property documentation. Many residents of Kabul had given up hope that their deeds could be found and are elated that legal copies of deeds can now be obtained. In some cases, the copies are used in the settlement of land disputes; in others, for proving property ownership to secure loans or for clarification of inheritance. The improvements in document storage and retrieval are real, but the system is not used by most people engaging in real estate transactions.

DISPUTE RESOLUTION

One step that cannot be overlooked in achieving tenure security is dispute resolution. In Afghanistan the Norwegian Refugee Council (NRC) operates the Information, Counseling and Legal Assistance (ICLA) program, whose counselors resolve land disputes. In addition to providing shelter and education, distributing aid, and managing camps for refugees and internally displaced persons, the NRC employs Afghan nationals as legal specialists and counselors. Free of charge, the ICLA has helped tens of thousands of people regain their land (Foley 2008). The ICLA does not import Western notions of jurisprudence, and the staff is skilled in handling small cases. Once the parties to a dispute are satisfied that their case, often perceived to be against a socially more powerful opponent, has been heard, they are encouraged to accept arbitration from a traditional *jirga* (tribal assembly) or shura, where a final ruling will be made. The ICLA imbues confidence in small claimants who face more powerful parties that they stand a fighting chance to regain their land via a jirga or a shura.

Conor Foley, a former program manager of the ICLA, believes that jirgas, in which all neighborhood or village males participate, or the more restrictive shuras, which comprise select elders, "are the closest thing to democratic institutions

256 Land and post-conflict peacebuilding

in Afghanistan today. They can reach decisions much faster than the official courts, are virtually cost-free, are less susceptible to bribery and are accessible to illiterate Afghans" (Foley 2004).[2] The ICLA earns legitimacy by infusing traditional, community-based institutions for dispute resolution with vitality and the added prestige of an international endorsement. Due to the international status of the NRC representatives, militia commanders and other power brokers may behave more civilly, and there may be less bloodshed. Yet Foley has no misconceptions about the paucity of justice in Afghanistan: "Such initiatives may help individuals, and may even have a role to play in strengthening civil society and holding the authorities to account, but they are no substitute for an effective justice system based on respect for the rule of law and human rights. Many of NRC's clients have still not obtained justice, and managing people's expectations is becoming an increasing problem. Conversely, the organisation's successes may attract more cases than the centres can handle" (Foley 2004).

ENVIRONMENTAL INITIATIVES: BAND-E-AMIR NATIONAL PARK

Afghanistan's urgent humanitarian needs and desperate living conditions make it difficult to undertake long-term development projects, even in an area as important as land administration. Environmental issues rank even lower on the political, social, and legal agendas, not only in Afghanistan but in many developing countries, where attempts to enact conservation programs by relying on a top-down approach have failed. Afghan officials have instead embraced a bottom-up strategy, in which local residents have a stake in the success of environmental protection.

The journalist Aunohita Mojumdar describes how the fond childhood memories of Mustafa Zahir, chief of the Afghan National Environmental Protection Agency (NEPA), contrast with grim, present-day realities:

> When Zahir was growing up, he recalls meeting people who had traveled thousands of kilometers out of a desire to breathe Kabul's invigorating air. Back then, Afghanistan was a tourist destination that enjoyed renown for its crystalline lakes, spectacular mountains, flowering gardens and fruit-laden orchards. Both affluent families and backpacking hippies visited. "Now," says Zahir, the grandson of Zahir Shah, the last king of Afghanistan, "if you breathe in the Kabul air, your lungs fill with poison" (Mojumdar 2009).

Kabul's toxic air stems from a population increase from 1.5 million in 2001 to 4.5 million in 2009 (Setchell and Luther 2009). The Afghan capital has become a megacity stripped of such basic natural resources as firewood. Residents burn

---

[2] Some researchers and Afghans use the term interchangeably (see J. D. Stanfield, Jennifer Brick Murtazashvili, M. Y. Safar, and Akram Salam, "Community Documentation of Land Tenure and Its Contribution to State Building in Afghanistan," in this book), which may reflect regional differences in usage.

the refuse they had collected for warmth, and the air is thick with the putrid odor of burned plastic jugs.

But in the Bamyan provincial highlands, Zahir finally has a reason for hope: in 2009 he announced the establishment of Afghanistan's first national park, Band-e-Amir Lakes, with six azure lakes separated by natural travertine dams. Thirteen villages within the park began a grassroots effort by establishing a protected area committee, with the help of the U.S.-based Wildlife Conservation Society (WCS) (Mojumdar 2009; Zahler et al. 2012). When WCS surveyed the area, it found the Siberian ibex, a type of wild goat; the urial, a species of wild sheep; wolves; foxes; and a snow finch, believed to be the only bird species endemic to Afghanistan (Smith 2009). Should a snow leopard—not reportedly seen in the country for years—be sighted, tourists would again trek "thousands of kilometers" to Afghanistan, as Zahir remembered, in the hope of catching a glimpse of the rare animal. A sighting would also boost the current efforts to obtain World Heritage status for the park.[3] USAID has noted:

> [S]pecies like the snow leopard are under pressure from excessive hunting, loss of key habitat, and illegal trade. Snow leopard pelts for sale in tourist shops can go for as much as [US]$1,500 each. International trade in species like the snow leopard is illegal under international law because snow leopards are globally endangered. Now that the snow leopard is protected under Afghan law, it is also illegal for Afghan nationals or internationals to hunt or trade the species within Afghanistan (USAID 2009b).

NEPA published the country's first protected species list at a critical time, in June 2009. The presidential decree banning the hunting of snow leopards in the country had expired the previous March.

In Western countries, the cadastre reflects the land policies of the central government. But a cadastre is not sufficient by itself; it is merely a tool within a hierarchy of land management functions. At the top is the land management system, which develops a national land policy and strategy. The land administration system, next in the hierarchy, implements that policy and strategy. Beneath that are subsystems for land tenure, taxation, utilities, and so forth. Finally comes the cadastre, which records boundary lines, surveyors' reports, land registration, and claims to land. This hierarchy is the conventional approach to land management, an arrangement adequate for most stable countries (Augustinus and Barry 2006).

Clarissa Augustinus, chief of UN-HABITAT's Land Tenure Unit, and Michael Barry argue that post-conflict societies like Afghanistan cannot follow this hierarchical model without incurring massive delay and expense, or without prolonging and exacerbating land crises. They advocate, instead, a local needs

---

[3] The UN Educational, Scientific and Cultural Organization administers the World Heritage Convention, which recognizes the world's exceptional sites of natural and cultural diversity. See http://whc.unesco.org.

258   Land and post-conflict peacebuilding

approach. For example, in the community-driven campaign to establish a protective area around Band-e-Amir Lakes, land management was most pressing. In other situations land tenure or land administration can come to the fore. The tendency in many international aid or development enterprises is to design a cadastre to fit the needs of a local settlement, then to take that model to the national level and attempt to create a single, overarching cadastral system that can suit every part of the country and take into account an underlying land policy. In post-conflict societies, "land policy is being developed at the local settlement level" (Augustinus and Barry 2006, 674). Cadastres must be established in order to record what is happening locally, and not wait for a national land policy to take shape. In Afghanistan, such a wait could be for decades.

NEXT STEPS: BRINGING CADASTRES TO THE FORE

Cadastres are land and property registries. In a nation where conflict or a major catastrophe has displaced large numbers of people, returning those people to their land is a key part of the effort to reconstruct the country. For post-conflict planners a cadastre remains the primary source of information about the broad spectrum of formal and informal rights and interests in land. Such information includes the identity of people who have interests in parcels of land; the interests themselves, such as the nature and duration of rights, restrictions, and responsibilities; and basic details about the parcel, including its location, size, value, and any improvements on it (FIG 1995).

A cadastre must fit the situation where it is applied because "land administration systems are reflecting the cultural and social context of the country in which they are operating" (Steudler, Rajabifard, and Williamson 2004, 4). Deed-based or title-based land registries have been unworkable in informal settlements, in countries where there is customary tenure, or in post-conflict situations, all of which are replete with competing land claims. Until now there has never been an internationally accepted standard or method for evaluating land administration systems.

One might think that cadastral information already serves as the foundation for post-conflict reconstruction and development aid. But providing a host nation with the technical and human resources is only half the challenge. Cadastres threaten those who want to maintain a status quo that cements their prestige, power, and profit. Not only criminals, terrorists, and insurgents, but also government officials, national elites, and their well-placed relatives can have ulterior motives to resist formalization of property regimes:

> Slum organizers, political bosses, and tribal chiefs can often view tenure regularization as eroding their privileged social and economic position. Municipal officials and ministries that exhibited near absolute power over land decisions do not easily give up control. Political sympathy for squatters is frequently low. Change, which improves the situation for some, will necessarily erode political,

Cadastres in Afghanistan **259**

cultural, and/or economic power for others. For all these reasons and more, the process is often complicated, political and violent (Durand-Lasserve and Royston 2002, 241).

While some foreign aid projects have modernized property regimes in developing countries, they have not insisted on transparent, digitized property data (Demarest 2008). It goes without saying that only analyzable cadastral data can guide effective post-conflict reconstruction toward sustainable development. In Afghanistan, it is at the local level that peoples' formal and informal rights and interests in land are known. And a new cadastral tool—one that can record local land policies, decisions, and claims—promises to make land administration an essential part of the international community's post-conflict reconstruction aid. That new tool is the Land Administration Domain Model.

LAND ADMINISTRATION DOMAIN MODEL

The inventive Dutch academicians Christiaan Lemmen, Peter van Oosterom, and Paul van der Molen, working with Clarissa Augustinus produced the Land Administration Domain Model (LADM).[4] The LADM is compelling because it makes explicit various types of land rights, restrictions, and responsibilities. It is flexible enough to record land tenure types not based on the traditional cadastral parcel—that is, customary, informal land rights such as occupancy, usufruct, lease, or traverse.

The LADM has reduced the complex database models that underlie title-based cadastres to the simple principle that a relationship (such as rights to land or customary tenure) always exists between land (spatial objects) and people. No matter how messy or difficult the world's land disputes, nothing falls outside this basic principle.

The LADM then translates these three categories—people, relationship, and land—into Unified Modeling Language to establish three classes for a cadastre: person, right, and spatial object, in that order. The LADM allows registration and maintenance of "relationships between people and land irrespective of the nature of the country's jurisprudence; this ability offers opportunities for the integration of statutory, customary, and informal arrangements within conventional land administration systems" (Lemmen et al. 2007, 7).

Because the LADM should be able to accommodate any legal framework of any culture, it allows great flexibility in describing the persons and places

---

[4] The LADM has garnered support from standardization and professional bodies such as FIG, the Open GIS Consortium, UN-HABITAT, and the Infrastructure for Spatial Information in Europe (van Oosterom et al. 2006). In February 2008 the International Organization for Standardization (ISO), the body responsible for determining all international standards, accepted the LADM as New Work Item Proposal 1954. After intensive review, in 2010 it became Draft International Standard (DIS) 19152 (ISO/TC 211 2010). At this writing (August 2012) the LADM is in Final Draft International Standard (FDIS) status, on track to become the world's first International Standard/Technical Specification for land administration by the end of 2012.

260   Land and post-conflict peacebuilding

involved and in the systematic recording of rights that are not title-based legal rights but are claims that may need adjudication. The LADM possesses the critical functionality to merge formal and informal land tenure systems, and urban and rural cadastres, into one data environment; it defines a reference model that covers all basic information-related components of land administration.

In brief, the LADM offers several features: a conceptual schema with five basic components (people and organizations, called parties in LADM terminology; parcels, called spatial units; property rights, called rights, responsibilities, and restrictions; surveying; and geometry and topology); a terminology for land administration—based on various national and international systems but kept as simple as possible in order to be useful in practice—that allows descriptions of practices and procedures from various jurisdictions; a basis for national and regional profiles of land administration; and the ability to combine land administration information from different sources in a coherent manner (Lemmen et al. 2009).

The LADM links spatial data from very different systems. In the past, linking such land information has been difficult, in part because of the database structure. Registering the myriad social tenures to land requires linking disparate data, and this is where the LADM excels. It is less a database than a word processor. Anything—even photographs, hand-drawn sketches, and oral testimony—can be put into a document, as long as it records all evidence relevant to a property and the rights that various people claim on it. Thus the LADM is especially suited to recording deeds. Furthermore, when using the LADM:

- Formal and informal tenure systems can be held in one data environment.
- The computer-based system can be converted to a paper-based one, and vice versa.
- Spatial information can be represented in existing geodetic networks and in new spatial frameworks.
- Spatial data can be linked to other systems.
- The computer environment is distributed and decentralized, with information simultaneously processed on multiple, geographically separated computers over a network, making the system usable both centrally and locally.
- Source data can be of disparate types, with different geospatial accuracies.
- Different tenures can be allowed to overlap.
- Places can be identified by a range of identifiers: parcels referenced to geographical coordinates, unreferenced parcels, lines, and points.
- Conflicts can be recorded, women's access to land can be ensured, and highly complex relationships can be described (Lemmen et al. 2007).

Land information systems should serve decision makers at national, regional, and local levels, with the emphasis on decentralized decision making. The basic concept behind the LADM is to produce and provide land registration (the administrative and legal component) and cadastral mapping referenced to geographical coordinates (the spatial component) for land administration in a decentralized environment. The model will allow better vertical coordination, between local interests and top-down information and policy guidance. In this way, national development policies can be harmonized with local programs (Lemmen et al. 2007). Thus the LADM facilitates the rehabilitation of both local and central governance.

The Social Tenure Domain Model (STDM), a subset of the LADM, is an informative annex in the International Organization for Standardization draft standard of the LADM. The STDM, as it stands, has the capacity to broaden the scope of land administration by providing a land information management framework that would integrate formal, informal, and customary land systems with administrative and spatial components. This is hugely important because "property, even real property, is not a thing. Property is a concert of rights, associated with the thing, that regulates relationships between people" (Demarest 2008, 265).

The STDM makes large projects, such as the reconstruction of Afghanistan, possible through tools that facilitate recording all forms of land rights (even claims), all types of rights holders, and all kinds of land and property objects, regardless of the level of formality. The STDM also goes beyond some established conventions by providing an extendable basis for an efficient and effective system of recording land rights. It focuses on land and property rights that are neither registered nor registerable, as well as overlapping claims that may have to be adjudicated in terms of who (the claimant), where (the location of the claim), and what (the right involved). Finally, the STDM's emphasis on social tenure relationships reflects the concept of a continuum of land rights promoted by the Global Land Tool Network, UN-HABITAT, and the international community generally (Lemmen et al. 2009) (see figure 1).

CONCLUSION

With a comprehensive repository of land information, decisions about tenure and environmental conservation can be made efficiently and equitably. Even in the

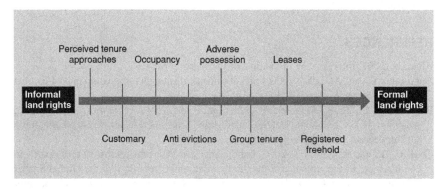

Figure 1. Land rights continuum
Source: UN-HABITAT (2008).

262 Land and post-conflict peacebuilding

absence of regional and national land policies, at the local level cadastres strengthen governance, further economic development, and institutionalize the rule of law—goals of the international community's post-conflict reconstruction efforts in Afghanistan. Where a cadastral system is in use, the rule of law is evident, and—according to Stig Enemark, president of FIG—"the system . . . acts as a backbone for society" (Enemark 2005, 8).

Although cadastres could be the deciding factor between success and failure for the international community's investment in post-conflict Afghanistan, they have not been reconstruction priorities in that destitute country. This is tragic, because the Afghan Geodesy and Cartography Head Office still boasts a cadastral division and has the capacity to conduct surveys. The office's analog cadastral surveying in the 1960s and 1970s was technically sound, and the staff has made considerable progress learning digital technologies in a GIS (geographic information system) laboratory over the past few years.

By recording the restrictions on environmentally harmful practices, and by assigning to a person or organization the responsibility for environmental stewardship, a cadastral system can visibly link environmental needs to human ones. The LADM promises the ability to record citizens' environmental concerns, rights, and interests, as well as the quasi-legal claims of landless people in tumultuous post-conflict environments so that they can be addressed, adjudicated, and later harmonized with regional and national land policies and administration. For large-scale post-disaster or post-conflict environments, the LADM merits close attention by the North Atlantic Treaty Organization, the United Nations, the U.S. Departments of State and Defense, USAID, and other entities seeking to move shattered nations from reconstruction to stability and then to sustainable development.

The Afghan environmental, economic, peacebuilding, and other initiatives discussed above, when recorded in cadastres, indicate that a key foundation of civil society is being built. If the sighting of a rare snow leopard in Afghanistan is sure to make headlines, the sighting of another rarity on the Afghan landscape—a cadastral survey party—is sure to make peace in that troubled country measurably closer to reality.

REFERENCES

Allan, N. 2007. Interview by the author of geographer. May 16.

Augustinus, C., and M. Barry. 2006. Land management strategy formulation in post-conflict societies. *Survey Review* 38 (302): 668–681.

Batson, D. E. 2008. *Registering the human terrain: A valuation of cadastre.* Washington, D.C.: National Defense Intelligence College Press. http://ni-u.edu/ni_press/pdf/Registering_the_Human_Terrains.pdf.

Cousins, B., and R. Kingwill. 2006. Land rights and cadastral reform in post-apartheid South Africa. Paper presented at the 9th International Conference of the Global Spatial Data Infrastructure (GSDI-9), Santiago, Chile, November 6–10. www.gsdidocs.org/gsdiconf/GSDI-9/abstracts/TS26.4abstract.pdf.

Demarest, G. 2008. *Property and peace: Insurgency, strategy, and the statute of frauds.* Fort Leavenworth, KS: United States Army Foreign Military Studies Office.

Cadastres in Afghanistan 263

Durand-Lasserve, A., and L. Royston. 2002. *Holding their ground: Secure land tenure for the urban poor in developing countries.* London: Earthscan.

Enemark, S. 2005. The land management perspective: Building the capacity. Paper presented at the ITC Lunstrum Conference, "Spatial Information for Civil Society: Capacity Building for the International Geo-information Society," Enschede, Netherlands, December 14–16.

FIG (International Federation of Surveyors). 1995. FIG statement on the cadastre—Summary. Copenhagen. www.fig.net/commission7/reports/cadastre/statement_on_cadastre _summary.html.

Foley, C. 2003. Afghanistan: The search for peace. Minority Rights Group International. www.minorityrights.org/download.php?id=45.

———. 2004. Legal aid for returnees: The NRC programme in Afghanistan. *Humanitarian Exchange* 26 (March). www.odihpn.org/report.asp?id=2610.

———. 2008. Housing, land, and property restitution rights in Afghanistan. In *Housing, land, and property rights in post-conflict United Nations and other peace operations: A comparative survey and proposal for reform*, ed. S. Leckie. Geneva, Switzerland: Centre on Housing Rights and Evictions.

Gall, C. 2006. Afghans, returning home, set off a building boom. *New York Times*, October 30.

Gebremedhin, Y. 2006. Legal issues pertaining to land titling and registration in Afghanistan: Land Titling and Economic Restructuring in Afghanistan (LTERA) Project. United States Agency for International Development. www.terrainstitute.org/pdf/USAID_LTERA _2006%20LEGAL_ISSUES_AFGHANISTAN.pdf.

IRIN (Integrated Regional Information Networks). 2003. Angola: Interview with Development Workshop director on land rights. IRIN Humanitarian News and Analysis, November 27. www.irinnews.org/report.aspx?reportid=47452.

———. 2007. Afghanistan: Environmental crisis looms as conflict goes on. IRIN Humanitarian News and Analysis, July 30. www.globalsecurity.org/military/library/news/ 2007/07/mil-070730-irin01.htm.

ISO/TC 211 (International Organization for Standardization/Technical Committee 211, Geographic Information/Geomatics). 2010. Resolutions from the 31st ISO/TC 211 plenary meeting in Canberra, Australia. Page 8. December 9–10. www.isotc211.org/ opendoc/211n3049/.

Lemmen, C., C. Augustinus, P. van Oosterom, and P. van der Molen. 2007. The Social Tenure Domain Model: Design of a first draft model. Paper presented at the International Federation of Surveyors Working Week, Hong Kong, May 13–17.

Lemmen, C., P. van Oosterom, H. Uitermark, R. Thompson, and J. Hespanha. 2009. Transforming the Land Administration Domain Model (LADM) into an ISO Standard (ISO 19152). Paper presented at the International Federation of Surveyors Working Week, Eilat, Israel, May 3–8. www.fig.net/pub/fig2009/papers/ts06a/ts06a_lemmen _oosterom_etal_3282.pdf.

Maassen, G. 2007. Interview by the author of chief of party to Land Titling and Economic Restructuring in Afghanistan. March 16.

Mojumdar, A. 2009. Afghanistan: Environmental protection initiative a sign of hope for reconstruction. *Eurasia Insight*, May 4. www.eurasianet.org/departments/insightb/ articles/eav050409a.shtml.

Rubin, B. R. 2006. Still ours to lose: Afghanistan on the brink. Washington, D.C.: Council on Foreign Relations. www.cfr.org/afghanistan/still-ours-lose-afghanistan-brink/ p11486.

264   Land and post-conflict peacebuilding

Safar, M. Y. 2007. Interview by the author of former chief of the cadastral department of the Afghan Geodesy and Cartography Head Office. March 10.

Setchell, C., and C. Luther. 2009. Kabul: A case study in responding to urban displacement. *Humanitarian Exchange* 45.

Smith, D. M. 2009. Afghanistan announces first national park: Despite ongoing conflict Afghans support environmental protection. *suite101.com*, June 24. http://ecosystem-preservation .suite101.com/article.cfm/afghanistan_announces_first_national_park#ixzz0JkE93AUB&D.

Stanfield, J. D. 2007. Community recording of property rights: Focus on Afghanistan. Paper presented at the annual conference and trade show of the International Association of Clerks, Recorders, Election Officials and Treasurers, Charlotte, NC, July 19.

Steudler, D., A. Rajabifard, and I. Williamson. 2004. Evaluation of land administration systems. *Land Use Policy* 21 (4): 371–380.

UK Defence Geographic Centre, Geographic Research Branch. 2006. *Summary of land ownership in Afghanistan.* Middlesex, UK.

UNECE (United Nations Economic Commission for Europe). 1996. Land administration guidelines: With special reference to countries in transition. ECE/HBP/96. Geneva, Switzerland. www.unece.org/fileadmin/DAM/hlm/documents/Publications/ land.administration.guidelines.e.pdf.

———. 2005. *Social and economic benefits of good land administration.* 2nd ed. London: Her Majesty's Land Registry.

UNEP (United Nations Environment Programme). 2003. UNEP report chronicles environmental damage of the Afghanistan conflict. January 29. http://new.unep.org/ Documents.Multilingual/Default.asp?DocumentID=277&ArticleID=3201&l=en.

UN-HABITAT (United Nations Human Settlements Programme). 2007. A post-conflict land administration and peacebuilding handbook. Volume 1, *Countries with land records.* Nairobi, Kenya. www.unhabitat.org/pmss/listItemDetails.aspx?publicationID=2443.

USAID (United States Agency for International Development). 2009a. Land titling and economic restructuring in Afghanistan: Projection completion report (2004–2009). http://pdf.usaid.gov/pdf_docs/PDACP698.pdf.

———. 2009b. National Environmental Protection Agency declares Afghanistan's first protected species list. Press release. June 3. http://afghanistan.usaid.gov/en/USAID/ Article/673/National_Environmental_Protection_Agency_Declares_Afghanistans_First _Protected_Species_List.

van Oosterom, P., C. Lemmen, T. Ingvarsson, P. van der Molen, H. Ploeger, W. Quak, J. Stoter, and J. Zevenbergern. 2006. The Core Cadastral Domain Model. *Computers, Environment and Urban Systems* 30 (5): 627–660.

World Bank. 2009. World Development Indicators. http://data.worldbank.org/country/ afghanistan.

Zahler, P., D. Wilkie, M. Painter, and J. C. Ingram. 2013. The role of conservation in promoting sustainability and security in at-risk communities. In *Governance, natural resources, and post-conflict peacebuilding,* ed. C. Bruch, C. Muffett, and S. S. Nichols. London: Earthscan.

Community documentation of land tenure and its contribution to state building in Afghanistan

J. D. Stanfield, Jennifer Brick Murtazashvili, M. Y. Safar, and Akram Salam

Turmoil for the past thirty years in Afghanistan has led to widespread insecurity, including in regard to land rights. While decades of conflict have severely weakened the formal justice system, this has not resulted in lawlessness. In the absence of effective formal authority, systems of land administration based on religious and customary practices have provided a measure of security.

Even before the 1979 Soviet invasion, when the authority of the Afghan state was at its apogee, the formal government was not actively involved in resolving land disputes. But when the state did exert its authority over land issues, it did so in an authoritarian manner, often redistributing massive amounts of land from one party to another.

This chapter explores various strategies employed by the government of Afghanistan, both historically and in contemporary times, as well as by foreign development assistance programs that aim to move the country out of a state of government failure and to enable the government to provide services to its citizens. It reports on a pilot project developed to encourage a sense of community ownership of locally crafted property records that document the right to use communally held rangeland and the ownership of privately held agricultural land. It presents suggestions for linking the administration of these records with the administration of property records in government agencies to forge stronger and more harmonious relations between rural people and the state. And it argues that community-state cooperation to provide a public service—in this case the documentation of land rights—can help minimize future conflicts over these land rights and fortify governance structures in general.

J. D. Stanfield is president of Terra Institute. Jennifer Brick Murtazashvili is an assistant professor in the Graduate School of Public and International Affairs at the University of Pittsburgh. M. Y. Safar is an Afghan cadastral survey and land administration specialist and a member of Terra Institute. Akram Salam is the general director of Cooperation for the Reconstruction of Afghanistan, an Afghan nongovernmental organization. The authors were members of or participated in Afghanistan's 2006–2007 Rural Land Administration Project.

266 Land and post-conflict peacebuilding

A FOOTHOLD FOR STATE BUILDING IN AFGHANISTAN

Informal arrangements at the village and clan levels about who has access to land, when, and for what purpose are far from perfect, but such arrangements have worked in the past, and even under the unstable conditions of the past thirty years have continued to function, particularly in rural areas, except in some places concerning use rights to rangeland. While citizens have had little contact with agencies of the state, and many view the state as hopelessly corrupt and irresponsible, informal mechanisms have provided land administration services in the absence of effective government rule (ICG 2007).

People involved in state building efforts in Afghanistan tend to view the relationship between formal and informal justice systems in zero-sum terms: the existence of legal systems based on customs undermines the authority of the formal government. Such a view is misplaced, however, in the context of Afghanistan, where the informal sector has demonstrated not only its ability to maintain records and mediate disputes in rural areas but also a willingness to cooperate with formal authorities.

The most common approach to state building focuses on creating formal government institutions, usually working from the top down and from the capital to the periphery. A key assumption is that new institutions and organizations must be created "from whole cloth [to create] missing state capabilities and institutions" (Fukuyama 2004, xi). This approach focuses on creating institutions and building capabilities that are largely absent in a failed state, beginning at the national level—with national elections, a constitution, and national policies that encourage a dynamic economy and multiparty political system for the country as a whole. Such an approach views a country like Afghanistan, which has been without a coherent central government for more than thirty years, as an institutional tabula rasa with no significant governing capabilities to build on.

A more productive approach is to ask which of the country's institutions could provide a foothold for state building projects (Brick 2008b). In Afghanistan, as in many weak states, the provision of public goods and services takes place in the absence of an effective centralized system of government (Bardhan 2005). Decision making and political and economic governance do take place, but may occur without the participation, consent, or awareness of the formal government. Economic and political activity does not grind to a halt because the state does not provide adequate services with the underpinning of formal law. Groups and individuals have much to gain by developing alternative institutions for providing public goods and services, particularly at the community level (Dixit 2004). It would seem wise to build upon this resilient governance capacity at the community level with a bottom-up approach that complements the top-down nation-building approach that has emerged from the failed-state analysis.

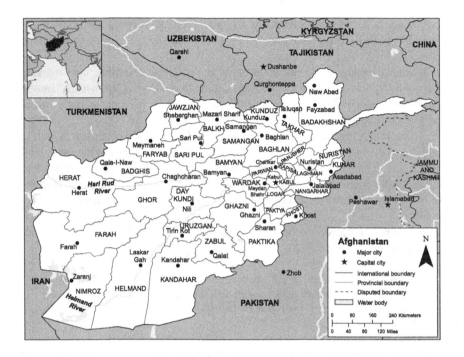

LAND ADMINISTRATION

An effective system of land administration is vital for the development of Afghanistan. Without effective property rights, incentives for innovation decline along with prospects for economic growth (North 1990; North and Thomas 1973). Current efforts to build an effective property and land management system go through the central government, without much regard for the far more pervasive and effective informal or customary system.

According to formal law, past and present, the Afghan judicial system is responsible for preparing and archiving deeds to land. During years of warfare, the physical state of these archives severely deteriorated, and the personnel who administered them fled or were killed. Compounding these physical challenges is the complex web of laws, regulations, and agencies administering land rights, making the system costly to utilize. As a result, court-prepared deeds document the rights to less than 10 percent of rural properties and less than 30 percent of urban properties.

Lack of a court-prepared deed does not necessarily result in acute tenure insecurity. Informal transactions, mediated by respected community leaders, are the primary mechanism through which individuals secure tenure rights. Some acquisitions involve privately drafted customary deeds, written transfer agreements that are witnessed by locally respected people but kept by the parties to

268 Land and post-conflict peacebuilding

the transaction and not recorded in any government office. Other transactions involve verbal agreements witnessed by family members and respected village elders.[1]

Such transactions do not occur daily in most villages, since land markets are generally not very active. The transactions that do occur are usually among family members or community residents who respect verbal agreements, particularly regarding inheritance or family or tribal transactions.

The recording of documents defining rights to real properties in public registries becomes important when there are multiple claimants to the same land and where land markets are more dynamic, such as in urban and peri-urban areas. Under such conditions, lack of documentation produces varying degrees of insecurity of tenure as perceived by the property holders or potential property holders.

Tenure is perceived to be more secure when rights to land are seen as both legitimate and legally valid:

> Secure rights to land and property depend on a combination of two key elements. The rights being claimed must be seen, first, as legitimate by the local population; and second, they must also be ascribed legality by the state (Toulmin 2006, 4).

Afghan community customs provide rules that are often more effective in guiding people's everyday lives than the country's formal laws and regulations. Rights to land may be recognized as legitimate by the community, as in the customary deeds described above, even though they are not documented in accordance with legally defined procedures.[2] Government officials may issue documentation of rights to land that is drawn up in strict accordance with legal requirements, even though it faces strong local opposition—such as allotment of land to a developer. In such cases, land rights may be legally valid yet not considered socially legitimate. Such situations may contribute to conflict.

Bringing about the conditions under which land rights can be recognized as both socially legitimate and legally valid is of critical importance for Afghanistan's development. To this end, the Afghan government made a cadastral effort to document landholdings between 1964 and 1977. This effort focused on applying formal law to adjudicate claims to land through field teams assembled and trained by a state agency, the Cadastral Survey. In Afghanistan,

---

[1] In many communities, illiterate villagers confirm transactions by inking their fingerprint on a document to signify agreement to a private contract not drawn up by a judge. This process is known as *shasht*. One of the greatest challenges in Afghanistan is the high rate of illiteracy in the rural population. Because of this, even if a streamlined land records system could be established, it is questionable whether many people would participate in it.

[2] See Sheleff (2000) for a useful discussion of the literature on customary law, and Zadran (1977) for a description of Pashtun customary law in Afghanistan.

as in some other countries, these technical field teams consulted with community leaders and landholders to identify boundaries and rights to land. However, following these consultations, the governmental agency responsible typically archived the information in centralized archives and used it in often distant governmental offices.[3]

Similar approaches in many countries have tended to focus on equipping and training field adjudication and survey teams. They also typically develop cadastral agencies for producing accurate parcel maps and promoting specialized government land registries for administering the legal documents that define property rights. If such an effort is attempted again in Afghanistan, the institutions carrying it out must find a new way to become connected to the people of Afghanistan. Only with a valid strategy will they be in a position to work toward their objectives and become equipped and trained to do their jobs properly, extending their services to the community typically through the use of information and communication technologies.

The court-administered system of land transaction deeds is not widely used in rural areas; instead, customary deeds are drawn up privately by the parties involved in the transactions. It is not likely that a sporadic involvement of the courts in formalizing land rights will manage to merge the legitimacy of customary transactions with the requirements for legal validity on the widespread basis needed.

STATE-BASED RURAL LAND ADMINISTRATION IN AFGHANISTAN

Afghanistan has a total land mass of 64.9 million hectares, of which 7.8 million are classified for agricultural use, including 3.3 million hectares of irrigable land. About one-half of this land is under cultivation.[4] Even with this underutilization of agricultural land, the agricultural sector continues to be a primary contributor to the nation's gross national product and to provide the largest number of jobs. It is essential to the economic development of the country, and its growth will be an important factor in the reduction of poverty.

Accurate land use statistics for Afghanistan are difficult to obtain. A 1993 study of land use indicated that for that year about 12 percent of the total land area of the country was available for agriculture. The amount of land currently available is somewhat lower, due to the almost continuous conflict as well as periodic droughts (FAO 1999; Alden Wily 2003b).

Rangeland

Millions of Afghan rural people, especially nomads, depend heavily on Afghanistan's approximately 30 million hectares of rangeland to survive. Rangeland is legally

---

[3] For a review of various approaches to land administration, including property records administration, see Burns et al. (2006).

[4] This section is drawn from Stanfield (2007) and Safar and Stanfield (2007).

270 Land and post-conflict peacebuilding

defined as public land and cannot be privately owned.[5] Families, clans, tribes, and nomadic groups use it to feed livestock, as a source of fuel and of medicinal and culinary herbs, and to move livestock from one place to another. Rangelands are also crucial water catchment systems. Their degradation can lead to erosion and lower the level of aquifers, negatively affecting both farmers and urban residents.

In recent decades, many rangelands have become degraded, and others have been converted to rainfed agriculture. In drought years and in low rainfall areas, this severely weakens the capability of the land to regenerate a stabilizing plant cover. Rangeland has decreased at the same time as demand for it has grown, and conflicts between farmers and pastoralists have increased. Evidence suggests that pastures are the principal focus of conflict in Afghanistan because they involve and affect more people than conflicts over farms or houses. Conflicts over pastureland may also inflame ethnic or other group tensions (Alden Wily 2004).

According to the Land Management Law of 2000, villagers have the exclusive right of use of community pastureland, which is defined in article 9 as "the area from where the loud voice of someone standing at the edge of the village can still be heard." Grazing areas that are beyond this boundary are called public pastures. In the past, village elders and tribal leaders met and agreed over the use of community pastures, and, in some cases, public pastures (Barfield 2004). In other cases, public pastures could be used by anyone at any time. These agreements were mediated informally, generally without the involvement of government authorities.

Customs and traditions relating to the use of community and public pastures are more tentative today than they were before the 1980s: due to the passage of time and the displacement of people, rights are often not clear and people's confidence in exercising them is often not high. Such instability and uncertainty provides fertile ground for conflicts over land use and tenure.

Agricultural land

Users of agricultural land face less confusion about their rights to the land than users of rangelands, but they typically do not have legally produced deeds to their properties. Most have either customary deeds, produced and witnessed locally, or no documentation at all (McEwen and Whitty 2006). This can create problems for rural people who return to their lands after leaving to find work or escape violence. While local knowledge can verify their land rights, lack of documentation can limit their access to credit and institutional assistance.

---

[5] Article 84 of the Land Management Law of 2000, states: "Pastures are public property, an individual or the State may not own pasturelands, unless otherwise stipulated by sharia [Islamic law]." It also states that pastures are to be reserved for public use by the villagers (such as for cattle grazing areas, graveyards, and threshing grounds).

The Amlak

During the reign of the Afghan king Mohammad Zahir Shah in the early 1960s, the Amlak Department was officially established within the Ministry of Finance to handle the government's interests in land. It was composed of the Directorate of State Properties, which was to manage state-owned land, and the Directorate for Private Properties for recording the allocation of state land to private owners. The Directorate for Land Surveying was also created, which was conventionally called the "directorate of land measurers"; measurers were assigned to prepare the sketches for land surface measurement for the calculation and collection of property taxes (Nasser 2005). During the bureaucratic reforms of Prime Minister Mohammed Daud Khan (1973–1974), the Amlak developed further and gained a great deal of independence within the Ministry of Finance.

Subsequently, to implement its plans for progressive land taxation and for an ambitious land reform program, the Daud government needed detailed information about agricultural landholdings. To this end, the Amlak was tasked in 1975 with the much enlarged responsibility of creating ownership records, based on declarations by each rural household of how much land the household owned. Updating this household-level information continues to be a task of the provincial Amlak offices.

In addition to recording landownership, the Amlak has the legal authority to administer the rights of the state in rangelands, which the law defines as state owned. This authority is only exercised sporadically, for example in response to conflicts among local users or unauthorized conversions of rangeland to agricultural land. Amlak officials do not normally get involved with local arrangements for rangeland use.

Thus the Amlak has been an instrument of the central government in land reform and taxation and has intermittently exerted the state's rights over rangeland. These efforts have had a mixed reception at the community level, due to resentment over taxes, land redistribution, and the extraction of rents for the use of rangelands. (Although the state claims ownership of rangelands, the rural population has traditionally considered them to be community lands.) Over the years, the Amlak, like most government agencies, has lost much of its authority in rural areas; it is largely disconnected from the lives of rural people.

The Cadastral Survey

In an effort that was institutionally separate from the Amlak, the government staffed and equipped sixteen regional Cadastral Survey directorates from 1964 to 1986. These directorates contained the records of surveys of 5,379 tax units conducted throughout the provinces.[6] The Cadastral Survey was installed in the

---

[6] A tax unit was a defined geographic area whose boundaries were established by the Ministry of Finance for property tax collection. Units normally coincided with village boundaries but could include a number of hamlets.

mid-1970s as a department within the Afghanistan Geodesy and Cartography Head Office, under the office of the prime minister, where it remains to this day.

By 1978, these surveys covered about one-third of Afghanistan's cultivated agricultural land, or about 4 million hectares. (Although small amounts of land were added to the Cadastral Survey through 1986, data are not available on the exact amounts surveyed during this period.) This enormous effort did not, however, lead to the establishment of a nationwide land registration system or to the issuance of formal title documents for the surveyed land parcels. The entry of an owner's name on survey forms was not official confirmation of ownership but rather a statement of probable ownership based on the data collected by the survey teams.

The population has had little contact with the regional cadastral offices. Cadastral and Amlak records have not been integrated. The Amlak does not use the cadastral records, and the courts also largely ignore them when preparing deeds. Thus, these land records have gradually lost their accuracy and potential usefulness.

The courts

The primary court system for documenting land transactions, which began in the early 1900s, continued during and after the Cadastral and Amlak surveys described above and is now the primary method of formally documenting landownership. Court-issued land documents are based on verbal descriptions of parcel boundaries; when agricultural land is involved, the court also asks the Amlak for verification of ownership. Provincial appeals courts maintain archives containing all court documents produced in their provinces, including land deeds (Stanfield, Reed, and Safar 2005). However, the judiciary and other agencies that administer property ownership information are weak. Figure 1 shows an example of extreme

Figure 1. Property documents in the Kabul Provincial Court Archives, 2003
Source: Photo by M. Y. Safar.

Community documentation of land tenure in Afghanistan   273

disorder in the archiving of property documents. Despite efforts to reorganize property document archives, the problem remains.

Given the web of people and agencies involved, formal documentation of land transactions is costly in terms of both time and money. For this and other reasons, it has been estimated that fewer than 10 percent of the owners of rural properties and fewer than 30 percent of the owners of urban properties have a court-issued deed (McEwen and Whitty 2006; LTERA 2006). Most people simply do not use this formal institutional structure.

CUSTOMARY COMMUNITY GOVERNANCE

The authority of the central Afghan government has rarely extended to the community level. Even the 2004 constitution's call for elected village councils has yet to be implemented. As a result, there is no formal government structure that extends beyond the district level, and villages have no legal representation to the state. In the absence of effective formal authority to resolve property disputes, customary procedures at the village level have emerged throughout the country.

Customary village authorities are not perfect or fully representative of their communities. Women, for example, are underrepresented and are often absent altogether from public meetings. Nonetheless, studies such as that conducted by the Asia Foundation and field experiences of the authors support the notion that citizens view these village authorities as effective and legitimate and trust them more than any other public organization in the country (Asia Foundation 2007). In the absence of an effective government, they remain the best available solution to problems of governance throughout rural areas of the country.

The definition of community can be complicated in Afghanistan, where concepts describing rural community life include *qarya* (often translated as "village"), *qishlāq* (usually meaning "settlement," from a Turkic root meaning "place of winter settlement"), *manteqa* (meaning "area"), and *mahalla* (meaning "neighborhood").[7]

While formal governance structures may be weak or nonexistent in many areas, some customary community structures are quite resilient. Often referred to as traditional or informal structures, they are not static but evolve over time. Afghanistan is an extremely diverse country in terms of geography and culture, and it is difficult to generalize about customary community governance systems, but certain patterns are common. Such systems are characterized by three main actors, whose roles may sometimes overlap:

- *Maliks* are local leaders who represent the community to government agencies and vice versa—for example, on issues relating to land and water.
- *Shuras* or (as they are known in Pashtun areas) *jirgas* are village councils that decide on family disputes and forge community consensus about needed

---

[7] For discussion of these terms, see Mielke and Schetter (2007); Brick (2008a); and Allan (2001).

274   Land and post-conflict peacebuilding

collective action, particularly in reference to the legitimate users of common lands and the legitimate holders of agricultural land.

- *Mullahs* are religious leaders who, in addition to providing religious instruction, interpret Islamic rules that guide behavior and dispute resolution, including those pertaining to inheritance of land and the legitimization of transfers of land rights.

The malik is a key figure in community governance in Afghanistan.[8] Chosen by the community but not formally elected, maliks are arguably the most important members of the Afghan national political system, although they do not hold formal political office (Nojumi 2002). In Afghanistan, community members historically have viewed their village leaders as self-made men who

> achieve their position through personality, not age or genealogical position . . . they create unity out of difference, or restore a previous unity . . . they are patrons, acting on behalf of trusting clients, but use their own initiative in action, risking their followers' disapproval; they speak to government as representatives rather than delegates (Tapper 1983, 56).

The term *malik* thus does not refer to a local government official. It is a descriptive title for those who achieve positions of influence in tribal or local governance (Hager 1983). Maliks are generally responsible for holding documents required or issued by government agencies that affect the community, such as royal decrees awarding land rights to the community or to certain families. Villagers view the malik as the person who represents them in official functions and interacts with the government.

Maliks tend to be literate people from prominent or well-respected families. They usually inherit the position from a father or grandfather who was also a malik. However, it is not uncommon for a malik to be unseated and replaced if members of the community are dissatisfied with his work. Through years of conflict and displacement, several prominent families that provided maliks and other village notables have left their communities and have not returned. In these areas, villages have selected new individuals to serve as maliks. Maliks do not act on their own. They represent community interests to the government and usually work alongside councils composed of mullahs and elders.

Shuras or jirgas (councils) convene from time to time in local communities and at times in regional gatherings. They are traditionally composed of family or clan elders, and have played important roles in resolving community, regional, and national conflicts and in establishing agreements about general policies

---

[8] Other names for malik in different parts of the country are *arbab, qaryadar, nomayenda, kalantar*, and *khan*. Most but not all maliks are men. During field research in 2007, Jennifer Brick interviewed a female malik in Balkh Province in northern Afghanistan. The deputy governor of Balkh Province also indicated during an interview that there were four female maliks in the province.

Community documentation of land tenure in Afghanistan 275

(Wardak 2003). They tend to support the actions of the malik, but it is highly unlikely that a malik could act unilaterally without the support of community elders. The maliks are influenced by the community councils, which serve a valuable purpose in holding the maliks accountable to the community as they deal with state institutions.

Maliks and shuras or jirgas have periodically organized to express opposition to a centralizing state (Brick 2008a). Amin Saikal and William Maley have argued that "given the difficulty of building a strong central state capable of restraining the impulses of powerful social groups, a governance system strongly based in community decision making structures has the best prospect of providing a degree of order and stability in the long-run" (Saikal and Maley 1991, 6). M. Nazif Shahrani argues that the strength of Afghan community organizations must be taken into account by the central government (Shahrani 1998). Yet, too often the central government has sought to replace these organizations rather than work with them.

Mullahs are local religious figures who have varying importance in Afghan communities; they are far more numerous than maliks. A community of 1,000 people is likely to have one malik but perhaps three or four mosques, each with its own mullah. While mullahs play an important role in adjudicating family disputes and giving advice about other family and community issues, they are also constrained in their actions by community shuras and maliks.

Maliks and shuras generally play a more important role than mullahs with regard to land administration, because land administration is seen as a more bureaucratic and procedural issue. Mullahs typically become key actors during the resolution of disputes, especially those regarding inheritance, with the support of other actors in the village. Some mullahs are influential in a wider range of community issues.

The nature of these village institutions has led Afghan village governance to be consensus-driven rather than dominated by one charismatic personality. The interactions of the three village governance institutions—maliks, shuras and jirgas, and mullahs—tend to hold separate village powers and thus prevent one from dominating. While they are far from perfect or perfectly representative, as discussed earlier, these organizations have represented community interests better than any alternative presented by the government of Afghanistan or other actors in the past century.

Maliks, supported by their village council and other leaders, meet regularly with the *woluswal*, or district governor, who is usually appointed by the provincial governor. The woluswal currently represents the lowest level of the Afghan state governance structure. The woluswal and the maliks exchange information about community and government activity. The woluswal also helps resolve disputes within a village or between villages when the disputants have been unable to come to a resolution themselves.

Almost every village in Afghanistan has a village council, a village leader, and a religious leader. Their names may differ, and so may the informal or customary laws they apply. In Pashtun areas, for example, *Pashtunwali* (Pashtun tribal code) may be used to resolve a dispute, while other areas may rely more heavily on

276 Land and post-conflict peacebuilding

religious law. But in most areas, there is a division of authority within communities that works to increase the accountability of these informal bodies to citizens.

Settled villagers cultivating agricultural land and maintaining livestock are not the only people who get into disputes over land rights. In many areas of Afghanistan, pastoralists move vast distances with their herds and use rangelands according to seasonal availability. While the exact figure is not known, they may number nearly 2 million. Afghan pastoralists are popularly called *Kuchi*, which literally means "to move."[9] The term includes not only Pashtun pastoralists but also other pastoralist communities, like the Baluch in the north. Being Kuchi, particularly for the Pashtun but also for the Baluch, refers not only to migration but to a code of dress, behavior, and dialect. Even settled Kuchi who have not migrated in several years still consider themselves to be Kuchi.

Kuchi communities are not necessarily fixed entities; families leave and rejoin as their needs dictate, depending on the availability of rangeland, agricultural land, pasture, and water and the traditions of migration. Several households typically migrate together, splitting from the community and rejoining it in the summer or winter area. This migration is not centrally organized but is determined at the household level. Communities provide security in numbers, provide support and labor opportunities for the poor, and serve as a pool of shared labor (Glatzer 1982). Kuchi-settled communities have a malik who typically represents their interests in the decision-making councils of regional gatherings of Kuchi clans, or in discussions with governmental officials.

A Kuchi community is defined in the National Multi-sectoral Assessment on Kuchi (de Weijer 2005) as a group of households that have the same winter and summer grazing area (*dasht*). One grazing area can contain more than one community. Generally, these communities have a clear, tribally based sense of identity and a clear leadership structure that includes a shura.

In Afghanistan as elsewhere, it is not uncommon for agriculturalists and pastoralists to compete over land and water rights. Groups may negotiate customary arrangements and mutually advantageous relations at one time, only to see them deteriorate when neither settled nor nomadic families have surpluses for trade or exchange. However, customary law still exists and, even when under pressure, settled and pastoral people are usually able to agree on use of pastures. Most such agreements were crafted during Zahir Shah's reign of the early 1960s, when many informal agreements were developed that allowed migrants seasonal access to pastures in exchange for a commitment that if their livestock interfered with crops, they would pay full compensation. "What these kinds of informal agreements suggest is that the potential for pastoral and settled people to reconcile their land interests does exist" (de Weijer 2005, 10).

It is important not to idealize customary arrangements, which can break down and can themselves be sources of conflict or lack legitimacy. But these

---

[9] In this chapter, the terms *Kuchi* and *nomad* are used interchangeably.

Community documentation of land tenure in Afghanistan   277

limitations do not invalidate the community-based approach to land administration as a general strategy.

THE RURAL LAND ADMINISTRATION PROJECT

While often weak or afflicted by tensions, both settled and pastoralist communities have developed structures for producing public goods and services for their members and even for resolving disputes over rangeland access. An effective way to help rebuild and strengthen Afghanistan would be for the central government to recognize these community structures. Future governments will likely be more successful if they build upon communities as the basic unit of government rather than treating them as an afterthought of centrally based public administration. Shahrani observes that Afghanistan

> must choose to build . . . [the] national state on the proven strengths of . . . "civil society," the powerful self-governing community structures that have reemerged as part of the . . . most recent struggles. . . . A national government must be committed to . . . guaranteeing the constitutional rights of community self-governance at the local, district, provincial, and regional levels throughout the country—that is, allowing local communities to run their own local civil, judicial, security and educational administrations by themselves (Shahrani 1998, 240).

State building efforts usually focus only on creating new institutions, including local institutions like the community development councils (CDCs),[10] assuming the absence of coherent governance from top to bottom. In Afghanistan, however, as discussed above, myriad customary institutions exist at the local level that provide a wide variety of valued political goods, including security, property dispute resolution, conflict resolution in general, representation of community interests to the government, and water and land resource management. These local institutions have proven resilient in many rural communities, and can provide a foundation for the reconstruction of links between the institutions of the central and provincial governments and village residents, who represent over 70 percent of the population of the country.

One attempt to link state and community governance mechanisms emerged in reference to the administration of rural land records. The 2006–2007 Rural Land Administration Project (RLAP) was based on the assumption that community-based administration of property records, supported by state institutions, was appropriate to existing Afghan conditions and could contribute to long-term rebuilding of state-community relations. It was defined as the administration of property records by local people—rather than by the district office of a central

---

[10] CDCs are sponsored by the Ministry of Rural Development and Reconstruction's National Solidarity Program to administer funds for infrastructure projects (Brick 2008a).

278 Land and post-conflict peacebuilding

land registry receiving petitions and recording transactions or periodically sending a team to communities to gather evidence of land transactions.

The hypothesis was that if people produced and controlled access to their own land records, they would feel more secure in formal land documentation and be more likely to use it and take care of it. Liz Alden Wily describes this approach as the "empowerment of people at the local level to manage their land relations themselves" and says, "Only when land administration and management is fully devolved to the community level . . . is there likely to be significant success in bringing the majority of land interests under useful and lasting record-centered management" (Alden Wily 2003a, 35).

This emphasis on community definition of rights and community administration of the records that document these rights does not mean that formal law and the role of district and provincial land agencies can or should be ignored. The community consultation approach must include the views of all community segments about who holds legitimate rights to land. To solidify security of tenure for the long term, it must strengthen the links between local and national systems of land records administration.

Community-based administration of rural land property rights

As discussed above, earlier attempts by the Afghan government to document rural landownership—through the Amlak, the Cadastral Survey, and the courts—failed to win the confidence of the general public. All three attempts started from classical conceptions of the government's role in providing the public with an integrated land registration system to identify the true owners of rural land.

The RLAP started, instead, by asking what rural people actually want in terms of information about property rights and how to satisfy this demand. Its experience suggests some practical components of a community-based administration of property rights in land.

The project began in June 2006, primarily focusing on community consultations to define legitimate rights to rangeland (Stanfield, Safar, and Salam 2008). Procedures were developed for documenting rights to communal pasturelands in four test sites through consultations with leaders such as maliks, village shuras, mullahs who are knowledgeable about traditional rangeland use patterns, and representatives of nomadic groups who share the same rangelands during certain times of the year.

The project developed a precise methodology for these village and nomadic entities to agree among themselves about who has the right to use what rangeland, for what purposes, during what times of the year. This approach to defining the operational rules for managing rangelands relies on decision making that is structured and regulated by the local community, within the broad legal framework of the state.

During this process, participants were able to resolve most differences of opinion, though this sometimes required lengthy discussions. In the few cases

Community documentation of land tenure in Afghanistan   279

in which agreement was not possible within a reasonable amount of time, the disputants were referred to nongovernmental organizations for continued mediation. The RLAP searched for agreements and found them or helped craft them on the spot, documented their features, and validated them through consultations with neighboring community leaders and district government officials.

Legitimate rights and valid rights

The RLAP distinguished between legitimate rights (supported by custom) and valid rights (supported by law).[11] A legitimate right to land is reached by consensus of the village shura, elders, maliks, mullahs, nomadic maliks, and heads of families. It could be called a customary right in other contexts, one which by tradition and custom is considered correct and acceptable by the community. Alden Wily suggests the following defining characteristics of legitimate or customary rights to land:

- Customary rights are often called informal rights, because they usually have not been formalized in writing.
- They change over time, and recognizing customary land tenure today means recognizing the norms and practices of today.
- One critical element of custom, which never changes, is that the frame of reference for decisions is the local community, not the government. Any practice or rule that is agreed on by the local community can be considered customary (Alden Wily n.d.).

By contrast, a valid right to land is described in a document prepared or validated according to a process established in state legislation and administered by state agencies. A valid right can also be legitimate, but if, for example, it was acquired through force or corruption, it might not be legitimate even if it was supported by legally valid documentation. The goal is that these two concepts will someday become equivalent, but that is not the case now. For now, the sorting out of legitimate rights to land is best centered in the community, while efforts are made to improve as quickly as possible the relations between communities and the state.

Following success in agreeing on rangeland rights in the RLAP's four test sites, villagers in the Naw Abad test site in Chardara District, Kunduz Province, suggested that the private holders of agricultural land in their village would be interested in using the same consultation and documentation procedures to document their rights to their irrigated agricultural land parcels in ways that would be recognized as legally valid by state institutions. Community elders and leaders invited the field team to work with them to reach consensus on the legitimate holders of private ownership rights to agricultural land.

---

[11] For rangelands, which are by definition public, the focus was on use rights and not ownership.

280 Land and post-conflict peacebuilding

Naw Abad is a Kuchi settlement based on irrigated agriculture and on large, tribally managed pastures close to the settlement as well as public pastures in the distant mountains. Village leaders were initially interested in working with the RLAP to document the legitimate rights of use of pasturelands, but then saw the relevance of the same methodology to the clarification of ownership of agricultural land, housing, and commercial parcels. This interest came in part from the difficulties experienced by some families in the recent past with returning migrants or their children or grandchildren, who claimed land in Naw Abad that had been used for many years by other people.

Regarding both communal rangeland and privately held agricultural land, the hypothesis gradually emerged that community interest in documenting land rights could be substantially increased if the documentation remained in the village, accessible to local people and under their control.

The project aimed to improve customary practices for administering rights to both types of land, based on the following hypotheses:

- A local consensus can be reached about the rights people that have to rangeland and agricultural land.
- This consensus can be strengthened through documentation witnessed by respected people from the community.
- This documentation can and should be maintained by the community.
- Information about rights to land, produced and maintained by the community but linked to government land administration agencies, can make a significant contribution to land tenure security under present Afghan conditions.

The use of a community-based property rights system does not make government agencies and the legal framework irrelevant. On the contrary, the reestablishment of positive community-state relations is critically important for a stable and resilient administration of property rights. The RLAP started with the community as a locus of rural land administration and management. However, a national program must be developed to strengthen the capacity of both communities and state agencies to carry out these functions if Afghanistan is to achieve a viable and effective governance system.

Community

The RLAP defined a community as a settlement with a locally known name that is served by a functioning CDC.[12] Most of the selected communities also had

---

[12] The RLAP selected villages that had at least two years of experience with a CDC, because it did not have the resources or time to work with village leaders to call a special shura together or to train shura members in formal record keeping. Elected village councils, as called for in the 2004 constitution, have not yet been established, but numerous villages have CDCs.

Community documentation of land tenure in Afghanistan 281

the services of an *arbab* (the equivalent of a malik in the project area), although the function of linking the community with outside agencies also is frequently carried out by an influential mullah.[13]

The RLAP did not invent the idea of community administration of land rights. The Ministry of Urban Development and the municipality of Kabul developed a similar approach for regularizing the tenure of some informal settlements in Kabul (LTERA 2006). Afghanistan's draft land policy states in section 2.2.4: "The government shall promote land tenure regularization in [informal settlements] in collaboration with relevant communities based on standards to be established by law" (Islamic Republic of Afghanistan 2007, 6). A 2007 review of land registration options for Afghanistan makes the following recommendation:

> Any future system for land registration should be rooted at the community level. The system will be able to draw upon community knowledge, practical understanding of local issues, and tried and tested (if sometimes imperfect) systems to resolve disputes. By directly engaging the community, the system will be viewed as transparent, equitable and legitimate. Also, implementation costs can be kept to a minimum and public access to records will be improved (McEwen and Nolan 2007, 23).

In other countries, similar ideas are being tested. For example, in Benin, village land tenure management committees have been adjudicating titles and administering the resulting property records (Delville 2006). And Tanzania's 1999 Village Land Act calls for village land committees to validate claims to land and village land registries to administer the land records, in coordination with their district counterparts.

The ADAMAP process for documenting land rights

Project staff and villagers held discussions on the viability of the community approach for documenting land rights and recording those rights in community land files. Discussions covered both rangeland (usually communally managed) and agricultural land (usually privately owned). Once village leaders agreed to the benefits of this activity, and the shura invited RLAP staff to move forward, documentation procedures were developed using a method called ADAMAP, which involved the following steps:

A: Ask for community cooperation.
D: Delineate the boundaries of different types of lands.
A: Agreements are prepared.
M: Meet, discuss, and approve the agreements and delineations.
A: Archive the agreements and delineations.
P: Prepare for the continual updating and security of property records.

---

[13] See Wardak, Zaman, and Nawabi (2007) for a discussion of the importance of local and regional religious leaders.

282 Land and post-conflict peacebuilding

ADAMAP builds on and formalizes traditional rules based on sharia (Islamic law) about land access and use that have eroded during years of conflict and disruption. The objective is to secure agreements, document legitimate use rights, and allow ready public access to these documents. For documenting rights to rangeland, the community's responsibilities include the following:

- Initial recording of traditional rights of access and use by both settled people and nomads.
- Mapping of rangeland parcel boundaries on large-scale satellite images (RLAP 2007).
- Preparation of appropriately witnessed agreements by relevant stakeholders.
- Storage of agreements and images in village-administered storage cabinets.

With slight modifications, this process is also feasible for certifying private ownership of agricultural land.[14] The village team prepares parcel specification forms, in consultation with the owners or their representatives, which are then reviewed and approved by a group of village elders. The team also delineates the boundaries of each parcel on a satellite map and gives it a unique identification number.

Copies of the documentation are filed with the provincial government. Parcel maps are digitized and copied into a geographic information system (GIS) for incorporation into appropriate databases and for cross-referencing at the community, district, province, and national levels. Procedures are also established to change these agreements when there is local consensus to do so.

In Naw Abad, the field team selected a block of one hundred privately owned parcels by inspecting satellite imagery and verified that the Cadastral Survey had maps and parcel cards available for those parcels (albeit from thirty years earlier). Through consultations with the owners of the parcels, boundaries were delineated on high-resolution Quickbird satellite imagery (provided by the National Geospatial-Intelligence Agency through the International Security Assistance Force in Kabul) plotted at the scale of 1:2,000. Each was assigned a unique number, and ownership and use information were noted for each on a parcel specification form. The names of subsidiary users, sharecroppers, or other users were also noted. A parcel-based information system emerged, using the model shown in figure 2.

To limit the likelihood of unauthorized modifications to the forms or maps, two procedures were devised:

1. A log book listed all parcel forms in sequence, with basic information about each, including ownership. Any subsequent modification of a form must be authorized by the shura and so indicated on the forms and in the log book.

---

[14] See McEwen and Nolan (2007) for suggestions for private parcel tenure recording.

Community documentation of land tenure in Afghanistan 283

Figure 2. Sample land record from the village of Naw Abad in Kunduz Province
Source: Photo by J. D. Stanfield.

284 Land and post-conflict peacebuilding

2. The delineated parcel maps were digitized, and the forms were digitally photographed. Subsequently these digital records were combined into a simple GIS and archived in an appropriate government agency.

Shura members from Naw Abad asked for satellite images of the village's remaining agricultural land and blank copies of the parcel forms, so that they could complete the file of maps and forms for all of the privately owned agricultural land.

The legal basis for community-based land administration

Community-based land administration should be supported by clear national policies and laws. At this point, such a comprehensive framework does not exist in Afghanistan. In its absence, the RLAP has drawn on three key documents.[15]

The 2004 Policy and Strategy for the Forestry and Range Management Sub-Sectors, approved by the Ministry of Agriculture, Irrigation and Livestock in 2005, states:

> The sub-sector partners shall adopt a community-based approach in forestry, range and wildlife management. This approach shall involve the transfer of effective management responsibilities for forestry and range resources within defined community geographical areas to communities in a manner which (i) creates value for community members (both in the form of productive resources— timber, firewood, better pasture, and as means of protecting natural resources from erosion), and (ii) develops within communities the capacities to organise, operate and sustain the improved measures with a minimum of support from outside (MAIL 2005, 2).

A clearer statement of land issues and policies needed to address them was contained in the draft 2007 Multi-ministerial Land Policy, produced by a commission in which the Ministries of Agriculture, Justice, and Urban Development and Housing were represented:

> 2.2.7 Issue: Proof of Rights to Land: In most cases, proof of land rights is based upon tax records, Amlak registration, customary deeds, formal deeds and local knowledge. Some formal deeds are suspect or fraudulent; in some areas registered deeds have been destroyed during the years of conflict. Under such a chaotic property rights situation, it is imperative for the government to establish a realistic and effective method of property clarification process. Best practices and the reality in the country inform that community-based property adjudication processes that utilize local knowledge can be effective vehicle [sic] to re-identify local ownership. 2.2.7 Policy

---

[15] The draft 2007 Multi-ministerial Land Policy and the 2008 Afghan National Development Strategy, both published subsequent to the RLAP's completion in 2007, were drawn upon by RLAP when the documents were in their draft forms.

Community documentation of land tenure in Afghanistan 285

- It is a national policy that landownership may be documented through a process of property clarification and certification process conducted at the community level.
- It is a national policy that recognition be given to customary documentation and legitimate traditional property rights affirmed by local knowledge, in accordance with a law to be issued to govern the regularization of property rights (Islamic Republic of Afghanistan 2007, 7).

Finally, the 2008 Afghan National Development Strategy calls for Afghanistan to

> create the capability to record and archive information about the customary deeds, if not actual copies of such deeds, at the local level in villages or combinations of villages, where local elders and respected people can oversee and verify the continuous accuracy of the locally archived property rights information (Islamic Republic of Afghanistan 2008, 29).

Even more important for the RLAP were the opinions of provincial appeals court judges in Kunduz and Herat provinces, who reviewed the ADAMAP procedures and resulting documentation.[16] These two judges advised that should such documentation be presented to them during a court case, they would treat it as significant evidence of rights. Both judges said that when they hear village land disputes, their first step is to require that the disputants get the opinions of their village shuras. The ADAMAP process includes documentation of the shura's views.

RESPONSES TO THE ADAMAP PROCESS

Villagers, community leaders, and district government staff have reacted positively to the ADAMAP method in three provinces (Kunduz, Takhar, and Herat), welcoming the help it offers both in verifying use rights (for communally held rangeland) and ownership (for privately held agricultural land) and in archiving the resulting documentation.

Villagers expressed satisfaction with the work done by the field teams, which included both project specialists and villagers. People saw that the process can lead to stable land relations and agreement about the legitimate users of rangeland, how these lands should be managed, and the responsibilities of communities and the state for the administration of documentation of both rangelands and agricultural lands.

Especially important for villagers is the preservation of documents in the village itself, which will enable them to address land problems that may arise in the future without the expense of traveling to consult distant government agencies. Several villages have established what they call a land administration room, located in the shura compound or in a mosque or cooperative office, where

---

[16] The author interviewed the appeals court judge in Kunduz in May 2007 and the appeals court judge in Herat in November 2006. Both individuals requested to remain anonymous.

286 Land and post-conflict peacebuilding

the parcel maps are put on public display and all records of rights to land are archived.

Community leaders in the Kunduz site appreciated the work on private land, as it gave landowners additional documentation beyond that which may have already existed, such as tax receipts from the Amlak. For pastureland, such documentation had not existed before, and the community agreements were perceived as an important means to formally register user rights.

Villagers have expressed confidence that they can now carry out the entire ADAMAP process—not only administering documentation that has already been produced, but also delineating pasture parcels, producing agreement forms, and producing a community register of private lands—and have expressed willingness to volunteer to teach the process to other villages.

A concern remains as to the government's involvement. Some villagers fear that in spite of documentation perceived as legal under sharia and customary law, the state may use for state projects some pasture areas that are presently used by community groups. This concern motivated villagers to urge the government to formally recognize the community rangeland agreements as legal documents. Villagers have also asked the government to recognize their shuras as responsible for local land administration. Shuras have asked the government to clarify which government entity is responsible for which type of land, so that they can effectively carry out this role. A clause in the rangeland agreement form states that villagers must not convert pastureland to agricultural use,[17] and the government must not implement projects on communal pastures without the community's consent. This clause was easily accepted by villagers in the test sites, and they expressed hope that the government will respect it as well.

Villagers have described the ADAMAP approach as a viable means to resolve conflicts between communities and the state over land. They have emphasized that formal documentation of user rights will provide the incentive to protect their pastures better and to invest in pasture improvement.

NEXT STEPS

The search for a community-based administration of property records is in part a recognition of the incapacity of the central state to effectively administer property records. This incapacity is rooted in the more general inability of Afghan regimes to establish a dominant central state. Communities of various sorts have resisted the centralized model. The current court-administered system of transaction deeds has proved to be of little interest to landholders.

---

[17] The shura in the Takhar test site has consistently regulated rangeland use. By verbal decree, it has forbidden any conversion of grazing land to agricultural use, and community groups strictly observe this decree. While this practice may not be widespread, it does show the potential influence of community decisions about rangeland use.

Community documentation of land tenure in Afghanistan 287

In light of the state's inability to provide a land administration service that is valued by the population, it may be time to build instead on the governance capabilities of local communities, which they have developed as a matter of survival.

> [I]n the name of creating national unity, the state under its various long- and short-lived regimes, systematically undermined the identity and local autonomy of distinct ethnic and sectarian communities. In response, the local communities saw the state as the main source of their oppression and they devised complex social mechanisms to insulate themselves from direct contact with government agents and agencies. . . . Local communities isolated themselves from corrupt government officials by creating community-based parallel power structures (that is, a strong Sharia-governed civil society) to resolve internal problems locally through their own trusted leaders, both religious and secular. It was indeed, these trusted local figures who emerged during the anti-Soviet jihad as the leaders and commanders of many local resistant units across the country (Shahrani 1998, 230).

The brief experiences of the RLAP showed that, at least in some local communities, there is a great commitment to and capacity for administering land records locally, as one aspect of a vibrant community-based governance system. This experience is an example of community self-governing capacities which, in small ways accumulated across the country, can form the basis for the rebuilding of Afghanistan.

Alden Wily argues that "democratisation of [land administration and management] should be an objective of all countries" (Alden Wily 2003a, 1). This principle is particularly relevant to Afghanistan as its citizens work to create a democratic political economy. A corollary is that the nearer the administration of property records is to landholders, "the more accessible, useable and used, cheaper, speedier and generally more efficient the system will be" (Alden Wily 2003a, 2). Of course, this approach cannot be carried to the extreme of every hamlet operating its own land registry, or else the system would be inordinately expensive. But particularly in Afghanistan, where state institutions are weak and not well connected to the population, reestablishing the confidence of the people in governing institutions, including land governing institutions, by making them transparent and observable at the local level, is of fundamental importance.

Improving state-community links

The state's potential contributions to community-based property records administration have not been extensively tested in practice. A key unresolved issue is the role of the judiciary. At present, judges prepare deeds, when asked, for rural property transactions after asking the Amlak to certify property ownership. It is conceivable that judges could consult with communities for such certification in the future. It is unknown whether such a consultation would encourage more rural people to ask judges to prepare title deeds. Any links between judges and community property records archives must be carefully worked out.

A second link between the community and the state could be the latter's offering of an archival service to safeguard copies of community-prepared property rights documentation. If this archiving is kept up to date, it would also facilitate judicial consultation of community records when preparing title deeds.

Figure 3 shows the information flows proposed by RLAP for the production and archiving of private land parcel specification forms and maps, in which communities keep the initiative but government agencies carry out monitoring, capacity building, supervision, and archiving. The capacities of government agencies for carrying out these functions have to be strengthened.

As a third link, state agencies could offer technical assistance to communities as they document ownership and use right claims—to help assure the validity of the information collected and its presentation in a more-or-less standard format.

A fourth potential link is the assembly by the Amlak of information about land use and approximate land values. On the parcel form, there is a place to specify the type of land. This item has two purposes: (1) to enable a statistical tabulation of data on types of agricultural land to support planning by the Ministry of Agriculture, Irrigation and Livestock; and (2) to help estimate the value of a land parcel based on its productive potential. This information can also be used by village shuras, which ask family heads for contributions (based on the size of their landholdings) to help pay for land record management, as many already do for payment to arbabs for their work.

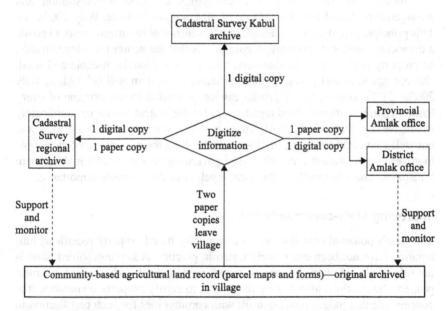

Figure 3. Information flows for parcel forms and maps relating to private land
Source: Diagram designed by Rural Land Administration Project staff.
Note: One paper copy of the land record is kept in village archive, one goes to the Cadastral Survey regional office, and one goes to the provincial Amlak office.

Further testing

The RLAP's experiences in regard to both communal pasturelands and privately held agricultural lands showed that the generation of written property records at the community level is feasible and that elders and landholders, at least in some villages, are willing to do much of the work of creating the records themselves. Part of villagers' enthusiasm for the process appears to derive from the awareness that they would retain and update the records themselves.

Government agencies can support this process by helping to build communities' capacity to administer property records, monitoring their work, providing backup digital archiving, providing plotted satellite images, and assisting with the formulation of rangeland improvement plans.

Despite the positive results of the RLAP experiment and its implications for how community-state relations can be strengthened, village by village, any extension of the approach will require additional testing. The ADAMAP methodology starts with asking community leaders whether they want to participate in the program. All communities contacted by the RLAP teams responded positively, although some required extensive explanation. This may not always be the case.

Further testing is also needed of methodologies for verifying ownership of croplands—for example, refining the role of village recording secretaries, designated by the community council to manage and archive maps and parcel forms, and establishing the training they need in procedures for maintaining and updating ownership records. Testing is needed to establish how much review the field teams' work needs and how to control unauthorized changing of parcel records. More work needs to be done to ensure the involvement of nomadic rangeland users and any state agency claiming ownership along with the local users of the land and village elders.

Other issues

Despite RLAP's success to date, many governance issues need consideration before a large community-based land administration program is rolled out. Many government officials in Kabul remain suspicious of community-oriented programs, despite the relative success of the community-oriented National Solidarity Program. The means for incorporating Kuchi input into the rangeland agreements have to be refined. Ways need to be found to ensure that community consultations incorporate all community segments, and not just the heads of large landowning families. The capacity to perform new functions supporting community land administration needs to be strengthened for staff in the Amlak and Cadastral Survey, as well as those in the Ministry of Agriculture, Irrigation and Livestock's Land Resources Department who are responsible for improving rangeland management, and the woluswali (district heads). There is a fundamental need for a more supportive legal and administrative framework with people committed to building new state-community relations. The RLAP has shown that a

290   Land and post-conflict peacebuilding

development program that operates in alignment with sharia law and custom is quite acceptable legally and culturally among provincial judges and rural community leaders.

REFERENCES

Alden Wily, L. 2003a. *Governance and land relations: A review of decentralisation of land administration and management in Africa.* London: International Institute for Environment and Development.

————. 2003b. *Land rights in crises: Restoring tenure security in Afghanistan.* Kabul: Afghanistan Research and Evaluation Unit. http://unpan1.un.org/intradoc/groups/public/documents/apcity/unpan016656.pdf.

————. 2004. *Looking for peace on the pastures.* Kabul: Afghanistan Research and Evaluation Unit.

————. n.d. *Customary land security programme pilot, Blue Nile State; Technical guideline number 1: A background to the process.* Khartoum: Government of Sudan.

Allan, N. J. R. 2001. Defining place and people in Afghanistan. *Post-Soviet Geography and Economics* 42 (8): 545–560.

Asia Foundation. 2007. *Afghanistan in 2007: A survey of the Afghan people.* Kabul. http://asiafoundation.org/publications/pdf/20.

Bardhan, P. K. 2005. *Scarcity, conflicts, and cooperation: Essays in the political and institutional economics of development.* Cambridge, MA: MIT Press.

Barfield, T. 2004. *Nomadic pastoralists in Afghanistan.* Washington, D.C.: World Bank Information Center.

Brick, J. 2008a. The political economy of customary village organizations in rural Afghanistan. Paper presented at the annual meeting of the Central Eurasian Studies Society, Washington, D.C., September 18–21.

————. 2008b. The political foundations of state-building and limited government in Afghanistan. Paper presented at the 66th Midwest Political Science Association Annual Meeting, Chicago, April 3–6.

Burns, T., C. Grant, K. Nettle, A.-M. Brits, and K. Dalrymple. 2006. *Land administration reform: Indicators of success, future challenges.* Wollongong, Australia: Land Equity International.

Delville, P. L. 2006. Registering and administering customary land rights: PFRs in West Africa. Paper presented to the World Bank Conference on Land Policies and Legal Empowerment of the Poor, Washington, D.C., October 31–November 3.

de Weijer, F. 2005. *National multi-sectoral assessment on Kuchi.* With support from A. Pinney, A. Assil, Z. Mehri, and S. Kabuli. Kabul: Ministry of Rural Rehabilitation and Development, in collaboration with the Ministry of Frontiers and Tribal Affairs and the Central Statistics Office.

Dixit, A. K. 2004. *Lawlessness and economics: Alternative modes of governance.* Princeton, NJ: Princeton University Press.

FAO (Food and Agriculture Organization of the United Nations). 1999. *Provincial land cover atlas of the Islamic State of Afghanistan.* Project AFG 90/002. Rome.

Fukuyama, F. 2004. *State-building: Governance and world order in the 21st century.* Ithaca, NY: Cornell University Press.

Community documentation of land tenure in Afghanistan 291

Glatzer, B. 1982. Processes of nomadization in west Afghanistan. In *Contemporary nomadic and pastoralist peoples: Asia and the North*, ed. P. C. Salzman. Studies in Third World Societies, No. 18. Williamsburg, VA: College of William and Mary, Department of Anthropology.

Hager, R. 1983. State, tribe and empire in Afghan inter-polity relations. In *The conflict of tribe and state in Iran and Afghanistan*, ed. R. Tapper. New York: St. Martin's Press.

ICG (International Crisis Group). 2007. *Afghanistan's endangered compact*. Brussels. www.crisisgroup.org/en/regions/asia/south-asia/afghanistan/B059-afghanistans-endangered -compact.aspx.

Islamic Republic of Afghanistan. 2007. Draft multi-ministerial land policy. Kabul.

———. 2008. Afghanistan national development strategy, governance and public administration sector reform, pillar II, good governance. Kabul.

LTERA (Land Titling and Economic Restructuring in Afghanistan). 2006. Informal settlements and land tenure issues: Report on pilot project Kabul District #7. Kabul: United States Agency for International Development.

MAIL (Ministry of Agriculture, Irrigation and Livestock). 2005. Policy and strategy for forestry and range management sub-sector. Kabul.

McEwen, A., and S. Nolan. 2007. Options for land registration. Working paper. Kabul: Afghanistan Research and Evaluation Unit.

McEwen, A., and B. Whitty. 2006. *Land tenure*. Kabul: Afghanistan Research and Evaluation Unit.

Mielke, K., and C. Schetter. 2007. Where is the village? Local perceptions and development approaches in Kunduz Province. *ASIEN* 104 (July): 71–87.

Nasser, A. H. 2005. *A brief history of the Amlak*. Kabul: Land Clarification Department of the Amlak.

Nojumi, N. 2002. *The rise of the Taliban in Afghanistan: Mass mobilization, civil war, and the future of the region*. New York: Palgrave Macmillan.

North, D. C. 1990. *Institutions, institutional change, and economic performance*. New York: Cambridge University Press.

North, D. C., and R. P. Thomas. 1973. *The rise of the western world: A new economic history*. New York: Cambridge University Press.

RLAP (Rural Land Administration Project). 2007. *Capacity building for land policy and administration reform, final report*. TA 4483-AFG. Manila, Philippines: Asian Development Bank / Department for International Development.

Safar, M. Y., and J. D. Stanfield. 2007. Cadastral Survey in Afghanistan. Project Report No. 4, Capacity Building for Land Policy and Administration Reform Project. TA 4483-AFG. Kabul: Asian Development Bank / Department for International Development.

Saikal, A., and W. Maley. 1991. *Regime change in Afghanistan: Foreign intervention and the politics of legitimacy*. Bathurst, Australia: Crawford House Press.

Shahrani, M. N. 1998. The future of the state and the structure of community governance in Afghanistan. In *Fundamentalism reborn? Afghanistan and the Taliban*, ed. W. Maley. New York: NYU Press.

Sheleff, L. 2000. *The future of tradition*. London: Frank Cass.

Stanfield, J. D. 2007. A study of the General Directorate of Land Management and Amlak of the Ministry of Agriculture, Irrigation and Livestock. Project Report No. 4, Capacity Building for Land Policy and Administration Reform Project, TA 4483-AFG. Kabul: Asian Development Bank / Department for International Development.

292 Land and post-conflict peacebuilding

Stanfield, J. D., J. Reed, and M. Y. Safar. 2005. *Description of procedures for producing legal deeds to record property transactions in Afghanistan*. Kabul: United States Agency for International Development, LTERA Project.

Stanfield, J. D., M. Y. Safar, and A. Salam. 2008. Community rangeland administration: Focus on Afghanistan. Paper prepared for the biennial congress of the International Association for the Study of the Commons, Cheltenham, UK, July 14–18.

Tapper, R. 1983. Introduction. In *The conflict of tribe and state in Iran and Afghanistan*, ed. R. Tapper. New York: St. Martin's Press.

Toulmin, C. 2006. Securing land rights for the poor in Africa—key to growth, peace and sustainable development. Paper prepared for the Commission on the Legal Empowerment of the Poor, International Institute for the Environment and Development, London.

Wardak, A. 2003. Jirgas: A traditional mechanism of conflict resolution in Afghanistan. http://unpan1.un.org/intradoc/groups/public/documents/APCITY/UNPAN017434.pdf.

Wardak, M., I. Zaman, and K. Nawabi. 2007. *The role and functions of religious civil society in Afghanistan*. Kabul: Cooperation for Peace and Unity.

Zadran, A. 1977. Socioeconomic and legal-political processes in a Pashtun village, southeastern Afghanistan. Ph.D. diss., State University of New York–Buffalo.

Title wave: Land tenure and peacebuilding in Aceh

Arthur Green

In Aceh, Indonesia, activities meant to improve land tenure security may have supported or may have undermined peacebuilding during the post-conflict, post-tsunami period of 2005 to 2009. Recent studies of property and resources in post-conflict scenarios have focused on the quantifiable economic value of resources and on how that value affects the escalation and relapse of violent conflict (Collier and Hoeffler 2004; Collier, Hoeffler, and Rohner 2009). However, many resources have political, cultural, and social value that renders them into powerful symbols that may be connected to the escalation and continuance of violence (Aspinall 2007). Such symbolic resources are often identified as central problems in intractable conflicts—especially where land or territory constitutes a symbolic homeland (Kahler and Walter 2006).

In 2005, the people of Aceh began recovering from both a twenty-nine-year secessionist conflict and the devastation of the 2004 Indian Ocean tsunami. Property and tenure systems were severely damaged by the conflict and tsunami (Kecamatan Development Program 2007; World Bank 2008). Although property rights and tenure security were not among the central issues negotiated in the peace process or among issues identified as problematic for demobilization, disarmament, and reintegration (World Bank 2006a), they were major concerns for many of the people involved in post-disaster recovery (Fitzpatrick 2005).

Many international donors, international nongovernmental organizations (INGOs), and state actors perceived the lack of state-issued land titles in these lowland areas to be a reflection of tenure insecurity and a central obstacle to tsunami recovery and future political and economic development (World Bank 2006b). In response to perceived tenure insecurity, donors offered technical resources and a budget of US$28.5 million for a state-administered land registration program called the Reconstruction of Aceh Land Administration System (RALAS). Partly

---

Arthur Green is a McGill Major and United States–Indonesia Society Fellow working on his doctoral dissertation in the Department of Geography at McGill University. His research examines how land reforms in post-conflict and legally pluralistic contexts affect access to resources and the dynamics of resistance, conflict, and peace.

294   Land and post-conflict peacebuilding

as a result of the early emphasis on post-disaster property issues, the existing narratives and examinations of property rights in Aceh emphasize post-disaster dynamics and judge the benefits and problems of RALAS in post-disaster terms (Harper 2006; Fitzpatrick 2008; Jalil et al. 2008; Deutsch 2009). There has been a failure to link post-disaster and post-conflict property issues (Burke and Afnan 2005).

This chapter examines some overlooked connections between property administration and violent conflict. Specifically, it examines how policy narratives concerning property and tenure security affected the design and success of the state-administered program for land registration and title issuance in Aceh. It argues that activities meant to improve land tenure security in Aceh came from politicized post-disaster narratives that marginalized post-conflict aspects of property administration. The resulting lack of consideration of post-conflict land- and property-administration issues may have not only limited RALAS's ability to issue titles and support tenure security but also undermined existing, secure tenure relations. The failure to frame tenure security as a post-conflict issue as well as a post-disaster one ultimately affected how tenure security was defined, how land tenure programs were designed to meet perceived challenges, and how these programs did or did not link to peacebuilding. The lessons learned in the case of Aceh pose broader questions about what difference the symbolic values of natural resources might make in post-conflict natural resource management, and specifically what difference a lack of attention to these symbolic values makes when land and property are linked to peacebuilding.

This chapter is not intended to support arguments for or against state-administered land titles, registration programs, and property systems. Ample debates over the merits and problems of transitions to state-administered property systems document how statutory land titles, land registration programs, and property systems can simultaneously emancipate some people and dispossess others (Scott 1998; de Soto 2000; Blomley 2003; Home and Lim 2004; Elyachar 2005; Otto 2009). These debates clearly indicate the lack of an efficient solution to property rights problems. They point to the need to move beyond ideological approaches to an investigation of the merits and problems of property systems in regard to specific situations, legal forms, and interests.

HISTORY OF THE CONFLICT

The Indonesian province of Aceh, also known as Nanggroe Aceh Darussalam, encompasses the northern tip of the island of Sumatra. From 1976 to 2005, this region was the site of a sporadic secessionist conflict between the Free Aceh Movement (Gerakan Aceh Merdeka, or GAM) and the government of Indonesia (GOI). Cyclical outbreaks of violence—combined with long-term intimidation, torture, and material dispossession of civilians—have claimed some 15,000 to 33,000 lives, paralyzed regional development, and polarized much of the population (Reid 2006; Schulze 2007).

Although the conflict in Aceh has sometimes been depicted as one based on one or more main cleavages, the violence is actually a result of a complex

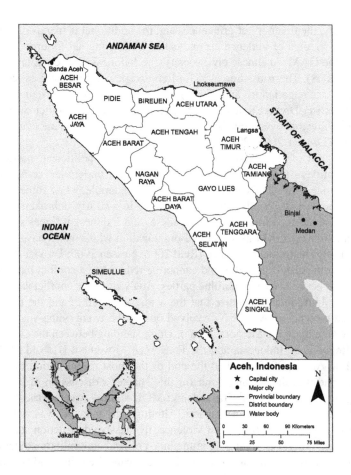

mix of contextual opportunities and issues. These issues include ethnonational territorial claims, a desire for local political autonomy, disputes over local distribution of hydrocarbon and resource revenues, and even personal vendettas. Adding further complexity are the issues of Acehnese cultural identity, recognition of Islamic principles of governance, and grievances involving justice and reparations for conflict-related crimes. The issues and the conditions that escalated and supported violent resistance in Aceh have changed over time with the strategic agendas of changing participants (Reid 2006; McCarthy 2007; Schulze 2007; Drexler 2008). GAM demands for amnesty and a special reintegration fund for former combatants, for example, contributed to the failure of the 2003 peace negotiations. Working toward a sustainable peace in Aceh has required confronting the complex overlap of elite and grassroots grievances, with changing participants and conditions that encourage violent resistance, and it has meant acknowledging the special needs of parties involved in the violence.

Even though previous peace processes have treated the GAM and the GOI as monolithic representatives of the Acehnese people and the Indonesian state,

296 Land and post-conflict peacebuilding

respectively, the diversity of grievances and the additional demands of the GAM and of the victims of violence are indicative of the internal fissures within and between the GAM, Acehnese civil society, the Indonesian military, and the GOI (Drexler 2008). These fissures, which often escape conflict analyses, contribute to failed peace negotiations and continue to pose obstacles to a sustainable peace. As Elizabeth F. Drexler notes, "Observations of the Aceh conflict over the last ten years show that oversimplified analyses of conflicts extend and even intensify violence" (Drexler 2008, 20).

Disregard of the internal complexities supports politicized narratives of group identities—narratives that have been used to undermine certain players and legitimize others in the conflict in Aceh. For example, while some narratives find the roots of the conflict and of the GAM in a nearly unbroken history of armed resistance to colonial Dutch, Japanese, and Indonesian forces since 1873, others identify the GAM as a criminal organization whose goals have little connection to this historical resistance (Reid 2006; Nessen 2006; Drexler 2008). But the conflict in Aceh is complex and cannot be reduced to a conflict based on any single issue between two monolithic parties. Analyses of the conflict and progress in peacebuilding must recognize that the actors involved in and the reasons for continued violence in Aceh have evolved during the twenty-nine-year conflict.

The signing of the Memorandum of Understanding between the Government of the Republic of Indonesia and the Free Aceh Movement (Helsinki MOU) in Finland, in August 2005, marked the end of the most recent period of violence in Aceh, and it is the starting point for this chapter's discussion of land tenure security and peacebuilding.[1] The Helsinki MOU signing was inextricably linked with the 2004 Indian Ocean tsunami. Although the tsunami was only one of many factors leading to the end of violence, its massive destruction set the stage for the peace process by changing immediate political and military strategies and the region's economic, social, and ecological landscape (Le Billon and Waizenegger 2007; Gaillard, Clave, and Kelman 2008; Renner 2013).

On the December 26, 2004, the Indian Ocean tsunami inundated the lowlands of Aceh, killing some 168,000 people and leaving 500,000 more homeless. In addition to the human death toll, it is estimated that some 300,000 land parcels, 250,000 homes, 15 percent of agricultural lands, over 2,000 schools, and 10,000 kilometers of roads were severely damaged or destroyed (Fitzpatrick 2005; Kenny, Fan, and Palmer 2006; Benny, Haroen, and Heryani 2006). Indonesian military operations from 2003 to 2004 had weakened the GAM, and unpublicized peace negotiations had begun at least as early as October 2004, but the tsunami allowed the GAM and the GOI to make public concessions on subjects that had been fundamental sticking points in the collapsed peace negotiations of 2003 (Schulze 2007). However, even though the tsunami allowed concessions and changed short-term opportunities for pursuing political and personal violence, many authors

---

[1] For the complete text of the Helsinki MOU, see www.aceh-mm.org/download/english/ Helsinki%20MoU.pdf.

recognize that the resulting peacemaking process did not address all the grievances of different groups in Aceh (Le Billon and Waizenegger 2007; Drexler 2008; Gaillard, Clave, and Kelman 2008; Renner 2013).

LAND TENURE SECURITY IN ACEH

In many post-conflict scenarios, clarifying and securing property rights are important steps in addressing the roots of the conflict, conflict-related grievances, and post-conflict conditions that may lead to relapses of violence (Unruh 2003). Even where property disputes are not the primary driver of violent conflict, the destruction of property systems can result in post-conflict disputes over resources and a return to violence. Reestablishing property rights and land tenure security is fundamental for meeting immediate recovery needs, enabling dispute resolution, laying the foundation for sustainable livelihoods, and enabling investment and economic development (USAID 2005). However, in post-conflict scenarios, the state often lacks legitimacy and is faced with existing traditions and informal systems that can undermine state territorial authority. Where the state itself is unreliable and is known for using its legal system to dispossess and undermine local claims to property, the problems with making the statutory legal system locally legitimate are numerous.

In Aceh, as in many post-conflict situations, the importance of disputes over property rights as a condition for the escalation and duration of violent conflict has changed over time. Although individual and communal property rights were not central to the escalation of violent conflict in 1976, the disruption over time of informal and formal property systems by violence, human rights abuses, and hydrocarbon resource exploitation have led to property rights grievances against the government (Fitzpatrick 2008).

Aside from the effects of the violent conflict on property rights, there are several problems with applying the Indonesian legal framework for property rights in Aceh. For example, the legal framework regarding communal property rights is unclear (Lindsey 2008). This lack of clarity means that application of the statutory system can create tenure insecurity and that elites or state officials can manipulate claims through the legal system or other means (Peluso 2005; McCarthy 2006). Indeed, the National Land Agency (Badan Pertanahan Nasional, or BPN) is locally perceived to be one of the most corrupt agencies in the country, and Indonesia has low overall performance in governance as measured by indicators such as Transparency International's Corruption Perceptions Index.[2]

The weak legal framework and resulting tenure insecurity are especially problematic for the post-conflict legal landscape of Aceh, where the Indonesian state's legitimacy as a sovereign power is still questioned by some former combatants. Indeed, as of 2008, the political, economic, ecological, and sociocultural

---

[2] For 2011, Indonesia was ranked 100th out of 183 (Transparency International 2011).

298   Land and post-conflict peacebuilding

value of land remained points of contention as changing regional laws, fees, taxes, and state claims transformed local ownership and locally acceptable understandings of property and tenure security (Fitzpatrick 2008). Underlying these challenges with implementation of the statutory legal framework is the fact that Aceh is a legally pluralistic community where property claims are often subject to contradictory legal traditions (Bowen 2003).

Land tenure security and legal pluralism

Residents of Aceh draw from multiple legal and normative traditions in their daily interactions. Many authors and Acehnese residents identify three working sets of laws or normative traditions that define tenure security and govern the use and ownership of property: *adat* (informal or customary institutions), statutory law (formal institutions), and Islamic jurisprudence and Islamic courts (Bowen 2003; Harper 2006). These three designations are also used to label practices for political purposes.

A number of other normative traditions should also be considered either directly relevant to property or at least important for defining the practices of the three main traditions in regard to property. For example, the informal property transactions that occur in peri-urban and urban areas do not neatly fit into one of the three major traditions. Also, in post-disaster Aceh international and local NGOs influenced property rights through such activities as community mapping, building narratives about property rights, intervening in property disputes, and adding discourses of natural or human rights to property debates. Proponents of one tradition tend to point to limitations and abuses in other traditions in order to justify changes that they feel are appropriate or that benefit themselves. Supporters of statutory titling contrasted what they considered the vagaries and inequities of customary laws (adat) with the supposed economic benefits of title, the state's ability to avoid and adjudicate violent disputes, and the protection that statutory law provides for the environment and for the rights of women, children, and members of minority groups.

But these three traditions are not autonomous, opposing, and constitutive of specific rights claims. There are many ways that the three traditions are interlinked, mutually constituted, and composed of overlapping practices. For example, adat is closely associated with Islamic jurisprudence in Aceh, and over time local communities have invested differing weight in flexible, equitable practices versus dogmatic religious principles (Bowen 2003). It is true, however, that the different traditions are associated with unique governance styles, economic relations, and cultural places, and parties sometimes use the traditions as political labels to differentiate and categorize hybrid legal practices and hybrid legal spaces in order to make potent political rights claims.

Statutory land law in Indonesia is based on the Basic Agrarian Law of 1960 (Law No. 5/1960), which lays out the basic rights to landownership and the legal processes for acquisition, management, and transfer of land, and for land dispute resolution. Rights to land include private ownership rights (*hak milik*, which is similar to landownership as recognized by freehold title), building rights (*hak guna bangunan*), rights of commercial exploitation (*hak guna usaha*), rights of use (*hak pakai*), rental rights (*hak sewa*), and communal land rights (*hak ulayat*, which recognize customary land and resource tenure). Statutory laws link to or recognize the authority of adat and Islamic jurisprudence in several different ways and at different scales of governance. The Indonesian state uses terms that derive from broader Islamic tenures. For example, the term *hak milik* comes from the Islamic term *mulk/milk* and describes "private full ownership" (Sait and Lim 2006, 12).

In Aceh, Islamic jurisprudence has long been intimately linked to adat and plays an important role in local decision-making processes (*musyawarah*) at the *gampong* (village) and *mukim* (aggregate of villages) levels. Islamic jurisprudence has commonly been considered an avenue for handling inheritance cases, and new regional laws (*qanun*[3]) and national laws have given Islamic jurisprudence larger governance capacities and a more formal role in decisions over land use, investments, the property rights of women and members of minority groups, and the use of land as financial collateral (Bowen 2003; Harper 2006). For example, through National Law No. 48/2007, Islamic courts (*mahkamah syar'iyah*) are given the authority to decide rightful heirs and guardians in inheritance cases, and the Islamic treasury (Baitu Mal Aceh) is given equal authority with the public trust (Balai Harta Peninggalan) to manage post-tsunami property where no legal heir has been identified. This incorporation and formalization of Islamic courts and jurisprudence into the different scales of government reflect and repeat some of the historical missteps and legal vagueness that occurred during previous attempts to regularize or register property and to formalize the diverse, informal traditions known as adat.

Adat practices are officially recognized in state law; however, this recognition can take many different forms in practice (Morse and Woodman 1988). This recognition might vary based on whether the state confers governance power on adat institutions or acknowledges such power, whether adat has sole or shared authority, or whether adat sanctions are rendered impotent or left intact. Additional dimensions that may make the recognition varied are whether adat has authority equal to that of the state and whether the power to appoint or change the composition of adat leadership requires state approval. The recognition of adat governance structures has been crucial to the decentralization of government in Indonesia and to the meeting of some identity claims in Aceh, but there has been a simultaneous drive to reorganize adat institutions so they fit seamlessly into the state. For example, the formalization of the gampong (village) and mukim (aggregate of villages) has

---

[3] *Qanun* refers to regional regulations as passed by the Regional House of Representatives (Dewan Perwakilan Rakyat Daerah) in Aceh. The capacity to create qanun was first granted by Law No. 18/2001 (Special Autonomy for the Province of Aceh as the Province of Nanggroe Aceh Darussalam) and was reaffirmed by Law No. 11/2006 (the Law on the Governing of Aceh).

300   Land and post-conflict peacebuilding

implications for the adjudication of property disputes. When communities are faced with formal, statutory title and legal concepts like hak milik, these communities lose the authority and power to enforce traditional punitive sanctions that may alienate property rights from individual owners or expel owners from the community.

One of the most important ways in which statutory laws interact with adat is in the recognition of communal property rights (hak ulayat). Statutory law recognizes communities' ability to allocate land, approve transfers, control use, and adjudicate land disputes (Harper 2006). But there are several problems with the clarity, implementation, and breadth of application of statutory laws regarding community property (Lindsey 2008). For example, communal lands are often subject not to the Basic Agrarian Law but to forestry laws, natural resource policy, and several bureaucratic layers inaccessible to locals. Searching for applicable laws regarding communal forests and forest-resource access in Aceh requires acknowledging the temporal sequence and ambiguities between the Basic Agrarian Law and laws on forestry, regional autonomy, and special autonomy for Aceh. In short, the relative simplicity of the Basic Agrarian Law framework overlooks how land is connected to resources, and it therefore contributes to disputes surrounding forests and communal resources (Eye on Aceh 2009).

Disputes with the government over communal resources were not part of the peace process, but they have been sources of local grievance in Aceh. Because there is no concept of adverse possession within Indonesian law, in some cases the state has failed to recognize communities' claims to land on which they have lived and paid taxes for more than forty years (Fitzpatrick 2008). In interviews with rural households in the Aceh Jaya region in 2007, these legal ambiguities were cited as a disincentive to the adoption of statutory law and as one of the reasons that titles have not successfully supplanted adat practices and the use of sale documents as deeds. That said, adat practices are sometimes defined by the state, so they should not be glorified as antecedent, customary practices that oppose the state (Li 2001; Burns 2004). Indeed, adat practices may incorporate statutory law; may consider the reaction of statutory law before local decisions are made concerning natural resources; or, in the case of "countermapping" and "weapons of the weak," may be reshaped by their resistance to the state (Peluso 2005; Bowen 2003).

The informal practices known as adat have resilience in Aceh because they are flexible, local creations that draw from but are independent of statutory law and Islamic jurisprudence. The fundamental point of agreement in all adat practices is the emphasis on local, flexible management and consensual mediations that can consider a multitude of factors outside the range of formal courts and freehold title rights. These practices vary over space and time, and by practitioner. Despite this diversity, adat commonly provides rights related to communal land (hak ulayat); customary ownership (*hak milik adat*); and use, including agricultural usage (*useuha*), rental usage (*sewa/kontrak*), sharecropping (*bagi hasil/mawaih*), pledge/pawn usage (*gadai/gala*), and cultivation (*numpang tanam*) (Harper 2006).

Although paper documents are not always used in adat processes, statutory titles or deeds (*akte jual beli*) can be important components of transactions and can support claims or formalize divisions in disputes. The broad, qualitative differences between statutory and adat practices in regard to process and definition of rights can be summarized as the social embeddedness of adat. Adat can work without or around formal titles and deeds, lower costs of tenure-security maintenance, and include particular rules concerning preemption and the transfer and sale of land. For example, land held under hak milik adat (typically rural and sometimes peri-urban land) may only be sold if first offered to neighbors and if third parties' ongoing right of access will be respected, may not be sold to outsiders, and may be appropriated by the community or community leader (*keucik*) as a community good (Fitzpatrick 2005; Harper 2006). These limits are not very different from statutory covenants, easements, and takings but are sometimes embedded in the unwritten traditions of a community and make little sense to statutory understandings of private property (Peluso 2005). Adat practices offer strong, flexible, and equitable tenure security for local needs, but without state recognition, adat tenure is usually insufficient as collateral for bank loans or as protection from state claims.

Land registration and the Torrens title system

Statutory titles often provide benefits in terms of tenure security against foreign claims and increased ability to alienate (that is, transfer) property. Moreover, in a capitalist land market, a well-maintained, accountable, and transparent title system that guarantees an indefeasible title can reduce time and costs normally associated with deeds systems. Because of these benefits, the main form of property administration currently endorsed in many development projects follows Hernando de Soto's claim that registration of property in state-administered title systems is fundamental to political and economic advancement (de Soto 2000).

The recommendation of de Soto is to implement some variation of the Torrens title system in order to register property. Developed in Australia, the Torrens system organizes the central management of titles and focuses on the state cadastre as the primary legal instrument for tenure security. But such a system is not costless, politically neutral, free of faults, or the only option for states that need to intervene in order to reinforce or guarantee tenure security. The process of creating geographically complete and accurate property-administration systems sometimes dispossesses politically marginal communities and forces new costs (such as taxes, transfer fees, and registration fees) onto poor communities that use informal practices (Home and Lim 2004). Such a system also requires that the state have the capacity and legitimacy to enforce the registration of property and property transactions. Furthermore, the economic and social costs of converting informal systems into state-administered title systems are often quite high and tend to disregard systems that are better able to interact with informal practices, such as those that emphasize deeds or that incorporate social-tenure models.

302 Land and post-conflict peacebuilding

Although some urban areas, peri-urban areas, and market-oriented rural communities may benefit from state registration in Torrens title systems, state titles can be inappropriate in rural and post-conflict areas that do not meet many assumptions regarding state legitimacy, land markets, or cost-benefits (Green 2008; Otto 2009). Moreover, some authors and activists argue that state-led registration and titling processes are synonymous with the dispossession of local property rights and the reorganization of social, cultural, and political relations (Scott 1998; Elyachar 2005; Moore 2005; Fauzi 2009). Indeed, the costs of maintaining centralized title systems that accurately reflect transactions, the absence of anticipated benefits among local populations, and the politicization of registration processes have historically undermined formal property systems (Smith 2003; Sowerwine 2004). Likewise, where everyday interactions deviate over time from centralized title systems, variations of the Torrens title system are unable to adequately mirror what is actually occurring with property transfers and ownership at the ground level. These concerns cast serious moral doubts on the utility and efficacy of allocating money to build centralized title systems immediately after conflicts when alternative deeds systems or informal networks can support tenure security.

Land tenure security after the tsunami and secessionist conflict

The extent to which property and formal or informal tenure systems were damaged by the tsunami and conflict is largely a geographic question. Tsunami effects were limited to lowland areas, whereas conflict intensity and effects were clustered in both areas that were and areas that were not affected by the tsunami (Kecamatan Development Program 2007). The wide array of tsunami- and conflict-related problems confronting land tenure security in Aceh included the destruction of the BPN (National Land Agency) offices, the death of several BPN staff, the destruction of field markers and boundary lines, promises of land for reintegration of former combatants, and disputed claims against the Indonesian state. In addition, there have been gender rights and inheritance issues resulting from deaths, tsunami- and conflict-refugee movement and resettlement, as well as inconsistencies between intact local practices and statutory law. Further problems included compensation for irrecoverably damaged land and property, the nebulous status of renters and squatters, and informal agreements regarding property use and ownership (Fitzpatrick 2005). Complicating these matters were the region's legal pluralism and the fact that land and property rights were potent political symbols that were especially problematic where the state's territorial control and right to tax were still disputed.

The legitimacy and the capacity of Indonesian state institutions was limited in the region, and informal institutions were the predominant basis of tenure security and property management. Of the 300,000 parcels affected by the tsunami, only 25 percent had titles issued by the state (Fitzpatrick 2005; Benny, Haroen, and Heryani 2006). Statutory law was most prevalent in the lowland cities, where the tsunami was most devastating. By killing several BPN officials and destroying existing titles, state registration offices, and field markers for plot identification, the tsunami threw the cadastral system into chaos (Benny, Haroen, and Heryani 2006). Some 80 percent of the damaged titles have been recovered by work at the Japan International Cooperation Agency, but these documents' lack of fidelity to activities on the ground may contradict community maps of claims and cause additional problems for tenure security. Lowland informal institutions were more resilient than the BPN-administered cadastre, but they suffered greatly from the loss of traditional property markers, of human knowledge surrounding use rights and informal arrangements, and of the overload of inheritance cases.

In the highlands and in some separatist areas, the tsunami had a limited impact. In these areas, formal institutions were largely superficial. Local resistance to statutory law and a lack of implementation capacity meant that statutory laws never supplanted local traditions in rural and conflict-prone areas. Likewise, in urban areas informal (but not always adat) arrangements regarding renters, squatters, and use rights tended over time to undermine the state cadastre's ability to reflect reality. There were many reasons why the state-administered cadastre was unable to make a permanent foothold in Aceh before the tsunami, including the history of colonial legal structures, economic costs of title registration and title maintenance, incompatibly of local customs and national legal systems, and corruption on the part of government officials. Lack of implementation capacity, lack of land markets, the GAM's territorial authority in some areas, and a general resistance to state institutions also impeded the cadastre.

Land tenure security was thought to be important for disaster recovery because it allowed agencies to establish camps and negotiate relocation of refugees, provide basic services, and identify and compensate owners of destroyed property. Furthermore, agencies were able to protect orphans' and widows' property rights, begin reconstructing houses, and mediate land-related disputes (BRR 2005; Fitzpatrick 2005). Encouraging land tenure security was also thought to support peacebuilding. It was argued that it provided the ability to give immediate access to basic and essential services, mediate conflict-related land disputes, resolve land-related grievances, provide land for reintegration of former combatants, and promote long-term goals of good governance and economic development equitable for women as well as men (Harper 2006).

Land tenure security in post-conflict Aceh appeared to be greater than in other post-conflict regions because there were intact village-level customary institutions for land management and because there were no significant secondary occupations of houses, and therefore fewer resettlement issues; no layered history of displacement and dispossession, and therefore fewer competing claims between local groups; and no significant commercial tourism developments on the coasts, and therefore fewer competing claims between commercial and local groups (Fitzpatrick 2005). Because they assumed that conflict-related land issues were minor, policy makers appeared to concentrate almost exclusively on post-disaster issues rather than post-conflict dynamics. The concepts and process were geared toward urban and post-tsunami recovery by a number of factors, including the development focus on urban areas with little international commercial investment, and the lack

304 Land and post-conflict peacebuilding

of immediate land disputes between communities and households, of conflict-related resettlement problems, and of understanding of the problems of the Indonesian legal framework regarding land and resource access. In fact, understanding how policy makers defined land tenure security is central to understanding how they pursued regional property administration and how this affected disaster recovery, post-conflict stabilization and transition, and long-term development.

Despite the widespread use of adat and the post-conflict resonance of the cultural and political representation of land in separatist struggle, the main emphasis of international donors and national agencies was on expanding the state-administered cadastre. Even before the Helsinki MOU was ratified in August 2005, international donors, INGOs, local activists, BPN, and the National Development Planning Agency (Badan Perencanaan dan Pembangunan Nasional, or BAPPENAS) identified land tenure security as a priority for post-disaster recovery, post-conflict reconstruction, and future regional development (Fitzpatrick 2005; Kenny, Fan, and Palmer 2006; Lindsey and Phillips 2005). In April 2005, the BAPPENAS Master Plan for Rehabilitation and Reconstruction in Aceh and Nias made specific mention of restoring titles and expanding the national land cadastre (BAPPENAS 2005). The BPN-administered land registration project called RALAS became the primary tenure-security program in the region. The goal of RALAS was to facilitate fair processes for land registration, improve state capacity to manage the cadastre, and digitize the cadastre and land register. Mandated to run from August 2005 to August 2008, RALAS was initially financed by a grant of US$28.5 million through the Multi-Donor Trust Fund for Aceh and North Sumatra. RALAS also received technical support from several other donors and INGOs.

As evidenced by early publications and public statements by officials, explicitly underlying the entire project were de Soto's assumptions that freehold title guaranteed by the state was the most secure form of land tenure security, allowed the state to protect individual property rights, gave license to reconstruct buildings, and liberated the "dead capital" of the poor as financial collateral. Additional assumptions have been that freehold title enabled more equitable treatment of women and orphans and permitted the state to mediate conflicting claims and disputes over lands (BRR 2005). However, for critics on the ground, the project's goal of registering 600,000 parcels seemed unrealistic and appeared to be an opportunistic effort to increase state control over lands and to generate new tax revenues.[4] Regardless of the underlying motives, RALAS took laudable steps to lower economic barriers to registration (for example, the Ministry of Finance waived taxes and fees), to incorporate adat through legislative reform, and to implement participatory methods for the delineation of property and adjudication of land claims (Benny, Haroen, and Heryani 2006; Kenny, Fan, and Palmer 2006).

Over time, however, problems surfaced, and the initiative met with limited success. Community-driven adjudication and mapping performed by NGOs and

---

[4] UN-HABITAT personnel, personal communication, Calang, Indonesia, June 11, 2006.

INGOs were not recognized by the BPN as valid for issuing titles; the early consultative communications between NGOs and the BPN ended; state claims over lands in Aceh Jaya and Aceh Besar dispossessed residents; activists from the Aceh Legal Foundation were arrested for assisting villages with claims from the conflict period that identified government dispossession or underpayment for land; and some neighborhoods were partially mapped and registered by the BPN, only to be left without titles (Fitzpatrick 2008; Deutsch 2009). By September 2009, fewer than 120,000 of the intended 600,000 land titles had been issued, with the majority being concentrated in urban areas (Deutsch 2009). Nearly 50 percent of the recipients of title certificates who were interviewed in a large-scale project assessment of RALAS did not feel that the certificate had improved their tenure security (Deutsch 2009).

Likewise, 50 percent of these respondents also recognized that the community demarcation and adjudication activities had not been fair, especially with regard to women's rights, due to the internal power dynamics that dominated such sessions. Not only did RALAS fail to resolve many of the lingering disputes over property, several disputes were caused by errors of land measurement or inadequate recording of ownership information on the titles. There were other issues regarding the government's role in land management, the clarification of land-transmission details, the mistreatment of women's claims to property rights even after issue of the title certificates, and the prospect of future transfer costs and taxes that remained unclear to a large portion of the residents of Aceh (Fitzpatrick 2008; Jalil et al. 2008; Deutsch 2009).

PEACEBUILDING IN ACEH

To what extent has peacebuilding been successful in Aceh? As of late 2011, Aceh appeared to be exiting the post-conflict transition phase and moving toward a consolidation of peace. But even as several grievances and conditions contributing to armed violence have been attended to, some roots of the conflict remain unaddressed. Though it is tempting to look at the current lack of armed violence in Aceh and proclaim peacebuilding success, several measures of peacebuilding progress suggest considering more and broader criteria (Paris 2004; Barnett et al. 2007). Indeed, Damien Kingsbury notes that although armed violence has decreased as a result of the Helsinki MOU and demobilization, disarmament, and reintegration, a commitment to the letter and the spirit of the peace agreement may still not guarantee a sustainable peace in Aceh (Kingsbury 2006). Broad changes in underlying social, political, and economic relations have been and remain necessary for a sustainable peace.

Keeping these changes in mind, this chapter adopts the United Nations Environment Programme's definition of peacebuilding—a definition consistent with peacebuilding approaches that move beyond peacemaking and peacekeeping to focus on transformation of the range of conditions that may lead to violence:

306 Land and post-conflict peacebuilding

Peacebuilding comprises the identification and support of measures needed for transformation toward more sustainable, peaceful relationships and structures of governance, in order to avoid a relapse into conflict. The four dimensions of peacebuilding are: socio-economic development, good governance, reform of justice and security institutions, and the culture of justice, truth and reconciliation (UNEP 2009, 7).

A number of organizations have been involved with peacebuilding in Aceh. The peacemaking process and resulting Helsinki MOU required the establishment of the Aceh Monitoring Mission (AMM) to monitor peacekeeping activities. The AMM and the related Commission on Security Arrangements began in September 2005 and ended in December 2006. At that time, the Communication and Coordination Forum for Peace in Aceh and the Commission on the Sustainability of Peace in Aceh took up where the AMM left off. The AMM improved the security situation, but reforms involving the political process and socioeconomic development were being handled by other INGOs and official agencies, such as BAPPENAS, the United Nations Development Programme's Emergency Response and Transitional Recovery Programme, and the International Organization for Migration.

Immediately after the peace deal was concluded, the International Organization for Migration and the World Bank provided support for "socializing the peace" through the Socialization Team, and in February 2006, the government formally established the Aceh Reintegration Board (Badan Reintegrasi-Damai Aceh, or BRA). The Socialization Team played a role in reintegrating some 2,000 former combatants and 400 former prisoners, and the BRA was responsible for economic and social assistance to conflict victims, aid to former combatants and political prisoners, reconstruction help for those who lost property, and compensation for victims and their families. In areas where the tsunami had a heavy impact, the duties of the BRA and the Rehabilitation and Reconstruction Agency (Badan Rehabilitasi dan Rekonstruksi, or BRR) sometimes overlapped. However, because the BRR was focused primarily on infrastructure and on the economic, psychological, and social dimensions of disaster recovery and reconstruction, it did not explicitly examine post-conflict issues or work with conflict victims.

In Aceh, peacebuilding is an ongoing process, with successes achieved over time. Demobilization, disarmament, and reintegration of former combatants, integration of GAM representatives into political parties, local elections in 2006, as well as the implementation of local autonomy with regard to Islamic governance and recognition of Acehnese culture by way of the installation of a ceremonial head of state (*Wali Nanggroe*) are all clear peacebuilding successes. Other achievements include the adoption of an official Acehnese flag and hymn, redistribution of hydrocarbon profits through direct payments and a shared fund, and general implementation of livelihood projects and infrastructure development. All of these successes have attendant problems, but there is general agreement on their positive results.

On the other hand, peacebuilding has been unsuccessful in establishing a Truth and Reconciliation Commission, supporting the Aceh Human Rights Council, equitably distributing reintegration funds, resolving seventeen problematic points of the Law on the Governing of Aceh, supporting the local government's delivery of basic services, and constructing a long-term peacebuilding plan that includes civil society. Not yet resolved are subprovincial demands to break free from Aceh Province and internal frictions among GAM members who continue to insist on a separatist state. Indeed, former combatants and the Aceh Transitional Committee (Komite Peralihan Aceh) are linked to violent criminal acts, kidnapping, and political intimidation in the region (Center for Domestic Preparedness 2009).

Connections between land tenure security and peacebuilding

Did activities meant to strengthen land tenure security support, create opportunities for, or hinder the success of peacebuilding in Aceh? Land and property rights were mentioned in the 2005 Helsinki MOU, the 2006 Law on the Governing of Aceh, and many post-disaster needs assessments. The effects of the tsunami and conflict on property and land tenure security were qualitatively different and geographically varied. Despite recognition of the geographic variation of local needs and the mention of land and property rights in the peace process, land-tenure security has been addressed primarily through the post-disaster-oriented RALAS project. This section outlines the ways in which land and property rights were addressed in the peace process. It then summarizes the design and implementation of the RALAS project and examines how RALAS and other land-security activities affected peacebuilding.

Land tenure security in the peace process

Article 3.2 of the Helsinki MOU outlines several general activities with regard to land and post-conflict peacebuilding and requires the following:

> 3.2.3: GoI and the authorities of Aceh will take measures to assist persons who have participated in GAM activities to facilitate their reintegration into the civil society. These measures include economic facilitation to former combatants, pardoned political prisoners and affected civilians. A Reintegration Fund under the administration of the authorities of Aceh will be established.
>
> 3.2.4: GoI will allocate funds for the rehabilitation of public and private property destroyed or damaged as a consequence of the conflict to be administered by the authorities of Aceh.
>
> 3.2.5: GoI will allocate suitable farming land as well as funds to the authorities of Aceh for the purpose of facilitating the reintegration to society of the former combatants and the compensation for political prisoners and affected civilians. The authorities of Aceh will use the land and funds as follows: a) All former combatants will receive an allocation of suitable farming land, employment or, in the case of incapacity to work, adequate social security from the authorities

308   Land and post-conflict peacebuilding

of Aceh. b) All pardoned political prisoners will receive an allocation of suitable farming land, employment or, in the case of incapacity to work, adequate social security from the authorities of Aceh. c) All civilians who have suffered a demonstrable loss due to the conflict will receive an allocation of suitable farming land, employment or, in the case of incapacity to work, adequate social security from the authorities of Aceh.

The Law on the Governing of Aceh, passed in 2006, was meant to provide legal follow-through related to the guidelines set out in the Helsinki MOU.[5] Although there are still unresolved complaints about deviations between the Helsinki MOU and the Law on the Governing of Aceh, the latter is currently the main legal foundation for confronting the origins and conditions of conflict in Aceh. Its most relevant sections for land tenure security are several articles from chapters 29 and 39:

XXIX, 213: (1) Every Indonesian citizen who is present in Aceh has right over land in accordance with the stipulation of law. (2) Aceh Government and/or District/city are authorized to regulate and manage the allotment, utilization and legal relationship in relation to the right over land by acknowledging, honoring and protecting the existing rights including the indigenous rights in accordance with the nationally prevailing norms, standards and procedures. (3) Right over land as meant in clause (2) covers the authorities of Aceh Government, District/ City to grant right to build and right of exploitation in accordance with the prevailing norms, standards and procedures. (4) Aceh Government and/or District/ City are obliged to conduct legal protection towards wakaf lands, religious assets and other sacred needs. (5) Further stipulation regarding the procedure for granting rights over land as meant in clause (1), clause (2) and clause (3) is regulated with Qanun which heeds the stipulation of law.

XXIX, 214: (1) Aceh Government is authorized to grant the right to build and right of exploitation for domestic capital investment and foreign capital investment in accordance with the prevailing norms, standards and procedures. (2) Further stipulation regarding the procedure for the granting of license as meant in clause (1) is regulated with Aceh Qanun.

. . .

XXXIX, 253: The Regional Office of National Land Agency in Aceh Provincial Region and the Office of District/City National Land Agency become Aceh and District/City Regional apparatus at the latest in the beginning of the Budget Year of 2008. (2) Further stipulation regarding the implementation of those meant in clause (1) is regulated by Presidential Regulation.

The Helsinki MOU clearly outlines the government's role in provisioning and replacing property. On the other hand, the Law on the Governing of Aceh

---

[5] For the complete text of the Law on the Governing of Aceh, see www.aceh-eye.org/ data_files/english_format/indonesia_government/indogovt_decrees/indogovt_decrees _2006_08_01_11.pdf.

Land tenure and peacebuilding in Aceh **309**

is more oriented toward outlining assignment to the Acehnese regional government of responsibility for respecting and protecting property rights. But according to a 2006 World Bank study on GAM reintegration needs, many of the GAM never left their communities, so land for reintegration was a moot point; 55.5 percent of the GAM had access to land, and most of the GAM combatants who were interested in farming were part of this group; most land access was facilitated through family holdings (63.8 percent), individual holdings (24.4 percent), or communal lands (7.4 percent); and land was only an issue for GAM returnees where it was also a disaster or conflict issue for receiving communities (World Bank 2006a). Because the provisions mentioned here apply specifically to former GAM combatant reintegration and because many of the combatants did not need land as part of reintegration aid, the ways in which land and the violent conflict were linked were sometimes ignored or deemphasized.

Reconstruction of Aceh Land Administration System (RALAS) in the peace process

Despite the previous references to land in the peace process, the main vehicle for implementing land tenure security was the disaster-focused RALAS project. RALAS rebuilt land administration offices, offered technical training, digitized cadastres and land records, and restored and expanded the land titles administered by the BPN. In addition, several other agencies were involved in advocating for and supporting property rights and community mapping. Some of the work outside RALAS included the extensive property rights studies performed by or on behalf of Oxfam and the International Development Law Organization, Fauna and Flora International's efforts in community mapping, and United Nations Human Settlements Programme (UN-HABITAT) materials developed to inform the population of their rights and the steps needed to register property. UN-HABITAT materials included a number of educational tools and forms that could serve as temporary statements of property ownership. Although these forms were distributed and occasionally filled out, they had no legal weight as evidence.

Land negotiations with resident communities were undertaken by BPN representatives and NGO and INGO staff to allow entire communities of tsunami refugees to relocate to land far from the coast. Legal assistance increased as mobile Islamic courts deployed primarily to tsunami-affected regions to assist communities that were puzzling through complicated inheritance and guardianship issues.

Human rights activists from the Aceh Legal Aid Institute (LBH-Aceh) played a significant role in distributing property rights materials and assisting victims of land expropriations that occurred during the conflict. LBH-Aceh alleged that during the conflict communities in East Aceh had been forced to sell their land at low prices to the plantation company PT Bumi Flora or, if they resisted the land purchase, be declared part of the separatist movement. These allegations led to the retaliatory July 2007 arrest of eight LBH-Aceh activists and to their August 2008 conviction on charges of "orally or in writing committing a violent

310   Land and post-conflict peacebuilding

act against the government" and "disseminating hate against the government."[6] This prosecution suggests that property expropriation may be much more prevalent than currently known, but that cases are rarely reported due to the political dynamics in the region.

The RALAS framework adapted official protocols for registering real property to the situation in Aceh. It experimented with community-driven adjudication (CDA), community mapping, and lowering registration costs to facilitate and legitimize the registration process. Registration occurred in several stages: location determination (village selection by the BPN and the BRR), community agreement, measuring and mapping (BPN validation), announcement, filing of rights and issuing of title certificates, and title certificate presentation. Community participation was largely limited to the stage called *community agreement*, wherein members of the community came to agreement regarding the demarcation of the parcel boundaries and recognition of parcel ownership (BPN 2005). The process empowered NGOs and INGOs as community-agreement facilitators, outlined specific types of complaints, and designated the parties to whom complaints should be addressed. In villages that were not selected by the BPN, other programs, such as the "district development program, Program for the Elimination of Urban Poverty, Local Government Innovation Foundation program or UNDP [United Nations Development Programme] or any other BRR endorsed programs" could implement the community-agreement phase (BPN 2005, 7).

Once delineation of property, ownership status, and a sketch of the parcels were agreed upon by the community and its facilitators, the BPN validated the community's work by checking the juridical and physical evidence on boundaries, ownership, and land types. In principle these participatory processes were meant to legitimize and expedite registration, but BPN staff would sometimes repeat mapping exercises because of inconsistencies between the participatory processes and the BPN's internal regulations or inconsistencies between the BPN's existing land register, the 80 percent of damaged titles returned to Aceh, and participatory mapping results (Fairall 2008; Deutsch 2009). Results of the BPN validation were publicly announced for thirty days, during which objections to any of the data could be presented. After this period, the title certificates were to be registered and issued by the BPN office and then presented through the adjudication committee to land owners.

All titles were registered in and issued from Jakarta. Unfortunately, the reliance on Jakarta to issue the titles caused delays in title distribution and sometimes resulted in changes to the boundaries outlined in participatory mapping (Fairall 2008). All titles registered through this processes were integrated into an electronic land information system to avoid future loss and to facilitate government management. The project also took steps to establish and protect women's and children's rights regarding inheritance, custodianship, and ownership of land. It did so by requiring

---

[6] Indonesian Penal Code, arts. 160 and 161.

women's participation in community adjudication and by outlining clear standards for custodianship and joint titling. In December 2008 all land administration duties were transferred from Jakarta to the Acehnese regional government.

RALAS certainly had positive effects, including the training of nearly 700 NGO facilitators and 500 BPN staff in CDA mapping methods, the establishment of new land offices, the clarification of property rights in urban areas, and the introduction of a digital cadastre (Deutsch 2009). But there were several criticisms of the RALAS process. These criticisms revolved mainly around choices in the targeting of communities, the exclusion of certain community segments, the irrelevance of the registration process to the cultural milieu, the ambiguity of the Indonesian legal framework concerning traditional and informal land and forest tenure, and the bureaucracy and corruption of the BPN. These criticisms can be generalized to land registration in the rest of Indonesia, but in Aceh there were additional conflict-related problems that undermined the process. The BPN was also responsible for implementing similar cadastral programs throughout Indonesia in its Land Management and Policy Development Project, but RALAS was unique to Aceh. Comparison of RALAS in Aceh to the Land Management and Policy Development Project throughout Indonesia shows that RALAS was much less effective than could be expected (Fairall 2008). World Bank staff and an Australian consultant attribute the differing results to a "mix of poor leadership, corruption and mistrust of the process by local land owners. Aceh has been in almost perpetual rebellion against Jakarta since colonial times, so this is not surprising" (Fairall 2008).

Although official recognition of the limited success of RALAS usually identifies bureaucratic bottlenecks and limited capacity on the ground as the main hurdles, there were clearly a number of other cultural, economic, and political disincentives to titling, which have been identified in this chapter. It seems that the policy makers focused on post-disaster issues because there was a lack of intra-communal disputes, state institutions, and immediate conflict-related problems with post-conflict resettlement. In terms of the symbolic value of land and trust in national government, the post-conflict land problems in Aceh were similar to land registration hurdles in many other post-conflict countries. If taken into consideration, these problems may have altered the way in which land registration was performed and land tenure security conceived in Aceh. Indeed, the assumption that instituting a state-administered land cadastre in a separatist region simply requires community participation and lowering of economic disincentives is naive at best and ideological at worst: naive in that many of the aid agencies and international consultants framed property rights as a post-disaster issue due to their lack of experience in post-conflict situations, and ideological in that this assumption is the result of overextending de Soto's ideas regarding formalization of property rights to rural and post-conflict scenarios. While de Soto's theory was used to justify RALAS, his theory was developed for peri-urban and urban communities (not rural land) and has been widely criticized for its failure to recognize specific political, geographic, cultural, and social dynamics regarding property rights. Despite

312   Land and post-conflict peacebuilding

the fact that RALAS identified ways for the community to participate in and to lower cost disincentives for land registration, the working concept of land tenure security and the goal of land registration themselves need to be reevaluated.

The RALAS emphasis on state land registration for tenure security is understandable from the standpoint of disaster recovery and international financial investment, but it ignores the post-conflict situation, strong existing tenure systems, local perceptions regarding the legitimacy of the Indonesian state, and contradictions in the national legal framework that weaken recognition of customary resource practices in a context of legal pluralism. Without a better grasp of the disincentives to land registration and the specific needs of different geographic areas, the RALAS program was bound to be only partially successful in its aims to increase tenure security through registration.

Despite all this, RALAS was necessary for increasing tenure security in some urban and tsunami-affected areas. Likewise, whether or not RALAS succeeded in increasing tenure security and issuing titles, the RALAS process and activities regarding property administration may have affected peacebuilding. Land tenure security was often mentioned as the foundation of the post-conflict society in Aceh, but the ways that property registration affected land tenure security and peacebuilding remain an open question. Did formal land registration provide tenure security? Did the process assist or hinder the restoration of basic needs and essential services, economic development and sustainable livelihoods, reconciliation, good governance, the reintegration of combatants, or the return and resettlement of refugees?

Basic needs and essential services

Although GAM reintegration did not require formal land-registration processes, the reconstruction of houses for many of the 500,000 tsunami refugees depended on RALAS. The tsunami affected urban areas where land markets existed and where informal practices and agreements were not as clear to survivors as the adat practices were in rural areas. Likewise, international organizations were not equipped to deal with local tenure systems. INGOs and donor agencies often required clear title in order to build new homes on land parcels. The emphasis of UN-HABITAT and others on providing some sort of temporary evidence of possession—even if not legally binding—assisted with the process of providing housing.

RALAS was not oriented toward rebuilding conflict-damaged property, and the BRA may have caused more problems than it resolved with its conflict-damage and victim-compensation schemes, but we need to consider what might have happened to the peace process if formalization of landholdings had not been performed in urban and tsunami-affected areas. Would the peace process have progressed if RALAS did not exist? Although there were problems—including riots in 2005 and 2006 directed at the BPN and the BRR for not moving fast enough to provide shelter and title—RALAS work paved the way for tsunami-refugee shelter and, one could argue, helped prevent a relapse of violent conflict.

Land tenure and peacebuilding in Aceh **313**

Evidence indicates that formalizing property rights was central to improving access to shelter and played a role in equitable distribution of aid. Claims backed by formal title allowed compensation for statutorily recognized property owners that often exceeded that paid to renters and others lacking formal titles. Also, the allocation of emergency housing and the rate at which neighborhoods could be rebuilt were contingent on the ability of groups to either prove their property claims with formal title or implement the RALAS titling procedures. In these ways, formalization of property rights helped prevent serious political backlash that could have derailed peacebuilding.

Economic development and sustainable livelihoods

In Aceh the RALAS project and formal property rights were explicitly linked to the ability to invest in land and to mortgage land to gain access to financial resources. Indeed, the BRR, politicians, and international organizations cited de Soto's problematic theory of land registration for empowering the poor as one of the main justifications for the RALAS project (BRR 2005). But despite anecdotal evidence of businesspeople in Banda Aceh and other urban areas mortgaging their land, most of the people in Aceh have alternative means to access temporary financial assistance—through social networks or arrangements involving, for example, cooperatives, forward sales of crop harvests, or mortgages on vehicles.

These arrangements are typically preferable for most of the poor and rural areas where communities do not want to risk the main source of their livelihoods or well-being (their land or homes) and cannot extract land that is embedded in social relations and obligations. Several bank representatives have expressed hesitation at taking land as collateral even if it is formally titled because the social relations and legal framework surrounding the land may limit its use and because it is difficult to value rural lands where there is no developed market. Robert Deutsch reported that "within the study sample, only about 2.5% of respondents reported accessing credit from commercial banks prior to receiving RALAS land titles, while nearly 7% took bank loans after the receipt of titles" (Deutsch 2009, 43). However, he notes, the small sample size does not account for such factors as a possible increase in investment and the lowering of collateral standards in the region due to the end of the conflict; nor did the study focus on areas where land markets already existed. There are plenty of examples of how formal registration has allowed investment in urban areas, but there is no clear evidence that livelihoods required formal land title or that the process of registering land has allowed the poor to access more resources or has encouraged international investment to the benefit of the peacebuilding process.

Reintegration of combatants and return and resettlement of refugees

Reintegration of GAM combatants was able to take place independently of the efforts to formally register land titles (World Bank 2006a). Most of the GAM

314   Land and post-conflict peacebuilding

accessed land through its communal adat networks and did not need to be relocated onto land with formal title in order to gain tenure security. Where formal title could help was in payment for property damage inflicted during the twenty-nine-year conflict and in resolution of land disputes between communities and government agencies. Communities that were forced to move or sell their land under threat during the conflict are refugees or have experienced violation of their property rights. When groups such as LBH-Aceh have supported communities with claims against the government, the allegations led to activists being severely punished. Publicized disputes with several communities over government-claimed land, local acknowledgment that lands had been taken but an absence of a climate deemed appropriate for pursuing these claims, the punishment of LBH-Aceh, and the ongoing political and personal violence in the region indicate that a minefield of conflict-related property claims still needs to be addressed.

Reconciliation

At a minimum, reconciliation with the government should address the different experiences of former GAM combatants versus those of local communities. Did the RALAS land titling process bring the GAM and the GOI into a cooperative relationship? Did it provide an avenue for resolution of local grievances with the government? The answer to the first question is outlined in the tax structure and the Law on the Governing of Aceh: land registration was a cooperative governance project, and it will establish a source of revenue to be shared between the GOI and the Aceh Party (formerly the GAM), which now runs local politics.

The community-driven adjudication process—where it was desired by the community and was successfully implemented—certainly built confidence in the capacity of the GOI to undertake projects with the locals' well-being in mind. Cynicism regarding the real reasons for land titling and the utility of the land titling process could be overcome where the community-driven process was meticulously followed and where local power dynamics were amenable to it. However, due to problems with implementation and local disincentives to registration, this process often failed to provide reconciliation between local communities and the government.

GOOD GOVERNANCE

By emphasizing participation, transparency, accountability, and monitoring, the land titling project in Aceh promoted positive principles of good governance. Moreover, it built capacities within communities to interact with the government, created digital systems (land cadastres and evidence) that were less susceptible than earlier recordkeeping systems to corruption, decentralized powers by transferring some of them to local political authorities, and provided alternative avenues for dispute resolution through BPN-appointed facilitators. What RALAS and the regional focus on property administration could not do was change the substantive

Land tenure and peacebuilding in Aceh   315

content of the rule of law by clarifying the ambiguous national legal framework regarding communal tenure and transitions of legal rights between adat and statutory systems. But promotion of local capacity and principles of good governance helped the peace process by encouraging responsible governance.

LESSONS LEARNED

The implementation of the RALAS land titling project in Aceh presents us with many lessons about post-conflict development and property administration. The RALAS project indirectly supported peacebuilding by supporting the meeting of basic needs and the delivery of essential services such as shelter, and by providing opportunities for reconciliation and good governance. But there was little real connection between land titling, on the one hand, and economic development, sustainable livelihoods, reintegration of combatants, or resettlement of conflict refugees, on the other. Ultimately, the project missed several opportunities to support peacebuilding and was itself limited by its lack of consideration of the conflict's effects on political, social, and economic relations surrounding land. Unique aspects of the Aceh conflict led experts to detach land titling from problems of violent conflict and to associate it more with tsunami refugees and tsunami damage. The success of the land titling project depended on the legitimacy of state institutions, adequate legal frameworks, understanding of local power dynamics, and accurate identification of incentives and disincentives to registration.

A number of lessons from Aceh might be generalized to other post-conflict situations. For example, in complex political emergencies, development programs should be wary of categorizing programs as post-disaster while conflict dynamics are still relevant. Specifically, it should never be assumed that land is free of cultural and political value or that all disputes between individuals or between individuals and institutions are openly presented in post-conflict scenarios.

Also, transparency, accountability, community participation, and monitoring can promote confidence in the process of adjudication and demarcation of property. Legal and financial accountability within the government hierarchy should be clearly established at the earliest possible date in order to prevent bureaucratic tension or hesitations in implementation. Likewise, the establishment of an independent monitoring institution and of requirements for regular disclosure can be more efficient and effective than reliance on existing institutions to self-police or monitor other institutions.

Furthermore, integrating INGOs and NGOs into government extension regarding property or the provision of essential services requires a clear legal framework. Time-limited and renewable laws can be issued by executive order to allow an immediate legal framework for such activities. The allocation of financial resources for land registration should be goal-oriented instead of time-oriented; there should be no expiring budgets that must be immediately used. There must also be clarification of the legal status of informal practices regarding property rights before property-registration programs are undertaken.

316 Land and post-conflict peacebuilding

Where informal or deeds-based systems are functioning, it is not necessary to immediately convert all land to a state-administered, centralized title system. Titling should be locally evaluated instead of broadly applied.

Finally, the use of social tenure domain models or simple registers that do not specify legal boundaries of property but allow institutions to build records of community locations may be better suited to financial limits and community needs in post-conflict transitions. Community participation in land demarcation and adjudication should be preceded by community-led assessment of needs and should identify methods of integrating women and members of minority groups into public forums that are more effective than simply mixing them with men and members of dominant groups.

In summary, a lack of consideration of conflict dynamics can lead to inappropriate timing and location of and methods for implementing land tenure security programs for peacebuilding. Although there were approaches that could have strengthened tenure security in Aceh while respecting the dynamics of communal property and factors surrounding violent conflict, alternatives to RALAS were never explored (Baranyi and Weitzner 2006). For example, an approach that did not focus on individual titles but that provided communities with communal title and with clear guidelines for internal dispute resolution and interaction with investors or aid agencies could have been less costly and more capable of meeting the demands of INGOs and NGOs, and could have allowed individual tenure security to remain flexible. Such an approach would also have had drawbacks, but it would have been more in line with a gradual, less confrontational strategy of land titling, and it would have been sensitive to post-conflict relations among individuals, communities, and the state.

REFERENCES

Aspinall, E. 2007. The construction of grievance: Natural resources and identity in a separatist conflict. *Journal of Conflict Resolution* 51 (6): 950–972.

BAPPENAS (Badan Perencanaan dan Pembangunan Nasional). 2005. *Master plan for the rehabilitation and reconstruction of the regions and communities of the Province of Nanggroe Aceh Darussalam and the Islands of Nias, Province of North Sumatra.* Jakarta.

Baranyi, S., and V. Weitzner. 2006. *Transforming land-related conflict: Policy, practice and possibilities.* Ottawa: International Land Coalition and the North-South Institute.

Barnett, M., H. Kim, M. O'Donnell, and L. Sitea. 2007. Peacebuilding: What is in a name? *Global Governance* 13 (1): 35–58.

Benny, H. Z. A., T. S. Haroen, and E. Heryani. 2006. Post-tsunami land parcel reconstruction in Aceh: Aspects, status and problems. Paper presented at XXIII FIG Congress, Munich, Germany, October 8–13.

Blomley, N. 2003. Law, property, and the geography of violence: The frontier, the survey, and the grid. *Annals of the Association of American Geographers* 93 (1): 121–141.

Bowen, J. R. 2003. *Islam, law, and equality in Indonesia: An anthropology of public reasoning.* Cambridge, UK: Cambridge University Press.

Land tenure and peacebuilding in Aceh 317

BPN (Badan Pertanahan Nasional). 2005. *Manual of land registration in the affected tsunami areas at Nanggroe Aceh Darussalam and Sumatra Utara: Reconstruction of Aceh Land Administration System (RALAS)*. Jakarta.

BRR (Badan Rehabilitasi dan Rekonstruksi). 2005. Aceh and Nias one year after the tsunami. In *One year report*, Executing Agency of the Rehabilitation and Reconstruction Agency for Aceh and Nias. Banda Aceh: Rehabilitation and Reconstruction Agency for Aceh and Nias.

Burke, A., and Afnan. 2005. Reconstruction in a conflict environment: Views from civil society, donors, and NGOs. In *Indonesian social development,* ed. P. Barron and L. Ashari. Jakarta: Department for International Development.

Burns, P. 2004. *The Leiden legacy: Concepts of law in Indonesia.* Leiden, Netherlands: Koninklyk Instituut Voor Taal Land.

Center for Domestic Preparedness. 2009. Aceh conflict monitoring update for December 2008–February 2009. In *Aceh conflict monitoring update.* Jakarta: World Bank.

Collier, P., and A. Hoeffler. 2004. Greed and grievance in civil war. *Oxford Economic Papers* 56 (4): 563–595.

Collier, P., A. Hoeffler, and D. Rohner. 2009. Beyond greed and grievance: Feasibility and civil war. *Oxford Economic Papers* 61 (1): 1–27.

de Soto, H. 2000. *The mystery of capital: Why capitalism triumphs in the West and fails everywhere else.* New York: Basic Books.

Deutsch, R. 2009. Indonesia Reconstruction of Aceh Land Administration System (RALAS) project: Project implementation and beneficiary assessment, 2008. Banda Aceh: Multi-Donor Trust Fund, World Bank.

Drexler, E. F. 2008. *Aceh, Indonesia: Securing the insecure state.* Philadelphia: University of Pennsylvania Press.

Elyachar, J. 2005. *Markets of dispossession: NGOs, economic development, and the state in Cairo.* Durham, NC: Duke University Press.

Eye on Aceh. 2009. *Challenges of forest governance in Aceh.* Banda Aceh.

Fairall, J. 2008. The aftermath. *ASM Magazine,* April 8.

Fauzi, N. 2009. Land titles do not equal agrarian reform. *Inside Indonesia* 98.

Fitzpatrick, D. 2005. *Restoring and confirming rights to land in tsunami-affected Aceh.* Oxfam / United Nations Development Programme. http://atdr.tdmrc.org:8084/jspui/bitstream/123456789/9479/1/20050714_Rights_Land_Tsunami_Aceh.pdf.

————. 2008. Women's rights to land and housing in tsunami-affected Aceh, Indonesia. Asia Research Institute Working Paper No. 3, ed. A. Reid, B. Nowak, P. Daly, and M. Feener. Singapore: Asia Research Institute / Oxfam International.

Gaillard, J.-C., E. Clave, and I. Kelman. 2008. Wave of peace? Tsunami disaster diplomacy in Aceh, Indonesia. *Geoforum* 39 (1): 511.

Green, A. 2008. Land title questions in Aceh. Paper presented at American Association of Geographers Annual Conference, Boston, April.

Harper, E. 2006. *Guardianship, inheritance and land law in post-tsunami Aceh.* Rome: International Development Law Organization.

Home, R. K., and H. Lim. 2004. *Demystifying the mystery of capital: Land tenure and poverty in Africa and the Caribbean.* London: Glasshouse Press.

Jalil, A., D. Silalahi, G. J. Aditjondro, S. K. Tarigan, Jufriadi, and Darmawan. 2008. The World Bank–financed Reconstruction of Aceh Land Administration System (RALAS). Medan, Indonesia: International NGO Forum on Indonesian Development. www.scribd.com/doc/24157433/working-paper-Penelitian-tentang-RALS-di-Aceh.

318 Land and post-conflict peacebuilding

Kahler, M., and B. F. Walter. 2006. *Territoriality and conflict in an era of globalization.* Cambridge, UK: Cambridge University Press.

Kecamatan Development Program. 2007. *2006 village survey in Aceh: An assessment of village infrastructure and social conditions.* Jakarta: Ministry of Home Affairs Community Development Office.

Kenny, S., L. Fan, and R. Palmer. 2006. The tsunami two years on: Land rights in Aceh. Briefing note. London: Oxfam International.

Kingsbury, D. 2006. *Peace in Aceh: A personal account of the Helsinki peace process.* Jakarta: Equinox.

Le Billon, P., and A. Waizenegger. 2007. Peace in the wake of disaster? Secessionist conflicts and the 2004 Indian Ocean tsunami. *Transactions of the Institute of British Geographers* 32 (3): 411–427.

Li, T. M. 2001. Masyarakat adat, difference, and the limits of recognition in Indonesia's forest zone. *Modern Asian Studies* 35:645–676.

Lindsey, T., ed. 2008. *Indonesia, law and society.* 2nd ed. Leichhardt, NSW, Australia: Federation Press.

Lindsey, T., and R. Phillips. 2005. Inheritance, guardianship, and women's legal rights in post-tsunami Aceh: The interaction of Syariah, adat and secular laws. Report to International Development Law Organization. December.

McCarthy, J. F. 2006. *The fourth circle: A political ecology of Sumatra's rainforest frontier.* Stanford, CA: Stanford University Press.

———. 2007. The demonstration effect: Natural resources, ethnonationalism and the Aceh conflict. *Singapore Journal of Tropical Geography* 28 (3): 314–333.

Moore, D. S. 2005. *Suffering for territory: Race, place, and power in Zimbabwe.* Durham, NC: Duke University Press.

Morse, B. W., and G. R. Woodman. 1988. *Indigenous law and the state.* Dordrecht, Netherlands: Foris.

Nessen, W. 2006. Sentiments made visible: The rise and reason of Aceh's national liberation movement. In *Verandah of violence: The background to the Aceh problem,* ed. A. Reid. Singapore: Singapore University Press.

Otto, J. M. 2009. Rule of law promotion, land tenure and poverty alleviation: Questioning the assumptions of Hernando de Soto. *Hague Journal on the Rule of Law* 1 (1): 173–194.

Paris, R. 2004. *At war's end: Building peace after civil conflict.* Cambridge, UK: Cambridge University Press.

Peluso, N. 2005. Seeing property in land use: Local territorializations in West Kalimantan, Indonesia. *Geografisk Tidsskrift* 105 (1): 1–15.

Reid, A. 2006. *Verandah of violence: The background to the Aceh problem.* Singapore: Singapore University Press.

Renner, M. 2013. Post-tsunami Aceh: Successful peacemaking, uncertain peacebuilding. In *Livelihoods, natural resources, and post-conflict peacebuilding,* ed. H. Young and L. Goldman. London: Earthscan.

Sait, S., and H. Lim. 2006. *Land, law and Islam: Property and human rights in the Muslim world.* London: Zed Books.

Schulze, K. 2007. GAM: Indonesia, GAM, and the Acehnese population in a zero-sum trap. In *Terror, insurgency, and the state: Ending protracted conflicts,* ed. M. Heiberg, B. O'Leary, and J. Tirman. Philadelphia: University of Pennsylvania Press.

Scott, J. C. 1998. *Seeing like a state: How certain schemes to improve the human condition have failed.* New Haven, CT: Yale University Press.

Smith, R. E. 2003. Land tenure reform in Africa: A shift to the defensive. *Progress in Development Studies* 3 (3): 210–222.

Sowerwine, J. 2004. Territorialisation and the politics of highland landscapes in Vietnam: Negotiating property relations in policy, meaning and practice. *Conservation and Society* 2 (1): 97–136.

Transparency International. 2011. Corruption perceptions index 2011. Berlin, Germany. http://cpi.transparency.org/cpi2011/results/.

UNEP (United Nations Environment Programme). 2009. *From conflict to peacebuilding: The role of natural resources and the environment.* Nairobi, Kenya. http://postconflict .unep.ch/publications/pcdmb_policy_01.pdf.

Unruh, J. D. 2003. Land tenure and legal pluralism in the peace process. *Peace and Change* 28 (3): 352–377.

USAID (United States Agency for International Development). 2005. *Land and violent conflict: A toolkit for programming.* Washington, D.C.

World Bank. 2006a. GAM reintegration needs assessment: Enhancing peace through community-level development programming. Washington, D.C.

———. 2006b. Indonesia: Reconstruction of Aceh Land Administration System (RALAS). Washington, D.C.

———. 2008. Aceh poverty assessment 2008: The impact of the conflict, the tsunami, and reconstruction on poverty in Aceh. Jakarta.

Beyond land redistribution: Lessons learned from El Salvador's unfulfilled agrarian revolution

Alexandre Corriveau-Bourque

Control of El Salvador's agricultural land has been the single most divisive issue in the country for the past two centuries. Revolts and insurgencies for which land was a dominant mobilizing narrative punctuated the time between the Salvadoran government's abolition of corporatist landholding in 1881–1882 and the civil war that ended with the Chapultepec Peace Accords on January 16, 1992. While there has been relatively little political violence directly associated with the land issue since 1992, the issue has not been resolved or removed from the public consciousness. The failure to address widespread rural landlessness and poverty is a lingering legacy of the post-accord period. However, instead of armed groups taking up these causes, civil society has emerged with more strength, thanks to the unprecedented opening of democratic space. The creation of such space through the peace accord and the United Nations–sponsored post-conflict peacebuilding is in itself revolutionary. Democratization has not ended rural poverty. But the peace agreement and post-conflict monitoring by the international community effectively demobilized the rebels and dismantled a notoriously repressive security apparatus—creating a new police force, reducing the size of the armed forces by more than half, and putting both under civilian control. The accord also was successful in transforming the Farabundo Martí National Liberation Front (Frente Farabundo Martí de Liberacíon Nacional, or FMLN) from a rebel military force into a viable political party.

However, the Chapultepec Peace Accords failed to produce revolutionary results, let alone a "negotiated revolution" (Karl 1992), when addressing the socioeconomic inequalities that have fuelled tensions in El Salvador. This is particularly true with regard to land distribution. Nearly two decades after the end of the civil war, rural poverty, violence, and landlessness remain a reality for Salvadorans. And while the conflict has ended, it can be argued that peace has not been consolidated. More Salvadorans died violently in the decade following the signing of the Chapultepec Peace Accords than in the last decade of the civil

---

Alexandre Corriveau-Bourque holds a master's degree from McGill University's Department of Geography.

322   Land and post-conflict peacebuilding

war (Wallace 2000; Bourgois 2001). Although the rate has fallen dramatically, as of 2008 El Salvador retained the dubious distinction of having one of the highest per capita murder rates in the world: 55.3 per 100,000 population (OSAC 2009). The interpersonal violence witnessed today remains fundamentally rooted in a history of brutal oppression and persisting poverty, inequity, and social disinvestment (Bourgois 2001).

Hopes of fixing such inequalities were linked to the negotiation of new land reforms through the peace accords.[1] As such, El Salvador's 1992–1997 Land Transfer Program, known as El Programa de Transferencia de Tierras (PTT), provides a unique lens to examine the challenges of managing expectations of resource access in a context of scarcity.

Land scarcity in El Salvador is of two types. The first, structural scarcity, emerges from a historical legacy of marginalization of the rural poor through the elite capture of valuable land resources, the violent repression of social movements by the state, and the redistribution of marginal lands to appease regular rural uprisings while perpetuating the cycles of poverty. Structural scarcity was formally cemented during the negotiation of the peace accords, when the FMLN acquiesced to the government's demand that the 1983 constitution be upheld, essentially preserving the landed elites' hold on the country's most valuable land. As a result, only lands that were willingly sold by former owners would be subject to distribution through the PTT. These limited lands were then made available to some (but not all) former combatants from both sides of the conflict and civilian supporters of the FMLN. The programs and reconstruction efforts left many of the rural poor (especially but not only excombatants and FMLN supporters) with a sense of unfulfilled revolutionary promise (Bourgois 2001; Binford 2002; Ozerdem 2009).

The second type of scarcity is physical, resulting from a growing population and a limited amount of viable agricultural land. This has led to settlement on marginal lands (such as hillsides and areas with poor soils) and an unsustainable intensification of agriculture on small parcels.

Faced with these fundamental constraints on potential land reform, the parties involved in El Salvador's peace negotiations and post-conflict peacebuilding process proved unable to build strong foundations for smallholder agricultural livelihoods or significantly address rural poverty. This case study examines the role of land as a political tool for post-conflict peacebuilding; it finds that the inability to move beyond the redistribution of land has limited prospects for stability and viable rural livelihoods.

This chapter presents an overview of land relations in El Salvador from the abolition of collective holdings in the 1870s and 1880s to state-led land reform in the 1980s, giving historical context to the structural and physical scarcities that shape contemporary land relations. It examines how the peace negotiations

---

[1]   As with most peace agreements, there were multiple rounds of negotiations and agreements that culminated in the Chapultepec Peace Accords in January 1992.

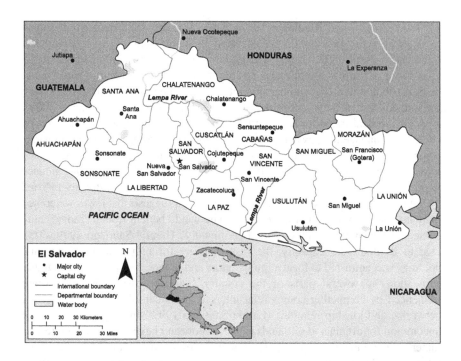

cemented structural scarcity as a condition for peace and identifies the challenges that undermined the PTT's potential for creating viable livelihoods for smallholder agriculturalists. It then discusses the inability of the peacebuilding process to address the wider issue of rural poverty and disenfranchisement, and ends with a review of lessons that can be learned from El Salvador's experience.

A CONTEXT FOR REBELLION

While the colonial and precolonial periods left an indelible trace on the social and economic structures of contemporary El Salvador, this chapter will primarily focus on the period beginning with the emergence of the Salvadoran coffee economy in the nineteenth century.

A liberalism-inspired movement among elites in recently independent El Salvador in the mid-nineteenth century sought to strengthen private holdings to increase the production of cash crops. In order to achieve these higher levels of production, the government passed a series of decrees from 1879 to 1882 designed to break up collective land holdings. According to an 1879 decree, farmers would be granted a private title if they could plant a quarter of their farms with coffee, cocoa, grape, agave, or rubber (Browning 1971). Those who did not plant these cash crops and continued planting food crops would eventually lose their right to cultivate the land. Credit was not provided by the central government, placing the burden of investment on individual farmers and the municipalities (Browning

324   Land and post-conflict peacebuilding

1971; Posterman and Riedinger 1987). The 1881 and 1882 decrees attempted to accelerate the process of privatization by abolishing *tierras communales* (customary-administered lands) and *ejidales* (municipally administered lands), eliminating all forms of collective and cooperative tenure. Ideally, land was to be redistributed to those who occupied it, and for some time, small farmers were the immediate beneficiaries of these reforms (Gould and Lauria-Santiago 2008).

This radical transformation undermined the security of tenure provided by communal management systems.[2] It was a catalyst for competition and divisions among members of the cooperative holdings, as individuals and families attempted to assert their claims to the best lands (Lauria-Santiago 1999). Adding nuance to the oft-reproduced historical narrative that this reform was uniformly resisted by indigenous communities, Aldo A. Lauria-Santiago suggests that it was welcomed by many indigenous and Ladino farmers, who would benefit from a "more secure ownership of lands that they farmed continually" (Lauria-Santiago 1999, 505). Due to limited state capacity, the responsibility for redistributing communal holdings was entrusted to local administrators and judges. The process was highly contentious in several parts of the country since the distribution was often influenced by competing commercial interests, political alliances, patron-client networks, and kinship relations (Lauria-Santiago 1999). In addition, it was not uncommon for officials to sell lands to speculators and large local landed interests rather than divide them into parcels and distribute them among the original inhabitants. Those with capital and knowledge of the law and the mechanisms of formal land tenure (such as titles, surveys, and bureaucratic procedures) used these tools to assert claims to former communal lands (Posterman and Riedinger 1987; Lauria-Santiago 1999). This may have led to immediate dispossession for some, but, as Jeffrey L. Gould and Aldo A. Lauria-Santiago reveal, a significant smallholder and peasant sector also emerged from the process and survived until the 1920s (Gould and Lauria-Santiago 2004).

The rapid growth of the coffee economy also played a significant role in transforming the country's rural landscape. However, its cultivation was limited to the rich, well-drained volcanic soils of the central and western highlands, where the population was most dense and competition for land was highest (Browning 1971; Dunkerley 1982). Due to high labor demands and start-up costs,[3] coffee production favored larger landholders who could dedicate more of their lands to the cash crop instead of to food crops. In the first two decades of the twentieth century,[4] the coffee boom drove up profits and increased the incentive

---

[2]   At the time of privatization, these systems were already under strain from increases in population, competition with neighbors, and the establishment of lucrative individual farms on collective holdings (Lauria-Santiago 1999).

[3]   Coffee requires a five-year maturation period between planting and the first harvestable crop.

[4]   Coffee made up on average 75 to 80 percent of all exports between 1900 and 1922, further rising to 92 percent through the remaining decade (Montgomery 1995).

El Salvador's unfulfilled agrarian revolution 325

for large landowners to expand their holdings and for mid-sized producers to consolidate their production (McReynolds 2002; Gould and Lauria-Santiago 2004).[5] This in turn put pressure on smallholders to sell their plots in these valued areas, squeezing out all other forms of agricultural production (Gould and Lauria-Santiago 2004, 2008). Increased profits allowed landowners to branch into other forms of agriculture—sugar, cattle, and cotton—in other parts of the country.

At the same time, El Salvador's population expanded rapidly, nearly doubling between 1880 and 1930. Within a few generations, small holdings became unviable as they were divided between heirs, reducing plots below subsistence level and forcing many farmers to seek wage employment or trade labor for land under the *colonato* system.[6] Smallholders were also susceptible to predatory lending from large landowners who took their lands if debts were not paid (Gould and Lauria-Santiago 2004).

By 1930, over 50 percent of adult men in western El Salvador had to hire out their labor because they did not have enough land to support themselves (Gould and Lauria-Santiago 2004, 2008). Increased landlessness in turn contributed to a larger labor pool, pushing down wages (Gould and Lauria-Santiago 2008). Ariane De Bremond estimates that as much as 40 percent of the country's land was concentrated in the hands of the landed elite in the decades following the dissolution of communal lands (De Bremond 2007).[7] Not only did more people depend on wage labor to support themselves, but relations between laborers and landowners deteriorated as coffee prices (and wages) plummeted in the late 1920s. Poor work conditions and a sense of recent dispossession, combined with increasing social distance from landowners, produced an environment that was ideal for organized resistance to emerge among *campesinos* (peasants) (Gould and Lauria-Santiago 2004, 2008).

The legal means of dispossession were also directly intertwined with the repressive mechanisms of the state. Between 1882 and 1932, at least five agrarian-based uprisings occurred in El Salvador's countryside, targeting symbols of the land reform (judges, local officials, and landowners) and those perceived to have benefited from it (Browning 1971; Lauria-Santiago 1999; McReynolds 2002). These uprisings were rapidly (and often brutally) quelled by state security forces, culminating in a massive campesino uprising in 1932, famously led by Farabundo

---

[5] A few particularly savvy mid-scale commercial producers benefited enormously from this growth in the sector and were able to join the elite through expansion, despite having emerged from relatively modest holdings (Gould and Lauria-Santiago 2008).

[6] Under the colonato system, landowners would grant peasants a small parcel of land for subsistence crops or food in exchange for their labor on the plantation. This institution was known to be particularly exploitative in that it was often characterized by a lack of wages and limited physical and social mobility, ensuring labor commitments to large landowners (Browning 1971; Simon and Stephens 1981; De Bremond 2007).

[7] Between 1880 and 1930, most of the concentration of land occurred in the western and central highlands. In eastern El Salvador (especially northern Morazán), most peasant farmers retained control over their lands during this period (Gould and Lauria-Santiago 2004, 2008).

326 Land and post-conflict peacebuilding

Martí. The army's crackdown on the rebels became known as La Matanza (the massacre) due to the killing of some 30,000 rebels and campesinos suspected of supporting them. The government also established a paramilitary force, the Guardia Nacional, which was designed to enforce the rule of law in rural areas but in practice was often the tool of landed elites. The Guardia Nacional was frequently used to disrupt campesino organizations and enforce vagrancy laws, essentially evicting those without formal title from their lands and forcing those with little or no land to work on large plantations (Browning 1971; Posterman and Riedinger 1987; Dunkerley 1990; De Bremond 2007).

Following La Matanza, the military government attempted to appease rural unrest by promising to redistribute lands to campesinos. From 1932 to 1979, the government redistributed a mere 62,000 hectares (ha) (Flores 1998). The program mostly legalized land occupations on a small number of properties that had not been effectively managed by their owners. Many of the plots given were of poor quality, and little credit or training was provided to the beneficiaries. It is estimated that most of those who received land were forced to abandon or sell it within a few years due to their inability to make payments or the exhaustion of the soil (Browning 1971). The coffee and cotton booms of the 1950s and 1960s, respectively, only further fuelled this process of land consolidation (see table 1).

By 1971, small farmers' access to land in productive areas of the country was primarily limited to rental and sharecropping arrangements with large landowners (Seligson 1995). Jeffrey M. Paige characterizes many of these arrangements as "starvation renting" (Paige 1996, 130).[8] Under this system, it is estimated that,

Table 1. Land transfers in El Salvador, 1932–1998

Total area	20,720 square kilometers (km²) or 2,072,000 hectares (ha)
Agricultural land*	15,560 km² or 1,556,000 ha
Population density in 2006	326 people/km²
Land transferred 1932–1979	~ 62,000 ha
Percentage of agricultural land controlled by the oligarchy in 1971	72–78%
Land transferred in the 1980s	295,694 ha
Percentage of agricultural land transferred in 1980s	17–20%
Land transferred 1992–1998	103,300–104,000 ha
Percentage of agricultural land transferred 1992–1998	~ 7%
Percentage of agricultural land transferred 1980s–1990s	~ 25%

Sources: Helms (1990); Flores (1998); McReynolds (2002); De Bremond (2007); FAO (2009); Ozerdem (2009); UNSD (2009).

* Agricultural land is defined as arable land that is under temporary or permanent pasture or crops or temporary fallow (UNSD 2009).

---

[8] A minimum of 2.4 hectares would be necessary to make a viable income through tenancy (renting, sharecropping, or participating in the colonato system) (Vidales 1993), but more than 82 percent of those engaged in tenant agreements held less than 1.4 hectares (Flores 1998).

El Salvador's unfulfilled agrarian revolution   327

of the 37 percent of the rural population who had access to land for cultivating crops for their own consumption or sale,[9] half were renters, *colonos*, or share-croppers operating on parcels of less than 1.4 ha (Seligson 1995; Flores 1998). Large landowners generally rented out the marginal, less productive areas of their properties. Those who owned their own land often fared little better: over half of the farms owned were on holdings of less than 1.4 ha, considered inadequate to sustain a family, forcing most smallholder farmers to seek employment on plantations (Paige 1996; Flores 1998; McReynolds 2002).[10]

The dispossession of the rural poor was so systematic that it is estimated that, between 1892 and 1971, the amount of land available to the majority of farmers was reduced, through concentration in the hands of the elite, from 7.4 ha per farmer to 1.5 ha (Durham 1979). Durham dispels the notion that population increase was a significant contributor to the reduction of average parcels for small farmers. According to his calculations, population changes over the same period of time only accounted for a 1.1 ha reduction, in addition to the 5.9 ha lost to elite concentration. Accounting for both these factors, average holdings for small farmers were reduced from 7.4 to 0.4 ha by 1971. To get a sense of the scale of the concentration of land, by 1971, 9 percent of privately owned farms encompassed 72.7 percent of the country's total agricultural land (Helms 1990; Flores 1998).[11]

---

[9]   This includes those who owned their land as well as those who had access through tenancy.

[10]   The level of pre-conflict landlessness has been vigorously debated in academia. A commonly used figure suggests that rural landlessness was at 65 percent (Simon and Stephens 1981). However, Mitchell A. Seligson argues that those measurements are based on an overly inclusive definition of landlessness (Seligson 1995). His more exclusive definition is based on an unusually conservative estimate of how much land is required to sustain a family (0.7 ha), and he eliminates most permanent laborers from his calculations. He argues that a 25 to 29 percent pre-conflict landless rate is a more reasonable estimate. Martin Diskin challenges Seligson's definition of landlessness as too restrictive and says it "employ[s] an extremely low limit for defining the land-poor" (Diskin 1996, 113). The more widely accepted measurement for land-poor owners is 1.4 ha, doubling Seligson's pre-conflict estimates from 25 percent to 50 percent of the rural landowning class (Diskin 1996; Paige 1996; Flores 1998). This framework derives its measurement from Roy L. Posterman and Jeffrey M. Riedinger's use of adequate tenure as a basis for establishing economic vulnerability (Posterman and Riedinger 1987). This framework focuses on the value of farming one's own lands (without having to pay rent or relinquish a portion of one's crops, which would diminish the returns from the land), therefore encompassing laborers and renters within the landless category. Diskin adds that due to low incomes, both permanent and temporary laborers are economically vulnerable in terms of the types of returns the agricultural sector brings them (Diskin 1996). Roberto Vidales estimates that those who farm rented land need at least 2.8 ha to have viable incomes (Vidales 1993). Another 30 percent of farms were smaller than 7 ha (Flores 1998).

[11]   Most of the large holdings were located in the densely populated western and central highlands (for coffee) and the coastal lowlands (for cotton).

328   Land and post-conflict peacebuilding

These policies of land concentration left only marginal, often isolated, mountainous, and generally unproductive lands available for smallholder settlement (Browning 1971; De Bremond 2007). It was unlikely that farmers and their families could subsist on these smallholdings without supplementing their income as seasonal laborers for the large plantations (Paige 1996).[12] These areas also tended to be neglected in terms of rural development (Browning 1971). It is no coincidence that the insurgencies of the 1970s emerged in these mountainous, marginal areas—the *departamentos* of Chalatenango, Cuscatlán, and Morazán—which remained FMLN strongholds throughout the civil war.

REBELLION AND LAND REFORM IN THE 1980s

Several insurgencies emerged in El Salvador's rural areas in the early 1970s in response to growing resentment of the military regime's repressive tactics against labor unions, campesino groups, academics, and anyone else who publicly called for economic, political, or social reform. The groups drew on a range of ideologies, from Catholic liberation theology to indigenous nationalism to socialism and communism (North 1981; McReynolds 2002; Ozerdem 2009). Most of these groups recruited from and were supported by the peasantry. As a result, they emphasized the need for transformative land reform as a mobilizing narrative to attract followers (Villalobos 1989). The respective movements gained traction following the 1972 presidential elections, which were widely believed to have been rigged in favor of the military regime's candidate, General Arturo A. Molina. The other candidate had built a coalition of centrist Christian Democrats, Social Democrats, and communists and had promised full-scale land reform, but narrowly lost. After the election, Molina pledged to enact some land reforms, following intensifying pressure from campesino organizations. It has been argued that the regime's subsequent failure to deliver on its pledges energized guerrilla groups, allowing them to escalate their low-intensity insurrection to more overt acts of rebellion (Posterman and Riedinger 1987; Paris 2004).

In October 1979, a group of reformist military officers led a coup against the military leadership and established a civilian-military junta, the first time since 1931 that El Salvador was not run exclusively by the military. The October junta fell apart in January 1980 as civilian members resigned over increasing repression by state security forces and the inability to come to a consensus on land reform. The military leaders, desperate for civilian partners, cajoled the

---

[12] David Browning describes this land as having thin and acidic soil, being subject to strong winds, and generally unsuitable to coffee farming, and therefore not of interest for capital investment by the government (Browning 1971). It was mostly settled by small-scale farmers, who had exhausted its productive capacity by 1879 through extensive deforestation and intensive cultivation and grazing. It is estimated that a farmer would need 10 ha of land on the poorest soils to sustain a family without outside work (Pearce 1986).

El Salvador's unfulfilled agrarian revolution **329**

Christian Democrats into joining a new junta, promising rapid progress on land reform (Posterman and Riedinger 1987). The junta found a willing patron for its land initiative in the United States, which had been pressuring El Salvador and other Latin American nations to address the land issue to undercut the growing potency of leftist political and military ideologies (Harris and Espinosa 1981).

In March and April 1980, two decrees making up the Ley Básica de la Reforma Agraria were announced, paving the way for what promised to be a significant overhaul of the country's agrarian system. The reform was to take place in three phases, targeting different types of landholdings and designed to redistribute them to different categories of the rural population.

Phase I expropriated all properties exceeding 500 ha in size and was to redistribute the lands to the permanent laborers, colonos, and renters of those properties, via the formation of cooperatives. The original owners were allowed to choose 100 to 150 ha to keep for their own purposes, while receiving compensation for the rest (Simon and Stephens 1981; Helms 1990; McReynolds 2002). The redistribution transferred 215,167 ha (about 15 percent of the country's agricultural land) to 36,697 families (Flores 1998). The program mostly benefited those who had been permanent laborers on the farms, to the exclusion of other categories of rural poor. This was a major source of criticism in that it did little for the most vulnerable under the economic conditions of the times (Simon and Stephens 1981; del Castillo 1997; De Bremond 2007; Ozerdem 2009). The transferred land was not necessarily prime agricultural land, with over 60 percent categorized as pasture or fallow land or inaccessible due to forests or mountainous terrain (Helms 1990).

Phase II targeted holdings of between 100 and 500 ha and was by far the most controversial, in that its implementation promised to break the landowning elite's monopoly over El Salvador's most productive lands, covering 30 percent of the country's coffee and cotton lands (Paige 1996; McReynolds 2002). Phase II was never implemented due to the overwhelming resistance of the landowners. This resistance demonstrates the limits to the compromise that powerful elites were willing to accept on the issue of land. Phase I reportedly only affected a small number of landowners (Posterman and Riedinger 1987). Members of the landowning elite showed themselves willing to accommodate limited reforms as long as the core of their holdings and wealth remained intact.

The landed elites' coup de grâce on this issue was the implementation of a cap on land holdings in the 1983 constitution. Despite significant pressure from the United States to implement the junta's agrarian reforms (which would cap holdings at 100 ha), the National Assembly passed a constitution placing the cap at 245 ha, protecting the vast majority of coffee, cotton, and sugar plantations (Paige 1996). Lands exceeding 245 ha were to be sold to poor campesinos within three years of the constitution's enactment or would be expropriated by the government. This provision remained mostly unenforced due to political pressure and the instability caused by the civil war. It was also largely flouted by owners, who often hid the size of their holdings (Kowalchuck 2003a).

330   Land and post-conflict peacebuilding

Phase III was a land-to-the-tiller program whereby all sharecroppers and tenant farmers were to become owners of the land on which they worked. However, most of these holdings were small and on agriculturally marginal lands, often not even large enough to provide subsistence. Binding the farmers to these small plots neglected the land use patterns that characterized rental arrangements. Prior to this reform, renters rarely worked a single plot intensively. Instead, they shifted from one site to another leaving former plots fallow for regeneration. On these plots, they produced mostly subsistence food crops rather than woody perennial cash crops like coffee. The parcelization of lands in this manner meant that these marginal lands would now be intensively worked, increasing farmers' dependence on expensive agricultural inputs such as fertilizer (Simon and Stephens 1981). It would also exacerbate environmental degradation due to erosion, which had been a problem for agriculture in these areas since the late 1800s (Browning 1971).

In addition, the bureaucratic process of applying for a title was reported to be so cumbersome and complicated that only 31 to 42 percent of the intended beneficiaries received their land (Posterman and Riedinger 1987). The legislature also decreed that land not claimed through the application process by June 1984 should revert back to the original owners. Many applications were rejected during the process. In the end, 42,489 families received land parcels during phase III; 69,605 ha of land was transferred, averaging 1.6 ha per family (Flores 1998).

Those who received land during phases I and III were to pay the government for their properties over a period of thirty years with a fixed annual interest rate of 6 percent. The first four years would be a grace period for principal and interest. While the banks were nationalized by the junta in order to ensure a flow of credit to the beneficiaries, the costs of the start-up for many of the cooperatives were driven up by the right-of-reserve clause of the phase I reform, which allowed the former owners to select which lands to keep. Many of the former owners also removed most of the agricultural equipment and livestock from the lands,[13] or selected the land with infrastructure built on it, undermining the potential productive value of the future cooperatives (Simon and Stephens 1981; Posterman and Riedinger 1987; Helms 1990).

In addition, the titling process for many of the properties was delayed due to bureaucratic inefficiency and a lack of capacity in the government's implementing body, the Salvadoran Institute of Agrarian Transformation (Instituto Salvadoreño de Transformacíon Agraria, or ISTA). This undermined the security of the holdings, limited the beneficiaries' ability to obtain credit for production, and denied them the flexibility to transfer or sell their land if they so chose (Simon and Stephens 1981; Posterman and Riedinger 1987). By 1987, many of the cooperatives had been abandoned due to violence, a collapse in global coffee prices, and lack of technical and financial support (Helms 1990). The cooperatives that

---

[13] Most of the lands from phase I were pasture lands that needed livestock to be efficiently productive (Simon and Stephens 1981).

El Salvador's unfulfilled agrarian revolution   331

persisted were burdened by the debt cycle that started in the 1980s; the beneficiaries of phase I owed US$228.5 million by 1997 (Kowalchuk 2003a).

The stated objectives of the land reform obscured an ulterior motive that was
revealed through its implementation. The land reform law was not only designed
to address the economic and social issues plaguing the country, it was also central
to the junta's counterinsurgency strategy. This explains why, on the same day that
it was decreed, a state of siege was announced under which the rights to free speech,
press, assembly, and habeas corpus were suspended (North 1981). The program
was to be implemented through the joint efforts of the ISTA and the military.

The reforms were received with resistance not only by the landowning class
but also by many of the intended beneficiaries, who were wary of the military's
role in the reform (Flores 1998). The military was dispatched to the phase I
properties (those exceeding 500 ha) to take them over for the purpose of redistribution; however, this process was accompanied by a repressive crackdown on
campesino organizations, unions, and the general population by the same security
forces. At the same time, attacks by right-wing paramilitary groups escalated,
frequently targeting the intended beneficiaries of the land reform with illegal
evictions, threats, abuse, and murder (Simon 1984; Helms 1990). Even government
figures supporting the reform were targets. The head of the ISTA was assassinated
along with two consultants less than a year after the reforms were announced.

The failure to implement phase II of the reform, and the lack of consultation
with campesino groups before and during the program's implementation, indicate
both a paternalistic approach to the agrarian issue and an underlying imperative to
manage the agrarian-based unrest, rather than a genuine commitment to addressing
the issues that fuelled the conflict. Therefore, the use of land reform as a counterinsurgency tactic was, in the end, too little, too late. As the junta began rolling
out its plans for land reform in 1980, the disparate guerrilla groups independently
fighting the government coalesced into the Farabundo Martí National Liberation
Front (Frente Farabundo Martí de Liberacíon Nacional, or FMLN), evoking the
name of the martyred leader of the 1932 campesino rebellion. By January 1981,
the FMLN was able to launch its first major coordinated offensive, throwing the
country into full-scale civil war.

By the end of the civil war, about 20 percent of the country's land had been
redistributed, making this the most significant redistribution of agrarian resources
and transformation of agrarian institutions since 1882. However, few who had
been landless or economically vulnerable before 1980 actually benefited from
the reform. Once again, the landed elites' manipulation of the state's judicial,
legislative, and security institutions ensured their continued control over the
country's most productive lands. This structurally imposed scarcity was combined
with insufficient technical and financial support for the intended beneficiaries,
reducing their chances of exploiting their holdings in efficient, sustainable ways.
Even though communally managed lands were reintroduced, excessive debt payments and lack of institutional support had trapped the intended beneficiaries in
a cycle of poverty.

332   Land and post-conflict peacebuilding

PEACE NEGOTIATIONS AND LAND REFORM IN THE 1990s

By 1989, the FMLN and the government had reached a military stalemate.[14] Popular support for both sides was waning, as the death toll rose (by the end of the conflict, over 75,000 people had been killed) and over one-quarter of the population was displaced. The economy was in tatters due to the guerrillas' attacks on the country's economic infrastructure and the military's scorched-earth tactics in rebel strongholds.

Seizing on the impasse and the shift in the American position vis-à-vis its support for the Salvadoran government, the United Nations offered to broker a peace deal. It was produced piecemeal, with the 1991 New York Agreement and 1992 Chapultepec Peace Accords containing the most significant provisions on agrarian reform. Although the peace accords as a whole were extensive and detailed, their provisions on social and economic reforms were sparse (del Castillo 1997; McReynolds 2002; De Bremond 2007; Ozerdem 2009).

Rhetorically, the FMLN insisted that agrarian reform had to be a central feature of any successful peace accord (Villalobos 1989). However, the negotiations rapidly revealed that no progress was likely to be made as long as sweeping reforms of the agrarian sector remained a central issue. The elite's fear of radical agrarian reform was one of the major impediments to progress on the peace accords. The Salvadoran government insisted during negotiations that agrarian reform would have to be accomplished by amending the constitution (which required approval by two successive National Assemblies), reducing the chance that it would pass (Karl 1992). As a condition for peace, the FMLN needed to recognize the 1983 constitution, which upheld the 245 ha ceiling on landownership. There was fear that pressing the issue further would spoil the peace process (Call 2002).

The FMLN spent most of its negotiating capital on assuring its political inclusion and establishing mechanisms for an overhaul of the security sector, both which it prioritized over social and economic reforms (Kowalchuck 2003a; De Bremond 2007). The elites' inflexibility on the issue of agrarian reform was

---

[14]   The Soviet Union's halt of arms sales to the Sandinistas in Nicaragua in 1989 reduced a major source of military support for the FMLN (Karl 1992; del Castillo 1997; Call 2002). This loss was further compounded by the Sandinistas' loss to a party unsympathetic to the FMLN in Nicaragua's 1990 presidential elections, eliminating one of the guerrillas' main financial supporters (Ozerdem 2009). The Salvadoran government, which had been propped up by billions of dollars in U.S. military and economic assistance during the Reagan administration, lost support in the United States due to reports of crimes against humanity by Salvadoran security forces. The turning point was the killing of six Jesuit priests and their housekeeper in November 1989 by a right-wing paramilitary group, a story that was widely covered in the global media. Combined with the diminishing relevance of the Soviet Union as a supporter of Latin American insurgency, it became increasingly difficult for the George H. W. Bush administration to justify its continued support for the Salvadoran regime (Karl 1992; Holiday and Stanley 1993; de Soto and del Castillo 1995).

El Salvador's unfulfilled agrarian revolution 333

strengthened by their continued control of the state apparatus; the FMLN recognized that failing to dismantle those structures would inevitably prevent any type of agrarian reform. The FMLN leadership's confidence in the ability of the post-conflict electoral process to bring about necessary social and economic reforms was articulated in a 1989 article in *Foreign Policy*, in which an FMLN commander wrote: "The FMLN does not fear elections. Under fair conditions the majority of Salvadorans would opt for revolutionary change." He added that holding these free elections would "require a change in the balance of military power in the country . . . so long as the military balance does not change, social change will be blocked because the army will always act to reconstitute its power" (Villalobos 1989, 118, 121–122).

The FMLN's acceptance of the 1983 constitution within the framework of the peace accords indefinitely suspended the possibility for substantial, widespread agrarian reform by ensuring an insurmountable land scarcity that helped legitimize claims that there was not enough land to meet the demands of the rural population (Seligson 1995).

FMLN negotiators instead focused on creating a mechanism to legalize tenancy in conflict zones as a means to consolidate their political gains. Near the end of the civil war, the FMLN and campesino organizations actively encouraged their supporters to occupy and start working lands previously held by others (those who did so were identified as *tenedores* in the peace accords) within the territories under FMLN's control (Chalatenango, Cuscatlán, and Morazán).[15] By negotiating to legalize their supporters' claims through the accords, they stood to gain political credibility among other landless and land-poor people, positioning themselves well for the elections set for 1994 (McReynolds 2002; De Bremond 2007).[16] Provisions were also made to facilitate soldiers' transition to civilian livelihoods—inevitable given the dismantling of the FMLN's military wing and the Guardia Nacional and the reduction in size of the military—by providing them access to land. From this perspective, the transfer of land in the 1990s can be interpreted partially as a process of disarmament, demobilization, and reintegration that happened to use land as a vehicle for reintegration rather than a genuine effort at land reform.

On the issue of tenedores, the Chapultepec Peace Accords guaranteed that the tenure situation found in conflict zones at the time of the signing of the accords would be respected, protecting the tenedores from eviction until they could receive

---

[15] Ironically, 60 percent of the lands identified by the FMLN for redistribution were located in Chalatenango, where most of the plots were already owned by small landholders with less than 3.5 ha each (Montgomery 1995).

[16] The peace accords established a cap on the number of beneficiaries for the PTT and other reintegration programs. Therefore, the selection of beneficiaries was often dependent on relationships with FMLN commanders and political alignments within the group, influenced by personal rivalries, and biased against women (Bourgois 2001; Binford 2002).

334   Land and post-conflict peacebuilding

formal title to the land they were occupying.[17] If the original landlord was unwilling to sell, they were given the right to stay on their current holding until another parcel could be found for them. However, the boundaries of the conflict zones within which this provision applied were not clearly spelled out in the agreement, and therefore, the number of tenedores and the lands to which they were entitled were subject to fierce negotiation after the Chapultepec Peace Accords were signed.

The Chapultepec Peace Accords also stated that the lands would be only made available if the original owners sold willingly—eliminating the prospect of expropriation, except for properties exceeding the 1983 constitution's 245 ha limit.[18] Like in the 1980s, landowners could choose which lands to sell. Not only did this limit the available land, driving up the price,[19] it guaranteed that it would be mostly marginal and relatively unproductive. Paige notes that the post-conflict stabilization of the rural areas and the subsequent increase in demand for land drove rents to new exploitative highs, further reducing the incentive to sell (Paige 1996).

The ambiguity in the Chapultepec Peace Accords was also a source of considerable post-accord tension and caused implementation delays. In order to accelerate the process, the government attempted to impose a cap on the amount of credit that would be made available to each beneficiary for the purchase of land. (The agreement established that credit would be made available, but not how much or on what terms.) The FMLN objected, arguing that this provision would limit the amount of land that could be purchased, especially as land prices were rising and the cap would be in the Salvadoran currency, the *colon*, which was subject to depreciation (del Castillo 1997; De Bremond 2007). The tension was also heightened by the government's perceived violation of the agreement in forcibly evicting tenedores from lands the FMLN claimed were within the conflict zones (Call 2002). In September and October 1992, the wrangling over these ambiguities reached its climax and almost ended the ceasefire. The FMLN halted the demobilization of its forces in protest, and the government responded in kind.

Many of these struggles can be attributed to political gamesmanship. The government stalled progress and limited access to land in order to undermine the FMLN's credibility as an unarmed political force. By releasing as few assets as possible, it would deny the FMLN a key victory that would have strengthened its support among the rural masses in the period leading up to the election (Córdova-Macías 2001; De Bremond 2007).

---

[17] According to Graciana del Castillo, one of the UN's chief architects of the PTT, guaranteeing the rights of the tenedores was intended to put pressure on the landlords to sell their lands, assuming that if they refused, the tenedores would still occupy the land for a long time before they were relocated (del Castillo 1997).

[18] State lands would also be made available for redistribution; however, these only amounted to 17,500 ha. Even six years after the signing of the accords, many properties exceeding the constitutional limit remained in the possession of elites (Kowalchuck 2003b).

[19] The high demand and low supply after the civil war caused land prices to multiply five or six times (McReynolds 2002; De Bremond 2007; Ozerdem 2009).

El Salvador's unfulfilled agrarian revolution 335

The impasse was resolved by a UN-brokered deal on October 13, 1992, that clarified many of these ambiguities and defused many of the tensions. This included a cap on the size of lands to which beneficiaries would be entitled, which would be determined on a sliding scale, depending on the quality of land (UNDPI 1995). Despite ardent protests by the FMLN that this cap would trap beneficiaries in the same patterns of poverty that existed before the civil war, the international community pressured both parties heavily to accept the deal. Under the PTT, the maximum amount of highest-quality land that could be acquired was 1.4 ha, while the lowest-quality land would be capped at 4.9 ha. The agreement reduced the number of beneficiaries requested by the FMLN, establishing that 25,000 tenedores and 22,500 excombatants (from both sides) would have access to benefits. It calculated a 50 to 65 percent shortfall in land to cover the (already reduced) number of beneficiaries, based on lands already made available prior to the October 13 agreement, but failed to establish how this was to be filled. The payment structure for the lands drew on the Ley Basica of the 1980s. Once again, the land would be sold, not given to the beneficiaries. Loan agreements from the Agricultural Development Bank were based on the category of beneficiary, with terms somewhat favoring former combatants (McReynolds 2002).[20]

However, even after the October 13, 1992, agreement, the implementation of the PTT progressed slowly for several reasons. First, there was insufficient financial commitment by the international community to support the programs. According to Alpaslan Ozerdem, there were signs of donor fatigue as early as 1993–1994, less than two years after the Chapultepec Peace Accords had been signed, hindering the government's ability to implement reintegration programs (Ozerdem 2009). The funding gap between what was pledged and what was actually donated for the period of 1993–1996 was US$600 million. The institutions also lacked the technical proficiency to deliver titles efficiently, and the process was slowed by an antiquated bureaucratic apparatus (del Castillo 1997; Call 2002; McReynolds 2002). Graciana del Castillo suggests that the slow implementation of titling reflected not only financial constraints but also a lack of institutional and political will to accommodate the beneficiaries of the PTT (del Castillo 1997).

This argument has some value, considering the systems put into place would ultimately undermine the future viability of beneficiaries' livelihoods. Although nothing in the October 13 agreement or Chapultepec Peace Accords stipulated this requirement, the government and lending agencies also refused to distribute production credit until the beneficiaries held a title; however, by October 1994, only one-quarter of intended beneficiaries had successfully received one. These delays significantly undermined the ability of beneficiaries to engage in viable, productive livelihoods. Without credit or titles, the intended beneficiaries were caught in limbo

---

[20] Tenedores would be entitled to 10,000 colones and would have a one-year grace period on payment of interest and principal. The interest rate was 18.5 percent over ten years. Former combatants were entitled to a five-year grace period and a 14 percent interest rate over ten years (McReynolds 2002).

336 Land and post-conflict peacebuilding

and had little incentive (or ability, given the lack of credit) to cultivate or improve their lands, since the security of their tenure was not guaranteed (de Soto and del Castillo 1995; del Castillo 1997).[21] Technical assistance was also scarce, which was particularly problematic since many of the combatant beneficiaries were unskilled in agriculture (Montgomery 1995; del Castillo 1997; Kowalchuck 2004; Ozerdem 2009).

The absence of technical assistance, the small size of parcels, the poor quality of land on which they were settled, delays in making production credit available, and the disproportionately slow growth of the agricultural sector due to policy neglect all contributed to the creation of a debt crisis for PTT beneficiaries and an exacerbation of the debt crisis for beneficiaries of the 1980s reform. In all, the agrarian debt of beneficiaries of both programs amounted to US$400 million by 1997. Of the US$400 million, beneficiaries of the PTT owed US$100 million (roughly US$2,800 per beneficiary), while beneficiaries from phase I of the 1980s plan owed as much as US$228.5 million (Kowalchuck 2003b). While the FMLN and campesino organizations mobilized politically in the mid-1990s to get the debt pardoned, many beneficiaries were ultimately compelled to sell their lands or hire themselves out as wage laborers. This has resulted in a reconcentration of land, as wealthy landowners have capitalized on individuals' financial vulnerability to buy back the lands (Kowalchuck 2004; Ozerdem 2009).

An important factor undermining the viability of the land transfer program was the disconnect between policy makers and the intended beneficiaries. Several critiques have been raised that campesinos, labor organizations, and nongovernmental organizations were marginalized by donors (such as the World Bank) and the government in the design of the PTT and the National Reconstruction Plan (Foley, Vickers, and Thale 1997; Córdova-Macías 2001; Call 2002). Even within the FMLN, rigid hierarchies and the educational gap between the leadership and the rank and file often left many FMLN supporters with the feeling of being underrepresented or left out of the FMLN's gains (Kowalchuk 2003a). After the conflict, many former combatants and civilian supporters (beneficiaries and non-beneficiaries) expressed a sense of disillusionment in the revolutionary leadership (Bourgois 2001; Binford 2002).

The sense of disillusionment in the post-conflict era needs to be examined in terms of the viability of the livelihoods created by the program. One of the lingering legacies of the peacebuilding process is the inability to stimulate economic opportunities in the rural areas, opportunities that would decrease dependence on land and the fickle agricultural sector. While the national economy grew at an average annual rate of 6.7 percent in the 1990s, the agricultural sector grew at a much slower 2.5 percent, indicating an asymmetrical commitment to development (Foley, Vickers, and Thale 1997). The post-conflict agricultural policies also failed to develop markets for small producers' goods. In fact, following the

---

[21] These delays also had severe long-term consequences. A 1999 study revealed that families who had received their PTT lands earlier had lower levels of malnutrition-induced stunted growth among children (Brentlinger et al. 1999).

El Salvador's unfulfilled agrarian revolution 337

civil war, the government embarked on a policy of importing most of its food in an attempt to drive down food prices in urban areas, despite the fact that small-holder agriculture is almost entirely directed toward the production of food. The artificially inflated colon also undermined the competitiveness of Salvadoran agricultural commodities (McReynolds 2002; Ozerdem 2009).

Some factors have emerged to mitigate these declines in the agricultural sector. Since the end of the conflict, remittances have overtaken export earnings and development aid from the United States as the primary source of foreign exchange in the country. By the end of the civil war, remittances accounted for over US$1.4 billion per year (Call 2002; Pedersen 2004). In addition, increased urban migration and nonfarm employment have diminished dependence on agricultural livelihoods.

By 1994, it was estimated that over 35 percent of the economically active population in rural areas was employed in the nonfarm sector (Lanjouw 2001). Participation in this economic sector has been correlated with lower rates of poverty than those for agricultural households, whether or not the latter own their land (Lanjouw 2001; González-Vega et al. 2004). Despite the presence of alternative opportunities, there remains a strong attachment to land as a safety net, so as nonfarm incomes increase, the demand for land also rises (González-Vega et al. 2004). In addition, Jeffrey Hopkins, Douglas Southgate, and Claudio González-Vega suggest that raising nonagricultural earnings decreases dependence on small-scale, environmentally unsustainable agriculture while providing more viable alternatives for poverty alleviation (Hopkins, Southgate, and González-Vega 1999). However, the ability to access these alternative livelihoods and the employment of better agricultural practices is dependent on educational levels, which remain low in El Salvador's rural areas (Hopkins, Southgate, and González-Vega 1999; Lanjouw 2001). Due to low availability of credit, personal savings and remittances appear to be a strong factor enabling households to diversify their livelihoods (Lanjouw 2001; González-Vega et al. 2004). The availability of nonfarm employment also varies by region. Close to San Salvador, as much as 50 percent of the economically active population derives income from the nonfarm sector, while the figure falls to under 25 percent in eastern departamentos, indicating a significant disparity in rural development (Lanjouw 2001).

While the period of rapid post-conflict economic growth witnessed a decrease in poverty levels (rural poverty declined to 49 percent in 2002), income inequality in El Salvador has worsened, as the poorest 20 percent of the population's share of national wealth diminished from 3 percent to 2.8 percent between 1991 and 2002 (USAID 2005). The rapid growth of the 1990s significantly slowed between 1998 and 2008, when the average annual growth of the gross domestic product declined to a 2.7 percent average from a 5.1 percent average in the preceding decade (World Bank 2009). In addition, poverty rates and inequality are expected to worsen due to the global financial crisis, as the flow of remittances is expected to diminish, eliminating a safety net upon which many poor Salvadorans depend (UNDP 2009). Claudio González-Vega and colleagues suggest that in periods of declining opportunities for nonagricultural income (opportunities that are often created through the

338   Land and post-conflict peacebuilding

flow of remittances), households become increasingly dependent on subsistence agriculture (González-Vega et al. 2004).

In addition to looking at the PTT from the perspective of land redistribution, it is also necessary to evaluate its effectiveness as a disarmament, demobilization, and reintegration program, for which it was designed. From a broad security perspective, the program successfully facilitated the transformation of the FMLN into a nonmilitarized political party. This abated tensions at the national level and eliminated the mechanisms through which the parties could wage further conflict. However, at an individual level, the economic insecurity of beneficiaries and the lack of consultation with excombatants have resulted in high rates of recidivism. While unfulfilled expectations regarding the transfer of land in Nicaragua's arms-for-land program resulted in the contras rearming, in El Salvador, a number of excombatants who were beneficiaries of the PPT were not able to go back into the FMLN and therefore joined armed gangs, known as *maras*, or private security firms (de Soto and del Castillo 1995; Paris 2004; Ozerdem 2009). Ozerdem and Philippe Bourgois suggest that violence has transformed from ideological and political conflict to criminality, yet this violence still revolves around the inequalities of the system, making El Salvador one of the world's most violent countries (Ozerdem 2009; Bourgois 2001).[22]

What is especially perplexing about these persisting problems is that the very structures of dispossession and inequality are being reproduced in a democratic environment in which free and fair elections have been held since 1997. What happened to Joaquin Villalobo's idealized social and economic revolution through the ballot box (Villalobo 1989)?

FACTORS AFFECTING THE OUTCOME OF LAND REFORMS

In terms of scale, the PTT of the 1990s accomplished half as much redistribution as the 1980 Ley Basica. This limited scope was primarily a result of the structural and physical scarcities that have constrained Salvadoran land programs since the 1930s. The threat of renewed violence during the negotiations enabled the government to maintain the 1983 constitution, which guaranteed the landed elites control over the country's most productive land.

However, it was political gamesmanship between the parties following the accords that ultimately undermined the effectiveness of the PTT. Much of this jockeying was due to the ambiguity of the original agreement, which allowed the conflicting parties to limit the effectiveness of the agreed-upon reforms. While international actors played a significant role in containing and resolving these tensions, the rapid onset of donor fatigue contributed to the weakening of the

---

[22]   Lisa Kowalchuck notes that there remains some state-led and private violence directly related to the land issue: police have teargassed, beaten, and jailed participants in land occupations, and civil society activists have been assaulted and threatened (Kowalchuk 2003b).

PTT. Land redistribution requires extensive and sustained capital and technical support—first, to process claims and ensure efficient titling, and second, to provide the technology, personnel, and capacity-building programs required to streamline often archaic bureaucratic processes and provide training for beneficiaries. Financing delays also impeded beneficiaries' access to credit and titles, slowing their recovery and prolonging their dependence on food aid. Despite its limited scope, if the PTT had had sufficient support, it could have established a firm foundation for smallholder agriculture in El Salvador and a basis upon which to build a rural economy.

Several authors compellingly argue that the neoliberal policies that framed the PTT and the post-conflict economy undermined the programs and perpetuated the issues that fuelled the civil war in the first place (Foley, Vickers, and Thale 1997; Paris 2004; De Bremond 2007; Ozerdem 2009). They identified the trend in the first UN peacekeeping efforts of the 1990s, particularly in Latin America (Guatemala, Nicaragua, and El Salvador). The United States and the World Bank pressured the governments of these countries in the late 1980s and early 1990s to liberalize their economies and political systems as a condition of aid. These authors argue that it was primarily the combination of the market-led agrarian reforms and the liberalization of government services that prompted speculation on the land markets, insufficient investment in the agricultural sector, and the decline in government services. By failing to provide viable alternatives to agriculture-based livelihoods, these policies essentially reproduced the systems of inequality that fuelled the conflicts in the first place.

Ultimately, the lack of depth of these programs merely perpetuated an ongoing cycle of smallholder poverty and dependence on wage labor. In addition, the measures for rural development implemented during the post-conflict peacebuilding efforts provided few viable alternatives to agricultural livelihoods, increasing dependency on remittances from family members living in urban areas or abroad.

LESSONS LEARNED

El Salvador's peace negotiations formalized the structures that maintained an asymmetric access to land resources, cementing the structural scarcity of land in El Salvador. Despite being flawed, the Chapultepec Peace Accords were a success in that hostilities were effectively ended between the government and the FMLN and paved the way for a conflict-wracked nation to move into a new period of political stability. The international community's close monitoring of the situation allowed external actors to intervene quickly enough when disagreements over ambiguities in the agreement threatened to undermine the peace process. Yet political stability was not effectively translated into the economic and social reforms necessary to address widespread poverty and a sense of disenfranchisement.

Disillusionment with this legacy can be attributed to the fact that the promise of addressing the country's long legacy of social and economic inequalities was linked almost entirely to the redistribution of land. Faced with the reality that a

340   Land and post-conflict peacebuilding

revolutionary redistribution of land could not occur, domestic and international actors took insufficient steps to ensure that the dividends of peace would be accessible to a wider range of Salvadorans. The process excluded the majority of the rural landless from these benefits, while failing to manage their expectations of future reforms by providing alternative opportunities. As a result, many rural poor people remain dependent on insufficient land and unequal labor relations in a weakened agricultural sector. An effort at rural development would have also increased the viability of beneficiaries' livelihoods by developing infrastructure and providing alternative employment to increase food security. Instead, long-term economic growth and social stability were neglected for the sake of short-term political stability.

Many of the criticisms of the programs of the 1990s are the same as those raised in previous generations, indicating not only an inability to fundamentally change the control over the institutions regulating land but also a disconnect between policy makers and local realities and priorities. El Salvador's land redistribution programs have often been criticized for failing to engage campesino groups in the decision-making process, thus threatening the sustainability of peace. Interventions have been carried out on behalf of intended beneficiaries instead of in partnership with them, further marginalizing them from the process. These programs would have been perceived as being more legitimate if donors and government had included local stakeholders in the decision-making process. However, building these relations of trust will require strong leaders on both sides to bridge the gaps resulting from generations of alienation.

CONCLUSION

Of the natural resources that fuel conflict, land is particularly imbued with a deep history of violence, control, dispossession, and especially grievance. In El Salvador, land and land-based resources (agricultural products) shaped the social and political struggles of the twentieth century. However, political opening, rapid urbanization, and remittances have transformed rural dynamics in the 1990s and 2000s. While net wealth has grown, disparities have also grown. Elite control over land has prohibited El Salvador's poor from becoming landowners. Land could have been used as a tool to build peace by giving campesino groups access to a resource that would provide them with a livelihood. On the other hand, the strong focus on redistributing land for livelihood generation led to the neglect of other options that could have contributed to stability and income generation for the rural poor. Resolving the roots of the problems that led to the civil war depended on an equitable redistribution of land, and because this was not achieved, addressing the pervasive problems of poverty and criminality will require a long-term commitment by the state and the international community that focuses on providing sufficient education and nonagricultural jobs for rural youth, access to credit for the creation of small businesses, market linkages for agricultural products, and measures to halt the pervasive environmental degradation in El Salvador.

El Salvador's unfulfilled agrarian revolution   341

REFERENCES

Binford, L. 2002. Violence in El Salvador: A rejoinder to Philippe Bourgois' "The power of violence in war and peace." *Ethnography* 3 (2): 201–219.

Bourgois, P. 2001. The power of violence in war and peace: Post–Cold War lessons from El Salvador. *Ethnography* 2 (1): 5–34.

Brentlinger, P. E., M. A. Hernán, S. Hernández-Diáz, L. S. Azaroff, and M. McCall. 1999. Childhood malnutrition and postwar reconstruction in rural El Salvador: A community-based survey. *Journal of the American Medical Association* 281 (2): 184–190.

Browning, D. 1971. *El Salvador: Landscape and society.* Oxford, UK: Oxford University Press.

Call, C. T. 2002. Assessing El Salvador's transition from civil war to peace. In *Ending civil wars: The implementation of peace agreements,* ed. S. J. Stedman, D. Rothchild, and E. M. Cousens. Boulder, CO: Lynne Rienner.

Córdova-Macías, R. 2001. Demilitarizing and democratizing Salvadoran politics. In *El Salvador: Implementation of the peace accords,* ed. M. S. Studemeister. Washington, D.C.: United States Institute of Peace.

De Bremond, A. 2007. The politics of peace and resettlement through El Salvador's land transfer programme: Caught between the state and the market. *Third World Quarterly* 28 (8): 1537–1556.

del Castillo, G. 1997. The arms-for-land deal in El Salvador. In *Keeping the peace: Multidimensional UN operations in Cambodia and El Salvador,* ed. M. W. Doyle, I. Johnstone, and R. C. Orr. Cambridge, UK: Cambridge University Press.

de Soto, A., and G. del Castillo. 1995. Implementation of comprehensive peace agreements: Staying the course in El Salvador. *Global Governance* 1 (2): 189–203.

Diskin, M. 1996. Distilled conclusions: The disappearance of the agrarian question in El Salvador. *Latin American Research Review* 31 (2): 111–126.

Dunkerley, J. 1982. *The long war: Dictatorship and revolution in El Salvador.* London: Junction Books.

———. 1990. *Latin America since 1930: Mexico, Central America and the Caribbean.* Cambridge, UK: Cambridge University Press.

Durham, W. H. 1979. *Scarcity and survival in Central America: Ecological origins of the Soccer War.* Stanford, CA: Stanford University Press.

FAO (Food and Agriculture Organization of the United Nations). 2009. *State of the world's forests.* www.fao.org/docrep/011/i0350e/i0350e00.HTM.

Flores, M. 1998. El Salvador: Trajectoria de la reforma agrarian, 1980–1998. *Revista Mexicana de Sociología* 60 (4): 125–151.

Foley, M. W., G. R. Vickers, and G. Thale. 1997. *Tierra, paz y participacion: El desarrollo de una politica agrarian de posguerra en El Salvador y el papel del Banco Mundial.* http://lasa.international.pitt.edu/LASA97/foleyspa.pdf.

González-Vega, C., J. Rodrígez-Mez, D. Southgate, and J. H. Maldonado. 2004. Poverty, structural transformation, and land use in El Salvador: Learning from household data. *American Journal of Agricultural Economics* 86 (5): 1367–1374.

Gould, J. L., and A. Lauria-Santiago. 2004. "They call us thieves and steal our wage": Toward a reinterpretation of the Salvadoran rural mobilization, 1929–1931. *Hispanic American Historical Review* 84 (2): 191–237.

———. 2008. *To rise in darkness: Revolution, repression and memory in El Salvador, 1920–1932.* Durham, NC: Duke University Press.

342   Land and post-conflict peacebuilding

Harris, K., and M. Espinosa. 1981. Reform, repression and revolution in El Salvador. *Fletcher Forum* 5 (2): 295–319.

Helms, M. W. 1990. The society and its environment. In *El Salvador: A country study*, ed. R. A. Haggerty. 2nd ed. Washington, D.C.: Library of Congress.

Holiday, D., and W. Stanley. 1993. Building the peace: Preliminary lessons from El Salvador. *Journal of International Affairs* 46 (2): 415–438.

Hopkins, J., D. Southgate, and C. González-Vega. 1999. Rural poverty and land degradation in El Salvador. Paper presented at the annual meeting of the American Agricultural Economics Association, Nashville, TN.

Karl, T. L. 1992. El Salvador's negotiated revolution. *Foreign Affairs* 71 (2): 147–164.

Kowalchuk, L. 2003a. Asymmetrical alliances, organizational democracy and peasant protest in El Salvador. *Canadian Review of Sociology and Anthropology* 40 (3): 291–309.

————. 2003b. Peasant struggle, political opportunities, and the unfinished agrarian reform in El Salvador. *Canadian Journal of Sociology* 28 (3): 309–340.

————. 2004. The Salvadoran land struggle through the 1990s: Cohesion, commitment and corruption. In *Landscapes of struggle: Politics, society and community in El Salvador*, ed. A. Lauria-Santiago and L. Binford. Pittsburgh, PA: University of Pittsburgh Press.

Lanjouw, P. 2001. Nonfarm employment and poverty in rural El Salvador. *World Development* 29 (3): 529–547.

Lauria-Santiago, A. A. 1999. Land, community, and revolt in late-nineteenth-century Indian Izalco, El Salvador. *Hispanic American Historical Review* 79 (3): 495–534.

McReynolds, S. A. 2002. Land reform in El Salvador and the Chapultepec Peace Accord. *Journal of Peasant Studies* 30 (1): 135–169.

Montgomery, T. S. 1995. *Revolution in El Salvador: From civil strife to civil peace.* Boulder, CO: Westview Press.

North, L. 1981. *Bitter grounds: Roots of revolt in El Salvador.* Toronto: Between the Lines.

OSAC (Overseas Security and Advisory Council, United States Department of State). 2009. *El Salvador 2009 crime and safety report.* www.osac.gov/pages/ContentReportPDF.aspx?cid=7772

Ozerdem, A. 2009. *Post-war recovery: Disarmament, demobilization and reintegration.* London: I. B. Tauris.

Paige, J. M. 1996. Land reform and agrarian revolution in El Salvador: Comment on Seligson and Diskin. *Latin American Research Review* 31 (2): 127–139.

Paris, R. 2004. *At war's end: Building peace after civil conflict.* Cambridge, UK: Cambridge University Press.

Pearce, J. 1986. *Promised land: Peasant rebellion in Chalatenango, El Salvador.* London: Latin America Bureau.

Pedersen, D. 2004. In the stream of money: Contradictions of migration, remittances, and development in El Salvador. In *Landscapes of struggle: Politics, society and community in El Salvador*, ed. A. Lauria-Santiago and L. Binford. Pittsburgh, PA: University of Pittsburgh Press.

Posterman, R. L., and J. M. Riedinger. 1987. *Land reform and democratic development.* Baltimore, MD: Johns Hopkins University Press.

Seligson, M. A. 1995. Thirty years of transformation in the agrarian structure of El Salvador, 1961–1991. *Latin American Research Review* 30 (3): 43–74.

Simon, L. R. 1984. Social ethics and land reform: The case of El Salvador. *Agriculture and Human Values* 1 (3): 33–36.

Simon, L. R., and J. C. Stephens. 1981. *El Salvador land reform, 1980–81: Impact audit.* Boston, MA: Oxfam America.

UNDP (United Nations Development Programme). 2009. *Overcoming barriers: Human mobility and development.* Human Development Report. New York: Palgrave Macmillan. http://hdr.undp.org/en/.

UNDPI (United Nations Department of Public Information). 1995. *The United Nations and El Salvador 1990–1995.* Vol. 4. New York: United Nations Publications.

UNSD (United Nations Statistics Division). 2009. Environmental indicators. http://unstats.un.org/unsd/environment/qindicators.htm.

USAID (United States Agency for International Development). 2005. El Salvador: Budget. www.usaid.gov/policy/budget/cbj2005/lac/sv.html.

Vidales, R. 1993. Small farmers in El Salvador, 1993: A comparison of landowners, renters, cooperative members, "finateros," and "tenedores." In *El Salvador agricultural policy analysis: Land tenure study*, ed. M. Seligson, W. C. Thiesenhusen, and M. Childress. Washington, D.C.: United States Agency for International Development.

Villalobos, J. 1989. A democratic revolution for El Salvador. *Foreign Policy* 74: 103–122.

Wallace, S. 2000. "You must go home again": Deported LA gangbangers take over El Salvador. *Harper's Magazine*, August.

World Bank. 2009. El Salvador at a glance. http://devdata.worldbank.org/AAG/slv_aag.pdf.

Institutional aspects of resolving land disputes in post-conflict societies

Peter Van der Auweraert

The international humanitarian and peacebuilding community's engagement with post-conflict land disputes—and with land issues more broadly—has grown considerably since the end of the Cold War, and especially since the Yugoslav conflicts of the 1990s.[1] Although interventions have mostly focused on conflicts that were accompanied by large-scale forced population movements, the notion that building a lasting peace often requires engagement with land issues is no longer as alien as it was ten or fifteen years ago (Leckie 2009; Moore 2010). Indicators of this greater recognition include an increase in normative work within the international community since that period,[2] as well as a growing number of handbooks, guidelines, and trainings that the international community continues to develop to assist its professionals in dealing with post-conflict and post-disaster land issues (Pons-Vignon and Lecomte 2004; UN-HABITAT 2007, 2010; Wehrmann 2008). This chapter is a modest contribution to wider efforts to improve knowledge sharing and integration of lessons learned from experiences in post-crisis land programming and other interventions.[3]

Land disputes are competing claims between or among individuals, communities, and state authorities about access to, control of, or use of certain pieces of land. All types of land can be subject to such competing claims, including urban land, rural land, constructed land, and land containing high-value natural resources.

Peter Van der Auweraert heads the land, property, and reparations division at the International Organization for Migration. Currently he is engaged in a United Nations–sponsored peace mediation effort on land and property issues in Kirkuk, Iraq.

[1] For the sake of readability, the remainder of this chapter will employ the term *international community* to refer to the international organizations and nongovernmental organizations that are active in humanitarian assistance and peacebuilding.

[2] A prime example is the 2005 United Nations Principles on Housing and Property Restitution for Refugees and Displaced Persons, better known as the Pinheiro Principles. This set of principles was endorsed by the United Nations Sub-commission on the Promotion and Protection of Human Rights on August 11, 2005.

[3] The Housing, Land and Property Working Group of the Global Protection Cluster is intended to play a key role in this respect. See www.humanitarianreform.org/Default .aspx?tabid=434.

346　Land and post-conflict peacebuilding

Not all land disputes require special attention in peacebuilding or post-conflict recovery efforts. Land disputes occur even in the most peaceful societies, and unnecessarily dramatizing those that pose little or no risk to the long-term peace can have as adverse an effect as ignoring land disputes that do pose a threat (Alden Wily 2009). The key consideration is whether a set of land disputes has the potential to derail or undermine short- or longer-term peacebuilding efforts and to reignite the conflict; this has to be assessed afresh in each post-conflict situation.

There are, however, a number of general factors indicating that a land dispute poses a threat to peace. A land dispute may be a threat to peace in a post-conflict situation if access to or control over the use of land or the natural resources underneath it was one of the root causes or drivers of the conflict; if the conflict was accompanied by mass displacement, and the cessation of violence is triggering a rapid return of the displaced population; if the conflict was accompanied by large-scale land grabbing by the belligerent parties or by the population itself (for example, in the case of sectarian conflict); if the conflict was accompanied by widespread destruction of homes or livelihoods; or if the conflict caused the collapse of pre-conflict dispute resolution mechanisms. It is when land conflicts pose a threat to long-term peace that the international community often steps in to assist with their resolution.

The chapter begins by reviewing institutional options for resolving post-conflict land disputes. It stresses the importance of first understanding the political aspects of land disputes before making institutional choices. Three proposals are then introduced to improve the integration of local political considerations into the dispute resolution process: (1) the development of a standard assessment methodology that focuses on specific social and political dynamics in a given land dispute situation; (2) the establishment of multidisciplinary teams to work on dispute resolution projects; and (3) the maintenance of robust political engagement after resolution policies have been approved. These three proposals are then reviewed and evaluated on the basis on their practicability. The chapter concludes by stressing the importance of conducting a detailed analysis of the dispute resolution process, using the Property Claims Commission in Iraq as an example.

OPTIONS FOR RESOLUTION OF LAND DISPUTES

Many types of institutional arrangements can be used to resolve post-conflict land disputes, with the local situation and the nature of the disputes being the principal factors that will determine what is likely to work best in a given situation.

One concrete option is the establishment of an ad hoc land or claim commission that has exclusive jurisdiction over a defined post-conflict land-dispute file. Recent such commissions include the Commission for Real Property

Institutional aspects of resolving land disputes 347

Claims of Displaced Persons and Refugees in Bosnia and Herzegovina,[4] the Property Claims Commission in Iraq,[5] and the Housing and Property Claims Commission in Kosovo.[6] Despite their common denomination, ad hoc commissions can strongly differ from one another—for example, in terms of the rules and procedures under which they operate and the constitution of their decision-making bodies, which can be entirely national, entirely international, or a mixture of both.

The local judicial system constitutes another possible institutional avenue for resolving post-conflict land disputes, although in most cases the courts will require significant additional resources to deal with the additional, often complicated caseload. In Colombia the national court system has played an important role in relation to land claims from internally displaced persons (Elhawary 2007).

Dispute resolution mechanisms that are based on customary law or tradition may also provide an institutional solution—where they exist, as they do in Côte d'Ivoire (McCallin and Montemorrow 2009). They will be especially relevant in countries where state institutions are weak or ineffective and where, in practice, land relations are mostly governed by customary law.

Finally, there are situations where a multi-institutional approach is the best available option. In Burundi, for example, post-conflict land disputes are addressed by the civil courts, the National Commission for Land and Other Properties, dispute resolution mechanisms based on customary law, and targeted community-based mediation efforts, usually supported by international or national civil society organizations (Theron 2009).

Political considerations

The political aspects of post-conflict land disputes should be one of the international community's central concerns in advising or programming. This holds

---

[4] The Commission for Real Property Claims of Displaced Persons and Refugees was created under Annex VII of the General Framework Agreement for Peace in Bosnia and Herzegovina, better known as the Dayton Peace Agreement. For a technical description of this commission, see IOM (2008). For an in-depth analysis, see Williams (2005).

[5] The Property Claims Commission was established in February 2010 to deal with land disputes emanating from widespread property confiscations and politically motivated expropriations by the Baath Party regime. The Property Claims Commission is the successor organ to the Commission for the Resolution of Real Property Disputes (CRRPD), established in 2006, which was itself a successor to the Iraq Property Claims Commission, established by the Coalition Provisional Authority in 2004. All three commissions had virtually the same mandate, but there were some important differences. On the CRRPD, see Van der Auweraert (2009). On the differences between the respective mandates of the Property Claims Commission and the CRRPD, see Van der Auweraert (2010b).

[6] The Housing and Property Claims Commission and the Housing and Property Directorate were both created by the United Nations Interim Administration Mission in Kosovo in 1999 (IOM 2008). For an assessment of the land and property situation in Kosovo, see Tawil (2009).

348 Land and post-conflict peacebuilding

true both when the international community is making or advising on the best institutional choices available and when it has been asked to provide support to the institutional arrangements chosen by local political leaders.

Usually the international community becomes involved in post-conflict land disputes where the conflict was accompanied by large-scale forced displacement and subsequent occupation of the displaced population's land by others. On the one hand, a durable solution for the displaced population is necessary, and on the other hand, a way must be found to prevent a reigniting of the conflict when returnees find their land occupied or controlled by others.

When looked at against this background, the core of such land disputes appears to be a clash of rights between the returnees and the current occupiers of the land. The principal challenge of resolving such a clash is to find ways of determining who holds the prevailing right over the land under dispute. For this a set of ground rules is necessary. The international community's principal normative framework in this respect is expressed in the 2005 United Nations Principles on Housing and Property Restitution for Refugees and Displaced Persons, better known as the Pinheiro Principles. This set of principles articulates a rights-based vision of land disputes that puts a heavy premium on the restitution of the rights of the displaced and hence on a return to the pre-conflict land situation.

Restitution, however, can be a problematic remedy for land and property rights violations, especially when there has been protracted displacement. There are instances where restitution would be neither just nor in the interest of peace (Ballard 2010). This would be the case, for example, where prior to the conflict land was concentrated in the hands of a small, elite group or where discriminatory land and property relations were at the center of the conflict. Furthermore, an exclusive focus on the question of rights may overlook the fact that for local people, land disputes involve many issues other than just differing opinions about who has the strongest right to the land in question. Those issues are often deeply political, and if they are important enough, they will strongly influence how local people proceed.

Four local issues are particularly common: a close connection between landholding and the ability to exercise political power; disputes over land that has important symbolic or emotional value; competing and incompatible visions of post-conflict economic development; and structural inequalities in relation to access to and control over land.

Connections between landholding and political power

A connection between landholding and the ability to exercise political power can play out at both the level of the people who control and govern the country, in which case large landholdings can be translated into far-reaching political power, and at the level of local communities, where differences in social status and influence are frequently linked to the size of landholdings, especially in agrarian societies. In such situations certain parties will often have used the conflict to fundamentally alter land relations and thereby political power structures. People who have succeeded

Institutional aspects of resolving land disputes 349

in doing this will usually be extremely reluctant to let go of their spoils of war and will rarely, if ever, accept abandonment of the land simply on the basis that someone else has a legally stronger right. A prime example are the recent conflicts in the Democratic Republic of the Congo, where control over land containing high-value natural resources played a key role in the ability and motivation of the different parties to engage in horrifically violent conflict (Prunier 2009).

Symbolically and emotionally valuable land

When land has significant symbolic or emotional value to its present or former owners or occupiers, communities may pressure parties in a land dispute not to relinquish their claims so as not to weaken the community's hold on a certain area.[7] For example, in the disputed Ninewa and Kirkuk provinces in Iraq, minority communities pressure former owners not to give up their claims even if the parties would be happy to opt for compensation instead. A similar situation has been playing out in Cyprus, where Greek Cypriots who lost property through the partition are being discouraged from accepting compensation for their loss rather than restitution (Gürel and Özersay 2006). For indigenous communities the relationship with ancestral land is often deeply interwoven with the community's identity and worldview.

Moreover, political entrepreneurs may use the symbolic or emotional value of land to continue agitating their fellow community members even after the cessation of violence. For example, when ethnic, tribal, national, or religious groups try to expand their power and influence in the new post-conflict society, any policy to resolve land disputes will need to integrate these symbolic or emotional aspects of land. A strictly rights-based approach, wherein a court or courtlike institution authoritatively declares who wins and who loses, will fail to durably resolve the dispute and may become a source of further or renewed violent conflict.

Competing visions of post-conflict economic development

When there are competing and incompatible visions of post-conflict economic development, a substantive choice must be made between those two visions, or the parties must arrive at a compromise that takes the visions of both sides into account. A typical example of this sort of situation is a clash between post-conflict leaders who support the expansion of agribusiness and subsistence farmers who are being pressured to give up their land (Daniel and Mittal 2009). In South Sudan, for example, land deals concluded between local power holders and foreign investors since the completion of the Sudanese Comprehensive Peace Agreement in 2005 threaten the land rights of small-scale farmers and farming communities (Africa Review 2011).

Such substantive choices underlying the resolution of post-conflict land disputes are not always openly debated, however. In Iraq, for example, the

---

[7] For an analysis of social identity, natural resources, and peacebuilding, see Green (2013).

350 Land and post-conflict peacebuilding

potential impact of large-scale land restitution on the equality of distribution of land among the population, or on land management more broadly, has received very limited attention. Mostly the establishment and workings of the Property Claims Commission are discussed only from the perspective of the right to a remedy for land and property rights violations committed by the former regime (Van der Auweraert 2010).

Structural inequalities

Structural inequalities with regard to access to and control over land are often a factor when former owners attempt to reverse land gains that the formerly dispossessed made during the conflict. The former owners may accomplish this by invoking the concept of restitution, which is central to the international community's normative framework for resolving land disputes. In such situations, policy discussions about how to resolve the land disputes should focus not only on the question of legal primacy, but also on the more fundamental question of whether or not to accept the land redistribution that has taken place during the conflict.

For example, in the case of Timor-Leste, the technical difficulties of determining what rights should prevail when there are competing land claims are often cited as a key reason why, more than ten years after Indonesia withdrew, the country still has no transitional or permanent land law. This argumentation, however, hides a much more fundamental dilemma and disagreement about how land should be distributed in the country. Primacy of Portuguese over Indonesian land titles and, especially, over current informal occupation would mean, for example, that in the capital, Dili, the majority of land would be owned by a few very large landowners. Recognition of the primacy of peaceful occupation over earlier, formal property titles, on the other hand, would result in a broad distribution of small pieces of land among the population currently living in the city (ICG 2010; Fitzpatrick 2002; Van der Auweraert 2008).[8]

Institutional choices

Regardless of the nature of its engagement with a given post-conflict land dispute, the international community should care about the foregoing political considerations for several reasons. First, understanding the political situation can help

---

[8] One common structural inequality that does not always have a direct link to the risk of more conflict is gender inequality with respect to access to and control over land— for example, when the local normative framework ties women's land rights to those of their husbands or other male relatives. Such situations violate the right to nondiscrimination on the basis of gender, which is enshrined in human rights conventions, and it may cause serious survival issues. Where the violent conflict has caused the number of female-headed households to rise, such households may end up with no livelihood possibilities unless the normative framework governing land is drastically changed (UNCHS 1999).

Institutional aspects of resolving land disputes   351

the international community to ensure that decision making regarding the dispute is as inclusive as possible. Unless it has a good grasp of who the different parties are, including their respective interests, power, and influence, it will have a hard time determining whether local decision-making processes are sufficiently diverse, or are exclusionary and dominated by the powerful few.

In Kirkuk, Iraq, for example, one key component of the United Nations Assistance Mission to Iraq's support to the local people's efforts to resolve multiple land issues has been to push for a decision-making process that equally involves all three main communities in the governorate (Arabs, Kurds, and Turkmen) and addresses the concerns of these three communities. Exclusionary decision-making processes, by contrast, can further inflame sectarian tensions.

The international community's use of its political leverage to advocate for an inclusive decision-making process can be crucial in situations where many factors work against inclusivity, such as a central government's desire to reassert itself after the conflict is over and to centralize power as much as possible,[9] or victorious leaders' belief that they do not need to consult anyone outside their own circles but should start by safeguarding their own interests. Although sometimes little space is available for the international community to promote inclusivity, frequently the post-conflict administration depends heavily on the international community for guidance and resources, giving it a window of opportunity to weigh in on the broadening of the decision-making process (Alden Wily 2009).

Another reason the international community should pay attention to political considerations is that in order to assess what type of institutional arrangements are likely to work best, it must be able to contextualize these arrangements in the local political landscape. Of course, in most post-conflict circumstances, local people will decide on the institutional arrangements to be used for addressing land disputes—as they should. It is not uncommon, however, for local people to look to the international community for technical advice and input in this respect. Moreover, the international community often has an important role in funding those institutional arrangements, and this will also require an assessment of the suitability and likely success of various institutional options.

For example, the international community should consider the legitimacy and authority that different institutional arrangements are likely to have in the local communities they need to operate in. No blueprints or guarantees exist in this respect, at least in part because authority and legitimacy tend to fluctuate over time and often witness dramatic changes during a conflict, so empirical assessments are necessary (NRC 2010). The international community is ill-advised to either look solely to state institutions or embrace traditional or customary dispute resolution mechanisms without first investigating how local people feel about the institutions in question.

---

[9] Centralization is not pursued only by local leaders. International initiatives also sometimes focus on the central government alone. With respect to Afghanistan, for example, see Jones (2010).

352   Land and post-conflict peacebuilding

An understanding of political considerations is also important for the establishment of new, special-purpose institutions like land commissions, which may need to have particular features to gain acceptance by local people who have particular expectations regarding dispute resolution mechanisms. For example, many Iraqi lawyers working with the Property Claims Commission in Iraq perceive mass claims-processing techniques as incompatible with due process, so the commission has been reluctant to embrace such techniques, even though they would considerably increase the efficiency and expediency of the commission's work.[10]

A related question that is difficult to assess without an understanding of the political situation is the extent to which available institutions are likely to have an inherent bias toward one of the parties in a land dispute and hence, without reform, may be unsuitable for playing an important role in resolving post-conflict land disputes. This can vary from one country to another. National courts, for example, may be subservient to large landowners' interests in one location but able to function in a neutral and objective way in another.

Finally, it is important for the international community to know where the resistance points are likely to be once the institutional arrangements start operating so it can play a constructive role in monitoring and in addressing problems that may arise in the process of resolving land disputes. One of the key challenges in the implementation of the proposed land restitution provisions in the Colombian Victims Law is likely to be resistance by local institutions that are dominated by large landowners and by commercial interests that stand to lose from a widespread restitution process for the benefit of the internally displaced population in Colombia (Blomqvist 2010).

It is not uncommon for resistance to land dispute resolution to continue throughout the implementation period. Such resistance can manifest itself in many different ways, from obstruction, to intimidation and bribery, to the use of violence to prevent the enforcement of decisions in particular land dispute cases. This is an area in which the international community can sometimes play both a preventive and a curative role, for example, by ensuring sufficient political engagement with those who are likely to disrupt the process of resolving land disputes. But, again, it can only do this if it has a clear understanding of the wider political picture, including the different stakeholders' positions, local standing, and likely political methods.

Such political engagement requires an extensive local network and sufficient staff and resources to continuously engage with this network throughout the implementation period. Projects that are intended to support policy implementation for land dispute resolution too often allocate their resources only toward the technical work, with little or no staff allocated to carrying out the political component of the effort.

---

[10] On the use of mass claims processing in post-conflict situations, see Holtzmann and Kristjánsdóttir (2007).

Three proposals

Three actions may improve the international community's ability to integrate local political considerations into its work of supporting resolution of post-conflict land disputes: the development of a standard assessment tool that focuses on specific social and political dynamics in a given land dispute situation; the establishment of multidisciplinary teams to work on dispute resolution projects; and the maintenance of robust political engagement after resolution policies have been approved.

Development of a political assessment tool

The existing humanitarian assessment tools with which the international community usually approaches programming and interventions for land dispute resolution tend to have two principal characteristics (OCHA 2009). First, they usually aim to obtain quantitative information, such as the number of land disputes; the number of houses destroyed or occupied by others; and the percentage of land that is owned, rented, or subjected to the right of use. Second, these tools usually address predominantly technical, legal matters, such as the extent to which the displaced population holds formal property titles, the legal regimes that govern land relations, and the types of titles people tend to have over land.

Although these types of assessment are, of course, relevant and important, they provide the international community with little or no information about such issues as the competing interests and views that exist around land and its use; about who the principal parties in the post-conflict land dispute file are, including their respective strengths and weaknesses; or about who the leaders and power holders are in relation to this file. In short, the picture that the international community develops with its current tools may hide from sight many crucial aspects of the setting in which resolution of the land disputes will take place. If assessment is purely quantitative, issues that are of great political importance for local people will at best appear as a distant background that attracts attention only when the issues interfere with planned policies and programs—at which time it may be too late to change course.

One answer to these limitations is the development of a new standard assessment tool that focuses on the specific social and political dynamics surrounding the post-conflict land disputes and land relations in a given situation. With this in its arsenal of humanitarian assessment tools, the international community can enter the complex world of land and land disputes with a proper map. Routine employment of a political assessment tool may have the additional benefit of pushing the international community to think harder about who will win and who will lose as a result of its proposals and projects, and about which parties are likely to resist or support the objectives it wants to pursue. This in turn may provide international organizations with a much clearer picture of what impact their programs and projects are likely to have—and not to have—and the extent to which they are likely to succeed or fail.

354 Land and post-conflict peacebuilding

Finally, a political assessment tool may help the international community to better understand that despite its self-perception as a nonpartisan and neutral party, local people may view the international community as very much a political player among others, not least because its actions frequently have a real effect on how power, wealth, and influence ends up being distributed in the new, post-conflict society. This is not, of course, a reason not to engage, but it is an important element that the international community needs to take into account when developing and implementing its projects and programs.

Political assessment is not a one-time exercise. Assessing the specific social and political dynamics surrounding post-conflict land disputes will need to be repeated over time because those dynamics are usually in flux, especially in a transition period. Depending on the available time and resources, such reassessment can range from a desk review of available literature combined with small-scale interviews of relevant parties to much broader and more time- and resource-consuming community consultation and observation processes.

Establishment of multidisciplinary teams

The international community tends to rely too strongly on legal-technical advice and expertise when addressing post-conflict land disputes, with a particular bias toward professionals with human rights backgrounds. Although having a certain background does not, of course, preclude approaching land disputes with multiple viewpoints in mind, an overreliance on people trained in a certain way of thinking risks leaving the international community with a too-narrow view of what the specific disputes are about and how they can be realistically resolved. Therefore, systematic efforts should be made to use multidisciplinary teams to address post-conflict land disputes.

The ideal composition of such teams would depend on the specific situation, but in almost all cases they would need to include specialists in the politics of peacebuilding and conflict resolution, development professionals specializing in land and land administration issues, people with a broad humanitarian background and experience, country specialists, and people with a legal background. Of course, the systematic use of multidisciplinary teams is not by itself sufficient: the leadership in the international community should also insist that any proposed policies or plans be adopted only if they clearly set out their likely political, economic, development, and societal consequences and effects. A multidisciplinary approach is likely to decrease the chance that the international community will fail to integrate broader political considerations into its engagement with a given post-conflict land dispute file.

Maintenance of robust political engagement

The international community has a tendency to reduce, if not abandon, robust political engagement once policies and programs for the resolution of post-conflict land disputes have been approved or adopted, and to focus exclusively on project

Institutional aspects of resolving land disputes   355

or program implementation, including technical support, capacity building, and assistance to vulnerable groups or individuals. In many post-conflict situations, however, there is more political work to be done after the local authorities have agreed to adopt particular laws or policies to resolve post-conflict land disputes.

The political struggle around the resolution of post-conflict land disputes is likely to continue throughout the period of implementation, and it has the capacity to derail, divert, or otherwise undermine what the policies backed by the international community are aiming to achieve. It is for this reason that the international community needs to ensure that implementation is systematically accompanied by sustained, robust political engagement with the relevant local parties. This would put the international community in a better position to anticipate and reduce the adverse effects that negative dynamics can have on the goals it is trying to achieve and to quickly adapt its approach to the almost inevitable changes the local political situation will undergo during the implementation period.

There are a number of ways in which ongoing political engagement can be achieved, and what works best will differ from one situation to another. Key conditions that need to be fulfilled in terms of the internal functioning of the international community include a sufficient political alignment among relevant international organizations on the broad goals of the land dispute resolution effort;[11] a shared knowledge and understanding of the political realities on the ground and of the role of the international community; good lines of communication among international parties, especially in the case of communication from the periphery to the center; and allocation of sufficient and capable resources to construct and maintain real local networks and continuously engage with them on the issues that arise during implementation. Securing resources to establish strong local networks and maintain those networks long enough to acquire deep local knowledge may be the most difficult. Retaining staff for a sufficient length of time is especially challenging in complex and difficult post-conflict situations, which are often also the most dangerous ones.

Not all parties within the international community need to play the same part in continuing political engagement. A division of labor can be imagined, for example, between the political sections of UN missions, on the one hand, and specialized agencies and implementing organizations, on the other. The former could be responsible for continuous political engagement with respect to the post-conflict land dispute file, and the latter could focus on providing technical

---

[11]   What these goals will turn out to be in a concrete situation depends on the interplay of various factors, including international community policy and practice, as expressed in international law, international soft law, guidelines, handbooks, and internal mandate and policy documents; the priorities and preferences of the donors engaged in the specific situation, and the resources they can make available; the type of international community organizations present on the ground; the policies developed and adopted by local leaders; and the socioeconomic, environmental, cultural, and political particularities of the local situation.

356 Land and post-conflict peacebuilding

support to the implementation of the relevant policies. Although the often divided and competitive nature of the international community does not facilitate creating and maintaining a platform for common political engagement, this is not, however, impossible to achieve. The still insufficient but nevertheless much improved degree of convergence achieved among humanitarian entities through the humanitarian reform process can serve as an inspiration in this respect.[12]

PRACTICABILITY

Clearly, the particular political features of a set of post-conflict land disputes are not the only factors that should influence which institutional arrangements are chosen and put in place. Additional factors depend in part on the objectives that institutional arrangements are expected to fulfill beyond the peaceful resolution of land disputes. These objectives can include reconciliation between the parties to the disputes or within affected communities, establishing the truth about the land rights violations that occurred during the conflict, and reestablishing the rule of law or the population's trust in the state and its institutions. In the case of peaceful resolution of land disputes, however, practicability is a factor that should have a deep impact on the international community's approach to institutional arrangements.

The term *practicability* refers to the institution's realistic ability to resolve post-conflict land disputes in a fair and just manner, on the basis of the applicable ground rules, and within a period of time that is acceptable to the parties involved. The question of practicability—and the related issues of what is needed in terms of reinforcement, capacity building, and additional material resources to ensure practicability—needs to be considered both before the decision on institutional arrangements is made and throughout the process of resolving the land disputes. Unless practicability has been an overriding concern in deciding on the institutional arrangements—trumping, for example, abstract ideas or beliefs about what institutional arrangements should look like—there is a heightened risk of inflated and unrealistic expectations and, more important, of failure to successfully resolve the land disputes at hand.

It is not uncommon for tension to arise between what international organizations regard as key components of the rule of law and the reality of dispute resolution methods and mechanisms on the ground. If ideology trumps pragmatic considerations about what is practicable in a given situation, then efforts to support the resolution of post-conflict land disputes are likely to be in vain or, even worse, counterproductive.[13]

---

[12] The ongoing humanitarian reform seeks to "improve the effectiveness of humanitarian response by ensuring greater predictability, accountability and partnership." For background, see www.humanitarianreform.org.

[13] For a discussion of the shortcomings of traditional rule-of-law programming, see Samuels (2006).

Institutional aspects of resolving land disputes 357

The international community can play an important role in injecting the issue of practicability into the local debate about how post-conflict land disputes should be addressed, especially in situations where local authorities lack the technocratic skills and expertise to seriously consider this issue or are too embroiled in substantive issues to spend much time on practicability concerns.

Posing the institutional question broadly

To make an effective practicability assessment of institutional choices in a given post-conflict situation, the international community must pose the institutional question broadly enough. First, it must address the question of whether the observed land disputes are a problem merely in and of themselves or are also an expression of a broader structural problem, such as land scarcity or incoherent or otherwise inadequate land regulation, management, or administration systems. In the former case it maybe that the only thing that needs to be put in place is a mechanism to peacefully resolve those disputes. In the latter case, adequate post-conflict policies to resolve the land disputes need to focus on measures to address the underlying structural issues. This also means that the institutional question needs to address much more than just the institutions that are required to resolve the land disputes.

In Burundi, for example, there is a direct relationship between land scarcity and the high number of land disputes. There is simply not enough available, usable land to fulfill the needs of a population that remains largely dependent on small-scale farming. Unless the structural issue of land scarcity is addressed, the frequency of land disputes is likely to remain high, even with the best dispute-resolution mechanisms in place (Huggins 2009).

Second, the international community must assess a variety of institutional routes that are available to resolve the land disputes in the given situation. It is important not to focus the assessment solely on state institutions, but to also look at other types of commonly used dispute resolution mechanisms, including, where they exist, customary-law based mechanisms. In many post-conflict countries, state institutions were never strong to begin with, and it is very unlikely that the conflict will have made them stronger. Moreover, in countries with a weak state structure, state institutions and state law rarely have much reach beyond the capital city or other urban areas. Therefore, a pragmatic approach to post-conflict land disputes needs to at least consider other dispute resolution mechanisms as well, even if they do not seem to respond to all human rights criteria.

Finally, the international community should consider not just dispute resolution mechanisms but also supporting institutions in the practicability equation. This is especially relevant when the available institutional options are limited to using existing state institutions, such as courts or tribunals, or establishing a new ad hoc national or international land commission. Including supporting institutions in the practicability equation is necessary both for determining whether a certain institutional route is feasible and for identifying what additional resources need

358 Land and post-conflict peacebuilding

to be allocated to ensure that the chosen institutional route will produce the sought outcomes.

The example of the Property Claims Commission (PCC) in Iraq illustrates that many institutions can be involved in resolving post-conflict land disputes, in addition to an ad hoc commission. The PCC was originally established in 2004 to resolve land disputes related to the Baath Party regime's forced displacement and expropriation policies. At the time of writing, the PCC had received almost 160,000 claims, out of which it had finally resolved approximately 40,000.[14] While the commission is the sole responsible organization for making decisions regarding the land disputes that come before it, a plethora of additional organizations are involved in the process of resolving the claims, as set out in figure 1 below.

For all the institutions that appear in figure 1, the same rule applies: the mandate of the PCC requires them to carry out additional work. As part of a practicability assessment, it would be necessary to ask whether these institutions have sufficient capacity for this additional work without additional funds or staff, or whether they require more resources in order to take on the extra responsibility. If questions about these issues are not posed at the outset, it is possible that foreseeable bottlenecks will not be addressed in time—as was the case with the PCC, whose progress was slowed in part by a lack of capacity and, in some cases, the unwillingness of supporting institutions to carry out their part of the work.

Posing the institutional question broadly enough is also important for carrying out the initial political assessment. The composition of support organizations and structures, the views and interests of their leadership, and their governance strengths and weaknesses in terms of political neutrality and transparency all will affect how they fulfill their roles in the land dispute resolution process.

Conducting a detailed analysis of the dispute resolution process

When local and international decision makers are assessing the practicability of a set of institutional arrangements, it is important that they have a full picture of what the process of resolving a land dispute under these institutional arrangements entails. They can most easily gain such an understanding by drafting a detailed process flow that exhaustively records the steps involved in resolving disputes. Such a process flow needs to start at the beginning—with the existence of two or more groups or individuals who have a dispute over a certain piece of land—then trace the path all the way to the moment when the dispute has been fully resolved.

There are multiple purposes for mapping out the process in such detail. The first is to enable policy makers to fully understand the complexities involved in resolving the land disputes, thereby preventing a situation in which such complexities are underestimated and predictable challenges and bottlenecks remain

---

[14] PCC internal statistics, July 2010 (available from the author).

Institutional aspects of resolving land disputes 359

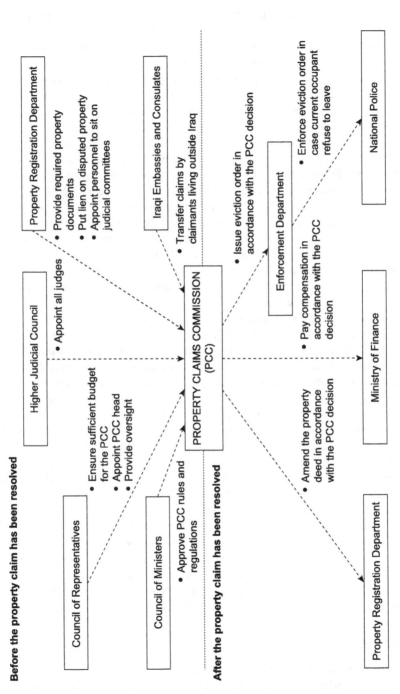

Figure 1. Institutional linkages with the Iraq Property Claims Commission

360 Land and post-conflict peacebuilding

out of sight when policy makers are determining which set of institutional arrangements is likely to work best in the given situation. For example, although at first a new land commission may seem to be a good idea, an examination of the detailed process may reveal that such a commission is unlikely to work in the situation at hand because it may take too long for the commission to become operational, or because it is unlikely that state institutions will be able to carry out their support functions in relation to the commission.

Second, detailed mapping of the dispute resolution process allows local and international decision makers to assess whether each step in the process is realistic and feasible—and if a step is not realistic or feasible, what, if anything, can be done to make it so. For example, if using the judicial route would require parties to the dispute to travel to the nearest court to file a complaint, and then to return multiple times during the court proceedings, it would be important to consider what exactly this would entail for the parties: How far would they need to travel? How long would they need to be away from their fields? Would they be able to afford transportation and accommodations? Would they have someone to tend their farms? If such hurdles are likely to appear, the next question that would need to be addressed is whether there are sufficient national or international resources available to assist the parties to the dispute with their access to the courts.

A third purpose for conducting a detailed process-flow analysis is to allow decision makers to make a realistic assessment of how long it will take to resolve all of the land disputes and to determine whether this duration is acceptable to the affected parties. For example, the PCC in Iraq was initially established to deal with the immediate influx of returnees to Kirkuk and other sensitive areas after the U.S.-led invasion of Iraq in 2003. The idea was that providing a peaceful route for the resolution of the many land disputes that were likely to emerge from this return would prevent private evictions and violence, and would provide previous owners the ability to rapidly resettle on their former land.

A detailed analysis of the process, accompanied by an assessment of the time it would take to resolve the expected caseload of disputes, would immediately have shown that the time frame of the returnees and that of the commission were dramatically out of sync. The returnees wanted their land back in a matter of months, but even under the best of circumstances, the commission would require many years to fully process the caseload that was likely to come before it. Although such findings would not necessarily have led decision makers to abandon the idea of establishing a land commission, they could have provoked consideration of interim measures and of additional routes for resolving at least some of the disputes in a faster, more efficient way.

CONCLUSIONS

The international community's role in assisting local parties with resolving post-conflict land disputes has the highest chance of success if it is fully grounded in local political and institutional realities. Interventions based on abstract rules

Institutional aspects of resolving land disputes   361

and principles usually yield few, if any, positive results unless their pursuit and application are grounded in what exists and what is realistically possible and attainable given local conditions. Ensuring the highest possible awareness of the local situation and of the limitations and possibilities it brings—before deciding how to engage with a given set of disputes—is the international community's best route to a successful contribution to the resolution of post-conflict land disputes.

REFERENCES

Africa Review. 2011. Unregulated S. Sudan land buys threaten rights, warns report. March 23. www.africareview.com/Southern+Sudan/-/1084032/1131252/-/jvpmnw/-/index.html.

Alden Wily, L. 2009. Tackling land tenure in the emergency to development transition in post-conflict states: From restitution to reform. In *Uncharted territory: Land, conflict and humanitarian action,* ed. S. Pantuliano. Rugby, Warwickshire, UK: Practical Action Publishing.

Ballard, M. 2010. Post-conflict property restitution: Flawed legal and theoretical foundations. *Berkeley Journal of International Law* 28:462–496.

Blomqvist, O. 2010. Colombia's land reform under a new president. *Open Democracy,* September 26. www.opendemocracy.net.

Daniel, S., and A. Mittal. 2009. *The great land grab: Rush for world's farmland threatens food security for the poor.* Oakland, CA: Oakland Institute.

Elhawary, S. 2007. *Between war and peace: Land and humanitarian action in Colombia.* London: Overseas Development Institute.

Fitzpatrick, D. 2002. *Land claims in East Timor.* Canberra, Australia: Asia Pacific Press.

Green, A. 2013. Social identity, natural resources, and peacebuilding. In *Livelihoods, natural resources, and post-conflict peacebuilding,* ed. H. Young and L. Goldman. London: Earthscan.

Gürel, A., and K. Özersay. 2006. *The politics of property in Cyprus.* Oslo, Norway: Peace Research Institute Oslo.

Holtzmann, H. M., and E. Kristjánsdóttir, eds. 2007. *International mass claims processes: Legal and practical perspectives.* Oxford, UK: Oxford University Press.

Huggins, C. 2009. Land in return, reintegration and recovery processes: Some lessons from the Great Lakes region of Africa. In *Uncharted territory: Land, conflict and humanitarian action,* ed. S. Pantuliano. Rugby, Warwickshire, UK: Practical Action Publishing.

ICG (International Crisis Group). 2010. Managing land conflict in Timor-Leste. Asia Briefing No. 110. September 9. www.crisisgroup.org/en/regions/asia/south-east-asia/timor-leste/B110-managing-land-conflict-in-timor-leste.aspx.

IOM (International Organization for Migration). 2008. *Property restitution and compensation: Practices and experiences of claims programs.* Geneva, Switzerland.

Jones, S. G. 2010. It takes the villages: Bringing change from below in Afghanistan. *Foreign Policy* 89 (3): 120–127.

Leckie, S. 2009. United Nations peace operations and housing, land, and property rights in post-conflict settings. In *Housing, land, and property rights in post-conflict United Nations and other peace operations,* ed. S. Leckie. Cambridge, UK: Cambridge University Press.

362 Land and post-conflict peacebuilding

McCallin, B., and M. Montemorrow. 2009. *Whose land is this? Land disputes and forced displacement in the western forest area of Côte d'Ivoire.* Geneva, Switzerland: Internal Displacement Monitoring Centre.

Moore, J. 2010. Africa's continental divide: Land disputes. *Christian Science Monitor,* January 30.

NRC (Norwegian Refugee Council). 2010. *Confusions and palava: The logic of land encroachment in Lofa County, Liberia.* Oslo. www.nrc.no/arch/img.aspx?file_id=9481898.

OCHA (United Nations Office for the Coordination of Humanitarian Affairs). 2009. *Assessment and Classification of Emergencies (ACE) project: Mapping of key emergency needs assessment and analysis initiatives, final report.* Geneva, Switzerland. www.humanitarianinfo.org/iasc/pageloader.aspx?page=content-subsidi-common-default&sb=75.

Pons-Vignon, N., and H.-B. Solignac Lecomte. 2004. Land, violent conflict, and development. OECD Development Centre Working Paper No. 233. Paris: Organisation for Economic Co-operation and Development.

Prunier, G. 2009. *Africa's World War: Congo, the Rwandan genocide, and the making of a continental catastrophe.* Oxford, UK: Oxford University Press.

Samuels, K. 2006. Rule of law reform in post-conflict countries: Operational initiatives and lessons learned. World Bank Social Development Papers. Paper No. 37. October. Washington, D.C.

Tawil, E. 2009. *Property rights in Kosovo: A haunting legacy from a society in transition.* New York: International Center for Transitional Justice.

Theron, J. 2009. Resolving land disputes in Burundi. *Conflict Trends* 1:3–10.

UNCHS (United Nations Centre for Human Settlements). 1999. *Women's rights to land, housing, and property in post-conflict situations and during reconstruction: A global overview.* Nairobi, Kenya: United Nations Human Settlements Programme. www.un-habitat.org/downloads/docs/1504_59744_Land.pdf2.pdf.

UN-HABITAT (United Nations Human Settlements Programme). 2007. *A post-conflict land administration and peacebuilding handbook.* Volume 1, *Countries with land records.* Nairobi, Kenya. www.unhabitat.org/pmss/listItemDetails.aspx?publicationID=2443.

———. 2010. *Land and natural disasters: Guidance for practitioners.* Nairobi, Kenya.

Van der Auweraert, P. 2008. The quest for solutions to Timor-Leste's land and property issues. *Migration,* July. http://publications.iom.int/bookstore/free/Migration_July%202008_EN.pdf.

———. 2009. Policy challenges for property restitution in transition: The example of Iraq. In *Reparations for victims of genocide, war crimes, and crimes against humanity,* ed. C. Ferstman, M. Goetz, and A. Stephens. Leiden, Netherlands: Martinus Nijhof.

———. 2010a. Displaced persons, squatters, land disputes, and land management in Iraq. Paper presented at "Toward a Land Management Policy for Iraq," a conference hosted by United Nations Human Settlements Programme and the World Bank, Beirut, Lebanon, May 27–28.

———. 2010b. Iraq updates its approach to former-regime related land and property claims. TerraNullius. March 10. http://terra0nullius.wordpress.com.

Wehrmann, B. 2008. *Land conflicts: A practical guide to deal with land disputes.* Eschborn, Germany: GTZ (Deutsche Gesellschaft für Technische Zusammenarbeit).

Williams, R. C. 2005. Post-conflict property restitution and refugee return in Bosnia and Herzegovina: Implications for international standard-setting and practice. *New York University Journal of International Law and Politics* 37 (3): 441–553.

Rebuilding peace: Land and water management in the Kurdistan Region of northern Iraq

Nesreen Barwari

Recent experiences in many conflict-affected areas have shown that reconstruction and development assistance can be used to support peace initiatives before a final resolution to conflict is achieved. In itself, reconstruction will not bring about peace, but it can make a contribution toward reducing the scope of the conflict and provide much-needed assistance to people who otherwise would be forced to leave their homes in search of relief and public welfare. It is a way of breaking the vicious circle of violence and poverty, especially for women-headed households and other vulnerable segments of the population.

The village reconstruction program in the Kurdistan Region of northern Iraq from 1991 to 2003 provided housing for internally displaced families and returning refugees, and removed obstacles that hampered equitable access to land, water for drinking and irrigation purposes, and a better quality of life. The program contributed to coordination between housing provision and peacebuilding efforts by increasing access to housing and contributing to its affordability, appropriateness, and sustainability. The program also provided input into relevant policy and strategy development by identifying innovative strategies for increasing opportunities for community consultation.

In the Kurdistan reconstruction program, communities led the process of bringing peace and development, and displaced families relearned their roles by becoming responsible for designing their own reconstruction efforts. It was their choice to return to their destroyed communities, to rebuild their homes, and to make improvements over what existed before.

This chapter provides an insider's view of reconstruction and development in the Iraqi Kurdistan Region, and examines the community-based approach—with its emphasis on localized decision making—as a model of coordinated municipal

---

Nesreen Barwari, a lecturer on planning and housing at Dohuk University, formerly served as minister of municipalities and public works in Iraq and minister of reconstruction and development for Kurdistan. She is the founder and chairwoman of Breeze and Hope, a nongovernmental organization (NGO) that promotes participatory democracy in the Kurdistan Region, and the president and chairwoman of Tolerancy International, an NGO that strives to foster stable secular democracies.

364 Land and post-conflict peacebuilding

development for addressing simmering land and property disputes in other parts of Iraq.[1]

ORIGINS OF THE PROBLEM

At the crossroads of Sunni and Shia Islam, Iraq was created out of the ruins of the Ottoman Empire in August 1921 (Fawcett and Tanner 2002). Eleven years later, Iraq received independence from the British Empire and became the state recognized today. In 1968, the Baath Party took power and eventually saw the ascendance of Saddam Hussein to the presidency. The Hussein regime engaged in a series of conflicts with the Kurdish population in the northern part of the state. In the 1970s, Saddam Hussein militarily destroyed scores of Kurdish villages, and in the 1980s, he used chemical weapons against Kurdish rebel populations (Cohen and Fawcett 2002).[2]

In March 1991, after Iraqi forces had been driven out of Kuwait by the U.S.-led Coalition Task Force, groups within Iraq launched a rebellion in both the north and the south of the country. In the face of a military campaign directed against them by the Iraqi army, over 450,000 Kurdish people fled to the Turkish frontier in a single week. By mid-April, another 1.5 million Kurds fled to Iran (see figure 1 for the location of various ethnic and religious groups in Iraq) (Fawcett and Tanner 2002).

The need for a safe haven

As images of desperate Kurds trapped in the mountains of northern Iraq continued to be televised worldwide, international pressure to find a solution mounted. At the beginning of April 1991, the idea of a safe haven for the Kurds inside Iraqi Kurdistan was proposed. After some deliberation, on April 5 the United Nations Security Council adopted Resolution 688, which insisted that "Iraq allow immediate access by international humanitarian organizations to all those in need of assistance" and authorized the Secretary-General to "use all resources at his disposal" to address "the critical needs of the refugees and displaced Iraqi populations" (UNSC 1991).

On April 10, members of the Coalition Task Force declared a no-fly zone in northern Iraq and assumed leadership of the relief effort (Barkey and Laipson 2005; Fawcett and Tanner 2002). Camps were established for the Kurds. The aim was to enable the Kurds' quick return to northern Iraq and then to turn the operation over to the United Nations. Within the United Nations, it was suggested

---

[1] This chapter is based upon the author's work with various United Nations agencies and later as a government cabinet minister in charge of reconstruction and development from 1991 to 2003 in the Iraqi Kurdistan Region.

[2] For a detailed history of Iraq, including the Hussein regime's actions in northern Iraq, see O'Leary, McGarry, and Salih (2005).

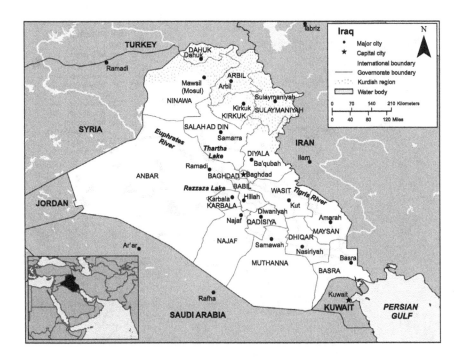

that the UN Office of the High Commissioner for Refugees (UNHCR) should lead the humanitarian operation and that the establishment of a safe haven in Iraq would be a substitute for the creation of refugee camps inside Iraqi territory. But UNHCR officials expressed concerned about the safety of Kurds returning to northern Iraq.[3] The Iraqi government had not provided any guarantees for their security. UNHCR therefore argued for a more gradual transition.

To encourage return, the coalition forces told the Kurds that UN guards would protect them, and they distributed hundreds of thousands of leaflets announcing that it was safe to go back. The desperate Kurds, blocked in the cold mountain passes on the Turkish border, soon started to return. In the first two weeks, nearly 200,000 refugees returned to Iraq.

The resettlement of millions of refugees and internally displaced persons could not have taken place without the active collaboration of nongovernmental organizations (NGOs). Their contributions included accompanying refugees back to their places of origin, designing and implementing quick-impact rehabilitation projects, and monitoring human rights.

---

[3] In a letter to the UN Secretary-General on May 17, 1991, High Commissioner Sadako Ogata expressed her "continued concern" for the security of the returnees. She explained that "nothing short of a negotiated settlement" accompanied by "international guarantees" could offer a lasting solution to the plight of the Kurds (UNHCR 1991; 2000, 217).

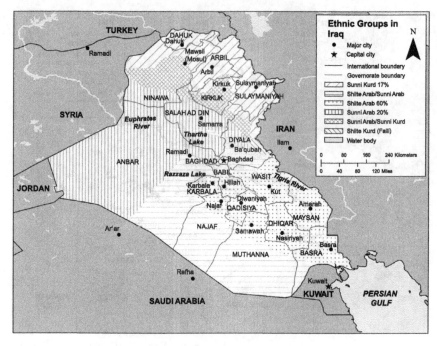

Figure 1. Ethnic and religious groups in Iraq
Source: University of Texas Libraries (1978).

Once the emergency relief phase was completed and rehabilitation and reconstruction were under way, UNHCR handed over its operation to other UN agencies, including the new UN Department of Humanitarian Affairs (DHA), which was set up to coordinate responses to humanitarian emergencies on the basis of UN General Assembly Resolution 46/182 of December 19, 1991. In 1998, DHA became the Office for the Coordination of Humanitarian Affairs.

The establishment of the safe haven in northern Iraq has often been regarded as a success, particularly because it allowed the return of hundreds of thousands of Iraqi Kurds to their homes. Initially, however, economic conditions in the Kurdistan Region were difficult. The region suffered from a double economic embargo—UN sanctions against Iraq as a whole and an internal embargo imposed by the Iraqi government. In the following years, security problems continued in the region, both as a result of power struggles between the two rival Kurdish factions and because of military incursions. There was violence in 1996, for instance, when Iraqi government forces briefly surrounded the city of Arbil. The region also experienced incursions by Iranian military forces and, on a larger scale, Turkish military forces, which on a number of occasions attacked places suspected of harboring members of the Kurdistan Workers' Party. In March 1995, Turkey sent 35,000 troops into the Kurdish Region. A survey by United Nations Human Settlements

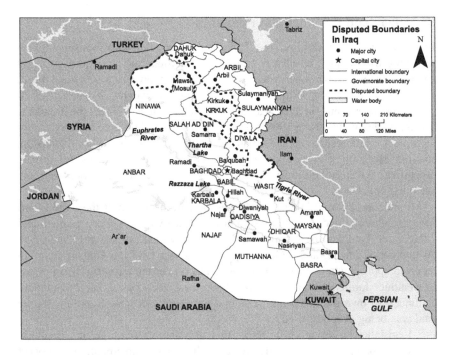

Figure 2. Iraqi political boundaries
Source: Adapted from a map produced by the ICG (2008).

Programme (UN-HABITAT) estimated the number of internally displaced persons in Kurdistan at 805,000 in October 2000 (UN-HABITAT 2001).[4]

In spite of these problems, rehabilitation and reconstruction work continued throughout the decade, and economic and security conditions gradually improved. Iraqi Kurdistan managed to establish a legitimate government long before the fall of the Hussein regime and ruled without conflict for more than five years, from 1997 until 2003. The Kurdistan Region (composed of the governorates of Arbil, Dahuk, and Sulaymaniyah) had a parliament, a government, and several political parties prior to the collapse of the Iraqi state on April 2003 (see figure 2 for political boundaries within Iraq).

---

[4] The Iraq Foundation concludes that "the deportation of Kurds and Turkomans from areas under government control, and particularly from the Kirkuk governorate, has left over 100,000 people from northern areas homeless and destitute" (Iraq Foundation 2001; see also HRW (2003)). The Austrian Centre for Country of Origin and Asylum Research and Documentation states that "an estimated 100,000 people ... were deported from government-controlled areas, especially from Kirkuk, Khanaqin, and Mosul. They were sent to Northern Iraq for several reasons, yet the majority of them were accused of having affiliations with the opposition parties in the north or abroad. Being a Kurd or Turkmen also sufficed as a reason" (ACCORD 2001, 57).

368 Land and post-conflict peacebuilding

Historical land administration patterns

Under the Ottoman Empire, the Turkish system of head-of-household land recording was adopted in what is now Iraq to facilitate the taxation of property and its transfer through inheritance and sale. Property owners were issued *tapus*, similar to deeds. Under British rule and the Iraqi monarchy, 90 percent of all arable, nontribal land in Iraq was surveyed and mapped. After the Baathists overthrew the monarchy in 1968, much agricultural land became the property of the state. Certain residential and urban properties remained in private ownership, and the Ministry of Justice continued to issue and update tapus for private properties. Privately held agricultural land was limited to 1,500 *donums* (375 hectares) per owner.[5]

Public agricultural lands came under the administration of the State Board for Agricultural Lands. They were distributed in two ways. Poor farmers and villages received rent-free distributions, and individual farmers received up to 50 donums (12.5 hectares). Groups or villages that held the land in common received approximately 120 donums (30 hectares) per ten farmers. Distributions to wealthier farmers or villages were made on a lease basis. The government continued to own the lands but permitted long-term occupation as long as the land was being properly used.

Legislation passed in 1970 decreed that all further distributions of agricultural land would be made as leaseholds.[6] Areas with sufficient precipitation to support rain-fed agriculture were scarce, and Iraq needed more agricultural production. A large-scale reclamation program began. This meant building canals and other irrigation infrastructure to convert dry areas into productive agricultural property. These leasehold distributions had the same characteristics as older distributions. They were transferable, had limited subdivision rights, and had inheritance rights. Payments from land leases were a significant source of revenue for the government.

New restrictions on the size of leaseholds were set by the presidential council in 1997. They were designed to limit the amount land that any one individual or group could hold. During the embargo period of 1990 to 2003, when international sanctions had a serious effect on agricultural production, the government of Iraq began a new program that gave land allotments free of rent for five years. The requirement for these free distributions was that the new landholders grow certain crops that had been embargoed. After five years, these allocations could become permanent leaseholds. Even though the Kurdistan Region was separated from the rest of the country in 1991, it continued to use Iraqi laws, including all rules related to land (Hajan 2009).

---

[5] The donum is a Middle Eastern unit used for measuring land areas, dating back to the Ottoman period. The actual size of a donum varies among Middle Eastern countries. An Iraqi donum is equivalent to 2,500 square meters.

[6] Agrarian Reform Law No. 117 of 1970. Available at http://faolex.fao.org/docs/pdf/irq38269.pdf.

The formal system of land registration that was in place prior to 1991 was not widely accepted by the Iraqi people. Because registration was not compulsory, many Iraqis did not bother to register land in the urban areas. A set of master plans created for the major cities in the 1980s comprised the majority of the information required for planning and parcel management. In the agricultural regions, however, registration of leases and transfers was done and records were kept.

Alongside these standard forms of ownership tenure were several classifications is Islamic customary tenure: *mulk*, individual full ownership; *miri*, state control and ownership with possible usage rights for individuals; *musha*, collective or tribal ownership; and *waqf*, a religious trust. Processes for dealing with customary tenure were different from those for standard forms of tenure. This issue was a delicate one for the Kurdistan reconstruction program, and it required innovative solutions. Reconstruction workers had to learn how the people dealt with land conflict and adopt aspects of this into the program implementation. Recognition of customary practices that were in line with the morals and values of the targeted communities helped avoid conflicts.

Unlike land rights, customary water rights had no specific statutory governance framework, and these water rights are tied to landownership. If a spring or a well was on a certain family's land, then they held control over that resource. Additionally, the tribe possessed an understanding of the management of the local water resources, such as allocation of certain amounts of the water for the village each day for household needs, and diversion of irrigation channels so other farmers could gain access to the water. In other words, the community managed how the water resources were allocated within the village, giving preference to landowners. These long-standing cooperation mechanisms allowed for a negotiation process and the political space to find agreement.

Recognition of traditional land management mechanisms also responded to the concern that given the scope and magnitude of property issues in Iraq, it was unlikely that all land disputes could be resolved through the ordinary court system, at least within a time frame that corresponded to the needs of the displaced. Moreover, from a wider peacebuilding perspective it may be preferable to resolve as many disputes as possible through voluntary, mediated outcomes and solutions rather than through imposed judicial or administrative decisions. Finally, the likely difficulties involved with enforcing judicial or administrative decisions against losing parties provide an argument in favor of an important role for traditional mechanisms in addressing property disputes.

CASE ANALYSIS

The speed with which the refugees fled Iraq was matched by that of their return. On April 18, 1991, the United Nations and Iraq signed an agreement allowing UN humanitarian centers to be established on Iraqi territory, and the refugees began to trek back home only six weeks after the start of the exodus. Their return to a devastated landscape and continuing insecurity presented a number of serious

370   Land and post-conflict peacebuilding

problems. At the end of August, large numbers of people were still without adequate shelter and in danger from the rigors of the oncoming winter. In a race against the clock, UNHCR launched one of its largest shelter programs ever.

Distribution of building materials was not started until October 15, when the population movements were sufficiently stabilized. This distribution had to be completed by mid-November to esure adequate shelter was built before the onset of winter. Although security considerations delayed implementation of the program, by October 30 some 1,600 trucks had crossed the border from Turkey to Iraq over mountain trails to deliver 30,000 metric tons of winter construction material to half a million people. Between October and December 1991, reconstruction work was carried out in more than 1,500 of the 4,000 villages that had been destroyed (CHC 2002).

The structure of the reconstruction program

The reconstruction program in the Kurdistan Region sought to help displaced persons, refuges, and communities to reclaim their lands and rebuild their livelihoods, crucial components for sustainable peace. It initially drew its funding from various UN and NGO programs, and in later years it also received money from the UN's Oil-for-Food Programme, with Iraqi oil sales financing the project. Responsibility for implementing the program also shifted over time, with one or another UN body and elements of the Kurdistan Regional Government always involved in coordination.

Ultimately, the program assisted over 800,000 internally displaced persons and members of vulnerable groups in more than 4,000 villages and small towns across the Kurdistan Region. According to UN-HABITAT, the program delivered more than 50,000 housing units; 1,200 primary and secondary schools; 260 health centers; 1,200 kilometers of water and sewage systems; 5,000 kilometers of access and internal roads for new settlements; 43 bridges; and 425 facilities to support agricultural and community activities (UN-HABITAT 2003). The project directly benefited some 50,000 families while improving the living conditions of over 1.3 million people, or close to 30 percent of the area's population. The program was also instrumental in helping to revive the economy by establishing and capacitating a vibrant local construction industry and creating some 80,000 jobs (UN-HABITAT 2003).

The program's comprehensive, integrated reconstruction and development assistance was offered to communities where conflict was relatively low. After learning from previous reconstruction programs run by the UN and NGOs, the leaders of this project strongly encouraged community involvement from the outset to ensure participation from internally displaced persons and members of disadvantaged groups. Engaging these local communities built a sense of ownership that would greatly increase the likelihood that the program would succeed over the long term and that internally displaced persons and refugees would be peacefully resettled.

When the implementers reached out to the communities, the program often acted as a filter to determine which communities were ready to commit to reconstruction and which ones were not. In some cases, villages that were initially unprepared to commit to the program would later renegotiate to receive reconstruction assistance.

The assistance included repair and reconstruction of housing and water supply systems, rehabilitation of agriculture, and revitalization of small enterprises to ignite the rebuilding process in the region. The communities themselves provided labor, and the program provided materials and technical assistance.

The overall objective of the program was to support the peace process by economically rejuvenating particularly those areas where the conflict was less intense, and where people had remained or to which they had returned.[7] It also supported the peace process by drawing internally displaced persons back to their homelands. When people are internally displaced, they are vulnerable to economic deprivation, often have difficulties with their new neighbors, and are prone to participation in the fighting. On the other hand, when internally displaced persons return to their place of origin, the distribution and management of resources becomes a significant challenge for their communities as the number of people competing for resources increases. The reconstruction program improved the availability of infrastructure and basic services—such as schools, health clinics, and roads—to entice people to return to their homelands from more sensitive areas and to help offset the effects of their return. By providing livelihood assistance, program leaders hoped to persuade people to cease fighting and instead to engage in productive activities and rebuild their lives. In other words, they hoped that the incentive of having something productive to do would be greater than that of active participation in the conflict.

While an area emerging from conflict is regaining its social and economic vigor, it becomes increasingly able to withstand the pressure of the warring parties and will, in turn, be able to exert pressure on the parties to refrain from conflict. After conflicts, when ostensibly demobilized fighters roam the countryside with few options, it is crucial to engage these individuals in productive activities through livelihood assistance. The reconstruction program created momentum toward peace. Program leaders understood that unless a general political solution was reached, full reconstruction could not take place. But they knew that by creating an atmosphere in which the number of people who are displaced and unemployed is reduced, they could gradually reduce the severity of the conflict. The program can thus be summed up in three words: return, investment, and employment.

Return of displaced people

One of the most severe challenges that the reconstruction program faced was the mass, spontaneous repatriation of refugees and internally displaced persons to

---

[7] *Conflict* here refers both to conflicts between the main Kurdish factions (and between families loyal to them), which lasted from 1994 to 1996, and to military attacks and incursions by the Turkish and Iranian armies into the border areas.

372   Land and post-conflict peacebuilding

their former homes. There are many scenarios in which Iraqi families became displaced. Some returned from work or school to find that their home was partially or totally destroyed. Some families were forcibly displaced by the armed forces. This happened in Iraq's Arabization process, when government forces or armed groups belonging to a political faction would force non-Arab people to leave their home, then force Arab people to live in the home under threat of death and to pay rent to the government of Iraq (Amnesty International 1999; Cohen and Fawcett 2002; Fawcett and Tanner 2002; HRW 2003).[8] In other cases, poor families were displaced when their homes were destroyed in the course of fighting.

In the 1980s, the Iraqi government launched a punitive campaign known as Anfal, which destroyed up to 4,500 Kurdish villages (HRW 1993; Isser and Van der Auweraert 2009). In 1988, tens of thousands fled into Iran and Turkey. Following a failed Kurdish uprising in early 1991, some 1.5 million Kurds sought temporary refuge in Iran and along the Turkish border. By the end of 1991, most Kurdish refugees had returned, but some 700,000 remained displaced within the Kurdistan Region. Many had been displaced two or more times, as fighting continued between Kurdish and Iraqi government forces. During 1992 and 1993, more Kurds were displaced by skirmishes and shelling along the confrontation line dividing the Kurdish zone from government-controlled Iraq, and government forces expelled many Kurds from their homes, driving them into the Kurdish zones. In 1994, about 100,000 previously displaced persons were able to return to their home villages, many of which had been destroyed during the Anfal but were being rebuilt with UN and NGO assistance. However, an estimated 600,000 persons remained displaced within northern Iraq. Of those, about 200,000 were not able to return to their places of origin in government-controlled Iraq or in border areas due to fears for their safety. The remainder was displaced from one area of the Kurdistan Region to another. Others fled areas subjected to shelling by Iraqi government forces or by Turkey (HRW 1995).

When displaced families return to their homes, they sometimes find someone else living there. Perhaps the new occupants had fled from another neighborhood and were unable to return to it because their own home was destroyed and the area was unsafe. Sometimes the new occupants refused to leave. Sometimes, having already damaged or gotten rid of most of the home's furnishings, they threatened to cause further damage or even destroy the home if the original occupants took legal action. Finally, sometimes a displaced family found that their home had been sold or rented without their consent and that the proceeds had gone to an individual or group that could not be found.

There was also an urgent need to adopt an interim policy on housing and land, grounded in international human rights principles and best practices. The establishment of the Kurdistan Ministry of Reconstruction and Development in 1992 to coordinate policy and programmatic efforts to resolve outstanding

---

[8]   For a historic overview of Iraq's Arabization policies, see Talabany (1999).

Land and water management in the Kurdistan Region of Iraq 373

housing and land issues was a major catalyst for solving the urgent need for shelter and, through shelter provision, for promoting peacebuilding.

Water resources

Land and water resources are the basis of livelihoods for many people in the Kurdistan Region, so access to these resources was a crucial component of reconstruction. With water resources being scarce in the region, special attention had to be paid to ensuring that every family received the required quota on the basis of UN standards. Communities would share water resources (such as a well or spring) within their tribe but also with neighboring villages. The program allowed for community members and neighbors to participate in a negotiating process to determine how decisions regarding water resources would be made fairly, when water could be extracted, and what quantity could be extracted. With drinking water, the communities had to establish a system to pump water into a tank and then to redistribute it, or they would have families form a queue for tap water. In turn, communities would monitor the water allocation to ensure that everyone received their allotted share and not excessively more. Over time, the communities could make adjustments to the system as necessary.

The government was not responsible for the daily management of water resources at the household and community levels. Communities took responsibility for managing water, while the government provided pumps, pipes, purification, and training. In some cases, a community member would drive a truck with a water tank to the water source, fill it to capacity, then drive it back to the village, where the water would be distributed equally. The trucking capacity would be provided by that village and not the government, so residents had to fully commit themselves to providing financial and labor resources over the long term. With more sophisticated systems, officials would train staff and provide spare parts, but would not operate the infrastructure. The goal was to improve the capacity of the communities, reach an agreement on allocation and access, and provide community residents with the right tools so they could operate the water system sustainably and for the long term.

Women were rarely directly involved in the process for negotiating allocation of water resources. A women-headed household would be represented by a male in-law, or the government would hold separate meetings for women so they could express their interests, especially related to daily water issues, then report back findings to the community leadership. Thus, in the case of water resources, women were allowed to enter the negotiating process and voice their concerns, albeit indirectly.

Women were very interested in water resources for daily household uses, and they were often concerned with distribution and allocation. They wanted to express their ideas and opinions because they were concerned about having enough water for their daily household activities. Typically, men were more interested in land issues because of the role of land in determining prestige and

374   Land and post-conflict peacebuilding

because of its high value in the tribe. Agriculturalists needed water for irrigation purposes, so the men would take an interest in water distribution for irrigation, but they were not as interested in water allocation for household activities.

Local culture

Reconstruction planners needed to respect the importance of the culture of honor (*sharaf*) in Iraq. Keeping one's word of honor and following through on promises, especially at the community level, is something that transcends cultural or religious differences and is key to strengthening ties among the community. This proved critical to all of the program's reconstruction efforts.

Tribalism, on the other hand, presented challenges. The tribe is an element of traditional communal identity that transcends the sect and is part of the fabric of civil society in Iraq. It is both a form of sociopolitical organization and a cultural identity based on notions of kinship, genealogy, honor, and autonomy. Tribes are a stable form of traditional collective identity and have weathered the storms of colonialism and modernity. Thinking about how communities understood their tribal identities allowed program leaders to have a window on how shared ideas about morality, honor, and the nature of society related to concepts of reconciliation and conflict resolution. Tribes are an entry point into Iraqi society and were key to efforts to promote democratic values and civil society in Iraq, including the rights of women and minorities (O'Leary 2008).

The community-based approach

Traditional tribal mechanisms for dialogue and conflict resolution were an important part of the program's activities to bring communities together.[9] They could produce enhanced understanding (*tafahom*), which could then lead to agreement (*tawafiq*), which could in turn lead to consensus (*ijma*).[10] It was a gradualist approach.

Village-level committees, anjommans

Government agencies could not successfully manage many of the problems and conflicts that arose during the reconstruction program in the Kurdistan Region. Therefore, new initiatives for cross-sectoral and integrated management of resources often included a committee formed at the village level, called an *anjomman*. The regional officials would coordinate with the local administration, which would in

---

[9]   This section was developed on the basis of the author's self reflection, insiders' views, and discussions and interviews with people who were heavily involved in the program (Salih 2009; Doski 2009; Hakim 2009; Khoshnaw 2009).

[10]   The term *ijma* is considered as a fundamental source of sharia by Sunni Muslims, while some Shia communities view it differently. When used in this chapter, the term means "consensus"; it is not used to invoke Islamic law.

Land and water management in the Kurdistan Region of Iraq 375

turn organize meetings with villages to initiate the establishment of the anjommans. The local administration would help with resolving disputes and would determine if a higher-ranked official was needed to mediate. Furthermore, the anjommans would receive assistance from the government and from UN agencies that provided resources, technical training, organization, and conflict-resolution techniques. With the establishment of an anjomman that was accepted by the community, the next step in the reconstruction and resettlement program could proceed.

The anjomman would consist of the prominent people within a community, including elders, established families, the largest landholders, educational professionals, religious authorities, at least one representative from each family, and any authoritative figures in the village. It would drive the reconstruction process, determining which villagers received which resources.

Agriculture and animal husbandry were the main economic drivers in the region, and these are closely tied to land and water resources. Decisions related to administration of land and water resources were processed in four procedural settings: negotiations between authorities and stakeholder representatives; small-group negotiations involving all affected stakeholders and facilitated by authorities; public hearings with affected stakeholders and interested NGOs; and public participation, facilitated by authorities, in which the specific form of involvement was open but guided by minimum requirements.

The objectives of community-based reconstruction programs in the Kurdistan Region were to build the capacity of communities so they could address their emergency needs, and establish effective community institutions that could carry out various emergency and development interventions and avoid conflicts. Organized, institutionalized communities could carry out many negotiations and development interventions, and the initiatives were flexible enough to meet the community's development needs.

When natural resources were being addressed in the reconstruction process, allocation of land and water resources determined not only how much land and water people received and when they received it, but also where and when to build schools, health clinics, and other infrastructure. The village anjomman would determine how to spend the financial resources available for reconstruction. Also, the collective decision-making process ensured that everyone would be represented and have a say.

Cooperation and dispute resolution

The reconstruction program's community-based initiatives were designed to provide support to displaced families and vulnerable segments of the society and to promote a comprehensive approach to resettlement. Land allocation, housing, and access to water were negotiated as a package. In some cases, interventions failed due to a lack of consensus on land or water allocations or distribution.

To achieve sustainable improvement, the initiative introduced and promoted the concepts of community participation in project design and implementation,

376　Land and post-conflict peacebuilding

as well as collective care and self-management by the community. Effective advocacy was required to encourage behavioral change, and policies that facilitated development needed to be promoted.

A community-based mechanism for resolving disputes was introduced as a component of the initiatives. With the support of staff from NGOs and UN agencies, the Communication for Behavioral Impact (COMBI) approach was used to assist in the planning, implementation, and monitoring of a variety of communication actions.[11] Furthermore, for alternative dispute resolution, this project adopted the traditional methods used by the particular tribe or village. Each of the thousands of villages covered by the project had its own methods for handling land and water disputes, mostly due to varying sociopolitical and economic factors in each village. In some cases, government officials would arrange a meeting with religious leaders to speak with them regarding an issue. If these religious leaders agreed with the government's plan, they would reach out to their followers to exert their influence and build consensus within the tribe. The influence of religion would help people in the tribe to resolve their disputes peacefully and to reach an agreement.

The government also reached out to prominent people in the villages, such as the leader of the anjomman, the largest landowner, or the headmaster of a school, to get them involved in alternative dispute resolution. Tribal leaders usually most of the land and have an extensive family as well. The tribal leaders would have influence over this family group and would be better able to win its cooperation with the program than a government official would be. Likewise, a landowner or water rights holder might negotiate differently with the anjomman than with a government official. For example, landowners might not take as hard of a stance regarding their desire for more resources if they are negotiating with their anjomman rather than with the government.

In some cases, people were very generous and offered land to refugees and returning internally displaced persons without any negotiations. On the other hand, if the returnees took over the land without negotiation or due process, then conflict or distributional issues would erupt and have to be resolved before they escalated. In most cases, each community agreed on the basic principles of the reconstruction program; this enabled alternative dispute resolution to work effectively.

If a village could not agree on the basic principles of the program, then the government would have to move on to the next village. Without agreement on a common platform, the resettlement process would not be successful and could cause grievances. Officials understood that these villages needed help and would

---

[11]　According to the World Health Organization, "COMBI is social mobilization directed at the task of mobilizing all societal and personal influences on an individual and family to prompt individual and family action. It is a process which blends strategically a variety of communication interventions intended to engage individuals and families in considering recommended healthy behaviours and to encourage the adoption and maintenance of those behaviours" (WHO 2004, 1).

Land and water management in the Kurdistan Region of Iraq 377

approach them in the next season, unless the village solved their differences first and reengaged with the government.

Functional and structural organization

The programs at the village level were managed by the anjommans and assisted by intersectoral support teams from the UN and NGOs that were incorporated informally into the local governance system. Municipal committees supported village facilities, and the UN agencies and NGOs built the capacity of the anjomman members for supervising the promotion and implementation of self-built projects and collective care.

The anjomman at the village level reported to the district center. The municipal representative in charge of the district was, in turn, a member of the provincial intersectoral support team that oversaw the implementation of basic development projects at the village level.

Community-based organizations were trained to use socioeconomic information based on the results of household socioeconomic surveys conducted at the village level. The organizations learned to update the information and use it for emergency preparedness and response and for development activities.

An important component of this system was the village fund managed by the village anjomman and funded through subscriptions, donations, and inputs from the public sector. In some villages, 50 to 70 percent of the amount of the village fund was raised from beneficiaries, who were charged fees to cover service costs.

Planning, performed jointly by community-based organizations and other partners, was based on village information, previous development experience, expert views, risk analysis, and analysis of facilitating factors and available resources. Monitoring and evaluation was to be agreed upon by stakeholders.

Cooperation, ownership, and accountability made the reconstruction program an overall success for the post-conflict period in the Kurdistan Region. The program formally closed in 2003 when financing through the Oil-for-Food Programme ended. However, it had a profound impact across the Kurdistan Region, as well as ramifications for future resettlement programs. It demonstrated the use of community-based methods to design programs and encourage cooperation over resource allocation and distribution. The anjomman process established by the resettlement program continues to solve land disputes in the present, showcasing the sustainability of this community-based program.

LESSONS LEARNED

The leaders of the successful Kurdistan reconstruction program learned much that can be helpful to groups who implement similar programs elsewhere. These lessons relate to prerequisites, area selection, first steps, the opportunities and risks presented by community-based initiatives, and balancing short-term efforts and long-term objectives.

378 Land and post-conflict peacebuilding

Prerequisites

A number of conditions are required for a successful peacebuilding reconstruction program. First, the program must have participation from major donors. It is especially important that the international community be actively involved.

Second, the formation of a multistakeholder group that includes multiple NGOs associated with the program has several advantages. Such a group provides vehicles for funding specific projects or activities within the comprehensive program and, of course, it increases the total amount of funding available. Most important, international aid groups provide a means for engaging a variety of countries and institutions in the peacebuilding measures. Also, a great deal of contact will occur between opposing sides in a conflict through representatives of the aid groups working in the country. Although this is unlikely to lead to a political settlement of the conflict, at an operational level such contact can pave the way for a great number of small-scale agreements that can reduce the levels of violence and ultimately support conflict resolution.

Third, the program should establish contact with all entities involved in reconstruction at the beginning and maintain this contact throughout the course of the program. Save the Children Fund, Caritas Switzerland, Christian Aid, the International Rescue Committee, Peace Winds Japan, Qandil Sweden, and other NGOs played key roles in Kurdistan, bridging gaps between government representatives and donor communities. Members of the U.S. Office of Foreign Disaster Assistance team in Kurdistan helped broker a deal between Kurdish and Iraqi government representatives in the summer of 1991, by which crops in Kurdish-controlled areas were harvested with Iraqi government combines and partially sold to Iraq. The particular activities each side permitted varied from one locality to another, but the program could proceed with a broad understanding of what could be done without interruption.

Fourth, a reconstruction program must maintain strict neutrality. It is vital that it not be used for political gain by either side in the conflict. Program structure can aid operational neutrality. As a general rule, funds should be used to rebuild only critical infrastructure of a noncontroversial nature and to provide assistance with reconstruction that can be administered locally by implementing agencies and rural cooperatives. Also it is important to avoid politically sensitive areas. It will not be possible to extend reconstruction activities to some locales.

Fifth, the importance of experienced staff cannot be overemphasized. The keys to a successful reconstruction program are innovation and the ability to adapt quickly to a changing situation.

Finally, innovative disbursement mechanisms are a must. Experience has shown that a mixed expenditure system—for example, with direct cash grants, distribution of building materials, and provision of matching funds—is a practical means of disbursing resources.

Area selection

When considering a reconstruction program, officials were often perplexed about how to decide which localities should be given preference during the initial stages. In some cases, they used maps and surveys to determine which communities to help first, and they would seek out these villages to involve them in the program. Also, the officials would survey an area where internally displaced persons would be resettled to ensure that it was free of landmines, was not disputed territory, and was not near border regions that are susceptible to invasions (MAG 2004).

The best strategy is to follow the people's lead. For example, the migration patterns of spontaneous returnees often give a clue as to which areas people consider safe. The people usually have much better knowledge about the local situation than governments or relief agencies. They will know when it is safe to return. Supporting returnees can then be an important first step in initiating reconstruction programs and beginning to make progress toward the long-term objectives.

Other areas to consider for initial assistance are communities that are on the periphery of the conflict zone but are cut off from the more vicious fighting, and thus are places where prospects for recovery seem the brightest; communities where internal conflict is minimal; areas that have been reoccupied after the locus of conflict has shifted; urban settlements where large concentrations of displaced persons have permanently resettled on their own; areas with a large concentration of women-headed households; and areas with the worst living conditions for priority groups.

In a parallel process, communities would sometimes seek out officials and ask to be incorporated into the reconstruction program. In these cases, the community leaders will have recognized a desire to return, resolved any internal tensions, and gained the support of the community to proceed with resettlement. A community that has initiated the process is generally more committed to implementing it by holding members accountable through tribal mechanisms. These projects often had the highest success rates and were sustainable over the long-term.

First steps

In a new reconstruction project, certain first steps will usually be necessary at the local level. The project must have sufficient capacity and established procedures to protect residents from arbitrary eviction, and it must establish protection measures for marginalized populations. Temporary allocations of land must be made for housing and commercial purposes. The area must be made free of landmines, and emergency-management plans must be in place. Finally, mass media and other information-dissemination mechanisms must be put in place.

Protection of records must also be a part of peacekeeping in the early stages. The UN Security Council resolution giving the UN authority to undertake peacekeeping operations in a country or territory should be written in such a way as

380 Land and post-conflict peacebuilding

to include physical protection of land records where land disputes are a key part of the conflict.

Potential and pitfalls of community-based initiatives

The case study of the Kurdistan reconstruction program and complementary analyses of regional and national level documents and reports on planning, participation, and natural resources management reveal the potential and a number of pitfalls of community-based reconstruction initiatives.

On the positive side, planning can help to integrate differing interests, and technical and participation procedures can be adapted to the nature and scope of the local problem. Through its cross-sectoral approach, participatory planning is open to addressing natural resource problems in various combinations and can help to coordinate problem-solving activities and decisions across resources—for example, addressing land and water issues in concert with each other.

The direct involvement of municipal staff in planning decisions makes local integration of decisions possible in relation to all dimensions of sustainability—ecological, economic, and sociocultural. The process involves checks and balances reaching across administrative sectors; relating to public and individual interests; and relevant to local and higher levels. It is sensitive to local conditions and recognizes which societal priorities cannot be enacted.

Participatory planning does not limit the circle of participants, and it can help to mobilize new or previously silent stakeholders. Consultative participation can be enhanced through the opening of planning processes at an early stage for problem definition and negotiations. The Kurdistan reconstruction program shows how public involvement can improve dissemination of information about local conditions. To some extent it can create local agreement and support for improved solutions when time and facilitation of the participation process allow a deeper discussion.

On the negative side, some problems in planning increase with improper implementation of participatory planning. Participation approaches that use only minimal requirements and procedures (by means of letters and reports, for example) do not facilitate a dialogue between resource users and authorities. Such minimal participatory procedures are not receptive to ideas that show up in the wrong phase of planning. When early consultations in operational planning are not open to the public, there is a tendency to filter away local concerns. Mobilizing people for strategic plans on the municipal level is difficult, and traditional procedures of participation do not sufficiently mobilize the existing local creativity and capacity for problem solving.

In rural areas individuals are important for networking among participants, for implementation of plans and programs, and for facilitating planning processes. Local organizations create important forums for debate and action as well. Rural municipalities have limited resources and therefore must rely on these local organizations. Even when rural municipalities are unable to contribute material resources, they can provide needed encouragement to local NGOs.

The traditional methods of communicating with the public—public meetings and exchanges of letters—do not provide an appropriate forum for conflict management and negotiations between participants. These methods tend to wash over differences, ride over those remaining silent, or lead to polarization when participants feel that they need to keep a defensive position. Constructive management of disagreements is important in small, rural communities where mutual dependence of the residents requires maintaining good relations.

Planners' roles are changing, and their skills need to be enhanced in several areas. According to the interviews conducted for this case study, many Iraqi planners still think that they do not have sufficient skills and practical experience to plan. There is a need for further education, for promoting on-the-job skill development, and for the employment of interdisciplinary capacities in planning. Planners also need training in interpersonal conflict management. Many leading planners in Iraq graduated two to three decades ago and have no education in interpersonal conflict and process management, unless they have developed such skills through their professional practice.

Finally, the shortage of financial and other resources makes a systematic evaluation of participation initiatives in Iraq unlikely. Thus, the advantages of participation often remain invisible. For the same reason, the lessons learned tend to remain localized and limited as the practical knowledge developed by individuals does not spread beyond the local setting.

Any institution contemplating a post-conflict reconstruction program must be aware of some of the operational realities and risks. At first the program will seem to be only barely viable, and progress will be ponderously slow. There may be long periods when it is impossible to disburse funds because the locus of conflict has shifted back into the community, or because people are simply unwilling to assume the financial risk of investing. There will also be occasional setbacks. These may mean temporary suspension of the program, and in some cases it may even be necessary to withdraw from certain localities for long periods of time. Problems from extremists on both sides can be expected.

Risks can be categorized as financial, political, and personal. Surprisingly, the financial risks are the least difficult and can be minimized with proper program design. Program monitoring based on performance to specific standards can provide a suitable means of keeping tabs on the program and ensuring that it meets the long-term objectives.

Short-term efforts; long-term objectives

It is important that work in post-conflict peacebuilding is not wasted in solely short-term measures—that project leaders think clearly about leveraging short-term interventions into longer-term outcomes.

Conceptual gaps between relief and development must be addressed. Any resettlement process, whether the planning horizon is short- or long-term, has to consider not only meeting urgent human needs but also the physical infrastructure

382   Land and post-conflict peacebuilding

problems that arise, including the need for adequate shelter for all. Experience proves that in post-disaster situations interventions are most effective when long-term effects add value to short-term efforts, and short-term efforts add depth to long-term effects. Long-term reconstruction and economic recovery should therefore begin while emergency relief actions are being undertaken to restore normalcy for displaced populations who are returning home or settling in new places. Strategic investment during the emergency and relief stages can contribute significantly to the building of a foundation for peace and development.

If properly planned and executed, reconstruction can play a significant role in reducing conflict and supporting long-term peace objectives. In itself, reconstruction will not bring about peace, but it can make a contribution toward reducing the scope of a conflict. At the same time, it can provide much-needed assistance to people who otherwise would be forced to leave their homes in search of relief and public welfare.

In fragile states, the challenges of management, organizational development, and technical capacity are often overlooked. When governments make bad decisions it is not always because of a lack of political will; a lack of management ability, organizational development, and technical capacity can also feed bad decisions. Capacity works at all levels—national, regional, and local—and building capacity requires education and training. People in organizations at all levels of the system must know about strategies to strengthen relationships, promote a shared vision, determine allocations of resources that are in line with national goals, and so on. Capacity includes the knowledge and skills that are necessary for ongoing management of an emerging system; building technical capacity involves training leaders at all levels of the system so they will understand how to implement their organizations' mandates under a clear set of rules and regulations.

Continued international support for direct assistance to senior-level managers at the national, regional, and governorate levels is crucial for ongoing capacity building. Funds should be directed toward one-on-one mentoring, or twinning, programs in which an outside expert with high-level management, technical, and organizational development experience is matched to a particular senior-level manager for a period of six months. A key tool that can be transferred to Iraqi managers is strategic planning. The international community can help to advance these capacities in order to mitigate the consequences of a lack of political will, and to strengthen emerging political capacity as technical capacity improves.

The Kurdistan reconstruction program developed a process whereby communities led efforts to bring peace and development, and displaced families relearned their roles, becoming responsible for designing their own reconstruction efforts and making improvements over what existed before. Earlier injustices were removed, conflicts were managed, and more than 50,000 families responded by voluntarily choosing to return to live in peace. It was their land, their home, and their life. It was their choice.

REFERENCES

ACCORD (Austrian Centre for Country of Origin and Asylum Research and Documentation). 2001. Iraq: 6th European Country of Origin Information Seminar, Vienna, 13–14 November 2000, final report. www.unhcr.org/refworld/docid/402d04e97.html.

Amnesty International. 1999. Victims of systematic repression. Washington, D.C. www.amnesty.org/en/library/info/MDE14/010/1999/en.

Barkey, H. J., and E. Laipson. 2005. Iraqi Kurds and Iraq's future. *Middle East Policy* 12 (4): 66–76.

CHC (Center for Humanitarian Cooperation). 2002. Population displacement scenarios of northern Iraq. Montclair, NJ. http://reliefweb.int/node/122526.

Cohen, R., and J. Fawcett. 2002. Iraq's displaced: A test for democracy. *International Herald Tribune*, December 28. www.brookings.edu/opinions/2002/1228iraq_cohen.aspx.

Doski, H. 2009. Interview by author of engineer and community manager for United Nations Human Settlements Programme, 1997–2003, March 9.

Fawcett, J., and V. Tanner. 2002. The internally displaced people of Iraq. Occasional paper. Washington, D.C.: Brookings Institution–SAIS (Johns Hopkins University School of Advanced International Studies) Project on Internal Displacement.

Hajan, S. 2009. Interview by author of director of the Agriculture Department of Summel, Iraq. March 10.

Hakim, F. 2009. Interview by author of Kurdistan Reconstruction Organization engineer. March 10.

HRW (Human Rights Watch). 1993. *Genocide in Iraq: The Anfal campaign against the Kurds.* New York. www.hrw.org/legacy/reports/1993/iraqanfal/.

———. 1995. *Iraq's crime of genocide: The Anfal campaign against the Kurds.* New York.

———. 2003. *Iraq: Forcible expulsion of ethnic minorities.* New York. www.hrw.org/en/reports/2003/03/13/iraq-0.

ICG (International Crisis Group). 2008. Oil for soil: Toward a grand bargain on Iraq and the Kurds. Middle East Report No. 80 (October 28). www.crisisgroup.org/~/media/Files/Middle%20East%20North%20Africa/Iraq%20Syria%20Lebanon/Iraq/80_oil_for_soil___toward_a_grand_bargain_on_iraq_and_the_kurds.

Iraq Foundation. 2001. Ethnic cleansing in Kirkuk. January 26. Washington, D.C.

Isser, D., and P. Van der Auweraert. 2009. Land, property, and the challenge of return for Iraq's displaced. Special Report No. 221. Washington, D.C.: United States Institute of Peace. www.usip.org/files/resources/1.pdf.

Khoshnaw, N. 2009. Interview by author of Kurdistan Reconstruction Organization engineer. March 12.

MAG (Mines Advisory Group). 2004. Iraq: Assisting returnees. February 5. Washington, D.C.

O'Leary, C. A. 2008. Statement made by professor at the School of International Service, and scholar in residence for the Middle East Initiative at the Center for Global Peace at American University, before the U.S. Senate Committee on Foreign Relations hearing: Iraq 2012. April 3.

O'Leary, B., J. McGarry, and K. Salih. 2005. *The future of Kurdistan in Iraq.* Philadelphia: University of Pennsylvania Press.

Salih, M. S. 2009. Interview by author of Dahuk mayor. February 28.

Talabany, N. 1999. *Iraq's policy of ethnic cleansing: Onslaught to change national/demographic characteristics of the Kirkuk Region.* www.internal-displacement.org/

384   Land and post-conflict peacebuilding

8025708F004CE90B/(httpDocuments)/032622FF4B21AC90802570B7005944D1/$file/
Talabani_report.pdf.

UN-HABITAT (United Nations Human Settlements Programme). 2001. *IDP site and family survey. Final report.* Nairobi, Kenya.

———. 2003. Reconstruction plan for shelter and urban development. Nairobi, Kenya.

UNHCR (United Nations High Commissioner for Refugees). 1991. Letter from Sadako Ogata to Secretary-General Javier Pérez de Cuéllar. May 17.

———. 2000. *The state of the world's refugees 2000: Fifty years of humanitarian action.* New York. www.unhcr.org/4a4c754a9.html.

University of Texas Libraries. 1978. Iraq: Distribution of religious groups and ethnic groups. Perry Castañeda Library Map Collection. Map No. 503930. www.lib.utexas.edu/maps/middle_east_and_asia/iraq_ethnic_1978.jpg.

UNSC (United Nations Security Council). 1991. Resolution 688. S/RES/688. April 5.

WHO (World Health Organization). 2004. Mobilizing for action: Communication-for-Behavioural-Impact (COMBI). http://archive.k4health.org/system/files/COMBI.pdf.

ADDITIONAL SOURCES

Although the following materials were not cited, they have been listed because they contributed to the conceptual development of the chapter.

Cohen, R. 2004. Status of internal displacement in Iraq. May 21. www.brookings.edu/interviews/2004/0521humanrights_cohen.aspx.

Cordesman, A. H. 1998. *Iraq after Saddam: Nation building and opposition movements.* Washington, D.C.: Center for Strategic and International Studies. http://csis.org/files/media/csis/pubs/981118_iraqnationoptions.pdf.

Dammers, C. 1998. Iraq. In *Internally displaced people: A global survey,* ed. J. Hampton. London: Earthscan.

HRW (Human Rights Watch). 1999. *World report 2000, Iraq.* www.unhcr.org/refworld/country,,HRW,,IRQ,,3ae6a8cdc,0.html.

———. 2003a. *World report 2003, Iraq and Iraqi Kurdistan.* www.hrw.org/legacy/wr2k3/mideast4.html.

———. 2003b. Human rights and Iraq's reconstruction. Memorandum to June 24 international donors meeting. http://reliefweb.int/node/128809.

———. 2004a. Iraq: In Kurdistan, land disputes fuel unrest. August 3. http://reliefweb.int/node/151543.

———. 2004b. *Claims in conflict: Reversing ethnic cleansing in northern Iraq.* Report No. 16 (4E). www.hrw.org/sites/default/files/reports/iraq0804.pdf.

Hussein, F., M. Leezenberg, and P. Muller, eds. 1993. *The reconstruction and economic development of Iraqi Kurdistan: Challenges and perspectives.* Amsterdam: Netherland-Kurdistan Society.

ICG (International Crisis Group). 2003. *War in Iraq: Managing humanitarian relief.* Middle East Report No. 12. Brussels, Belgium. www.crisisgroup.org/~/media/Files/Middle%20East%20North%20Africa/Iraq%20Syria/Lebanon/Iraq/War%20in%20Iraq%20Managing%20Humanitarian%20Relief.

IRIN (Integrated Regional Information Networks). 2004. Iraq: Political, ethnic tensions halt IDP resettlement in Kirkuk. IRIN Humanitarian News and Analysis, October 25. www.irinnews.org/Report.aspx?ReportId=24256.

Land and water management in the Kurdistan Region of Iraq 385

Leckie, S. 2004. Addressing housing, land, and property rights in post-conflict settings: A preliminary framework for post-conflict Iraq. Presentation at the FIG Commission 7 meeting "Symposium on Land Administration in Post-Conflict Areas," Geneva, Switzerland, April 29–30.

Marr, P. 2004. *A modern history of Iraq*. Boulder, CO: Westview Press.

Stigall, D. E. 2009. Refugees and legal reform in Iraq: The Iraqi Civil Code, international standards for the treatment of displaced persons, and the art of attainable solutions. *Rutgers Law Record* 34 (1): 1–30.

United Nations. 1995a. United Nations consolidated inter-agency humanitarian programme in Iraq: Extension of the cooperation programme for 1995–1996. DHA/95/74. March. Geneva, Switzerland.

————. 1995b. United Nations consolidated inter-agency humanitarian programme in Iraq: Mid-term review. September. Geneva, Switzerland.

United Nations Assistance Mission for Iraq. 2003. Map of IDP movement trend in the three northern governorates. No. 1. UNHCR Refworld. June. www.unhcr.org/refworld/docid/46ce916d1f.html.

United Nations Cluster on Refugees and Internally Displaced Persons and the United Nations Country Team. 2004. Draft strategic plan for IDPs in Iraq. August.

United Nations Commission on Human Rights. 1998a. Question of the violation of human rights and fundamental freedoms in any part of the world, with particular reference to colonial and other dependent countries and territories. Report on the situation of human rights in Iraq, submitted by the Special Rapporteur, Mr. Max van der Stoel, in accordance with Commission Resolution 1997/60. E/CN.4/1998/67. www.unhchr.ch/Huridocda/Huridoca.nsf/(Symbol)/E.CN.4.1998.67.En?OpenDocument.

————. 1998b. *Report of the Representative of the Secretary-General, Mr. Francis M. Deng, submitted pursuant to commission resolution 1997/39. Addendum: Guiding principles on internal displacement*. E/CN.4/1998/53/Add.2. February 11. www.unhcr.org/refworld/docid/3d4f95e11.html.

United Nations High Commissioner for Refugees. 1993. *The state of the world's refugees 1993: The challenge of protection*. New York: Penguin Books. www.unhcr.org/4a4c6da96.html.

————. 2003. UNHCR's operations in Iraq update. December 19. Geneva, Switzerland.

United States Committee for Refugees and Immigrants. 1995. U.S. Committee for Refugees world refugee survey 1995. Washington, D.C.

————. 1996. U.S. Committee for Refugees world refugee survey 1996. Washington, D.C.

————. 1997. U.S. Committee for Refugees world refugee survey 1997. Washington, D.C.

————. 1998. U.S. Committee for Refugees world refugee survey 1998—Iraq. Washington, D.C. www.unhcr.org/refworld/country,,USCRI,,IRQ,,3ae6a8b748,0.html.

————. 1999. U.S. Committee for Refugees world refugee survey 1999—Iraq. Washington, D.C. www.unhcr.org/refworld/country,,USCRI,,IRQ,,3ae6a8cc34,0.html.

————. 2000. U.S. Committee for Refugees world refugee survey 2000—Iraq. Washington, D.C. www.unhcr.org/refworld/country,,USCRI,,IRQ,,3ae6a8d020,0.html.

————. 2001. U.S. Committee for Refugees world refugee survey 2001—Iraq. Washington, D.C. www.unhcr.org/refworld/country,,USCRI,,IRQ,,3b31e16413,0.html.

————. 2002. U.S. Committee for Refugees world refugee survey 2002—Iraq. Washington, D.C. www.unhcr.org/refworld/country,,USCRI,,IRQ,,3d04c15514,0.html.

Transboundary resource management strategies in the Pamir mountain region of Tajikistan

Ian D. Hannam

The Republic of Tajikistan, the smallest and most isolated of the new nations of formerly Soviet Central Asia, experienced ten years of civil conflict in the 1990s that debilitated the country socially, economically, and environmentally. Since 2000 political violence has ended, and there have been efforts to improve the condition of Tajikistan's natural resources, which suffered extensive damage during the long conflict. The Pamir mountain region of eastern Tajikistan was one of the most adversely affected areas in the years following Soviet occupation. Its natural environment was severely degraded, and the region saw a substantial increase in poverty.

John Heathershaw reports that post-Soviet, post-conflict Tajikistan is an understudied and poorly understood case in the conflict studies literature (Heathershaw 2009). This chapter discusses a sustainable land management program introduced into the Pamir region under a joint international–Tajik government project, which has been catalytic in a number peacebuilding actions, including capacity building, reconciliation, and societal transformation activities. The Pamir project has brought many parts of the Pamir community together to solve its resource management problems, and the main outcome has been a long-term natural resource strategy for the region that includes legal, policy, and institutional elements. The progress made in the Pamir region of Tajikistan has generated valuable regional and transboundary natural resource management norms and guidelines that can be adapted to similar mountain environments in other parts of the world.

Ian D. Hannam is an adjunct associate professor at the Australian Centre for Agriculture and Law, University of New England, Australia, and chair of the International Union for Conservation of Nature Commission on Environmental Law Specialist Group for Sustainable Use of Soil and Desertification. The study upon which this chapter is based was carried out in the context of the Global Environment Facility (GEF), United Nations Environment Programme (UNEP), and United Nations University (UNU) project on "Sustainable Land Management in the High Pamir and Pamir-Alai Mountains Project—An Integrated and Transboundary Initiative in Central Asia." The chapter reflects only the views of the author, not those of GEF, UNEP, or UNU.

388 Land and post-conflict peacebuilding

This chapter begins by outlining the historical context of conflict in Tajikistan, highlighting the role of foreign influence in both Tajikistan's factious politics and more recent peacebuilding efforts. The chapter then focuses in on the Pamir mountain region as a unique microcosm for the study of sustainable natural resource management and community development. The author outlines the PALM project (formally known as the Sustainable Land Management in the High Pamir and Pamir-Alai Mountains project) noting its effects on local governance, poverty, resource management, and transboundary relations. The chapter concludes with mentions of relevant international and regional environmental laws and policies, and lessons learned from PALM and general peacebuilding efforts in the Pamir mountain region.

ARMED CONFLICT AND ITS AFTERMATH

With a population of approximately 7 million and virtually no arable land, Tajikistan is the poorest of the new republics of Central Asia, and because its natural resources are severely degraded it has a difficult economic future.

The ten-year civil conflict that debilitated the nation erupted at the time of independence, when groups that had been out of power since the establishment of Soviet authority reemerged. These power groups won initial elections but were prevented from taking office by others who had enjoyed power in the Soviet Union and who had Russian backing to maintain power. The worst part of the ensuing civil conflict ended in 1993 with a settlement that provided for a sharing of power between the elected government and the opposition, but sporadic fighting continued (Beeman 1999).

Decades of Soviet control over Tajikistan meant that few institutional mechanisms were in place to manage political diversity, and the new leaders had little experience in the practice of political compromise (Barnes and Abdullaev 2001). Violence was the means for gaining political dominance. This problem was exacerbated by the involvement of external powers that directly or indirectly supported the different factions. With an interest in the outcome of the civil war, those powers became secondary parties to the conflict. Later, however, they became vital resources to the peace process.

On June 27, 1997, in Moscow, the president of Tajikistan, Emomali Rahmonov, and opposition leader Sayeed Abdullo Nuri signed the peace agreement on Establishment of Peace and National Accord in Tajikistan. The agreement addresses constitutional amendments, government reforms, and the amendment of some laws, including election laws.

As a result of the conflict in Tajikistan, between 40,000 and 100,000 people died, hundreds of thousands became disabled, livelihoods were lost, approximately one million people became refugees or were internally displaced, and more than 50,000 homes were destroyed. Economic damage was estimated at US$7 billion (Toshmuhammadov 2004). But even before the civil war, socioeconomic development was unbalanced, and had been for some seventy years. The country was

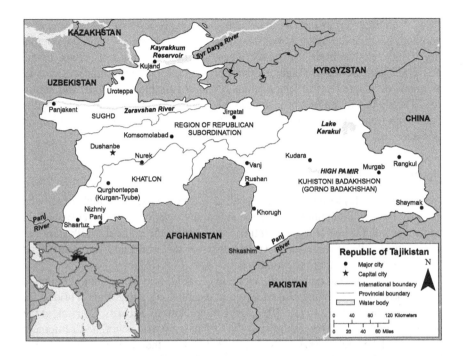

essentially a "raw materials–producing agrarian appendage of industrially developed regions of the former Soviet Union" (Toshmuhammadov 2004, 9). At the beginning of the 1990s, according to Deutsche Bank, Tajikistan held the lowest ranking for economic development and resource potential among the Commonwealth of Independent States (Toshmuhammadov 2004).

Since 2000, countrywide order has emerged in Tajikistan, and the 1997 peace agreement between the parties in the civil conflict has held. Superficially Tajikistan's emergence from conflict appears to be a case of successful international intervention for liberal peacebuilding, but the Tajik peace is characterized by authoritarian governance. Zamira Yusufjonova's view is that one of the main obstacles to complete reconciliation is an almost exclusive concern in the Tajik peace process for institutional reform—to the neglect of social psychological issues (Yusufjonova 2005). She contends that the peace process lacks the relational dimension of peacebuilding, which centers on reconciliation, forgiveness, and trust building.

CASE ANALYSIS

Under United Nations parameters, peacebuilding consists of a wide range of activities associated with capacity building, reconciliation, and societal transformation (Boutros-Ghali 1992). It is a long-term process that occurs after violent conflict has slowed down or come to a halt, and after peacemaking and peacekeeping.

390   Land and post-conflict peacebuilding

In post-conflict Tajikistan, at least two basic peacebuilding discourses were adopted: the elite *mirostroitelstvo* (Russian for "peacebuilding") and the popular *tinji* (Tajik for "wellness" or "peacefulness"). Studies conducted between 2003 and 2005 indicate that a singular definition of Tajik peacebuilding was elusive as practices adapted to the relationships between multiple discourses and identities. The studies found that peacebuilding is a complex and dynamic process that entails the legitimation and shared acceptance of new relationships of power (Heathershaw 2007).

Political reconciliation

Internationally Tajikistan plays the role of a transit state, in which peace and stability have to be maintained for the safe transportation of the energy carriers and other natural resources of Central Asia. During the conflict, Tajikistan was at the crossroads of interests of superpowers of the world and the region, and this exacerbated the internal situation.

The international community, including Russia, Iran, other donor countries, and Tajikistan's neighbors, played a role in establishing a negotiation bridge for political reconciliation. In late 1992, the United Nations Security Council, at the request of member states, authorized the UN to support a negotiated settlement (Barnes and Abdullaev 2001). UN officers first took up their functions in Tajikistan in January 1993 (Toshmuhammadov 2004), and the UN later sponsored the inter-Tajik negotiations, which began in April 1994 and resulted in completion of the peace agreement three years later.

The peace agreement embraced a wide range of cooperative actions for an orderly conciliation of the crisis, including formation of the Commission on National Reconciliation, which was responsible for leading the nation toward parliamentary and presidential elections; legalization of United Tajik Opposition parties and integration of their armed units into the Tajik Army; and the holding of national parliamentary and presidential elections. All of these provisions of the peace accords have been put into effect, followed by enactment of a decree that formally dissolved the reconciliation commission on the grounds that it had completed its mission.

One of the main factors in the civil war in Tajikistan was the uneven distribution of power among representatives of individual regions of the republic. Prior to the collapse of the Soviet Union, top government positions were usually held by designees from the northern (Leninabad) clan. This imbalance of power was built upon support from Moscow. With the disintegration of the Soviet Union, no regional political group was strong enough to govern the country alone. The peace agreement provided for a redistribution of power in line with a formula according to which the opposition would hold 30 percent of offices at all levels. Some analysts believe that the continuing imbalance of power remains a major challenge to the maintenance of peace and harmonious relations in the years ahead (Toshmuhammadov 2004; Mullojanov 2005).

Economic rehabilitation

Tajikistan, and in particular the Pamir mountain region, still faces many challenges as a consequence of the civil war. These difficulties of the transitional period are connected with land degradation and loss of environmental amenities, a high poverty rate among migrant laborers and the general population, weak social protections, and the decline of the municipal economy. Poverty currently affects over half of the population, and employment opportunities are limited. Between 400,000 and 1 million people leave the country in search of work each year. Food security, sufficiency of power supplies, communication difficulties, and natural resource management are critical issues (GOT 2002).

Notwithstanding these challenges, Tajikistan has maintained peace and stability in recent years, and its national reconciliation policy has continued. Due to the peace process, political, economic, social, and environmental reforms are now being successfully implemented. Tajikistan is moving toward democratization of the society and transition to a market economy. A new constitution was adopted in 1994,[1] a standing parliament was established and is functional, and six political parties are active in the country. The gross domestic product is increasing, and the national currency is reasonably stable.[2] Under Tajikistan's international open-door policy, foreign relations are broadening, and the republic's international prestige is increasing.

Despite implementation of several long-term programs aimed at post-conflict rehabilitation, however, progress is hampered by Tajikistan's limited budget. Under the circumstances, aid from the international community is essential.[3] As in many complex humanitarian emergencies created by conflict, a wide range of international agencies and nongovernmental organizations have worked with their Tajik counterparts to address the political, legal, humanitarian, socioeconomic, and security dimensions of the conflict and its aftermath (Barnes and Abdullaev 2001).

Conditions in the Pamir mountain region

Internationally the Pamir mountain region has been viewed as vitally important to peacebuilding in and the future economic development of Tajikistan because

---

[1] The constitution of Tajikistan was adopted on November 6, 1994, and amended by referendum on September 26, 1999, and June 22, 2003. It is the supreme law of the Republic of Tajikistan.

[2] According to World Bank data, the gross domestic product of Tajikistan expanded at an average rate of 9.6 percent between 2000 and 2004, but by March 2007, 53 percent of Tajikistan citizens were still living below the poverty line (World Bank n.d.).

[3] For example, the Islamic Development Bank, as of 2004, has provided Tajikistan with loans of US$60 million and grants of US$1.6 million; the European Bank for Reconstruction and Development and the International Financial Corporation have provided Tajikistan with a loan of US$14 million for the development of small and medium-sized businesses; and in 2003 a UN appeal resulted in the receipt of 172,000 tons of humanitarian aid worth US$116 million from thirty-nine countries (Toshmuhammadov 2004).

392 Land and post-conflict peacebuilding

of its rich natural assets and unique opportunities for economic, social, and ecological development. Numerous peaks, with altitudes ranging from 5,000 to 7,000 meters, deliver water to the Panj-Amu Darya River basin, making rich agricultural production possible farther downstream in the semi-arid lowlands. Although the deep valleys of the Pamir Mountains are only thinly populated, they are home to several ethnic groups that practice irrigated agriculture. The highland meadows in the Eastern Pamirs are used mainly to raise livestock. Among the region's most important assets are rich natural resources, potential for hydropower generation, scenic beauty that could attract tourists, and comparatively high educational standards based on the unifying vision of the Ismaili culture of Shia Islam in extensive parts of the region (Breu and Hurni 2003).

During the Soviet era, settlement and population growth were actively promoted within the Pamir mountain region of east Tajikistan for border security reasons: it is an extremely isolated area at the crossroads between China (to the east), Pakistan (to the south), Afghanistan (to the west), and Kyrgyzstan (to the north). Moscow heavily subsidized the region by providing goods and services at minimal prices, and these subsidies supported the development of an entire economic and natural resource management system that was unrelated to the limited natural carrying capacity of the region's ecological resources. Traditional land use systems were replaced by collective farms that were often assigned the sole purpose of breeding livestock for distant markets in the Soviet Union. At the same time, large numbers of pastoralists of Kyrgyz ethnic descent who had been living in the High Pamirs were forced to abandon their traditional transhumant herding lifestyle and to take up permanent residence in newly constructed small towns located at altitudes of over 3,000 meters.

Following the collapse of the Soviet Union in 1991, subsidies were immediately withdrawn, and the lopsided economy was deprived of markets and exchange relations. Unemployment increased dramatically with government retrenchment and the closure of inefficient state industries: some 80 percent of the population was either unemployed or underemployed, with little or no income earning opportunity. Poverty became widespread, livelihoods focused on survival rather than economic development, and a high level of external humanitarian support was needed. The civil war led to further deterioration of human and natural resources.

Establishment of the PALM project

Since the peace agreement was signed in 1997, the Tajik government has promoted post-conflict confidence building and national reconciliation, and international agencies have provided funding for conflict resolution activities (Mullojanov 2001). Consistent with these goals, between 2004 and 2007 the inhabitants of the Pamir Mountains and the Tajik government partnered with the Global Environment Facility and United Nations Environment Programme to establish the PALM project. The United Nations University is the implementing agency for the project, and the Committee on Environment Conservation of the Government

Transboundary resource management strategies in Tajikistan   393

of Tajikistan and the State Agency on Environment Protection and Forestry of Kyrgyzstan were designated as national collaborative partners (PALM 2008). The PALM project has made significant contributions to the political, social, and ecological aspects of peacebuilding in the Pamir mountain region in particular, and in Tajikistan in general. Its long-term environmental and development goal is:

> [T]o restore, sustain, and enhance the productive and protective functions of the transboundary ecosystems of the High Pamir and Pamir-Alai mountains of Tajikistan and Kyrgyzstan, so as to improve the social and economic well-being of the rural communities and households utilising the region's ecosystem resources to meet their livelihood needs, while preserving its unique landscape and globally important biodiversity (PALM 2011, 13).

The various components of the PALM project address land degradation and poverty in a manner that has brought communities of the Pamir mountain region and the national government together by using cooperative and participatory processes, including discussion and problem-solving meetings, training and capacity-building workshops, and joint field excursions and investigations. The project also has adopted a transboundary approach, with Tajikistan and Kyrgyzstan working together to take responsibility for ecosystem resources and to improve the technological, institutional, policy, and legislative environment for the mountain communities.

A regional strategy and action plan for sustainable development of the mountain region was prepared through a participatory process involving community members, the government, and other stakeholders. To ensure implementation of the strategy, participatory community-based resource assessment, land use planning, and micro-projects were conducted at selected hot spots in the region. These community activities mobilized many additional resources to encourage as wide an adoption of these initiatives as possible. The entire project comprised five components related to sustainable land management: improvement of the legal, policy, institutional, and planning environment; capacity building; poverty alleviation; evaluation of impact and identification of lessons so the project could be replicated; and project management (UNEP 2005).[4]

The centerpiece of the PALM project was the Pamir-Alai Transboundary Strategy and Action Plan (PATSAP), which applied various peacebuilding actions in its development. Following a procedure defined by United Nations University, a multidisciplinary team of international, national, and local experts undertook data collection and prepared baseline reports (UNU 2009). Environmental reports

---

[4] Other aspects of the project included enhancing capacities for project-specific activities, implementing adaptive research, and mobilizing cofinancing resources; working with existing pilot sites rather than scaling up project activities; developing generic guidelines for replicating the project's experience; and emphasizing project management and performance monitoring and reporting rather than development of an integrated decision-support system based on GIS (geographic information system).

394   Land and post-conflict peacebuilding

covered ecosystems, land management and livelihoods, and the indirect driving forces of change in land resource management in the Pamir region. Given the importance of grazing to livelihood, considerable resources were allocated to obtaining information on how the mountain communities managed pastures. Economic investigations reviewed the local economy, globalization, trade, markets, public services, and energy infrastructure. The PATSAP summarized best practices and suggested measures for land rehabilitation, identifying priority areas for treatment and recommending long-term land rehabilitation projects.

Governance, principles, and ethics

The 1997 peace agreement gave insufficient emphasis to the reform of constitutional and governance structures. The Commission on National Reconciliation was responsible for overseeing implementation of the agreement and recommending constitutional amendments and post-war legislation, with technical assistance provided by the UN (Barnes and Abdullaev 2001). To address issues of governance, the PALM project incorporated participation, accountability, predictability, and transparency into its project activities to obtain a better perspective on the rights of Pamir people, to recognize their capacity to make decisions that directly affect their lives, and to hold the government accountable for its actions (Nzongola-Ntalaja 2002).

Moreover, the PALM project promoted the value of a comprehensive legal framework as a foundation for governance in the region. The fundamental principles of good governance advocated by the Organisation for Economic and Co-operation and Development (OECD 1997) formed the basis for the strategic tools prepared for the specially formed Tajik Legal Task Force, which was responsible for investigating governance issues, including:

- Transparency, participation, and accountability.
- Fairness and equity in dealings with citizens.
- Efficiency and effectiveness of services.
- Clarity and transparency of laws and regulations.
- Consistency and coherence in policy formation.
- Respect for the rule of law.
- Standards of ethical behavior.

Project training workshops emphasized that governance encompasses much more than just government responsibilities (GEF, UNEP, and UNU 2008). Law and institutional frameworks, participation, accountability, and efficacy were regarded as essential for creating legitimacy for and achieving compliance with post-conflict rehabilitation efforts in the Pamir mountain region.

To create the best chance possible for good governance to be put into practice in the region, the PALM project promoted fundamental legal principles of international natural resource law: equitable and reasonable utilization, the duty of cooperation, dispute prevention and resolution, and compliance. This approach was consistent with a peacebuilding process that begins to develop a civil society infrastructure composed of both traditional social institutions and newer nongovernmental organizations. For the Pamir region it was also important to facilitate reintegration of former Tajik refugees in Afghanistan and to settle local disputes while addressing a range of other social needs (Barnes and Abdullaev 2001).

Project leaders investigated the possibility of establishing a transboundary protected area to maintain ecological balance and preserve biodiversity in the Pamir area because they perceived this to be an important mechanism for furthering positive international economic and political relations for this isolated and ecologically unique region. Worldwide, protected areas have grown in significance not only for the purpose of safeguarding complex ecosystems but also to make possible new forms of economic development and to recognize the value of local cultures and traditions (Kemp, Parto, and Gibson 2005; Schulz 2007).

The principles of a regional governance system for natural resource management were used by the Legal Task Force to establish the methodology for implementing the natural resource management aims and economic and social objectives of the PALM project. Using an ecological approach, the task force became more aware of the links among multiple natural resources, including drainage basins, air, soil, and water. This approach was beneficial to the peacebuilding effort because it necessitated regular interaction among various communities of the region and among people from all facets of the project. For example, in the development of the transboundary legal and institutional framework, the ecosystem approach made all concerned more aware that the native species of the Pamirs and their habitats are interconnected and that certain human activities place the ecological environment under stress. Further, the inclusive transboundary approach, with its focus on joint management, led to better management opportunities for the mountain region by internalizing the consequences of the natural resource management policies developed through this process (Benvenisti 2002).

Improving the legal and regulatory framework for sustainable land management

Earlier studies in the Pamir region had identified many gaps in and constraints on the enabling legal, policy, and institutional environment at the regional, national, and local government levels (Hannam 2006a, 2006b). These problems grew from the lack of consultation between groups, institutional dysfunction, and a general lack of trust between different sectors of government and society. The Legal Task Force was aware of these problems when it reviewed the national laws and regulations in relation to the sustainable land management and ecosystem objectives for the Pamir Mountains (GEF, UNEP, and UNU 2008).

The development of the regional Natural Resource Management Governance Framework was significant as a peacebuilding activity. This framework included national laws, policies, and institutional requirements for implementing sustainable

396 Land and post-conflict peacebuilding

land management, as well as the transboundary law necessary for managing the natural resources of the Pamir mountain region. It relied heavily on the building of partnerships and trust (PALM 2008).

Methodological research guidelines

The methodological research guidelines that the Legal Task Force used to formulate the legal, policy, and institutional framework for sustainable land management proved to be a valuable communication tool because they were based on a series of procedural steps for locating, analyzing, and interpreting legislative, policy, and institutional information (Hannam 2006a; University of New England 2009). As the guidelines were applied, opportunities arose to address a number of key post-conflict issues, including ways to improve the sharing of information and knowledge, as well as the use of multidisciplinary working groups to identify common problems and devise solutions and reforms. Application of the guidelines also highlighted relationships and interdependence between different levels of environmental law and policy. Because of the authoritarian approach of the Russian era, not may local people knew about the role of international, national, regional, and local environmental law. Although the methodological research guidelines were developed specifically for the PALM project, Tajik officials supported their adoption as standard administrative government procedure for environmental law and policy reform within the country as a whole.

Legislation and policy

Various international and national studies of the Tajik mountain environment have identified many sustainable land management issues (Breu and Hurni 2003; Centre for Development and Environment 2005). These were used in the implementation of the methodological research guidelines.

The Legal Task Force gathered additional information by examining strategic materials (such as land management studies, environmental reports, and government reports) and paying particular attention to their objectives, recommendations, and conclusions. Again, this procedure was critical to capacity building and reconciliation because it relied on cooperation between different groups of Tajik people. Together, these groups decided on benchmarks of important environmental problems relevant to sustainable management of the mountain environment; established indicators of the types of legal and institutional elements required for each level of law to effectively manage each sustainable land management issue in the future; made comparisons between individual laws and the legal and institutional profiles of each area of law; and identified future areas for legal, policy, and institutional reform.

An aspect of the PALM project that engendered enthusiasm among the Tajik officials was the opportunity to see the outcome of their work contributing to the development of global mountain law and policy, which is still in its infancy,

Transboundary resource management strategies in Tajikistan 397

with few mountain-specific legal instruments currently in force at the national level (Fodella and Pineschi 2002; Hannam 2006a). Tajik officials were excited at the prospect of contributing to something outside their own country. In this regard, using the methodological research guidelines to investigate legal, policy, and institutional problems and to develop a new and more appropriate system of law for the Pamir mountain region gave those involved a sense of pride, achievement, and hope. It increased the urgency of achieving peace and harmony and of achieving many goals that were important to their daily lives, including:

- Improving resource utilization and environmental protection, sustainable management of ecosystems, and prevention of land degradation.
- Creating regulations that are enforceable.
- Removing uncertainty of land tenure in the Pamir region and ensuring that land use rights were restored for rural communities.
- Ensuring that the land use decision-making system and rural land management activities of the Pamir region are linked with the national environmental legislative and policy system, but not overridden by the latter.
- Removing institutional limitations to the implementation of the legal, policy, and regulatory framework for sustainable land management.

Two of the ongoing barriers to change in Tajikistan have been a lack of coordination among national institutions and sector agencies and a paucity of regional rules to ensure uniformity in approach to the management of the Pamir region as a distinct biogeographical and ecological unit (Breu and Hurni 2003). Substantial overlap existed between many organizations in their administrative, legislative, and policy responsibilities for land management. The national law and policy framework that evolved in the immediate post-conflict period was highly sectoral and did not recognize integrated land use management in the Pamir region. Through the PALM project, it was realized that without the benefit of an effective common-boundary, transjurisdictional agreement achieving consistent land use and conservation goals for the entire Pamir region would be difficult.

Transboundary issues

Delicate negotiations have been under way between the Tajik and Kyrgyz governments to finalize transboundary natural resource management arrangements within the Natural Resource Management Governance Framework for the Pamir region. The transboundary arrangements are viewed as critical for the economic development of the region because if implemented properly they would help overcome many of the post-Soviet issues still affecting the mountain region. The very nature of a transboundary approach—"any process of cooperation across boundaries that facilitates or improves the management of natural resources to the benefit of all parties in the area concerned" (Griffin et al. 1999, 21)—is that it engenders coop-

398   Land and post-conflict peacebuilding

eration and communication among the occupants of a transboundary region and can go a long way toward harmonization of relationships in the region.

Engaging in transboundary activities is another effective way of consolidating the peacebuilding process because of its focus on sharing resources, ensuring that communities and other stakeholders benefit from a sustainable use of resources, countering inequitable resource distribution associated with unfair land and resource appropriation, and optimizing the distribution of benefits from natural resource use for economic development.

International and regional environmental law and policy instruments

Tajikistan has ratified a number of international treaties that include procedures that are important to peacebuilding in the Pamir region, including the Convention on Biological Diversity, the Framework Convention on Climate Change, and the Convention to Combat Desertification (PALM 2008). Various procedures in these multilateral treaties, when applied in conjunction with national legislative provisions, play an important role in improving economic, human, and environmental conditions. The Legal Task Force took these conventions into account when it was engaged in the evaluation and participative processes associated with implementation of the methodological research guidelines and development of the Natural Resource Management Governance Framework (University of New England 2009).

Convention on Biological Diversity

The Legal Task Force looked to many articles of the Convention on Biological Diversity for direction for managing the ecology of the Pamir mountain environment and as an indicator of the reduction in biological diversity, mostly due to habitat loss and land degradation, that resulted from activities in the post-Soviet conflict period.[5] In particular, the Legal Task Force used various articles of the convention relating to environmental, economic, and social benefits of conserving biodiversity to recommend changes to individual natural resource laws related to management of the Pamir region.

The obligations outlined in article 6, for example, were used in the preparation of implementation strategies and measures for conservation of biological diversity. The strategies highlighted important links between different methods of conserving biodiversity in the Pamir, and how they could benefit ecotourism, improve land management, and mitigate the effects of climate change. To successfully reflect national obligations found in the Convention on Biological Diversity in the Pamir transboundary framework, and to reach consensus on standards and rules for

---

[5] For the text of the UN Convention on Biological Diversity, see www.cbd.int/convention/text/.

Transboundary resource management strategies in Tajikistan 399

conservation, the Legal Task Force consulted with community groups. To achieve the full benefits of the convention in the peacebuilding process, the mountain communities had to be directly involved in discussions concerning conservation and sustainable use of biological resources.

Framework Convention on Climate Change

Consistent with the United Nation's position on the effects of human-induced changes to the global climate system, the PALM project used the processes of the UN Framework Convention on Climate Change in deciding how the terrestrial ecosystems of the Pamir mountain region could be effectively used as a sink for greenhouse gases.[6] Using the objective articulated in article 2 of the convention ("to achieve stabilization of atmospheric concentrations of greenhouse gases at levels that would prevent dangerous anthropogenic interference with the climate system") and its key principles (expressed in article 3), which encourage parties to protect the climate system for the benefit of present and future generations, various precautionary and mitigation measures were derived through consultation and participatory processes that discussed a sustainable development approach to land use in the region. These measures were then included in the strategy and action plan, or PATSAP (PALM 2008).

In particular, the PATSAP documented agricultural activities of the Pamir region that were considered to be a source of greenhouse gases, including changes in land cover and land use that contributed emissions of greenhouse gases through vegetation destruction, biomass burning, livestock keeping, and cultivation using organic manure and nitrogenous fertilizers (PALM 2008). The PATSAP also acknowledged that Tajikistan has a responsibility to improve its legal, policy, and institutional systems to protect the climate system of the country for the benefit of present and future generations, and Tajik officials realized that precautionary measures are necessary for minimization of the causes of climate change.

Convention to Combat Desertification

The basic objective of the UN Convention to Combat Desertification was applied in the PALM project to reduce land degradation, rehabilitate degraded land, and reclaim desertified land (PALM 2008), using the same cooperative and participatory processes mentioned above.[7] The type of action required of the Pamir communities to combat desertification and mitigate the effects of drought highlighted an important synergistic relationship between the obligations of the three conventions. Specific sustainable land management techniques were included in the

---

[6] For the text of the UN Framework Convention on Climate Change, see http://unfccc.int/essential_background/convention/background/items/1349.php.

[7] For the text of the UN Convention to Combat Desertification, see www.unccd.int/convention/text/pdf/conv-eng.pdf.

400 Land and post-conflict peacebuilding

PATSAP and the Natural Resource Management Governance Framework to combat desertification and control land degradation. These derived from community participation activities to decide on mechanisms to combat desertification, which used various procedures under the Convention to Combat Desertification as a guide.

Over time the Tajik government will implement strategies to combat land degradation in the Pamir mountain region that use an integrated approach to address the physical, biological, and socioeconomic aspects of land degradation and drought (UNU 2009). The ability of Tajik government programs to control these problems in the Pamir region is dependent on a successful education and capacity-building program to build confidence and expertise.

Regional treaties

The Framework Convention on Environment Protection for Sustainable Development in Central Asia (Ashkhabad, Turkmenistan, June 22, 2006) and, for members of the Commonwealth of Independent States, the Convention on Frontier Cooperation (Bishkek, Kyrgyzstan, October 10, 2008) specify the importance of interrelations between biodiversity and various technologies on conservation of mountainous systems. When it was developing the Natural Resource Management Governance Framework, the Tajik Legal Task Force considered the role of these instruments in improving land management processes, including the establishment of rules on protection and rational use of land resources in the High Pamir and Pamir-Alai mountains. However, because greater utilization of the procedures of these instruments depends on closer dialogue and cooperation between the governments of Kyrgyzstan and Tajikistan on transboundary issues, the full benefit of these instruments may not be realized for some time yet. Still, the participatory and cooperative processes involved in discussing the objectives and the role of these instruments benefit peacebuilding in the Pamir region and in Tajikistan as a whole.

LESSONS LEARNED AND NEXT STEPS

Through the two phases of the PALM project (project development and project implementation), the Tajik government and the communities have worked together, slowly improving their knowledge of sustainable land management and how it can be applied at the local and regional levels. The process has helped to improve trust and harmony between different groups as they have come together to solve mutual problems of livelihood and environmental security. Continued financial, political, and technical support from international organizations is important to expand the conflict resolution and peacebuilding capacities of Tajikistan's civic organizations and their ability to engender dialogue and political participation and to ensure protection of rights (Mullojanov 2001).

Although there have been many positive outcomes of the PALM project, various constraints affect the rate of progress, including interagency rivalries

Transboundary resource management strategies in Tajikistan 401

and power struggles, and limitations on the availability of human, technical, and financial resources. The PALM project experience indicates that involving all stakeholders makes it possible to take advantage of more optimal options for problem resolution, including the participation of the community to solve common natural resource usage problems that threaten livelihoods. After nearly four years, through the efforts of the PALM project, Tajikistan now has a better appreciation of the international economic and ecological value of the Pamir region because of its unique ecotype and its potential for ecotourism.

International agencies' involvement with the Tajik people has been important in providing them with skills to undertake activities that directly contribute to the peacebuilding process, including conflict resolution programs with political parties, public movements, and civic organizations. It is important that the good work of the PALM project continue with even greater focus on activities that bring people together and build trust and cooperation for identifying and solving problems.

Political developments in Tajikistan will depend on the nature of sociopolitical relations in the country, the maintenance of geopolitical equilibrium in the region, and the evolution in the interests of superpowers such as the United States, Russia, and China.

A number of direct global environmental benefits will continue to accrue from the PALM project, including the development of replicable sustainable land management guidelines that can be used to address natural resource management problems in similar high-altitude mountain regions. In this way, Tajikistan, while going through an internal process of peacebuilding and addressing its own critical natural resource management problems, can connect with and make a contribution to the outside world.

REFERENCES

Barnes, C., and K. Abdullaev. 2001. Politics of compromise: The Tajikistan peace process. *Accord*, March.

Beeman, W. O. 1999. The struggle for identity in post-Soviet Tajikistan. *Middle East Review of International Affairs* 3 (4): 100–105.

Benvenisti, E. 2002. *Sharing transboundary resources: International law and optimal resource use.* Cambridge, UK: Cambridge University Press.

Boutros-Ghali, B. 1992. *An agenda for peace.* New York: United Nations.

Breu, T., and H. Hurni. 2003. *The Tajik Pamirs: Challenges of sustainable development in an isolated mountain region.* Bern, Switzerland: Centre for Development and Environment, University of Bern.

Centre for Environment and Development. 2005. *Synthesis report: Baseline survey on sustainable land management in the Pamir-Alai Mountains.* Bern, Switzerland: Institute of Geography, University of Bern.

Fodella, A., and L. Pineschi. 2002. Environmental protection and sustainable development of mountain areas. In *International law and protection of mountain areas*, ed. T. Treves, L. Pineshi, and A. Fodella. Milan, Italy: Giuffrè Editore.

402   Land and post-conflict peacebuilding

GEF (Global Environment Facility), UNEP (United Nations Environment Programme), and UNU (United Nations University). 2008. *GEF/UNEP/UNU Sustainable Land Management in the High Pamir and Pamir-Alai Mountains Project—An Integrated and Transboundary Initiative in Central Asia: Inception report.* Washington, D.C.

GOT (Government of Tajikistan). 2002. *Economic development programme for Tajikistan until 2015.* Dushanbe, Tajikistan.

Griffin, J. D., S. Cumming, M. Metcalfe, M. t'Sas-Rolfes, and J. Singh. 1999. *Transboundary natural resource management in southern Africa: Main report.* Washington, D.C.: Biodiversity Support Program, World Wildlife Fund.

Hannam, I. D. 2006a. *Synthesis report: The legal, policy and institutional aspects of sustainable land management in the Pamir-Alai mountain environment.* Washington, D.C.: Global Environment Facility.

———. 2006b. *Transboundary regulatory frameworks and institutional arrangements: The legal, policy and institutional aspects of sustainable land management in the Pamir-Alai mountain environment.* Washington, D.C.: Global Environment Facility.

Heathershaw, J. 2007. Peacebuilding as practice: Discourses from post-conflict Tajikistan. *International Peacekeeping* 14 (2): 219–236.

———. 2009. *Post-conflict Tajikistan: The politics of peacebuilding and the emergence of legitimate order.* London: Routledge.

Kemp, R., S. Parto, and R. B. Gibson. 2005. Governance for sustainable development: Moving from theory to practice. *International Journal of Sustainable Development* 8 (1–2): 12–30.

Mullojanov, P. 2001. Civil society and peacebuilding. *Accord*, March.

———. 2005. Party building in Tajikistan. *Central Asia and the Caucasus—Journal of Social and Political Studies* 2 (32): 88–96.

Nzongola-Ntalaja, G. 2002. UNDP role in promoting good governance. Seminar for the international guests at the Congress of the Labour Party of Norway, November 9.

OECD (Organisation for Economic Co-operation and Development). 1997. *Final report of the ad hoc working group on participatory development and good governance.* Parts 1 and 2. Paris.

PALM (Sustainable Land Management in the High Pamir and Pamir-Alai Mountains). 2008. Sustainable Land Management in the High Pamir and Pamir-Alai Mountains— An Integrated and Transboundary Initiative in Central Asia: Project brief. Bishkek, Kyrgyzstan.

———. 2011. *Strategy and action plan for Sustainable Land Management in the High Pamir and Pamir-Alai Mountains.* Bishkek, Kyrgyzstan. www.ehs.unu.edu/palm/file/get/8238.

Schulz, A. 2007. Creating a legal framework for good transboundary water governance in the Zambezi and Incomati river basins. *Georgetown International Environmental Law Review* 19 (2): 117–183.

Toshmuhammadov, M. 2004. Civil war in Tajikistan and post-conflict rehabilitation. Paper presented at the Hokkaido University Slavic Research Center, 21st-century COE Program, "Making a Discipline of Slavic Eurasian Studies: Meso-Areas and Globalization," Sapporo, Japan.

UNEP (United Nations Environment Programme). 2005. Sustainable land management in the High Pamir and Pamir-Alai Mountains—An Integrated and Transboundary Initiative in Central Asia. Global Environment Facility (GEF) grant request, draft full project brief. www.ehs.unu.edu/file/download/3478.

University of New England. 2009. *Methodological research guidelines for legal task forces for analysing the capacity of legal, policy and institutional aspects of sustainable land management in the High Pamir and Pamir-Alai mountain environment.* Armidale, Australia.

UNU (United Nations University). 2009. *Strategic analysis of regional development and environmental issues.* Adapted from M. Giger, S. Mathez-Stiefel, and C. Ott, *Sustainable Development Appraisal* (2003). Bern, Switzerland: United Nations University / Centre for Development and Environment, Eastern and Southern Africa Partnership Programme.

World Bank. n.d. Tajikistan. http://data.worldbank.org/country/tajikistan.

Yusufjonova, Z. 2005. Peacebuilding in Tajikistan. The Beyond Intractability Project. University of Colorado. www.beyondintractability.org/case_studies/tajikistan.jsp?nid =5304.

PART 4

Laws and policies

Introduction

Specific tools and techniques for managing post-conflict land issues, such as those described in part 3, must be applied in a manner that takes into account local laws, legal traditions, and policies in order to resolve disputes sustainably, make lasting change, and lay the foundation for a durable peace. Where inequitable access to and distribution of land was a contributing cause of the conflict, it is often necessary to review and revise the national legal and policy framework in order to identify causes of discrimination and exclusion. Even where grievances over land were not a contributing cause to the conflict, such review and revision may be necessary to support livelihoods and economic development. In both instances, it is important to consider not only the formal statutory and regulatory framework, but also any relevant traditional or customary norms and institutions, as well as Islamic law traditions in the countries where they are practiced.

An improved post-conflict legal and policy framework is also important to guarantee the protection of housing, land, and property (HLP) rights and to prevent arbitrary interferences with those rights, such as forced evictions. With the recent spread of large-scale land acquisitions in post-conflict countries, effective laws and policies have gained renewed importance.

The five chapters in this part examine the opportunities and conditions for developing, revising, and implementing land laws and policies in post-conflict countries, as well as the challenges that face post-conflict countries and the institutions providing assistance. Together they highlight the need for a broad view of law and policies that encompasses statutes and regulations, administrative practices, custom, and (where relevant) Islamic norms and institutions.

Laws and policies addressing return and restitution—discussed in detail in part 2 of this book—often link to broader questions of suitable post-conflict frameworks for land administration. The first two chapters in this part focus on efforts to create a suitable legal framework for land management in post-conflict Cambodia. In "Title through Possession or Position? Respect for Housing, Land, and Property Rights in Cambodia," Rhodri C. Williams discusses widespread post-conflict violations of HLP rights in Cambodia and the challenges associated with the implementation of a legal framework for the protection of those rights. Two decades after the 1991 Paris Peace Agreements, insecure land tenure, rapid urbanization, and forced evictions continue to create internal displacement, threaten people's livelihoods, and potentially undermine national stability. Williams examines the roles of the Cambodian authorities, domestic nongovernmental organizations (NGOs), and international organizations in the failure over the past decade to engender full respect for HLP rights and to guarantee accountability for abuses in accordance with the provisions of Cambodia's groundbreaking 2001 Land Law.

408   Land and post-conflict peacebuilding

Manami Sekiguchi and Naomi Hatsukano take a different view of developments in Cambodia. In "Land Conflicts and Land Registration in Cambodia," they provide a historical overview of land regime changes, land disputes, and the failure of management policies since the fall of the Khmer Rouge in 1979. Analyzing the evolution of the Cambodian legal and policy framework, they highlight how the merging of overlapping legal systems has contributed to ambiguity and to the contestation of land rights. Sekiguchi and Hatsukano are particularly critical of what they characterize as international actors' failure to incorporate customary norms, institutions, and practices into statutory frameworks, particularly the 2001 Land Law. The authors conclude by stressing the practical importance of incorporating customary law into the legal and policy frameworks governing land management in post-conflict countries, which usually have limited human resources and less implementation capacity.

Legal pluralism—the de facto and often deliberate coexistence of multiple legal systems (statutory, customary, and religious)—is both an opportunity and a challenge for post-conflict societies. The opportunities for applying customary and religious law arise largely from some post-conflict governments' lack of capacity to enforce their laws and to exert their will in remote parts of the country. Local familiarity with and the perceived legitimacy of customary and religious law help to ensure its application and people's adherence to it. However, locally legitimate laws may conflict with national laws and international human rights obligations—for example, regarding the rights of women and minority populations. Another challenge arises from the potential for conflicts with formal legal instruments, such as international treaties, national constitutions, peace agreements, national laws, and subnational ordinances.

In "Legal Frameworks and Land Issues in Muslim Mindanao," Paula Defensor Knack examines the complex relationship between land laws and land conflict deriving from the demand of Muslims from Autonomous Mindanao to set up an expanded autonomous entity (the Bangsamoro Juridical Entity), from the current Autonomous Region in Muslim Mindanao. Defensor Knack traces the roots and evolution of the conflict from the colonial period, through the Spanish and American regimes, to the two peace agreements, in 1976 and 1996, that led to the creation of the Autonomous Region in Muslim Mindanao. She explores the political aspects of the territorial dispute, economic and livelihood issues, and a number of key legislative and constitutional law debates that have been of central significance to peace negotiations. Defensor Knack concludes that for political and social stability to be achieved in post-conflict Mindanao, a clear definition of territorial and jurisdictional boundaries is necessary for genuine autonomy in contrast to outright secession, which is prohibited by the constitution.

Like customary law, Islamic law can play a substantial and often synergetic role in land law. In "Unexplored Dimensions: Islamic Land Systems in Afghanistan, Indonesia, Iraq, and Somalia," Siraj Sait points out that people often conflate Islamic law and customary law governing land, and he describes Islamic land management tools as applied in four Islamic post-conflict countries with dissimilar economic, political, and legal systems and institutions. Sait considers the political risks and human rights trade-offs (particularly regarding gender) associated with the adoption of Islamic land management practices and laws in post-conflict Muslim societies. He argues that it is possible for Islamic tenure models to be effective tools to secure HLP rights while respecting women's rights, and contends that the failure of peacebuilding institutions to consider Islamic law and institutions following conflict is both a mistake and a missed opportunity. Sait concludes that the appropriate use of Islamic land management tools has the potential to enhance peacebuilding through the application of flexible, practicable, and locally familiar solutions.

Customary law can be particularly important in post-conflict societies that lack a well-established statutory framework. In "Customary Law and Community-Based Natural Resource Management in Post-Conflict Timor-Leste," Naori Miyazawa examines the critical role played by the customary law system of *tara bandu* in the post-conflict recovery of Timor-Leste. The application of customary law—which was recognized by the newly established government—has enabled villages to manage natural resources for daily use and to adapt rules to specific local conditions. Miyazawa concludes by highlighting the priority that the government places on developing statutory laws and combining them with customary law in a multilayered system for managing natural resources.

In sum, this part highlights three key lessons regarding how laws and policies can help to resolve land tenure issues and strengthen post-conflict peacebuilding. First, the establishment of a clear legal framework for land tenure and management is important, but it is also necessary that such a framework engage constructively with customary and (where appropriate) Islamic norms and institutions. Second, international organizations and NGOs can provide substantial assistance in the development and implementation of land laws and policies, including the incorporation of international standards and best practices, but they also need to demonstrate openness to local legal traditions and contextual issues. This lesson echoes a core observation from the analysis in part 2 on the application of the Principles on Housing and Property Restitution for Refugees and Displaced Persons (also known as the Pinheiro Principles) in responses to displacement and dispossession. Third, resolution of land disputes needs to be tailored to the local context and can often benefit from the integration of traditional institutions. These lessons are important to the development, revision, and implementation of laws and policies governing return, restitution, and longer-term HLP rights.

Title through possession or position? Respect for housing, land, and property rights in Cambodia

Rhodri C. Williams

Two decades after the 1991 Paris Peace Agreements, widespread violations of housing, land, and property (HLP) rights represent a new threat to Cambodia's fledgling stability. Despite domestic and international efforts to protect HLP rights through legislative reform and institutional capacity building, respect for these rights has deteriorated during this period according to almost any indicator.

In the countryside, home to approximately 85 percent of the Cambodian population, landholdings are increasingly skewed, with hard-pressed subsistence farmers often forced to sell to urban speculators who hold large plots of arable land idle. Although rural land was relatively equitably distributed in the 1980s, landlessness subsequently mushroomed from 13 percent in the late 1990s to 20 percent in 2004. Meanwhile, programs meant to distribute land back to the rural poor have not been implemented. A prominent nongovernmental organization (NGO), the Cambodian Center for Human Rights, has seen land disputes rise to "human rights and social problem number one" for rural Cambodians participating in its regular public forums (Cambodian Center for Human Rights 2006a, 2).

Insecure rural tenure and landlessness have exacerbated encroachment on forest lands inhabited by Cambodia's indigenous population, much of these lands have already been devastated by years of unregulated logging and resource exploitation. The most visible result of rural impoverishment has been migration from the countryside to Cambodia's cities, and particularly to the capital, Phnom Penh. Rural migrants have swelled the ranks of the urban poor, creating a population of unskilled casual workers who live in informal settlements under unremittingly poor conditions and with precarious tenure. Although Cambodia has experienced sustained economic growth since the 1991 peace agreement, the benefits have accrued primarily to wealthier, urban segments of the population, and flight from the relatively stagnant countryside has intensified pressure on the urban settlements where migrants tend to congregate (World Bank 2006b).

Rhodri C. Williams is a human rights lawyer who specializes in land and forced-migration issues. An earlier version of this chapter appeared as a Center on Housing Rights and Evictions occasional paper in November 2008.

412   Land and post-conflict peacebuilding

Facing competition between the housing needs of urban residents and the development plans of large commercial interests, local authorities have consistently sided with the latter. As a result, many long-term residents of urban neighborhoods have faced relocation under legally dubious circumstances, ranging from inadequately compensated expropriations to violent forced evictions. In Phnom Penh, 11,000 families, or approximately 55,000 people, were evicted between 1998 and 2003, under circumstances that frequently violated their rights and impaired their standard of living (Asian Coalition for Housing Rights 2005). Today it is estimated that approximately 70,000 people are threatened with forced eviction in Phnom Penh, and at least 150,000 people live in fear of eviction from their homes and land nationwide. Increasing numbers of Cambodia's poor currently live under conditions perhaps most aptly described as internal displacement.

This chapter provides an overview of developments with regard to HLP rights in Cambodia, focusing on the last decade—a period during which international engagement with these issues has been both more intense and more controversial than during the immediate aftermath of Cambodia's political transition in the early 1990s (Williams 2008). An overview of the current political and legal context for implementing HLP rights is followed by a brief historical description of the lingering effects of collectivization, displacement, and privatization during the decades prior to the 1991 peace settlement. Next, the chapter provides an overview of more recent efforts by the Cambodian authorities, domestic NGOs, and international organizations to improve respect for HLP rights in contemporary Cambodia, as well as outstanding problems and obstacles. Finally, the chapter concludes with recommendations for international and domestic actors.

BACKGROUND: DEMOCRACY, PATRONAGE, AND HUMAN RIGHTS IN CAMBODIA

The problems of insecure tenure and inequitable access to HLP resources in Cambodia are exacerbated by structural factors such as demographic pressure, the lingering effects of decades of conflict, increasing urbanization, and persistent rural and urban poverty. However, much of the problem is also political. One of the main barriers to equitable HLP access, as well as the exercise of many other human rights, is the persistence of unaccountable and corrupt patronage-based networks that hold power at all levels of government.

Since the destruction of Cambodia's economy and the killing of much of its skilled workforce by the Khmer Rouge regime (1975–1979), successive Cambodian governments have struggled to staff and finance local administration and provide public services. In many cases, this was achieved through delegations of power to existing local authorities, which created layers of bureaucrats whom the government could not afford to pay. This in turn led to a revival of traditional Cambodian practices in which public servants buy their offices from more powerful patrons (Chandler 2000). In order to pay their debts—and make

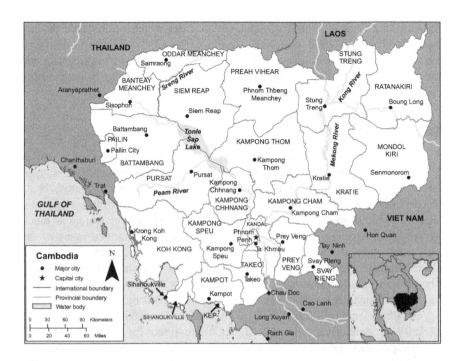

ends meet—officials are then tacitly expected to skim public proceeds and impose unofficial fees for services.

The prevalence of corruption in contemporary Cambodia dictates that access to many essential public services, ranging from issuance of land title certificates to medical treatment and education, tends to be contingent on the payment of bribes that are often unaffordable to the poor (Nissen 2005). These conditions also undermine the rule of law, resulting in the selective and arbitrary application of legal protections by courts vulnerable to political pressure and bribery. Perhaps most significantly, economic liberalization has increased the value of housing, land, and natural resources, drawing them further into competition among ordinary Cambodians, who see them as prerequisites for subsistence, and the rich and powerful, who view them as commodities subject to speculation and trade. As a result, genuine progress in the protection of HLP rights is likely to require a confrontation with entrenched political practices and powerful vested interests.

Cambodia is currently governed by the Cambodian People's Party (CPP), headed by long-standing prime minister Hun Sen. The CPP is the direct successor to the communist regime that ruled Cambodia from the fall of the Khmer Rouge in 1979 until the transition to multiparty democracy under the 1991 peace agreement. This agreement formally reconciled the CPP with opposition elements and led to UN-administered multiparty elections in 1993. Although the CPP failed to win a majority in the 1993 elections, it maintained de facto power through its control of local patronage networks and later resorted to intimidation and outright

414   Land and post-conflict peacebuilding

military attacks on its political opponents in order to regain and hold de jure power in the 1998, 2003, and 2008 elections. The CPP continues to dominate the political environment today. Despite the promises of the peace agreement and the nation-building efforts of the 1990s, the Cambodia of today has made little progress in adopting the rule of law and genuinely democratic governance.

The role of the international community

The record of the international community in discouraging human rights abuses in Cambodia has been mixed. On one hand, international observers have enjoyed largely unobstructed access to the country and cooperation with a vigorous NGO sector. International organizations have also had a great deal of leverage, not least by virtue of the fact that international aid continues to constitute as much as half of Cambodia's gross domestic product. Cambodia ratified many of the major multilateral human rights treaties as early as 1992, including the International Covenants on Civil and Political Rights and on Economic, Social and Cultural Rights. The UN transitional administration, set up to administer the first Cambodian elections, included a human rights component that was succeeded by an institutionalized Special Representative of the Secretary-General for Human Rights in Cambodia, as well as a local office of the UN High Commissioner for Human Rights.

Despite these promising conditions at the outset, international and domestic pressure has not succeeded in stemming human rights violations in Cambodia. The international community, comprising numerous international humanitarian and development agencies, NGOs, and bilateral donors, is vulnerable to criticism for at least two tendencies that have undermined its effectiveness in addressing HLP and other violations.

First, international organizations frequently appear to emphasize process over outcomes, with observation of the forms of human rights and democracy taken at face value. The most notorious example may be the 1997 coup de force in which the CPP unleashed a military assault on a rival political party, summarily executing much of its leadership and driving it underground (HRW 1997). Cambodia's application for membership in the Association of Southeast Asian Nations (ASEAN) was suspended as a result—but only until the next year's elections gave the CPP a fresh (albeit disputed) mandate. This approach gives rise to concern that elements of the international community have tacitly accepted the CPP's heretofore illiberal approach to democracy and human rights as the price to be paid for the fundamental stability it has brought to Cambodia after decades of conflict.

A second concern involves the tendency of the international community to focus on Cambodia's HLP issues from a development perspective, in a manner that can marginalize discussion of the government's human rights obligations. For example, the Consultative Group, an important annual meeting between the Cambodian government and bilateral donors, framed Cambodia's natural resources and land issues almost exclusively in terms of human development and governance

Housing, land, and property rights in Cambodia   415

(World Bank 2006a). While pro-poor development is undoubtedly crucial, explicit reference to and recognition of the obligations to respect and comply with human rights duties is vital to ensuring that development is inclusive and occurs within a framework that prioritizes participation, citizen empowerment, and human dignity.

The legal framework for HLP rights in Cambodia

Concerns about respect for human rights are particularly salient with regard to housing rights, which have been, at best, tangentially covered in a developing legal framework that is primarily concerned with safeguarding property interests. Cambodia is obligated under the terms of the International Covenant on Economic, Social and Cultural Rights to protect the right to adequate housing by all appropriate means, including the adoption of legislation and the provision of judicial remedies. This treaty entails state obligations to affirmatively guarantee security of land tenure and facilitate access to housing that is affordable, habitable, accessible, culturally adequate, appropriately located, and provided with adequate services and infrastructure. According to the UN Committee on Economic, Social, and Cultural Rights, such measures to ensure equitable access to housing should also extend to land (UN CESCR 1991):[1]

> Within many States parties increasing access to land by landless or impoverished segments of the society should constitute a central policy goal. Discernible governmental obligations need to be developed aiming to substantiate the right of all to a secure place to live in peace and dignity, including access to land as an entitlement (UN CESCR 1991, art. 8(c)).

The most important protection guaranteed by the right to adequate housing is security of tenure, or legal protection against forced evictions, which have been defined as "permanent or temporary removal against their will of individuals, families and/or communities from the homes and/or land which they occupy, without the provision of, and access to, appropriate forms of legal or other protection" (UN CESCR 1997, 3). Under international law, evictions are lawful only under exceptional circumstances, in situations where they serve a compelling public interest and where all feasible alternatives have been explored in a process of genuine consultation with those affected. In cases where evictions are deemed justified, they must comply with the principle of proportionality and incorporate procedural protections, including adequate notice, the full disclosure of relevant information, ongoing consultation, and the availability of effective complaint procedures. Under no circumstances should excessive force be used.

---

[1] With regard to housing, the committee recommends that states "establish housing subsidies for those unable to obtain affordable housing, as well as forms and levels of housing finance which adequately reflect housing needs" (UN CESCR 1991, art. 8(c)).

416 Land and post-conflict peacebuilding

Evictions must not render individuals homeless or vulnerable to the violation of other human rights. Therefore the government must ensure that adequate alternative housing and land is provided, in consultation with the affected families. Where these requirements are not met, victims of forced eviction are entitled to a legal remedy, even in cases where they did not enjoy full ownership rights to their homes (UNCHR 1993).[2]

Forced evictions that occur in the context of rapid development have been recognized as a growing threat to the exercise of housing rights in Cambodia and beyond (Kothari 2006a). Where such evictions affect large populations, as in Cambodia, it is necessary to inquire whether the state is contributing, through its actions or inaction, to human rights violations giving rise to the emergence of an internally displaced population.

To date in Cambodia, the international community has sought to address the effects of tenure insecurity and forced evictions primarily by sponsoring legislative and institutional measures to protect property rights. Since the 1993 elections, international donors have invested significant resources and efforts in drafting processes that resulted in a 2001 update of Cambodia's Land Law as well as numerous related regulations and decrees. On the basis of this legal regime, international organizations have supported an ambitious scheme to demarcate, register, and administer all of Cambodia's land. However, such efforts have often failed to recognize the complementarity of development goals and human rights standards. Meanwhile, the concrete impact of donor projects continues to be limited by the unaccountability of the politically connected beneficiaries of illegal land transfers. Without greater emphasis on human rights compliance, painstakingly drafted laws and standards will be bypassed, and forced evictions, expropriations, and concessions of land and other natural resources to powerful interests will continue.

Codification processes are undoubtedly a crucial first step in securing the observation of HLP rights in Cambodia. Domestic laws can, at the very least, force irregularities into the open and provide an important practical basis for ordinary citizens to understand and realize their rights. However, unless such legal drafting is accompanied by unified international insistence that legislative rules be applied consistently, impartially, and in the spirit of Cambodia's international obligations, donor-sponsored laws run the risk of becoming Potemkin villages, adopted to placate international critics but disappointing the expectations of ordinary Cambodians. The former Special Representative of the Secretary-General for Human Rights in Cambodia, Yash Ghai, provoked debate by advocating that international organizations in Cambodia begin more actively advocating respect for human rights:

---

[2] The UN Commission on Human Rights condemned the practice of forced evictions as a "gross violation of human rights" and urges governments to provide remedies to those forcibly evicted (UNCHR 1993, para. 1).

Housing, land, and property rights in Cambodia   417

It is not sufficient to rely on technical assistance and capacity building. . . . Nor are new laws or suddenly created institutions the panacea, for the Government has disregarded laws or, through abuse, turned them to its own partisan advantage, and it has set up new institutions instead of making existing ones work (UNHRC 2006, 4).

HLP rights in Cambodia in historical perspective

Customary law governing land rights in Cambodia traditionally provided that legitimate possession followed the occupation and use of land. In a country dependent on rice farming, peasants were entitled to hold land they had cleared and cultivated, but they lost all claims to land they had stopped using. The French, who colonized Cambodia in the mid-nineteenth century, attempted to replace such use-based rights of possession with title-based rights of ownership, but were largely unsuccessful outside of the cities. Cambodia became independent after World War II and maintained a policy of nonalignment during the early years of the Cold War. However, by the early 1970s, Cambodia had allied itself with the U.S. war effort in neighboring Viet Nam and found itself facing an increasingly powerful domestic communist insurgency, the Khmer Rouge.

In 1975, Phnom Penh fell to the Khmer Rouge, which introduced a radical regime of collectivization, whereby Cambodia's cities and traditional institutions were abandoned and the entire population was forced to work the land. Within weeks, Cambodia's urban areas had been entirely evacuated. Educated Cambodians were singled out for summary execution, and the rest of the population was put to work under inhuman conditions on collective farms. All housing and land became the property of the state, and property records were systematically destroyed. During the five-year reign of the Khmer Rouge, an estimated 1 to 2 million people—as much as a fifth of the population—were murdered or died of overwork, starvation, and disease.

In 1979, Viet Nam responded to a series of border clashes with the Khmer Rouge by invading Cambodia. The Khmer Rouge leadership was driven across Cambodia's western border into Thailand and replaced by a Vietnamese-backed communist regime, the People's Republic of Kampuchea (PRK). Although the PRK promised to allow those displaced by the Khmer Rouge to return to their homes, they did not renounce the collectivization of land, and they initially blocked return to the cities, confiscating prime urban real estate for their own high officials. In response to this and other PRK policies, many educated former urban dwellers also fled to Thailand, forming an alliance of necessity with the remnants of the regime that had sought to exterminate them. During the 1980s, Cambodia became one of the Cold War's last proxy conflicts, with the PRK (backed by Viet Nam and the Soviet Union) locked in a military stalemate with rebel elements in Thailand (backed by China and, tacitly, the United States).

Beginning in the mid-1980s, the PRK undertook pragmatic reforms, including decollectivization of land and property and the granting of concessions to exploit

418   Land and post-conflict peacebuilding

natural resources. The administration of these tasks was delegated to local functionaries, resulting in haphazard implementation. Land distribution in particular tended to be skewed by patronage ties but nevertheless resulted in a broadly equitable distribution of land, from which most rural households benefited. Exploitation of timber and other resources fell under the control of local military units that enjoyed unrestricted access to wilderness areas.

In 1989, the PRK began a transition from communism that began with changing the country's name to the State of Cambodia (SOC) and renaming the ruling communist party the Cambodian People's Party (CPP). The authorities also privatized housing and land, a reform carried out with the implicit intent of cutting off claims by the 360,000 Cambodians then in exile by vesting title in whoever happened to be occupying their former homes or lands at the time. The introduction of a formal market in land came as a shock to a society where decades of conflict had inhibited the gradual transition from customary use-based land tenure to title-based ownership rights that had been seen in other developing countries (CDRI 2001). As a result, privatization was often a free-for-all, with title issuance in both urban and rural contexts contingent on bribes and political influence, and many smallholders dispossessed or forced into debt.

By the late 1990s, fewer than 15 percent of the estimated 4 to 5 million applications for registration dating from this time had been processed, in part because of widespread refusal to pay unofficial fees up to one hundred times greater than the official price of registration (CDRI 2001). The resulting legal ambiguity left many small farmers exposed to outright land grabbing or subject to distress sales of their property at low prices. Meanwhile, the lack of other attractive domestic investment opportunities in Cambodia encouraged land speculation by the wealthy, which rendered idle large agricultural plots in the midst of increasing rural landlessness. The situation was aggravated by a nearly unregulated program of land concessions for the purpose of commercial exploitation by private enterprises. At their height, such concessions took up over one third of Cambodia's most productive land, and they continue to restrict access to a large proportion of the country's arable fields (Leuprecht 2004).[3]

Meanwhile, the end of the Cold War led to a political transition in Cambodia in the form of the 1991 Paris Peace Agreements. This treaty ended the war between the CPP and opposition factions based in Thailand and set out a framework for UN-administered elections. Although the agreement called for the repatriation of the 360,000 Cambodian refugees from camps in Thailand, no specific provision was made for the restitution of their homes, lands, and properties. In fact, although repatriation was successfully carried out, attempts merely to provide returnees with land for farming were frustrated by uncooperative local authorities and widespread landmine contamination. These factors contributed in turn to the present problem of rural landlessness. In 1992, the SOC formalized its

---

[3] Much of the land held under concession has yet to be developed or exploited by the beneficiary firms.

Housing, land, and property rights in Cambodia **419**

reallocation of property rights by passing a land law extinguishing all pre-1979 rights to land.

Control of HLP resources has been an important factor in the exercise of political power in post-conflict Cambodia. By locking in control over the ownership and allocation of land and homes before the Paris Peace Agreements, the CPP not only denied these assets to its political opponents but also rewarded the functionaries within its own patronage network. The political nature of the CPP's allocation and privatization programs dictated that HLP resources were diverted away from ordinary citizens and farmers to the benefit of the political elite. The way in which land distribution and privatization programs were implemented emphasized the primacy of political connections, rather than possession or need, in securing and defending rights to HLP resources. The effect was to decrease access to land rather than to increase it.

The long-term results of this approach to HLP resources have been negative. Tenure insecurity has increased inequality, both between the stagnant countryside and the relatively prosperous cities, and between subsistence farmers whose informal landholdings are under constant threat and urban speculators whose acquisitions are recognized and protected by the state. As a result, the World Bank has noted that Cambodia's post-conflict economic growth has been accompanied by an unusually marked rise in inequality, and that failure to achieve more equitable growth could hinder both further economic progress and the achievement of Cambodia's Millennium Development Goals (World Bank 2006b).

THE 2001 LAND LAW REGIME AND OBSTACLES TO ITS IMPLEMENTATION

The Land Law of 1992 included a prospective mechanism for acquisition of land by prescription. This provision allowed those who peacefully used land for five years to apply for a title, but the extent to which the provision was effective in increasing access to land is unclear (EWMI 2003).[4] Meanwhile, human rights observers noted that general protection of HLP rights continued to deteriorate after the 1993 elections and the departure of the UN transitional authority. Large-scale land acquisitions (often referred to as land grabbing), forced evictions, and unregulated concessions of land and other natural resources for exploitation contributed to a general perception that high-ranking political and business interests were conspiring to "eat the kingdom" (Leuprecht 2004, 36).

In the late 1990s, international donors encouraged the drafting of new legislation to better regulate land issues. The resulting 2001 Land Law created a legal framework that went a long way, on paper, toward securing rights to land and housing. It recognized acquisitive possession by those who had begun their occupation at least five years prior to its passage, but stipulated that future land

---

[4] Lack of awareness of an application requirement limited the effectiveness of this provision.

420   Land and post-conflict peacebuilding

distribution was meant to take place through a more organized system of officially administered "social land concessions" rather than individual self-help. It also protected existing property rights by conditioning expropriation on public-interest grounds, legal process, and "fair and just compensation." In one of its most innovative provisions, the law also recognized indigenous groups' collective ownership rights to their traditional lands. Over the long term, all of these rights are to be protected by a comprehensive titling and demarcation regime in which all of Cambodia's land is to be registered and mapped.

The drafting process for the 2001 Land Law set a Cambodian precedent in terms of transparency and consultation of affected groups, but it was initiated primarily by international organizations—including the Asian Development Bank, which had imposed economic conditionality measures—and it had an uncertain level of commitment from the Cambodian government (Simbolon 2002). Moreover, even at the time of its promulgation, the 2001 Land Law was viewed only as "a blueprint for reform" that would require the passage of at least fifteen government regulations ("sub-decrees" in Cambodian legal parlance) in order to be fully operational (EWMI 2001, 1). As a result, the process of drafting and approval of sub-decrees has caused significant delay in the application of the 2001 Land Law (World Bank 2004).

The justification for the 2001 Land Law was framed almost exclusively in terms of the need to implement the protection of property set out in the 1993 constitution, completing the transition from collective socialist tenure forms to market-compatible ownership rights (EWMI 2001). However, the law also has serious implications in terms of the Cambodian authorities' general constitutional obligation to respect their subjects' human rights "as stipulated in the United Nations Charter, the Universal Declaration of Human Rights, and the covenants and conventions related to human rights."[5] Nevertheless, where the Land Law could facilitate an increased degree of respect for property rights if fully implemented, its provisions on their own would not be sufficient to ensure full respect for broader HLP rights, and particularly the right to adequate housing.

A further challenge to full implementation of the Land Law and broader protection of HLP rights is the ongoing lack of capacity and resources at the central level. De facto or even de jure control over complicated HLP issues is often delegated to local authorities without sufficient guidance or oversight, reinforcing their tendency to exercise power in unaccountable and corrupt ways. While the Cambodian government routinely condemns official corruption and malfeasance, it takes few concrete steps to actually prevent or remedy such practices. As a result, although domestic NGOs have brought abuses to light and international donors have supported legal drafting processes to address them, the Cambodian authorities have largely failed to fulfill their corresponding responsibility: enforcement of the law in light of their human rights obligations. This failure is manifested in a number of interrelated problems, including lack of

---

[5] Constitution of the Kingdom of Cambodia, ch. III, art. 31.

Housing, land, and property rights in Cambodia 421

accountability for violations of HLP rights, failure to act in accordance with the law, lack of demarcation of land, irregular expropriations, urban forced evictions, failure to secure access to rural land and urban housing, and failure to secure the HLP rights of vulnerable groups.

Lack of accountability for past and ongoing violations of HLP rights

Many of Cambodia's most powerful civilian and military officials have been credibly accused of abusing their authority in order to acquire land and other natural resources for their personal enrichment (Global Witness 2007, 2009). Accusations of land grabbing and irregular allocations run throughout the political spectrum and extend from the central authorities in Phnom Penh down to local political bosses. Some holders of dubiously acquired land have allegedly granted it in the form of economic concessions to domestic enterprises or foreign investors, while others exploit it themselves or simply engage in speculation, indefinitely excluding poor subsistence farmers from large swaths of Cambodia's increasingly scarce productive land.

The prevalence of such practices undermines the rule of law and aggravates rural poverty and landlessness. Without the return of much or all of the land that has been lawlessly appropriated since the early 1990s, the government's plans for land distribution to the poor and vulnerable are likely to fail. Furthermore, local authorities responsible for identifying land currently available for distribution in the form of social land concessions have tended to point out unproductive and inaccessible plots rather than risk exposing more productive tracts that are lying fallow as a result of their own or others' illegal claims (World Bank 2004).

The 2001 Land Law framework includes a number of mechanisms for freeing up arable land for social concessions. The most obvious source of land for distribution is degraded forest, but sole reliance on this category would create additional pressure on Cambodia's remaining healthy forest areas, many of which are already threatened by logging and agro-industry concerns. Another potential source of land is a mechanism in the Land Law for reviewing pre-2001 economic concessions that would allow territory granted in excess of a set maximum size to be taken back, or for concessions to be revoked where no development has taken place within set time limits.[6] However, there has been little progress so far in the process, as strict enforcement would involve challenging the powerful interests, often close to the government, that allocated and received the concessions.

The third available mechanism for recouping land for distribution involves a review process for land disputes that would allow the identification and redemption

---

[6] Chapter 5 of the 2001 Land Law sets out conditions for economic land concessions, including a maximum size of ten thousand hectares and a requirement that each concession be exploited in the manner agreed within twelve months of its issuance. Failure to comply with these conditions can render a concession null and void under article 18, requiring the concessionaire to vacate the property under article 19.

422   Land and post-conflict peacebuilding

of illegal confiscations and transfers. As with review of economic concessions, this process represents an acid test of the political establishment's commitment to the rule of law, given that it has benefited at virtually all levels from irregular transactions in land. In practice, the formal review mechanism under the Land Law is widely viewed as having failed. A system of cadastral commissions set up in support of the broader titling process under the 2001 Land Law has made some headway in resolving local boundary disputes, but has proved unable to resolve more than a fraction of the hundreds of pending complaints involving land grabbing by powerful people.

In light of this limited progress, both the international community and domestic NGOs were taken by surprise by a February 2006 royal decree on the formation of a new National Authority for Land Dispute Resolution. A subsequent decree appointed a membership for the new body that was a compendium of CPP powerbrokers and, in the words of one observer, a "who's-who of the regime's biggest land-grabbers."[7] Although the new National Authority appeared to have the political clout to tackle many of the most controversial cases, concerns remain about the potential for its members to abuse their position to protect their own past transgressions from scrutiny. However, given that the National Authority was announced just days prior to the 2006 Consultative Group, observers speculate that the initiative may have simply been meant to deflect international criticism of the failure of the cadastral commissions to resolve high-profile disputes.

Failure to act in accordance with law

Cambodian authorities often proceed without reference to the Land Law and other relevant regulations in carrying out important actions affecting HLP rights. While this may be in part because of unfamiliarity with the legal regime, many observers infer that the authorities simply wish to be able to continue to act as they see fit without having their hands tied by rules. The government's demonstrated disregard for the law has undermined public confidence in the new Land Law regime, which was built up through painstaking efforts to consult affected parties and proceed transparently (Adler, Porter, and Woolcock 2008).

Some of the most drastic examples of the failure of Cambodian authorities to act within the law have been provided in the context of urban evictions. For instance, in 2004 and 2005, the municipal authorities in Phnom Penh sought the eviction of residents of Koh Pich Island who claimed to have acquired valid legal interests to their lands through possession, in accordance with the 2001 Land Law. Despite the fact that the cadastral commissions have exclusive jurisdiction over cases involving such unregistered property rights, the authorities sought and won a judicial eviction order, bypassing the 2001 Land Law entirely (Kothari 2006b).

---

[7] Sub-decree on the Composition of the National Authority for Land Dispute Resolution, Ref. No. 168, March 16, 2006.

Housing, land, and property rights in Cambodia **423**

The Cambodian authorities have also flouted the Land Law regime by selling prime urban land occupied by public institutions to private investors through land exchanges or swaps. Although such public institutions are, by definition, located on inalienable state public land, they have been sold to private investors in exchange for a promise to rebuild them elsewhere. Technically, public properties that have lost their public-interest use can be converted to state private property by special legislation and sold.[8] However, cases have involved functioning police stations, hospitals, and university campuses where, in some cases, hundreds of employees and their families had lived for decades (Kothari 2006b). Alienation of such manifestly public-interest institutions is not only illegal under the Land Law but has led to numerous forced evictions, in violation of Cambodia's international obligations.

Even ostensibly protective actions such as the provision of alternative land to persons evicted from informal settlements take place without reference to law. In June 2006, some 1,200 families were forcibly relocated from settlements near the Bassac River in central Phnom Penh to undeveloped land in villages twenty kilometers away without receiving even minimal information about who owned the land they were to occupy, whether or how the authorities acquired it, how long they were entitled to remain, whether public services and utilities would be provided, and whether they would eventually be eligible to receive title (Cambodian Center for Human Rights 2006b). The families continue to live on the resettlement land in dire circumstances, without access to potable water, sanitation, health facilities, or other basic services and infrastructure.

Lack of demarcation

One of the fundamental challenges to protecting property interests of all kinds in Cambodia is the lack of demarcation of land. Under the Land Law regime, virtually all rights and obligations adhering to land and property depend on its classification in one of four broad categories: individually owned property, collectively owned indigenous land, state-owned property available for sale or concession ("state private land"), or inalienable state-owned property ("state public land"). State private land is meant to be available for both economic land concessions to business interests and social land concessions for the poor and vulnerable.

Although previous registration programs were initiated under the French and the SOC, they were never fully implemented. Until its discontinuation in September 2009, an internationally sponsored Land Management and Administration Project (LMAP) worked together with the domestic authorities on an ambitious agenda of legal drafting, capacity building, dispute resolution, land management, and, crucially, land titling and registration. The titling program had focused on the main agricultural areas in Cambodia, where the bulk of the population lives.

---

[8] Cambodia Land Law of 2001, arts. 15–16.

424   Land and post-conflict peacebuilding

Using trained teams of Cambodian surveyors, LMAP proceeded on the basis of on-site work in communes and issued nearly 1.24 million titles by the time the program was discontinued (World Bank 2011). However, the process had been expected to take ten to fifteen years with estimates of unregistered titles in Cambodia initially running as high as 8 million.

The LMAP program's primary focus on privately owned agricultural property meant that urban poor communities with legal rights to apply for title under the 2001 Land Law remained vulnerable to urban land grabbing. The failure to address sensitive urban demarcation issues was ultimately LMAP's undoing. As described in a 2009 NGO report, World Bank officials on a June 2008 supervision mission failed to question government LMAP officials' classification of the entire Phnom Penh neighborhood of Boeung Kak as state land (Grimsditch and Henderson 2009). When the Bank reacted to this criticism by seeking to extend greater measures of social and economic protection to LMAP land adjudication in "disputed urban areas," the government of Cambodia withdrew its support for the project (World Bank 2009). The resulting forced evictions led to the case being referred to the World Bank Inspection Panel as an alleged violation of the World Bank's resettlement policy (Bugalski 2010). The panel eventually found that significant violations of the policy had occurred (World Bank 2011).

In the wake of LMAP, a number of other contested categories of rural land, such as inalienable state public land and protected indigenous areas, are likely to indefinitely remain without dispositive boundaries. This issue is of particular significance for households occupying land in the expectation that their occupation will result in title, in accordance with the system for land acquisition that was carried over from the 1992 Land Law. According to some estimates, as many as one-third of such families may ultimately find themselves occupying state public land (World Bank 2006b). This is likely to lead to situations in which some households are recognized as titleholders, while neighbors who held land under identical circumstances face eviction without compensation and even legal sanctions.[9]

Others likely to suffer as a result of the delay include indigenous minorities and other groups that practice shifting agriculture. Studies have shown that one of the most common forms of land grabbing has been the acquisition of lands that were within the known domain of subsistence farming communities but lying fallow and thus apparently unused at the time (CDRI 2001). Because of their political marginalization and limited understanding of the law and their rights, indigenous

---

[9] Such severe potential consequences of unlucky squatting derive from the fact that such squatters effectively fall under provisions of the Land Law meant to hold land grabbers and illegal concessionaires to account. Under article 18 of the 2001 Land Law, "any entering into possession of public properties of the State" is null and void "irrespective of the date of the creation of possession." Article 19 of the 2001 Land Law provides for uncompensated eviction in such cases as well as penalties for "intentional and fraudulent" acquisition of state public property.

Housing, land, and property rights in Cambodia **425**

groups have been one of the easiest targets for land grabbers. This gives rise to concerns that "there will be little land left to title" by the time registration programs arrive in Cambodia's highlands and forests (Leuprecht 2004, 24).

Lack of demarcation of alienable state private land also undercuts the reliability of past and current transactions involving state land. A series of government orders and sub-decrees in 2005 sought to address these problems by setting up a system of provisional classification of state land by local working groups as a basis for allowing such transactions pending final registration.[10] However, demarcation under these regulations is explicitly preliminary, and significant legal uncertainty is likely to attend all public and private investment in Cambodia's large expanses of unmapped land for years to come.

Irregular expropriations

Urban land in Cambodia has come under enormous pressure, particularly in the capital, Phnom Penh. Insecure tenure and landlessness has led many rural families to migrate to urban areas, where they congregate in informal settlements in order to access wage labor markets. While some of the earlier urban migrants may have claims under the Land Law to urban plots they have occupied since before 2001, the more recent arrivals are typically only able to find space as tenants.

Faced with these mounting residential needs, the municipal authorities of cities such as Phnom Penh are also presiding over a real estate boom, in which large investors are eager to develop high-end housing, hotels, and retail space. In Phnom Penh, as in many other developing cities, "the main political and economic actors are also the main land and [real] estate speculators" (Kothari 2006b, 15). It is therefore unsurprising that the government has regularly supported development over low-income housing, singling out the poorest and most vulnerable urban residents for eviction.

As mentioned above, evictions of urban residents with legal claims to title over properties they have occupied for years often involve apparent and even blatant violations of the 2001 Land Law. For instance, the 2005 clearance of Koh Pich Island in Phnom Penh affected many long-term residents presumptively entitled under the Land Law to register ownership of the plots they had lawfully possessed for years. However, rather than formally expropriating these rights or even challenging their existence through appropriate legal channels, the government harassed residents, insisted that they had to leave, and, when pressed, offered ad hoc compensation worth one-tenth of the land's estimated market value (CLEC-PILAP 2005).

Significant legal questions regarding expropriation remain unresolved. First, pending demarcation, claims of rights based on possession depend on a disputable assertion that the land involved is either private land or state private land, which

---

[10] Sub-decree on State Land Management, No. 118 ANK/BK, October 7, 2005.

426 Land and post-conflict peacebuilding

can be alienated, rather than belonging to one of the categories of state public land, which cannot.[11] Second, the provisions of the 2001 Land Law regulating expropriation are vague and formally require the passage of enabling legislation or regulations.[12] However, pending the completion of the legislative and regulatory framework, Cambodia remains bound by its broader international law obligations to ensure that its citizens are neither arbitrarily deprived of their property and possessions nor subjected to forced eviction and associated violations of the right to adequate housing. Any regulations or policies regarding expropriation must accord in full with these obligations under international human rights law.

Urban forced evictions

Cambodian authorities' failure to respect international obligations is even more pointed where no domestic law exists. This is currently the case with regard to urban communities that do not have arguable claims to title over the land they occupy. Under international law, even tenants in informal settlements enjoy the right to adequate housing, which entails the right to consultation and process, appeal against removal from their homes, remedies for forced evictions, and an expectation that the government will take steps to regularize their tenure and provide adequate infrastructure, services, and utilities in their neighborhoods. However, although the Cambodian authorities have adopted policies reflecting these obligations, they clearly do not view themselves as bound by them in practice.

Cambodia's national commitment to housing rights began in 2001 with the formulation of a National Housing Policy, which was subsequently adopted and includes provisions on financing and construction of low-income housing (Kothari 2006b). However, the extent to which this policy will shape urban planning in Cambodia is unclear. For instance, although the policy provides that housing programs should be included as an element of urban master plans, a master plan for Phnom Penh has been developed in a contemporaneous process that has suffered from a near complete lack of transparency or consultation with affected groups (Kothari 2006b).

In a move more immediately relevant to jeopardized urban settlements, on the eve of the July 2003 national elections, Prime Minister Hun Sen announced a policy of upgrading 100 poor communities every year for five years. This policy has been implemented in a few isolated cases where slum communities were provided assistance in improving their residential situations. However, it is generally deemed a failure, with implementation falling far short of the "systematic, large-scale programme to tackle slum upgrading" that would signify a real commitment to meeting Cambodia's adequate-housing obligations (Kothari 2006b, 15). Meanwhile evictions of urban poor communities have continued unabated, particularly in

---

[11] A list of categories of state public land is given in article 15 of the 2001 Land Law.

[12] Cambodian Land Law of 2001, art. 5: "An ownership deprivation shall be carried out in accordance with the forms and procedures provided by law and regulations."

Housing, land, and property rights in Cambodia 427

Phnom Penh. In a particularly sad irony, in 2006 the Phnom Penh authorities evicted 168 families who had received UN-HABITAT support in upgrading their own community in 1991. Their homes on the grounds of the Monivong Hospital were traded away in a dubious land swap (COHRE 2006).

Local and international scrutiny of forced evictions in Phnom Penh sharpened in 2006 with the violent forced eviction of the Sambok Chab community, who were living near the Bassac River waterfront (De Launey 2006). Although this community had existed since the 1990s, the land they occupied was claimed by a private company. Immediately prior to the eviction date, a Phnom Penh city official stated that an organized relocation was to take place and that title to plots of land and subsidized water would be provided to Bassac residents at peri-urban locations (Chhoeurn 2006).

In an interview, a representative of the Bassac community voiced concerns, noting that those who rented space instead of owning shacks—up to 80 percent of the population—were categorically excluded from relocation benefits.[13] The new land plots were believed to be completely bereft of services and utilities and were so far outside the city center that commuting costs would amount to twice the average daily income of local residents. The community leader feared violence in the short term, noting that with only five days to go most of the community remained unaware of the impending evictions. Over the long term she predicted that those relocated would sell their land plots to speculators and drift back to other urban slums, while the rest would be rendered at least temporarily homeless.

Some 1,200 families, comprising 6,000 people, were forcibly relocated to a site, Andoung, more than twenty kilometers from central Phnom Penh by early June 2006. The eviction itself involved intimidation and force, and additional concerns were raised by the conditions at the resettlement site. Both domestic and international observers referred to the situation as a humanitarian emergency (Kothari and Jilani 2006):

> One household occupies less than five by five meters. Most families take shelter under plastic sheets or other makeshift materials, not sufficient to provide privacy and dignity. Only a few families have received tarpaulins. Muddy water standing in pools created by heavy rainfalls is used for washing and cleaning. The municipality provides only two or three trucks of drinkable water a day. There are not enough provisional toilets. Public health service is not available on a regular basis. Medicine is distributed by some NGOs only. Located more than 20 kilometers from their former homes, most people have lost their meager income making opportunities and many are already starving. There is no administration of this site and security is not guaranteed: People do not leave their small huts for fear that others will take their few belongings. The most vulnerable groups, including women, infants and children, older people, disabled people and people living with

---

[13] The information in this paragraph was derived from an interview with a community leader of the Tonle Bassac community conducted by the author, April 27, 2006.

428 Land and post-conflict peacebuilding

HIV/AIDS are already affected by this precarious situation and their condition is at high risk of worsening (Cambodian Center for Human Rights 2006c).

Forced evictions and relocations, such as those inflicted on the Sambok Chab community, constitute unambiguous breaches of Cambodia's international obligations. Although Cambodia should pass and implement laws necessary to prevent such violations in future, it is also under a current obligation to provide remedies to those it has already harmed. Numerous observers have also recommended an immediate moratorium on urban evictions and relocations as the only way to ensure that Cambodia abides by its obligations pending the drafting of binding rules.

The situation of the Bassac evictees has quickly deteriorated, with many children suffering from malnutrition and preventable diseases. In a move described by an expert as "rubbing salt in the wound," adults have not been allowed to register locally, so they are unable to access services and exercise other rights. In the words of one observer of conditions at the resettlement site:

> Not only have the adults and children ... lost access to basic healthcare and education services to which they are entitled, they have effectively been disenfranchised ... they can't register to vote, even children can't register at schools as they have no fixed address. ... They have effectively become noncitizens, non-people (Barton 2006).

Still formally citizens of Cambodia, yet vulnerable and disenfranchised as a result of their displacement, the former Bassac residents increasingly fit the definition of internally displaced persons; this underscores the obligation of the authorities to provide them with assistance and to protect their legal rights (UNCHR 1998).

The Cambodian authorities are not the only ones to blame for the problem, however. Although international lending institutions such as the World Bank and the Asian Development Bank have insisted on the application of protective resettlement guidelines in development projects in Cambodia, these guidelines often go unimplemented or are poorly implemented in practice, and many bilateral donors do not formally require resettlement safeguards to be a part of the development projects they fund.[14] According to experts, large-scale investors such as China and Viet Nam have never imposed any resettlement conditions, while it was not until 2005 that the Japan International Cooperation Agency, one of the biggest donors in Cambodia, adopted standards requiring some degree of compensation to those displaced by resettlement. Even when resettlement policies are required by donors, however, this does not relieve the Cambodian government

---

[14] For a positive example of resettlement guidelines, see Asian Development Bank (1995, 2011). In Cambodia, these guidelines are often not properly implemented for Asian Development Bank–funded projects, such as the National Highway 1 project.

Housing, land, and property rights in Cambodia   429

of its obligation to codify resettlement standards in a legislative framework that would bind both domestic and international investors and donors.

Failure to secure access to rural land and urban housing

Cambodia has received a great deal of criticism for violating HLP rights by failing to respect existing tenure, whether through rural land grabbing or urban forced evictions. The government's failings also include a persistent inability to prospectively make adequate land and housing accessible to Cambodia's most impoverished and vulnerable groups. So far, efforts to secure such affirmative rights to housing and land have focused almost exclusively on the countryside.

The primary means envisioned for delivering land to the poor under the 2001 Land Law is the granting of social land concessions. The purpose of these concessions is defined vaguely in the Land Law as to "allow beneficiaries to build residential constructions and/or to cultivate lands belonging to the State for their subsistence" (art. 49). A March 2003 sub-decree provided a good deal more detail, setting out a number of goals, including the provision of "land for residential purposes to poor homeless families" and agricultural land "to poor families for family farming."[15] The sub-decree also provided for considerable decentralization of the selection and administration processes for such concessions. Concerns about the capacity of local officials to distribute land effectively motivated a World Bank project to analyze the potential impact of land reform and to identify ways to increase the effectiveness of social concessions (World Bank 2004).

This evaluation process has delayed the actual granting of social concessions but is meant to ensure that once implementation begins, it will significantly benefit the rural poor and landless. It remains unclear why the anticipated impact of social concessions is likely to remain limited to the countryside. The World Bank has justified the exclusively rural focus of social-concession implementation by referring to the role of land as a crucial safety net for Cambodia's still over-whelmingly rural population:

> In the long term, . . . only improved non-farm income can meet the country's employment demand. Those opportunities are not yet available in sufficient quantity, which means that land access still matters, particularly for the most vulnerable. Demography will put increasing pressure on cities to plan growth. The development of the housing policy and pilot projects in planning and settle-ment upgrading point the way to improved urban land management (World Bank 2004, 2).

To the extent that the country can be said to have an unofficial housing policy for the poor, precedent suggests that it consists of removing them from

---

[15]   Sub-decree on Social Land Concessions, No. 19 ANK/BK, March 19, 2003, art. 3.

430 Land and post-conflict peacebuilding

central urban land of interest to developers and leaving them to their own devices on unimproved plots so distant from their former work sites that they will eventually find their way back to other urban slums. As the World Bank has noted elsewhere, the populations of urban informal settlements are probably already undercounted, and the problem is likely to be exacerbated as the country continues to urbanize. These circumstances justify the creation of "specific policies and programs for the urban poor, to a significant degree distinct from those designed for the rural poor" (World Bank 2006b, 48). Indeed, the failure of the LMAP to prioritize urban housing issues is seen as one of the key factors in its 2009 termination (World Bank 2011). While there may be grounds for prioritizing the needs of the rural landless in the overall planning of social land concessions, this should not entail excluding the urban poor entirely. If social land concessions are not an appropriate device for meeting prospective urban housing needs, this should be clearly established, and alternative policies with a meaningful chance of having an impact should be identified.

Failure to secure the HLP rights of vulnerable groups

Two specific groups within Cambodian society are particularly vulnerable to violations of their HLP rights. The first is female-headed households. In a broad sense, women are seen as having relatively equal rights to men in Cambodian society (World Bank 2006b). Although the mass murder under the Khmer Rouge regime created a high proportion of potentially vulnerable female-headed households in the 1970s, women appear to have been allocated land on an equal basis during the PRK reforms of the 1980s, and to date they have by and large retained this land. Early results from the LMAP titling program gave some credence to the idea that the property of married couples is more likely to be formally owned by women than men (LMAP 2005).[16]

On the other hand, there is evidence that female heads of household own smaller plots of land than men, have fewer opportunities to increase the amount of land they hold, and are at greater risk of becoming landless (CDRI 2001). Women have a lower likelihood of receiving a basic education and are underrepresented in many vocational areas. Although poor women often do take on significant income-generating activities outside the home, they tend to receive less pay than men and are still expected to take responsibility for most domestic tasks (World Bank 2006b). These factors seem to translate into a general lack of bargaining power for women, vis-à-vis men, in negotiating crucial HLP matters such as land purchases, loans, access to basic services, and terms of relocation (Kothari 2006b).

---

[16] According to a 2005 report, 70 percent of the nearly 300,000 properties registered at the time were jointly owned by married couples, while a further 18 percent were registered in the wife's name and only 6 percent in the husband's name (LMAP 2005).

Housing, land, and property rights in Cambodia **431**

A second vulnerable group in Cambodia is indigenous people—a small minority population that primarily inhabits the country's forested northeastern highlands. The 2001 Land Law explicitly recognizes indigenous groups' collective rights to the lands they have traditionally occupied, but these provisions cut very much against the grain of Cambodia's historical approach to its indigenous communities, which have faced repression, forcible relocation, and predatory resource exploitation on their lands since before independence. Likewise, although the Land Law specifically protects indigenous rights to shifting (or swidden) agricultural practices, the tendency throughout the region had previously been to outlaw such practices on the pretext that they lead to environmental damage (Simbolon 2002).[17]

During the 1990s, the Cambodian military presided over such extensive and uncontrolled logging of the country's forests that concerns arose about complete deforestation and environmental devastation. As a result, moratoria on logging in forest concessions and transportation of logs were imposed in 2002. However, allegations of illegal logging continue, and timber clearing is still allowed on economic land concessions. Grants of profoundly oversized concessions in the country's northeast appear to represent another attempt to bypass Cambodia's forest management controls and impinge further on indigenous land (Leuprecht 2004). Indigenous groups are also vulnerable to fraud and to being intimidated into selling or giving away title to land. Despite the fact that individual sales of collectively held land are illegal under the Land Law, courts in northeastern Cambodia have upheld ostensible sales of such land that are based on outright deception and bribery (HRW 2001).[18]

Perhaps most threatening, rural poverty in other parts of Cambodia has led an increasing number of landless farmers to settle in the northeast, where they seek jobs in concession areas and clear forests for farming. The presence of such settlers is tacitly approved by the Cambodian government, which despite its rhetoric about indigenous rights, appears to view development and colonization of the northeast as important goals.

Misunderstanding of swidden farming systems also creates the risk of local authorities classifying indigenous lands as degraded forest suitable for distribution through social land concessions, which encourages more migration and creates greater pressure on the few remaining indigenous areas. Local unwillingness to enforce the Land Law has been exacerbated by delays in the preliminary demarcation of indigenous land and the promulgation of an implementing sub-decree related to indigenous land (Kothari 2006b).

---

[17] Swidden agriculture was outlawed in neighboring Laos and Viet Nam after being blamed for erosion that more likely occurred as a result of logging and agricultural settlement.

[18] One case involved the purchase of 1,200 hectares of indigenous land by a general who bribed district officials to steal the property from villagers by pressuring them to thumbprint title documents they had not read and by offering gifts such as bags of salt in exchange (HRW 2001).

432   Land and post-conflict peacebuilding

Most observers agree that social land concessions, which assume eventual distribution to individual farmers, would not be an appropriate response to the loss of land collectively held by indigenous people. However, unless the Cambodian authorities are prepared to begin rigorously enforcing the provisions of the Land Law barring illegal acquisition of land and invalidating individual sales of indigenous land outside the community, indigenous people will face increasing dispossession and displacement. Many displaced indigenous people are likely to migrate to urban centers, swelling the ranks of indigent migrants there. As most indigenous people cannot speak the language of the Khmer majority in Cambodia, they are likely to suffer from extreme marginalization and associated social problems. Simply put, "If not addressed as a matter of priority, the land alienation problem is likely to result in the destruction of indigenous culture" (NGO Forum on Cambodia 2004, 6).

CONCLUSIONS

Many of Cambodia's HLP rights abuses are related to its relatively recent transition to peace, democratic government, and a market economy. The sudden exposure of Cambodia's largely rural population to globalized markets in land and other natural resources after two decades of conflict and international isolation have radically destabilized local understandings of how HLP resources are to be valued and legitimately held (CDRI 2001). Although considerable progress has been made, the polarizing effects of insecure tenure remain a threat to Cambodia's political stability and to its people's welfare and livelihoods.

The government of Cambodia has cooperated with the international community in developing policies, legislation, and institutions meant to safeguard HLP rights and ensure equitable access to HLP resources. However, it has failed to give effect to this new framework, and it has responded to domestic and international criticism with a blend of conciliatory public gestures, occasional intimidation, and precious little action (LICADHO 2006). Although a process of titling and registration of property interests was initiated, its abrupt cancellation in September 2009 denied its benefits to those most in need, such as Cambodia's embattled urban slum dwellers and indigenous minorities. Moreover, registration and dispute resolution efforts to date have failed to redress land grabbing by the rich and powerful.

In sum, a basic framework now exists for redressing the worst HLP violations of the past twenty years and for working toward protection of the rights of the country's poorest and most vulnerable citizens. Both domestic and international organizations should insist on the completion and implementation of this framework in the spirit of Cambodia's human rights obligations. Giving effect to these standards will require the government to confront powerful vested interests and ubiquitous patronage practices, but failing to do so will further undermine the broader effort to establish the rule of law in Cambodia.

In light of these realities, the highest priority of the government of Cambodia should be to arrest the most socially destructive HLP practices that are occurring now. A crucial first step would be to place a moratorium on transfers of land traditionally occupied or used by indigenous people until all regulatory and institutional preconditions have been met for the administration of indigenous land in accordance with the 2001 Land Law and Cambodia's international obligations. Ideally, such measures would include a review of recent transactions in order to determine their compatibility with the law.

Another urgent measure that should be undertaken is suspension of evictions from and clearances of informal settlements, whether by official or private actors, until the regulatory and institutional preconditions have clearly been met for relocation processes to be decided on and implemented in a manner that will avoid human rights violations in the form of forced evictions and arbitrary displacement.

In all cases where forced evictions or other human rights violations have resulted in the involuntary displacement of Cambodians from their homes or places of habitual residence, those affected should presumptively be treated as internally displaced persons in the sense of the UN's 1998 Guiding Principles on Internal Displacement. Specifically, such persons should not be discriminated against in the exercise of any of their rights and freedoms as a result of their displacement. They should also receive protection and humanitarian assistance from the authorities of Cambodia in order to both mitigate their specific vulnerabilities during displacement and to bring about an end to their displacement through voluntary return or resettlement and reintegration.

Likewise, in cases in which land or property has been illegally appropriated, held in concession, or diverted from its lawful possessors or users, the primary concern of the Cambodian authorities should be to bring about the immediate disgorgement of such land or property in order to return it to its lawful possessors or users or make it available to socially vulnerable groups in the form of social land concessions. The work of institutions mandated to resolve disputes should be supported in order to ensure uniform application of the law in all cases. While those responsible for illegal appropriations and diversions of land should be held legally accountable, care should be taken to avoid either politicization of such processes or undue delay in the return of land determined to have been illegally acquired or held.

Steps should also be taken to ensure equitable prospective access to HLP resources for the poor, landless, and socially vulnerable. The social land concession provisions of the 2001 Land Law should be activated as soon as procedures have been put in place to ensure their effective and transparent implementation. Prospective measures should not be limited to rural areas. Cambodia is obliged to take concrete measures to provide the urban poor with adequate housing, whether through social concessions, upgrading, or other means.

While the government of Cambodia bears the primary responsibility for ensuring respect for rights to land and housing, international organizations in Cambodia should do more to support the development of effective domestic land management and dispute resolution institutions. The credibility of the laws and institutions that the international community has invested in to date will continue

434   Land and post-conflict peacebuilding

to be undermined unless these begin to function consistently, transparently, and in the spirit of Cambodia's human rights obligations. In particular, future registration and titling programs should be implemented in a manner that prioritizes the provision of secure tenure to those urban and rural communities currently most vulnerable to forced evictions.

REFERENCES

Adler, D., D. Porter, and M. Woolcock. 2008. Legal pluralism and equity: Some reflections on land reform in Cambodia. J4P Briefing Note. April. www-wds.worldbank.org/external/default/WDSContentServer/WDSP/IB/2008/05/15/000333038_20080515040808/Rendered/PDF/436870BRI0J4P01Box0327368B01PUBLIC1.pdf.

Asian Coalition for Housing Rights. 2005. *ACHR activities during the 2004 year*. New Delhi, India.

Asian Development Bank. 1995. *Involuntary resettlement: Policies and strategies*. Manila, Philippines. www.adb.org/sites/default/files/pub/1995/involuntary_resettlement.pdf.

————. 2011. Involuntary resettlement safeguards: A planning and implementation good practice source book—Draft working document. March. http://beta.adb.org/sites/default/files/ir-good-practices-sourcebook-draft.pdf.

Barton, C. 2006. Life in limbo for Phnom Penh's evicted poor people. *Phnom Penh Post*, November, 17–30.

Bugalski, N. 2010. The World Bank struggles with its resettlement policy in Cambodia. TerraNullius. August 16. http://terra0nullius.wordpress.com/2010/08/16/the-world-bank-struggles-with-its-resettlement-policy-in-cambodia/#more-789.

Cambodian Center for Human Rights. 2006a. Public forum. Quarterly report for March 29–June 17.

————. 2006b. CCHR demands from Phnom Penh City Hall to guarantee the rights of the deported Sambok Chab villagers to health and adequate housing. Press release. June 9.

————. 2006c. Relocation of Sambok Chab villagers threatens a humanitarian crisis—Phnom Penh City Hall must now guarantee the basic human rights. Press release. June 22. www.cchrcambodia.org/media/files/press_release/87_202_en.pdf.

CDRI (Cambodia Development Resource Institute). 2001. Social assessment of land in Cambodia. Working Paper No. 20. Phnom Penh.

Chandler, D. 2000. *A history of Cambodia*. Boulder, CO: Westview.

Chhoeurn, M. 2006. Interview by author of vice governor of Phnom Penh municipality. April 27.

CLEC-PILAP (Community Legal Education Center Public Interest Legal Advocacy Project). 2005. Koh Pich case description. February 28.

COHRE (Centre on Housing Rights and Evictions). 2006. Human rights violations imminent in Phnom Penh due to Cambodian government's development initiatives. Media release. July 3.

De Launey, G. 2006. Poor Cambodians face relocation. *BBC News*. May 3.

EWMI (East-West Management Institute). 2001. Southeast Asia: Cambodian land reform project. *EWMI Briefing* 1 (2).

————. 2003. *Land law of Cambodia: A study and research manual*. Phnom Penh.

Global Witness. 2007. *Cambodia's family trees: Illegal logging and the stripping of public assets by Cambodia's elite*. Washington, D.C. www.globalwitness.org/sites/default/files/pdfs/cambodias_family_trees_low_res.pdf.

Housing, land, and property rights in Cambodia **435**

———. 2009. *Country for sale: How Cambodia's elite has captured the country's extractive industries.* www.globalwitness.org/sites/default/files/library/country_for_sale_low_res_english.pdf.

Grimsditch, M., and N. Henderson. 2009. *Untitled: Tenure insecurity and inequality in the Cambodian land sector.* Phnom Penh: Bridges Across Borders Southeast Asia / Jesuit Refugee Service; Geneva, Switzerland: Centre on Housing Rights and Evictions. www.babcambodia.org/untitled/untitled.pdf.

HRW (Human Rights Watch). 1997. *Cambodia: Aftermath of the coup.* New York.

———. 2001. Cambodia: Verdict a setback for indigenous land rights. Press release. March 30.

Kothari, M. 2006a. *Basic principles and guidelines on development-based evictions and displacement.* Phnom Penh Cambodia: Office of the High Commissioner for Human Rights.

———. 2006b. *Report of the Special Rapporteur on adequate housing as a component of the right to adequate standard of living—Addendum: Mission to Cambodia.* Geneva, Switzerland: United Nations Human Rights Council. March 21.

Kothari, M., and H. Jilani. 2006. UN experts condemn lack of respect for human rights shown in eviction of Bassac residents in Cambodian capital. Press release. June 29.

Leuprecht, P. 2004. *Land concessions for economic purposes in Cambodia: A human rights perspective.* Phnom Penh: Office of the High Commissioner for Human Rights.

LICADHO (Cambodian League for the Protection and Defense of Human Rights). 2006. Sparrows released during vigil at Prey Sar prison near Phnom Penh. Press release. July 10.

LMAP (Land Management and Administration Project). 2005. *Land management and administration project (LMAP) land registration data analysis.* Phnom Penh: Government of Cambodia.

NGO Forum on Cambodia. 2004. *Land alienation from indigenous minority communities in Ratanakiri.* Phnom Penh.

Nissen, C. J. 2005. *Living under the rule of corruption: An analysis of everyday forms of corrupt practices in Cambodia.* Phnom Penh: Center for Social Development.

Simbolon, I. 2002. Access to land of highland indigenous minorities: The case of plural property rights in Cambodia. Working Paper No. 42. Halle, Germany: Max Planck Institute for Social Anthropology.

UN CESCR (United Nations Committee on Economic, Social and Cultural Rights). 1991. General Comment 4: The right to adequate housing (art. 11(1) of the Covenant).

———. 1997. General Comment 7: The right to adequate housing (art. 11.1 of the Covenant); Forced eviction.

UNCHR (United Nations Commission on Human Rights). 1993. Resolution No. 1993/77. March 10.

———. 1998. *Report of the Representative of the Secretary-General, Mr. Francis M. Deng, submitted pursuant to commission resolution 1997/39. Addendum: Guiding principles on internal displacement.* E/CN.4/1998/53/Add.2. February 11. www.unhcr.org/refworld/docid/3d4f95e11.html.

UNHRC (United Nations Human Rights Council). 2006. A statement to the Human Rights Council by the Special Representative of the Secretary-General for Human Rights in Cambodia, Mr. Yash Ghai. September 26.

Williams, R. C. 2008. Stability, justice, and rights in the wake of the Cold War: The housing, land and property rights legacy of the UN Transitional Authority in Cambodia.

436   Land and post-conflict peacebuilding

In *Housing, land, and property rights in post-conflict United Nations and other peace operations: A comparative survey and proposal for reform*, ed. S. Leckie. Cambridge, UK: Cambridge University Press.

World Bank. 2004. *Cambodia: Assessment of potential impacts of "social land concessions."* Washington, D.C.

———. 2006a. Cambodia: Government and donors agree opportunity to benefit from deeper reforms is now. Press Release 2006/295/EAP.

———. 2006b. *Cambodia: Halving poverty by 2015? Poverty assessment 2006.* Washington, D.C.

———. 2009. Statement from the World Bank on termination by Royal Government of Cambodia of the land management and administration project. Press release. September 6.

———. 2011. World Bank Board of Executive Directors considers Inspection Panel report on Cambodia Land Management and Administration Project. Press release. March 8.

Land conflicts and land registration in Cambodia

Manami Sekiguchi and Naomi Hatsukano

Land policy—specifically, providing security of ownership—has been a key to post-conflict peacebuilding in Cambodia since 1979, which marked the end of the Pol Pot regime. However, the attempt to reform the legal system has been so rapid that there has been little chance to incorporate the traditional legal concepts rooted in local society with more modern concepts of land law. As a result, land policy has become a quilt of overlapping systems, some reaching back centuries, some recent: customary law, the French Civil Code, socialism, private ownership under modern law, and land registration systems.[1]

Land management in Cambodia has been significantly influenced by foreign donors' promotion of legal standards and systems that prevail in their own countries. Adding yet another layer of legal rules, the resulting ambiguity has led to an increasing number of disputes over landownership and threatens the long-term development of the country. It also fosters government corruption; and the weakest members of society, whose only claim to ownership is based on customary practice, are the most likely to be displaced from their land. It is important for both recipient countries and foreign donors to recognize the importance of the role of customary law and promote a legal system that considers customary legal concepts rooted in the societies of recipient countries.

Manami Sekiguchi graduated from the Department of International Studies, Graduate School of Frontier Sciences, at the University of Tokyo. Naomi Hatsukano is a research fellow at IDE-JETRO (Institute of Developing Economies, Japan External Trade Organization). The authors would like to express their gratitude to Youk Ngoy from the Royal University of Law and Economics and Nobuo Sambe from the Japan International Cooperation Agency. The authors would also like to express appreciation to Zonta Club of Tokyo I for its research grant supporting this project's field survey.

[1] *Modern* is used here to designate the legal system that many donors have encouraged Cambodia to adopt in the past twenty years, i.e., a legal regime that supports a free market, protection of private property, civil liberties, and open elections. Specific to the topic of this chapter, such a regime promotes private ownership of land and the recognition of that right through legal titling and the official registration of ownership. The term does not imply any superiority to traditional or customary Cambodian legal systems. Rather, it embodies a set of legal practices that can, and should, complement traditional law.

438   Land and post-conflict peacebuilding

This chapter reviews the changing land regimes in Cambodia, from customary law to the French Civil Code, to the destruction of private ownership in the Pol Pot era, to the socialist regime of the 1980s, and to the return of a market economy and private ownership of land in the 1990s. It then analyzes the land disputes that have proliferated due to the ambiguity of rights defined by the conflicting systems. The chapter next examines the failures of the overall land management regime, focusing on the legal system, policy implementation, and dispute settlement bodies. It then discusses the impacts of foreign donors on post-conflict land policy in Cambodia.

CHANGING LAND REGIMES

Under ancient customary law, all land in Cambodia was recognized as the property of the king. People enjoyed the right of possession, which means that they could cultivate land freely. As long as they cultivated continuously, their right of possession was recognized. If the land was not cultivated for three years, the possessor lost the right. This rule applied for centuries, until the colonization by France in the twentieth century (Rendall, Tremblay, and Baars 2003; Pel et al. 2005).

In 1920, during the French colonial period, Cambodia adopted the French Civil Code. Private ownership of land was first recognized in the law. At the same time, possession was still recognized under the Civil Code. After independence from France in 1953, the Western property system remained. According to the 1962 census, 76.9 percent of farm families had documents to prove their land rights issued by the land department, of which 84 percent had been recognized as land owners (Pel et al. 2005). At the same time, there were areas where customary law remained. Cambodia thus entered a transient period in which both modern ownership and the right of possession existed side by side.

Cambodia experienced a bloody purge during the Khmer Rouge regime (Democratic Kampuchea), led by Pol Pot, from April 1975 to January 1979. Private ownership was abolished, and all records related to landownership were destroyed. After the Khmer Rouge fell, the succeeding regime (People's Republic of Kampuchea), supported by Viet Nam, established a socialist economy—in which all land belonged to the state—that lasted through the 1980s. Under the land distribution system called *krom samaki*, farmers were divided into groups to share land, labor, and animals, and land was distributed to those groups regardless of ownership or possession before 1979 (Amakawa 2001a, 2001b).

In 1989, following the withdrawal of Vietnamese troops, a new government was formed, and it began to institute a market economy under the new constitution and a program of land reform. In 1989 the Instruction on Implementation of Land Use and Management Policy was adopted, and ownership of residential land was recognized. This instruction also recognized the right of possession on cultivated land. The 1992 Land Law went further by permitting ownership of residential land. In August 2001 the National Assembly enacted the 2001 Land Law, which expanded ownership of all types of land (Amakawa 2001b; Pel et al. 2005).

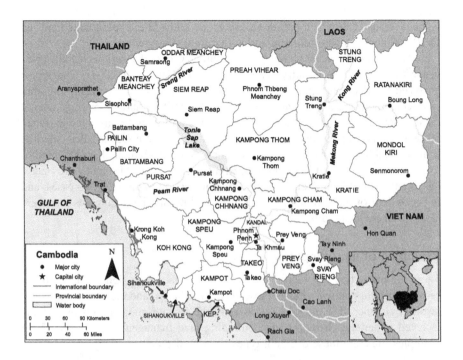

Although the government has tried to reconstruct and improve land management since 1989, there have been problems with both the legal system itself and the implementation of its laws. More than 80 percent of the Cambodian population lives in rural areas, where customary law still predominantly prevails. The government failed, in particular, to properly introduce the modern legal system of private ownership in those parts of the country. Beginning in the 1990s, rapid economic growth caused land in rural areas to increase in value and become a target for investors. It became crucial for those holding land under customary law to gain legal title to it to prevent losing it. At the same time, many people were not accustomed to the newly introduced modern system based on the idea of strict ownership. The attempt to rapidly introduce a modern legal system caused confusion and misunderstanding about how legal rights to land could be obtained, leading to numerous disputes.

ANALYSIS OF LAND DISPUTES

Conflicts over land have increased in Cambodia because of the ambiguity of land rights. Recently, as the price of land has risen, disputes over landownership have occurred among the people and villages. And there is a trend of land disputes escalating into violence involving government authorities. For example, one of the typical land disputes involves unregistered lands that become the object of economic land concessions even though people live on the lands. An economic land concession

440 Land and post-conflict peacebuilding

is a land transfer in which private investors are allowed to exploit state lands up to 10,000 hectares for industrial and agricultural development.

According to a report by the NGO Forum on Cambodia, serious land disputes occur throughout the country (NGO Forum on Cambodia 2009). The report analyzed 173 disputes reported in local newspapers in 2008.[2] The average number of affected households in a land dispute is 188 families, and the average size of the disputed area is 276 hectares, while 43 percent of disputes involved less than 50 hectares. The highest numbers of land dispute cases were seen in Sihanoukville, Kampot, and Kandal provinces. The largest cases, in which more than 200 families were involved, occurred in Ratanakiri, Kratie, and Banteay Meanchey provinces. Disputants had official documents to prove ownership in only 2 of 86 cases, and in nearly half of the complaints individuals had no official documents that were recognized by local authorities.

Examples of land disputes

There are many types of land disputes in Cambodia. Most significant are those between people within a village, those between villages, and those that ultimately result in violence. The underlying causes of the disputes are conflicts over rights received under the changing and conflicting land management regimes. Three examples illustrate these different types of land disputes.

Disputes between people in Village P (Siem Reap Province)

In 1987, the commune chief distributed land to one villager (Party A) under the framework of *krom samaki*. When Party A sold the land in 2004, four families (Party B) claimed they had owned the land before 1987, and requested a share of the sale price. The district government granted Party B's request (Pel et al. 2007).

Disputes between villages (Takeo Province)

In 1979, after the Pol Pot regime collapsed, the government of the People's Republic of Kampuchea distributed uncultivated land to Village C under *krom samaki*. In 1983, the district governor decided to redistribute the property to Villages D and E. Villages D and E were issued a certificate for the land in 1986. The chief of Village C disputed the certificate, but the area was occupied and cultivated by Villages D and E. In 2000 the new chief of Village C reignited the dispute by allowing villagers to cultivate the area and keep out Villages D and E. The provincial court decided in 2005 that Village C had to withdraw from the land, but the property is still in dispute.[3]

---

[2] The newspapers are the *Phnom Penh Post* (English), the *Cambodia Daily* (English), *Koh Santepheap* (Khmer), and *Rasmay Kampuchea* (Khmer).

[3] This description relies on the authors' interviews with stakeholders in three villages in December 2008.

Violent dispute among people (Banteay Meanchey Province)

In 1997, approximately 200 families (Party F) started to live in Village Q near the Thai border after the area was demined. In 1998, one man (Party G) applied for a title for the land on which Party F, the 200 families, lived. The General Department of Cadastre and Geography and the provincial court awarded the title of ownership to Party G in 1999. Party F disputed the decision, and representatives from the Ministry of National Assembly Senate Relations and Inspection investigated. In 2000, the commune chief issued a letter certifying that Party F had been living in the area, and in 2001, the district cadastral office stated that Party G's title was not valid. But the conflict escalated, and five villagers from Party F died in an attempted eviction in March 2005 (CHRAC 2005).

Causes of land disputes

The examples above illustrate several important problems in managing land in post-conflict Cambodia:

- Inconsistent decisions by different levels of institutions.
- Lack of valid legal documents to prove ownership, possession, or distribution, which leads to evictions without compensation, even if parties have possessed the land for a long time.
- Clash of claims based on the 2001 Land Law versus the customary law of possession.
- Lack of standards to recognize past land use.
- Inefficient dispute resolution systems, driving Cambodians to take matters into their own hands.

FAILURE IN LAND MANAGEMENT POLICIES

Land disputes are the result of a complex web of failures within land management policies in the post-conflict era following 1979. It is necessary to analyze the causes of those failures from the perspective of the legal system itself, its implementation, and dispute settlement bodies.

Legal system

The greatest problem for land management policies in Cambodia is that modern legal systems do not allow for consideration of customary law. In Cambodia it has been traditionally considered that the people could possess the lands of the king by using them continuously. The legal concept of private ownership was not introduced to Cambodian society until the colonial period. Enabling people to claim ownership of land regardless of continuous use was completely different from the customary concept of the right of possession. But it was not a problem

442   Land and post-conflict peacebuilding

at that time, before the Pol Pot regime, because land transactions were infrequent, and most people kept using their land in the traditional way.

The customary concept remained in the legal policies and land management systems in the reconstruction process begun after the Pol Pot regime. The 1989 Instruction on Land Use and Management Policy, for example, allows the right of possession on agricultural lands. The 1992 Land Law allowed citizens to gain ownership of land through possession for five years (art. 74), and the 2001 Land Law tried to finish this practice by promoting modern landownership. But the 2001 Land Law, while allowing people to submit five years of possession to be recognized for ownership (arts. 29–30), also required that the possession should be started before promulgation of the 2001 Land Law. In reality, although most land was not transformed to ownership after five years of possession, and those unregistered lands have been subject to disputes, the 2001 Land Law does not clarify the relations with previous norms and laws that allowed customary possessions even before five years passed. This uncoordinated legal regime has caused confusion about when and how the ownership of land can be recognized.

As the examples above illustrate, opposing parties in land disputes often base their claims on different legal grounds. It is quite common for one party to claim possession of land over a long time and another party to claim modern ownership with an official document for the same land. Those with legal titles of ownership usually have an advantage in such disputes. Even though most people in Cambodia still follow the customary legal concept of possession without valid legal documents, modern legal concepts of ownership dominate in the present legal policies and systems and fail to give appropriate consideration to the social impacts of customary laws of possession. For example, in land conflicts involving the eviction of residents for economic development by the state or private sectors, people who possessed lands for certain periods without legal titles often fail to receive reasonable compensation.

In replacing the right of possession, the 2001 Land Law prepared new systems, such as the social land concession (art. 17 and ch. 5) and collective ownership for indigenous people (ch. 3, pt. 2), to protect the land for the poor and the indigenous people who are most vulnerable.[4] The social land concession provides that vulnerable people receive unused state private land for their family farming.[5] Collective ownership for indigenous people allows them to continue traditional shifting cultivation (swidden agriculture). These provisions in the 2001 Land Law were prepared after consultation with international organizations and

---

[4]   Indigenous people live throughout the country. However, a greater number of indigenous people in Ratanakiri and Mondulkiri provinces maintain their lives in a traditional way. The total indigenous population is around 150,000.

[5]   There are two types of state land in Cambodia: state public land and state private land. State public land cannot be sold to the private sector and remains for public use only. State private land can be transferred to the private sector (2001 Land Law, ch. 2).

Land conflicts and land registration in Cambodia   443

nongovernmental organizations (NGOs), and were welcome when the law was promulgated (Simbolon 2002). However, the law stipulated only the framework; realizing those articles was another matter. The government has provided social land concessions only for a limited group of people. As for the indigenous people, because of delays in adopting the implementing sub-decree, only pilot project villages and some very remote villages were able to protect their land. Thus these systems have had only a small effect in protecting customary land use.

Policy implementation

There have been several problems with land management practices. First, the officials failed to record the land distribution arrangements made under *krom samaki*. Because the 1992 Land Law allows people to claim ownership through possession for five years, it is imperative to prove when parties began their period of possession. However, it is rare for people in rural areas to have a document proving when they got their land from the government in the 1980s under *krom samaki*. The lack of objective evidence in the form of documents makes landownership and possession rights unclear and causes complications in land disputes.

Second, there have been problems with the implementation of the land registration system. Land registration started in 1989 based on the Instruction on Land Use and Management Policy, and the 1992 Land Law set out the requirements for acquiring ownership through possession. This registration system is called *sporadic registration*. The system created under the Land Law of 2001 is called *systematic registration*. Thus the country has had two parallel processes for registration.

Sporadic registration

Under sporadic registration, an individual in possession of land initiates the process of registering. Rather than following an overall plan (for example, a government mandate to register all land in an area), individuals register their property, plot by plot. The system is expensive and complicated, and out of the reach of the majority of poor Cambodians. Applicants cannot receive certificates for ownership even after the registration process; instead they can receive a certificate of possession, which constitutes official recognition that the land belongs to the specified person.[6]

The key problem with sporadic registration is that the government failed to provide information on how to register land. The 1992 Land Law does not mention how to meet the requirements to qualify for ownership through possession. Besides the lack of information, people who attempted to register were sometimes asked to pay an extra fee from the officers because of budget shortfalls

---

[6] When the land registered in sporadic registration is targeted in systematic registration, the land is surveyed again with more accuracy.

444 **Land and post-conflict peacebuilding**

at the district level. The lack of information also impeded the progress of registration. While approximately 4.5 million people applied, it is estimated that only 51,000 people were able to obtain certificates of possession up to 1998 (Pel et al. 2005).

Systematic registration

Under the more efficient and less expensive systematic registration created in 2001, the government designates areas to be registered. All land in the area is surveyed, land documents are analyzed, and titles are granted for parcels. Systematic registration is the more efficient, equitable, and comprehensive method in theory.

The government and some donors supported the earliest efforts of the Ministry of Land Management, Urban Planning and Construction (MLMUPC) to start systematic registration using the latest facilities and satellite pictures. Its pilot project started in 1995, several years before the 2001 Land Law came under discussion.

In 2002, the Land Management and Administration Project (LMAP) officially started with support from the World Bank, Germany, Finland, and Canada. LMAP's overall goals are to reduce poverty, promote social stability, and stimulate economic development by improving land tenure security and promoting the development of efficient land markets. LMAP took the leading role in (1) the development of national policies, a regulatory framework, and institutions for land administration; (2) the issuance and registration of titles; and (3) the establishment of an efficient and transparent land administration system. And, indeed, LMAP succeeded in some respects. It established the Council of Land Policies, prepared necessary sub-decrees, and issued more than 1.1 million titles in the systematic registration in fourteen provinces.

But LMAP itself had limited capacity (Grimsditch and Henderson 2009). First, under the process of LMAP, the lands that are most likely to be disputed are not the target of systematic registration. The people who really needed a title and who were facing land disputes had no access to this program. Second, the delay in state land mapping made it difficult to register the private land near state land or within state land. Third, LMAP had no procedure to register land of indigenous people. The 2001 Land Law promised that indigenous people could register their collective ownership to protect their traditional shifting cultivation. But people had to wait until May 2009, when the Sub-decree on Procedures for Registration of Land of Indigenous Communities was approved. Before this sub-decree, more and more indigenous people's land was sold to outsiders, and their traditional land use was destroyed.

The government terminated World Bank financing of the LMAP on September 2009, because the two parties "could not come to agreement on whether LMAP's social and environmental safeguards should apply in some of the disputed urban areas" (World Bank 2009, 3). After that, the government and other donors (but

Land conflicts and land registration in Cambodia 445

Table 1. Authorities to which stakeholders referred land disputes cases in 2008

Type	%
Local authorities (village, commune, and district)	87.86
District/*khan* cadastral commissions	4.05
Provincial/municipal cadastral commissions	5.78
National Cadastral Commission	2.31
National Authority for Land Dispute Resolution	8.09
Provincial courts	27.17
Appeals court	6.36
Supreme Court	3.47
National Assembly	5.78
Prime Minister's cabinet	27.75
Provincial hall	49.71
Others	23.70

Source: NGO Forum on Cambodia (2009).
Note: Multiple answers are allowed because stakeholders may visit as many institutions as they think can support them.

not the World Bank) continued the land titling project. This showed that registration in the remaining areas will be more and more difficult as the titling project goes on. The pace of registration will get slower when attempts are made to register the disputed or potentially disputed areas, because it will take more time to survey the land and to settle disputes.

Dispute settlement bodies

People involved in land disputes have resorted to various institutions for resolution (see table 1 for disputes in 2008). Among these institutions, cadastral commissions, the National Authority for Land Dispute Resolution (NALDR), and the courts are the formal institutions that play an important role in dispute settlement. People tend, however, to resort to several authorities or institutions, both formal and informal, because some formal institutions cannot respond quickly enough.

The cadastral-commission system is a dispute settlement institution for resolving disputes over unregistered land.[7] It has a three-layered process consisting of the district/*khan* cadastral commissions (DKCCs)[8], the provincial/municipal cadastral commissions (PMCCs), and the National Cadastral Commission (NCC). Whereas the NCC decides cases of land disputes, the DKCCs and the PMCCs try to negotiate agreements between parties (Adler et al. 2006). Thus, in a DKCC, representatives of districts/khan, village authorities, and elders become conciliators

---

[7] The functions of a commission were defined by the Organization and Functioning of the Cadastral Commission, Sub-decree 47 of August 21, 2002, and Prakas 112 of August 21, 2002, Guidelines and Procedures of the Cadastral Commission.
[8] A khan is a subdivision of a municipality.

446   Land and post-conflict peacebuilding

(Pel et al. 2005). They facilitate land disputes when parties file disputes or when disputes are found in the process of sporadic registration. If the parties cannot reach an agreement in the DKCC, the dispute will be forwarded to the PMCC for further conciliation. If conciliation fails in a PMCC, the case is sent to the NCC (Adler et al. 2006). The NCC hears disputes, makes decisions about the validity of evidence and testimony, and renders a binding decision, subject to the parties' right to judicial appeal. The Sub-decree on the Organization and Functioning of the Cadastral Commission allows parties to appeal to the court within thirty days.

An NGO report in 2005 pointed out that the tri-level commissions had serious weaknesses, such as inadequate budgets and human resources, political bias, and a prolonged conciliation process (Pel et al. 2005). As of the end of 2007, the cadastral-commission system had received 4,689 cases of land disputes, of which 1,439 cases had been resolved (NCC 2008). Although the cadastral-commission system has played a role in the facilitation of land disputes, it has not been able to keep up with the increasing number of land disputes.

The NALDR was established in 2006 within the Council of Ministers to solve land disputes that were too difficult to resolve through existing cadastral institutions.[9] It receives complaints of land disputes from people and governmental institutions such as the MLMUPC, the Ministry of Justice, the Ministry of Interior, and the NCC. The land disputes sent from the NCC are the most common and are mostly concerned with state-owned public land (NALDR 2007). From its beginning to 2009, the NALDR had received 1,271 cases, of which 120 cases were solved and 127 cases were in the process of solution. Additional cases totalling 972 were not initially brought to the NALDR, because these cases were to finish processes of other other institutions, such as the NCC and the court system. The investigative teams for settling disputes include NALDR staff, provincial governors, and officers from relevant ministries. After their field surveys and discussion with team members, they decide the case and implement the decision.

There is also a formal judicial dispute resolution mechanism. It is important because a cadastral commission is not a formal judicial body, and its staff are not trained for adjudication; instead, its main role is facilitation. NALDR is not the institution to overturn the decisions by the court either. However, the judicial system does not work well; many reports by NGOs and international organizations have described corruption in the Cambodian judicial system (Calavan, Briquets, and O'Brien 2004; MacLean 2006; World Bank 2004). Therefore the court's ability to solve land disputes in a peaceful and fair manner seems weak. In the dispute between villages in Takeo Province, discussed above, the provincial court failed to order the enforcement of verdicts and mediate compromise settlements, so the dispute is still unresolved. In the dispute among people that resulted in violence in Banteay Meanchey province, also described above, the appeals court claimed it could decide the case based only on officially recognized documents and did

---

[9] NALDR was established by Royal Decree No. NS/RD/0206/067, February 26, 2006.

ROLE OF FOREIGN DONORS

Since the 1990s, foreign donors have helped to establish land management policies in Cambodia. In the 1980s, Cambodia received little assistance from Western countries due to the perception that the Cambodian government was not legitimate. Until the establishment of United Nations Transitional Authority in Cambodia by the Paris Peace Agreement in 1991, Cambodia had to reconstruct its society and create a land management system by itself. Even though the 1992 Land Law was enacted shortly after the peace agreement, the government drafted the law.

In the 1990s, donors began to assist Cambodia in many areas, including institution building. The 2001 Land Law, for example, was drafted as part of a project in the agriculture sector sponsored by the Asian Development Bank. Many international organizations, bilateral donors, and NGOs joined that consultative process. The World Bank and bilateral development agencies from Germany, Canada, and Finland have assisted the Cambodian government in drafting a new registration system and policies, providing a new technology to demarcate land, and training the staff engaged in land registration. The assistance of those donors has been significant and has helped Cambodia transition to a nation ruled by modern law.

Behind this assistance, there was hope that the introduction of a modern legal system in Cambodia would stimulate investment from abroad and help to reduce poverty. In the late 1990s, donors were overly optimistic about how easily a modern legal system could be introduced and the progress that could be made in land registration. In reality, systematic registration has not progressed as they had expected. Despite some provisions of the 2001 Land Law that attempted to protect those possessing land under customary law, the lack of coordination between the two legal systems has caused confusion. The registration project has succeeded only in limited areas, and most land in Cambodia is still under the rule of customary law. This uncoordinated land management system has caused land disputes, and parties with legal titles under the modern legal system commonly have advantages over parties who have engaged in continuous land use. Although the donors intended a quick reconstruction of Cambodia, the introduction of a new legal system was too rapid, resulting in a threat to people's livelihoods through a loss of lands in land disputes.

If implementing a modern system were to succeed in Cambodia, it had to prepare a feasible alternative system to secure the rights of people who have used the land in customary possession, because to implement systematic registration all over the country at once was impossible. It was necessary to provide a reasonable transition in which information was disseminated to the people. In addition, there must be a simpler way to legally recognize people's customary land use and convert it to modern ownership. For example, though sporadic registration has been generally neglected since systematic registration started, it

448 Land and post-conflict peacebuilding

could serve as a supplementary process in the areas where systematic registration has not been implemented.

A society ruled by modern law cannot be achieved instantly. Cambodia has received substantial support from developed countries and multilateral organizations, but it has had many difficulties in navigating the post-conflict period. For such countries, it takes longer for people and society to accept substantial change, and there is no short cut.

LESSONS LEARNED

It is essential to take a society's customary law into account when establishing a new legal system in the post-conflict period. The case of Cambodia illustrates the difficulties of introducing a modern legal system rapidly to a society that has traditionally followed customary law, especially when the society possesses little implementation capacity and minimal human resources. The first post-conflict land management policies based on modern law, the 1992 Land Law, and the sporadic registration system all acknowledged customary law. In the 1990s Cambodia began to be influenced by foreign donors who wanted to promote a modern legal system more rapidly, as seen in the 2001 Land Law, leaving the effects of previous laws and policies ambiguous. This rapid shift of legal frameworks has caused confusion among the people and land disputes in Cambodian society.

Cambodia's experience indicates the importance of taking time to review existing laws at the local level before introducing new laws, policies, and systems. Even though legal records and systems were devastated by armed conflict, customary rules and systems remain and play significant roles. In introducing the new laws, policies, and systems in post-conflict countries, it is therefore important to consider their impacts and establish statutory legal systems that can coexist with customary law. If foreign donors promote the introduction of modern legal systems that are common in their own countries, they also need to consider the roles of customary laws and assist the beneficiary country to rebuild its customary legal systems.

REFERENCES

Adler, D., K. Chhim, H. Path, and H. Sochanny. 2006. *Towards institutional justice? A review of the work of Cambodia's Cadastral Commission in relation to land dispute resolution.* Phnom Penh: Deutsche Gesellschaft für Technische Zusammenarbeit (GTZ). www.worldbank.org.kh/pecsa/resources/25.towardsinstitutionaljustice_eng.pdf.

Amakawa, N. 2001a. Kanbojia ni Okeru Kokuminkokka Keisei to Kokka no Ninaite wo Meguru Funsou. In *Kanbojia no Fukkou Kaihatsu*, ed. N. Amakawa. Kenkyu Sousho No. 518. Chiba, Japan: Institute of Developing Economies, Japan External Trade Organization.

———. 2001b. Nouchi Shoyuu no Seido to Kouzou—Poru Poto Seiken Houkaigo no Saikouchiku Katei. In *Kanbojia no Fukkou Kaihatsu*, ed. N. Amakawa. Kenkyu Sousho No. 518. Chiba, Japan: Institute of Developing Economies, Japan External Trade Organization.

Calavan, M., S. Briquets, and J. O'Brien. 2004. Cambodia corruption assessment. August 19. United States Agency for International Development / Casal and Associates. www.globalsecurity.org/military/library/report/2004/cambodian-corruption-assessment.pdf.

CHRAC (Cambodian Human Rights Action Committee). 2005. Case study: Eviction of 21 March 2005 at Kbal Spean Village, Poipet, Banteay Meanchey. www.licadho-cambodia.org/reports/files/73CHRACKbalSpeanReport.pdf.

Grimsditch, M., and N. Henderson. 2009. *Untitled: Tenure insecurity and inequality in the Cambodian land sector.* Phnom Penh: Bridges Across Borders Southeast Asia / Jesuit Refugee Service; Geneva, Switzerland: Centre on Housing Rights and Evictions. www.babcambodia.org/untitled/untitled.pdf.

MacLean, L. 2006. National integrity systems: Transparency International country study report; Cambodia 2006. Berlin, Germany: Transparency International. http://saatsaam.info/kh/images/stories/NonMedia/2008/August/n-536-en.pdf.

NALDR (National Authority for Land Dispute Resolution). 2007. 2007 first half-year report on the activities and achievements of the National Authority for Land Dispute Resolution. No. 194/07 R. NLDA.

NCC (National Cadastral Commission). 2008. Cadastral commission list for 2007 [Tarang Robaykar procham chnam 2007 roboh kanahkamakar soriya dai]. Phnom Penh.

NGO Forum on Cambodia. 2009. Statistical analysis on land dispute occurring in Cambodia 2008. Phnom Penh. http://www.ngoforum.org.kh/docs/publications/LIP_Land_Dispute_2008_Eng.pdf.

Pel, S., P.-Y. Le Meur, S. Vitou, L. Lan, P. Setha, H. Leakhena, and I. Sothy. 2007. Land transactions in rural Cambodia: A synthesis of findings from research on appropriation and derived rights to land (Siem Reap, Kampong Thom, Sihanoukville and Rotanak Kiri). Phnom Penh: Centre d'Etude et de Developpment Agricole Cambodgien and Groupe de Recherche et d'Echanges Technologiques.

Pel, S., Y. Yonekura, S. So, and K. Saito. 2005. Land issue study in Cambodia: Landlessness, land disputes and project affected people. Phnom Penh: Centre d'Etude et de Developpment Agricole Cambodgien and Japan International Volunteer Center.

Rendall, M., J. Tremblay, and P. Baars. 2003. *Land law of Cambodia: A study and research manual.* Phnom Penh: East-West Management Institute.

Simbolon, I. 2002. Access to land of highland indigenous minorities: The case of plural property rights in Cambodia. Working Paper No. 42. Halle, Germany: Max Planck Institute for Social Anthropology.

World Bank. 2004. Cambodia at the crossroads: Strengthening accountability to reduce poverty. Report No. 30636-KH. Washington, D.C. http://siteresources.worldbank.org/INTCAMBODIA/Resources/Cover-TOC.pdf.

———. 2009. Cambodia land management and administration project: Enhanced review report. http://siteresources.worldbank.org/INTCAMBODIA/147270-1174545988782/22303366/FINALERMREPORT.pdf.

Legal frameworks and land issues in Muslim Mindanao

Paula Defensor Knack

Mindanao, the second largest island grouping in the Philippine archipelago, has experienced lengthy conflict over land, resources, and identity. It is the only island grouping with a large Muslim population, while the rest of the country is predominantly Christian.

Territorial conflict in Mindanao began in the sixteenth century, when Spain conquered northern Mindanao and a small part of southern Mindanao from the sultanates or royal kingdoms of Sulu and Maguindanao. After years of revolts, the Philippine war for independence from Spain broke out in 1898. This was overtaken later that year by the Spanish-American War, which resulted in America's purchase of the Philippines from Spain. Mindanao was subdued by American forces, but conflict between the Moros and American-sponsored Christian migrant settlers and workers from other islands continued, resulting in laws legalizing confiscation of lands owned by the Moros, large-scale land acquisitions (also referred to as *land grabbing*), and prejudice against and marginalization of the Moros.[1] After Philippine independence from American rule in 1946, temporary calm ensued. However, in the 1960s, conflict resumed between Moros and Christian settlers, giving rise to a secessionist movement.

In the 1970s, a war of independence was launched by the Moro National Liberation Front (MNLF). Twenty years of negotiation, beginning with the Tripoli

---

Paula Defensor Knack is a former assistant secretary for lands and legislative affairs of the Philippine Department of Environment and Natural Resources, former head of national policy studies and legal specialist of the World Bank-AusAID Land Administration Management Program in the Philippines, and former legal adviser to the Philippine Permanent Representation to the Organization for the Prohibition of Chemical Weapons. The views expressed in this chapter are those of the author and do not necessarily represent those of the Philippine government.

[1] The term *Moro*, as used in this chapter, refers to Muslim inhabitants of Mindanao, who share a distinct culture and history. However, in other contexts, the term may hold a different meaning. See Yuri Oki, "Land Tenure and Peace Negotiations in Mindanao, Philippines," in this book. Oki uses the term *Moro* to refer to Muslims who are involved in insurgency due to their discontent with the central government of the Philippines and their desire for autonomy.

452   Land and post-conflict peacebuilding

Agreement in 1976 and culminating in a second peace agreement in 1996, put a temporary stop to the conflict. In 2008, the government and the Moro Islamic Liberation Front (MILF) signed the Memorandum of Agreement on Ancestral Domain (MOA-AD),[2] which marked a significant step in the Moro quest for a homeland by setting up the Bangsamoro Juridical Entity (BJE). Publication of the proposed area of the BJE sparked vehement public opposition, however, because the territory overlapped with non-Muslim regions and was determined without consultation of affected Christian communities. The Supreme Court ruled in *Province of North Cotabato v. GRP* (Government of the Republic of the Philippines) that this entity violated the constitution.[3]

This chapter discusses the complex legal framework for resolving the struggle over land and natural resources in Mindanao. It demonstrates how conflicting laws and policies inherited from colonial regimes have added another layer of complexity to the conflict and made the achievement of lasting peace more difficult. A comprehensive understanding of such frameworks is crucial in preventing a return to conflict and achieving stable political and social regimes in post-conflict countries.

The chapter is organized as follows: The first part reviews the relationship between the legal framework and the land conflict in Mindanao; the second part reviews the historical roots of the conflict. The third discusses the peace agreements and the creation of the Autonomous Region in Muslim Mindanao (ARMM); the fourth discusses the passage of the Indigenous Peoples Rights Act (IPRA) and its impacts on the legal framework; and the fifth discusses critical land issues arising from the 2008 MOA-AD. The chapter concludes by reviewing lessons learned.

LAND LAWS AND CONFLICT

Land conflicts are complex and politically charged, and their resolution requires attention to both substance and process. The framework of secular and religious laws and regulations of a post-conflict country can help create stability or cause a relapse into conflict. An adequate legal framework arising from the harmonization of relevant laws is essential for a peace agreement to provide just and equitable distribution of power, income, and resources.

Land laws are often determined by powerful national and regional interests. When a bill is introduced proposing to allocate land, expand jurisdiction, or give security of tenure to certain groups, powerful groups compete to influence the drafting of the law and often deliberately insert loopholes. In the Philippines, powerful politicians come from landed families with strong ties to business. In the ARMM, land is a major source of conflict among clans and of grievances that have driven the secessionist movement.

---

[2] The full name of the agreement is the Memorandum of Agreement on the Ancestral Domain Aspect of the GRP-MILF Tripoli Agreement on Peace of 2001. For its text, see www.ucd.ie/ibis/filestore/Kuala%20Lumpur%20Agreement.pdf.

[3] G.R. No. 183591, October 14, 2008.

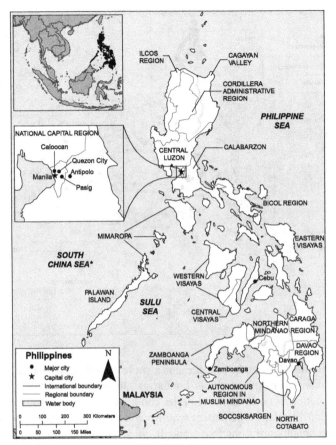

* The South China Sea is also known as the West Philippine Sea.

Land laws and policies hold the key to the social and economic well-being of a post-conflict region. Consistent land laws and secure land tenure encourage stability and reduce the risk of renewed conflict. However, the legal framework established in the peace agreements to resolve the land dispute in Mindanao is inadequate to provide genuine autonomy and peace.

Peace negotiators are presumed to be informed on basic constitutional and land issues affecting negotiations. This is essential in the Philippines, where land laws are a complicated product of several colonial and postcolonial regimes and where the functions of government agencies often overlap. If parties to negotiations consent to boundary agreements they know will be impossible to implement, they are not acting in good faith. This can lead to mistrust between the parties and can inhibit or even prevent further negotiations. Conflicting laws should be acknowledged at the outset, and all possible solutions drafted prior to negotiations for a peace agreement. Should an element to the agreement require legislation, this should be clearly communicated.

454 Land and post-conflict peacebuilding

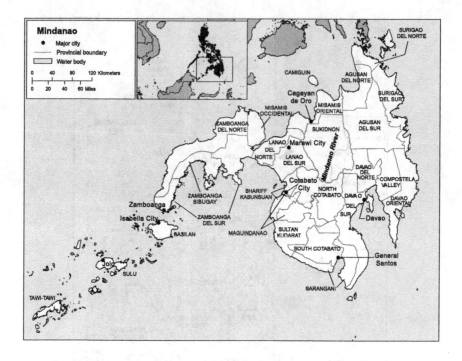

Constitutional amendments present a more complex issue than laws. If a proposed peace agreement entails numerous amendments of the constitution, then the solution is no longer within the competence of the negotiating parties. Even one constitutional amendment requires widespread consultation of citizens. If the amendments are numerous enough, they could require the drafting and ratification of an entirely new constitution. Amendments that deal with territorial integrity, foreign affairs, trade relations with other countries, natural resource management that involves territorial waters, or defense cannot be the subject of bargaining during peace negotiations, as these are defining characteristics of a state. A peace agreement that cannot be carried out breeds more conflict. Hence, transparency and thorough comprehension of relevant national and international laws must characterize peace negotiations.

The gap between broad constitutional principles and current land laws, policies, and practice can be vast. Such is the case in the Mindanao conflict, which has spanned generations and lasted through several constitutions and the terms of several presidents. Problems such as poverty, underdevelopment, and lack of secure land tenure prevail despite the passage of several national land policies intended to address them. The longer the conflict, the more difficult it is to reconcile new laws with existing ones into a coherent legal framework. A key post-conflict priority, therefore, must be to establish a coherent legal framework to guide institutions in implementing the provisions of the peace agreement. The legal framework has important implications for the return, recovery, and

Legal frameworks and land issues in Muslim Mindanao   **455**

reintegration of people affected by conflict. It can help establish territorial boundaries, create a political and economic structure, secure land tenure (and thus sustainable livelihoods), and provide a clear way to settle property claims. Lack of a coherent legal framework to address post-conflict land and property issues can threaten a fragile peace.

In the Philippines, resolution of land conflicts requires consultation among government agencies with overlapping functions. The ARMM in Mindanao, which is the only region in the country with a dominant Muslim population, has its own institutions and laws within the Philippine constitutional framework. The rest of Mindanao, with a Christian majority, is governed by national land laws. Resolving the land dispute in Mindanao requires thorough consideration of the constitution; national, regional, and ARMM laws; the mandates of various government agencies; and even sharia (Islamic law, which applies only in the ARMM and is limited to family and personal relations).

Peace agreements state broad principles and cannot possibly enumerate all pertinent laws and regulations, especially in situations where multiple legal systems are in effect with various modes of dispute settlement. Without a coherent legal framework to implement peace agreements, one that reconciles existing laws with subsequent ones, grievances are likely to accumulate, making the resumption of conflict likely and peace negotiations more difficult.

HISTORICAL BACKGROUND

Mindanao's conflict areas are in the southwestern and central areas of the island and are predominantly Muslim. The term *Moros* was first used to describe the Muslim inhabitants of Mindanao by the Spanish, who colonized the Philippines beginning in the sixteenth century, because they reminded the Spanish of the Moros (Moors) from North Africa who ruled Spain for 800 years. Today, *Moro* or *Bangsamoro* (Moro people) is the generic name for thirteen tribes, a quarter of the population of Mindanao, who share a belief in Islam and a distinct culture and history. According to the 2001 census of Mindanao, 71.77 percent of the population are Christians and migrant settlers and their descendants; 28.23 percent are Moros; and 5 percent are Lumads, indigenous people of Mindanao who are not Muslim (Bacaron 2010).[4] The use of the term *indigenous* to describe Muslims is controversial, as not all Muslims want to be considered indigenous.

Key eras in Mindanao history include the sultanate era (1310–1565), the Spanish colonial era (1565–1898), and the American colonial era (1898–1946). The Philippines became independent on July 4, 1946.

---

[4] The percentages derived from the 2001 census are taken directly from Bacaron (2010) and exceed 100 percent. The author attributes this discrepancy to the transient nature of the Lumads, who are Christians but also wish to be classified as Lumad in view of their claim to ancestral domain and for purposes of qualifying as participants in government programs.

456　Land and post-conflict peacebuilding

The sultanates of Mindanao

Islam was brought to the Philippines in 1310 by Arab traders, Sufis (Muslim mystics), Muslim missionaries, and other travelers who followed the trade routes from Arabia overland through Central Asia and then overseas to India, China, and Southeast Asia. The Islamization of the Philippines was eventually interrupted by Spanish colonists and missionaries (Majul 1973; Jubair 1997).

Islam changed politics, governance, economic systems, social structures, and justice systems. The sultanates of Sulu and Mindanao were established in the fifteenth century and had diplomatic and trade relations with other Asian countries (Jubair 1997; Majul 1973), who recognized them as independent and sovereign. Arts, textiles, pottery, and jewelry found in Mindanao came from as far away as the Middle East.

The Spanish regime

Ferdinand Magellan, a Portuguese navigator financed by Spain, sighted the Philippines in 1521. Spain made the Philippines a formal colony in 1565, establishing Manila, on the island of Luzon, as the capital in 1571. The conquerors were unable, however, to subjugate the sultanates in Mindanao, which had a more advanced social structure than the societies in Luzon and Visayas, and the sultanates were left largely alone.

Spain introduced Christianity, significant church influence in government, a unified government except for Mindanao, and a code of law. One of the new doctrines that Spain introduced was the regalian doctrine, which enabled the Spanish crown to claim all land not registered as private property.[5] The regalian doctrine lives on in the present constitution of the Philippines, in article XII, (entitled "National Economy and Patrimony") National Economy and Patrimony, which reserves for the state ownership of all natural resources other than agricultural lands, and the power to explore, develop, and utilize those resources.

Under the regalian doctrine, the government owned the land, and the Church administered it. Spanish religious orders and charitable organizations were given *encomiendas*—labor trusteeships or land grants measured by the number of indigenous people placed under their control—by the Spanish crown. The encomienda did not confer land tenure, but it gave the holder absolute control of indigenous people living within it, with the power to require them to contribute labor and a large share of their crops. Indigenous people who did not wish to pay tribute moved into the interior, away from the colonizers (Caballero 2002). Those who were educated in Europe, known as *ilustrados*, were critical of the abuse of the Spanish rulers and friars, and often led revolts (Agoncillo 1990; Constantino 1975; Rafael 1994). Eventually, the encomiendas were partitioned into smaller landholdings (though still sizeable by today's standards) known

---

[5] The issue of the regalian doctrine resurfaced in the 2008 MOA-AD controversy.

as *haciendas*, which Spanish friars obtained as land grants from the crown, donations from converts, or payments for debts, or purchased at very low prices from indigenous people (Caballero 2002; Gaspar 2000).

To strengthen their hold on the population, the Spaniards worked to Christianize the indigenous population and recruited them as troops in the conflict against the Moros. The Moros in turn raided Spanish territories, especially those along the coast occupied by Christianized indigenous people, who came to be known as Filipinos. This marked the beginning of mistrust and conflict between Christians and Moros. Filipinos were rewarded by the Spaniards with vast tracts of land, while the Moros, because of their opposition to the Spanish regime, were not. The trend of Christians owning more land than Moros even in Mindanao continued after the arrival of the Americans.

In 1898, Filipinos launched a nationwide armed revolution against the Spanish. When the Spanish-American War began later that year, the Filipinos allied with the Americans, and the Moros of Mindanao reasserted their authority over areas vacated by the Spaniards. The Philippine revolutionary government had difficulty in asserting its authority in Mindanao, and conflicts between Moros and Filipinos emerged (Gomez 2001; Tolibas-Nuñez 1997; Fowler 1985; Gowing 1970; Jubair 1997; Majul 1973; Fast and Richardson 1979).

The American regime

The Spanish-American War ended with Spain ceding the Philippines to the United States for a payment of US$20 million. Mindanao was included in the treaty, although Spain had never fully conquered the island and thus in the eyes of many had no right to cede it. As it was clear that the United States was not going to grant independence to the Philippines, Filipinos in Luzon launched a campaign against American forces in 1898 that lasted until 1902. The Americans quickly learned of the distrust between Moros and Christians and decided to pit one group against the other to prevent them from joining forces to resist U.S. rule.

The Americans were concerned about the legitimacy of their sovereignty over the Moro country, particularly the Sulu sultanate. On August 20, 1899, General John C. Bates and Sultan Jamalul Kiram II of Sulu signed the Kiram-Bates Treaty. In it, the United States was recognized as the sovereign power over the Sulu Archipelago, and in turn recognized the rights and dignity of the sultan and the *datus* (chieftains of noble descent) (Jubair 1997).

On April 9, 1900, General Bates informed the Sulu sultan that the agreement had been accepted by the president of the United States, except for the article regarding the practice of slavery. But the U.S. Congress did not ratify the treaty, on the grounds that the sultan and his people were polygamous. Under American law, the treaty was not valid, but the sultan did not understand this and thought of the Americans as friends. The Western concept of sovereignty was also alien to the Moros, and the sultan failed to appreciate its complex and far-reaching implications (Jubair 1997).

458   Land and post-conflict peacebuilding

While the Philippine-American War ended in 1902, members of the Katipunan, a revolutionary secessionist organization, continued to battle the Americans. Other Filipino revolutionaries struggled among themselves for leadership of the fight against the United States. The Americans had earlier promised to respect the sovereignty of the sultanates if the Moros remained neutral during this power struggle, but as soon as U.S. forces began to win against the Filipino revolutionaries, they proceeded with the conquest of Mindanao. The Moros fought until 1913, when they succumbed to the superior force of the Americans.

The Moros lost not only sovereignty but also their lands. New laws— regarding land registration, declaration of public land, mining, cadastral surveys, creation of agricultural colonies, procedures for private acquisition of alienable and disposable public land, and land settlements—were often imposed without understanding the Moro culture and drastically reduced the lands owned by the Moros (Quevedo 2003). Many land laws which deprived indigenous people, especially Moros who had not obtained title to communally owned ancestral lands, were established during the American period. Among these laws were Commonwealth Act No. 141 or the Public Land Act, which gave Christians more homestead lots than Muslims;[6] Public Act No. 718 of 1903, which voided all property of the Moro sultans unless recognized by the colonial government; and Public Act No. 926 of 1903, which declared unregistered lands to be in the public domain and open to Christian homesteaders. Land title registration was established as conclusive evidence of ownership of land. The application of American land policy caused many Muslims to lose their traditional land rights (McKenna 2008). Though it failed to destroy the Moros' traditional societies and political structures, American rule modified them by abolishing the power and privileges of their ruling elite (Pertierra and Ugarte 2002; McFerson 2002).[7] Armed conflicts erupted between Christians and Moros over agricultural land.

The onset of the Great Depression prompted the sugar industry and labor unions in the United States to press for Philippine independence so that cheap sugar and labor from the Philippines would not end up in the United States. The first attempt at legislation calling for Philippine independence—the 1933 Hare-Hawes-Cutting Act—passed the U.S. Congress over President Herbert Hoover's veto, but was rejected by the Philippine legislature on grounds that it allowed U.S. control over naval bases after independence. The 1934 Tydings-McDuffie Act, known as the Philippine Independence Act, passed both the U.S. Congress and the Philippine legislature with the provisions on U.S. naval bases deleted. It established the Commonwealth of the Philippines, which would be self-governing with foreign policy and certain other areas remaining under U.S. control, and provided for a ten-year transition to independence (Dolan 1991).

---

[6] This law remains the major public land law and provides the legal basis for land use classification at the national level.

[7] Further readings on the American regime in the Philippines include Miller (1990), Fowler (1985), and Salman (2001).

Legal frameworks and land issues in Muslim Mindanao 459

During the 1935 constitutional convention, 120 Moro datus of Lanao drafted the Dansalan Declaration, expressing their desire not to be included in the Philippines independence agreement:

> [W]e do not want to be included in the Philippines for once an independent Philippines is launched, there would be trouble between us and the Filipinos because from time immemorial these two peoples have not lived harmoniously together. Our public land must not be given to people other than the Moros (*Philippine Muslim News (Manila)* 2 (2): 7–12, July 1968, cited in Kamlian (2003), 3).

Subsequently, the 1935 Philippine constitution, which is mostly a copy of the U.S. Constitution, was passed, and Manuel Quezon became the first elected president. The Commonwealth administration pushed for the economic development of Mindanao. Poor people from Luzon and the Visayas, most of them Christians, settled in Mindanao—generally under the homestead policy, which was used and abused to secure ownership or control of land. Some settlers farmed the land themselves or recruited others to work it under various tenancy or labor arrangements; others acquired vast tracts of land as an investment (Gutierrez and Borras 2004). Land laws were manipulated to enable big businesses to establish plantations in Mindanao, which often paid Christian workers far more than Moros. Resettlement programs and plantations set the stage for major conflicts as rural Muslims and Lumads were further marginalized. If occupants refused to leave and the landowner was influential, occupants were evicted by force (McKenna 1998). This pattern of marginalization, loss of land, and neglect significantly limited development opportunities for the Moro people, and this lack of opportunity continues today.

PEACE AGREEMENTS AND THE CREATION OF AN AUTONOMOUS REGION

The current phase of the Moro rebellion has been led by the MILF. Land remains the central issue, though the actors have changed somewhat. The MNLF, the first and largest armed separatist group, commanded 30,000 troops at its peak in the 1970s (Gershman n.d.; David 2003). The MILF is more religion-oriented and began as a splinter group of the MNLF. Its major grievance is the continued socioeconomic underdevelopment of and discrimination against the people who live in Mindanao, particularly in the Sulu Archipelago.

The Tripoli Agreement of 1976 and the ARMM

In the 1960s, students and nationalists, mostly young Moro men, started the modern movement for Moro secession (Caballero-Anthony 2007).[8] Their grievances included

---

[8] For a discussion of the Mindanao conflict from the perspective of secessionist theory, see Biehl (2009).

460 Land and post-conflict peacebuilding

discrimination against Moros, poverty, and inequality due to marginalization of Moros caused by Christian migrants in Mindanao. The movement gained popular support after the eruption of violence in Cotabato in 1969–1971 and in response to the declaration of martial law in 1972 by President Ferdinand Marcos. In 1976, the government and the MNLF signed the Tripoli Agreement, which provided for an autonomous region in the southern Philippines and for the structure of the executive branch of government, which was to be followed by additional peace agreements for the region. Control of foreign policy remained with the central government, but the autonomous region was allowed its own economic and financial infrastructure. Upon the signing of the agreement, a provisional government was established, followed by a formal declaration of an autonomous government and ceasefire. While the Tripoli Agreement was implemented by various laws under President Marcos during the martial law regime, Moros claim that it was not genuinely implemented. In 1977, hostilities broke out again, though they were not as intense as those prior to the ceasefire.

During the term of President Corazon Aquino, the 1987 constitution was ratified. Three sections of article X of that constitution have particular bearing on national sovereignty and the autonomous region:

> Section 1. The territorial and political subdivisions of the Republic of the Philippines are the provinces, cities, municipalities, and barangays. There shall be an Autonomous Region in Muslim Mindanao and the Cordilleras as hereinafter provided.
> . . .
> Section 15. There shall be created autonomous regions in Muslim Mindanao and in the Cordilleras consisting of provinces, cities, municipalities, and geographical areas sharing common and distinctive historical and cultural heritage, economic and social structures, and other relevant characteristics within the framework of this Constitution and the national sovereignty as well as territorial integrity of the Republic of the Philippines.
> . . .
> Section 21. The preservation of peace and order within the regions shall be the responsibility of the local police agencies which shall be organized, maintained, supervised, and utilized in accordance with applicable laws. The defense and security of the regions shall be the responsibility of the National Government.

The national government, in granting autonomy to a region in Mindanao and dealing with secessionist groups such as the MNLF or the MILF, must contend with constitutional and statutory limitations (Brillantes and Tiusongco 2005). Subsequently, Presidential Decree No. 1681 provided for the Regional Assembly and the Regional Executive Council; this was the final step in the framework of the autonomous government. Local legislative councils were also established. The creation of the autonomous region aimed to enhance the attainment of peace and order, accelerate socioeconomic development, and resettle those displaced by conflict.[9]

---

[9] For further reading on a framework for autonomy, see Coronel Ferrer (2001).

Legal frameworks and land issues in Muslim Mindanao   461

Republic Act (RA) No. 6734, known as the Organic Act, was passed in 1989 and serves as the constitution of the ARMM. The executive branch is headed by a regional governor and vice-governor; the Regional Legislative Assembly is the policy-making body; and for its judiciary, an appellate court was created to oversee the sharia courts in the ARMM, whose jurisdiction is limited to personal and family relations among Muslim residents. Consistent with the Tripoli Agreement, it was submitted in a plebiscite to the people of the thirteen provinces and nine cities proposed for inclusion. However, only four agreed to be part of the ARMM: Lanao del Sur, Maguindanao, Sulu, and Tawi-Tawi.

To address unresolved issues related to autonomy and to strengthen and expand the ARMM, RA No. 9054 was passed in 2001 (Tanggol 2005). According to the MOA-AD of 2008, discussed later in this chapter, the expanded geographical scope of the ARMM under RA No. 9054 constitutes the Bangsamoro homeland, a highly contentious issue as this includes areas with large Christian populations.

The 1996 peace agreement

Violence in Mindanao continued despite the passage of the Organic Act. In 1996, during the term of President Fidel Ramos, the MNLF and the Philippine government signed a peace agreement that was considered the most comprehensive attempt to end this violence. In accordance with the earlier Tripoli Agreement, it provided that legislative power in the ARMM—with the exclusion of issues such as foreign affairs, national security, and defense—was to be exercised by a regional legislative assembly. The agreement was to be implemented in two phases. Phase 1 consisted of a three-year transition period and the establishment of the Special Zone of Peace and Development; the Southern Philippine Council for Peace and Development, assisted by the Advisory Council; and the Southern Philippines Development Authority. Phase 2 involved amending or repealing the Organic Act by requiring a plebiscite to determine the establishment of a new autonomous government and its area of coverage (Brillantes and Tiusongco 2005).

The implementation of the peace agreement was hampered by lack of funds for reconstruction and by the national government's unfulfilled development promises. The agreement has been criticized as having a flawed concept of autonomy, restricting the political authority of the ARMM government, leaving the status of sharia law ambiguous, and failing to provide institutional and legal safeguards to ensure just and equitable socioeconomic development (Bauzon 1999). On the positive side, some members of the original MNLF entered regional politics, and many were integrated into the Armed Forces of the Philippines.

The MILF's demands differ from those of the MNLF in that the MILF wants a more significant role for sharia law and demands that the government address the issue of land distribution. Although it did not take part in the Jakarta talks that led to the peace agreement between the government and the MNLF, the MILF did participate in the truce that was in place at the time. However, the

462 **Land and post-conflict peacebuilding**

government accused the MILF of taking advantage of the truce to build up its troops and armaments and consolidate territory (Honasan 2000). This situation was aggravated by the kidnapping of Filipinos and foreigners by the faction Abu Sayyaff (Honasan 2000). Consequently, President Joseph Estrada's administration launched an all-out attack on the MILF in 2000 and captured several of its camps, including Camp Abubakar, the largest.

President Estrada was ousted in 2001 and replaced by President Gloria Macapagal-Arroyo. In 2001, the government and the MILF signed a ceasefire. The MILF had earlier agreed to put aside its demands for independence in order to obtain progress on the rehabilitation of conflict-ravaged areas, the implementation of previous agreements between the MILF and the government, and the economic development of Mindanao (Gershman n.d.).

THE INDIGENOUS PEOPLES RIGHTS ACT

Another key part of the legal framework governing land issues in Mindanao is RA No. 8371, known as the Indigenous Peoples Rights Act (IPRA), which was signed into law in 1997 after heavy lobbying in Congress. It gave indigenous peoples the right to ancestral domain lands and enabled indigenous cultural communities or indigenous peoples to obtain CADTs (certificates of ancestral domain title). It also made it possible to grant title to land regardless of its existing classification and use and regardless of whether it is considered alienable or disposable under land laws.

The IPRA was heralded not only for addressing the exploitation of indigenous people, but also for its guarantee that they could be full-fledged partners in the development agenda of the Philippines (Erasga 2008; Tongson and McShane 2004). However, while it gave indigenous peoples unprecedented rights to exploit and use natural resources in ancestral domain lands, Justice Reynato Puno argued in a separate opinion to the Philippine Supreme Court ruling in *Cruz v. Secretary of Environment and Natural Resources* that it "introduced radical concepts into the Philippine legal system which appear to collide with settled constitutional and jural precepts on state ownership of land and other natural resources."[10] The IPRA contravened important laws relating to land classification, forestry, protected areas, mining, and environmental protection on public lands. It also conflicted with the government's policy of promoting mining to augment the national income.[11]

The IPRA received support from various interest groups, including indigenous people's groups, human rights groups, and industry lobbyists. But its critics predicted that it would empower the state to control the exploration and development of

---

[10] G.R. No. 135385, December 6, 2000. See also the separate opinions of Justices Panganiban and Vitug for detailed arguments that the IPRA violates the constitution and public land laws dating back to the Spanish regime.

[11] Based on the author's experience.

Legal frameworks and land issues in Muslim Mindanao 463

natural resources and consequently would disempower indigenous people from freely using the resources in their ancestral domains, result in legalized land grabbing by indigenous peoples, and promote fraudulent ancestral domain claims (Erasga 2008). Indigenous people were also among the law's strongest critics, claiming that the privatization implied by the process of granting titles would enable foreign companies to more easily obtain ancestral land, and would sow disunity within communities (Vargas 2004).

Another critique of the IPRA is that one of its provisions excludes from ancestral domains those property rights that preexisted the passage of the IPRA (Tauli-Corpus and Alcantara 2005). Because of this, mining companies licensed under the 1995 Mining Act continue to operate legally in these domains despite opposition by indigenous peoples.

A 2003 report by the UN Special Rapporteur on the Situation of Human Rights and Fundamental Freedoms of Indigenous Peoples documented serious human rights violations in several countries including the Philippines. The report discussed human rights implications for indigenous communities of economic activities such as large-scale logging, open-pit mining, multipurpose dams, agri-business plantations, and other development projects. Of particular concern are the devastating long-term effects of mining operations on the livelihood of indigenous peoples and on their environment (Stavenhagen 2003).

Shortly after the passage of the IPRA, a former member of the Supreme Court, Isagani Cruz, filed a petition before the Supreme Court assailing the constitutionality of the IPRA on three main grounds: (1) that it violated state ownership of natural resources based on the regalian doctrine; (2) that it deprived the state of control over the exploration and development of natural resources; and (3) that it threatened to deprive private owners of title to their land. Despite extensive deliberations, the Supreme Court remained tied on the issue; in December 2000, it dismissed the petition (*Inquirer Mindanao* 2008).

During the period between the passage of the IPRA and the Supreme Court's nondecision on its constitutionality, the Department of Environment and Natural Resources in Manila received numerous reports of conflict between indigenous people and mining firms and between different indigenous groups over territorial boundaries. Business groups complained, while some businesses are said to have encouraged indigenous peoples to file CADTs on lands covered by their mining permits to prevent future challenges by other indigenous peoples.[12]

The Department of Environment and Natural Resources convened a task force of land experts to draft a guide to reconcile the IPRA with various national and local laws and regulations relating to land. Aspects of the IPRA directly conflicted with the National Integrated Protected Areas System Act, the Mining Act, the Comprehensive Agrarian Reform Program, and other national and local laws. One or two laws could be reconciled; but the Local Government Code,

---

[12] Based on the author's experience.

464   Land and post-conflict peacebuilding

which delegates the power to approve development plans to local government units, was incompatible with the concept of ancestral domain. Ancestral domains were not provided for in the drafting of land laws, due to the regalian doctrine, which was part of the 1935, 1973, and 1987 constitutions. The task force, therefore, recommended restraint on the issue of ancestral domain and opted to wait for the resolution of the Supreme Court case.[13]

To prevent escalation of tensions between government agencies and indigenous people, the task force reported this recommendation to the Senate Committee on Environment. It was brought to the attention of the task force that many of the original Lumads in Mindanao had decades earlier voluntarily migrated to other regions to seek education or better work opportunities. It could not be generalized that they were displaced forcibly or by conflict. They have since been replaced by both Moros and Christians, some of whom have established title to their lands. Hence, the issue of identifying the original indigenous peoples entitled to file CADTs was highly problematic.

THE 2008 MOA-AD

In 2008, during the administration of President Arroyo, the Memorandum of Agreement on Ancestral Domain (MOA-AD) was signed by the government and the MILF. The main issue in the negotiations was the MILF's claim of territorial rights based on ancestral domain (Tumirez 2005; Jacinto 2007; Usman and Kabiling 2007). It was not a final peace agreement but a significant step in that direction. It provided for the territory of the Moro people and the powers of the autonomous government. Its most controversial provisions relate to the definition of Bangsamoro people, the establishment of the Bangsamoro Juridical Entity (BJE), the associative relationship between the government of the Philippines and the BJE (suggesting the creation of two different states), the planned expanded geographical scope of the ARMM, the BJE's right to enter into economic and trade relations with other countries, and sharing by the national government and the BJE of income from natural resources.

These provisions were challenged by the governor of an adjacent province before the Supreme Court in the case *Province of North Cotabato v. GRP*. The Supreme Court ruled that the BJE was far more powerful than the ARMM and declared the MOA-AD unconstitutional. The decision stated in part:

> It is not merely an expanded version of the ARMM, the status of its relationship with the national government being fundamentally different from that of the ARMM. Indeed, BJE is a state in all but name as it meets the criteria of a state laid down in the Montevideo Convention, namely, a permanent population, a defined territory, a government, and a capacity to enter into relations with other states.

---

[13] Based on the author's experience. The task force later disbanded with the change in government.

Legal frameworks and land issues in Muslim Mindanao   465

Even assuming *arguendo* that the MOA-AD would not necessarily sever any portion of Philippine territory, the spirit animating it—which has betrayed itself by its use of the concept of association—runs counter to the national sovereignty and territorial integrity of the Republic.

The defining concept underlying the relationship between the national government and the BJE being itself contrary to the present Constitution, it is not surprising that many of the specific provisions of the MOA-AD on the formation and powers of the BJE are in conflict with the Constitution and the laws.[14]

Addressing the issue of territorial integrity and secession in international law, the Supreme Court stated: "While the MOA-AD would not amount to an international agreement or unilateral declaration binding on the Philippines under international law, respondent's act of guaranteeing amendments is, by itself, already a constitutional violation that renders the MOA-AD fatally defective."[15]

Three key issues were identified during the peace negotiations between the government of the Philippines and the MILF on the MOA-AD: the standard for identifying indigenous people, the geographical scope (and proposed expansion) of the ARMM, and who has the right to control and use natural resources within it.

The standard for identifying indigenous people

The MOA-AD, under paragraph 3 of the Concepts and Principles section, defines ancestral domain and ancestral land as

> those held under claim of ownership, occupied or possessed, by themselves or through the ancestors of the Bangsamoro people, communally or individually since time immemorial continuously to the present, except when prevented by war, civil disturbance, force majeure, or other forms of possible usurpation or displacement by force, deceit, stealth, or as a consequence of government project or any other voluntary dealings entered into by the government and private individuals, corporate entities or institutions.

Even before the MOA-AD, the ancestral domain issue had proved divisive nationwide. There was difficulty in reaching a consensus as to which groups in the Philippines qualified as indigenous. In Mindanao, several tribal groups can be identified. It is common knowledge that both Lumads and Moros were the original inhabitants of Mindanao. However, the definition of ancestral domain in IPRA used the phrase "since time immemorial," which in the case of Mindanao would date back to the sultanates. Acknowledging a historical injustice committed centuries ago to Moros, and relying on the most recent law (IPRA) to lend legality to the establishment of territory for the Moros, has far-reaching implications.

---

[14]   G.R. No. 183591, October 14, 2008, p. 4.
[15]   G.R. No. 183591, October 14, 2008, p. 5.

466 Land and post-conflict peacebuilding

The current geographical scope of the ARMM does not correspond with the territory of the sultanates. Thus, the proposed expansion of the ARMM under the MOA-AD is problematic. It covers part of the territory of the sultanates, whose heirs are living and whose provinces adjacent to the ARMM are predominantly Catholic and opposed to inclusion in an expanded ARMM. Officials of the National Commission of Indigenous Peoples—the government agency primarily responsible for issues relating to indigenous peoples and the titling of their ancestral domains—told an interviewer in 2002 that the question of whether Moros should be considered indigenous people was uncertain and needed further discussion (Caballero 2002).

People in other regions have raised the following questions: If Moros as original inhabitants are indigenous to Mindanao, what about the Lumads, who were also original inhabitants of the region and some of whom, like the Moros, were displaced by warlords and by conflict between the government and other armed groups? Are all original inhabitants of other regions also to be considered indigenous people and, as such, entitled to ancestral domain claims under IPRA? In a region characterized by protracted armed conflict, it would be difficult or impossible to determine who migrated voluntarily and who was forcibly displaced. Moreover, fraudulent land titles abound in the region. Since armed conflict began, there has been no systematic attempt to rectify land records, as government officials often belong to warring clans with old grievances against each other and the ARMM government has been characterized by weak institutions and poor governance.

The proposed expansion of the ARMM

The main objectives of the MOA-AD were to amend the 1989 Organic Act that established the ARMM to expand its geographical scope and give land to the Moros as ancestral domain. It was the most recent in a series of additions to the territory of the ARMM, which ultimately grew to include the provinces of Sulu, Maguindanao, Lanao del Sur, Tawi-Tawi, Zamboanga del Norte, Zamboanga Sibugay, and Basilan (except Isabela City); Marawi City; six municipalities in Lanao del Norte; hundreds of villages in the provinces of Sultan Kudarat, Lanao del Norte, and North Cotabato that voted to become part of the ARMM in 2001; and two municipalities in Palawan. The proposed expansion generated widespread opposition, as many cities, municipalities, and provinces adjacent to the ARMM had refused to join the ARMM twice in the past and many non-Moro indigenous people's ancestral domains are located within the area.

Widespread opposition to the MOA-AD arose among Muslims and Christians alike. Public uproar followed when a major newspaper published a map of the proposed expanded ARMM, which encroached on non-Muslim regions (*Philippine Daily Inquirer* 2008a). According to the heir of the Sultan of Sulu, Sultan Esmail Kiram, the MOA-AD included as ancestral domain territory that was originally part of the Sultanate of Sulu. He questioned the true intention of the government and whether it was encouraging more conflict between Moros and Christians in Mindanao, while expressing disgust over the lack of prior consultation on the proposed expansion (*Philippine Daily Inquirer* 2008b). Politicians whose jurisdictions were threatened demanded an injunction from the Supreme Court against the signing of the MOA-AD.

The MOA-AD did not mention the Philippine constitution at all but referred instead to a "basic law" (*Philippine Daily Inquirer* 2008a), which created confusion as to whether it referred to the constitution or sharia law. Considering the Organic Act as the constitution of the autonomous region, the MOA-AD appears to be intentionally ambiguous as to its source of authority to cede territory beyond the provisions of the constitution, which requires an amendment of the Organic Act.

Just a few hours before it was due to be signed in Malaysia, the MOA-AD was declared unconstitutional by the Supreme Court because it had not been subjected to popular consultation (*Province of North Cotabato v. GRP*). The court enjoined respondents and agents from signing the MOA-AD and similar agreements in the future. According to Joaquin Bernas, Dean Emeritus of Ateneo Law School in Makati City, Philippines, a mere memorandum of agreement cannot cede the territory of a sovereign state. No territorial dispute, no matter how well-meaning parties to the negotiations are, can be settled when the peace agreement directly contravenes the provisions of the constitution. It would require an amendment of the Organic Act that created the ARMM, or even an amendment of the constitution (*Philippine Daily Inquirer* 2008c), and several amendments to or repeal of laws affecting land, natural resources, and regional government.

Control and use of natural resources

Complicating the dispute over land are the natural resources found on and under the land. In 2002, 29 percent of the ARMM was covered by forest (De La Paz and Colson 2008), while agricultural land accounted for 25.9 percent. Coconut, corn, banana, rubber, coffee, cacao, tubers, roots, and bulbs are key crops in the region (NSO 2008). Both logging and armed conflict have resulted in severe deterioration of forest cover. Forest and other public lands have also been illegally titled as private property, mostly by warlords.

Mindanao, like the rest of the country, is rich in metallic and nonmetallic minerals, including lead, zinc, ore, iron, copper, chromite, magnetite, gold, marble, salt, sand, gravel, silica, clay, and limestone (Mindanao Economic Development Council 2010). Mindanao's mineral resources account for nearly half of the country's gold reserves and 83 percent of its nickel reserves (see figure 1). Mindanao's mineral production amounted to 13.5 billion Philippine pesos in 2004 (approximately US$240 million), or about 25.5 percent of national output (Neri 2006). The potential for revenue from mineral mining may be even larger given that production has been hampered by armed conflict and by concerns about environmental damage. Furthermore, from 1996 to 1997, the mining industry suffered setbacks, with cases questioning the constitutionality of the Mining Act and the problems and controversies brought about by the passage of IPRA. From

468 Land and post-conflict peacebuilding

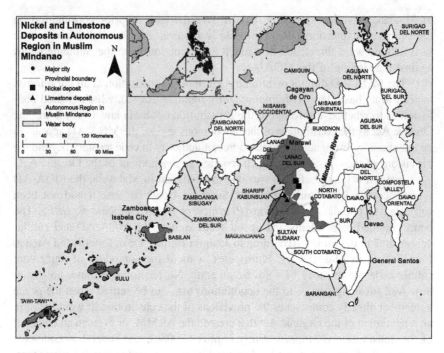

Figure 1. Nickel and limestone deposits in Mindanao
Source: MGB (2010).

2004 to 2005, a rise in global exploration spending and metal prices marked renewed interest of investors in the mining industry.

From the time the IPRA was passed, the mining industry—which the national government under President Arroyo strongly promoted in order to speed up economic growth—has strongly protested its implementation and at one time threatened to lobby Congress for its repeal. The Chamber of Mines, an industry association, warned of the potential that foreign mining firms could withdraw due to the vagueness of the IPRA and insufficient government commitment to the mining industry (Asian Development Bank 2002).[16] In 1998, the National Commission of Indigenous Peoples issued several administrative orders exempting all leases, licenses, contracts, and other forms of concession within ancestral domains existing prior to the promulgation of the implementing rules and regulations of the IPRA from the requirement of free and prior informed consent of indigenous peoples under IPRA.

The claim that the entire ARMM is ancestral land of the Moros is problematic, considering that the ancestral domain argument is used to circumvent not only the regalian doctrine of the constitution but the very provisions of the constitution

---

[16] One of the challenges of implementing the IPRA is identifying which groups are truly indigenous to a place.

Legal frameworks and land issues in Muslim Mindanao 469

on national territory itself, resulting in the dismemberment of Philippine territory. The objective of the MOA-AD is not just to award certificates of ancestral domain to Moros, but also to allow them to exploit and develop the mineral resources under the land and have trade relations with other countries. Unless the constitution and the Organic Act establishing the ARMM are changed, these issues will remain unresolved. In addition, extensive public consultation must be conducted in adjacent non-Muslim areas that would be affected by the proposed ARMM expansion.

Following the regalian doctrine, the constitution (art. XI, sec. 2) is clear that all land in the Philippines and all minerals underneath it belong to the state. The government's position is that ancestral domain gives indigenous people the right to use surface land but not the resources underneath. However, the MNLF has argued that the MOA-AD was supposed to implement the 1996 peace agreement, which stated that the exploration, utilization, and development of land and minerals in the autonomous region would be vested in the regional autonomous government.

This provision explicitly mentioned strategic minerals, which were to be defined later. The MNLF has contended that both sides should have a say in this definition, and has argued that the government violated the peace agreement by unilaterally identifying these minerals and limiting the autonomous government's jurisdiction over minerals and natural resources through an amendment of RA No. 6734, the Organic Act of the ARMM, by RA No. 9054 (Conde 2001). The government identified the following strategic minerals and other strategic resources as exempt from the ancestral domain agreement: uranium; coal, petroleum, and other fossil fuels; all potential sources of energy, such as lakes, rivers, and lagoons, and national reserves; aquatic resources; and forest and watershed reservations. In enumerating these resources, the government referred to the regalian doctrine in the constitution, which is repeated in other constitutional provisions on territory, national economy, and patrimony.

ARMM officials have expressed their desire to amend laws including RA No. 9054, the Organic Act of the region, so that the regional government can have full control over the region's natural resources. A representative of Lanao del Sur in the Regional Legislative Assembly said that while the ARMM government "has control and supervision over the exploitation, utilization, development and protection of the mines and minerals and other natural resources within its area, it has no control over mining and use of uranium, petroleum, and other fossil fuels, mineral oils, and all sources of energy." He also stated that RA No. 9054 specifically exempted "national reservations already delimited by authority of the central government or national government and those that may be defined by an Act of Congress," depriving the ARMM of "the right to manage their natural resources, specifically their strategic minerals" (*Inquirer Mindanao* 2010).

LESSONS LEARNED

A new peace panel was formed under President Benigno Aquino in 2010. The head of this panel has referred to the need to amend the constitution (Conde 2010), but any proposed amendment of the provisions on national territory is still subject

470 Land and post-conflict peacebuilding

to the approval of the Christian majority in areas proposed for expansion of the ARMM. Local government units that would be affected by the proposed expansion are also likely to vote against it in a plebiscite, setting the peace process back. In 2010, the MILF issued contradictory statements that Moros want to establish their own sub-state and that they are abandoning their bid for an independent state (*Philippine Daily Inquirer* 2010a, 2010b, 2010c).

Ongoing peace negotiations can benefit from the valuable lessons this challenging process has yielded thus far. In negotiating for peace in Mindanao, the parties need to uphold the constitution, specifically the provisions on national territory, patrimony, and economy. No written agreement between the parties can be effectively implemented if territorial boundaries are ambiguous. Land is crucial to the identity, culture, and livelihood of a people, and the land laws governing classification and reclassification, ownership, and transfer are all based on the constitution. In the case of Mindanao, this problem is compounded by the fact that the population is predominantly Christian and expansion of the ARMM is a sensitive, even explosive political issue. Expansion would need the consent of adjacent regions in a plebiscite, as specified in the constitution. Any peace agreement that disregards the constitution would have little chance of succeeding. If a proposal would require a constitutional amendment, this must be made clear during negotiations.

The difference between autonomy and secession must be kept clear. International law sets no rules for secession, but the criteria defining a state, as laid down in the 1933 Montevideo Convention on the Rights and Duties of States, are a permanent population, a defined territory, a government, and the capacity to enter into relations with other states.[17] Any agreement or other legal instrument that grants all of these powers raises questions as to whether it is conferring on an entity the status of a state. The MOA-AD attempted to give all of these powers to the ARMM, but it was never implemented due to the intervention of the Supreme Court. Other Philippine provinces have permanent populations, defined territories, and provincial governments. The reason that the Supreme Court found the MOA-AD unconstitutional was that the memorandum also granted the BJE its own autonomous government, and the capacity to enter into foreign relations with other states. While the MOA-AD ostensibly sought to expand the BJE, the Supreme Court held that the new authority that was granted by the MOA-AD was tantamount to secession, and thus unconstitutional. Secession cannot be disguised as the expansion of the territory of an autonomous region granted by a peace agreement. Any such expansion should be subjected to extensive public consultation among the residents of the areas affected.

Multiplicity of land laws is a major problem in the Philippines, including the ARMM. This problem is exacerbated by the presence of warlords who have been repeatedly accused of land grabbing, and even gaining title to environmentally protected areas.[18] The immediate cancellation of fraudulent and illegal land titles

---

[17] For the text of the convention, see www.jus.uio.no/english/services/library/treaties/01/1-02/rights-duties-states.xml.

[18] Based on the author's experience.

Legal frameworks and land issues in Muslim Mindanao 471

in ARMM should be a priority to retrieve public lands and protect critical natural resources. This can only be achieved if the warlords and their private armies are disbanded and if warlords are included as parties to the peace negotiations. Reconciling these claims will require cooperation between the executive branch in Metro Manila and local governments. Seasoned high-level peace negotiators for the government with vast know-how and experience with the parties and issues of the conflict can promote credibility and build confidence in the process, especially when backed by a multidisciplinary group of experts. The MILF must control its own ranks, and particularly rogue members. Warlords should also be included in the peace negotiations. Both parties must participate in negotiations in good faith and with respect for the mutually agreed ceasefire. Whether this will happen remains to be seen. Indeed, a new peace deal between the GRP and the MILF creating a Bangsamoro region with a parliamentary form of government was announced in October 2012, but immediately encountered constitutional issues requiring a long process of amendments to succeed.

REFERENCES

Agoncillo, T. 1990. *History of the Filipino people*. Quezon City: R.P. Garcia.

Asian Development Bank. 2002. Indigenous peoples/ethnic minorities and poverty reduction: Philippines. Manila. www.adb.org/sites/default/files/pub/2002/indigenous_phi.pdf.

Bacaron, M. A. 2010. Indigenous conflict resolution mechanisms in Mindanao: Is their institutionalisation the answer? *Asian Journal of Public Affairs* 3 (1): 49–59.

Bauzon, K. E. 1999. The Philippines: The 1996 peace agreement for the southern Philippines; An assessment. *Ethnic Studies Report* 17 (2): 253–280.

Biehl, E. D. 2009. The Philippine conflict in Muslim Mindanao and the Sulu Archipelago from the perspective of secessionist theory [Der philippinische Konflikt in Mindanao und dem Sulu-Archipel aus sezessionstheoretischer Perspektive]. *Journal of Current Southeast Asian Affairs* 1:97–99.

Brillantes, A., and J. Tiusongco. 2005. Institutional and politico-administrative responses to armed conflicts. *Philippine Journal of Public Administration* 49 (1–2): 1–39.

Caballero, E. 2002. Basis of conflict in ARMM in relation to land and resources. Technical report. Philippine Environmental Governance Project, Department of Environment and Natural Resources, and United States Agency for International Development. http://ecogovproject.denr.gov.ph/Downloads/Technical_reports/BASIS_OF_CONFLICT_IN_ARMM.pdf.

Caballero-Anthony, M. 2007. Revisiting the Bangsamoro struggle: Contested identities and elusive peace. *Asian Security* 2:141–161.

Conde, C. 2001. New ARMM law to deepen Mindanao's troubles. *Bulatlat*, July 22–28. http:bulatlat.com/archive1/023ARMM%20Law.html.

———. 2010. Marvic Leonen: Aquino's noteworthy choice of Mindanao peace negotiator. *Dateline Manila*, July 16. http://asiancorrespondent.com/carlosconde/aquino%E2%80%99s-noteworthy-choice-of-mindanao-peace-negotiator.

Constantino, R. 1975. *The Philippines: A past revisited*. Quezon City: Tala Publication Services.

Coronel Ferrer, M. 2001. Framework for autonomy in Southeast Asia's plural societies. Working Paper 13. Singapore: Institute of Defense and Strategic Studies. www.rsis.edu.sg/publications/WorkingPapers/WP13.pdf.

472 Land and post-conflict peacebuilding

David, R., Jr. 2003. The causes and prospect of the southern Philippines secessionist movement. Master's thesis, Naval Postgraduate School.

De La Paz, M. C. G., and L. Colson. 2008. Population, health, and environment issues in the Philippines: A profile of the Autonomous Region in Muslim Mindanao (ARMM). Washington, D.C.: Population Reference Bureau.

Dolan, R. 1991. *Philippines: A country study.* Washington, D.C.: Federal Research Division, Library of Congress.

Erasga, D. 2008. Ancestral domain claim: The case of the indigenous people in Muslim Mindanao (ARMM). *Asia-Pacific Social Science Review* 8 (1): 33–44.

Fast, J., and J. Richardson. 1979. *Roots of dependency.* Quezon City: Foundation for Nationalist Studies.

Fowler, D. 1985. The Moro problem: An historical perspective. Master's thesis, Naval Postgraduate School.

Gaspar, K. 2000. *The Lumad's struggle in the face of globalization.* Davao City: Alternate Forum for Research in Mindanao.

Gershman, J. n.d. Self-determination in conflict profile: Moros in the Philippines. *Foreign Policy in Focus.* Washington, D.C.: Interhemispheric Resource Center / Institute for Policy Studies. www.scribd.com/doc/20589646/Moros-in-the-Philippines.

Gomez, H. 2001. *The Moro rebellion and the search for peace: A study on Christian-Muslim relations in the Philippines.* Zamboanga City: Silsilah Publications.

Gowing, P. 1970. *Muslim Filipinos: Heritage and horizon.* Quezon City: Foundation for Nationalist Studies.

Gutierrez, E., and S. Borras. 2004. *The Moro conflict: Landless and misdirected state policies.* Washington, D.C.: East-West Center.

Honasan, G. 2000. On peace and insurgency: President Estrada and the conflict in Mindanao. *Kasarinlan* 15 (2): 237–244.

Inquirer Mindanao. 2008. Ancestral domain vs regalian doctrine. October 6.

———. 2010. ARMM execs seek control of natural resources. March 4.

Jacinto, A. 2007. Manila resumes peace talks with MILF. *Arab News*, October 24. www.arabnews.com/node/304908.

Jubair, S. 1997. *A nation under endless tyranny.* 2nd ed. Lahore, Pakistan: Islamic Research Academy.

Kamlian, J. 2003. Ethnic and religious conflict in southern Philippines: A discourse on self-determination, political autonomy and conflict resolution. Islam and human rights fellow lecture, School of Law, Emory University.

Majul, C. A. 1973. *Muslims in the Philippines.* Quezon City: University of the Philippines Press.

McFerson, H., ed. 2002. *Mixed blessing: Impact of the American colonial experience on politics and society in the Philippines.* Vol. 41 of *World View of Social Issues.* Westport, CT: Greenwood Press.

McKenna, T. 1998. *Muslim rulers and rebels: Everyday politics and armed separatism in the southern Philippines.* Berkeley: University of California Press.

———. 2008. *The origins of the Muslim separatist movement in the Philippines.* New York: Asia Society. http://asiasociety.org/countries-history/conflicts/origins-muslim -separatist-movement-philippines.

MGB (Mines and Geosciences Bureau, Republic of the Philippines). 2010. Geology and mineral distribution map of the Autonomous Region in Muslim Mindanao. Department of Environment and Natural Resources. Quezon City.

Legal frameworks and land issues in Muslim Mindanao 473

Miller, S. C. 1990. *Benevolent assimilation: The American conquest of the Philippines, 1899–1903*. New Haven, CT: Yale University Press.

Mindanao Economic Development Council. 2010. Mindanao. www.medco.gov.ph/mindanao.asp.

Neri, R. 2006. NEDA's economic and social report on Mindanao. Presentatation to Joint RDC-Cabinet meeting, July 8.

NSO (National Statistics Office, Republic of the Philippines). 2008. A review of the agriculture sector in autonomous region in Muslim Mindanao. www.census.gov.ph/data/sectordata/sr04119tx.html.

Pertierra, R., and E. F. Ugarte. 2002. American rule in the Muslim south and the Philippine hinterlands. In *Mixed blessing: The impact of the American colonial experience on politics and society in the Philippines*, ed. H. M. McFerson. Westport, CT: Greenwood Press.

Philippine Daily Inquirer. 2008a. Analysis: Self-inflicted dismemberment. August 8.

——. 2008b. Muslims, Christians to stage protests vs. govt-MILF deal. August 3.

——. 2008c. The controversial GRP-MILF MOA. August 11.

——. 2010a. MILF abandons bid for independent state. September 23.

——. 2010b. MILF says gov't needs cha-cha to form sub-state for Muslims. September 23.

——. 2010c. Moros want own "sub-state." September 23.

Quevedo, O. 2003. Injustice: The root of conflict in Mindanao. Paper presented at the 27th General Assembly of the Bishops' Businessmen's Conference, Taguig, Metro Manila Philippines.

Rafael, V. 1994. *Contracting colonialism: Translation and Christian conversion in Tagalog society under early Spanish rule*. Durham, NC: Duke University Press.

Salman, M. 2001. *The embarrassment of slavery: Controversies over bondage and nationalism in the American colonial Philippines*. Berkeley: University of California Press.

Stavenhagen, R. 2003. *Human rights and indigenous issues*. Report of the Special Rapporteur on the Situation of Human Rights and Fundamental Freedoms of Indigenous Peoples. New York: United Nations Economic and Social Council, Commission on Human Rights.

Tanggol, S. 2005. Democratization, governance and poverty alleviation in the autonomous region in Muslim Mindanao. *Philippine Journal of Public Administration* 49 (1–2): 40–58.

Tauli-Corpus, V., and E. Alcantara. 2005. *Engaging the U.N. Special Rapporteur on indigenous people: Opportunities and challenges; The Philippine mission of the UN Special Rapporteur on the Situation of Human Rights and Fundamental Freedoms of Indigenous People, December 2–11, 2002*. Baguio City: Tebtebba Foundation.

Tolibas-Nuñez, R. 1997. *Roots of conflict: Muslims, Christians and the Mindanao struggle*. Makati City, Philippines: Asian Institute of Management.

Tongson, E., and T. McShane. 2004. Securing land tenure for biodiversity conservation in Sibuyan Island, Romblon, Philippines. Paper presented at the EGDI and UNU-WIDER Conference, "Unlocking Human Potential: Linking the Informal and Formal Sectors," September 17–18.

Tumirez, A. 2005. *Ancestral domain in comparative perspective*. Washington, D.C.: United States Institute of Peace.

Usman, E. K., and G. D. Kabiling. 2007. Philippines: Muslim leaders welcome peace move. *Manila Bulletin*, August 14.

Vargas, M. 2004. Indigenous groups decry 7 years of IPRA law. *Bulatlat*, October 24–30. www.bulatlat.com/news/4-38/4-38-indigenous.html.

Unexplored dimensions: Islamic land systems in Afghanistan, Indonesia, Iraq, and Somalia

Siraj Sait

A common dilemma confronting post-conflict interventions in Muslim societies is whether, or to what extent, to engage with Islamic normative systems and perforce Islamic political dynamics. Will entertaining Islamic arguments add another layer of volatility, frustrate reform, and embolden radicals? Will Muslims intuitively resist universal principles and demand authenticity even at the expense of durable peacebuilding and development? Will canvassing medieval Islamic doctrines, like other customary norms, unravel the hard-won development consensus and jeopardize human rights? Widespread anxieties such as these may reflect the false premises and dichotomies—universal versus Islamic, secular versus faith-oriented, modern versus traditional—that sometimes permeate post-conflict resource management discourses.

Islamic arguments are a distinctive stream of thought that cannot always be subsumed within an all-encompassing "customary, informal, and alternative" category. At the same time, the role of Islamic ideas should not be exaggerated, given the dynamic relationship between Islamic, secular, customary, and state norms where there is legal pluralism. This chapter does not advocate for exclusive or automatic Islamic solutions where Muslims live; rather, it suggests that where Islamic components can be fitted into overall universal strategies, they must be deployed when appropriate, and this deployment must be accompanied by a realistic political assessment of the risks and opportunities. Muslims in post-conflict situations have natural resource concerns, needs, and challenges that are similar to those of any other post-conflict community, so they are likely to welcome global approaches that are adapted to their setting.

Exploration of Islamic best practices is not necessarily aligned with a fundamentalist, ideological, or even pro-faith agenda because Islamic development

---

Siraj Sait is reader and head of law research at the University of East London (UK), where he coordinates the Human Rights and the Islamic and Middle East Studies programs. A former state prosecutor on human rights in India, he recently worked with the United Natioins Human Settlements Programme supporting the launch of the Global Land Tool Network. The author acknowledges the research contributions of Clarissa Augustinus and Hilary Lim.

476   Land and post-conflict peacebuilding

tools can and do work alongside and within secular frameworks and with equal effectiveness (An-Na'im 2008). Notwithstanding the political risks and inherent limitations in using Islamic approaches, a pragmatic, flexible, and inclusive strategy should be able to harness potential tools when they are applicable and appropriate (Sait and Lim 2006; Global Land Tool Network 2006). Although Islam is recognized as a distinctive contributor rather than just another morphing custom, it exhibits internal diversity and mostly combines with customary, secular, state, and other norms and practices to operate through a hybridity of systems.

The short case studies from Afghanistan, Indonesia, Iraq, and Somalia in this chapter offer an opportunity to reflect on the potential of positive Islamic conceptions relating to natural resource management in familiar countries that represent some of the geographical, jurisprudential, and sociopolitical diversity within the Muslim world. The sketches arise out of the author's work with the Global Land Tool Network and the United Nations Human Settlements Programme (UN-HABITAT) since 2003.

Despite a common faith among their majority populations, these four countries have dissimilar socioeconomic trajectories and political narratives, which have prompted the promulgation of distinct laws with differing Islamic law inputs, as well as the creation of particular social, cultural, and political institutions. Contrasts between the rural parts of Somalia and the urban centres of Iraq, for example, could not be more striking. Given the staggering number of Muslim communities and the numerous manifestations of faith among Muslims, attempts to establish a global Islamic post-conflict natural resource management framework would be futile. However, where common theology and language intersect with shared experiences, comparative studies and cross-fertilization of ideas can yield useful perspectives.

The Islamic resource management tools under the lens here are property rights for cultivators of barren (*mawat*) land, Islamic endowments (*waqf*) adapted for community welfare, robust individual usufruct (*tassaruf*) rights over state land, and Muslim collective tenures. (A glossary of Islamic terms is presented as an annex to this chapter.) Such tools have been part of the legendary pursuit, ambitious yet elusive, of global initiatives aimed at strengthening land access, food security, and environmental sustainability (Augustinus 2009; Deininger 2003). These tenure models have been around for many centuries, coexisting with turbulent and violent histories, so it is likely that they will work well in post-conflict natural resource management. Mawat land has been used for reintegration of displaced people, the permanent dedication of waqf has been a bulwark against war-triggered change in political leadership, tassaruf rights have endured in spite of state succession battles, and Islamic cooperatives have been havens during civil wars and other conflicts.

Islamic dimensions of land management are often disregarded because of preconceptions about the incoherence of their content and about the political risks of deploying them. The four country studies, each exemplifying an Islamic concept, are therefore followed by responses to four questions: What are the political risks of entertaining Islamic arguments? Is there added value in differentiating Islamic

Islamic land systems 477

from other customary practices? Can Islamic methods help resolve disputes? And what are the human rights and gender trade-offs to be made in an investment in Islamic land management practices?

AN ISLAMIC NATURAL RESOURCE MANAGEMENT FRAMEWORK

It is widely assumed that mawat, waqf, tassaruf, and Sufi cooperatives—all regular Islamic tenures—are adaptable as tools for post-conflict natural resource management, but they have yet to be fully evaluated by research. A modest objective of this chapter is to provide a set of research questions for the study of these tools.

Mawat, waqf, tassaruf, and Sufi cooperatives are distinctly and uniquely Islamic. The descriptor *Islamic* is more accurate than *Muslim* because these are not merely Muslim practices but are consciously derived from Islamic law. Even where colonial and modernist reforms created new tenure types and terminology, the Islamic tenures are influential as concepts, if not always as practice, in many parts of the Muslim world. Reclamation of mawat is a centuries-old practice developed through Islamic jurisprudence. The waqf antedates the English trust, and many experts have argued that it inspired the trust (Cattan 1955; Gaudiosi 1988). The tassaruf is derived from classical Islamic law and has its own unique rules and no obvious equivalent in Roman law (Hamoudi 2008a). The Somali Sufi cooperatives are also consciously derived from Islamic principles.

There is no unified field branded as an Islamic natural resource management framework, but pieces of such a framework emerge from a set of overlapping themes, key concepts, practices, and principles. The framework can be drawn from well-established fields of international law, particularly human rights and humanitarian law, and from emerging fields such as Islamic jurisprudence on environmental protection and sustainable development (Khadduri 1966; An-Na'im 1990; Baderin 2003; Hashmi 2002; Al-Zuhili 2005; Hasan 2006). It would encompass the objectives of Islamic law, explicit Koranic verses, practices of the Prophet's generation (*sunna*), and subsequent jurisprudential peace and development doctrines. Islamic post-conflict and environment studies are evolving, and this presents opportunities to forge new approaches and develop fresh perspectives (Huda 2010; Sait 2007; Sait and Lim 2006).

Islamic doctrines often support natural resource management, particularly in post-conflict situations. Waqf can be dedicated for specific groups or purposes, including land development, waterways, and environmental protection. Mawat land reclamation or land grants (*iqta*) by the state can facilitate greater land access and better post-conflict resource management. Reserves (*hima*) can be established for public welfare, for example, or for conservation and management of rangelands, forests, watersheds, and wildlife. Within such reserves, development, deforestation, grazing, and hunting may be prohibited or regulated. Inviolable sanctuaries or zones (*harim*) for protection of human, animal, or particular plant life can be set up. UN agencies, civil society groups, and land management experts have been working successfully with such tools (Sait 2008).

478   Land and post-conflict peacebuilding

The most ambitious Islamic laboratory on land matters took shape during the Ottoman Empire (Aytekin 2009). During the sixteenth and seventeenth centuries, the empire's influence straddled several continents, including Western Asia, North Africa, and Southeastern Europe. An assumption is often made that Islamic land law was most evolved in regions formerly within the Ottoman sphere, namely the Middle East and North Africa. This is partly true; the Ottoman Land Code of 1858 continues to echo conceptually or in the law in many Middle Eastern and North African countries, including Iraq, and given the Islamic web of tenures, a broad knowledge of Islamic law and Ottoman practice is vital for the understanding a particular tenure.

Somalia, however, did not come under direct Ottoman influence, and its varied Islamic heritage is evident. Afghanistan was not part of the Ottoman Empire either, but the mawat case study demonstrates how Islamic ideas have flowed freely within the Muslim world even outside the empire. And Aceh, part of present-day Indonesia, was an Ottoman ally as an independent sultanate but did not import Ottoman law because the Acehnese had developed their own customary interpretation of Islamic principles. Given this legal pluralism, it is difficult to map out an Islamic natural resource management framework.

The Islamic philosophy driving the four tools discussed here is as important as the tools themselves. Obligations regarding philanthropy, fairness, and poverty alleviation are influential. Two important ideas are at play: the rights of individuals and the responsibility of state. First, natural resources are subject to divine ownership—a sacred trust—and humans are responsible for their just, equitable, productive, and responsible use. Therefore Islamic practices, from inheritance patterns to microfinance, provide access rights to a broad range of beneficiaries, including women, children, landless people, and minorities.

Second, the concept of access to natural resources under Islamic systems has implications far beyond the material domain as it stresses responsibility, poverty alleviation, and redistribution. In the Islamic welfare state, the public treasury has a specific mandate to support the poor and landless and to ensure fairness and redistribution. State funds comprise not only tax revenue but also individual contributions to the poor (*zakat*) and other donations. The state is expected to fund access to natural resources for the poor, and the principle of public interest (*maslaha*) requires the state to act in the interest of human welfare.

Unease over the seemingly unpredictable substantive and political outcomes of ventures with Islam is not exclusive to external interveners or commentators; it is often demonstrated also in the ambivalence within many Muslim societies. The recent uprisings in Tunisia, Egypt, Libya, and Bahrain did not yield a definitive answer to the recurring probe: Where or what is the Islamic dimension? There are many Islams, with liberal, conservative, or fundamentalist agendas, official (state-selected) or informal (mostly blending with custom). Islam may be under the surface, simmering or irrelevant. Islam is negotiated among competing perspectives and stakeholders in relation to both its role within society and how it is interpreted and applied. Generalizations about Muslims, who constitute about one-quarter of the world's population (Pew Research Center 2009), are based on the assumption of their shared beliefs, but their experiences are heterogeneous, as are their ideas about religion and politics.

Islam deals with post-conflict issues head-on. Many researchers have it that the Islamic concept of peace (*salaam*), like the Judeo-Christian understanding of shalom, signifies more than cessation of hostilities and extends to a dynamic state of consciousness, wholeness, and balance (Sait and Lim 2006; Bouta, Kadayifci-Orellana, and Abu-Nimer 2005; Rogers, Bamat, and Ideh 2008). Koranic verses extensively refer to the sanctity of life, the importance of peace, and the imperative of fairness and equity. They emphasize compassion, mercy, individual responsibility toward fellow beings and nature, and the unity of and interconnectedness of all creation. Faith-based values contemplate transformational change, justice, and reconciliation. For Muslims, Islam is a religion of peace—within, with God, toward all human beings, and with nature (Bouta, Kadayifci-Orellana, and Abu-Nimer 2005; Rogers, Bamat, and Ideh 2008).

Islamic faith principles and Islamic individuals, organizations, and institutions regularly play positive roles in peacebuilding and development in religious as well as nonreligious settings (Bouta, Kadayifci-Orellana, and Abu-Nimer 2005; Rogers, Bamat, and Ideh 2008). These leaders and organizations have limitations, of course, but they often provide legitimacy, access to networks, and a means of mobilization (Appleby 2003). Theological resources and activities, including interfaith dialogue, can be vital in all three major stages of conflict intervention: prevention, mitigation, and post-conflict reconstruction. Religion can integrate and sequence peacebuilding and natural resource management priorities.

Shifting from an Islam-as-trigger-of-conflict frame to an Islam-as-potential-support-mechanism approach requires peeling away several layers of skepticism. Some view Islam as a violent religion. They are alarmed by the shrill interpretation of jihadist doctrine by a tiny minority who are political extremists. Others extol Islam's peace message. They refer to core Islamic texts and the practices of the overwhelming majority of Muslims. It may not be necessary to arbitrate this intercivilizational debate if Islamic peacebuilding approaches are promoted not as faith-based strategies but as strategies that can be used pragmatically by believers, agnostics, and atheists alike to achieve certain shared objectives.

In addressing implementation challenges, this chapter makes a distinction between political Islam and developmental Islam. Political operatives regularly use Islam as a manifesto to achieve certain political ends, sometimes in concert with exclusionary and violent methods. Whether it is a revival of an idealist past, a critique of Western policies, or a cynical ideological ploy, politicized Islam divides Muslims on tactics and objectives (Tibi 2002). The overwhelming majority of Muslims are not interested in the Islamic state or in jihad for revenge, for their priorities are their personal faith, their livelihood, stability, and the rights encompassed within an Islamic developmental framework. What often works for them are practical Islamic community-driven conflict-resolution tools such as mediation (*sulh*), conciliation (*wasta*), and arbitration (*tahkeem*) (Irani and Funk

480   Land and post-conflict peacebuilding

1998; Abu-Nimer 2003), alongside an impressive array of culturally supported mechanisms. This chapter explores whether the fear of political Islam can be offset by the promises of developmental Islam, the latter being of far greater significance to the real lives of Muslims.

CASE STUDIES

One reason Islamic principles have failed to inspire tough-minded strategists is that theories of Islamic natural resource management have mostly been discussed in the idealized abstract without consideration of the politics of their implementation, or vice versa. For each of these short case studies, this chapter poses four questions about the content and use of Islam in post-conflict natural resource management. The first query relates to the political risks of employing Islamic strategies. The second question is whether there is added value or utility in recognizing these laws or practices as Islamic instead of subsuming them in the broader category of customary norms. The third issue is whether or how Islamic methods can help resolve disputes, including those over natural resources. The final question relates to possible human rights compromises arising out of these Islamic investments, particularly violation of the rights of women and minorities.

Barren (mawat) land in Afghanistan

A primary focus for post-Taliban reconstruction in Afghanistan is land reform. Driven by a broader agenda of modernization and change, interventions have sought to retract Taliban land laws, which were assumed, without examination, to be a medieval hodgepodge. The Taliban had introduced retrograde and brutal policies, which many saw as a perversion of Islam and which were condemned across the Muslim world. Yet overthrowing the Taliban is not the same as repudiating Islam, and well-meaning efforts toward secularization created tensions and backlash even from Afghan moderates (Suhrke 2007). A ready-made draft modern land code conjured by some of the world's leading land experts did not get the expected traction. As it turned out, the Western-supported Afghan government did not consider all Taliban legislative forays to be simply ideological trash. Some Taliban laws, such as the Land Management Law of 2000, had retained or codified positive features of Islamic land law that had predated the Taliban (Sait 2005).

The Afghan Land Management Law of 2000 refers to numerous Islamic land tenures and strikingly declares that the distribution of dead, or mawat, land (*mowat* in Afghanistan) is one of its key objectives. Few international consultants seem to have understood what this meant or grasped its dramatic implications for land reform in a country such as Afghanistan. It was an invitation to landless persons to claim access, even ownership, of empty lands—lands not owned or used by anyone—that are located away from development and are otherwise passed off as state lands. At stake was a retenuring of a large proportion of Afghanistan. Except for private, state, pasture, and endowment (waqf) lands, the land law had deemed all deserts, mountains, hills, rivers, arid and rocky lands, and jungles to be mawat. This had the potential to revive swaths of wasteland as well as provide land access to the displaced and the landless after the conflict ended. Mawat creatively offered opportunities for regularizing informal and squatter settlements through innovative use of the doctrine.

Redistribution of barren land is an established Islamic economic and legal process for the revival of dead, barren, or wasteland. Revival of mawat land has been a central feature of Islamic economic history and has also been used historically to generate rights of access to unused streams and rivers (Haque 1984). It is distinguished from the concept of a land grant (iqta), whereby the state gives land to deserving or favored people. Mawat reclamation is not at the discretion of the state but is a right exercised by the individual.

Mawat is derived from the Islamic conception of landownership, which is largely linked to land use. It incentivizes productivity and censures waste through a use-it-or-lose-it approach. Sohrab Behdad explains that while private property rights are protected generally, an individual who uses land will have priority over another who has failed to use it (Behdad 1989). In theory, unworked land cannot be owned. Such was the vigor of the argument against hoarding of and exploitation through land that classical theorists argued that excess land could not be rented out without the landlord's inputs, though this ruling was pragmatically overturned rather quickly (Sait and Lim 2006).

Although mawat is an Islamic tenure, its rules are defined by community practice and custom. It is seen as a natural way of improving food security, providing employment, sustaining communities, and fostering community cohesion. Unlike mere possession of *terra nullius*, where the emphasis is on the empty nature of land, it is productive activity on mawat land that creates rights. Ottoman approaches to mawat land exhibited both creativity and flexibility driven by encouragement for the cultivation and use of land. Thus undeveloped land at a particular distance from any town or village, in accordance with Islamic legal theory, could be enlivened through cultivation or other acts, such as irrigation. The occupier who reported effective use of such land and received the permission of the state would be granted rightful possession.

Afghan land law, far from being a primitive hodgepodge as assumed, has a developed and sophisticated mawat doctrine. Under Hanafi Islamic jurisprudence, which is applicable in Afghanistan, for land to be designated as mawat, it must satisfy several criteria: its ownership history must be unknown, there must be a lack of cultivation and construction, and it must be a particular distance from development (Gebremedhin 2006). The designation signifies more than a mere right to adverse possession. It is also distinguished from *mahlul*, a designation for uncultivated land that allows the state to reallocate property if the holder of title leaves it uncultivated for a period of three years. In the case of mawat, it is not the state but the individual who possesses the rights.

482   Land and post-conflict peacebuilding

Strict rules determine what may be considered wasteland. The Land Management Law, true to Ottoman practice and Hanafi doctrine, required that an application relating to rights over mawat land be made to the head of state. Still, the application of this project presented tricky questions. How should barren land be defined? At what distance from developed land should the mawat land lie? What acts should constitute reclamation of land? How was the land to be redistributed? War, control by organized crime syndicates, and the disarray of land institutions created a fluidity in which these issues did not receive adequate attention.

The Karzai government did not challenge the authenticity of mawat, it merely indicated that it did not know how to implement it in the current climate. Karzai, who as president was designated to approve allocation, issued a decree in 2002 (Decree No. 99) that froze the distribution of virgin and barren land by government ministries and agencies. Furthermore, distribution of rural land (including arable state land) to landless farmers was prohibited, presumably because of concerns about corruption and nepotism in land distribution. The international community could have seized on the opportunity to implement the mawat law, but there was no real dialogue about it (Gebremedhin 2007).

Another reason for internal resistance to distribution of mawat land is that the Afghan government was not enthusiastic about relinquishing the state lands under its control. The Afghan Civil Code treats mawat as state property even though there is a difference between barren unowned property and state property, and therefore reclamation has dual tenure transfer implications: it not only converts property from mawat to a license to use (which leads to full rights) but also releases the land from the competing land hunger of the Afghan government.

Land interventions in Afghanistan have mostly focused on titling and private ownership, and land development for the poor is rare. Expansion of the land base through reclamation of barren land would be welcome. Mawat can be a pro-poor tool that benefits the landless, internally displaced persons, and members of other targeted categories of people, but it is equally possible that some people will manipulate it as an opportunity for land grabbing. Internally displaced persons and returnees in Afghanistan face formidable odds. In their long absence, their original homes have often been destroyed and their lands occupied by other displaced families or by powerful warlords or other local elites. Access to land through mawat can be a fresh start. There was an opportunity for developing a reliable, equitable, and transparent mechanism for operationalizing mawat. However, lack of familiarity with the mawat doctrine, as well as absence of political will, sank the prospects for establishment of an innovative pro-poor form of land tenure for displaced and landless Afghans.

Waqf in Indonesia

In post-conflict and post-tsunami Indonesia, the destruction of land records was a tragic backdrop of local leaders' and international relief organizations' rethinking of land tenure relations. The reconstruction of land records, often from communal

Islamic land systems   483

memory, accompanied a renewed focus on individual and joint titling, as well as the customary tenures (*adat*).[1] Another dimension, Islamic law, was often marginalized by external interveners because of their hypothesis that it is amalgamated within adat.

One example of an innovative Islamic land tenure system is the flexible endowment (waqf) in Aceh (Bowen 1988). The Islamic endowment is a key institution that incorporates vast areas of land in the Muslim world. At one time a staggering one-third of Ottoman land was held in trust; wherever a Muslim community existed, one was likely to find a waqf (Sait and Lim 2006). Though modern reforms in several Muslim countries abolished, nationalized, or strictly regulated endowments, the waqf concept remains influential and is being reinvigorated.

At its heart, the waqf is closely tied to Islamic philanthropic principles, with care for orphans, widows, and old, sick, and landless people featuring regularly on the list of waqf objectives. Though the waqf is distinct from the charitable obligation that finds expression in zakat (a levy on Muslims for distribution to the poor and needy that is one of the five pillars of Islam), it flows from the same principles, and it thrives in post-conflict challenges.

Throughout history, the waqf was intended as a third sector of civil society, which existed independently of both the state and the profit-making private sector. As Jennifer Bremer notes, "The oldest civil society institution, the *waqf* or Islamic endowment, combined the features of a philanthropy, a social service agency, and albeit indirectly, a political voice competing with that of a ruler" (Bremer 2004, 5). For centuries in Afghanistan existing waqfs (or more properly in plural: *awaqf*) were revisited and new waqfs created by civil society to fill the gap in state or external funds. The waqf model was used in Aceh to purchase land for educational institutions, graveyards, mosques, and community centers. Waqfs emerged as an important resource to offer tsunami victims support during the emergency and beyond.

Islamic endowments (*wakaf* or *tanoh wakeueh* in Indonesia) are of considerable significance in Aceh, as in other parts of the Muslim world. Article 215 of the Indonesian Compilation of Islamic Law (Kompilasi Hukum Islam, or KHI) refers to waqf as "a legal act whereby a person or a group of persons or a legal body donate part of their wealth either permanently or for a set period for religious purposes and/or other public purposes in accordance with Islamic teachings." Rules determine who can donate a waqf, who can receive it, what can be donated, and which purposes are in accordance with Islamic law (sharia).

Although there is a national body for waqf management (Badan Wakaf Indonesia), under the 2006 Law on Governing Aceh, local authorities regulate and protect waqfs. Land is normally donated as waqf to the head of the village and the religious leader, who are then responsible for management of the land. In Aceh, waqfs have been created not only by individuals but also by community members in a village.

---

[1] For a review of land management in post-conflict and post-disaster Aceh, see Arthur Green, "Title Wave: Land Tenure and Peacebuilding in Aceh," in this book.

484 Land and post-conflict peacebuilding

The waqf in Indonesia is innovative in several dimensions, partly catalyzed by the profound post-conflict and post-tsunami experiences. A frequently cited limitation of waqfs has been their inflexibility, particularly because of the rule of perpetuity. The "once a waqf, always a waqf" rule was intended as a protection against takeover by the government or other parties, but over generations fragmentation, corruption, and waste often seeped in. The 2004 Indonesian waqf law paves way for temporary waqfs. In a departure from conventional waqf jurisprudence, the Indonesian Islamic endowment does not insist on perpetuity; it can be a trust created for a specified period. It envisages not only contributions from individuals but also collective donations. The reference to "waqf material" implies that it can be land or any other immovable property, and cash waqfs can be an important source of credit, with the endowed capital lent to borrowers.

In principle, land donated in the form of waqf cannot have its status changed or be used for any purpose other than that specified in the waqf document. This rule posed particular problems because the conflict and then the tsunami changed facts on the ground. Also, most registered waqf documents and many land managers and witnesses perished in the tsunami disaster. Disputes arose over changes of land use and beneficiaries. For example, could endowed dried out swamps be converted into housing for poor despite contrary waqf objectives, which were now not possible? Could heirs of the original habitants of housing reclaim waqf land, though the waqf is nonhereditary (IDLO 2008)?

A series of community meetings were held, and a spate of innovative Islamic advisory opinions (fatwas) stated that where the land could no longer be used for the designated purpose because of the natural disaster, it could be exchanged or traded on the basis of the Islamic legal maxims of necessity and public interest. Land and property belonging to tsunami victims who had no heirs would be transferred to the Muslim community through the state welfare treasury. It was ironic that it was fatwas, which frequently hit the headlines because of their obscurantist views, that augmented and liberalized waqf jurisprudence in Aceh.

The waqf in Indonesia has developed in tandem with adat and reflects local and community support. Though it falls directly within the jurisdiction of Aceh's Islamic courts, it is usually first addressed through negotiation, often with the assistance of the local religious office. A 2008 International Development Law Organization report details some of the waqf land negotiations in post-tsunami Aceh (IDLO 2008). A school building was planned for waqf land without any arrangement for compensation; the dispute was resolved through negotiation, with another piece of land given instead. Another parcel of waqf land, which was previously a cultivated rice field, became a site for a mosque. Similarly, burial grounds, a government medical center, and community centers were all built on waqf land, through negotiations and arbitration, and with clearance from the Islamic court where needed. Waqf lands have often been transformed into residential neighborhoods, schools, and community centers with the intervention of communities and through innovative use of waqf procedures, but very little of this has been documented.

Usufruct rights (tassaruf) in Iraq

Reconstruction of post-Saddam Iraq proceeds on the premise that modernizing the land laws could strengthen private property. However, it is estimated that over three-fourths of land in Iraq is state controlled, and the rest shows skewed private landholding patterns. Whether there is cause for despair depends on perspectives on usufruct (tassaruf) rights, which pertain to an estimated 70 percent of state lands (Wiss and Anderson 2008).

To negotiate, let alone reform, Iraqi land management systems requires fluency with Ottoman land tenure, which influences Iraq as well as the 1953 Iraqi Civil Code. Both draw heavily on Islamic law. Current-day land experts can learn from the Iraqi government's abortive attempt in the 1950s to redistribute extensive lands—an effort that stalled due to legal, political, and socioreligious objections.

The two main categories of land in the 1858 Ottoman Land Code were *mulk* and *miri*, which approximate individually owned and state land. The other main tenures are endowment land (waqf), barren land (mawat), public land (*matruke*), and uncultivated, lapsed land (mahlul). Miri land is land registered in the name of the state, but in practice belongs to the individual who has the right to develop and use it. Miri land constituted the vast majority of agricultural land in the Ottoman Empire for which farmers paid taxes. The classical Ottoman land tenure framework thus made a fundamental distinction between the right to cultivate land (tassaruf) and absolute ownership of land (*raqaba*).

There are several striking features of tassaruf. It is neither a customary practice of access nor a concession, but a full-fledged right to use, exploit, and dispose of miri land. Thus the term *tassaruf* is used in other contexts to denote control over assets (such as zakat or charity funds) or the right of a partner to dispose of certain property that is not his or her own as if it were private property. The state cannot ordinarily take such land back and must compensate the rights holder if it does; nor can private parties infringe on the user's rights. Volume 3 of the Iraqi Civil Code regulates property rights such as tassaruf (Stigall 2004). These rights were so strong that the distinction between tassaruf and full ownership appeared blurred. In practice, if the state was willing, a claim over the property could be upgraded to full ownership.

Usufruct rights may be diluted or even lost if individuals fail to pay their taxes or if they violate the relevant laws. Most significantly, a user who abandons the land loses rights over that piece of land. Miri land that is never used becomes mawat land, and the rights go to the individual who reclaims the land. On the other hand, if miri land is abandoned for three years, it becomes lapsed land (mahlul), and another person can apply to use it. It is an oversimplification to say that ownership can be proved by deeds and that tassaruf rights are not registered, for this may not be true. The Islamic continuum of land tenure recognizes land use, rewards productivity, and promotes food security.

Tassaruf rights are also inherited. Unlike privately owned property, which is subject to fixed compulsory shares under Islamic dispensation, miri land can

486 Land and post-conflict peacebuilding

be bequeathed or transferred in any manner. Female heirs can get shares equal to those of males, or even exclusively. Thus the transfer of tassaruf rights can compensate women for the lesser inheritance shares under Islamic rules, though there is no research on this. Technically, miri property cannot be subdivided, so land consolidation and adjustments regularly take place. Upon the tassaruf holder's death, the right is assigned to the holder's heirs. If they choose not to accept the tassaruf, it is auctioned to the highest bidder.

Tassaruf also promotes access to land and security for a wider range of people. The state has an obligation under public interest (maslaha) to ensure productive use of land to the maximum benefit of the largest number of people, particularly the landless and the poor. Few external commentators and consultants have appreciated the significance of the Iraqi Civil Code of 1953, which despite several amendments and additional laws still prevails. Several Iraqi experts argue that respect for the Iraqi Civil Code is "more or less like American reverence to the Constitution. In Iraq, constitutions come and go, they are politically motivated, they are hard to take as seriously, but the Civil Code is central to the legal theology" (Hamoudi 2008a, 14; Jwaideh 1953). Others find the Iraqi civil law system to be "a sophisticated, modern system, which [in spite of some needed amendments] is more than capable of addressing the need of displaced persons and those who have lost property" (Stigall 2009, 3). It has worked well in practice and is ingrained in the sociojuridical consciousness of the Iraqi polity.

The Iraqi Civil Code is a blend of continental civil law and Islamic law. It was drafted by the leading Muslim jurist Abd al-Razzaq al-Sanhūrī, who was then the dean of the Iraqi Law College. Its substance was taken largely from Islamic law, Egyptian law (which borrowed from the French Civil Code), and Ottoman legacy; in it the three are almost seamlessly stitched together (Arabi 1995). Knowledge of Islamic and Ottoman influences are critical to an understanding of Iraqi law. Dan E. Stigall, exploring Iraqi property laws and quoting from Sait and Lim (2006), argues

> Although secular legal institutions have long held sway in modern Iraq, the importance of Islam should be kept in mind when pondering contemporary legal institutions—even the most seemingly secular. This is not only because Islamic law still exists as a subsidiary source of law under the Iraqi Civil Code, but also because it allows one to better appreciate the cultural context of Iraqi law and the legal issues under consideration. As Sait and Lim note when discussing property law in the Middle East "a lack of engagement with the internal Islamic dialogue risks creating land systems that are bereft of authenticity and legitimacy and thereby of effectiveness and durability" (Stigall 2008, 2).

At a 2010 Iraqi land conference organized by UN-HABITAT and the World Bank, a comment was recorded by local participants: "We are legal experts in Iraq. We are not starting from scratch. Study the principles given to us by the Ottomans and find solutions in them" (World Bank and UN-HABITAT 2010). Iraq has been erroneously viewed as a clean slate or a stage for modernist land

Islamic land systems 487

experiments that ignore the country's history and influences. Most land consultants are unaware of tassaruf rights, or if they are aware of them, they merely footnote them as leaseholds or refer to such rights as ownership. Tassaruf rights probably endured the conflict in Iraq without the external commentators knowing of their existence. The Iraqi land code and civil courts are dealing with land matters in Iraq, but to ignore the legal culture in which this takes places diminishes the prospects of success for land reform.

Islamic land cooperatives in Somalia

In addition to promoting responsible individual landownership, Islamic law facilitates collective tenures. Muslim societies are comfortable with joint titling and shared tenures. Land consolidation is a Muslim way of life; it is used, for example, in postinheritance adjustments to prevent land fragmentation and maintain viability. Islamic finance products such as microfinance and insurance are predicated on pooling of resources.

In Somalia it is Sufism, the mystical stream of Islam, that provides an intriguing case study of the Muslim cooperative as a community-based tenure. Somalis have long practiced traditional clan lineage rights with respect to use of and access to resources, and clans fiercely protect their land and resource base. Because Somalis are overwhelmingly Muslim, their customary practices (*xeer*) are inclined toward Islamic principles and dealt with through traditional and Islamic dispute resolution mechanisms.

Modernist reformers in Somalia, who viewed the clan system as backward and divisive, began curbing clan-based practices through the 1973 Unified Civil Code before the 1975 Land Reform Act technically abolished customary tenure (Unruh 1995). Scientific socialism was introduced to transform informal collective land tenures into state enterprises and associations, which were projected as a model that synthesized Islamic, customary, and communist models. The state cooperatives were doomed because the rights of several categories of people, such as the pastoralists, were ignored, and excessive bureaucracy, corruption, rigidity, and mismatch of users and resources took their toll. However, there are still cooperatives in the country, working with mixed results, while the push for individual title yielded uncertain gains for poorer communities (Besteman 1989).

The impact of Sufism in Somalia has varied over time, and much of it has been indirect (Lewis 1998; Vikor 1993). The tension between Sufism and conventional Islam has many twists (most Somalis formally belong to the Shafi Sunni school), but Sufism remains influential in many parts. Various Sufi orders command large followings in Somalia, especially the Qadiriya, the Ahmadiya, and the Salihiya. Each order, or *tariqa* ("path" or "way"), is a vibrant community that is also a sociopolitical, economic, and spiritual organization.

The history of Somali tariqas provides a compelling narrative of how Islam created the basis of innovative Islamic land cooperatives. Sufi leaders who came to Somalia to found the Salihiya order in 1880, for example, sought to establish

488 Land and post-conflict peacebuilding

communities among the clan-based Somali society. By all accounts, these "saints" were well received and were offered uncultivated land that they used as a base and from which they expanded. The spiritual and political reasons for Somali receptivity towards these saints must have been the latter's spiritual status and perceived neutrality in clan disputes. Membership in the Sufi community is theoretically a voluntary matter unrelated to kinship. Each order has its own hierarchy that creates an alternative to kin-group dynamics. The Sufi communities thus both acted as a buffer between competing clans and promoted spiritual allegiances above clan differences, with mixed success.

The Sufi communities put the lands given to them to good use and expanded their landholdings through productive use and reclamation of empty land (mawat) by cultivation. Though the precise nature of land rights in Somalia is underresearched, these communities lived by Islamic principles that influenced property relations. These communities were preaching and not only practicing Islamic family law, including laws governing inheritance, but also promoting an Islamic economic ethos through equitable land access, rights to grazing land, access to water points, and sharing of responsibilities as well as profits and losses.

Beyond their religious and political activities, such communities used the fertile land along the Shabelle and Jubba rivers to establish farming communities with cooperative cultivation and harvesting. The tariqa was used as an organizational framework for the agricultural community to practice and transmit its way of life and religion. Knut Vikor argues that the spiritual communities were accompanied by scholar groups that debated and refined their methods of organization, in keeping with their interpretation of Islamic economic, political, and spiritual principles (Vikor 1993).

An influential report on Somalia by Gregory Norton, drawing on the limited literature available and quoting from Hoben (1988), describes tariqa land tenures:

> [Tariqas], . . . which have been active in Somalia for centuries, had an important influence on the development of land tenure. . . . These communities became the focus of "significant agricultural settlements" in the middle years of the 19th century and came into existence in large numbers in the first two decades of the 20th century. The founders of the settlements sometimes received land from lineage heads or were given land to establish a buffer between rival lineages, whose disputes they mediated; the land was owned collectively but cultivated individually. The settlements reportedly ranged in size from a few hundred to over 8,000 members and together encompassed 20,000 to 40,000 individuals in the period from around 1900 to 1940. . . . Hoben claims that the lasting significance of these settlements is that they established "an alternative model of land tenure and social political relations to the dominant, faction ridden clan model" and "provided security and access to resources for displaced, low status people, who could not easily obtain resources and be absorbed into the overarching clan system" (Norton 2008, 86–87).

Commentators and researchers on Somalia frequently complain that because of instability, land analysis in the country is informed by very limited original

Islamic land systems **489**

fieldwork on natural resource management. The Norton study complains that there is "relatively little comment on this (Islamic) development in the general historical and land-related literature on Somalia" (Norton 2008, 85). A closer examination of Muslim cooperatives may or may not deliver a replicable contemporary model, but it would demonstrate that property relations and land management can be developed with reference to faith principles in post-conflict situations. Islamic law is the dominant political discourse in Somalia, so using innovative Islamic ideas to reach universal goals may turn out to be practical.

ANALYSIS OF CASE STUDIES

These Islamic land tenure narratives from post-conflict Afghanistan, Indonesia, Iraq, and Somalia stand in striking contrast to the usual dispatches, which deemphasize Islamic dimensions. However, these case studies present selective, partial views in several respects. They do not fully explain Islamic tools within a cogent land analysis or an explanation of each country's pluralist land systems. The identification of these land tenure systems does not imply that these tools are working or even capable of working, and the case studies do not provide the intervener or practitioner guidance on how to develop technical capacity or negotiate political risks. No systematic or rigorous evaluation of these land tenure systems' design, impact, scale, or replicability has been carried out. This is a serious knowledge gap.

This analysis aims to move research forward by addressing four questions that overhang the case studies: What are the political risks of entertaining Islamic arguments? What is the value of differentiating Islamic from other customary land tenure systems? How can Islamic methods of dispute resolution help? And what human rights trade-offs may be involved in an investment in Islamic land tenure options, particularly with regard to gender?

Political risks

Land is political, and it does not become any less so when Islamic inputs and post-conflict situations are added to the cauldron. Yet the surprise from the case studies is the lack of noticeable links between political Islam and developmental Islam. None of the tools outlined in the case studies are part of hegemonic or even antagonist campaigns by Islamist national liberation movements, terrorists, or Islamist political groups. On the contrary, the armed or ideological movements appeared distinctly disinterested in an Islamic land rights ethos, apparently because of the threat to existing powerful monopolies posed by democratic and economic empowerment.

The approaches of developmental Islam often challenge political Islam, as well as other forces, to cater to broader community interests. It is often the secular or moderate forces that seek to lobby political Islam to yield to developmental Islam, but there can be unintended outcomes. On one hand, the Islamic nature of the land tools makes it convenient to legitimize them, lobby for them, and

490 Land and post-conflict peacebuilding

disseminate them. On the other, there can be a range of reactions from Muslim political groups—from skepticism to hijacking of initiatives. Donors and the international community can also be resistant to the use of Islamic approaches.

In Afghanistan, the so-called warlords, political operatives, land mafia, opium contractors, corrupt officials, and private speculators jointly opposed mawat land distribution because it undermined their illegal and extortionist land businesses. Land redistribution was an element of the Taliban's political agenda, though it was not a high priority. Mawat is found in the 2000 Afghan land law enacted by the Taliban, and it has been in play as a legal concept and practice for much longer. Appearing in the civil codes of the 1970s, mawat is seen not as a democratic, dictatorial, socialist, Taliban, or mujahideen concoction, but as an Islamic right. This does not mean that Islamic land practices exist in a political vacuum or are always politically neutral. It may well be that the Taliban's promotion of mawat reclamation was part of its political agenda.

The Salihiya tariqa of Somalia, which established the collectives, were also known for their anticolonial struggle. Examples from Hezbollah in Lebanon, the Muslim Brotherhood in Egypt, and Hamas in the Palestinian territories show how social welfare activities can be part of political platforms.

Though there has been concern in the past over religious management of waqfs, the fatwas over waqf matters in Indonesia have not been seen as politicalized outputs. Indonesian faith-based organizations, such as Nahdlatul Ulama and Muhammadiyah, may compete with each other over control of some waqfs as part of their welfare mandates, but the waqf is not their political platform.

Although there are worrying trends in the use of political Islam as an ideology or agenda for power struggles, the vast majority of Muslims use Islam quite the opposite way—for individual peace, harmony, and righteousness in this world and the hereafter. Further research would identify the stakeholders in Islamic land management and their roles, capacities, and objectives in servicing Islamic tools.

Reluctance to entertain Islamic options in post-conflict situations has as much to do with perceptions of the relative utility of those options as it does with skepticism about faith in general or unease about Islam in particular. To many, Islamic law is simply a medieval, monolithic, rigid, autonomous, and unfair system with inequitable outcomes that is driven by a fundamentalist agenda. Indeed, there are several contentious areas of Islamic law—such as gender equality, minority rights, and aspects of criminal law. The controversial interpretations of jihad as a license for unregulated violence are much protested by the overwhelming majority of Muslims, but they sour the appetite for Islamic law among non-Muslims.

Some parts of Islamic law may appear doctrinal, technical, or even abstract, but a significant proportion of Muslims see most of it as geared toward practical goals and subject to *ijtihad* (personal reasoning). Islam is particularly strong when it comes to natural resource management.

For most Muslims, Islamic law is the "epitome of the Islamic spirit, the most typical manifestation of the Islamic way of life, the kernel of Islam itself" (Khadduri and Liebesny 1955, 28). There is debate about and critique of both

Islamic land systems   491

Islamic law and negative portrayals of Islamic law, regardless of the faith of protagonists. There is also a trend toward deemphasising the Islamic-law-as-divine-trumping approach, with several recent commentaries suggesting that Islamic law is merely the use of religious resources through human choices and thus not very different from secular or state law (An-Naim 2008; Odeh 2004). The absoluteness of Islamic law is a myth. Pluralism and hybridity are more realistic frames for understanding applications of the law.

Regardless of whether the encounter is with political Islam or developmental Islam, the religious dimension has the propensity to politicize the debate. The line between religion and politics may be blurred, or interventions may have unintended political consequences. However, avoidance of Islamic discourse only abandons the field to the obscurantists, fundamentalists, and extremists. Challenging restrictive interpretations or divisive approaches empowers communities not only in material terms by addressing land rights but also psychologically by letting their voices be heard.

Differentiation of Islamic from customary land tenure systems

Islam is a primary determinant not only of collective identity but also of national constitutions and legal systems. The 2004 Afghan and 2005 Iraqi constitutions leave no room for doubt that Islamic law has primacy. The Somali draft constitution replacing the 1979 constitution emphasizes that all measures are to be sharia compliant. The 1945 Indonesian constitution does not hold Islam to be the only religion, but Aceh has special status and has imposed Islamic law.

However, land analyses of these countries do not pay adequate attention to Islamic dimensions of land management, subsuming them, instead, within the catch-all category of "customary, informal, and alternate" norms and practices. Typical reports on the fifty-seven countries that are members of the Organization of the Islamic Conference deal with custom but do not usually mention Islam. This is a strategic blunder, and the conflation of custom and Islam is specious and anthropologically obfuscating. Whatever the extent and form of Islamic law in a particular Muslim society, in the consciousness of much of the Muslim world, land tenure regimes and concepts are generally constructed with reference to sharia principles.

Islamic tenures differ from customary tenures in several respects—sources, methodology, nature, legal status, and impact. Most constitutions and laws make this differentiation, despite the complex symbiotic relationship between religion and custom. Islamic law recognizes custom (*urf*) unless it directly contravenes Islamic principles. Specific national or local customs, such as adat (Indonesia), xeer (Somalia), *pashtunwali* (Afghanistan), and Arab tribal customs (Iraq), influence the form that the Islamic law takes. In most Muslim societies, a complex and sometimes contentious relationship exists between particular conceptions of Islamic law and other forms of law—state or customary. In many Muslim societies, Islamic and customary norms are seen as almost fused together and a conscious effort is required to distinguish the two.

492   Land and post-conflict peacebuilding

Islam thus needs to be recognized as distinct from but closely related to custom. An exclusive treatment of Islamic manifestations, as seen in the case studies, could provide a misleading picture because secular state law and custom often operate alongside Islamic law to influence or determine tenure categories. An analysis of Afghan law and legal practice will point to legal pluralism and hybridity (Wardak 2004). Whatever the claims of the Iraqi constitution with respect to Islamic law, its practice has to reflect the larger ethnic, tribal, sectarian, and religious composition of the Iraqi people, and their practices as brought out in the Shia-Sunni-Kurd divisions (Jackson 2006; Rabb 2008). These issues, dealt with during the drafting of the constitution, continue to echo in Iraqi politics (Stilt 2004).

Muslim countries do not present a simple dichotomy of Islamic versus non-Islamic laws. Islamic legal principles generally coexist and overlap with social constructions of race, gender, family, kinship, and the global community through customary norms as well as state secular laws. Irene Schneider notices a clear hierarchy with respect to the different types of discourses found in Afghanistan (Schneider 2007). The secular discourse has been widely ignored, just like the discourse of statutory law. Islamic discourse enjoys the highest prestige, superior even to customary discourse. Yet Islamic law manifests itself in a variety of ways owing to choices between competing norms and methodologies—though there are certain agreed Islamic principles. On the other hand, Islamic laws function alongside a host of other legal cultures through a multiplicity of relationships. Islamic laws sometimes absorb or negotiate foreign elements and at other times conflict with them.

There is considerable divergence among Muslim countries with regard to the form and extent of Islamic law in their legal and political systems, and Islamic law is itself pluralist. Muslims are either Sunni (as in Afghanistan, Indonesia, and Somalia) or Shia (Iran) or both (Iraq). Among Sunnis, laws and practices are dependent on which one of the four jurisprudential schools (*maddhab*) they adhere to, for example Shafi (Somalia and Indonesia) or Hanafi (Iraq and Afghanistan). Following the same school does not lead to identical outputs, for there are other variables. The Somali Sufis follow mystical streams of Islam that offer their own particular approaches, which are very different from conventional Somali Islam. Norton notes that none of Somalia's sharia courts appear to follow a specific maddhab; Somalis are flexible in applying their personal readings according to their existing knowledge of the Koran and Islam (Norton 2008).

Classical Sunni and Shia schools reconciled diversity within their legal theories and material law. Selection between two competing concepts (*takhayyur*) and combination of concepts (*talfīq*) were strategies for improvising legal solutions and achieving equity. Though the Hanafi Sunni school of law officially prevails in Afghanistan, the Afghan Family Law Code of 1977 contains solutions from the Maliki school of law, especially with regard to divorce. Best-practice approaches may thus lead to cross-fertilization and innovation.

Specific historical and colonial contexts, state ideology, and the relationship between Islam and secular and customary laws matter. For example, the formal legal system of Afghanistan is a rich but complex matrix of influences: Western (particularly French) legal thinking, Marxist agendas (owing to Soviet reforms in the 1970s), and all hues of Islamic jurisprudence. To focus on Islamic law or statutory law alone is to miss how the uncodified customary law, or even the predominating pashtunwali (Pashtun customary law), influences how land is owned and transacted, as established through community practice and group dynamics. A civil law may abolish a practice, such as the bride price, but it may continue as a custom. Colonial fingerprints are seen in all the case studies as well.

Indonesia is one place where "differing ideas of justice," or "multiple norms," prevail; it is the site of long-standing, diverse efforts to shape lives in an Islamic way, but also of even longer-standing and more diverse efforts to shape them according to local complexes of norms and traditions (Bowen 2003, 4). Dutch colonial legal policy privileged the supposedly indigenous customary law, adat, using the reception theory, which held that Islamic rules had the force of law only where they had been received or integrated into the local tradition. Tensions about which regime should govern Indonesia's Muslims give rise to debates at all levels of society about the appropriate role for adat, sharia, and state laws (Cammack 2000).

Customary land tenure, as in Somalia, can appear to be chaotic to the outsider, and there are disputes over its role in the modern world. However, as Michael Van Notten proposes, "customary law is still very much alive. People tend to follow it. They abhor the statutory laws made by politicians and only obey them when forced. Much of the political turmoil in Africa is caused by the fact that Africans find statutory laws oppressive; abolishing statutory laws, many believe, would end much of that political turmoil" (Van Notten 2005, 10). Legal pluralism caused by state reforms can create multiple claims and complicate resolution of tenure disputes. In Somalia, state-sponsored legislative and policy shifts from customary tenure systems to the state system in the 1970s resulted in many instances of multiple claims to land (Unruh 1995). Sharia has also had a substantial influence on the uncodified custom or social contract (xeer), given the long history of Islam in Somalia. Conversely, xeer plays a role in sharia as urf—a custom that is acceptable as long as it does not contradict Islamic principles.

To dismiss Islamic principles as yet another set of customs is to miss the range of opportunities that faith-based approaches can bring to the table that customary law ordinarily cannot. At the same time, to consider Muslim communities to be determined exclusively by religion is to forget a common adage: Islam is influenced by society as much as it influences society. As Mark Cammack asks of a legislative development: Is this "Islamization of Indonesia or Indonesianization of Islam?" (Cammack 1997, 143). Of course, this dynamic differs from country to country, and in some cases custom may be stronger than religion, or religion may be best dealt with as religious custom. To engage with Islamic dimensions is to acknowledge Islam's relationship with other legal, quasi-legal, and informal systems that can be equally important.

494   Land and post-conflict peacebuilding

Dispute resolution

When new disputes over natural resources emerge in post-conflict situations, the formal legal institutions often are not strong enough to resolve them. In Muslim post-conflict situations, the appeal of Islamic justice is strong. Ali Wardak notes that nearly 80 percent of Afghan rural people have virtually no access to the formal justice system (Wardak 2006, 376), and women and minorities are particularly shut out. In these cases Islamic and customary systems, if they are not active already, reemerge.

There is no singular, all-encompassing dispute resolution mechanism. Just as land rights are governed by more than one legal regime, dispute resolution methods are pluralist. The Bonn Agreement states that Afghanistan's judicial system will be rebuilt in accordance with Islamic principles, international standards, the rule of law, and Afghan legal traditions. However, the pashtunwali customary law has generated its own community-based dispute resolution mechanisms that are based on Islamic principles. The traditional *jirgas* and *shuras* are widely accepted informal institutions that settle disputes by ensuring that the involved parties reach agreement. Likewise, in Aceh land disputes are mostly resolved through consultation at the village level.

When the Somali state collapsed in 1991, much of the population returned to the traditional legal system. It was strongest in rural areas and border regions where the government had been weak. Somali customary law (xeer) predated and survived colonial times and endured through Somali state formalization. The Islamic courts became popular in Somalia because they were procedurally flexible, brought in various constituents, and adopted the guiding principles of negotiation and mediation. Norton quotes a survey that shows that the combination of Islamic law, mediation, xeer, and relevant state laws can create a workable, "'win-win' resolution to a case that all parties will accept" (Norton 2008, 156).

In post-conflict situations, the distinct Islamic conflict-resolution mechanisms lead to much-needed confidence building and trust, and they offer sustainable resolution (Irani and Funk 1998; Abu-Nimer 2003). The concepts of mediation and conciliation are emphasized in the Koran; and the Ottoman Code, which attempted to codify sharia principles, referred to conciliation in contracts. Liz Alden Wily identifies three sets of Afghan mediators for community dispute resolution in property cases: neighbors and elders, the local mosque council, and the chair of the council (Alden Wily 2003). In many instances all three will be used in the same case. To ignore these community-based procedures that operate in most Muslim countries is to miss out on the totality of land law in action.

In Aceh, Afghanistan, and Somalia, primarily in rural areas, customary methods are the first level of dispute resolution. Traditionally, disputes and conflicts in Somali society are resolved through recourse to xeer, an unwritten code of conduct that is agreed on and applied locally by clans in each area, through a gathering of senior elders. Decentralized clan networks interpret and enforce it. The clans

Islamic land systems 495

use a mix of traditional and Islamic dispute resolution discourse that is based on broad communitarian principles of precedent, fairness, and justice. Unwritten sets of moral and social rules form the basis for resolution of issues arising within or between clans or subclan groups. Elders, chosen on basis of their knowledge, do not create the law; they discover customs and at the same time reach a compromise that is favored by most. If they are unable to do so, they can bring in an elder from another clan to settle the dispute (Van Notten 2005).

In the continuing civil war in Somalia, confiscation of property and denial of property rights between clans and subclans has been a frequent occurrence. Negotiations toward ending hostilities and exchanging prisoners have included clauses related to the return of looted property and access to grazing land in times of drought. For example, if more rain fell in the land of one clan, a guest community attracted by the pasture would be responsible for protecting the lives and livestock of the host community. Farmers' committees and other organized fora could help with these processes, but in their absence, the xeer offers common guidelines on restitution and the protection of life and property. New xeer rules are developed to address unforeseen occurrences, so the system is a dynamic and evolving one.

Custom and Islamic law are thus symbiotic fields. The community adjudicators are village elders as well as Muslims. Somali Islamic law applies to personal matters such as marriage and inheritance, and the common law of xeer applies to land disputes generally, so there is considerable overlap. The enforceability of the Somali system arises out of the clan approach of involving the extended family, not merely the individual, in decisions. Any compensation or punishment ordered has to be paid or served by the individual, or that person's extended family becomes liable. If a settlement is not agreed on at this stage, a *xeer-beegti*, or jury, may be appointed to pass judgment on a given case, with each party being expected to accept the verdict. The principle of mutual self-interest binds subclans into insurance groups that enforce community decisions or ostracize a perpetual offender. To survive, outlaws can seek membership in another clan.

In Afghanistan a *loya jirga*, or grand council, gathers periodically to decide on important national issues that are central to social and political order, sovereignty, and national unity. Smaller regular jirgas resolve land disputes and clarify property issues in accordance with customary and Islamic laws. Jirga members are also elders, and in southeastern Afghanistan they have at their disposal the *arbakai* (messengers), community police that operate as the tribal security system. The arbakai implement the jirga's decisions, secure the territory of the tribe or the community, and take action against those who perform illegal acts (Tariq 2004).

An in-depth study of the implementation of customary laws in Afghanistan indicates that the competence and legitimacy of village councils stem from their renowned negotiating skills. Laws regarding crimes against property require restoration as well as apologetic behavior on the part of the offender. The formal apology process involves the Islamic clerics and the elders, who take "the culprit to the family of the aggrieved party with a Qur'an [Koran], one or more sheep, money,

496 Land and post-conflict peacebuilding

rice, wheat, oil or other food stuffs, and a request for forgiveness" (International Legal Foundation 2004, 16). A party who rejects the decision of the community elders is dismissed from the tribe. Conflicts over land arising out of inheritance problems, preemption rights, and the return of occupied land are resolved in this way. Land disputes between villages are also handled by jirgas through mediation between representatives and elders from the two villages and from other villages.

Islamic and customary institutions seem to often act in concert. Courts are careful not to encroach on the power of local religious or tribal leaders, and they often refer matters to the village elders or tribal councils for resolution according to customary law. The judges then incorporate the decisions of tribal councils into their formal opinions. Only when resolution of a dispute is not possible at the village council level does the case enter the primary courts. Unfortunately, statutory and indigenous dispute resolution methods relating to different tenure systems create multiple and potentially contradictory layers. And despite their popularity and efficiency, customary dispute resolution mechanisms should not be romanticized because they often favor wealthier elites, men, and dominant ethnic groups.

In Aceh, the syariah court system (based on Islamic principles) has jurisdiction over inheritance, guardianship, waqf, the legal status of missing persons, and other matters. Although it does not have jurisdiction over land rights per se, it may make landownership determinations when formed as part of a larger inheritance dispute. In 2004 the chief justice of the Indonesian Supreme Court endorsed an increase in the jurisdiction of the syariah courts over civil matters, so long as this jurisdiction was authorized by provincial regulations. In 2005, a fatwa specifically asked that matters relating to landownership and inheritance go to the Islamic courts. The syariah courts in Aceh are therefore key in land matters. In addition, a survey undertaken by the United Nations Development Programme (UNDP) showed that the syariah court system is regarded as considerably more trustworthy and transparent than the system of the general courts (UNDP 2003). UNDP also reports that the quality of recordkeeping is far better in the syariah courts than in the general courts (Fitzpatrick 2008).

Although it is the primary authority on Islamic law throughout Indonesia, the compilation of law known as KHI is a nonbinding guide, and judges may refer to other sources of law, including, in Aceh, fatwas or secular laws passed by the regional legislature. John Bowen argues that the civil and Islamic judiciaries have sought to integrate local property systems into national and Islamic legal frameworks (Bowen 1988). The Islamic courts in Indonesia therefore should not be considered in isolation from their political context. Islamic courts in both Afghanistan and Aceh are influenced by the decrees and policies of the president or cabinet that impact Islamic land law—for example in relation to mawat and women's rights.

The ideology of the Islamic courts and their relationship with the people also depends on who the judges are—or where they come from. In Aceh, the syariah courts come under the Ministry of Religious Affairs rather than the Department of Justice (as the regular secular courts do). Most Somali sharia judges are educated solely through informal religious studies in Somalia. A few

Islamic land systems 497

judges have formal Islamic training from Sudan, Egypt, or Saudi Arabia as well. Therefore, Somali Islamic courts do not operate according to any strict formal procedure, but they do adhere to general Islamic principles. In Afghanistan, most Islamic court judges (*qadis*) are products of a twelve-year Islamic education. The elites who studied law at the Faculty of Islamic Law at Kabul University seem to be reluctant to enter the Afghan Islamic judiciary, in part because of their lack of specialization in the field. With support and training, the Islamic courts have the potential to respond to housing, land, and property issues.

In Somalia, Islamic court functions cover civil matters, including registering marriages and divorces, determining inheritance rights, and settling disputes (Le Sage 2005). Unlike Aceh, Somalia has no definitive body of guiding Islamic principles but appears to use general Koranic principles—for example, on the importance of trustworthy witnesses (Norton 2008). Though limited information is available on the Islamic courts' land cases in Somalia, the courts do register land documents.

In most Muslim countries, a dynamic and pluralist legal framework—with overlapping customary, Islamic, and secular laws—is evident. As discussed earlier, Islamic principles along with international standards, the rule of law, and customary law will be used to rebuild Afghanistan's judicial system. In Aceh, the syariah courts, while based on Islamic principles, are considered the benchmark for determining and applying customary law (adat). And in Somalia, sharia court judges assert that there is no conflict between Islamic law and traditional Somali clan law (xeer). They claim that Somali culture and Islam are fully integrated and that thus no conflict was possible (Le Sage 2005). Islamic law is seldom applied exclusively, rather Islamic principles are applied in concert with existing legal frameworks.

Human rights and gender tradeoffs

The four case studies support a range of innovative land rights mechanisms for diverse groups of people. The tools exhibited are widely acknowledged as pro-poor tools for landless people that provide both land access and tenure security. In contrast to charity, the rights created are grounded in law and enforced through or against the state. An extensive literature shows judicial supervision of registered land rights through mawat, waqf, and tassaruf under Islamic systems. These are not merely individual rights. Landholders must exercise the rights responsibly and productively or the rights will be assigned to someone else more deserving.

All four Islamic tools are in theory gender-responsive, inclusive, and non-denominational. There is no requirement in any of these tools that the beneficiary be Muslim or male (except in the case of the Islamic cooperatives, where ostensibly religion is a primary bond). Tassaruf and reclamation of mawat arise out of land use, rather than gender or religious beliefs. The waqf is a gender-responsive Islamic land tenure that has traditionally included women as creators, managers, beneficiaries, and users (Sait and Lim 2006). Often beneficiaries of waqfs are widows and children, including orphans, as in Aceh. Waqfs can also be set up by non-Muslims, or by

498   Land and post-conflict peacebuilding

Muslims for non-Muslims. However, there is a gaping hole in research as to how these tools work or would work in practice, particularly in patriarchal societies.

Whether tassaruf or mawat reclamation is gender-responsive depends on wider socioeconomic practices, and in a cooperative the nature of gendered land relations depends on broader ideas about the role and status of Muslim women. There is nothing to prevent women from reclaiming land or seeking usufruct rights, except patriarchy, of course.

Because tassaruf is usufruct over state (miri) land, it is useful to consider historical gendered ownership patterns. Colin Inber notes that historically miri land was generally held and passed down by males, but that the changing demography of the Ottoman Empire, as well as willingness to allow more state land into individual productive use, made it possible for women to gain access (Inber 2010). The rules were the same for men and women—the landholder had to pay taxes, cultivate the land, and be accountable. The interesting twist is that women could inherit tassaruf in miri land without the limitations of Islamic inheritance rules, since these did not apply to miri land. With women working more than before, the tools become more gender-neutral, at least in theory.

The key Islamic legal materials generally support women's right to acquire, hold, use, administer, and dispose of property. Muslim women—unmarried, married, divorced, or widowed—have extensive independent rights to property under Islamic law and human rights. There is explicit recognition in the Koran of women's rights to property acquired through purchase, inheritance, *mahar* (property transferred to the wife from the husband as security for marriage), and other transactions. There are no restrictions on the property a Muslim woman can purchase out of her earnings, on the gifts she may receive from her natal family or her husband's family, or on the endowment she may enjoy as a beneficiary of a waqf. In all these respects, she is entitled to equal treatment with male members of the family (Sait and Lim 2006).

However, there are difficulties in terms of fixed Islamic inheritance rules and patriarchal customs practiced in the name of Islam. In Aceh, Afghanistan, Iraq, and Somalia, women are working for their rights within the Islamic framework through social action, political campaigns, and ijtihad, an acknowledged Islamic interpretative process.

In all four countries, and generally in Muslim societies, Islamic law offers far greater rights for women than customary practice. A striking example is the property rights of widows, which are vital in post-conflict and post-disaster situations. Judgments in inheritance cases after the tsunami in Aceh saw the sharia courts grant more rights to widows than traditional courts. When widows' property rights are violated in Afghanistan and Somalia, it is a triumph of customary practices over Islamic norms. For example, the traditional Afghan concept of honor applies to protection of both women and property but can lead to situations in which women are treated as property (Kamali 1985). Another example is *tanazul*, a customary practice in which even the reduced female inheritance share is renounced in favor of a male member of the family; this practice has over time been incorporated into the Islamic legal process (Moors 1995).

Islamic land systems   499

The Islamic courts in post-tsunami Aceh debunk several stereotypes. They are proceeding on the basis of the Indonesian constitutional guarantee against discrimination in the absence of any gender-specific terminology in either the marriage law or the KHI. Property rights for women are closely related to marriage and inheritance. Under Islamic law a man can often divorce more easily than a woman, who often needs a judicial decree. But an interesting statistic in post-tsunami Aceh, recorded in 2004, is that an overwhelming majority of those granted divorce were women (UNDP 2003).

In Afghanistan, the civil code allows women to obtain dissolution of their marriage by the court if certain conditions are met. An Afghan man can marry additional wives if certain conditions are met, such as equal treatment of wives, financial capacity to provide maintenance, and lawful benefit from a second or third marriage—for example, to produce children in the case of the infertility of the first wife. In practice these conditions are said to be flouted. Another problematic area is the dowry (mahar), a payment that the groom pays to the bride in cash or property, or promises to pay as financial security in the future. In Afghanistan the dowry is paid by the groom or his family to the head of the bride's household, not to the woman. This practice, called *walwar*, is un-Islamic and illegal, but it continues as a customary practice.

In Somalia, in the absence of formal courts, women "are often not well served" by customary mechanisms, "and customary law has not always kept pace with social changes, though it remains inherently flexible" (Norton 2008, 13). Little research has been done on the gender-responsiveness of Islamic courts in Somalia, though basic information out of the more stable judicial systems of the Somaliland and Puntland regions indicates that there are opportunities for enforcement of Islamic women's rights. Nevertheless, as in Afghanistan, strong customary patriarchal attitudes and the fluidity of civil war have conspired to keep women marginalized. Unlike Indonesia, which signed the Convention on the Elimination of All Forms of Discrimination against Women without reservations, and Afghanistan, which followed, Somalia has not ratified the convention. Yet, the existence of female saints in Somalia, the high social respect for women, their role in the economy, and their participation in Islamic land cooperatives and other cooperatives points to hidden information. The limited research does indicate that Somali women are creating innovative tenures (for example, mother-son partnerships) to circumvent patriarchal structures (Besteman 1995).

The challenge to women's access to justice in Somalia comes from their exclusion from legal proceedings. Where procedural processes of settling property disputes are based on mediation and willingness to reach a compromise, accessibility for Somali women is restricted (IDMC 2008). This is part of the larger issue of women's participation in post-conflict situations and their role in resolution (Nakaya 2003).

Afghan rural women also have limited access to formal courts and mostly do not play an active role in jirgas (though there were 114 women on the loya jirga). However, there have been recommendations that women's shuras (consultations) be institutionalized as part of gender mainstreaming (Ayyubi 2006;

500 Land and post-conflict peacebuilding

Wordsworth 2008). In Aceh, campaigns are underway for women to be able to serve as judges and for a 30 percent quota for women holding office in political parties. Women's groups are active in Aceh, and to a lesser extent in Afghanistan; there is little documentation of women's civil society organizations in Somalia.

Equal rights for women are a complicated platform in some Muslim societies. Islamic feminists prefer the term *equity* to *equality* because of concerns that Western human rights will dissolve distinctive Islamic gender roles. Working within Islamic discourses, Muslim women and men are seeking ways to reconcile universal and Islamic human rights principles.

In post-conflict situations, the priorities for women are shelter, access to health care and education, and access to credit and livelihood strategies. These are general needs, but they are often articulated as basic Islamic rights too, despite the customary challenges. As Muslim women have become more assertive and visible in their enhanced roles and reclamation of rights, they have taken recourse to Islamic sources to demand more rights on the basis of gender-responsive interpretations (Sait and Lim 2007). The four gender-neutral Islamic land tools could lead to greater opportunities for Muslim women to access land.

FACTORS AFFECTING OUTCOMES

Afghanistan, Aceh, Iraq, and Somalia share Islam as a religion but exhibit numerous differences arising out of their particular histories, local conflict dynamics, and sociopolitical and economic outlook and reforms. These case studies offer glimpses of potential land management tools rather than the full-fledged investigations that are needed. However, several common factors affecting deployment of Islamic strategies emerge from the studies.

Knowledge gaps

Awareness of and use of information on Islamic land management, particularly in post-conflict situations, has been very limited. Participants in key multistakeholder meetings are confused about usufruct rights in Iraq; Afghanistan has frozen the redistribution of barren land because of a lack of distribution mechanisms; the creative transformation of waqfs in Aceh is largely undocumented; and researchers on Somalia have lost the research thread on cooperatives. It is not clear how predictable or durable Islamic principles are as they step into the vacuum of formal legal authority in post-conflict situations. Research on Islamic land management should focus not only on specific land management concepts but on principles such as accountability, universality, philanthropy, productivity, and distribution, which are embedded in the social consciousness of most Muslims.

Legal pluralism

A key challenge is to develop a sound and widely accepted pluralistic legal basis for land rights management. The role of Islamic land law in Muslim societies

Islamic land systems 501

should not be exaggerated, as it exists in tandem with customary and secular land regimes. Yet distinguishing Islamic principles from other customary norms may be necessary to counter injurious customary practices, just as legal pluralism offers choices and opportunities for positive interpretations of some Islamic doctrines. An exclusive appreciation of Islamic principles is often as futile as negation of them. Where differences between competing norms and practices arise, protocols to harmonize and resolve incompatibilities and to promote access to land need to be developed.

Community-led approaches

The legitimacy and durability of Islamic land management principles are driven not by their religious appeal but by their acceptance and use by the people. Community practices develop and operationalize these land management tools. The use of Islamic strategies thus requires working with a range of local Muslim leaders for peacebuilding and development.

Ideally the use of Islamic principles will be an empowering experience that gives voice to ordinary people rather than being just an ideological exercise for the few. Islamic law can have positive implications for land rights, but traditional structures, fundamentalist agendas, and conservative interpretations of Islamic law often combine to diminish such rights, particularly for women. Therefore, listening to internal civil society debates and participating in positive interpretation strategies with Islamic scholars are vital to the viability of Islamic land law.

Alternative dispute resolution mechanisms

Using pluralistic approaches is not merely about being open to beneficial faith-based ideas, but also about engaging with Muslim personnel and harnessing Islamic and customary systems of conflict resolution, which often overlap. These alternative or parallel methods can be sophisticated, efficient, flexible, quick, and cheap. Because they are based on the cultural and religious values of the community, these strategies have retained popular support and legitimacy. They are diverse, with sources ranging from irregular religious scholars who issue fatwas to institutionalized Islamic courts. They are capable of translating the extensive property rights in the Koran and other Islamic sources into practical guarantees. Addressing the philosophy, capacity, resources, procedures, and effectiveness of Islamic courts is one way of ensuring their support for equitable access to land, and of raising questions about possibly negative gender impacts.

Abuse of religion

For all the positive scenarios celebrating Islamic principles, the reality is that Islam can be misused for political ends or to frustrate the land rights of others. Therefore, a coherent methodology for using faith-based approaches needs to be developed that engages with religious resources in a nondenominational, professional, and objective manner (Global Land Tool Network 2006).

502   Land and post-conflict peacebuilding

Planners need to consider which Islamic tools should be used, and when and how they should be used; then they must apply their conclusions on a case-by-case basis. Although faith-based principles are respected for their integrity and authenticity, they must be harmonized with well-acknowledged human rights and development principles. Therefore, the testing of tools must involve both egalitarian Islamic benchmarks and international principles.

LESSONS LEARNED

The existence of tools of Islamic land law does not guarantee their success. The tools have to be located within the dynamic interplay between ideas, customary practices, and formal prescription that is the hallmark of an inclusive, flexible, and results-driven methodology. These tools are not static. They are constantly evolving and being tested by communities.

Most commentators and interveners in Afghanistan, Aceh, Iraq, and Somalia have failed to detect these Islamic land tools because they were not looking for them or were uncritically discounting their relevance. Whether or not the tools ultimately work, decision makers need to be asking questions about the relationship between Islamic land law and customary and state laws, the historical role of Islamic land tenures, and the implications of Islamic philanthropic obligations and financial traditions. They need to know how social structures affect property regimes, particularly in relation to women, and they need to understand community-based conflict-resolution mechanisms. It is beneficial for planners to be acquainted with ijtihad, the Islamic practice of personal reasoning, and to understand its usefulness for the development of pro-poor land management tools. Finally, keeping in mind the roles of various stakeholders, including the state, strategists should consider the implications of Islamic land management practices for environmental sustainability, promotion of land rights, and protection of human rights generally.

Well-intended post-conflict land interventions are often overly selective and miss potential breakthrough strategies. In Afghanistan, the Islamic redistributive principle perished without the support of interveners. In Iraq, heavily funded big hitters of the global land agenda lacked understanding of Islamic land tenures. In Aceh, fatwas were generating creative endowment solutions while the international community's attention was elsewhere, and Somali cooperatives have been similarly overlooked.

Another side effect of the avoidance of the Islamic arguments and faith-based leaders is the attempted secularization of the land agenda in Muslim communities. Even with the drawbacks of existing Islamic and customary systems of property, reform is best carried out with sensitivity for these systems; otherwise it risks alienating the people for whom it is intended. Unsuccessful reforms of customary systems can create tenure confusion and accentuate land conflict. Sustainable peacebuilding and natural resource management requires solutions that are close to people's experiences, and research shows that faith-based players can make a

Islamic land systems **503**

positive contribution to the securing of land, property, and housing rights. At the same time, care should be taken to involve players who may not subscribe to particular religious views or approaches.

In some cases, Islamic mechanisms are straightforward and enjoy sufficient demand and the necessary support. However, other Islamic tools are complicated, and a series of activities and outputs may be needed before the tools are ready for implementation. It might be necessary to clarify and disseminate doctrines, convert them into policy or laws, create institutions or procedures, generate capacity through training, and develop strategies for design, implementation, monitoring, and evaluation. The use of Islamic tools may involve a wide range of stakeholders, from policy makers and land professionals to representatives of civil society, including women, researchers and trainers, experts on Islamic land law, and traditional Muslim scholars (Global Land Tool Network 2006).

Where potentially cost-effective Islamic tools are innovative, pro-poor, and respectful of women's rights, a professional plan for their implementation or upscaling should be put in place. Strategic decisions in Muslim post-conflict situations should be based on an assessment of the added value of engaging with Islamic ideas over customary norms or statutory laws, as well as evaluation of resources, capacity, and risks.

REFERENCES

Abu-Nimer, M. 2003. *Nonviolence and peace building in Islam: Theory and practice.* Gainesville: University Press of Florida.

Alden Wily, L. 2003. *Land rights in crisis: Restoring tenure security in Afghanistan.* Kabul: Afghanistan Research and Evaluation Unit. http://unpan1.un.org/intradoc/groups/public/documents/apcity/unpan016656.pdf.

Al-Zuhili, W. M. 2005. Islam and international law. *International Review of the Red Cross* 858:269–283.

An-Na'im, A. A. 1990. *Toward an Islamic reformation: Civil liberties, human rights, and international law.* Syracuse, NY: Syracuse University Press.

———. 2008. *Islam and the secular state: Negotiating the future of shari'a.* Cambridge, MA: Harvard University Press.

Appleby, S. 2003. Retrieving the missing dimension of statecraft: Religious faith in the service of peace-building. In *Religion: The missing dimension of statecraft,* ed. D. Johnston and S. Sampson. New York: Oxford University Press.

Arabi, O. 1995. Al-Sanhūrī's reconstruction of the Islamic law of contract defects. *Journal of Islamic Studies* 6 (2): 153–172.

Augustinus, C. 2009. Land governance in support of the MDGs: Responding to new challenges. Paper presented at "Improving Access to Land and Shelter," World Bank and International Federation of Surveyors conference, Washington, D.C., March 9–10.

Aytekin, A. 2009. Agrarian relations, property, and law: An analysis of the Land Code of 1858 in the Ottoman Empire. *Middle Eastern Studies* 45 (6): 935–951.

Ayyubi, S. 2006. Conflict resolution in Afghanistan and the role of women in formal and informal justice. In *Conflicts and conflict resolution in Middle Eastern societies: Between*

504   Land and post-conflict peacebuilding

tradition and modernity, ed. H.-J. Albrecht, J.-M. Simon, H. Rezaei, H.-C. Rohne, and E. Kiza. Berlin: Duncker and Humblot.

Baderin, M. 2003. *International human rights and Islamic law*. Oxford, UK: Oxford University Press.

Behdad, S. 1989. Property rights in contemporary Islamic economic thought: A critical survey. *Review of Social Economy* 47 (2): 185–211.

Besteman, C. 1989. *Land tenure in the Middle Jubba: Customary tenure and the effects of land registration in Somalia*. Madison, WI: Land Tenure Center, University of Wisconsin–Madison.

———. 1995. Polygyny, women's land tenure, and the "mother-son partnership" in southern Somalia. *Journal of Anthropological Research* 51 (3): 193–213.

Bouta, T., S. A. Kadayifci-Orellana, and M. Abu-Nimer. 2005. *Faith-based peace-building: Mapping and analysis of Christian, Muslim, and faith-based actors*. The Hague, Netherlands: Clingendael Institute.

Bowen, J. R. 1988. The transformation of an Indonesian property system: *Adat*, Islam, and social change in the Gayo highlands. *American Ethnologist* 15 (2): 274–293.

———. 2003. *Islam, law, and equality in Indonesia: An anthropology of public reasoning*. Cambridge, UK: Cambridge University Press.

Bremer, J. 2004. Islamic philanthropy: Reviving traditional forms for building social justice. Paper submitted at "Defining and Establishing Justice in Muslim Societies," the 5th annual conference of the Center for the Study of Islam and Democracy, Center for the Study of Islam and Democracy, Washington, D.C.

Cammack, M. 1997. Indonesia's 1989 Religious Judicature Act: Islamization of Indonesia or Indonesianization of Islam? *Indonesia* 63:143–168.

———. 2000. *Dossier 22: Inching toward equality: Recent developments in Indonesian inheritance law*. London: Women Living under Muslim Laws.

Cattan, H. 1955. The law of waqf. In *Law in the Middle East*, ed. M. Khadduri and H. Liebesny. Washington, D.C.: Middle East Institute.

Deininger, K. 2003. *Land policies for growth and poverty reduction*. A World Bank policy research report. Oxford, UK: World Bank / Oxford University Press.

Fitzpatrick, D. 2008. Managing conflict and sustaining recovery: Land administration reform in tsunami-affected Aceh. Aceh Working Paper No. 4. Singapore: Asia Research Institute.

Gaudiosi, M. M. 1988. The influence of the Islamic law of waqf on the development of the trust in England: The case of Merton College. *University of Pennsylvania Law Review* 136:1231–1261.

Gebremedhin, Y. 2006. Legal issues pertaining to land titling and registration in Afghanistan: Land Titling and Economic Restructuring in Afghanistan (LTERA) Project. United States Agency for International Development. www.terrainstitute.org/pdf/USAID_LTERA _2006%20LEGAL_ISSUES_AFGHANISTAN.pdf.

———. 2007. *Capacity building for land policy and administration: Land tenure and administration in rural Afghanistan, legal aspects*. Manila, Philippines: Asian Development Bank.

Global Land Tool Network. 2006. *Developing Islamic land tools*. Nairobi, Kenya: United Nations Human Settlements Programme.

Hamoudi, H. A. 2008a. Baghdad booksellers, Basra carpet merchants, and the law of God and man: Legal pluralism and the contemporary Muslim experience. *Berkeley Journal of Middle Eastern and Islamic Law* 1 (1): 83–126.

Islamic land systems **505**

———. 2008b. Legal change and Iraq. *Opinio Juris*, June 20. http://opiniojuris.org/2008/06/20/legal-change-and-iraq/.

Haque, Z. 1984. *Landlord and peasant in early Islam: A study of the legal doctrine of muzaraa or sharecropping.* Islamabad, Pakistan: Islamic Research Institute Press.

Hasan, Z. 2006. Sustainable development from an Islamic perspective: Meaning implications and policy concerns. *Islamic Economics* 1 (19): 3–18.

Hashmi, S. 2002. Interpreting the Islamic ethics of war and peace. In *Islamic political ethics: Civil society, pluralism, and conflict*, ed. S. Hashmi. Princeton, NJ: Princeton University Press.

Hoben, A. 1988. The political economy of land tenure in Somalia. In *Land and society in contemporary Africa*, ed. R. Downs and S. Reyna. Hanover, NH: University Press of New England.

Huda, Q. 2010. *Crescent and dove: Peace and conflict resolution in Islam.* Washington, D.C.: United States Institute of Peace.

IDLO (International Development Law Organization). 2008. Legal provisions and regulations on *wakaf*. Rome.

IDMC (Internal Displacement Monitoring Centre). 2008. Housing, land and property rights in the south central Somalia: Preliminary assessment and proposed strategies for expanded approaches. Geneva, Switzerland: Displacement Solutions.

Inber, C. 2010. Women as outsiders: The inheritance of agricultural land in the Ottoman Empire. In *Religious divide: Women, property, and the law in the wider Mediterranean (ca. 1300–1800)*, ed. J. Sperling and S. K. Wray. London: Routledge.

International Legal Foundation. 2004. *The customary laws of Afghanistan.* Kabul.

Irani, G., and Funk, N. 1998. Rituals of reconciliation: Arab-Islamic perspectives. *Arab Studies Quarterly* 20:53–74.

Jackson, S. 2006. Legal pluralism between Islam and the nation-state: Romantic medievalism or pragmatic modernity. *Fordham International Law Journal* 30 (1): 158–176.

Jwaideh, Z. E. 1953. The new civil code of Iraq. *George Washington Law Review* 22:176–185.

Kamali, M. H. 1985. *Law in Afghanistan: A study of the constitutions, matrimonial law and the judiciary.* Leiden, Netherlands: E. J. Brill.

Khadduri, M. 1966. *The Islamic law of nations: Shaybani's Siyar (Kitab al-siyar al-kabir).* Baltimore, MD: Johns Hopkins University Press.

Khadduri, M., and H. Liebesny. 1955. *Law in the Middle East.* Vol. 1. Washington, D.C.: Middle East Institute.

Le Sage, A. 2005. *Stateless justice in Somalia: Formal and informal rule of law initiatives.* Report for the Centre for Humanitarian Dialogue. Geneva, Switzerland.

Lewis, I. M. 1998. *Saints and Somalis: Popular Islam in a clan-based society.* London: Haan.

Moors, A. 1995. *Women, property and Islam: Palestinian experience, 1920–1990.* New York: Cambridge University Press.

Nakaya, S. 2003. Women and gender equality in peace processes: From women at the negotiating table to postwar structural reforms in Guatemala and Somalia. *Global Governance* 9:459–476.

Norton, G. 2008. *Land, property, and housing in Somalia.* Oslo: Norwegian Refugee Council.

Odeh, L. A. 2004. The politics of (mis)recognition: Islamic law pedagogy in American academia. *American Journal of Comparative Law* 52:789–824.

506   Land and post-conflict peacebuilding

Pew Research Center. 2009. *Mapping the global Muslim population: A report on the size and distribution of the world's Muslim population*. Washington, D.C.

Rabb, I. A. 2008. "We the jurists": Islamic constitutionalism in Iraq. *University of Pennsylvania Journal of Constitutional Law* 10 (3): 527–579.

Rogers, M. M., T. Bamat, and J. Ideh, eds. 2008. *Pursuing just peace: An overview and case studies for faith-based peacebuilders*. Baltimore, MD: Catholic Relief Services.

Sait, S. 2005. Islamic land law in Afghanistan: Innovative land tools and strategies. Paper presented at "New Legal Frameworks and Tools in Asia and Pacific," an expert group meeting on secure land tenure. United Nations Economic and Social Commission for Asia and the Pacific, World Bank, United Nations Human Settlements Programme, and International Federation of Surveyors. Bangkok, December 8–9. www.fig.net/commission7/bangkok_2005/papers/3_2_sait.pdf.

———. 2007. Islamic microfinance in post-crisis countries: The unofficial developmental discourse. Paper delivered at Harvard Law School, Cambridge, MA, April 14.

———. 2008. *The relevance of Islamic land law for policy and project design*. Washington, D.C.: World Bank.

Sait, S., and H. Lim. 2006. *Land, law and Islam: Property and human rights in the Muslim world*. London: Zed Books.

———. 2007. Accidental Islamic feminism: Dialogical approaches to Muslim women's inheritance rights. In *Feminist perspectives on land law*, ed. H. Lim and A. Bottomley. London: Glasshouse.

Schneider, I. 2007. Recent developments in Afghan family law: Research aspects. *ASIEN* 104 (July): 106–118.

Stigall, D. E. 2004. From Baton Rouge to Baghdad: A comparative overview of the Iraqi Civil Code. *Louisiana Law Review* 65:131–138.

———. 2008. A closer look at Iraqi property and tort law. *Louisiana Law Review* 68 (3): 765–822.

———. 2009. Refugees and legal reform in Iraq: The Iraqi Civil Code, international standards for the treatment of displaced persons, and the art of attainable solutions. *Rutgers Law Record* 34 (1): 1–30.

Stilt, K. 2004. Islamic law and the making and remaking of the Iraqi legal system. *George Washington International Law Review* 36:695–756.

Suhrke, A. 2007. Reconstruction as modernisation: The "post-conflict" project in Afghanistan. *Third World Quarterly* 28:1291–1308.

Tariq, M. O. 2004. Community-based security and justice: Arbakai in Afghanistan. *Institute of Development Studies Bulletin* 40 (2): 20–27.

Tibi, B. 2002. *The challenge of fundamentalism: Political Islam and the new world disorder*. Berkeley: University of California Press.

UNDP (United Nations Development Programme). 2003. *Access to justice: A review of the justice system in Aceh, Indonesia*. New York.

Unruh, J. D. 1995. The relationship between indigenous pastoralist resource tenure and state tenure in Somalia. *GeoJournal* 36:19–26.

Van Notten, M. 2005. *The law of the Somalis*. Trenton, NJ: Red Sea Press.

Vikor, K. 1993. Sufi brotherhoods in Africa. In *The History of Islam in Africa*, ed. N. Levtzion and R. L. Pouwels. Athens: Ohio University Press.

Wardak, A. 2004. Building a post-war justice system in Afghanistan. *Crime, Law and Social Change* 41:319–341.

Islamic land systems 507

————. 2006. Structures of authority and local dispute settlement in Afghanistan. In *Conflicts and conflict resolution in Middle Eastern societies: Between tradition and modernity*, ed. H.-J. Albrecht, J.-M. Simon, H. Rezaei, H.-C. Rohne, and E. Kiza. Berlin: Duncker and Humblot.

Wiss, M., and M. Anderson. 2008. *The unique forms and rights of Iraqi real property law: A primer for those interested in transacting business in Iraq.* London: International Bar Association.

Wordsworth, A. 2008. *Moving to the mainstream: Integrating gender in Afghanistan's national policy.* Kabul: Afghanistan Research and Evaluation Unit.

World Bank and UN-HABITAT (United Nations Human Settlements Programme). 2010. Proceedings of the "Toward a Land Management Policy for Iraq" Conference, Beirut, Lebanon, May 27–28.

508 Land and post-conflict peacebuilding

ANNEX
Glossary of Islamic Terms

adat: customary law

Ahmadiya: one of several Sufi orders

arbakai: community police that operate as the tribal security system, meaning "messengers"

fatwa: an Islamic advisory opinion

Hanafi: a school within the Sunni branch of Islam

harim: inviolable sanctuaries or zones for protection of human, animal, or plant life

hima: a reserve; an area set aside for the conservation and management of rangelands, forests, watersheds, and wildlife

ijtihad: personal reasoning

iqta: land grants

jirga: a traditional dispute resolution mechanism, which operates at the tribal level

Kompilasi Hukum Islam: (Indonesian) Compilation of Islamic Law; also referred to as KHI

loya jirga: grand council that decides on national issues central to social and political order, sovereignty, and national unity

maddhab: a Muslim jurisprudential school

mahar: dowry; a payment of cash or property a groom pays, or promises to pay, to the bride

mahlul: uncultivated, lapsed land; a designation for uncultivated land that allows the state to reallocate property if the holder of title leaves it uncultivated for a period of three years

Maliki: a school within the Sunni branch of Islam

maslaha: the principle of public interest which requires the state to act in the interest of human welfare

matruke: public land

mawat: barren land, wasteland; in Afghanistan, **mowat**

miri: land owned by the state

mulk: individually owned land

pashtunwali: customary law of the Pashtuns

qadi: Islamic court judge

Qadiriya: members of the Qadiri Sufi order

raqaba: absolute ownership of land

salaam: the Islamic concept of peace

Salihiya: one of several Sufi orders

Shafi: a school within the Sunni branch of Islam

Shia: a branch of Islam

sharia: Islamic law

shura: consultation or traditional dispute resolution mechanism, which operates at the tribal level

Sufism: the mystical branch of Islam; includes the orders of Ahmadiya, Qadiriya, and Salihiya

Sufi cooperatives: a Muslim collective land tenure model

sulh: mediation

sunna: the body of Islamic custom and practice based on the Prophet Muhammad's words and deeds

Sunni: a branch of Islam; includes the orders of Hanafi, Hanbali, Maliki, and Shafi

tahkeem: arbitration

takhayyur: picking and choosing legal rules from a variety of sources

talfiq: combination of concepts

tanazul: a customary practice in which the share of female's inheritance is renounced in favor of a male member of the family

tariqa: Islamic religious order, under Sufism, meaning "path" or "way"

tassaruf: individual usufruct rights over state land

urf: a custom that does not contradict Islamic principles

walwar: contrary to Islamic principles, the customary practice of the groom paying a *mahar*, or dowry, to the head of the bride's household and not the bride

waqf: an Islamic trust or endowment, often involving landownership (plural: **awaqf**); in Indonesia, **wakaf** or **tanoh wakeueh**

wasta: conciliation

xeer: customary law (Somalia)

xeer-beegti: a jury

zakat: a levy imposed on Muslims for charitable distribution to the poor and needy; one of the five pillars of Islam

Customary law and community-based natural resource management in post-conflict Timor-Leste

Naori Miyazawa

The concept of the commons has evolved since the publication of Garrett Hardin's article "The Tragedy of the Commons" in *Science* (Hardin 1968). Hardin argued that degradation of the environment is likely when sizable numbers of individuals use resources in common. He used the example of pastures in Britain. A pasture is open to all, and many herders directly benefit from grazing their animals there. A rational herder may be motivated to add more animals, continually seeking more benefit. But as more and more animals are released to pasture, the pasture becomes barren. Pursuing this logic, Hardin argued that exhaustion of common resources is inevitable unless the property is owned by a public or private entity that can regulate access to pasture.

Hardin's theory accelerated the development of a dichotomy between the public and private sectors in environmental management, especially in developing countries. This contributed to a denial of the value of the customary and indigenous management of natural resources that operated until governmental authorities put Hardin's theories into practice (Murota and Mitsumata 2004).

However, subsequent research has pointed out that Hardin's paper was based on a misconception of the common system. Social scientists and anthropologists who grasped the characteristics of community-based management of natural resources revealed that many common systems still exist globally, and that the systems successfully manage and conserve natural resources on a community basis (McCay and Acheson 1987; Murota and Mitsumata 2004). Elinor Ostrom, who shared the 2009 Nobel Prize in Economics, examined various practices of managing common-property resources around the world from political and socioeconomic viewpoints. In a historical analysis, she presented eight conditions under which the commons can work in the long term and joint management of natural resources can succeed (Ostrom 1990).

Naori Miyazawa is a lecturer and researcher at the Graduate School of Arts and Sciences at the University of Tokyo. From 2001 to 2005, she was the country project manager for Timor-Leste for the International Development Center of Japan and the director for Timor-Leste for Adventist Development and Relief Agency. In this chapter, she has drawn on her personal experience managing these projects and living in Timor-Leste.

512   Land and post-conflict peacebuilding

A society's customary law and community-based land management processes are influenced by political and social changes in the post-conflict situation, yet little research on customary law focuses on post-conflict settings. This case study analyzes the role of customary law and community-based management for land and natural resources in post-conflict Timor-Leste. It discusses how the customary law system of *tara bandu* has been affected by the conflict and the roles it has played in post-conflict recovery.

BACKGROUND OF RESEARCH

The author worked in post-conflict Timor-Leste with three organizations—an international nongovernmental organization (NGO), a university, and a consultancy organization—from 2001 to 2005. During this period, environmental management measures were implemented by the United Nations and the Timorese government, but the immediate effects of such measures were limited. For example, the UN and the government set up signboards banning tree cutting as part of a nationwide forest-conservation campaign. The signs said, "Do not cut trees. Let us conserve the forests for the future." However, the signs failed to stop people from cutting trees. Indeed, trees were cut down even in locations adjacent to such signboards.

In contrast, community-based actions for natural resource management were more effective. It has been frequently observed that communities effectively manage natural resources by utilizing customary law. The community did not put up signs like the governmental authorities did, but erected altars made of tree branches and other natural objects. These customary practices nearly stopped the harvesting of natural resources by residents in the protected areas. Customary law was regulating the use of natural resources by Timorese people, especially in the rural areas. It was once again guiding local decisions, collective action, and enforcement systems.

Research focus

In order to analyze how natural resources should be managed after a conflict, the author considers the relationship between two major stakeholders: civil society (customary law, community, and international organizations) and government. Companies are a third major stakeholder. The balance of the three stakeholders in a state unaffected by conflict differs from the balance in a post-conflict situation. Figure 1 shows that the relationship of the stakeholders is balanced during a stable period in a democratic country. Figure 2 depicts the lack of balance among the stakeholders in a post-conflict society. In post-conflict Timor-Leste, the role of civil society—community, customary law, NGOs and international organizations—became larger than it was under stable circumstances, and the roles of the government and companies became smaller. This study focuses on the relative functions of these elements of civil society and government in natural resource management in post-conflict Timor-Leste.

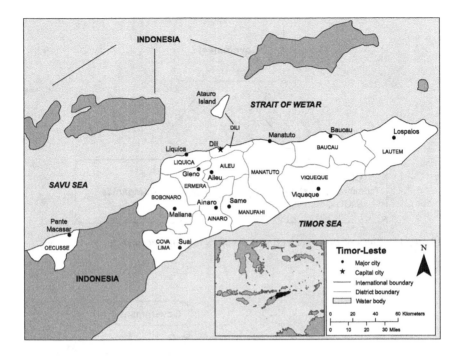

Definitions

This study uses C. K. Allen's definition of customary law: "Native customary law means a rule or a body of rules regulating rights and imposing correlative duties, being a rule or a body of rules which obtains and is fortified by established native usage and which is appropriate and applicable to any particular cause, action, suit, matter, disputes, and includes also any native customary law" (Allen 1939).

Though there is a wide range of definitions of community, this research defines community as a geographical distribution of individuals because people in Timor-Leste have close ties to the geographical area in terms of natural resource management. This is a slight adaptation of Ernest W. Burgess's definition of community: "social groups where they are considered from the point of view of the geographical distribution of the individuals and institutions of which they are composed" (Burgess 1967, 144). Community is thus the geographical distribution of people at the village (*suco* in Tetum, the local language of Timor-Leste) and hamlet (*aldeia* in Tetum) levels.

This study adopts the following definition of *the commons*: 1) institutionalized systems for the collective management of natural resources, and 2) the natural resources commonly owned and used (Mitsumata, Morimoto, and Murota 2008). According to this definition, customary law is included in the commons in Timor-Leste because communities have applied customary law to manage common pool natural resources. Customary law is particularly applied to common land and forests that community members share.

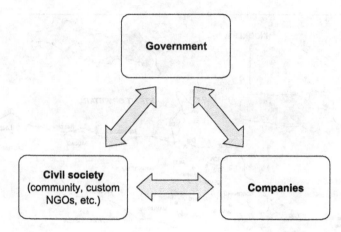

Figure 1. Roles of three societal stakeholders in a balanced state

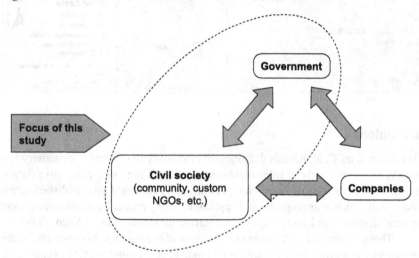

Figure 2. Shift in balance of stakeholder roles in a post-conflict society (Timor-Leste)

Nature and history of the conflict

Timor-Leste was colonized by Portugal in the seventeenth century. The pro-independence party, the Revolutionary Front for an Independent Timor-Leste (Frente Revolucionária de Timor-Leste Independente, or FRETILIN), declared the independence of Timor-Leste in 1975 after the territory was decolonized in 1974. Subsequently Indonesia invaded the territory and occupied it until 1999. The Indonesian government was interested in Timor-Leste's natural resources, especially the oil and gas reserves in the Timor Sea. During the Indonesian occupation, resistance continued in the form of guerrilla combat, which was waged mostly in the countryside (Candio and Bleiker 2001). Indonesian forces committed large-scale human rights violations such as murders, rapes, torture, and forced relocation on a massive scale. Indonesian repression is asserted to have resulted in the deaths of about 200,000 East Timorese, or approximately one-quarter of the population (Shalom, Chomsky, and Albert 1999).

In the August 1999 popular election, 78.5 percent of East Timorese voters opted for independence from Indonesia. Immediately after announcement of the ballot result, the Indonesian military and pro-Indonesian militia groups went on a rampage in Timor-Leste and destroyed an estimated 70 percent of the territory's infrastructure (Tee 2000). The death toll was estimated to be about six hundred people, though the UN conceded that the number could have been much higher (Candio and Bleiker 2001). Timor-Leste became independent in May 2002.

THE EFFECTS OF ARMED CONFLICT ON NATURAL RESOURCES

Serious problems for the environment emerged in post-conflict Timor-Leste: destruction of infrastructure, decrease in forest area, lack of effective law and policy, and loss of human and technical resources that weakened state capacity.

During the twenty-four years of Indonesian administration, natural resources were exploited for short-term profit. The Portuguese and Indonesian regimes "denied, or at least failed to encourage, a constructive role for local communities in the management and conservation" of resources (McWilliam 2003, 308). This followed decades during which the Indonesian occupation not only depleted the resources of the physical environment but also weakened the social structure by which communities had managed and protected natural resources. The effects of bombings and forced resettlement practices by Indonesian governmental authorities also contributed to the changes in the environment and social structure (Aditjondro 1994a, 1994b). The forced resettlement of the population to roadside areas and other more controllable places detached people from their sacred lands and community forests (Anderson and Deutsch 2001).

The independence of Timor-Leste brought to light the country's environmental problems. As indicated in table 1, 192,250 hectares of forest cover were lost between 1972, before the Indonesian invasion, and 1999, the year Timor-Leste voted for independence (Sandlund et al. 2001). This represents a 30 percent reduction in forest cover over the period—a deforestation rate of roughly 1.1 percent per year, nearly four times higher than the global average of 0.3 percent (FAO 2005).

Two major factors contributed to deforestation from 1975 to 1999. First, the Indonesian military's counterinsurgency activities included regular burning of forests

Table 1. Pre- and post-conflict forest cover in Timor-Leste

	Dense forest (ha)	Sparse forest (ha)	No forest (ha)	Total (ha)
1972 (before conflict)	321,542	324,558	624,546	1,270,646
1999 (after conflict)	207,654	246,196	816,796	1,270,646

Source: Sandlund et al. (2001).

516   Land and post-conflict peacebuilding

Figure 3. Depleted forest on hillsides around Dili, Timor-Leste's capital city
Source: Photo by author (2003).

to flush out opposition forces and "to reduce protective cover and concomitant opportunities for ambush" (McWilliam 2003, 316). Second, the Indonesian administration and Indonesian companies pursued logging for export, especially of high-value timber such as sandalwood and teak. Timor-Leste's timber resources were virtually monopolized by Indonesian business interests (Aditjondro 1994b). The hillsides around Dili, Timor-Leste's capital city, depicted in figure 3, were once covered in forest and home to marsupial mammals; now only a few trees remain.

Armed conflict negatively influences not only natural resources themselves but also environmental management systems. It disrupts state institutions and mechanisms of policy coordination, which in turn increases the likelihood of poor management and illegality (UNEP 2009). As a consequence of the conflict in Timor-Leste, the government there has faced a policy and regulation gap, a human resources shortage, financial resource limitations, and a lack of baseline information.

Policy and regulation gap

After the withdrawal of the Indonesian government in 1999, the United Nations Transitional Administration in East Timor (UNTAET) undertook state building and administrative activities until 2002, including establishment of environmental

Customary law and community-based management in Timor-Leste 517

regulations.[1] In principle, UNTAET adopted the policies formally applied during the Indonesian administration, including laws and regulations on forest conservation. However, those policies were sometimes ineffective due to the changes in the post-conflict situation (MAFF 2004).

Later, the national legislature started to transform the transitional regulations established by UNTAET into national regulations. Currently the government of Timor-Leste is in the process of formulating a range of policies, laws, decrees, and regulations related to the environment and natural resource management. Throughout this process, there have been periods when policies and regulations proved inefficient or the law did not function effectively. Environmental law that covers pollution control and the Environmental Impact Assessment Law were finally promulgated in February 2011, nearly ten years after independence. As of February 2011, the land law was still being debated in parliament.

Human resources shortage

Timor-Leste has also faced a structural human resources shortage. During the Indonesian administration, most civil servants in management positions were Indonesian personnel, partly because the Indonesian authorities intentionally kept Timorese out of senior management positions in the government. There was little opportunity for Timorese public servants to develop their capacity as senior-level managers.

After the popular election in 1999, over 7,000 Indonesian public servants fled Timor-Leste in the chaos of the ensuing violence (UNDP 2003). This situation created a vacuum in the public service, with a limited number of qualified personnel available in the administration. For example, the National Directorate of Forestry and Water Resources (NDFWR) of the Ministry of Agriculture, Forestry and Fisheries (MAFF) had only fifty-seven staff covering the entire country, or roughly 19 percent of the number of staff during the Indonesian administration. Only seven of the fifty-seven—or some 12 percent of NDFWR staff members— had a bachelor's degree in forestry; the education level of most staff was senior high school level (MAFF 2007).

Financial resource limitations

The government of Timor-Leste has faced severe budget constraints after independence was decided in 1999, and these constraints have impacted the budgets

---

[1] There have been three subsequent UN peacekeeping missions to Timor-Leste: the UN Mission of Support in East Timor (May 2002–May 2005), a peacekeeping mission to assist the newly independent state; the UN Office in Timor-Leste (May 2005–August 2006), which supported capacity building, democratic governance, and the observance of human rights; and the UN Integrated Mission in Timor-Leste (established in August 2006), whose mandate includes supporting the government in strengthening stability, promoting democratic governance, and facilitating political dialogue among stakeholders.

518   Land and post-conflict peacebuilding

of MAFF, NDFWR, and the Department of Forestry. For the years 2002 to 2011, the cumulative sum of the annual budgets for the state of Timor-Leste totaled nearly US$4.4 billion (MOF n.d.). During this same period, the cumulative sum of MAFF's annual budgets totaled US$128 million, less than 3 percent of the state budget. The NDFWR and the Department of Forestry had similarly restricted budgets. The NDFWR's annual budget was US$199,000 between 2001 to 2004, and the Department of Forestry's 2011 budget was US$555,159, only 4 percent of the MAFF's annual budget (MAFF 2004; MOF n.d.). In light of these financial constraints, it was important for the ministry to have a strategic partnership with other institutions, including international organizations and NGOs that provided assistance with environmental management.

Lack of baseline data

Data related to the environment were not properly maintained during the conflict. Therefore, there is limited accurate baseline information to consult for the purpose of policy and project formation. This poses a major challenge for the government of Timor-Leste in planning, analyzing, and formulating environmental policy.

Accurate forest inventories, data on biodiversity, and land classifications delineating clear boundaries between forest and nonforest areas were nonexistent (MAFF 2004). The resulting uncertainty has made it more difficult to attract attention from donors and has caused delays in project implementation. For example, when a reforestation program was implemented with MAFF, the discussions on where public and private forest boundaries should be located caused substantial delays in program implementation.

In light of these needs, in 2001 the United Nations Development Programme (UNDP) and the Norwegian Institute for Nature Research published *Assessing Environmental Needs and Priorities in East Timor* to provide basic data on environmental resources (Sandlund et al. 2001).

FRAMEWORKS FOR ENVIRONMENTAL REGULATION

Natural resources are key to the long-term sustainability and prosperity of Timor-Leste and its local communities. In 2001, the agricultural sector employed 80 percent of the population, contributing 40 percent of the gross domestic product and 90 percent of foreign exchange (da Costa 2001),[2] and agriculture was the main source of income in 94 percent of villages (East Timor Transitional Authority 2001). With 86 percent of the people living in rural areas and 80 percent dependent

---

[2] Petroleum exploitation in the waters southeast of Timor-Leste in the mid-2000s reshaped Timor-Leste's economy. As of 2011, the oil sector contributes 95 percent to the country's gross domestic product and accounts for most of its foreign exchange (World Bank n.d.a).

Customary law and community-based management in Timor-Leste **519**

on agriculture, forestry, and fisheries (World Bank n.d.b), rural communities continue to rely directly on natural resources for their daily life. For example, people depend on forests for a variety of medicinal and food items, as well as building and household materials (Sandlund et al. 2001).

United Nations environmental regulation framework

While the transitional administrator of Timor-Leste, UNTAET, was working on state building and administrative activities from 2000 to 2002, it also established two main interim regulations for natural resource management. The first regulation (Regulation 17/2000) was to ban illegal logging of wood and the burning of forests. The second regulation (Regulation 19/2000) provided for the protection of fifteen areas designated as "protected wild areas" of natural importance.

For illegal logging, a differential scale of penalties was established. Individual loggers were to be charged up to US$5,000, and business entities who violated the regulations were to be fined up to US$500,000. However, people continued to log wood and burn forests despite the UNTAET prohibitions. The penalty system, with its large fines, was impractical, and the regulation became unenforceable (McWilliam 2003).

Customary law for land and natural resource management: Tara bandu

A system of customary law called tara bandu, on the other hand, is well-practiced in Timor-Leste and provides protection for natural resources. In Tetum, the term *tara bandu* means "prohibition (*bandu*) by hanging (*tara*)." Tara bandu is a community-based natural resource management system based on traditional sociopolitical structures at the village and hamlet levels.

The three steps of tara bandu

Through observation and interviews with communities in Dili, Ainaro, and Liquiçá from 2001 to 2005, the author identified three major steps as the core mechanism for the practice of tara bandu: initiation, announcement, and enforcement.

First, specifically prohibited activities are determined at a public meeting of community members. Tara bandu typically prohibits the burning of forests, the cutting of trees, collection of forest products, agricultural harvests, and hunting and fishing in a forbidden zone for a defined period of time, as well as a broad variety of other activities.

Second, the community conducts a public ceremony to announce its enactment of the determined prohibition. A ritual authority figure takes the leading role in conducting the ceremony. The ceremony consists of a set of ritual forms: an altar is established, an animal is sacrificed, and the animal blood is poured over the land. Items are hung on the altar to inform the community about the prohibition. For

Figure 4. *Tara bandu* inception ceremony in Dili
Source: Photo by author (2004).

example, a lighter hung from a cross made out of tree branches may signify a ban on burning forests in a designated area. Such altars can be found in most areas.

Figure 4 depicts a ritual ceremony for announcing regulations by tara bandu. The man in the center holding a megaphone is a traditional leader. The community had decided to prohibit the cutting and burning of trees on the hill behind the altar, which was made of leaves and tree branches. A lighter was hung on the altar at this time, to indicate that tree burning was prohibited. A goat was sacrificed for the gods during the ceremony, and blood from the sacrificed goat was sprinkled over the land.

Third, as an enforcement mechanism, fines are determined by the community leaders and are imposed on any individual who is caught violating the regulation. Violators usually pay their fines in kind—by giving the community leaders an animal, for example—but sometimes they pay in cash. For example, if someone cut trees from the prohibited areas, the violator must pay the determined fines or provide his or her animal to the community leaders. The collected animals and cash fines are pooled and maintained by the community leaders for future ritual ceremonies.

There is strong compliance with regulations established in this manner. For example, when a public works project cut palm trees protected by tara bandu without permission from customary village authorities in the Oecusse District, the district government paid the mandated fine to the affected communities (Meitzner Yoder 2003).

Historical background of *tara bandu*

Following independence from Indonesia, a strong movement to reestablish customary practices for land and natural resource management emerged. Tara bandu is said to have been practiced before the Portuguese colonial era, and its key elements persisted through the Portuguese colonial era (Taylor 1999). Natural resource management by customary practices faded during the Indonesian occupation (Meitzner Yoder 2003), when the Indonesian administration replaced ritual authorities with Indonesian forestry officers to approve tree felling. Ritual authorities maintained their role only in conducting the annual agricultural rituals (Meitzner Yoder 2007). The customary system was also weakened by population relocation and social disruption (MAFF and Oxfam 2004).

The resurgence of customary law resulted from a perceived crisis of forest-resource depletion following the 1999 popular election and ensuing violence. Communities faced a severe shortage of wood materials when they needed to rebuild their homes, many of which were mostly destroyed by fire during the crisis in 1999. In 2001 and 2002, communities started to take the initiative by enacting harvesting restrictions in locally protected or sacred forests. For example, from 2001 to 2004, fifteen out of eighteen villages (over 80 percent) in Oecussi District held tara bandu ceremonies (Meitzner Yoder 2007).

Local perception of the environment

The practice of tara bandu is closely related to cultural perception of the environment. Local people perceive the environment as a cultural resource inherited from the ancestors, and they are tied to their land for reasons beyond its productive purpose: "It is a place where the life of the clan is invested, the place where the history of the existing lineage can be found, the site of ancestors' graveyards, the place of a clan's sacred altar and other cosmologically related affairs" (Anderson and Deutsch 2001, 21).

This perception of the environment is closely linked with the enforcement mechanism of tara bandu. The people believe that someone who violates the prohibition set by tara bandu will be cursed. During interviews the author conducted in Ainaro in 2004, community members mentioned such curses: "He died by snakebite because he cut trees from a prohibited area"; "He died after suffering from an unknown fever because he harvested products from a forbidden area." This local belief facilitates the people's strong compliance with the regulations implemented by customary leaders.

Leadership for the practice of customary law

Core leadership for the practice of tara bandu is taken by the *lia nain*, a descendant of a chief. A respected individual within the community, the lia nain enforces proper treatment of nature by drawing on accumulated local knowledge. He takes a key role in supernatural aspects of the tara bandu mechanism and in maintaining order for ritual.

522   Land and post-conflict peacebuilding

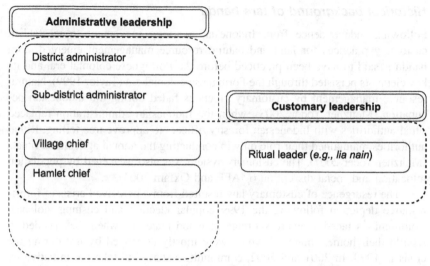

Figure 5.   Conceptual relationships between administrative and customary leadership

The village chief and hamlet chief also play leadership roles in managing land and natural resources through customary law. Historically the role of chief was a hereditary position, but since independence the chiefs have been chosen by election. In the absence of effective law for landownership and land registry, the chief of the village, or *chefe de suco* (in Tetum), serves as a key figure in unofficial land markets. A chefe de suco may witness documents, maintain copies of documents, and even issue documentary acknowledgments of land rights. Most parties to land transactions are aware of the land administrative role of the chefe de suco, but are less sure of the role of the Land and Property Directorate, the government entity that is officially responsible for land transactions. Usually the chefe de suco consults with local authorities when a purported transaction takes place on land claimed as customary land; this seems particularly to be the case in transactions involving outsiders or foreigners (Fitzpatrick, McWilliam, and Barnes 2008).

Administrative leaders are officials appointed by the government. In some areas, administrative leaders play a leadership role in customary practice as well. The customary regulations can be enforced as long as the government empowers customary authorities and supports their enforcement mechanisms. If customary authorities have no leadership in enforcing customary law, such law will not be effective. (The leadership struture for the practice of the customary law is shown in figure 5.)

Strengths and limitations of tara bandu mechanism

Because it originates locally, tara bandu makes it easy for community members to enforce rules and adjust them according to environmental and social conditions. The practice is also straightforward for communities because the environment is closely related with local beliefs and other aspects of local culture. Thus tara bandu is familiar to local people and widely acceptable to them.

Figure 6. Tara bandu ceremony in Dili with the then-president and then-prime minister of Timor-Leste in attendance
Source: Photo by author (2004).

Tara bandu has certain limitations, however. Sometimes customary authorities have difficulty resolving intervillage disputes. Because tara bandu does not bind people from adjacent areas or villages who did not participate in its establishment, violations committed by nonparticipating villages are not covered by its restrictions (Cardinoza 2005). Thus it is necessary for leaders to collaborate with other villages, particularly those with common boundaries, when establishing tara bandu regulations. All neighboring villages should be invited to attend the meetings and ceremonies. In the event that collaboration fails, government officials provide support for mediation.

Another limitation is that sometimes a community cannot afford the materials for the ceremony, and there is a tendency to delay declaring a rule by tara bandu until the community can arrange for the required ritual materials (Cardinoza 2005). To address this problem, the government and NGOs occasionally provide material support to communities—sometimes even supplying the goat to be used for the sacrifice. Government officials' attendance at tara bandu ceremonies, as depicted in figure 6, increases the legitimacy of customary leaders and customary law. Figure 6 shows a symbolic ceremony in which government authorities and a customary leader intermingle. When a community organizes a tara bandu ceremony, they usually invite governmental officers to attend the ceremony.

524   Land and post-conflict peacebuilding

LANDOWNERSHIP AND LAND DISPUTES

The land tenure system in Timor-Leste is closely related to the way natural resources are managed in rural areas. Most of the land is governed by customary law and not registered formally. In 2008 Timor-Leste had a population of 1.1 million. However, there were fewer than 47,000 formal land titles, of which 2,709 were from the Portuguese colonial era and 44,091 were issued during the Indonesian era (Hohe and Nixon 2003). Customary authorities generally recognize land boundaries and transactions, and land tenure systems are related to ancestral origin (D'Andrea 2003), although as of October 2011 there is no statutory framework that recognizes customary land in Timor-Leste. Origin groups have de facto authority over land allocation, including permission for the clearing and cultivation of new land (Fitzpatrick, McWilliam, and Barnes 2008). Further, a multilevel ownership system has been practiced in Timor-Leste—that is, the land itself and other things existing above the land are sometimes owned by different people. For example, trees planted on a certain tract of land may be owned by one person, while the land itself can have a different owner.

The bulk of the forests are managed by communities in Timor-Leste. According to a 2005 assessment of global forest resources (FAO 2005), 33 percent of forests in Timor-Leste are designated as public and 67 percent as private. Privately owned forests are forests managed by communities. This private-ownership figure is much higher than that in neighboring countries: the 2005 assessment deemed 96 percent of forests in South and Southeast Asian nations as publicly owned, and only 3 percent as privately owned.

These disparate ownership figures reflect confusion about immovable property in Timor-Leste. A draft land law approved by the Council of Ministers in March 2010, entitled the Special Regime for the Determination of Ownership of Immovable Property, would offer this clarification: "Any immovable property acknowledged by the community as being of their common and shared use, by a group of individuals or families, organized in accordance with local practices and customs shall be considered as community property" (article 25.1).

In areas designated for annual cultivation of food crops, an individual group member can farm a specific plot. At the end of the cultivation period the individual claim is relinquished, and the land reverts back to communal property. In some places with privileged access for group members only, individuals or households may control portions of land. Some areas are set aside as sacred land, and use or access are forbidden; these areas are closely associated with ritual or spiritual prohibitions. Sometimes, however, the boundaries of forests, pasturelands, and agricultural land are unclear and land conflicts ensue (Fitzpatrick, McWilliam, and Barnes 2008).

According to research conducted in 2004 for the Timor-Leste Land Law Program, which included interviews with 162 government officials and community members, the people of Timor-Leste prefer to resolve land conflicts at the local level if at all possible. The tendency is to take land disputes first to elders (*katuas*) at the family or hamlet level, then, if necessary, to a village- or subdistrict-level mediation forum (see figure 7). Most people prefer to avoid the

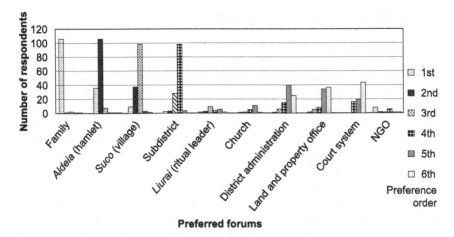

Figure 7. Order in which land disputes are taken to forums in Timor-Leste
Source: Urresta and Nixon (2004).

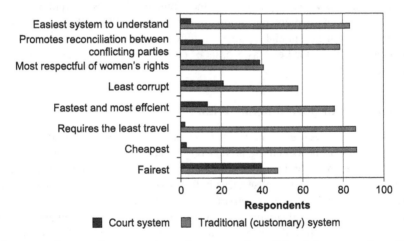

Figure 8. Community perceptions of courts and traditional (customary) conflict resolution systems in Timor-Leste
Source: Urresta and Nixon (2004).

formal court system and the mediation framework of the government's Land and Property Office (Urresta and Nixon 2004). This shows the population's overall preference for land conflict resolution that occurs through customary means.

The same research also demonstrates a strong overall perception among the population that customary conflict resolution systems are better than the courts. The data show that the customary systems are more easily understood by local community members; are believed to more effectively promote reconciliation between conflicting parties; are considered less corrupt, cheaper, faster, and more efficient than the courts; and require less travel than court proceedings (see figure 8).

526 Land and post-conflict peacebuilding

REGULARIZATION OF CUSTOMARY LAW

The new government of Timor-Leste has recognized the importance of customary law and has emphasized its significance in various rules and regulations. It began by highlighting the value of customs in the Timor-Leste constitution. Article 4 of the constitution reads: "The State shall recognize and value the norms and customs of Timor-Leste that are not contrary to the Constitution and to any legislation dealing specifically with customary law." Regarding the environment, article 61 of the constitution reads: "1. Everyone has the right to a humane, healthy, and ecologically balanced environment and the duty to protect it and improve it for the benefit of the future generations. 2. The State shall recognize the need to preserve and rationalize natural resources."

Tara bandu was also integrated into forestry and watershed policy and strategy by Ministry of Agriculture, Forestry and Fisheries (MAFF). A key strategy document recognizes tara bandu as "an inherent part in the development of local ordinances to protect the forest-watershed areas" (MAFF 2004, 38). The Special Regime for the Determination of Ownership of Immovable Property (i.e., the land law) was approved by the Council of Ministers, although it is still before the parliament for approval, as of October 2011. If the land law is adopted without substantial change, customary practice will be recognized in the land law of Timor-Leste as a basis of community property and community representation.

Advantages to governmental authority

The MAFF has been encouraging the revival of tara bandu for both technical and political reasons, benefiting both governmental authority and customary leaders. The government of Timor-Leste faces a critical shortage of human resources, and the demand for technical services in forestry and watershed management far exceeds the supply. Although MAFF has limited knowledge and capacity for overseeing forests, local communities possess many years of accumulated knowledge and practice. In order to overcome those resource constraints, government officials have recognized tara bandu as a cost-effective mechanism for managing natural resources (D'Andrea 2003). Also, the new government has a strong incentive to differentiate itself from previous Indonesian rule. The Indonesian government did not recognize the role of communities in natural resource management. The newly established government is displaying an explicitly different approach by recognizing the role of customary law.

Advantages to customary leaders

Communities have experienced a severe scarcity of natural resources and have sought ways to restore those resources. They have recognized that if the power of customary leaders is regained, it will be possible to control diminishing resources.

Such revitalization of the customary law system requires legitimizing of the authority of customary leaders.

Regularization of customary leaders' authority has also provided a new channel for these leaders to voice their concerns to the state. When communities implement customary practice, government officials attend the ceremony as well as the meetings preceding it. On such occasions, community leaders discuss their concerns—about boundary issues, government support, and other matters—with the government officials.

Communities in Motaulun, a village in the Liquiçá district, started to implement tara bandu in May 2003. In an interview with Claudia D'Andrea, village leaders said that they decided to implement tara bandu in reaction to the power vacuum of 1999–2001 (D'Andrea 2003). They took inspiration from the new constitution and felt that it was important to start with fresh legislation in the new era of independence.

FACTORS CONTRIBUTING TO REVIVAL OF CUSTOMARY LAW

When armed conflict limited state capacity in Timor-Leste, many of the measures taken by the UN or the government were insufficient to achieve their intended aims. Furthermore, mechanisms imported by the UN lacked the benefit of local knowledge and legitimacy, and thus were not always reasonable given local conditions. Lack of resources on the part of the government also posed challenges for the enforcement of regulations.

In contrast, natural resource management methods based on customary law are often sufficiently equipped to function in such situations. The government of Timor-Leste would have been unable to effectively manage natural resources during the immediate post-conflict period if customary law had not been used proactively by local communities. It was therefore in the government's interest to elevate the role of customary law. Thus customary law retained substantial legitimacy in Timor-Leste as governmental authority grew, in contrast to many other developing countries that were not affected by conflict, where customary law tends to lose legitimacy as the government becomes stronger. (See figure 9 for conceptual graphs comparing the function of governmental administration to the function of customary law governing natural resources in developing countries not affected by conflict and in post-conflict Timor-Leste.)

Internal factors

A number of internal factors contributed to the revival of customary law. *Internal factors* mean internal issues for community members. First, dependence on natural resources for daily life is high in Timor-Leste, where 80 percent of the population lives in rural areas. When community members are directly affected by environmental deterioration and receive direct benefit through better environmental management, they have more incentive to manage natural resources effectively

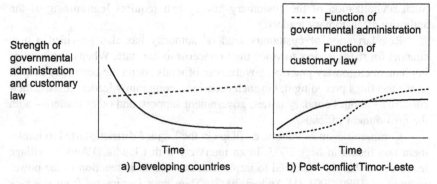

Figure 9. Conceptual graph illustrating the relative roles of governmental administration and customary law governing natural resources in developing countries not affected by conflict and in post-conflict Timor-Leste

to maintain their daily life than those who do not benefit directly from the availability of natural resources.

Communities possess accumulated knowledge and customs for managing natural resources. For example, when the author interviewed customary leaders in Ainaro in December 2003, they mentioned that a landslide had happened because trees from a particular zone had been cut down. The customary leaders and other community members possessed such historical knowledge because it had been passed down by word of mouth from generation to generation.

Customary leaders have an important role in establishing, implementing, and enforcing customary law. For instance, when a community is deciding whether to open a prohibited forest for harvesting, a customary leader assesses the maturity of the trees by using a traditional chisel to check the thickness of the tree bark. On the basis of this assessment, the community then decides on the timing for opening the forests for logging.

Regulations under customary law are closely related to local beliefs and are shared as norms among community members. In rural areas, a high level of compliance with regulations based on customary law is ensured by community members. Community members who violate the rules not only are punished by a fine, but they are subject to a curse, according to local beliefs. In contrast, in the capital city, Dili, where large numbers of foreigners and migrants from other districts share fewer norms and practices of customary law, compliance with rules of customary law is lower.

Monitoring of regulations is ensured by community members. For example, in Sacoco, a hamlet of the village Ponilale, located in the Ermera District, the community elects four or five monitors in a community-wide vote (D'Andrea 2003). The people who are elected take responsibility for monitoring resources for a given period of time and report offenses to the customary leaders (D'Andrea 2003).

Customary leaders also act as negotiators with external parties such as foreigners, government officials, and representatives of NGOs and international organizations. For example, a Portuguese owner of a coffee plantation

Customary law and community-based management in Timor-Leste **529**

in the Liquiçá district told the author in a September 2002 interview that he had negotiated with customary leaders over maintenance of his coffee plantation.

Finally, because customary law is applied in a specific area, normally at a village level, communities can easily adjust the rules according to changes in environmental conditions observed by the community.

External factors

Several external factors have also contributed to the revival of customary law in Timor-Leste. *External factors* mean the issues derived from external power or relationships beyond the community. First, the new government has a strong incentive to distinguish the independent administration from previous Indonesian rule. For example, the new government decided to use Portuguese and Tetum instead of Indonesian as official national languages, even though less than 25 percent of the population speaks Portuguese and the Indonesian language is understood among the educated population. While the Indonesian government replaced community leaders who had managed natural resources with Indonesian forestry officers, the newly established government recognizes the role of the community and its customs in natural resource management in the statutory law. The statutory recognition was important to legitimize the role of the customary leader, as well as the rules and regulations established by customary law.

Furthermore, with independence came an administrative vacuum. After 7,000 Indonesian public officers fled Timor-Leste in 1999, the administration did not have enough officials with the necessary skills. At the same time, communities faced a severe scarcity of natural resources needed for their daily life. This set the stage for governmental recognition of tara bandu.

Finally, not only the new government but also international organizations and NGOs have promoted tara bandu as an effective means of natural resource management. A UNDP report recommends that traditional laws and customs should be incorporated into environmental legislation (Sandlund et al. 2001). Haburas, a local environmental NGO, calls tara bandu "traditional ecological wisdom" and has supported communities' revival of tara bandu (GEP n.d.). Haburas supports the practice by facilitating government and international organizations' participation in tara bandu ceremonies organized by communities. Previously, customary leaders did not have extensive contact with external parties such as international organizations. NGOs have linked customary leaders and external parties to achieve better implementation of customary law.

IMPLICATIONS FOR POST-CONFLICT NATURAL RESOURCE MANAGEMENT

This chapter reveals that the customary law for natural resource management in Timor-Leste, tara bandu, has had prominent roles in the country under the sociopolitical transition following the end of conflict in Timor-Leste. The research

530 Land and post-conflict peacebuilding

also found that tara bandu was functioning for natural resource management during this period and has started to be integrated into state legislation. When government capacity is limited in a post-conflict situation, environmental policies implemented by the government and international community can fail to achieve the desired effect. In Timor-Leste, gaps were identified between policies on the one hand and, on the other, actual conditions in the community, capacity limitations related to law enforcement, and structural problems such as a lack of human resources.

Although the government has needed time to establish effective environmental laws and policies and to take efficient measures, communities started to revitalize tara bandu and to manage natural resources by local methods fairly soon after the conflict. The newly established government had limited capacity and faced difficulty in managing natural resources effectively when it was not relying on customary law. For natural resource management to be improved quickly, it was imperative for the state to engage local knowledge and practice, and to promote local participation and ownership. The use of customary law was a way to address the urgent agenda of the transitional government. In fact, the government has begun incorporating customary law into other national policies. Customary law is based on local ecology and social structure, and it thus provides a way to manage natural resources in a locally adaptable manner. It widely reflects the local community's structure, its social norms and values, and its concept of land and natural resource management.

In Timor-Leste, increasing the role of customary law was effective in part because the government had insufficient administrative capacity to enforce modern methods for natural resource management after the conflict. However, statutory law also needs to be developed, and the timing of the integration of modern law and customary law early on is important. Multilayered management systems can be quite effective in the management of natural resources. Thus government must recover the capacity to manage statutory law after conflict while strengthening the weak aspects of customary law and supplementing them with other methods of management. During the post-conflict period, assistance should be given not only to government administration but also to communities that enforce customary law to manage natural resources.

REFERENCES

Aditjondro, G. J. 1994a. From Memo to Tutuala: A kaleidoscope of environmental problems in East Timor. In *East Timor: An Indonesian intellectual speaks out*, ed. H. Feith and E. Baulch. Deakin, Australia: Australian Council for Overseas Aid.

———. 1994b. In the shadow of Mount Ramelaw: Some sketches of East Timorese culture. In *East Timor: An Indonesian intellectual speaks out*, ed. H. Feith and E. Baulch. Deakin, Australia: Australian Council for Overseas Aid.

Allen, C. K. 1939. *Law in the making*. London: Oxford University Press.

Anderson, R., and C. Deutsch, eds. 2001. East Timor: Perceptions of culture and environment; Summary of full paper. In *Sustainable development and the environment in East*

Customary law and community-based management in Timor-Leste 531

Timor: Proceedings of the conference on sustainable development in East Timor, 25–31 January 2001. Timor-Leste: Timor Aid.

Burgess, E. W. 1967. Can neighborhood work have a scientific basis? In *The city*, ed. R. E. Park, E. W. Burgess, and R. D. McKenzie. Chicago: University of Chicago Press.

Candio, P., and R. Bleiker. 2001. Peacebuilding in East Timor. *The Pacific Review* 14 (1): 63–84.

Cardinoza, M. 2005. Reviving traditional NRM regulations *(tara bandu)* as a community-based approach of protecting carbon stocks and securing livelihood. In *Carbon forestry: Who will benefit? Proceedings of workshop on carbon sequestration and sustainable livelihoods*, ed. D. Murdiyarso and H. Herawati. Bogor Barat, Indonesia: Center for International Forestry Research.

da Costa, H. 2001. Agriculture, comparative advantage, and macro economy. In *East Timor: Development challenges for the world's newest nation*, ed. H. Hill and J. M. Saldanha. Canberra, Australia: Asia Pacific Press.

D'Andrea, C. 2003. The customary use and management of natural resources in Timor-Leste. Discussion paper prepared for "Land Policy Administration for Pro-Poor Rural Growth," workshop, Dili, December.

East Timor Transitional Authority. 2001. *Suco survey*. Dili.

FAO (Food and Agriculture Organization of the United Nations). 2005. *Global resources assessment 2005*. Rome.

Fitzpatrick, D., A. McWilliam, and S. Barnes. 2008. Policy notes on customary land in Timor Leste. *East Timor Law Journal*, November 20.

GEP (Goldman Environmental Prize). n.d. Demetrio do Amaral de Carvalho: East Timor; Environmental policy. www.goldmanprize.org/node/95.

Hardin, G. 1968. The tragedy of the commons. *Science* 162:1243–1248.

Hohe, T., and R. Nixon. 2003. *Reconciling justice: "Traditional" law and state judiciary in East Timor*. Report prepared for the United States Institute of Peace. January. www.gsdrc.org/docs/open/DS33.pdf.

MAFF (Ministry of Agriculture, Forestry and Fisheries, Democratic Republic of Timor-Leste). 2004. *Policy and strategy: Forestry and watershed subsector*. Dili.

———. 2007. *First national report: Land degradation in Timor-Leste*. Dili.

MAFF (Ministry of Agriculture, Forestry and Fisheries, Democratic Republic of Timor-Leste) and Oxfam. 2004. *Study on lessons learned in implementing community-level agriculture and natural resource management projects in Timor-Leste*. Dili.

McCay, B., and Acheson, J. 1987. *Question of the commons: The culture and ecology of communal resources*. Tucson: University of Arizona Press.

McWilliam, A. 2003. New beginnings in East Timorese forest management. *Journal of Southeast Asian Studies* 34 (2): 307–327.

Meitzner Yoder, L. S. 2003. Custom and conflict. Discussion paper prepared for a regional workshop on "Land Policy and Administration for Pro-Poor Rural Growth," Dili, December.

———. 2007. Hybridising justice: State-customary interactions over forest crime and punishment in Oecusse, East Timor. *Asia Pacific Journal of Anthropology* 8 (1): 43–57.

Mitsumata, G., S. Morimoto, and T. Murota. 2008. *New frontiers in commons research: Communal use of mountains, grasslands, seas, and rivers*. Tokyo: University of Tokyo Press.

MOF (Ministry of Finance, Democratic Republic of Timor-Leste). n.d. Timor-Leste budget transparency portal. www.budgettransparency.gov.tl/publicTransparency/transparency

532   Land and post-conflict peacebuilding

Navigation;jsessionid=3EF3257D945316C7AB654905DBA95A38?fiscalYearId=72&is Inflow=false.

Murota, T., and G. Mitsumata. 2004. *Iriairinya to commons*. [In Japanese.] Tokyo: Nihonhyoronsya.

Ostrom, E. 1990. *Governing the commons: The evolution of institutions for collective action*. New York: Cambridge University Press.

Sandlund, O. T., I. Bryceson, D. de Carvalho, N. Rio, J. da Silva, and M. I. Silva. 2001. *Assessing environmental needs and priorities in East Timor*. Dili, Timor-Leste: United Nations Development Programme–Dili; Trondheim, Norway: Norwegian Institute for Nature Research.

Shalom, S., N. Chomsky, and M. Albert. 1999. East Timor: Questions and answers. *Z Magazine*, October. www.zcommunications.org/east-timor-questions-and-answers-by-noam-chomsky.

Taylor, J. G. 1999. *East Timor: The price of freedom*. London: Zed Books.

Tee, E. 2000. It's a difficult birth of a new nation. *Straits Times*, February 13.

UNDP (United Nations Development Programme). 2003. Recovery, Employment and Stability Programme for Ex-combatants and Communities in Timor-Leste (RESPECT). Annex 11 to UNDP Timor-Leste Programme Package Document. New York.

UNEP (United Nations Environment Programme). 2009. *From conflict to peacebuilding: The role of natural resources and the environment*. Nairobi, Kenya. http://postconflict .unep.ch/publications/pcdmb_policy_01.pdf.

Urresta, E., and R. Nixon. 2004. *Report on research findings and policy recommendations for a legal framework for land dispute mediation*. Dili: Timor-Leste Land Law Program.

World Bank. n.d.a. Making natural resource management more transparent in Timor-Leste. http://web.worldbank.org/WBSITE/EXTERNAL/COUNTRIES/EASTASIAPACIFICEXT/ TIMORLESTEEXTN/0,,contentMDK:22988462~pagePK:141137~piPK:141127~theSit ePK:294022,00.html.

———. n.d.b. Rural development & agriculture in Timor-Leste. http://web.worldbank.org/ WBSITE/EXTERNAL/COUNTRIES/EASTASIAPACIFICEXT/EXTEAPREGTOPRUR DEV/0,,contentMDK:20534357~menuPK:3127810~pagePK:34004173~piPK:34003707 ~theSitePK:573964,00.html.

PART 5

Lessons learned

PART 5

Lessons learned

Lessons learned in land tenure and natural resource management in post-conflict societies

Jon Unruh and Rhodri C. Williams

Since the mid-twentieth century, armed conflict has changed: instead of involving wars between different countries, armed conflict is more likely to involve governments and opposition groups; moreover, it usually occurs in regions where people depend on land and natural resources for their livelihoods. Of the thirty-seven armed conflicts under way in 2011, for example, only one was interstate, nine were internationalized internal armed conflicts, and thirty-four were located in developing agrarian economies (Themnér and Wallensteen 2012; UCDP n.d.). And in all but three of the more than thirty intrastate conflicts that occurred between 1990 and 2009, land-related issues played a substantial role (UNFT 2012; Alden Wily 2009). The shift to intrastate conflicts in resource-dependent regions has increased the associated risks: studies show that conflicts related to natural resources are more likely to relapse than those that are not, and do so twice as quickly (UNFT 2012).

In Afghanistan, where agriculture is the main source of livelihoods and 80 percent of households rely directly on natural resources for their livelihoods, land and water are the principal causes of local disputes.[1] Such disputes, which can become violent, have exacerbated the wider war and have complicated and weakened efforts to promote peace in the country. In Africa, 48 percent of civil conflicts that occurred during the first decade of this century were in areas where access to rural land matters deeply to the survival of the majority of the population (UNFT 2012; Alden Wily 2009). The conflict in Darfur, for example, is inextricably intertwined with competition over water and fertile land, and climate change is expected to exacerbate competition over these scarce resources (UNEP 2009).

Jon Unruh is an associate professor of geography at McGill University. Rhodri C. Williams is a human rights lawyer who specializes in land and forced-migration issues. Some material in this chapter is based on the authors' personal experiences, and several sections were informed by internal, unpublished reports developed by Jon Unruh for the World Bank.

[1] More than half of Afghan respondents to a 2007 Oxfam survey reported that land and water are the main causes of local disputes. Several other studies, including surveys conducted by the Independent Afghan Human Rights Commission and the Asia Foundation, corroborated these results (Waldman 2008).

536   Land and post-conflict peacebuilding

In Colombia, which has been plagued by agrarian conflicts throughout its history, land has both sparked and funded conflict for several decades. Between the early 1980s and 2000, paramilitaries acquired approximately 50 percent of the country's most fertile and valuable land, and conflict between paramilitaries and guerrilla groups has led to the displacement of between 2 and 4 million Colombian peasants (Elhawary 2009).

Land and natural resources often contribute to conflict and are affected by conflict; thus, to achieve lasting peace, the post-conflict peacebuilding process must address the origins of conflict that are related to land and natural resources, the impacts of the conflict on the natural resource base, the challenges of displacement, and long-term development: all of these require careful attention to land-related issues, including land rights.

Even where land and natural resources are not central to the onset and conduct of conflict, they are crucial to post-conflict peacebuilding. Land affects livelihoods; macroeconomic recovery; governance; trust in government; and the reintegration of conflict-affected populations, including former combatants. A solid system of land management can strengthen governmental credibility and promote the rule of law; in addition, authoritative guarantees of tenure security help foster investment in and productive use of land resources (Collier et al. 2003). Despite its importance to many aspects of peacebuilding, however, land issues have been addressed unevenly in peacebuilding processes.

Post-conflict peacebuilding is often complicated by land and property issues that develop during and immediately after armed conflict. Typical conflict-related damage includes exploitation of valuable natural resources (often to finance the conflict); degradation of forests and agricultural lands; and destruction of public buildings, infrastructure, and homes. Lingering tensions often manifest themselves in competition for land and resources—and there is often a surge in competing claims to land and property, particularly as returning populations assert their rights. Eager to restart the economy, governments often grant large land concessions for agricultural production or natural resource extraction, sparking conflict with smallholders. The demands created by returning refugees, members of the diaspora, internally displaced persons (IDPs), and even members of the international assistance community can lead to acute housing shortages. Finally, land records may have been damaged, destroyed, or falsified in the conflict, creating obstacles to the resolution of disputes.

The chapters in this book underscore the critical role of land and land rights in the recovery from armed conflict. Taken together, these twenty-one chapters—based upon case studies from seventeen countries—illustrate a familiar lesson: although there are beneficial approaches to engaging with land rights—and, more broadly, addressing land issues—there is no one template for doing so success-fully. The variables are too numerous and the contexts too individual; moreover, land issues are too embedded in other aspects of sociopolitical recovery. Nevertheless, the experiences recounted in this book offer broad lessons that are relevant to future post-conflict scenarios. Drawing upon the analyses in this book and the broader literature, this chapter identifies lessons in conceptualizing and addressing post-conflict land tenure, management, and related issues.

The problems that arise in efforts to address post-conflict tenure security, particularly in developing countries, can be grouped into four broad categories: legal ambiguity, legal pluralism, disputes, and land recovery. The first four sections of this chapter address these categories, highlighting experiences and insights drawn from the case studies presented in this book. The chapter then proceeds with a discussion of the coordination and sequencing of interventions during the peacebuilding process, identifying approaches to managing land in post-conflict situations.

LEGAL AMBIGUITY

Legal ambiguity, one of the most immediate and obvious land-related problems in post-conflict situations, leads to confusion about a variety of legal and administrative issues, from the boundaries between parcels to the status of conflicting claims on the same parcel. The link between such confusion and tenure insecurity is clear (Bruce, Migot-Adholla, and Atherton 1994).

In the wake of conflict, legal ambiguity typically takes one of four forms:

- *Unclear rights of access to and use of natural resources.* When rights holders claim conflicting use or access rights, when customary and statutory rights differ, and when resource management systems are inconsistent, tensions can arise. Concessions that are granted on the basis of ambiguous, contested, or dated rules may exclude or antagonize local communities, particularly where such rules give concessionaires the right to deny communities access to land or land-based resources. In fact, many rebel groups and certain governments issue concession contracts of questionable legitimacy, which generates conflicts between claimants, users, and uses.
- *Confusion about which institutions govern land.* Particularly where postcolonial elites have retained the rules that once granted colonial authorities sweeping control of any lands not held under formal title, the disposition of rights to government land; public land; and tribal, indigenous, or community land is often unclear or misunderstood. Ambiguity is especially likely in rural areas, where customary administrative units (such as clan homelands and chieftaincies) and statutory administrative units (at the national and subnational levels) overlap. Where the distinctions between government land, public land, and tribal, indigenous, or community lands are unclear, ownership is often contested, particularly between local residents and returnees. In addition, local residents may misunderstand (and therefore oppose) attempts to survey land.
- *Disputes related to individual ownership of land.* The process by which individuals acquire deeds, titles, or other government-issued, land-related documents is often unclear, may involve many steps, can be easily corrupted, and can be especially difficult if land has historically been held under customary

538   Land and post-conflict peacebuilding

tenure. Controversies often arise when the rules governing the inheritance of land make it difficult to determine who is the rightful heir. In post-conflict situations, squatters may lay claim to land under rules of adverse or acquisitive possession, creating particular concerns when original claim holders have been forced to vacate land as a direct result of conflict.[2] When fraudulent, coerced, or ambiguous land transfers are widespread, the competing claims that arise undermine tenure security, and thereby inhibit investment and growth.

- *Overlapping, incomplete, inconsistently applied, or outdated policies regarding land and property.* Particularly where statutory and customary systems intersect, confusion over which norms apply can impede governance of land and property. Incomplete and inconsistently applied regulations create additional barriers to effective land use and development. Finally, pre-conflict regulations may not fully reflect post-conflict reality.

Among the examples of legal ambiguity considered in this book is the relationship between Indonesian statutory law and the *adat* (customary) institutions of Aceh. As discussed by Arthur Green, tensions have arisen over three issues: (1) the extent to which Indonesia's formal recognition of adat practices confers governance power on adat institutions; (2) whether adat authority is exclusive or is shared with statutory institutions; and (3) whether changes in the composition of adat leadership structures require state approval (Green 2013*).[3] In another example, Allan Cain notes that in post-conflict Angola, the occupation of land has been contested where local officials had a practice of approving bills of sale themselves, as a matter of expedience, because the process of obtaining formal title to surface rights from provincial governments was arduous and inaccessible to the majority of inhabitants (Cain 2013*).

In Afghanistan, mistrust of the central government's motivations have run so high that communities engaged in efforts to register their land were uncertain which would entail greater risk: seeking state recognition or avoiding it (Stanfield et al. 2013*). In the Philippines, the Supreme Court held that sweeping rights granted in Mindanao under the 1997 Indigenous Peoples Rights Act (1) directly contradicted laws on land classification and environmental protection and (2) conflicted with the government's policy of promoting mining to augment national income (Defensor Knack 2013*); this ruling reflects a common tension between the goals of maximizing economic growth and protecting the rights of indigenous people.[4]

---

[2] The terms *adverse possession* and *acquisitive possession* refer to rules in common law and civil law, respectively, which set out legal conditions (that may vary by jurisdiction) under which those who use land that does not belong to them may eventually be recognized as lawful owners.

[3] Citations marked with an asterisk refer to chapters within this book.

[4] See also Oki (2013*).

Lessons learned **539**

These and other examples of legal ambiguity highlight a number of lessons. First, in post-conflict situations, land tenure is often messy and chaotic; at the same time, domestic and international capacity, financial resources, and expertise may be extremely limited. International and domestic actors have sometimes responded to such scenarios by attempting to resolve all outstanding land issues at once. For example, proposals have been put forward for temporary international assumption of responsibility for virtually the whole spectrum of land and property administration (UN-HABITAT 2007). But in Bosnia and Herzegovina, when international administrators assumed such responsibilities to prevent discriminatory land allocations, their own lack of capacity created a bottleneck that not only failed to halt such allocations but also inhibited legitimate investment (Williams 2013a*). The reality is that it is often counterproductive to attempt to quickly resolve post-conflict chaos, and that such chaos is often best managed until peace consolidation has advanced and capacity has increased (Fitzpatrick 2002).

A less ambitious—and often practical—approach to the fluidity of the post-conflict legal environment is to issue authoritative legal interpretations, executive instructions, or decrees to deal with specific categories of problems as they arise, rather than to undertake a full legislative review and reform process too quickly. When such rulings are developed through a consultative process and broadly disseminated, they can preempt certain kinds of disputes that occur in large volume, and allow others to be resolved outside of court.

Many of the land-related issues in post-conflict Liberia, for example, are highly contested, volatile, and potentially serious enough to undermine the peace process; thus, they need to be dealt with quickly. Among the issues that would likely benefit from specific legal rulings are the following:

- The legal distinction between government land, public land, and land held under tribal land deeds.
- Which rights are and are not included in a concession.
- Whether the years of conflict count toward the occupancy requirement for adverse possession.
- What constitutes a bad-faith or good-faith land transfer.
- Which laws are still to be applied—including old laws and received laws.[5]
- The precise legal steps for acquiring land deeds.
- The allocation of authority over land matters between statutory and customary institutions.
- The legality of previously issued concessions.

Approaches that involve rulings on specific issues, however, need to be implemented with some caution. In post-conflict Sierra Leone, attempts to increase

---

[5] The term *received laws* refers to those laws or parts of laws that are imported from another country—either during a colonial period, out of expediency, or because of lack of capacity on the part of the receiving country.

540   Land and post-conflict peacebuilding

legal clarity by surveying boundaries led to renewed violence in some cases (Unruh 2008), suggesting that for some actors, ambiguity is desirable because it allows ongoing negotiation of overlapping land uses and claims. Ambiguity also reflects the fact that in customary systems, boundaries are not always clearly and permanently demarcated, but may take the form of zones that vary in use and precise location over time, and that have different meanings for various members of different groups.

In the wake of conflict, ambiguity regarding squatters' rights to land and other resources poses a significant problem in both rural and urban areas. In some cases, squatters attempt to establish claims not only through adverse possession but by planting trees or making other improvements. Meanwhile, evictions—particularly if they are carried out on a large scale, or involve excombatants or others who have been encouraged or allowed to settle on available property—may lead to social unrest. For instance, Cain describes the risks created by the fact that excombatants in Angola often lacked access to sufficient land to sustain their livelihoods (Cain 2013*). Rhodri C. Williams notes that in Bosnia, controversial land allocations, which favored the occupants of homes that were claimed by displaced persons, were used to dampen the political fallout that resulted when such occupants were eventually evicted (Williams 2013a*). In many cases, squatters feel that they have little to lose, and occupy land in the hope that any resulting dispute will result, at a minimum, in some form of compensation.

The low tenure security inherent in squatting can also lead to excessive exploitation of resources, including timber, minerals, and rubber, as in post-conflict Liberia (Smucker 2005; IRIN 2005). Because of the movement of IDPs, cities are also subject to an influx of squatters during and after conflict (Buchanan-Smith and McElhinney 2011; Assaf and El-Fil 2000; Bahir 2010; Williams 2011). In cities where IDPs have created informal settlements, a potentially constructive response to squatting is to engage squatters in development planning by offering them secure tenure in exchange for sweat equity and voluntary compliance with planning rules (Williams 2011). Generally, successful approaches to squatting depend on increasing tenure security and providing income sources, with the latter tending to follow from the former (Galiani and Schargrodsky 2010; Salas 1986).

In sum, in post-conflict situations where capacity is low, the best approach to legal ambiguity may be to gradually increase clarity by issuing binding legal interpretations, executive instructions, and decrees that allow specific problems to be resolved within the context of the existing legislative framework. It is crucial, however, to consult with affected parties in advance, to determine how they are likely to perceive, be affected by, and react to such measures. Consultation with vulnerable or potentially volatile groups—including IDPs, women, youth, squatters, excombatants, and members of ethnic, political, and religious groups—are particularly important. Broad dissemination of legal interpretations, executive instructions, and decrees is also important, to maximize their preventive effect on latent conflicts.

LEGAL PLURALISM

Legal pluralism is one of the most prominent features of post-conflict land tenure. In a pluralistic setting, difference types of laws—including ad hoc, customary, religious, and statutory (often localized)—coexist and function in parallel (Kamphius 2005; Plunkett 2005).[6]

In some contexts, legal pluralism may simply represent the accrued effects of long-standing legal ambiguities of the types described in the previous section. In Mindanao, for example, where differing legal systems coexist, Islamic courts may initially apply sharia to resolve a land dispute, but the decision may be appealed to the Supreme Court, which would apply statutory legislation (Oki 2013*). In Afghanistan, where different legal frameworks have been imposed successively over the past three decades—on the basis of tribal, communist, Islamic, and capitalist norms, among others—the situation is more complex (Sait 2013*). In many parts of the country, the combination of political insecurity and coercion, along with the inconsistent application of laws by successive regimes, has undermined the credibility of land laws and dispute resolution bodies (Batson 2013*).

Afghanistan illustrates both the opportunities and the challenges associated with legal pluralism. On the one hand, by offering locally legitimate rulings that are free and accessible even to illiterate villagers, land administration systems that integrate religious and customary practices have provided a measure of tenure security at times when the state has been unable to do so (Stanfield et al. 2013*). On the other hand, under such systems, rules may be applied inconsistently—in particular, in ways that favor local ethnic or economic elites (Batson 2013*). Nevertheless, such systems have broad appeal in post-conflict situations. In post-conflict Timor-Leste, for example, in the absence of a statutory regime governing land, customary legal structures have been crucial in addressing environmental problems (Miyazawa 2013*).

Alternative forums for land-related disputes offer advantages not only at the interpersonal level but also at the intergroup level. The complexity of the Abyei border dispute between Sudan and South Sudan, for example, has rendered it particularly intractable: the opposing parties had to first agree on the borders of the territory and then on the process for resolving the dispute before they could address the question of which side would gain control over the territory. Despite rulings from a number of early forums (including the Abyei Boundary Commission), the dispute remains unresolved; nevertheless, the decisions of these forums made it easier for the government of Sudan to accept the subsequent decision of the Permanent Court of Arbitration—at least initially (Salman 2013*).[7]

---

[6] For further consideration of the concept of legal pluralism, see Merry (1988) and Griffiths (1986).

[7] The problems associated with Abyei were still ongoing at the time of writing, primarily because of continued disputes over oil and the inability of local tribes to reach agreement on land-related issues. On September 27, 2012, Sudan and South Sudan signed agreements on oil and agreed to demilitarize their borders, but these agreements did not resolve the disputes associated with Abyei or other border regions.

542　Land and post-conflict peacebuilding

In their exploration of the advantages and disadvantages of legal pluralism, Ruth Meinzen-Dick and Rajendra Pradhan note that pluralistic arrangements may offer more robust enforcement structures, may be more readily adapted to changing circumstances, and may help empower parties affected by a conflict (Meinzen-Dick and Pradhan 2013). Meinzen-Dick and Pradhan also observe that different parties may indeed have legitimate claims under different legal systems, and that pluralism allows individuals to cite the law that best supports their claim to a plot of land. Finally, they caution that attempting to clarify property rights by upholding the legitimacy of one legal system (such as statutory law) over others risks reigniting conflict between parties that rely on different normative bases for their claims.

A particular challenge presented by legal pluralism is forum shopping, in which disputants choose between a number of coexisting normative orders and institutions, seeking the forum that they believe offers the most advantageous arena in which to pursue property rights claims. Like legal pluralism itself, forum shopping offers both advantages and disadvantages. On the one hand, it creates considerable room for negotiation within the political-legal sphere (Lund 1996); moreover, if claimants believe that their options are not confined by rigid and uncompromising legal structures, they may be less likely to engage in violence (Berry 1993). On the other hand, such flexibility can also generate conflicting legal decisions from different bodies relying on different principles. Furthermore, where customary forums are no longer viewed as legitimate, the lack of enforcement mechanisms (beyond the expectation of voluntary compliance) may heighten the risk that forum shopping will be exploited as means of legitimizing land grabbing (Corriveau-Bourque 2010).

In some cases, forum shopping can be converted from a horizontal arrangement, in which parties can choose from different but equal forums, to a vertical arrangement, in which parties who are unsatisfied by the results from the first (usually customary) forum appeal to a second, superior (usually statutory) forum (Unruh 2003). Afghanistan, where disputants may move from customary systems, such as the tribal Pashtunwali system, to the formal court system, offers an example of vertical forum shopping (Mason 2011).

As is the case with legal ambiguity, post-conflict governments and the international community may attempt to rationalize legal pluralism too quickly, by introducing a single legal framework for land governance. The relatively rapid imposition of one set of rules has caused problems, however. In Sierra Leone, for example, a quickly developed and implemented land policy reform conflicted with customary forms of post-conflict tenure to such an extent that the reform process was reinitiated, to ensure that it more effectively embraced the realities of post-conflict land tenure (Renner-Thomas 2010; Foray 2011). Moreover, the preservation of customary rules and institutions can reduce land-related conflict, particularly in post-conflict situations. To succeed, rationalization of the tenure system must be a long-term endeavor.

Lessons learned 543

A growing number of states formally recognize customary legal systems, sometimes specifically for land and sometimes more generally. The 2002 constitution of Timor-Leste, for example, recognizes customary law and calls for customary law to be incorporated into national law (Miyazawa 2013*). Customary law is a cost-effective way to handle natural resource issues—in particular, because it encourages intervillage dispute resolution and provides local communities with an additional avenue for voicing their concerns to the central government. Manami Sekiguchi and Naomi Hatsukano point out that although Cambodia's 2001 Land Law included mechanisms designed to formalize customary law and to recognize indigenous land rights, international pressure for quick reform led to the imposition of provisions that did not adequately conform to the nature of Cambodian customary rules (Sekiguchi and Hatsukano 2013*). Williams argues, however, that the government of Cambodia has been reluctant to be held accountable to any rules—statutory or customary—in making decisions regarding land and other resources (Williams 2013b*).

It is worth noting in this context that although governments are often inclined to apply statutory systems exclusively, international human rights law recognizes the rights of indigenous and traditional communities to land held under customary tenure.[8] As a consequence, states need to find approaches to land tenure that respect land held under customary forms of ownership. The processes for formally recognizing multiple legal orders governing land and property need not be rigid, however. Recovery from armed conflict occurs amid significant social change; in such contexts, the various sets of norms that coexist in a legally pluralistic setting may evolve over time, responding to contingencies as they arise. In fact, as several studies have noted, statutory law may gradually infiltrate customary law and other nonstatutory norms over time, until nonstatutory law comes to resemble state law (Michaels 2005; Merlet and Bastiaensen 2012; Peleikis 2006). And the reverse can also occur, in which statutory law borrows concepts and

---

[8] International and regional courts have interpreted rights to culture, property, and life in ways that limit the state power to void customary claims to land. See, for example, *Saramaka People v. Suriname*, Inter-American Court of Human Rights, November 28, 2007, Preliminary Objections, Merits, Reparations, and Costs, Series C No. 172, paras. 89–99 (finding that failure to recognize indigenous land tenure constituted a violation of the right to property under article 21 of the American Convention on Human Rights); *African Commission on Human and Peoples' Rights, Centre for Minority Rights Development (Kenya) and Minority Rights Group (on behalf of Endorois Welfare Council) v. Kenya*, no. 276/03, November 25, 2009, paras. 196–205 (interpreting article 14 of the African Charter on Human and Peoples' Rights to require states to recognize rights of indigenous communities to legal ownership of their ancestral territory); *Human Rights Committee, Chief Bernard Ominayak and the Lubicon Lake Band v. Canada, Communication*, no. 167/1984, 38th session, February 14, 1984, UN Doc. CCPR/C/38/D/167/1984, 1990, paras. 32.2–33 (finding that expropriation of territory of an indigenous band violated their right to culture under article 27 of the International Covenant on Civil and Political Rights); Miranda (2012); Anaya and Williams (2001).

544   Land and post-conflict peacebuilding

symbols from other normative orders (Silliman 1985; Hayden 1984). Indeed, as John Griffiths asserts, legal pluralism may create a dynamic in which statutory and nonstatutory law eventually unite, in a pattern that renders legal pluralism instrumental to the process of nation building (Griffiths 1986).

Change that occurs through the interaction between customary and statutory law is not always slow and incremental, however. Michael S. Lund has argued, for example, that when negotiation is central to tenure conflicts, "open moments" arise during which significant social rearrangements may occur (Lund 1996). An open moment is defined as a period when the room for "situational adjustment is great and hence where the capacity to exploit it is crucial for the actors" (Lund 1998, 2). During and after conflict, legitimacy, authority, and rules are much more fluid and open than perhaps at any other time; in such contexts, social relationships may evolve rapidly, to reflect the pace of overall societal change. Open moments are thus likely to occur in the course of peace processes, when the sociopolitical forces associated with recovery challenge many aspects of legitimacy, authority, and rules, including those associated with tenure.

Although it has been suggested that state recognition of legal pluralism merely adds a layer of complexity to an already chaotic situation (Griffiths 1986), it can be argued that post-conflict scenarios are already inherently messy, and that measures likely to promote stabilization should be given greater priority than efforts to impose legal certainty by assigning primacy to statutory law. Particularly where state legitimacy and capacity are low, it may be important, in the course of a peace process, for the state to accord some degree of recognition to legal pluralism with respect to land and property. Siraj Sait has noted, for example, that Islamic land law can play a significant and positive role where state legitimacy and capacity to implement and enforce statutory land law are limited. Indeed, under such circumstances, states effectively depend on local communities to administer land (Sait 2013*). In Timor-Leste, for example, significant commitment to customary legal institutions has allowed for flexible management of natural resources that is grounded in local conditions (Miyazawa 2013*). And in Ethiopia, after several decades of civil conflict, legal pluralism has been formally recognized in a number of important domains: article 78 (5) of the constitution, for example, accords full recognition to customary and religious courts of law where both contesting parties consent to the forum (Unruh 2005a). Finally, in El Salvador's Chapultepec Peace Accords and in the General Peace Agreement for Mozambique (and subsequent legislation regarding land), state recognition of legal pluralism was a primary means of facilitating the reintegration of much of the population into productive activities (de Soto and del Castillo 1995; Unruh 2006).

When Sierra Leone's civil war ended in 2002, there was little interaction between nationwide statutory and local customary tenure systems or between the many forms of customary tenure practiced in the country's 149 chiefdoms (GOSL 2005). Such pluralistic arrangements were a significant obstacle to commercial investment; rule of law; gender equity; and the reintegration of excombatants,

Lessons learned **545**

refugees, and IDPs. In 2005, with the goal of attracting foreign and domestic investment, the government of Sierra Leone established the Lands Commission to modernize laws on commercial land use—particularly in the provinces, where customary law predominates.[9] The commission identified three key problems: legal pluralism, the low level of contact and communication between chiefdom leaders, and the failure to disseminate statutory or customary land tenure decisions. The commission concluded that improved communication and the publication of decisions would enable different chiefdoms to make use of approaches to land issues that had been adopted by the state and by other chiefdoms, which would facilitate the eventual harmonization of tenure administration between chiefdoms (LRC 2004). Unfortunately, these conclusions were not taken far enough in the new law—and, as noted earlier, an improved law was under development at the time of writing (Foray 2011).

In sum, legal pluralism and the forum shopping that may arise from it are problematic, potentially useful, and inevitable in post-conflict situations. In states characterized by low capacity and low legitimacy, there may be no choice but to recognize the results of normative processes that local populations accept, understand, and implement. State recognition of legal pluralism entails risk, however, where compliance with decisions made by customary bodies breaks down, or where forum shopping remains entirely horizontal and characterized by clashing and incompatible claims, instead of becoming a vertical process based on appeals to bodies that all parties to a dispute accept as legitimate.

After the immediate post-conflict period, when legal pluralism may be resistant to significant regulation, the establishment of a constructive long-term relationship between statutory and customary norms—one that allows for legal certainty, respect for human rights, and the affirmation of a shared normative framework—should occur in a way that respects and reflects the local context. Often, such a relationship will develop spontaneously, when dispute resolution requests overwhelm one or more forums, and the forums in question begin requiring disputants to submit their requests to another forum. This pattern fosters the transition from a horizontal to a vertical arrangement, with the consequent advantages noted earlier.

DISPUTES

Post-conflict situations generally feature numerous disputes over land, which vary in type and origin. Examples include disputes between pastoralists and farmers, between large- and small-scale landowners, and between returnees and squatters; disputes that predate the conflict may also flare up. A number of factors contribute to the pervasiveness of land disputes in the post-conflict context, including weak government capacity; low tenure security; legal ambiguity; legal pluralism; and

---

[9] Land Commission Act, 2005.

546 Land and post-conflict peacebuilding

the resettlement of excombatants, refugees, and IDPs. A high number of land disputes can clog the legal system, adding further tension to an already unstable post-conflict situation. In post-conflict Burundi, for example, an overwhelming number of land disputes have generated a case backlog and threatened peace: between 2006 and 2011, the National Commission for Land and Other Goods, which was set up to reduce the burden on the courts, closed 4,701 files; 2,680 were outstanding (Baribeau 2011).

Timely resolution of land-related disputes is crucial to post-conflict reconciliation. It is also one of the foundations of economic recovery; in particular, dispute resolution supports livelihoods, food security, and self-reliance. Finally, to avoid further instability and resource degradation, it is essential to resolve disputes in ways that are seen as legitimate and equitable (Unruh 2002, 2003).

Disputes that occur in post-conflict situations characterized by legal pluralism and by tensions between different categories of tenure rights tend to fall into three categories, each of which requires its own set of solutions: (1) disputes between parties that are both operating within the statutory tenure system; (2) disputes between parties that are both operating within one or more customary tenure systems; and (3) disputes in which one party is relying on the statutory system and the other on customary systems.[10] These types overlap somewhat: for example, two claimants operating within the customary system may jointly seek resolution in the statutory system. Disputants may also attempt to use aspects of tenure systems other than those they would ordinarily use. Nesreen Barwari notes, for example, that in northern Iraq, returnees and secondary occupants used traditional mediation mechanisms, which were not necessarily their own, to resolve land disputes (Barwari 2013*). Barwari concludes that in addition to responding to concerns about overloading the court system, this approach reflected the difficulty of enforcing judicial or administrative decisions against losing parties. As noted earlier, however, tensions arising from legal pluralism in the tenure system may be aggravated in the wake of conflict.

Land disputes within the statutory system

Where post-conflict land disputes play out entirely within the statutory tenure system, many issues can arise. During and after conflict, land is often sold and resold with little or no reference to evidence of original ownership, registration, or proper transfer procedures. Titles, deeds, land records, registries, and archives are often destroyed in the conflict. Where documents supporting claims do exist,

---

[10] It is also possible to categorize disputes according to the parties—that is, (1) between individuals and the state, (2) between individuals and companies (which may, for example, involve alleged land grabbing), and (3) between individuals and other individuals (for example, squatters and original owners, or owners granted rights to the same piece of land by different regimes).

Lessons learned 547

they may be fraudulent or inaccurate.[11] Courts are overwhelmed with land disputes, and conflicts are exacerbated by clashing documentation and evidence. While the disputes slowly make their way through the legal system, the government is often trying to rebuild the economy, and may be granting concessions without adequate demarcation and without ensuring that no competing claims exist. Even where attempts are made to search the records, dysfunctional registry systems may render full title searches impossible; moreover, when land is held under customary tenure, it is not usually reflected in registries.

Given a high volume of disputes and the likelihood of legal ambiguities in the prevailing tenure system, attempting to resolve all land disputes through case-by-case judicial adjudication may not be feasible.[12] Although cases that raise vital issues of precedent, that are related to acute problems, or that may affect the interests of powerful political actors may require individual attention, most disputes can be assigned to categories and addressed through tailored, ad hoc legal approaches—thereby reducing the burden on courts and the time, resources, and effort needed to hear and decide each case.

In Mozambique, for example, new legal regulations made it possible to resolve a number of dispute categories en masse. One such issue, the standing of returning Portuguese colonists and their descendants to make land claims, led the prime minister's office to determine that claims based on colonial-era law were not valid; as a result, a significant number of cases were dismissed from court. In a move that led to the exclusion of additional cases, clear rules were adopted regarding properties that had been abandoned by their residents because of the conflict. Disputes arising from the allocation, as stipulated in the peace accord, of specific lands to particular users were resolved through compensation.

Finally, the Mozambican government excluded from court jurisdiction disputes resulting from transactions that had been made in bad faith. Before the conflict, such transactions had primarily involved the seizure of land and property from users who lacked formal title by those who were able to obtain formal title. In such cases, the bad faith involved the failure, on the part of the title applicant, to provide current occupants with the required notice of the pending application. After the conflict, however, disputes involving bad faith were more likely to occur between holders of conflicting title documents; although the documents in question may have been valid, the transactions that led to them may have occurred in bad faith (for example, the transactions may have been coerced, or may have occurred without due process). The post-war law does not nullify titles that were improperly issued to land already occupied by someone else under customary ownership; instead, the law provides for titles to be reversed for failure

---

[11] This was the case, for example, in Bosnia, Cambodia, Croatia, Liberia, and Sierra Leone. See, for example, MOJ (2010), Davuth (2003), and USAID Liberia (2010).

[12] Bosnia, for example, experienced more than 200,000 property claims after the conflict (Williams 2013a*).

548 Land and post-conflict peacebuilding

to comply with the business or development plan under which title was granted (*MPPB* 1997).

The Mozambican government also categorized claims so as to decrease the volume of disputes and make land available for restitution. To this end, the government notified 2,500 applicants that article 46 of the 1998 Land Law required them to resubmit any land applications (for title or concessions) still pending. Although applicants were notified through letters and radio announcements, the rate of renewal was low; as a result, the initial twelve-month renewal period was extended an additional three months in 1999, and a further four months in 2000. At the end of this period, the government archived all applications that had not yet been renewed, leaving open the possibility of individual renewal through July 2001. In August 2001, DINAGECA (Direcção Nacional da Terras, the national department responsible for land rights registration and mapping) cancelled the remaining applications, including 1,234 applications for more than 3 million hectares of prime agricultural land in Zambezi Province alone (Norfolk and Liversage 2003). The cancellations facilitated the restitution of significant tracts of land to communities that lost it under questionable circumstances before, during, and after the conflict (Tanner 2002).

Another approach to reducing the burden on the court system is to create temporary tribunals, separate from the ordinary judicial system, that hear only conflict-related land and property cases. This approach is common in mass-claims situations where large, conflict-related caseloads risk overwhelming ordinary institutions and imposing hardship and delay on claimants. Uganda, for example, as part of its peace process, created a tribunal system to handle the large number of land disputes (World Bank 2009). And a manual advising national legislators on IDP issues recommends setting up such "facilitated procedures" in a number of situations related to both property claims and documentation:

> Procedures before ordinary courts and adjudicatory bodies tend to place the primary burden of proof on the initiator of a case . . . who must bring evidence and establish the facts in that particular case. Such procedures normally involve elaborate and time-consuming fact-finding and may be subject to multiple appeals. In situations of mass displacement in which patterns of dispossession are similar across cases and generally can be documented, such elaborate fact-finding procedures not only are unnecessary but also impose a high burden in terms of production of formal evidence, expense, time, and uncertainty on claimants who often are already impoverished and traumatized by their experience (Brookings–Bern Project on Internal Displacement 2008, 176).

When setting up a new institution to handle land disputes, it is important to ensure that it reflects local political realities. As Peter Van der Auweraert notes, the establishment of such an institution can be perceived as beneficial to some parties and detrimental to others, particularly where parties are not aware of or engaged in the process (Van der Auweraert 2013*). The decision to create new institutions to deal with land issues should be made, however, only after an analysis of stakeholders' views of existing institutions (both statutory and customary) that could play such roles. Dan E. Stigall argues that where local judicial bodies demonstrate sufficient capacity and are culturally embedded—as in Iraq, for example—any new institution should be grounded in the existing system, to ensure legitimacy and acceptance (Stigall 2013*).

Where state capacity is low, customary institutions can be given the authority and requisite training to undertake functions normally handled by the state. In Timor-Leste, for example, the state empowered the adat tenure system to handle land disputes, removing some of the burden from the courts in rural and peri-urban areas (Miyazawa 2013*). Similarly, in northern Iraq, the government facilitated the dispute resolution work of local *anjommans*—bodies consisting of elders, members of established families, landholders, teachers, and religious authorities (Barwari 2013*). Approaches that engage local actors who are familiar with customary forms of dispute resolution and land administration effectively provide a free good to the state.

Land disputes within the customary system

Although customary authorities are typically successful at brokering disputes within customary systems, the ability of customary systems to manage land disputes may break down under post-conflict tensions. In Liberia, for instance, ethnic tensions between settlers (descendants of the freed American slaves who founded the country) and indigenous groups have complicated the return of IDPs. In Monrovia and other areas, settlers who fled during the conflict are returning to claim land that they had "abandoned" and that was in many cases occupied by IDPs (Williams 2011).

In both India (Bavinck 1998) and Sierra Leone (Unruh 2006), customary law officers have been empowered to apply both statutory and customary rules, as well as ad hoc solutions, in order to mediate disputes. Where the losing party has the option of ignoring a decision (because it lacks the legitimacy accorded to negotiations that take customary rules into account), such approaches offer considerable flexibility in resolving cases where statutory adjudication often fails to hold.

In Liberia and Timor-Leste, intergroup political conflicts have, in some cases, manifested themselves as land disputes; in other cases, political conflicts have included a land dispute dimension through which larger political issues are being contested. When broad political issues are at stake, state involvement can undermine the capacity of customary institutions to resolve disputes. In some cases, however, external support can build the capacity of customary systems to resolve disputes. In Liberia, Mozambique, and Uganda, for example, the governments set up community-based documentation systems to help resolve inter- and intracommunity land disputes. But because community members were often ill-equipped to resolve the initial disputes that had to be addressed to complete the documentation process, simply establishing community-based systems was

550   Land and post-conflict peacebuilding

not always enough. Provided with basic legal education and paralegal support, however, communities made significantly more progress (Knight et al. 2012).

Land disputes involving statutory and customary systems

In post-conflict situations, disputes may arise when squatters in urban and peri-urban areas occupy land owned by others, under either statutory or customary tenure. The vast majority of disputes between parties holding statutory and customary land rights occur, however, when states grant concessions to commercial entities and customary rights holders dispute the legality, legitimacy, and transparency of such transfers. Although foreign investment has the potential to spur development and provide revenues to fund government operations, much of it has been used for industrial-scale agriculture or mining—activities that may not be compatible with the traditions, needs, or rights of local communities, and that generate an increasing number of disputes (Huggins 2011).[13]

In Africa, where most of the large-scale land acquisitions by foreign investors have been centered, 46.6 million hectares of arable land were acquired in large-scale land acquisitions between October 2008 and August 2009, reflecting a tenfold increase over the amount of land acquired during the previous decade (Kachingwe 2012; Ghatak n.d.). In South Sudan, as much as one-tenth of the arable land may have been committed to large-scale investors before the country even became formally independent in July 2011 (Deng 2011). Sierra Leone has been the site of even more extensive acquisitions: according to internal UN analyses, 82 percent of the country has been allocated for mining exploration or exploitation, and 17 percent of the arable land is under agricultural concessions.[14]

Largely because of its 1998 Land Law, which vastly expands the rights of smallholders to claim land (Hanchinamani 2003), Mozambique has had some success in dealing with post-conflict disputes involving statutory and customary tenure systems. First, the Land Law recognized the possibility that the rights of smallholders who occupied land under customary rules would be upheld, to the detriment of commercial applicants (Tanner 2002); in addition, the process of requiring reapplication for pending commercial rights to land, mentioned earlier, included consultations with local communities or individuals occupying the land in question. A second and more innovative option offered by the law was designed

---

[13] Large-scale land acquisitions have increased dramatically since the global food crisis of 2007–2008, which increased both the volatility of food commodity prices and worldwide demand for land. Before the onset of the crisis, large-scale land acquisitions totaled 4 million hectares annually, but 2008–2009 saw 56 million hectares of large-scale acquisitions (Deininger and Byerlee 2011). As of this writing, much of the land in large-scale concessions is being used to produce biofuel. For a classification of land grabbing, see Borras and Franco (2012).

[14] See Provost and McClanahan (2012).

to attract and retain investment by encouraging both foreign and domestic investors to negotiate directly with local communities. (Where occupants were absent because of colonial-era or wartime dislocation, the reoccupation of land triggers the requirement for negotiation, which is meant to further both dispute resolution and investment goals.) Under the new law, the rights accorded to customary smallholders both empowered and encouraged them to retain a significant role in natural resource management and conflict resolution, and to set limits on the areas available to private investors (Tanner 2002; Hanlon 2002; Norfolk and Liversage 2003).

Under what is known as the open-border model, a statutory commercial rights system can coexist with customary rights, including community rights of occupation; what makes the coexistence possible is a partial transfer of rights, based on a negotiated arrangement (Tanner 2002; Norfolk and Liversage 2003; Hanlon 2002; *MPPB* 1997).[15] The use of such a model is especially important in Mozambique, where there is no land in the country that has not been claimed by a local community in some form (De Wit 2002).

Conflict between nomadic pastoralists and sedentary farmers is another source of tension between statutory and customary systems. In the central highlands of Afghanistan, for example, the nomadic Kuchi and the settled Hazara communities have vied for access to land and pasture since the late nineteenth century. For more than a century, successive governments have attempted to replace customary with statutory tenure systems; some have favored the Hazara, and most have favored the Kuchi. From 2006 to 2008, the Afghan government attempted to resolve the conflict by allowing community landholdings to be formally recognized, which benefited the Hazara, while also creating a system to allow seasonal access to pasture, which benefited the Kuchi. Unfortunately, the larger national conflict exacerbated violence in the area, so the new reforms have not yet had much effect (Alden Wily 2013).

Sudan has experienced similar conflict, and the roots of the fighting in Darfur lie, in part, with tensions between pastoralists and farmers. Between 1987 and 1989, drought sparked fighting between sedentary non-Arab farmers and nomadic Arab herders. When the herders were backed by the central government in Khartoum, it marked the first time that Arab groups across the country had unified over a particular issue. In the decades since, both sides have viewed the conflicts in Darfur primarily as a fight over land, and attempts by nomadic Arab herders to establish statutory land claims in areas where customary systems had previously been in force exacerbated conflict along ethnic lines, with the government and Arab herders on one side, and rebel groups (made up of farmers) on the other (Tubiana 2007).

---

[15] The term *open borders* refers to the legal recognition of the boundary of a specific community; the border is "open" in the sense that investors are permitted to negotiate for rights within the boundary (Tanner 2002).

552   Land and post-conflict peacebuilding

LAND RECOVERY

Where land grievances fueled conflict or arose from fighting and displacement, aggrieved individuals and groups are likely to demand the recovery of their land. Post-conflict restitution of rights to housing, land, and property (HLP) has become an increasingly common component of peace agreements, and tends to be viewed, by both domestic and international observers, as an indicator of respect for human rights (Williams 2007). As a result, parties negotiating ceasefires and peace accords are increasingly likely to face politically difficult decisions about land and property: given the value and inherently limited nature of land, any effort to secure land resources for conflict-affected populations will necessarily require concessions from other groups.

The most concrete manifestation of the trend toward addressing HLP in post-conflict situations is the United Nations Principles on Housing and Property Restitution for Refugees and Displaced Persons (also known as the Pinheiro Principles)—a soft-law standard that asserts the right to post-conflict property restitution. The principles, which are anchored in international law, set out steps that states should take to give effect to this right (ECOSOC 2005). Although the Pinheiro Principles represent a step in the right direction, state actions do not consistently support the international trend toward the assertion of greater post-conflict rights to recovery of land and other assets. One reason is that many parties to armed conflict regard property seized from opposing forces as (1) territory that was won and should be controlled for strategic purposes, and (2) spoils of war that can be parceled out to supporters and patronage networks, to secure their continued loyalty. Another reason is that the permanent expulsion of particular population groups is often one of the goals of ethnic or sectarian conflict; thus, the confiscation and occupation of property left by fleeing minorities is viewed as crucial to preventing their return and thereby consolidating wartime gains. As the case of Bosnia illustrates, even where parties are willing to yield, on paper, to international demands to restore land, preventing such restoration may actually be a key post-conflict goal on the part of former combatant groups (Williams 2013a*).

Criticism of restitution-centered approaches to post-conflict land issues has been growing, not only because such programs are difficult to implement but also because of more principled concerns. For instance, Samir Elhawary and Sara Pantuliano observe that attempts to restore the status quo ante may be counterproductive where pre-conflict land relations were unjust, inequitable, politically destabilizing, or economically unsustainable (Elhawary and Pantuliano 2013*). Faced with hundreds of thousands of returning refugees and IDPs and insufficient land to accommodate everyone, post-conflict Rwanda applied an approach that reflected the general spirit of the Pinheiro Principles but compromised with regard to their implementation (Bruce 2013*). Although most observers continue to defend the utility of restitution-based approaches

Lessons learned **553**

in specific post-conflict circumstances,[16] there is now wide agreement among both academics and practitioners that land recovery must be understood more broadly.

Because conflict-based displacement tends to accelerate existing patterns of demographic change, including migration from rural to urban areas (de Waal 2009), IDPs and refugees may have little incentive to return or to seek to recover land that they left behind. Indeed, in light of the tendency for IDPs and refugees to become stranded indefinitely in provisional and unsatisfactory settlements established by humanitarian agencies—as well as the legal uncertainty, land grabbing, and forced evictions that often characterize immediate post-conflict situations—access and secure tenure to land and housing at the site of displacement is often the most pressing need. Regardless, however, of whether land and tenure rights pertain to the place of return or to the site of displacement, negotiating such rights is a delicate process. Efforts to understand the land-related needs and vulnerabilities of conflict-affected populations, and to develop nuanced approaches to land recovery, raise crucial issues, a number of which are addressed in the following five subsections.

Consultation and land recovery

Consultations with affected populations are key to the effective design and implementation of post-conflict land recovery efforts. Although such consultations can be time-consuming and complicated by questions of representativeness and manipulation, they are necessary not only as a matter of human rights but also as a matter of sound policy (Brookings–Bern Project on Internal Displacement 2008). Policy arguments for conducting a consultative process as a prelude to the development of post-conflict land measures include the following:

- Consultation helps to ensure that the populace is committed to the approach.
- Consultation creates an opportunity for those most affected by land issues to help develop nuanced understandings of problems and suggest innovative solutions to them.
- Consultation can help raise awareness of the statutory rules and procedures that protect HLP rights.
- By allowing different views of land issues to be aired, consultation potentially facilitates their peaceful resolution.
- Between the time that the need for new laws or policies is identified and the passage and implementation of those laws or policies, consultation can be used both to build political momentum and to manage public expectations.

---

[16] See McCallin (2013*), for example.

554 Land and post-conflict peacebuilding

The last item deserves particular mention. In the immediate aftermath of conflict, legal, financial, administrative, and material capacity to manage land issues is often lacking, and individuals and groups may have no choice but to make decisions about their HLP rights and claims largely on their own (Unruh 2003). In Rwanda, for example, during the mass repatriation that occurred between 1994 and 1997, the government's failure to articulate clear land policies or consult with stakeholders encouraged conflict-affected parties to take things into their own hands, in some cases through violent takeovers of property (Huggins 2004). To avert such outcomes, the state must protect against the most serious forms of conflict and opportunism that can arise when governance capacity is low; engaging in stakeholder consultations helps ensure that the state is perceived as taking an active role in resolving land issues (Unruh 2003, 2005b). At the same time, however, the state and the international community must communicate that it will take some time (often years) for reforms and results to emerge. National and regional workshops are one way to make the public aware that its concerns are being heard and that serious work is under way.

The experiences of four countries—Mozambique, Timor-Leste, Sierra Leone, and Angola—provide lessons about consultation and land recovery. In Mozambique, a three-year national consultation involving numerous stakeholders produced a successful land law but was criticized for being time-consuming.[17] Questions were also raised about (1) state attempts to control the debate; (2) the standing of former Portuguese colonists to claim restitution; and (3) the role of foreign donor agencies, embassies, and nongovernmental organizations in the process. In light of the significant natural resource and agricultural export opportunities at stake, political maneuvering (including occasional foreign involvement) over issues such as the privatization of state land and zoning to distinguish commercial land from customary areas was often intense, rendering outcomes more unpredictable (Unruh 2004b).

Unlike Mozambique, which used an exhaustive consultative process to develop a single, comprehensive post-conflict land law, Timor-Leste proposed numerous laws early in the post-conflict period to address specific topics, including land dispute mediation, land and title registration, land and title restitution, formal and traditional rights, requirements for foreign owners to comply with the Timor-Leste constitution, state property administration, and the cadastre system. Accordingly, separate consultative processes were initiated for each piece of draft legislation. These individual processes were more rapid than a single, comprehensive process would have been, but they were also repetitive, as a new process had to be undertaken (albeit in a more streamlined form) each time new legislation was proposed. In Timor-Leste, the political controversies associated

---

[17] Although the consultative process took three years, the development of Mozambique's new land law took four years from beginning to end—which is comparatively rapid in comparison to Sierra Leone (which, as of October 2012, had been without a new land law for seven years) and Timor-Leste (thirteen years).

Lessons learned **555**

with the development of land laws centered on the initial skepticism, on the part of the Ministry of Justice, toward sustained consultative processes.[18]

Sierra Leone's approach, which was similar to that of Timor-Leste, called for several laws, instead of only one; these included the 2000 Legal Practitioners Act (amended in 2004 and 2005), 2003 Restitution: The Chaytor Committee, the 2004 Commercial Use of Lands Act, the 2004 Local Government Act, the 2005 National Lands Policy, and the 2005 Lands Commission Act (Unruh 2008). While the topics differ from those addressed by Timor-Leste, both countries opted to divide the messy particulars of post-conflict land tenure and management into more easily managed components, and to engage in consultation on those particular components. Although the overall amount of time spent on consultation may have been longer in Timor-Leste and Sierra Leone than in Mozambique, the case-by-case approach allowed Timor-Leste and Sierra Leone to identify topics that required immediate attention (restitution in Timor-Leste, and commercial land use in Sierra Leone) and to focus on those priorities.

In Angola, by contrast, the development of the initial post-conflict land legislation involved little stakeholder consultation—and the consultation that did occur, spontaneously or with the assistance of nongovernmental organizations, was not clearly reflected in the final result. Cain notes that the failure to actively solicit public input, which stemmed largely from a desire to resolve land issues quickly, left the government unaware of tensions that had been simmering over land that had been abandoned as early as the 1970s, in the context of a previous civil conflict. Although Angola's 2001 decree on IDP resettlement (Norms on the Resettlement of the Internally Displaced Populations[19]) and the land and planning laws drafted in 2002 were intended to have included consultation and participatory planning, Cain observes that lack of coordination undermined public participation (Cain 2013*).

A number of the other chapters in this book expand on the issue of consultation. Barwari, for example, notes that a community-based consultative process was crucial to the reintegration of IDPs in northern Iraq after the 1990–1991 Gulf War. She points out that early efforts to actively solicit local input and constructively manage disagreements paid off: the local anjomman consultation structure successfully and sustainably resolved land disputes, provided information about conditions for return, and marshaled local support for development projects even after funding from the Oil-for-Food Programme had dried up (Barwari 2013*). Alexandre Corriveau-Bourque points out that in post-conflict El Salvador, the government's failure to consult *campesinos* (peasants) fostered a new sense of disenfranchisement, stoking the potential for future conflict (Corriveau-Bourque 2013*).

---

[18] As of October 2012, most of the legislation had yet to be formally adopted.
[19] Council of Ministers Decree Number 1/01, 2001.

556 Land and post-conflict peacebuilding

Community participation, along with transparency, accountability, and monitoring, can promote confidence in the adjudication and demarcation of property. Green notes that before substantive issues are addressed, a community-led needs assessment should be conducted in such a way as to effectively integrate women and minorities into the process. He also argues that establishing an independent monitoring institution and requiring regular disclosure can be more effective for ensuring public participation than relying on existing institutions to police themselves (Green 2013*). On the basis of his experience promoting sustainable land management in the Pamir Mountains Project in Tajikistan, Ian D. Hannam observes that by helping to improve trust and harmony between different groups, participatory approaches allow joint resolution of shared problems related to livelihoods and environmental security (Hannam 2013*). The benefits of participatory processes reflect broader lessons on the importance of engaging affected communities and individuals as part of the peacebuilding process (Nichols, Muffett, and Bruch 2013).

Evidentiary issues

In post-conflict situations, the presentation and evaluation of evidence to support asserted rights to land is important in both statutory and customary regimes for managing land. Broadly, the production of evidence involves making logical connections between observed reality and the interpretations and inferences linking that reality to specific claims. Thus, bringing evidentiary meaning to an observation or purported fact involves constructing an argument to support a connection (Murphy 2003). The "argument" notion of evidence is important: all land claims require the construction of an evidence-based argument. Even the existence of full statutory title is only an argument whose evidentiary basis can be contested as easily as claims that are based, for example, on the notion that particular lands belong to the members of a particular tribe, ethnic group, or religion.

In Liberia, the problem of missing, incomplete, destroyed, or fraudulent documentation has reduced the evidentiary value of statutory documents and increased the value of nondocumentary evidence in land disputes (Pichel et al. 2012). Similar circumstances prevailed after the 1999 withdrawal of Indonesian forces from Timor-Leste: because most documents relating to land and property had been destroyed, reliance on statutory title became more problematic (Marquardt, Unruh, and Heron 2002). Moreover, because most land held by local communities had never been formally titled, customary tenure was of more importance to many segments of the population, particularly in rural and peri-urban areas. In response to these circumstances, rural state officials and customary smallholders agreed, at least for the immediate post-conflict period, on what would constitute valid evidence for a land claim. The initial devaluation of documentary evidence vis-à-vis customary evidence, which was based on the agreement between the state and customary smallholders, not only allowed greater harmonization between the statutory and customary land tenure systems but also presented an opportunity to incorporate this compatibility into the reform of Timor-Leste's land law (Unruh 2006).

Although efforts to follow through with this opportunity have not been without issue, the lesson is that such opportunities do arise and can be capitalized on. At a minimum, Timor-Leste's experience suggests that caution should be exercised in the application of statutory evidence rules that either bar admissibility on the basis of factors other than relevance and probative value, or that unduly constrain the way evidence is collected, discovered, or researched on the basis of criteria other than ethical concerns.[20] In post-conflict Angola, for example, elites exploited the lack of formal documentation by selectively marshaling historical evidence (in the form of colonial-era maps), and thereby asserting control over the central highlands—the country's agricultural breadbasket (Unruh 2012).

While institutions and procedures for resolving land disputes must be effective, they need not be exclusively statutory. In post-conflict situations where effective and legitimate statutory institutions are lacking, traditional forms of landscape-based evidence are often used, particularly in support of claims based on occupation. For example, the intentional planting of trees—in particular, perennial fruit-bearing trees—is a widely accepted means of asserting legitimate occupation in a number of customary settings (Raintree 1987; Meinzen-Dick et al. 2002; Otsuka et al. 2001; Rocheleau and Edmunds 1997).[21] In the contested landscapes of the Middle East, where mutually legitimate institutions to resolve competing claims are lacking, tree planting has played a powerful informal role as evidence in both Palestinian and Israeli land claims (Cohen 1993). The potency of tree planting as evidence for land claims is underscored by the fact that in Liberia, Sierra Leone, and other post-conflict situations, groups such as women, tenants, and migrants are subject to legal restrictions on tree planting (Unruh 2008, 2009).

Although planting trees may be one way to substantiate claims, clearing land is an even more persuasive means of creating evidence of occupation. Despite the risk of deforestation posed by clearing, the practice remains widespread, in part because it is so effective. Where land adjudication institutions are weak, it is hard to imagine a more visible way not only to assert a claim but also to preempt counterclaims and obviate the need for institutionalized dispute resolution. Among the places where effective institutions are lacking and clearing has been used as evidence of occupation are Cameroon (Delville 2003), the Philippines (Uitamo 1999), Sierra Leone,[22] Uganda (Mulley and Unruh 2004; Aluma et al.

---

[20] For a discussion of customary and statutory evidentiary considerations in land disputes in Guatemala, see Bailliet (2003).

[21] For an annotated bibliography on trees and tenure, see Fortmann and Riddell (1985).

[22] This observation is based on fieldwork conducted by Jon Unruh in Sierra Leone in 2005.

558 Land and post-conflict peacebuilding

1989), and Zambia (Unruh, Cligget, and Hay 2005). Finally, unregistered papers attesting to the local validity of transactions (André 2003; Delville 2003) are yet another means of transforming landscape evidence into legal or quasi-legal arguments.

In the context of post-conflict land tenure, what tree planting, clearing, and unregistered documents have in common is that they are (1) reactions to the absence of clear, effective, fair, and affordable statutory institutions and procedures, and (2) an affirmation of the relationship between evidence and tenure security.

In post-conflict Mozambique, standards for customary evidence in the case of land disputes have been tested by the particularly difficult relationship between large commercial interests and the smallholder sector. These two groups often claim the same land, but under different regimes of authority, legitimacy, and proof, raising complex and potentially destabilizing questions about what forms of evidence are legitimate and persuasive. After the conflict, research found that forms of customary evidence that were more compatible with statutory notions of occupation tended to be favored (Unruh 1997). So, for example, planted trees became particularly important, both because they represented clear sociohistorical evidence and because they were consistent with statutory definitions of occupation (*MPPB* 1997; Norfolk and Liversage 2003; Pancas 2003; Kloeck-Jenson 1998). The Mozambican Land Commission incorporated the results of this research into its deliberations on land policy reform; as a result, article 9 of the 1997 Land Law stated that customary forms of evidence were to be treated as equivalent to evidence asserted through written title (Negrão 1999; Norfolk and Liversage 2003).

Many chapters in this book address evidentiary issues. At the level of general policy, Elhawary and Pantuliano recommend that land registration systems in post-conflict situations take legal pluralism into account, which includes recognizing communal forms of land governance (Elhawary and Pantuliano 2013*). Although standards such as the Pinheiro Principles reflect broad acceptance of such approaches, observers have noted that it is still important to ensure that land registration systems are (1) developed on the basis of consultation with local communities; (2) designed to meet their needs; and (3) designed to preserve, rather than supplant, the central characteristics of traditional land administration regimes.[23]

Although a locally sensitive approach to the development of local land registries is necessary, it should be followed by efforts to create some degree of integration with the central government's land management framework. In Afghanistan, the failure to take this step led to the gradual erosion of the accuracy of previous cadastral surveys, thus limiting their usefulness. As J. D. Stanfield and his colleagues note, local Afghan communities have developed sustainable procedures for documenting local landownership and land use rights, largely on

---

[23] See, for example, Alden Wily (2009).

the basis of customary evidence (Stanfield et al. 2013*). The self-contained nature of this system obviates the need to spend time and money traveling to provincial capitals to consult with government agencies, but it also reflects a deep-seated ambivalence about the role of government, which is viewed as both the ultimate guarantor of rights and as a system of potentially predatory and overreaching institutions. In a context such as Angola, where many rural residents do not own their land but where wealth is nonetheless tied to it, Cain notes that it is particularly important that local registration systems reflect local institutions, procedures, and practices, rather than the interests of national elites or outsiders (Cain 2013*). In Cambodia, a well-meaning effort to create tenure security through a registration program that admitted customary evidence was frustrated by the failure to assign priority to those land users who were most vulnerable to land grabbing—namely, small-scale rural farmers (Sekiguchi and Hatsukano 2013*).

Capacity building

Post-conflict situations are typically characterized by a wide variety of training and capacity-building needs related to land and property rights. Statutory systems are often crippled by the death or displacement of qualified staff, as well as by the destruction of facilities and official records. Even where customary institutions fill in the gap, their legitimacy and capacity may also have been weakened by conflict and displacement.

Various approaches have been used to address the needs of a recovering land management structure. In Angola, Sierra Leone, and Timor-Leste, for example, such efforts involved locating professionals (at different levels, and in different locations throughout the country) who had previous land and property administration experience. Bosnia, in contrast, relied on previous staff—which meant that in some cases, the local administrative authorities who had reallocated property left behind by fleeing minority groups were responsible, by default, for implementing post-conflict restitution laws that required them to reverse their wartime decisions and reinstate individuals and families displaced during the conflict (Williams 2007).

Where qualified staff did not exist before the conflict or can no longer be located, both short-term initiatives (such as rebuilding a cadastre) and long-term management (for example, administering the cadastre after donor funding ceases) often require training. Given both the weakness of post-conflict education systems and the amount of study necessary to qualify for work in land administration, however, training can be time-consuming. Mozambique, Sierra Leone, and Timor-Leste met this challenge by creating or reinstituting training and research units that were connected to in-country universities; the goal was not only to train land management professionals but also to promote research in areas related to land reform. Establishing such centers at national universities also meets two longer-term objectives: first, research capacity related to land reform will remain relevant for years, as the focus shifts to development and urban planning. Second,

560 Land and post-conflict peacebuilding

the rapid creation of a cadre of researchers can be crucial to fieldwork supporting proposed reforms throughout the country. In both Mozambique and Timor-Leste, particular donors took the lead in building land administration capacity and opened offices at the newly created research units they had helped to fund.

In Liberia and other countries, the administrative, technical, and judicial components required to handle land matters are underdeveloped, overstretched, or scattered among various ministries. Some countries have dealt with the need to develop new administrative units and procedures by identifying and reallocating capacity and mandates within existing land and property institutions. In Timor-Leste, for example, specific functions from various ministries were relocated to the Directorate of Land and Property within the Ministry of Justice, which provided a focal point for coordinating donor- and UN-supported projects. In Mozambique and Sierra Leone, the necessary institutions were in place but lacked the required physical infrastructure and trained personnel. Efforts to revive institutions crippled by conflict are expensive, and donors often bear the costs (Unruh 2009).

The development of land administration systems should not be regarded as a separate goal in the post-conflict phase but should instead be directly tied to peacebuilding priorities. In Timor-Leste, the U.S. Agency for International Development (USAID) working in collaboration with the Timorese government, developed land titling and registration policies. By integrating land management issues into its aid program, USAID hoped to revitalize and stabilize the economy and support the growth of democratic institutions (USAID 2004). In Aceh, in contrast, despite donors' efforts to address the risks posed by post-tsunami tenure insecurity, land registration efforts were not integrated with parallel efforts to support economic development, sustainable livelihoods, reintegration of combatants, and the resettlement of IDPs; as a result, donors missed the opportunity to support these peacebuilding aims (Green 2013*).

Finally, a note of caution: donors must ensure that their support for a recovering land and property system does not yield arrangements that exceed the financial and administrative capacity of the receiving country. Sierra Leone, for example, initially requested numerous institutional, training, administrative, and infrastructural components for its tenure system that would have been more appropriate for a developed country, and that would have been unsustainable after the withdrawal of donor support. Instead, donors provided a more modest level of support that they believed would be more easily sustained (Unruh 2005b).

Women and land recovery

With men having been killed in combat, imprisoned, displaced, or stigmatized by their participation in conflict, post-conflict societies typically have a higher proportion of female-headed households. And because women often face discrimination under both statutory and customary law, attention to women's land rights is crucial. Perhaps the most pervasive form of discrimination against women

Lessons learned 561

involves restrictions on their ability to inherit land or to assert title to it in the case of a husband's death (Wanyeki 2003). Discrimination can take many other forms, however, all of which limit women's ability to access land and dispose of it in ways that are necessary to both survival and self-reliance in post-conflict situations.

Because of discrimination, women tend to have lower literacy, experience more severe poverty, and enjoy fewer livelihood options; they also have less knowledge about their land rights than men. In Cambodia, for example, under land distribution reforms carried out in the 1980s, women and men initially benefited relatively equally; today, however, because they are less able to obtain agricultural loans and inputs (such as seeds, fertilizers, and pesticides) and to contest attempts to seize their land, women are more at risk of losing land than their male counterparts (Williams 2013b*). In fact, generally speaking, women are less able to defend their land rights and more vulnerable to land grabbing (Unruh and Corriveau-Bourque 2010). Afghanistan and South Sudan are among the many post-conflict situations in which such patterns have been identified (Rashid, Jan, and Wakil 2010; McMichael and Massleberg 2010).

Despite the attention that donors give to community involvement in reconstituting post-conflict land rights, representatives such as elders, chiefs, and lineage heads rarely speak for women, or adequately understand or respond to the problems that female-headed households face. As a result, female-headed households returning to reoccupy land may require particular assistance when asserting or claiming both customary and statutory rights (Unruh and Corriveau-Bourque 2010).

Land and the reintegration of former combatants

Reintegrating excombatants into civilian society—particularly through the provision of nonmilitary occupations and income sources—is a pillar of peacebuilding and post-conflict community development.[24] Given that most violent conflicts occur where livelihoods substantially depend on land and natural resources, the provision of sufficient and appropriate land can be critical in the reintegration of former combatants. Typically, 50 percent of former combatants participating in reintegration programs choose agriculture; in some cases, the proportion is as high as 80 percent. Access to land can be a limiting factor for such programs (UNEP 2012), however, and can thereby undermine the implementation of reintegration provisions in peace agreements.

---

[24] The allocation of land to excombatants has to be balanced against the needs of other vulnerable groups that would benefit from the recovery of land (especially women, youth, and IDPs). Appearing to favor excombatants over other groups will inevitably lead to new disputes, creating the potential for further violence and conflict (Douglas et al. 2004; UNEP 2012).

562   Land and post-conflict peacebuilding

For example, El Salvador's 1992–1997 land transfer program (Programa de Transferencia de Tierras, or PTT), which was undertaken after the civil war, redistributed lands that the original owners willingly sold to the program. The PTT then sold the lands to a capped number of former combatants from both sides of the conflict. The PTT also facilitated the transformation of the FMLN (Frente Farabundo Martí para la Liberación Nacional), the rebel military force, into a nonmilitarized political party.

Many problems undermined the efficacy of the PTT. Much of the land distributed was of poor quality, and there were limits on the amount of land that could be obtained through the program. Also, between the government's lack of technical capacity to deliver titles efficiently, lack of political will, and refusal to distribute agricultural production credits and technical assistance until beneficiaries held title (which was difficult to obtain), excombatants were often left with insecure tenure, little incentive to improve the land, and insufficient skills to achieve productive livelihoods in agriculture. The combination of economic insecurity, residual societal inequity, and inability to return to the FMLN led many excombatants to join armed gangs or private security firms (de Soto and del Castillo 1995; Paris 2004; Özerdem 2009).

COORDINATING AND SEQUENCING INTERVENTIONS

Given the diverse and profound needs, competing visions, and powerful peacebuilding potential associated with land, it can be difficult to determine, after conflict, where to begin. Because essential land-related measures—such as reforming tenure policies and laws, rebuilding registries and cadastres, and resolving disputes—may require years to achieve, it is critical to begin addressing land issues early in the peacebuilding process, and sometimes even before conflict is over. Even in the immediate aftermath of conflict, many steps can be taken to lay the foundation for longer-term development and reforms.

Table 1 highlights approaches to seven aspects of land management—legal ambiguity, legal pluralism, land disputes, land recovery, land policy reform, capacity building, and land allocation—that can be undertaken during the two principal stages of the peace process (immediate aftermath and peace consolidation). The diversity of approaches reflects the diversity of contexts: both timing and approach should be tailored to the needs, capacities, and opportunities of the particular context.

It is often necessary to proceed along parallel tracks: developing and reforming the legal framework governing land, rebuilding cadastres and other information management systems, resolving disputes, and building institutional capacity. Designing post-conflict initiatives that work toward a variety of objectives in parallel provides both resilience (in case one activity stalls) and opportunities for synergy (among the activities).

In Timor-Leste, the Ita Nia Rai ("Our Land") project—undertaken between 2007 and 2012, with support from USAID and in partnership with the Timorese

Table 1. Approaches to managing land in post-conflict situations

	Immediate aftermath	Peace consolidation
Legal ambiguity	Assess the degree of ambiguity associated with statutory and customary law and the interactions between them, including the extent of fraud, knowledge of laws, public trust in laws, and the emergence of conflict-related approaches to law. Instead of attempting to impose clarity, focus on managing ambiguity and chaos in land rights. In particular, (1) assign priority to the issuance of authoritative legal interpretations, executive instructions, and decrees that can be used to quickly manage broad problems as they arise, and (2) broadly disseminate them, in order to maximize their preventive effect on latent conflict. Examples include the following: Whether the years of conflict are to be included in claims of adverse possession. What constitutes bad-faith versus good-faith transactions. The legality of previously issued concessions. The state's legal recognition of certain customary institutions. The fate of lands subject to secondary occupation. Engage in consultations, with both prominent and marginalized stakeholders, regarding their primary land-related concerns, reaction to decrees, etc. Among the stakeholders who should be consulted are internally displaced persons (IDPs); women; youth; squatters; excombatants; and members of ethnic, political, and religious groups.	Through the development and implementation of laws and regulations, move toward the resolution of remaining legal ambiguities, giving priority to those that are causing problems. At the same time, resist the temptation to bring clarity to all forms of ambiguity: some ambiguities have uses for certain groups or support certain purposes, and attempting to eliminate them entirely may cause conflict. Move forward with institutional reform.
Legal pluralism	Given that in the wake of conflict, national law will have limited legitimacy and national institutions limited capacity, provide formal recognition of customary tenure systems even if they are at odds with state law: harmonization with statutory law is a subsequent process. Options include (1) recognizing customary forms of evidence as legal for claims; (2) providing limited statutory recognition to nonstatutory forums for land allocation, use, and the resolution of land disputes, even if they are not part of customary systems; and (3) considering the recognition of religious approaches to land rights where doing so would not encourage divisiveness.	Instead of attempting to prohibit certain forums outright, encourage a gradual shift from forum shopping based on multiple equal forums to more of an appeals format. Examine the intersections between statutory, customary, and other norms that shape land administration to identify commonalities, points of contradiction and contention, and legal gaps. The goal is to establish a constructive long-term relationship between statutory and nonstatutory norms that supports legal certainty, respect for human rights, and a shared normative framework.

Table 1. (*cond't*)

	Immediate aftermath	*Peace consolidation*
Land disputes	Establish separate land courts or tribunals, or significantly expand the capacity of the existing court system, in order to handle the surge in land disputes.	As the national court system recovers and the number of land disputes drops, transition from land courts or tribunals to an integrated court system.
	Recognize the potential outcomes of forum shopping (for example, among customary, religious, and ad hoc approaches) for dispute resolution.	Continue to formally recognize the outcomes of forum shopping under different rule-of-law systems, while evaluating how such systems might be integrated into the national court system.
	Explore the potential for programs under which donors and nongovernmental organizations would support alternative dispute resolution, including mediation.	Reduce the use of alternative dispute resolution.
	Consider using decrees or legal rulings to handle broad categories of disputes, such as bad-faith transactions made during the conflict, and issues associated with secondary occupation.	Move away from addressing land issues through decrees and legal rulings—by, for example, legally assigning termination dates to decrees, so they cannot be abused as the peace process proceeds.
	Apply specific articles of existing law to solve immediate problems, such as right of reversion.	Consider legally establishing a date beyond which certain conflict-related disputes will no longer be heard (e.g., land claims made by members of the returning diaspora and by those who belonged to the losing side in the conflict).
Land recovery	Consult with affected populations regarding restitution, focusing on the following:	Integrate local and customary land registries with national registries.
	Achieving buy-in from the populace.	
	Developing innovative solutions and a nuanced understanding of problems.	Continue with restitution programs, establishing a date by which conflict-related restitution programs will end.
	Educating the populace about statutory protections of land rights.	
	Airing different views, and thereby facilitating peaceful resolution of disputes.	
	Building political momentum and containing expectations.	
	Demonstrating that the state is moving forward to address land issues.	
	To address fraudulent, missing, destroyed, or incomplete documentation, take quick legal action to revamp evidentiary rules for land claims.	
	Assess the restitution needs of vulnerable populations, including women, marginalized ethnic groups, squatters, and excombatants.	
	Begin to reintegrate insurgent and other forces.	

Land policy reform	Assess the functionality of the statutory and customary land management and administration systems.	Complete land policy reforms; this includes the following:
	Assess the presence and functionality of other approaches to land rights (for example, ad hoc approaches that are related to religion or to the authority of warlords, or that arose during the conflict or as a consequence of neglect).	Completing consultations and evaluating the results. Moving from consultation to legal drafting. Widely disseminating drafts of the new land policy. Initiating political, parliamentary, and other processes for passage.
	Initiate consultations to support reforms that will connect, harmonize, or support positive interactions between statutory and customary land administration systems.	Develop either an overarching land law covering all issues, or a number of laws that address specific problems (the second approach may proceed more quickly). Engage donors to fund and provide technical assistance for specific components of the reform process.
Capacity building	Locate and hire technical staff from pre-conflict land and property institutions, avoiding those who were in leadership positions and were complicit in developing or implementing divisive land policies.	Expand training efforts by establishing training programs in land and property administration institutions as well as in universities, and by sending students to neighboring countries for training.
	Establish training programs through national universities, ensuring that they foster the skills necessary to interact with customary systems and authorities. As an interim approach, consider asking donors to conduct rapid training that is aligned with the most pressing needs.	Assign priority to placing trained staff in rural areas, where they can work directly with customary authorities on land issues. Seek donor funding for the infrastructural aspects of capacity building (for example, surveying, developing cadastres, and purchasing computers and other equipment).
Land allocation	Establish temporary forms of, and rights to, occupation for squatters, IDPs, excombatants, and others who are unable to return to their areas of origin in the near term.	Move from temporary forms of and rights to land occupation toward permanent rental, leasing, and sharecropping arrangements in a land market, where land can be bought and sold as a commodity.
	Develop secure forms of renting, leasing, sharecropping, and lending to (1) provide the landless with agricultural land, housing, and shelter (as appropriate), and (2) provide tenure security for landowners.	

566 Land and post-conflict peacebuilding

Ministry of Justice—strengthened property rights despite the absence of a national land law. During the Indonesian occupation of Timor-Leste (1975–1999), much of the rural population had been forcibly displaced; and during Timor-Leste's war for independence from Indonesia, land records were destroyed. After independence, returning Timorese settled where they could.

In 2002, when the transitional UN peacekeeping administration transferred control of the country to a nascent Timorese government, there was no statutory system in place for administering land rights, there was substantial confusion about who owned which lands, and it was unclear what legal framework should be used to regulate land. The fragile post-conflict state was subject not only to conflicting legal influences (remnants of both the Portuguese colonial system and the years of Indonesian occupation), but also to competing interests: some groups, for example, wanted to privatize all land, and commercial entities that held concessions for coffee production wanted to protect their contracts. Finally, particularly in rural areas, the customary resource and land management system continued to play a strong role in land administration and management.

The goals of the Ita Nia Rai project were to strengthen land policy, law, and regulations; to assist with the surveying, registration, and titling of land; to implement land administration and information systems; to develop dispute resolution mechanisms and capacity; and to increase public awareness of land issues (USAID Timor-Leste n.d.). With technical support from the project, a new land law was developed and submitted for legislative consideration, but it languished in parliament.

As part of its effort to survey and register land across the country,[25] the Ita Nia Rai project used local media and community meetings to familiarize communities with the project and its goals. Data collection teams visited each neighborhood, documenting who claimed each parcel of land and taking photographs of the claimaints; noting the global positioning system coordinates and photographing the markers that defined the corners of each land parcel; and compiling relevant information about the history or ownership of the land. Where neighbors disagreed regarding the boundaries or there were competing claimants, the team recorded the disputed boundaries and identified the competing claimants. Aerial photography was then used to create master maps of each community, on which all parcels (including disputed ones) were delineated; the maps also included photos of the recorded claimants. The maps were displayed in a local public place for thirty days, during which residents could verify their claims and correct errors.

From the beginning, the project gave priority to parcels that were not in dispute, while encouraging community members to discuss and resolve disputes.

---

[25] The project was initially intended to survey and register all land in the country, but the Ministry of Justice, USAID, and the other partners agreed to focus on urban and peri-urban areas, largely because there was as yet no land law that defined the legal status of customary land tenure regimes.

There was a conscious effort on the part of project staff to avoid creating incentives to contest ownership (for example, by making funds available to provide compensation); instead, the project provided local staff trained to mediate disputes, along with the necessary space for such mediation to occur. The Ita Nia Rai project collected information on more than 50,000 parcels, with an overall dispute rate of less than 10 percent (Ita Nia Rai 2012). In 2011, an executive decree formalized all undisputed private claims to land; by December of that year, landowners received their first certificates of land registration (Tetra Tech ARD n.d.).

Even though some disputes remained unresolved by the end of the project, and despite the fact that Timor-Leste still lacks a land law, the open discussion of landownership encouraged by the project led to the local resolution of many disputes; in addition, by transparently producing a new and wide-ranging national cadastre covering both urban and peri-urban areas, the Ita Nia Rai project improved tenure security.[26] Legal approaches to land and land rights issues in post-conflict societies are essential to long-term security; as the Ita Nia Rai project demonstrates, however, parallel methods can usefully bolster such approaches.

CONCLUSION

Post-conflict situations are frequently characterized by weakened and chaotic statutory land administration systems and vigorous but fluid customary tenure regimes, both operating in a larger context that includes new normative rules set out in peace accords, political wrangling over land and other resources, and pressure from international actors with diverse interests in the outcome of the peace process. While this constellation carries risks, it also represents real opportunities for resolving disputes, strengthening livelihoods, improving governance, and, ultimately, laying the foundation for a durable peace.

Post-conflict initiatives to reformulate the national laws, policies, and institutions that govern land need to look beyond the confines of ministries and missions; instead, such efforts should focus on institutions and processes that are developing on the ground, so as to draw legitimacy from them. Without this purposeful connection, local, regional, and national tenure institutions risk evolving in different directions. With such a connection, however, new frameworks can be designed to support approaches that already work and to strengthen ongoing reintegration and development. As experiences in Afghanistan and elsewhere show, an approach that bolsters local land management institutions can be an important part of rebuilding trust in government after conflict-induced state collapse (Stanfield et al. 2013*).

Following conflict, there is a window of opportunity to reform land tenure and administration. During this time, the international community can provide

---

[26] In 2011, the Ministry of Justice assumed full responsibility for the management of the Ita Nia Rai project.

568   Land and post-conflict peacebuilding

invaluable assistance by helping to resolve important or contentious issues in ways that are compatible with human rights obligations and development best practices. Such efforts may include crafting laws that support the livelihoods of the poor, as was the case in Ethiopia (Unruh 2005b), Mozambique (Unruh 2004a, 2004b), and Nicaragua (Barquero 2004). In some cases, such as Mozambique, the post-conflict period provides an opportunity to supplant an inequitable and problematic tenure system while systematically addressing the problems that the system had created, both before and during the conflict. In practice, this entailed setting a date after which the new, fairer system was used for all new title applications, while making separate efforts to resolve preexisting problems—by, for example, cancelling titles and concessions that had been acquired in bad faith.

In post-conflict countries, the rudimentary recovery of livelihood patterns in the immediate post-conflict lull gradually gives rise to the need for a full-fledged property rights system. The resulting surge of land tenure problems may continue for as many as five years after fighting has stopped, and may become particularly acute when international peacekeeping forces depart. Although some post-conflict countries have successfully pursued innovative approaches to tenure problems, others have had difficulty. And while the elements that make for a well-functioning tenure system in both developed and developing countries are known, the primary question for post-conflict situations is how to capitalize on the window of opportunity that is often present and assemble the elements in a workable format and in a timely fashion. Thus, while it may be tempting to import approaches that have worked elsewhere, either in whole or in part, it is crucial to keep in mind the importance of both local context and the particular types of vulnerability that can result from both conflict and displacement. In the post-conflict context, some issues—such as rampant opportunism, individual and group grievances, and near-term food security—will be magnified after a conflict; other issues, such as those related to the taxation of land and property, may have less immediate priority.

Finally, while certain solutions may seem attractive in theory, it is crucial to anticipate and focus on issues that may arise in practice. For instance, given that land and property transactions go on, as a matter of necessity, with or without governmental laws or decrees, if registry offices freeze land and property transactions while updating their records and procedures, a black market in land and property is likely to result—because land and property transactions within a population cannot, in reality, be frozen. Similarly, the prolonged absence of effective courts or other dispute resolution mechanisms may also create incentives to participate in black market alternatives. Although delays are likely inevitable in efforts to reform tenure systems in the wake of conflict, well-publicized consultation programs can encourage parties to potential transactions to adopt a wait-and-see approach, providing valuable time and political space for the formulation of effective solutions.

As the twenty-one chapters in this book illustrate, land offers both serious challenges and vital opportunities in post-conflict situations. Land disputes are

Lessons learned 569

often long-standing and difficult to resolve; post-conflict states have limited capacity and legitimacy for managing land; and wartime actions can exacerbate tensions. But it is possible to tailor solutions to specific situations, and thereby support livelihoods, economic recovery, human rights, local governance, and overall peacebuilding goals. Despite consistently being one of the most difficult tasks in post-conflict peacebuilding, effectively addressing land tenure and management can alleviate a powerful source of tension and help prevent conflict relapse.

REFERENCES

Alden Wily, L. 2009. Tackling land tenure in the emergency to development transition in post-conflict states: From restitution to reform. In *Uncharted territory: Land, conflict and humanitarian action*, ed. S. Pantuliano. Rugby, Warwickshire, UK: Practical Action Publishing.

————. 2013. Resolving natural resource conflicts to help prevent war: A case from Afghanistan. In *Livelihoods, natural resources, and post-conflict peacebuilding*, ed. H. Young and L. Goldman. London: Earthscan.

Aluma, J., C. Drennon, J. Kigula, S. W. Lawry, E. S. K. Muwaga-Zake, and J. Were. 1989. *Settlement in forest reserves, game reserves and national parks in Uganda: A study of social, economic, and tenure factors affecting land use and deforestation in Mabira Forest Reserve, Kibale Forest Reserve, and Kibale Game Reserve/Corridor*. Madison: Land Tenure Center, University of Wisconsin. http://minds.wisconsin.edu/handle/1793/31704.

Anaya, S. J., and R. A. Williams, Jr. 2001. The protection of indigenous peoples' rights over lands and natural resources under the Inter-American human rights system. *Harvard Human Rights Journal* 14:33–86.

André, C. 2003. Custom, contracts and cadastres in north-west Rwanda. In *Securing land rights in Africa*, ed. T. A. Benjaminsen and C. Lund. London: Cass Publishing.

Assaf, G., and R. El-Fil. 2000. Resolving the issue of war displacement in Lebanon. *Forced Migration Review* 7:31–33.

Bahir, A. L. 2010. Challenges and consequences of displacement and squatting: The case of Kore area in Addis Ababa, Ethiopia. *Journal of Sustainable Development in Africa* 12 (3): 261–285.

Bailliet, C. 2003. Property restitution in Guatemala: A transitional dilemma. In *Returning home: Housing and property restitution rights of refugees and displaced persons*, ed. S. Leckie. Ardsley, NY: Transnational Publishers.

Baribeau, G. 2011. Land conflict in Burundi: A strategic review of programming. Washington, D.C.: Search for Common Ground. www.sfcg.org/programmes/burundi/pdf/BDI_EV_Feb12_Land%20Conflict%20in%20Burundi%20A%20Strategic%20Review%20of%20Programming.pdf.

Barquero, R. 2004. *Access to land in post-conflict situations: A case study in Nicaragua*. Rome: Food and Agriculture Organization of the United Nations.

Barwari, N. 2013. Rebuilding peace: Land and water management in the Kurdistan Region of northern Iraq. In *Land and post-conflict peacebuilding*, ed. J. Unruh and R. C. Williams. London: Earthscan.

Batson, D. E. 2013. Snow leopards and cadastres: Rare sightings in post-conflict Afghanistan. In *Land and post-conflict peacebuilding*, ed. J. Unruh and R. C. Williams. London: Earthscan.

570   Land and post-conflict peacebuilding

Bavinck, M. 1998. "A matter of maintaining peace." State accommodation to subordinate legal systems: The case of fisheries along the Coromandel coast of Tamil Nadu, India. *Journal of Legal Pluralism* 40:151–170.

Berry, S. 1993. *No condition is permanent: The social dynamics of agrarian change in Sub-Saharan Africa.* Madison: University of Wisconsin Press.

Borras, S. M., Jr., and J. C. Franco. 2012. Global land grabbing and trajectories of agrarian change: A preliminary analysis. *Journal of Agrarian Change* 12 (1): 34–59.

Brookings–Bern Project on Internal Displacement. 2008. *Protecting internally displaced persons: A manual for law and policymakers.* Washington, D.C.: Brookings Institution.

Bruce, J. W. 2013. Return of land in post-conflict Rwanda: International standards, improvisation, and the role of international humanitarian organizations. In *Land and post-conflict peacebuilding,* ed. J. Unruh and R. C. Williams. London: Earthscan.

Bruce, J. W., S. E. Migot-Adholla, and J. Atherton. 1994. The findings and their policy implications: Institutional adaptation or replacement? In *Searching for land tenure security in Africa,* ed. J. W. Bruce and S. E. Migot-Adholla. Dubuque, IA: Kendall/Hunt Publishing.

Buchanan-Smith, M., and H. McElhinney. 2011. City limits: Urbanisation and vulnerability in Sudan; Nyala case study. With H. Bagadi, M. A. Rahman, A. Dawalbeit, A. Dawalbeit, M. Khalil, and B. El Din Abdalla. London: Humanitarian Policy Group. www.odi.org.uk/resources/docs/6515.pdf.

Cain, A. 2013. Angola: Land resources and conflict. In *Land and post-conflict peacebuilding,* ed. J. Unruh and R. C. Williams. London: Earthscan.

Cohen, S. E. 1993. The politics of planting: Israeli-Palestinian competition for control of land in the Jerusalem periphery. Geography Research Paper No. 236. Chicago, IL: University of Chicago Press.

Collier, P., L. Elliot, H. Hegre, A. Hoeffler, M. Reynal-Querol, and N. Sambanis. 2003. *Breaking the conflict trap: Civil war and development policy.* World Bank Policy Research Report. Oxford, UK: Oxford University Press.

Corriveau-Bourque, A. 2010. Confusions and palava: The logic of land encroachment in Lofa County, Liberia. Oslo: Norwegian Refugee Council. www.nrc.no/arch/img.aspx?file_id=9481898.

———. 2013. Beyond land redistribution: Lessons learned from El Salvador's unfulfilled agrarian revolution. In *Land and post-conflict peacebuilding,* ed. J. Unruh and R. C. Williams. London: Earthscan.

Davuth, L. 2003. Country report: Cambodia. Phnom Penh, Cambodia: Permanent Committee on GIS Infrastructure for Asia & the Pacific. www.fig.net/cadastraltemplate/countryreport/Cambodia.pdf.

Defensor Knack, P. 2013. Legal frameworks and land issues in Muslim Mindanao. In *Land and post-conflict peacebuilding,* ed. J. Unruh and R. C. Williams. London: Earthscan.

Deininger, K., and D. Byerlee. 2011. *Rising global interest in farmland: Can it yield sustainable and equitable benefits?* With J. Lindsay, A. Norton, H. Selod, and M. Stickler. Washington, D.C.: World Bank. http://siteresources.worldbank.org/INTARD/Resources/ESW_Sept7_final_final.pdf.

Delville, P. L. 2003. When farmers use "pieces of paper" to record their land transactions in Francophone rural Africa: Insights into the dynamics of institutional innovation. In *Securing land rights in Africa,* ed. T. A. Benjaminsen and C. Lund. London: Cass Publishing.

Deng, D. K. 2011. *The new frontier: A baseline survey of large-scale land-based investment in Southern Sudan.* Researched by Generation Agency for Development and Transformation–Pentagon and the South Sudan Law Society. Report 1/11 (March). Oslo: Norwegian People's Aid. www.npaid.org/filestore/NPA_New_Frontier.pdf.

de Soto, A., and G. del Castillo. 1995. Implementation of comprehensive peace agreements: Staying the course in El Salvador. *Global Governance* 1 (2): 189–203.

de Waal, A. 2009. Why humanitarian organizations need to tackle land issues. In *Uncharted territory: Land, conflict and humanitarian action*, ed. S. Pantuliano. Rugby, Warwickshire, UK: Practical Action Publishing.

De Wit, P. 2002. Land conflict management in Mozambique: A case study of Zambezia Province. Rome: Food and Agriculture Organization of the United Nations. www.fao.org/DOCREP/005/Y3932T/y3932t05.htm.

Douglas, I., C. Gleichmann, M. Odenwald, K. Steenken, and A. Wilkinson. 2004. *Disarmament, demobilisation and reintegration: A practical field and classroom guide.* Frankfurt, Germany: German Technical Co-operation, Gesellshaft für Technische Zusammenarbeit, Norwegian Defence International Centre, Pearson Peacekeeping Centre, and Swedish National Defence College. www.acus.org/files/publication_pdfs/82/0401-DDR_Guide.pdf.

ECOSOC (Economic and Social Council, United Nations). 2005. Economic, social, and cultural rights. E/CN.4/Sub.2/2005/17. www.unhcr.org/refworld/docid/41640c874.html.

Elhawary, S. 2009. Between war and peace: Land, conflict and humanitarian action in Colombia. In *Uncharted territory: Land, conflict and humanitarian action*, ed. S. Pantuliano. Rugby, Warwickshire, UK: Practical Action Publishing.

Elhawary, S., and S. Pantuliano. 2013. Land issues in post-conflict return and recovery. In *Land and post-conflict peacebuilding*, ed. J. Unruh and R. C. Williams. London: Earthscan.

Fitzpatrick, D. 2002. Land policy in post-conflict circumstances: Some lessons from East Timor. New Issues in Refugee Research Working Paper No. 58. Geneva, Switzerland: Office of the United Nations High Commissioner for Refugees.

Foray, K. M. 2011. Draft National Land Policy for Sierra Leone. National Land Policy Reform Project, Ministry of Lands, Country Planning and the Environment. Freetown, Sierra Leone.

Fortmann, L., and J. Riddell, with S. Brick, J. Bruce, A. Fraser, N. Garcia-Pardo, and R. Labelle. 1985. *Trees and tenure: An annotated bibliography for agroforesters and others.* Madison, WI: Land Tenure Center; Nairobi, Kenya: International Council for Research in Agroforestry. http://pdf.usaid.gov/pdf_docs/PNAAT387.pdf.

Galiani, S., and E. Schargrodsky. 2010. Property rights for the poor: Effects of land titling. *Journal of Public Economics* 94 (9–10): 700–729.

Ghatak, S. n.d. Land acquisition is rampant in Asia, Africa and Latin America, conclusion drawn by recent reports. Rome: Food and Agriculture Organization of the United Nations. http://typo3.fao.org/fileadmin/user_upload/fsn/docs/HLPE/Land_grab_ghatak.pdf.

GOSL (Government of Sierra Leone). 2005. National land policy. Freetown.

Green, A. 2013. Title wave: Land tenure and peacebuilding in Aceh. In *Land and post-conflict peacebuilding*, ed. J. Unruh and R. C. Williams. London: Earthscan.

Griffiths, J. 1986. What is legal pluralism? *Journal of Legal Pluralism* 24:1–52.

Hanchinamani, B. 2003. The impact of Mozambique's land tenure policy on refugees and internally displaced persons. *Human Rights Brief* 7 (2): 10–12, 16.

572 Land and post-conflict peacebuilding

Hanlon, J. 2002. The land debate in Mozambique: Will foreign investors, the urban elite, advanced peasants or family farmers drive rural development? London: Oxfam.

Hannam, I. D. 2013. Transboundary resource management strategies in the Pamir mountain region of Tajikistan. In *Land and post-conflict peacebuilding*, ed. J. Unruh and R. C. Williams. London: Earthscan.

Hayden, R. M. 1984. A note on Caste Panchayats and government courts in India: Different kinds of stages for different kinds of performances. *Journal of Legal Pluralism* 22: 43–52.

Huggins, C. 2004. Land access issues in post-genocide Rwanda. Rome: Food and Agriculture Organization of the United Nations.

———. 2011. A historical perspective on the "Global Land Rush." Rome: International Land Coalition.

IRIN (Integrated Regional Information Networks). 2005. Liberia: Ex-fighters making money from latex refuse to leave rubber plantation. IRIN Humanitarian News and Analysis, April 19. www.irinnews.org/Report/53970/LIBERIA-Ex-fighters-making-money-from -latex-refuse-to-leave-rubber-plantation.

Ita Nia Rai. 2012. Data and statistics. March 8. http://itaniarai.mj.gov.tl/eng/data.html.

Kachingwe, N., with contributions from S. Ambrose, R. Tripathi, and C. Gatundu. 2012. From under their feet: A think piece on the gender dimensions of land grabs in Africa. Johannesburg, South Africa: ActionAid. www.actionaid.org/sites/files/actionaid/actionaidfromundertheirfeet.pdf.

Kamphius, B. 2005. Economic policy for building peace. In *Postconflict development: Meeting new challenges*, ed. G. Junne and W. Verkoren. Boulder, CO: Lynne Rienner.

Kloeck-Jenson, S. 1998. Locating the community: Local communities and the administration of land and other natural resources in Mozambique. Paper presented at the Cape Town Conference on Land Tenure Issues, University of Cape Town, South Africa, January 27–29.

Knight, R., J. Adoko, T. Auma, A. Kaba, A. Salomao, S. Siakor, and I. Tankar. 2012. *Protecting community lands and resources: Evidence from Liberia, Mozambique and Uganda.* Executive summary. Rome: International Development Law Organization; Washington, D.C.: Namati. www.idlo.int/Publications/CommunityLandReport1.pdf.

LRC (Law Reform Commission, Sierra Leone). 2004. Annual report 2003. Freetown. http://lawrefcom.sl/2003.pdf.

Lund, M. S. 1996. *Preventive diplomacy: A strategy for preventing violent conflicts.* Washington, D.C.: United States Institute of Peace.

———. 1998. Struggles for land and political power: On the politicization of land tenure and disputes in Niger. *Journal of Legal Pluralism* 40:1–22.

Marquardt, M., J. Unruh, and L. Heron. 2002. Land policy and administration: Assessment of the current situation and future prospects in East Timor; Final Report. Dili: United States Agency for International Development / Government of Timor-Leste. http://pdf.usaid.gov/pdf_docs/PNACS142.pdf.

Mason, W. 2011. *The rule of law in Afghanistan: Missing in inaction.* New York: Cambridge University Press.

McCallin, B. 2013. The role of restitution in post-conflict situations. In *Land and post-conflict peacebuilding*, ed. J. Unruh and R. C. Williams. London: Earthscan.

McMichael, G., and A. Massleberg. 2010. Landmines and land rights in Southern Sudan. Geneva, Switzerland: Geneva International Centre for Humanitarian Demining.

Lessons learned 573

Meinzen-Dick, R., A. Knox, F. Place, and B. Swallow, eds. 2002. *Innovation in natural resource management: The role of property rights and collective action in developing countries.* Baltimore, MD: Johns Hopkins University Press.

Meinzen-Dick, R., and R. Pradhan. 2013. Legal pluralism in post-conflict environments: Problem or opportunity for natural resource management? In *Governance, natural resources, and post-conflict peacebuilding,* ed. C. Bruch, C. Muffett, and S. S. Nichols. London: Earthscan.

Merlet, P., and J. Bastiaensen. 2012. Struggles over property rights in the context of large-scale transnational land acquisitions: Using legal pluralism to re-politicize the debate. Discussion Paper 2012.02. Antwerp, Belgium: Institute of Development Policy and Management. www.agter.asso.fr/IMG/pdf/2012-02_dp_merlet_bastiaensen _legal-pluralism.pdf.

Merry, S. E. 1988. Legal pluralism. *Law and Society Review* 22 (5): 869–896.

Michaels, R. 2005. The re-*state*-ment of non-state law: The state, choice of law, and the challenge from global legal pluralism. *Wayne Law Review* 51:1209–1259.

Miranda, L. A. 2012. The role of international law in intrastate natural resource allocation: Sovereignty, human rights, and peoples-based development. *Vanderbilt Journal of Transnational Law* 45 (3): 785–840.

Miyazawa, N. 2013. Customary law and community-based natural resource management in post-conflict Timor-Leste. In *Land and post-conflict peacebuilding,* ed. J. Unruh and R. C. Williams. London: Earthscan.

MOJ (Ministry of Justice, Republic of Croatia). 2010. Real property registration and cadastre project: Final project report. Zagreb. www.uredjenazemlja.hr/web//uploads/ assets//dokumenti_eng/final_analisys/Final_Project_Report_ENG_.pdf.

MPPB (Mozambique Peace Process Bulletin). 1997. After NGO lobbying, new land law increases peasant rights. October 1.

Mulley, B. G., and J. D. Unruh. 2004. The role of off-farm employment in tropical forest conservation: Labor, migration, and smallholder attitudes toward land in western Uganda. *Journal of Environmental Management* 71 (3): 193–205.

Murphy, P. 2003. *Evidence, proof, and facts.* Oxford, UK: Oxford University Press.

Negrão, J. 1999. The Mozambican land campaign, 1997–1999. Paper presented at the Conference on the Associative Movement of Mozambique, Maputo, December 1999. www.caledonia.org.uk/land/mozambiq.htm.

Nichols, S. S., C. Muffett, and C. Bruch. 2013. Fueling conflict or facilitating peace: Lessons in post-conflict governance and natural resource management. In *Governance, natural resources, and post-conflict peacebuilding,* ed. C. Bruch, C. Muffett, and S. S. Nichols. London: Earthscan.

Norfolk, S., and H. Liversage. 2003. *Land reform and poverty alleviation in Mozambique.* Pretoria, South Africa: Human Sciences Research Council.

Oki, Y. 2013. Land tenure and peace negotiations in Mindanao, Philippines. In *Land and post-conflict peacebuilding,* ed. J. Unruh and R. C. Williams. London: Earthscan.

Otsuka, K., S. Suyanto, T. Sonobe, and T. P. Tomich. 2001. Evolution of land tenure institutions and development of agroforestry: Evidence from customary land areas of Sumatra. *Agricultural Economics* 25 (1): 85–101.

Özerdem, A. 2009. *Post-war recovery: Disarmament, demobilization and reintegration.* London: I. B. Tauris.

Pancas, M. 2003. Mozambique access to land. Paper presented at the Land and Food Security Seminar, Copenhagen, Denmark, December.

574 Land and post-conflict peacebuilding

Paris, R. 2004. *At war's end: Building peace after civil conflict*. Cambridge, UK: Cambridge University Press.

Peleikis, A. 2006. Whose heritage? Legal pluralism and the politics of the past: A case study from the Curonian Spit (Lithuania). *Journal of Legal Pluralism* 53–54: 209–237.

Pichel, F., P. B. Sayeh, A. Thriscutt, and O. Kemeh-Gama. 2012. Implementing an affordable, rapid deployment land records management solution for Liberia. Paper presented at the Annual World Bank Conference on Land and Poverty, Washington, D.C.

Plunkett, M. 2005. Reestablishing the rule of law. In *Postconflict development: Meeting new challenges*, ed. G. Junne and W. Verkoren. Boulder, CO: Lynne Rienner.

Provost, C., and P. McClanahan. 2012. Sierra Leone: Local resistance grows as investors snap up land. *Guardian*, April 11. www.guardian.co.uk/global-development/poverty -matters/2012/apr/11/sierra-leone-local-resistance-land-deals.

Raintree, J. B., ed. 1987. *Land, trees and tenure: Proceedings of an international workshop on tenure issues in agroforestry, Nairobi, May 27–31, 1985*. Nairobi, Kenya: International Centre for Research in Agroforestry; Madison, WI: Land Tenure Center.

Rashid, S. R., M. Jan, and M. Wakil. 2010. Landmines and land rights in Afghanistan. Geneva, Switzerland: Geneva International Centre for Humanitarian Demining. www.gichd.org/fileadmin/pdf/ma_development/wk-landrights-oct2010/LMAD-wk -Afghanistan-case-study-Nov2010.pdf.

Renner-Thomas, A. 2010. *Land tenure in Sierra Leone: The law, dualism and the making of a land policy*. Central Milton Keynes, UK: AuthorHouse.

Rocheleau, D., and D. Edmunds. 1997. Women, men and trees: Gender, power and property in forest and agrarian landscapes. *World Development* 25 (8): 1351–1371.

Sait, S. 2013. Unexplored dimensions: Islamic land systems in Afghanistan, Indonesia, Iraq, and Somalia. In *Land and post-conflict peacebuilding*, ed. J. Unruh and R. C. Williams. London: Earthscan.

Salas, C. 1986. *Jamaica Land Titling Project: Feasibility report*. Washington, D.C.: Inter-American Development Bank.

Salman, S. M. A. 2013. The Abyei territorial dispute between North and South Sudan: Why has its resolution proven difficult? In *Land and post-conflict peacebuilding*, ed. J. Unruh and R. C. Williams. London: Earthscan.

Sekiguchi, M., and N. Hatsukano. 2013. Land conflicts and land registration in Cambodia. In *Land and post-conflict peacebuilding*, ed. J. Unruh and R. C. Williams. London: Earthscan.

Silliman, G. 1985. A political analysis of the Philippines' Katarungang Pambarangay system of informal justice through mediation. *Law and Society Review* 19 (2): 279–302.

Smucker, P. 2005. Liberian gold rush threatens forest preserve. *New York Times*, March 2. www.nytimes.com/2005/03/01/world/africa/01iht-forest.html?pagewanted=all.

Stanfield, J. D., J. Brick Murtazashvili, M. Y. Safar, and A. Salam. 2013. Community documentation of land tenure and its contribution to state building in Afghanistan. In *Land and post-conflict peacebuilding*, ed. J. Unruh and R. C. Williams. London: Earthscan.

Stigall, D. E. 2013. Refugees and legal reform in Iraq: The Iraqi Civil Code, international standards for the treatment of displaced persons, and the art of attainable solutions. In *Land and post-conflict peacebuilding*, ed. J. Unruh and R. C. Williams. London: Earthscan.

Tanner, C. 2002. Law-making in an African context: The 1997 Mozambican land law. FAO Legal Papers Online No. 26. Rome: Food and Agriculture Organization of the United Nations.

Tetra Tech ARD. n.d. Highlight of the month: Strengthening property rights in Timor-Leste. www.tetratechintdev.com/intdev/index.php?option=com_k2&view=item&id=460:highlight -of-the-month-strengthening-property-rights-in-timor-leste&Itemid=55&lang=us.

Themnér, L., and P. Wallensteen. 2012. Armed conflicts, 1946–2011. *Journal of Peace Research* 49 (4): 565–575.

Tubiana, J. 2007. Darfur: A war for land? In *War in Darfur and the search for peace*, ed. A. de Waal. Cambridge, MA: Global Equity Initiative, Harvard University.

UCDP (Uppsala Conflict Data Program). n.d. UCDP Conflict Encyclopedia. Uppsala University. www.ucdp.uus.se/database.

Uitamo, E. 1999. Modeling deforestation caused by the expansion of subsistence farming in the Philippines. *Journal of Forest Economics* 5 (1): 99–122.

UNEP (United Nations Environment Programme). 2009. *From conflict to peacebuilding: The role of natural resources and the environment.* Nairobi, Kenya. http://postconflict .unep.ch/publications/pcdmb_policy_01.pdf.

———. 2012. *Greening the blue helmets: Environment, natural resources and UN peacekeeping operations.* Nairobi, Kenya. http://postconflict.unep.ch/publications/ UNEP_greening_blue_helmets.pdf.

UNFT (United Nations Interagency Framework Team for Preventive Action). 2012. *Land and conflict: Toolkit and guidance for preventing and managing land and natural resources conflict.* New York. http://postconflict.unep.ch/publications/GN_Land_Consultation.pdf.

UN-HABITAT (United Nations Human Settlements Programme). 2007. *A post-conflict land administration and peacebuilding handbook.* Vol. 1 of *Countries with land records.* Nairobi, Kenya.

Unruh, J. D. 1997. The role of land conflict and land conflict resolution in a peace process: Mozambique's return to agriculture. *Refuge* 16 (6): 28–33.

———. 2002. Local land tenure in the peace process. *Peace Review* 14 (3): 337–342.

———. 2003. Land tenure and legal pluralism in the peace process. *Peace and Change* 28 (3): 352–376.

———. 2004a. Mozambican land law issues: Foreign owner compliance with laws reserving the right to ownership of land to nationals/the state; and land title restitution experiences, strategies, and options. Burlington, VT: Associates in Rural Development East Timor Land Law Program.

———. 2004b. Rural property rights in a peace process: Lessons from Mozambique. In *WorldMinds: 100 geographical perspectives on 100 problems*, ed. D. G. Janelle, B. Warf, and K. Hansen. Dordrecht, Netherlands: Kluwer Academic Publishers.

———. 2005a. Changing conflict resolution institutions in the Ethiopian pastoral commons: The role of armed confrontation in rule-making. *GeoJournal* 64:225–237.

———. 2005b. *Land tenure and its relationship to food security and investment in postwar Sierra Leone.* Rome: Food and Agriculture Organization of the United Nations.

———. 2006. Land tenure and the "evidence landscape" in developing countries. *Annals of the Association of American Geographers* 96 (4): 754–772.

———. 2008. Land policy reform, customary rule of law and the peace process in Sierra Leone. *African Journal of Legal Studies* 2 (2): 94–117.

———. 2009. Land rights in postwar Liberia: The volatile part of the peace process. *Land Use Policy* 26 (2): 425–433.

576 Land and post-conflict peacebuilding

———. 2012. The interaction between landmine clearance and land rights in Angola: A volatile outcome of non-integrated peacebuilding. *Habitat International* 36 (1): 117–125.

Unruh, J. D., L. Cligget, and R. Hay. 2005. Migrant land rights reception and "clearing to claim" in Sub-Saharan Africa: A deforestation example from southern Zambia. *Natural Resources Forum* 29 (3): 190–198.

Unruh, J., and A. Corriveau-Bourque. 2010. Landmines and land rights in conflict affected countries. Policy Brief. Geneva, Switzerland: Geneva International Centre for Humanitarian Demining. www.gichd.org/fileadmin/pdf/publications/Landmines-LR-2011/Landmines-LR-Policy-Brief-Dec2010.pdf.

USAID (United States Agency for International Development). 2004. USAID strategic plan for East Timor: A new nation moving forward; 2005–2009. http://pdf.usaid.gov/pdf_docs/PDACD442.pdf.

USAID Liberia (United States Agency for International Development–Liberia). 2010. Proposed Threshold Country Program (TCP) for land tenure. March 12. http://liberia.usaid.gov/node/86.

USAID Timor-Leste (United States Agency for International Development–Timor-Leste). n.d. Timor-Leste. http://timor-leste.usaid.gov/sites/default/files/ARDfactsheet.pdf.

Van der Auweraert, P. 2013. Institutional aspects of resolving land disputes in post-conflict societies. In *Land and post-conflict peacebuilding*, ed. J. Unruh and R. C. Williams. London: Earthscan.

Waldman, M. 2008. Community peacebuilding in Afghanistan: The case for a national strategy. Oxfam Research Report. Oxford, UK: Oxfam International. www.oxfam.org/sites/www.oxfam.org/files/community_peacebuilding_in_afghanistan_report_feb08.pdf.

Wanyeki, L., ed. 2003. *Women and land in Africa: Culture, religion and realizing women's rights.* London: Zed Books.

Williams, R. C. 2007. The contemporary right to property restitution in the context of transitional justice. ICTJ Occasional Paper Series. New York: International Center for Transitional Justice.

———. 2011. Beyond squatters' rights: Durable solutions and development-induced displacement in Monrovia, Liberia. Norwegian Refugee Council Thematic Report. Oslo: Norwegian Refugee Council. www.nrc.no/arch/_img/9568756.pdf.

———. 2013a. Post-conflict land tenure issues in Bosnia: Privatization and the politics of reintegrating the displaced. In *Land and post-conflict peacebuilding*, ed. J. Unruh and R. C. Williams. London: Earthscan.

———. 2013b. Title through possession or position? Respect for housing, land, and property rights in Cambodia. In *Land and post-conflict peacebuilding*, ed. J. Unruh and R. C. Williams. London: Earthscan.

World Bank. 2009. *Uganda: Post-conflict land policy and administration options— The case of northern Uganda.* Report No. 46110-UG. Washington, D.C. https://openknowledge.worldbank.org/handle/10986/3071.

APPENDIX 1
List of abbreviations

ABC: Abyei Boundaries Commission (Sudan)
ACORD: Association for Cooperative Operations Research and Development
AJOC: Abyei Joint Oversight Committee (Sudan)
AMM: Aceh Monitoring Mission (Indonesia)
APS: Abyei Police Service (Sudan)
AR: Army regulation (United States)
ARMM: Autonomous Region in Muslim Mindanao (Philippines)
ASEAN: Association of Southeast Asian Nations
AUHIP: African Union High-Level Implementation Panel (Sudan)
BAPPENAS: National Development Planning Agency (Badan Perencanaan
   dan Pembangunan Nasional) (Indonesia)
BJE: Bangsamoro Juridical Entity (Philippines)
BPN: National Land Agency (Badan Pertanahan Nasional) (Indonesia)
BRA: Aceh Reintegration Board (Badan Reintegrasi-Damai Aceh)
   (Indonesia)
BRR: Agency of Rehabilitation and Reconstruction for Aceh and Nias
   (Badan Rehabilitasi dan Rekonstruksi) (Indonesia)
CAURWA: Community of Indigenous People of Rwanda (Communauté
   des Autochtones Rwandais)
CDA: community-driven adjudication
CDC: Community Development Council
CERP: Commander's Emergency Response Program (United States)
COMBI: Communication for Behavioral Impact
CPA: Comprehensive Peace Agreement (Sudan)
CPP: Cambodian People's Party
CRA: Cooperation for the Reconstruction of Afghanistan
CRRPD: Commission for the Resolution of Real Property Disputes (Iraq)
CSO: civil society organization
DFID: Department for International Development (United Kingdom)
DHA: United Nations Department of Humanitarian Affairs
DKCC: district/*khan* cadastral commission (Cambodia)

578 Land and post-conflict peacebuilding

DPA: Dayton Peace Agreement on Bosnia-Herzegovina
ESI: European Stability Initiative
EU: European Union
FAO: Food and Agriculture Organization of the United Nations
FCA: Foreign Claims Act (Iraq)
FIG: International Federation of Surveyors (Fédération Internationale des Géomètres)
FMLN: Farabundo Martí National Liberation Front (Frente Farabundo Martí de Liberacíon Nacional) (El Salvador)
FRETILIN: Revolutionary Front for an Independent Timor-Leste (Frente Revolucionária de Timor-Leste Independente)
FTAA: financial or technical assistance agreement
GAM: Free Aceh Movement (Gerakan Aceh Merdeka) (Indonesia)
GEF: Global Environment Facility
GIS: geographic information system
GOI: Government of Indonesia
GOS: Government of Sudan
GOSS: Government of Southern Sudan (prior to July 9, 2011); Government of South Sudan (as of July 9, 2011)
GRP: Government of the Republic of the Philippines
HLP: housing, land, and property
IACA: International Agreements Claims Act (Iraq)
ICC: Iraqi Civil Code
ICCPR: International Covenant on Civil and Political Rights
ICESCR: International Covenant on Economic, Social and Cultural Rights
ICLA: Norwegian Refugee Council's Information, Counselling and Legal Assistance program
IDP: internally displaced person
IGAD: Intergovernmental Authority on Development
INGO: International nongovernmental organization
IPRA: Indigenous Peoples Rights Act (Philippines)
ISAF: Interim Security Force for Abyei (Sudan)
ISO: International Organization for Standardization
ISTA: Salvadoran Institute of Agrarian Transformation (Instituto Salvadoreño de Transformacíon Agraria) (El Salvador)
JIU: Joint/Integrated Units (Sudan)
JMOC: Joint Military Observer Committee (Sudan)
KHI: Compilation of Islamic Law (Kompilasi Hukum Islam) (Indonesia)
LADM: Land Administration Domain Model
LBH-Aceh: Aceh Legal Aid Institute (Indonesia)
LMAP: Land Management and Administration Project (Cambodia)
LTERA: Land Titling and Economic Restructuring in Afghanistan
MAFF: Ministry of Agriculture, Forestry and Fisheries (Timor-Leste)
MILF: Moro Islamic Liberation Front (Philippines)

List of abbreviations   579

MINITERE: Ministry of Land, Environment, Forestry, Water and Mines (Rwanda)
MLMUPC: Ministry of Land Management, Urban Planning and Construction (Cambodia)
MNLF: Moro National Liberation Front (Philippines)
MOA-AD: Memorandum of Agreement on Ancestral Domain (Philippines)
MOU: memorandum of understanding
NALDR: National Authority for Land Dispute Resolution (Cambodia)
NATO: North Atlantic Treaty Organization
NCC: National Cadastral Commission (Cambodia)
NCP: National Congress Party (Sudan)
NDFWR: National Directorate of Forestry and Water Resources (Timor-Leste)
NEPA: National Environmental Protection Agency (Afghanistan)
NGO: nongovernmental organization
NPA: New People's Army (Philippines)
NRC: Norwegian Refugee Council
OCHA: United Nations Office for the Coordination of Humanitarian Affairs
OHR: Office of the High Representative (Bosnia and Herzegovina)
PALM: Sustainable Land Management in the High Pamir and Pamir-Alai Mountain project (Tajikistan)
PATSAP: Pamir-Alai Transboundary Strategy and Action Plan (Tajikistan)
PCA: Permanent Court of Arbitration
PCC: Property Claims Commission (Iraq)
PMCC: provincial/municipal cadastral commission (Cambodia)
PRK: People's Republic of Kampuchea (Cambodia)
PTT: Land Transfer Program (Programa de Transferencia de Tierras) (El Salvador)
RALAS: Reconstruction of Aceh Land Administration System (Indonesia)
RLAP: Rural Land Administration Project (Afghanistan)
RPA: Rwandan Patriotic Army
RPF: Rwandan Patriotic Front
RRTF: Reconstruction and Return Task Force (Bosnia and Herzegovina)
RS: Republika Srpska (Bosnia and Herzegovina)
SAF: Sudanese Armed Forces
SFRY: Socialist Federal Republic of Yugoslavia
SOC: State of Cambodia
SOFA: status of forces agreement
SPLA: Sudan People's Liberation Army
SPLM: Sudan People's Liberation Movement
STDM: Social Tenure Domain Model
UK: United Kingdom
UN: United Nations
UNDP: United Nations Development Programme
UNECE: United Nations Economic Commission for Europe

580 Land and post-conflict peacebuilding

UNEP: United Nations Environment Programme
UN-HABITAT: United Nations Human Settlements Programme
UNHCR: United Nations High Commissioner for Refugees
UNISFA: United Nations Interim Security Force for Abyei
UNITA: National Union for the Total Independence of Angola (União Nacional para a Independência Total de Angola)
UNMIS: United Nations Mission in Sudan
UNSC: United Nations Security Council
UNTAET: United Nations Transitional Administration in East Timor
USAID: United States Agency for International Development
WCS: Wildlife Conservation Society

APPENDIX 2
Author biographies

Nesreen Barwari is a citizen of Iraq and resident of its Kurdistan Region. Barwari, a lecturer on planning and housing at Dohuk University, formerly served as minister of municipalities and public works in the government of Iraq (2003–2006) and the former minister of reconstruction and development in the Kurdistan Regional Government in Erbil, Kurdistan-Iraq (1999–2003). She is the founder and chairwoman of Breeze and Hope, a nongovernmental organization (NGO) that promotes democracy in the Kurdistan Region; the president and chairwoman of Tolerancy International, an NGO that strives to foster stable secular democracies; and the development director at Ranj Company, a development, investment, and construction company in Iraq. Barwari has also worked with various United Nations agencies in program and management positions. She holds a bachelor's degree in architectural engineering and urban planning from Baghdad University and a Master of Public Administration in public policy and management from the Harvard University Kennedy School of Government. Barwari has also completed two years in a Ph.D. program at the University of British Columbia School of Community and Regional Planning and is finalizing her dissertation with the Faculty of Spatial Planning at Dortmund University.

Douglas E. Batson is a political geography analyst at the National Geospatial-Intelligence Agency of the United States and is a staff member of the Foreign Names Committee of the U.S. Board on Geographic Names. He holds a master's degree in education from Boston University and a bachelor's degree in geography from Excelsior College. Batson previously worked for the U.S. Geological Survey and the U.S. Department of Justice and is retired from the U.S. Army Reserve.

John W. Bruce has worked on land policy and law in developing countries for forty years, primarily in Africa, including ten year's residence in Ethiopia and Sudan. He holds a J.D. from Columbia Law School and an S.J.D. from the University of Wisconsin–Madison. Bruce is a former director of the Land Tenure Center at the University of Wisconsin–Madison, and between 1996 and 2006 he served at the World Bank in a dual capacity as senior counsel for land law

582   Land and post-conflict peacebuilding

in the Legal Department and as senior land tenure specialist in the Agriculture and Rural Development Department. Bruce currently heads the consulting firm Land and Development Solutions International. He has published extensively on land policy and law, most recently the book *Land Law Reform: Achieving Development Policy Objectives* (World Bank, 2006) and the strategic overview paper "Land and Business Formalization for Legal Empowerment of the Poor" (U.S. Agency for International Development, 2007).

Allan Cain is an architect and specialist in project planning and urbanization. He has an undergraduate degree in environmental studies from the University of Waterloo in Canada and completed his graduate studies at the Architectural Association in London and further specialist studies at Harvard University and the University of Colorado–Boulder. Cain has over thirty-five years of professional experience in developing countries, twenty-eight of those in Angola during and after the conflict there. He has participated in several program evaluations and missions for the United Nations, European Union, and World Bank. Cain is the director of Development Workshop, which operates in Canada, France, and Angola, and he serves as the Canadian Honorary Consul to Angola, an officer of the Order of Canada, and a board member for several development institutions. He has lectured at universities in Angola, Canada, Norway, South Africa, the United Kingdom, and the United States. He has published numerous articles and is working on a forthcoming book titled *Planning with Vulnerable People in Turbulent Times*.

Alexandre Corriveau-Bourque holds a master's degree from McGill University's Department of Geography. His thesis research examines the intersections between land tenure systems in post-war Liberia and the impact these intersections have on perceptions of security. Corriveau-Bourque has recently published some of his findings on post-war land tenure systems in Lofa County, Liberia, with the Norwegian Refugee Council. His research interests include relations between the informal sector and the state; legal pluralism; food security; and disarmament, demobilization, and reintegration.

Samir Elhawary is a research fellow in the Humanitarian Policy Group at the Overseas Development Institute. He is currently researching the evolving role of humanitarian action in conflict-affected emergencies, with a particular focus on the interface between humanitarianism and politics. He also works on stabilization and the links between security and development. Previously his work focused on the role of natural resources in armed conflict, and he was engaged in various initiatives to promote conflict sensitivity in the extractive industry.

Arthur Green is a professional educator, researcher, and land tenure specialist with consulting experience in several countries in sub-Saharan Africa, Central America, and Southeast Asia. His consulting focuses on forestry, agricultural production, legal aspects of land reform, and participatory mapping. As a McGill

Major Fellow and a fellow of the United States–Indonesia Society, he is currently finishing a doctorate in geography at McGill University. His research areas include property rights, legal geography, post-war and post-disaster reconstruction, natural resource tenure, land policy administration and reform, participatory mapping, food security, and sustainable livelihoods in the context of change.

Ian D. Hannam is an adjunct associate professor at the Australian Centre for Agriculture and Law, University of New England, Australia. He is chair of the Specialist Group for Sustainable Use of Soils and Desertification at the International Union for Conservation of Nature's Commission on Environmental Law. Hannam acts as a specialist consultant on environmental law and policy reform for various agencies within the United Nations system. Over the past thirty years he worked in many countries, including China, the Czech Republic, Iceland, Kyrgyzstan, Mongolia, Serbia, Tajikistan, and Thailand. He is widely published in international journals and has written books and specialist articles on a number of environmental topics, including climate change, sustainable land use management, ecosystem management, and natural resource governance.

Naomi Hatsukano has been a research fellow in the Southeast Asian Studies Group II at the Area Studies Center of the Institute of Developing Economies in Japan since 2003. She studied in Phnom Penh as a visiting researcher at the Royal University of Law and Economics, Cambodia, from 2007 to 2009. Hatsukano holds a master's degree in international studies and a bachelor's degree in law from the University of Tokyo.

Paula Defensor Knack is one of the Philippines' leading experts on land management and policy. Previously she has served as assistant secretary for lands and legislative affairs in the Philippine Department of Environment and Natural Resources, legal specialist and head of national policy studies in the AusAID-World Bank Land Administration Management Project, chair of the panel of experts on Toxic and Hazardous Wastes in Former U.S. Military Bases under the Office of the President, chair of the National Gender and Development Focal Point System, head of the Legislative Liaison Systems under the Office of the President, advisor to the speaker of the House of Representatives, deputy chief of staff in the Senate, and legal and scientific advisor to the Philippine Permanent Representation to the Organization for Prohibition of Chemical Weapons at The Hague. Defensor Knack holds bachelor's degrees in social sciences and law from the University of the Philippines and a master's degree in sustainable resource management from the Technical University of Munich.

Barbara McCallin works as a housing, land, and property adviser at the Geneva-based Internal Displacement Monitoring Centre of the Norwegian Refugee Council. Her current research focuses on addressing housing, land, and property issues in informal land tenure contexts. She contributed to the interagency publication *Handbook on Housing and Property Restitution for Refugees and*

584   Land and post-conflict peacebuilding

Displaced Persons: Implementing the Pinheiro Principles. McCallin is currently cochair of the housing, land, and property subgroup of the Global Protection Cluster Working Group, and she recently coauthored the report "Whose Land Is This? Land Disputes and Forced Displacement in the Western Forest Area of Côte d'Ivoire." Previously she worked in Mali and Bosnia and Herzegovina for the Office of the United Nations High Commissioner for Refugees and the Organization for Security and Co-operation in Europe; there she played an active role in the carrying out of the Property Legislation Implementation Plan. She graduated from the Institut d'Études Politiques d'Aix-en-Provence, and she has a master's degree in public international law from the University of Aix-en-Provence.

Naori Miyazawa worked as the head of office with the United Nations Office for Project Services in Tokyo from 2004 to 2008. From 2001 to 2005, she worked with various institutions in Timor Leste, including international nongovernmental organizations, managing post-conflict reconstruction and recovery, development, and environmental projects. Her experiences in Timor-Leste include a lectureship at the national university in the field of environmental studies. Prior to her tenure in Timor-Leste, she researched environmental governance issues in East Asia with the Environment and Sustainable Development Programme of United Nations University; her research is published in several articles. Miyazawa holds a Ph.D. in international studies from the University of Tokyo, where she is currently a lecturer. She holds a master's degree in environment and development from the University of London.

Jennifer Brick Murtazashvili is an assistant professor at the Graduate School of Public and International Affairs at the University of Pittsburgh. She is finishing a book on village and customary governance in rural Afghanistan, for which she conducted interviews and focus groups in more than thirty Afghan villages across six provinces. She has also managed democracy assistance for the U.S. Agency for International Development in Uzbekistan and drafted legislative materials for the new Afghan parliament as a consultant for the United Nations Development Programme in Kabul. Murtazashvili has lived in various parts of Central Eurasia, primarily Uzbekistan and Afghanistan. She holds a Ph.D. in political science and a master's degree in agricultural and applied economics from the University of Wisconsin–Madison.

Yuri Oki holds a master's degree in international relations from the University of Tokyo. For her master's dissertation, titled "Seeing Ethnologic Attributes as a Conflict Prevention Lens," she conducted a survey on peacebuilding in Mindanao, Philippines. Oki's general interests lie in the dynamics of post-conflict development, conflict prevention, and peacebuilding. Her current focus is land tenure and land resource management under a comprehensive scheme of peacebuilding.

Sara Pantuliano is head of the Humanitarian Policy Group at the Overseas Development Institute. A political scientist with extensive experience in programming in conflict and post-conflict situations, she is currently focusing on underexplored dimensions of displacement, particularly the role of land in return and reintegration processes and in displacement in urban contexts. Prior to joining the Overseas Development Institute, she led the United Nations Development Programme's peacebuilding unit in Sudan, brokered and managed a high-profile post-conflict response in Sudan's Nuba Mountains, and was a resource person and observer at the Intergovernmental Authority on Development's Sudan peace process. Pantuliano holds a Ph.D. in politics and has lectured at the University of Dar es Salaam.

M. Y. Safar is an Afghan topographical and cadastral surveyor, land tenure specialist, and member of the Terra Institute. He has more than forty years of professional experience in the surveying, classification, clarification, registration, and administration of land. A former deputy of the Afghan Geodesy and Cartography Head Office and director of the Cadastral Department, Safar has worked in Afghanistan on health, water, and sanitation for various agencies, including the United Nations Children's Fund, the United Nations Human Settlements Programme, the U.S. Agency for International Development, the World Bank, the Asian Development Bank, and UK Children in Crisis. He has completed studies at Kandahar National Cadastral Survey Vocational School, the Survey Training Institute in Hyderabad, and Gadja Mada University in Indonesia, where he earned a certificate in remote sensing for land use mapping and planning.

Siraj Sait is reader and head of law research at the University of East London, where he coordinates the human rights and Islamic and Middle East studies programs. A graduate of Harvard Law School, the University of Madras, and the University of London, Sait is a former state prosecutor on human rights in India, has served as trustee of the Commonwealth Human Rights Initiative, and has been a consultant for Minority Rights Group International, the office of the United Nations High Commissioner for Refugees, and the United Nations Children's Fund. He recently worked with the United Nations Human Settlements Programme, supporting the launch of the Global Land Tool Network, which he currently serves as a member of its international advisory board. Sait is a member of the Centre on Human Rights in Conflict. His publications include *Land, Law and Islam: Property and Human Rights in the Muslim World* (with H. Lim, Zed Books, 2006) and *The Policy Makers Guide to Women's Land, Property, and Housing Rights* (United Nations Human Settlements Programme, 2006).

Akram Salam, who is from Kabul, has twenty-five years of experience working with Afghan and international nongovernmental organizations and with the United Nations as a community mobilizer, construction engineer, and coordinator and director of refugee camps in Pakistan and Afghanistan. The organizations he has worked with include Deutsche Gesellschaft für Technische Zusammenarbeit, Architectes Sans Frontières, the United Nations Human Settlements

586   Land and post-conflict peacebuilding

Programme, the U.S. Agency for International Development, the University of Nebraska–Omaha, the Academy for Education Development, and the Afghan Independent Human Rights Commission. Salam currently directs an Afghan nongovernmental organization called Cooperation for Reconstruction of Afghanistan. He has published a textbook under the title of *Steel Work* (Manpower Training Program, 1991). Salam holds a bachelor's degree in civil engineering from Kabul University and speaks Dari, Pashto, and Turkish in addition to English.

Salman M. A. Salman is an academic researcher and consultant on water law and policy. Until December 2009, he worked as lead counsel and water law adviser with the legal vice presidency of the World Bank. Before joining the World Bank, he was a legal officer with the United Nations International Fund for Agricultural Development. Prior to that, he was a lecturer at the Law School of the University of Khartoum in Sudan. Salman is the author, coauthor, or editor of ten books and has published over fifty articles and book chapters on various issues in water law and policy. Some of his books have been translated into and published in Arabic, Chinese, French, and Russian. Salman obtained his LL.B. from the University of Khartoum Law School and holds an LL.M. and a J.S.D. from Yale Law School.

Manami Sekiguchi graduated from the Department of International Studies in the Graduate School of Frontier Sciences at the University of Tokyo. Her interests lie in rural development in Cambodia, particularly the establishment of farmers' organizations such as agricultural cooperatives and water users' associations. She has also conducted research on land resource management in Cambodia, especially concerning how a dysfunctional landownership system affects land conflicts among people.

J. D. Stanfield is a land tenure specialist with over thirty-five years of experience in teaching and international development research, and has provided technical assistance relating to land issues through the Land Tenure Center at the University of Wisconsin–Madison and the Terra Institute. Stanfield has also provided technical assistance and conducted applied research relating to land tenure and land administration issues through programs funded by the Asian Development Bank, Inter-American Development Bank, World Bank, U.S. Agency for International Development, and United Nations Human Settlements Programme in over twenty countries, including Afghanistan, Albania, the Bahamas, Brazil, Chile, Nicaragua, the Republic of Georgia, and Trinidad and Tobago. He is president of the Terra Institute and codirector of its program for building linkages between communities and key stakeholder organizations for resolving land and other resource issues. Stanfield holds a Ph.D. in communication from Michigan State University and is senior scientist emeritus at the University of Wisconsin–Madison.

Dan E. Stigall is currently a trial attorney in the U.S. Department of Justice, Office of International Affairs, where he assists in formal cooperation efforts

Author biographies **587**

between the United States and countries throughout the Middle East, Africa, and Asia. He has also served as a military attorney in Europe and the Middle East and throughout the United States, and has held assignments as a special assistant U.S. attorney in both Kentucky and Virginia. Stigall holds an LL.M. with highest honors in international and comparative law from George Washington University School of Law and a J.D. and bachelor's degree from Louisiana State University. He is the author of a book titled *Counterterrorism and the Comparative Law of Investigative Detention* (Cambria, 2009) and of numerous law review articles on issues related to international and comparative law.

Jon Unruh is an associate professor in the Department of Geography at McGill University. Since the early 1990s, his research and policy work have focused on post-conflict land tenure in the developing world. His work focuses on conflict resolution, land law and policy, legal pluralism, approaches to reconciling customary and formal tenure systems, and agriculture in post-war and peacebuilding contexts. Unruh's research and policy experience includes work in Cameroon, Central America, Ethiopia, Liberia, Madagascar, Mozambique, Peru, Sierra Leone, Somalia, Timor-Leste, Uganda, Zambia, and Zanzibar. Unruh holds a bachelor's degree in environmental studies from the University of Kansas–Lawrence, a master's degree in environmental studies from the University of Wisconsin–Madison, and a doctorate in geography and rural development from the University of Arizona.

Peter Van der Auweraert is head of the Land, Property, and Reparations Division at the International Organization for Migration. He is engaged in a United Nations–sponsored peace mediation effort on land and property issues in Kirkuk, Iraq. Previously, Van der Auweraert was executive director of Avocats Sans Frontières, an international nongovernmental organization working on access-to-justice issues in post-conflict and transitional countries in Africa, the Middle East, and Southeast Asia. He has also held a visiting lectureship in international criminal and public law at the University of Turku in Finland. Van der Auweraert holds an LL.M. in international law from the University of London and a first degree in law from the University of Antwerp. He has published on transitional justice and post-conflict land and property issues in English, French, Spanish, and Dutch.

Rhodri C. Williams is a human rights consultant with expertise on forced displacement, land, and property rights issues. He has over ten years experience providing technical advice and analysis in numerous settings, including Bosnia, Cambodia, Colombia, Cyprus, Georgia, Liberia, Serbia, and Turkey. Williams has worked as a consultant for numerous international and nongovernmental organizations, including the Brookings Institution, the International Center for Transitional Justice, the Norwegian Refugee Council, the United Nations Development Programme, and the United Nations Human Settlements Programme. From 2000 to 2004 he worked in Bosnia and Herzegovina for the Organization for Security

588   Land and post-conflict peacebuilding

and Co-operation in Europe, coordinating legal policy and field monitoring of the post-war restitution process. Williams holds a master's degree in geography from Syracuse University and a J.D. from New York University, and he is a member of the New York State Bar. He has lectured, published, and commented widely on land and property issues in humanitarian, transitional justice, and development settings; some of his writings appear on his blog, TerraNullius, at http://terra0nullius.wordpress.com.

APPENDIX 3

Table of contents for
Post-Conflict Peacebuilding and Natural Resource Management

This book is one of a set of six edited books on post-conflict peacebuilding and natural resource management, all published by Earthscan. Following is the table of contents for the full set. Titles and authors are subject to change.

HIGH-VALUE NATURAL RESOURCES AND POST-CONFLICT PEACEBUILDING
Edited by Päivi Lujala and Siri Aas Rustad

Foreword
Ellen Johnson Sirleaf

High-value natural resources: A blessing or a curse for peace?
Päivi Lujala and Siri Aas Rustad

Part 1: Extraction and extractive industries

Introduction

Bankrupting peace spoilers: Can peacekeepers curtail belligerents' access to resource revenues?
Philippe Le Billon

Mitigating risks and realizing opportunities: Environmental and social standards for foreign direct investment in high-value natural resources
Jill Shankleman

Contract renegotiation and asset recovery in post-conflict settings
Philippe Le Billon

Reopening and developing mines in post-conflict settings: The challenge of company-community relations
Volker Boege and Daniel M. Franks

590   Land and post-conflict peacebuilding

Diamonds in war, diamonds for peace: Diamond sector management and
kimberlite mining in Sierra Leone
Kazumi Kawamoto

Assigned corporate social responsibility in a rentier state: The case of Angola
Arne Wiig and Ivar Kolstad

Part 2: Commodity and revenue tracking

Introduction

The Kimberley Process at ten: Reflections on a decade of efforts to end the
trade in conflict diamonds
J. Andrew Grant

The Kimberley Process Certification Scheme: A model negotiation?
Clive Wright

The Kimberley Process Certification Scheme: The primary safeguard for the
diamond industry
Andrew Bone

A more formal engagement: A constructive critique of certification as a means
of preventing conflict and building peace
Harrison Mitchell

Addressing the roots of Liberia's conflict through the Extractive Industries
Transparency Initiative
Eddie Rich and T. Negbalee Warner

Excluding illegal timber and improving forest governance: The European
Union's Forest Law Enforcement, Governance and Trade Initiative
Duncan Brack

Part 3: Revenue distribution

Introduction

Sharing natural resource wealth during war-to-peace transitions
Achim Wennmann

Horizontal inequality, decentralizing the distribution of natural resource
revenues, and peace
Michael L. Ross, Päivi Lujala, and Siri Aas Rustad

The Diamond Area Community Development Fund: Micropolitics and
community-led development in post-war Sierra Leone
Roy Maconachie

Direct distribution of natural resource revenues as a policy for peacebuilding
Martin E. Sandbu

Part 4: Allocation and institution building

Introduction

High-value natural resources, development, and conflict: Channels of causation
Paul Collier and Anke Hoeffler

Petroleum blues: The political economy of resources and conflict in Chad
John A. Gould and Matthew S. Winters

Leveraging high-value natural resources to restore the rule of law: The role of
the Liberia Forest Initiative in Liberia's transition to stability
Stephanie L. Altman, Sandra S. Nichols, and John T. Woods

Forest resources and peacebuilding: Preliminary lessons from Liberia and
Sierra Leone
Michael D. Beevers

An inescapable curse? Resource management, violent conflict, and peacebuilding in the Niger Delta
Annegret Mähler

The legal framework for managing oil in post-conflict Iraq: A pattern of abuse
and violence over natural resources
Mishkat Al Moumin

The capitalist civil peace: Some theory and empirical evidence
Indra de Soysa

Part 5: Livelihoods

Introduction

Counternarcotics efforts and Afghan poppy farmers: Finding the right approach
David M. Catarious Jr. and Alison Russell

The Janus nature of opium poppy: A view from the field
Adam Pain

Peace through sustainable forest management in Asia: The USAID Forest
Conflict Initiative
Jennifer Wallace and Ken Conca

Women in the artisanal and small-scale mining sector of the Democratic
Republic of the Congo
Karen Hayes and Rachel Perks

592 Land and post-conflict peacebuilding

Forest user groups and peacebuilding in Nepal
Tina Sanio and Binod Chapagain

Lurking beneath the surface: Oil, environmental degradation, and armed conflict in Sudan
Luke A. Patey

Part 6: Lessons learned

Building or spoiling peace? Lessons from the management of high-value natural resources
Siri Aas Rustad, Päivi Lujala, and Philippe Le Billon

LAND AND POST-CONFLICT PEACEBUILDING
Edited by Jon Unruh and Rhodri C. Williams

Foreword
Jeffrey D. Sachs

Land: A foundation for peacebuilding
Jon Unruh and Rhodri C. Williams

Part 1: Peace negotiations

Introduction

The Abyei territorial dispute between North and South Sudan: Why has its resolution proven difficult?
Salman M. A. Salman

Land tenure and peace negotiations in Mindanao, Philippines
Yuri Oki

Part 2: Response to displacement and dispossession

Introduction

The role of restitution in post-conflict situations
Barbara McCallin

Land issues in post-conflict return and recovery
Samir Elhawary and Sara Pantuliano

Return of land in post-conflict Rwanda: International standards, improvisation, and the role of international humanitarian organizations
John W. Bruce

Table of contents **593**

Post-conflict land tenure issues in Bosnia: Privatization and the politics of reintegrating the displaced
Rhodri C. Williams

Angola: Land resources and conflict
Allan Cain

Refugees and legal reform in Iraq: The Iraqi Civil Code, international standards for the treatment of displaced persons, and the art of attainable solutions
Dan E. Stigall

Part 3: Land management

Introduction

Snow leopards and cadastres: Rare sightings in post-conflict Afghanistan
Douglas E. Batson

Community documentation of land tenure and its contribution to state building in Afghanistan
J. D. Stanfield, Jennifer Brick Murtazashvili, M. Y. Safar, and Akram Salam

Title wave: Land tenure and peacebuilding in Aceh
Arthur Green

Beyond land redistribution: Lessons learned from El Salvador's unfulfilled agrarian revolution
Alexandre Corriveau-Bourque

Institutional aspects of resolving land disputes in post-conflict societies
Peter Van der Auweraert

Rebuilding peace: Land and water management in the Kurdistan Region of northern Iraq
Nesreen Barwari

Transboundary resource management strategies in the Pamir mountain region of Tajikistan
Ian D. Hannam

Part 4: Laws and policies

Introduction

Title through possession or position? Respect for housing, land, and property rights in Cambodia
Rhodri C. Williams

594 Land and post-conflict peacebuilding

Land conflicts and land registration in Cambodia
Manami Sekiguchi and Naomi Hatsukano

Legal frameworks and land issues in Muslim Mindanao
Paula Defensor Knack

Unexplored dimensions: Islamic land systems in Afghanistan, Indonesia, Iraq, and Somalia
Siraj Sait

Customary law and community-based natural resource management in post-conflict Timor-Leste
Naori Miyazawa

Part 5: Lessons learned

Lesson learned in land tenure and natural resource management in post-conflict societies
Jon Unruh and Rhodri C. Williams

WATER AND POST-CONFLICT PEACEBUILDING
Edited by Erika Weinthal, Jessica Troell, and Mikiyasu Nakayama

Foreword
Mikhail Gorbachev

Shoring up peace: Water and post-conflict peacebuilding
Jessica Troell and Erika Weinthal

Part 1: Basic services and human security

Introduction

The role of informal service providers in post-conflict reconstruction and state building
Jeremy Allouche

A tale of two cities: Restoring water services in Kabul and Monrovia
Jean-François Pinera and Robert A. Reed

Conflict and collaboration for water resources in Angola's post-war cities
Allan Cain and Martin Mulenga

Thirsty for peace: The water sector in South Sudan
Sam Huston

Table of contents 595

Community water management: Experiences from the Democratic Republic of the Congo, Afghanistan, and Liberia
Murray Burt and Bilha Joy Keiru

Environmental management of the Iraqi marshlands in the post-conflict period
Chizuru Aoki, Ali Al-Lami, and Sivapragasam Kugaprasatham

Part 2: Livelihoods

Introduction

Irrigation management and flood control in post–World War II Japan
Mikiko Sugiura, Yuka Toguchi, and Mona Funiciello

Refugee rehabilitation and transboundary cooperation: India, Pakistan, and the Indus River system
Neda A. Zawahri

Despite the best intentions? Experiences with water resource management in northern Afghanistan
Jennifer McCarthy and Daanish Mustafa

Water's role in measuring security and stabilization in Helmand Province, Afghanistan
Laura Jean Palmer-Moloney

Part 3: Peace processes, cooperation, and confidence building

Introduction

The Jordan River Basin: A conflict like no other
Munther J. Haddadin

Transboundary cooperation in the Lower Jordan River Basin
Munqeth Mehyar, Nader Khateeb, Gidon Bromberg, and Elizabeth Ya'ari

The Sava River: Transitioning to peace in the former Yugoslavia
Amar Čolakhodžić, Marija Filipović, Jana Kovandžić, and Stephen Stec

Transnational cooperation over shared water resources in the South Caucasus; Reflections on USAID interventions
Marina Vardanyan and Richard Volk

Water security and scarcity: Potential destabilization in western Afghanistan and Iranian Sistan and Baluchestan due to transboundary water conflicts
Alex Dehgan, Laura Jean Palmer-Moloney, and Medhi Mirazee

596 Land and post-conflict peacebuilding

Water resources in the Sudan North-South peace process and the ramifications
of the secession of South Sudan
Salman M. A. Salman

Part 4: Legal frameworks

Introduction

Management of waters in post-Dayton Bosnia and Herzegovina: Policy, legal,
and institutional aspects
Slavko Bogdanovic

The right to water and sanitation in post-conflict legal mechanisms: An
emerging regime?
Mara Tignino

Part 5: Lessons learned

Harnessing water management for more effective peacebuilding: Lessons learned
Jessica Troell and Erika Weinthal

LIVELIHOODS, NATURAL RESOURCES, AND POST-CONFLICT
PEACEBUILDING
Edited by Helen Young and Lisa Goldman

Foreword
Jan Egeland

Managing natural resources for livelihoods: Helping post-conflict
communities survive and thrive
Helen Young and Lisa Goldman

Part 1: Natural resource conflicts, livelihoods, and peacebuilding approaches

Introduction

Social identity, natural resources, and peacebuilding
Arthur Green

Swords into ploughshares? Access to natural resources and securing
agricultural livelihoods in rural Afghanistan
Alan Roe

Forest resources in Cambodia's transition to peace: Lessons for peacebuilding
Srey Chanthy and Jim Schweithelm

Post-tsunami Aceh: Successful peacemaking, uncertain peacebuilding
Michael Renner

Manufacturing peace in "no man's land": Livestock and access to natural resources in the Karimojong Cluster of Kenya and Uganda
Jeremy Lind

Resolving natural resource conflicts to help prevent war: A case from Afghanistan
Liz Alden Wily

Part 2: Innovative livelihoods approaches in post-conflict settings

Introduction

The opportunities and challenges of protected areas in post-conflict peacebuilding
Carol Westrik

A peace park in the Balkans: Cross-border cooperation and livelihood creation through coordinated environmental conservation
J. Todd Walters

Mountain gorilla ecotourism: Supporting macroeconomic growth and providing local livelihoods
Miko Maekawa, Annette Lanjouw, Eugène Rutagarama, and Douglas Sharp

The interface between natural resources and disarmament, demobilization, and reintegration: Enhancing human security in post-conflict settings
Glaucia Boyer and Adrienne Stork

From soldiers to park rangers: Post-conflict natural resource management in Gorongosa National Park
Matthew F. Pritchard

Mitigating conflict in Sierra Leone through mining reform and alternative livelihoods programs for youth
Andrew Keili and Bocar Thiam

Linking to peace: Using BioTrade for biodiversity conservation and peacebuilding in Colombia
Lorena Jaramillo Castro and Adrienne Marie Stork

Part 3: The institutional and policy context

Introduction

Fisheries policies and the problem of instituting sustainable management: The case of occupied Japan
Harry N. Scheiber and Benjamin Jones

Developing capacity for natural resource management in Afghanistan: Process, challenges, and lessons learned by UNEP
Belinda Bowling and Asif Zaidi

598   Land and post-conflict peacebuilding

Building resilience in rural livelihood systems as an investment in conflict prevention
Blake D. Ratner

Improving natural resource governance and building peace and stability in Mindanao, Philippines
Cynthia Brady, Oliver Agoncillo, Maria Zita Butardo-Toribio, Buenaventura Dolom, and Casimiro V. Olvida

Commerce in the chaos: Bananas, charcoal, fisheries, and conflict in Somalia
Christian Webersik and Alec Crawford

Part 4: Lessons learned

Managing natural resources for livelihoods in post-conflict societies: Lessons learned
Lisa Goldman and Helen Young

ASSESSING AND RESTORING NATURAL RESOURCES IN POST-CONFLICT PEACEBUILDING
Edited by David Jensen and Steve Lonergan

Foreword
Klaus Töpfer

Placing environment and natural resource risks, impacts, and opportunities on the post-conflict peacebuilding agenda
David Jensen and Steve Lonergan

Part 1: Post-conflict environmental assessments

Introduction

Evaluating the impact of UNEP's post-conflict environmental assessments
David Jensen

Environment and peacebuilding in war-torn societies: Lessons from the UN Environment Programme's experience with post-conflict assessment
Ken Conca and Jennifer Wallace

Medical and environmental intelligence in peace and crisis-management operations
Birgitta Liljedahl, Annica Waleij, Björn Sandström, and Louise Simonsson

Thinking back-end: Improving post-conflict analysis through consulting, adapting to change, and scenario building
Alexander Carius and Achim Maas

Part 2: Remediation of environmental hot spots

Introduction

Salting the Earth: Environmental health challenges in post-conflict reconstruction
Chad Briggs and Inka Weissbecker

Remediation of polluted sites in the Balkans, Iraq, and Sierra Leone
Muralee Thummarukudy, Oli Brown, and Hannah Moosa

The risks of depleted uranium contamination in post-conflict countries:
Findings and lessons learned from UNEP field assessments
Mario Burger

Linking demining to post-conflict peacebuilding: A case study of Cambodia
Nao Shimoyachi-Yuzawa

Part 3: Restoration of natural resources and ecosystems

Introduction

Restoration of damaged land in societies recovering from conflict: The case of
Lebanon
Aïda Tamer-Chammas

Ecological restoration and peacebuilding: The case of the Iraqi marshes
Steve Lonergan

Haiti: Lessons learned and way forward in natural resource management projects
Lucile Gingembre

Peacebuilding and adaptation to climate change
Richard Matthew and Anne Hammill

Part 4: Environmental dimensions of infrastructure and reconstruction

Introduction

Addressing infrastructure needs in post-conflict reconstruction:
An introduction to alternative planning approaches
P. B. Anand

Mitigating the environmental impacts of post-conflict assistance: Assessing
USAID's approach
Charles Kelly

Challenges and opportunities for mainstreaming environmental assessment
tools in post-conflict settings
George Bouma

600   Land and post-conflict peacebuilding

Environmental assessment as a tool for peacebuilding and development: Initial lessons from capacity building in Sierra Leone
Oli Brown, Morgan Hauptfleisch, Haddijatou Jallow, and Peter Tarr

Natural resources, post-conflict reconstruction, and regional integration: Lessons from the Marshall Plan and other reconstruction efforts
Carl Bruch, Ross Wolfarth, and Vladislav Michalcik

Making best use of domestic energy sources: The Priority Production System for coal mining and steel production in post–World War II Japan
Mikiyasu Nakayama

Road infrastructure reconstruction as a peacebuilding priority in Afghanistan: Negative implications for land rights
Jon Unruh and Mourad Shalaby

Evaluating post-conflict assistance
Suppiramaniam Nanthikesan and Juha I. Uitto

Part 5: Lessons learned

Natural resources and post-conflict assessment, remediation, restoration, and reconstruction: Lessons and emerging issues
David Jensen and Steve Lonergan

GOVERNANCE, NATURAL RESOURCES, AND POST-CONFLICT PEACEBUILDING
Edited by Carl Bruch, Carroll Muffett, and Sandra S. Nichols

Foreword
Óscar Arias Sánchez

Natural resources and post-conflict governance: Building a sustainable peace
Carl Bruch, Carroll Muffett, and Sandra S. Nichols

Part 1: Frameworks for peace

Introduction

Reducing the risk of conflict recurrence: The relevance of natural resource management
Christian Webersik and Marc Levy

Stepping stones to peace? Natural resource provisions in peace agreements
Simon J. A. Mason, Damiano A. Sguaitamatti, and Pilar Ramirez Gröbli

Considerations for determining when to include natural resources in peace agreements ending internal armed conflicts
Marcia A. Dawes

Table of contents **601**

Peacebuilding through natural resource management: The UN Peacebuilding Commission's first five years
Matti Lehtonen

Preparing for peace: A case study of Darfur, Sudan
Margie Buchanan-Smith and Brendan Bromwich

Part 2: Peacekeepers, the military, and natural resources

Introduction

Environmental experiences and developments in United Nations peacekeeping operations
Sophie Ravier, Anne-Cécile Vialle, Russ Doran, and John Stokes

Crime, credibility, and effective peacekeeping: Lessons from the field
Annica Waleij

Environmental stewardship in peace operations: The role of the military
Annica Waleij, Timothy Bosetti, Russ Doran, and Birgitta Liljedahl

Taking the gun out of extraction: UN responses to the role of natural resources in conflicts
Mark B. Taylor and Mike Davis

Military-to-military cooperation on the environment and natural disasters: Engagement for peacebuilding
Geoffrey D. Dabelko and Will Rogers

Civil-military coordination and cooperation in peacebuilding and natural resource management: An enabling framework, challenges, and incremental progress
Melanne A. Civic

Part 3: Good governance

Introduction

Burma's ceasefire regime: Two decades of unaccountable natural resource exploitation
Kirk Talbott, Yuki Akimoto, and Katrina Cuskelly

Taming predatory elites in the Democratic Republic of the Congo: Regulation of property rights to adjust incentives and improve economic performance in the mining sector
Nicholas Garrett

Process and substance: Environmental law in post-conflict peacebuilding
Sandra S. Nichols and Mishkat Al Moumin

602   Land and post-conflict peacebuilding

Post-conflict environmental governance: Lessons from Rwanda
Roy Brooke and Richard Matthew

Corruption and natural resources in post-conflict transition
Christine Cheng and Dominik Zaum

Stopping the plunder of natural resources to provide for a sustainable peace in
Côte d'Ivoire
Michel Yoboue

Sartor resartus: Liberian concession reviews and the prospects for effective
internationalized solutions
K. W. James Rochow

Social benefits in the Liberian forestry sector: An experiment in post-conflict
institution building for resilience
John Waugh and James Murombedzi

Preventing violent conflict over natural resources: Lessons from an early
action fund
Juan Dumas

Part 4: Local institutions and marginalized populations

Introduction

Legal pluralism in post-conflict environments: Problem or opportunity for
natural resource management?
Ruth Meinzen-Dick and Rajendra Pradhan

The role of conservation in promoting sustainability and security in at-risk
communities
Peter Zahler, David Wilkie, Michael Painter, and J. Carter Ingram

Integrating gender into post-conflict natural resource management
Njeri Karuru and Louise H. Yeung

Indigenous peoples, natural resources, and peacebuilding in Colombia
Juan Mayr Maldonado and Luisz Olmedo Martínez

Part 5: Transitional justice and accountability

Introduction

Building momentum and constituencies for peace: The role of natural
resources in transitional justice and peacebuilding
Emily E. Harwell

Peace through justice: International tribunals and accountability for wartime environmental wrongs
Anne-Cecile Vialle, Carl Bruch, Reinhold Gallmetzer, and Akiva Fishman

Legal liability for environmental damage: The United Nations Compensation Commission and the 1990–1991 Gulf War
Cymie Payne

Reflections on the United Nations Compensation Commission experience
Lalanath de Silva

Part 6: Confidence building

Introduction

Environmental governance and peacebuilding in post-conflict Central America: Lessons from the Central American Commission for Environment and Development
Matthew Wilburn King, Marco Antonio González Pastora, Mauricio Castro Salazar, and Carlos Manuel Rodriguez

Promoting transboundary environmental cooperation in Central Asia: The Environment and Security Initiative in Kazakhstan and Kyrgyzstan
Saba Nordström

The Perú and Ecuador peace park: One decade after the peace settlement
Yolanda Kakabadse, Jorge Caillaux, and Juan Dumas

Transboundary collaboration in the Greater Virunga Landscape: From gorilla conservation to conflict-sensitive transboundary landscape management
Johannes Refisch and Johann Jenson

Part 7: Integration of natural resources into other post-conflict priorities

Introduction

Consolidating peace through the "Aceh Green" strategy
Sadaf Lakhani

Natural resource management and post-conflict settings: Programmatic evolution in a humanitarian and development agency
Jim Jarvie

Mainstreaming natural resources into post-conflict humanitarian and development action
Judy Oglethorpe, Anita Van Breda, Leah Kintner, Shubash Lohani, and Owen Williams

604   Land and post-conflict peacebuilding

Using economic evaluation to integrate natural resource management into Rwanda's post-conflict poverty reduction strategy paper
Louise Wrist Sorensen

Mitigating natural resource conflicts through development projects: Lessons from World Bank experience in Nigeria
Sandra Ruckstuhl

Natural resources and peacebuilding: What role for the private sector?
Diana Klein and Ulrike Joras

Part 8: Lessons learned

Fueling conflict or facilitating peace: Lessons in post-conflict governance and natural resource management
Sandra S. Nichols, Carroll Muffett, and Carl Bruch

Index

NOTE: Page numbers with *f* indicate figures; those with *t* indicate tables.

Abd al-Razzāq al-Sanhūrī, 210, 486
Abu Sayyaf, 76x
Abyei Boundaries Commission (ABC), 25
  mandate and process, 35, 40–42
  membership, 34, 56
  report, 35–41, 44*f*, 55–56
Abyei territorial dispute (Sudan/South
    Sudan), 23, 25–65, 541n7
  Abyei Addis Ababa Agreement, 59–62
  Abyei Agreement, 49–51, 56
  Abyei Boundaries Commission (ABC)
    Report, 25, 34–41, 44*f*, 55–56
  Abyei Joint Oversight Committee
    (AJOC), 59–60
  Abyei Protocol, 25, 29, 30–34, 52, 56,
    58, 61
  Addis Ababa Agreement, 27–28, 30,
    33n18
  boundary disputes, 25, 26, 30–35
  clashes and military operations, 38,
    48–50, 52–54
  Interim Security Force for Abyei
    (ISFA), 59–61
  international actors, 25
  Joint Military Observer Committee
    (JMOC), 59
  Kadugli agreements, 48–50, 55
  map, 27
  oil revenues, 33–34, 39, 42
  Pastoralist Migration agreement, 60
  PCA arbitration tribunal award, 39–45,
    55–56

  referendum on status, 33–34, 45–48,
    56–57
  residence criteria, 46–48, 52, 56–57
  return of refugees, 60
  timeline, 62–65
  traditional rights, 41–45, 56–58, 60
  UN Interim Security Force for Abyei
    (UNISFA), 61
  UN Mission in Sudan (UNMIS), 38,
    49, 52–54
  See also South Sudan; Sudan
Aceh (Indonesia), 242, 293–316
  Aceh Monitoring Mission (AMM), 306
  capacity building, 560
  community welfare endowments
    (*waqf*), 482–484, 490, 500, 502
  customary property rights (*adat*),
    297–301, 494–495, 538, 549
  dispute resolution, 494–497
  formal land rights, 297–300, 302–303
  GAM reintegration goals, 306–307,
    309, 312, 313–314
  Helsinki Memorandum of
    Understanding, 296–297, 306,
    307–309
  Indian Ocean tsunami of 2004, 242,
    293, 296, 302–303, 312, 484
  Islamic law, 299, 478, 482–484, 490,
    491
  Law on the Governing of Aceh of
    2006, 308–309, 483
  legal pluralism, 298–301

606 Index

map, 295
promotion of good governance,
  314–315
Reconstruction of Aceh Land
  Administration System (RALAS),
  242, 293–294, 304–305, 307,
  309–316
secessionist conflict, 293, 294–297, 302
state-led cadastre systems, 301–305
syariah court system, 496–497
tenure security, 293–294, 297–305,
  307–309
womens property rights, 499
acquisitive possession, 538
ADAMAP process, 242
  Afghanistan, 281–286, 289
  definition, 242n1
adverse possession, 538
Afghanistan, 8, 245–262, 287, 535
  ADAMAP process, 281–286, 289
  Afghan Civil Code, 482
  Afghan Family Law Code of 1977, 492
  agricultural land, 269, 270, 272, 276,
    279, 551
  Amlak Survey, 271, 286, 288, 290
  Band-E-Amir National Park, 257–258
  Cadastral Survey, 268–269, 271–272,
    288f, 289
  cadastre system, 241, 246, 248,
    257–262, 558
  capacity building, 265, 266, 287
  community-based land administration,
    241–242, 246, 248, 251–256,
    265–290, 567
  community development councils
    (CDCs), 277, 280–281
  customary documentary evidence,
    558–559
  customary governance, 245–246,
    273–277, 495
  customary land rights, 248, 250–251,
    266–269, 494–497
  dispute resolution programs, 255–256,
    494, 495–496, 551
  environmental degradation, 249–250,
    256–257
  formal legal system, 267–269, 272–273,
    286–289, 458, 482, 492

illiteracy rates, 268n1
Information, Counseling, and Legal
  Assistance (ICLA) program, 255–256
insurgency, 7, 10, 245
Islamic law, 408–409, 476, 478,
  480–482, 490–493
land grabbing, 12–13, 254
Land Management Law of 2000,
  480–482, 490
Land Titling and Economic Restructuring
  in Afghanistan (LTERA) program,
  252–255
legal pluralism, 541, 542
loya jirga, 495
makhzan rehabilitation program, 254–255
map, 15, 247, 267
mapping projects, 251–252
Multi-ministerial Land Policy, 284–285
National Development Strategy, 285
National Solidarity Program, 289
NCR ICLA restitution project, 111
pastoralist communities, 269–270, 276,
  278–279
Policy and Strategy for the Forestry and
  Range Management Sub-Sectors, 284
population explosion, 249, 256–257
redistribution of barren (*mawat*) lands,
  480–482, 490, 500, 502
refugee and IDP returns, 117, 248–249,
  395
Ring Road, 13
Rural Land Administration Project
  (RLAP), 251–252, 277–281,
  284–290
secular norms, 492
state-community links, 287–289
state property, 482
tenure security, 250–254, 268
womens property rights, 499–500, 561
African Commission on Human and
  Peoples Rights, 113
African Union
  Convention for the Protection and
    Assistance of Internally Displaced
    Persons, 106–107
  Great Lakes Pact of 2006, 95, 106,
    108, 113
  Peace and Security Council, 53

Index 607

African Union High-Level
  Implementation Panel on Sudan
  (AUHIP), 48n43, 51, 59, 60–61
agriculture, 1, 3, 535–536
  agrarian-based uprisings, 325–326, 328
  dispute resolution, 550–551
  FAO recommendations on plot size, 122
  food insecurity, 14, 550n13
  landscape-based evidence, 557–558
  large-scale/commercial agriculture, 1,
    13, 323–328, 348–349, 352, 536,
    550–551
  pastoralist communities, 269–270, 276,
    278–279, 551
  redistribution of barren (*mawat*) lands,
    480–482, 490, 500, 502
  subsistence farming, 1, 323, 325–328,
    338, 411, 421, 424–425, 551
  swidden farming systems, 431
  Timor-Leste, 518–519
Alden Wily, Liz, 278, 279, 287
Alexander, Jocelyn, 10
Allan, Nigel, 249
Allen, C. K., 513
alternative local regimes, 10
alternative tenure approaches, 2, 10
Alusala, Nelson, 131
ancestral domain lands, 73–87, 462–469
Angola, 15, 171–203, 538, 540
  capacity building, 201, 559
  civil war of 1975–2002, 171, 187, 189,
    198–199
  Cold War, 187
  colonial policies, 180–186
  contract labor laws, 180–182
  customary land rights, 178–180, 184
  evidentiary documents, 557, 559
  extractive industries, 171
  independence war, 171, 184–186
  Institute for the Social Reintegration of
    Ex-Combatants, 194n9, 196–197
  internal displacement, 187, 189–193
  land allocation reforms, 11–12, 96–97,
    187–188, 197–198, 200–202
  Land Law of 1992, 187–188, 197
  Land Law of 2004, 97, 197–198, 200
  landmines, 13, 189, 199
  map, 15, 179

natural resource management, 202
  Norms on Resettlement of Displaced
    Populations, 194
  occupation in good faith of peri-urban
    land, 189–193, 197–198, 200,
    201–202
  post-conflict resettlement programs,
    193–197, 538
  restitution, 555
  Revolt of Catete, 182
  slave trade, 180–181
  state lands, 186–187
Aquino, Benigno, III, 84n, 469–470
Aquino, Corazon, 73, 75–76, 460
Arabi, Oussama, 218
Arroyo, Gloria Macapagal, 72, 80, 81n,
  85, 464, 468
Arusha Peace Accords, 96, 124–125, 128,
  140–142
  on new villages, 129–131
  UN Assistance Mission for Rwanda, 132
Ashdown, Paddy, 163
Asian Development Bank, 420, 428, 447
assets, 4
Association for Cooperative Operations
  Research and Development
  (ACORD), 130–131, 135
Association of Southeast Asian Nations
  (ASEAN), 414
Augustinas, Clarissa, 257–258
Autonomous Region in Muslim Mindanao
  (ARMM), 72, 74–76, 82–84, 408
  Abbu Sayyaff faction, 462
  Bangsamoro Juridical Entity, 408, 452,
    461, 464–465, 470
  expansion proposals, 465–466, 470
  identification of indigenous people,
    465–466
  legal framework, 451–471
  map, 453
  Memorandum of Agreement
    (MOA-AD), 72–73, 80–82, 84–85,
    452, 464–469
  natural resources, 467–469
  Organic Act, 72, 74, 461, 466, 467, 469
  secessionist movement, 452–455,
    459–462
autonomy (definition), 470

608 Index

Bali, Ash, 215
the Balkans. *See* Bosnia and Herzegovina
Bangsamoro Juridical Entity (BJE), 408,
452, 461, 464–465, 470
Ban Ki-Moon, x
Barry, Michael, 257–258
Barwari, Nesreen, 243, 555, 569
Basic Principles and Guidelines on the
Right to a Remedy and Reparations
for Victims (UNGA), 101–102
Bates, John C., 457
Batson, Douglas E., 241, 569
Behdad, Sohrab, 481
Bender, Gerald J., 182
Berhanu, Kassahun, 35n21
Bernas, Joaquin, 467
Bosnia and Herzegovina, 96, 145–171
capitalism, 154
civil war of 1992–1995, 147–149
Commission for Real Property Claims
of Displaced Persons and Refugees,
346–347
compensation programs, 103
customary land rights, 149–152, 168
Dayton Peace Accords, 96, 148–149,
154
dispossession of land and property, 15,
147–148
economic development, 163–164
ethnic cleansing and segregation,
147–148, 155–156, 158–161, 552
ethnic groups, 146, 147*f*, 158*f*
European integration, 152–153,
163–168
high-value natural resource extraction,
148
international actors, 167–171, 539
land management agreements, 2
landmines, 148, 155, 166
land use, 150*f*
Laws on Construction Land, 164–165
map, 15, 146
Property Law Implementation Plan,
156–157, 163–164
Reconstruction and Return Task Force
(RRTF), 155–157, 161
resettlement, 149, 153, 155–168,
170–171

restitution, 3, 99, 101n2, 102,
112–113, 148–149, 153,
155–158, 163, 165, 170,
540, 547n12, 559
return, 153–157, 160–167
socialist legacy, 145, 146, 148,
151–152, 164
tradition of tolerance, 167
urbanization, 155, 168–169, 171
Bourgois, Philippe, 338
Bowen, John, 496
Bremer, Jennifer, 483
Browning, David, 328n
Bruce, John W., 96, 569–570
Burgess, Ernest W., 513
Burundi
dispute resolution, 347, 546
land scarcity, 357
map, 15
National Commission for Land and
Other Properties, 347, 546
NCR ICLA restitution project, 111
Rwandan refugees, 136
Bush, George H. W., 332n

cadastre systems
Aceh (Indonesia), 301–305
Afghanistan, 241, 246, 257–262, 288
Cambodia, 422, 441, 445–447
See also land records
Cain, Allan, 11–12, 96–97, 538, 540,
555, 559, 570
Cambodia, 407, 411–434, 437–448
Cambodian People's Party (CPP),
413–414, 418–419
civil conflict, 417–419, 438, 447
commercial land development schemes,
13, 439
corruption and patronage-based power,
412–423, 432–433
Council of Land Policies, 444–445
customary land rights, 408, 417,
438–439, 441–443, 447–448, 543
deforestation, 430
dispute resolution, 422, 445–447
economic land concessions, 439–340
forced evictions and relocations, 412,
415–417, 421–423, 425–429, 433

Index 609

housing, land, and property (HLP) rights, 407, 411–434
  human rights, 414, 415
  inadvertent squatters, 424n
  indigenous population, 411, 420, 423–424, 431–432, 442–443, 444
  international actors, 414–417, 419, 420, 428–429, 432–434, 444–445, 447–448
  international treaty obligations, 414, 415, 426
  Khmer Rouge, 412, 413, 417, 430, 438
  land and property reforms, 101n2, 102, 417–419, 559
  land grabbing, 418, 419, 421, 424–425
  Land Law of 1992, 438, 442, 443, 447, 448
  Land Law of 2001, 407, 408, 416, 419–433, 438, 442–444, 447, 448, 543
  landlessness, 411, 418–419, 429–431
  Land Management and Administration Project (LMAP), 423–424, 430, 444–445
  land registration and titling, 423–425, 432–434, 437–448
  map, 15, 413, 439
  market economy, 432
  Millennium Development Goals, 419
  National Authority for Land Dispute Resolution, 422, 445–446
  National Housing Policy, 426
  Paris Peace Agreements of 1991, 418–419, 447
  Peoples Republic of Kampuchea (PRK), 417, 438, 440
  restitution, 101n2, 102
  social land concessions, 421–422, 423, 429–430, 432, 442–443
  swidden farming systems, 431
  urban migration, 411, 425, 432
  women and female-led households, 430, 561
Cambodian Center for Human Rights, 411
Cammack, Mark, 493
Cao, Diogo, 180

capacity building, 11, 118, 241, 559–560, 562, 565*t*
CARE International, 135
Carson, Rachel, 246
Castillo, Graciana del, 334n17, 335
Centre on Housing Rights and Evictions, 107
coal, 78, 79–80
coalbed methane, 79–80
coffee production, 324–325
collective land rights, 110, 476–477, 487–490, 500, 502
  See also customary land rights
Colombia, 536
  dispute resolution, 347, 352
  land grabbing, 112
  National Land Restitution Plan, 107
  Victims Law, 352
commercial agriculture. *See* large-scale/ commercial agriculture
Commission for Real Property Claims of Displaced Persons and Refugees, 346–347
the commons, 513
  See also customary land rights
Communication for Behavioral Impact (COMBI), 376
community development councils (CDCs), 277n10, 280–281
community land, xiv
  See also customary land rights
Community of Indigenous People of Rwanda (CAURWA), 135
community participation. *See* participatory approaches
compensation, 112
  development-induced displacement, 106
  displacement and dispossession, 103, 118
conflict minerals, 88
  See also mineral resources
conflict relapse, 2, 7
consultative participation, 380
Continental civil law tradition, 210, 217–219, 230–233
  duress, 230–231
  lésion, 231–232
  negotiorum gestio, 232–233

610 Index

Convention for the Protection and Assistance of Internally Displaced Persons (Kampala Convention), 106–107
Convention on Biological Diversity, 398–399
Convention to Combat Desertification, 399–400
Cooperation for the Reconstruction of Afghanistan (CRA), 253
coordination of interventions, 562–567
copper, 78, 79, 80, 88
Corriveau-Bourque, Alexandre, 242, 555, 570
corruption, 4, 9, 13n, 201
  Aceh (Indonesia), 303, 311, 314, 484
  Afghanistan, 254, 255, 482
  Bosnia and Herzegovina, 163
  Cambodia, 412–423, 432–433, 437, 446
  Mindanao (Philippines), 24, 83, 85, 87, 88
  Somalia, 487
  transparency, 201, 254
  Transparency International Corruption Perceptions Index, 297
Côte d'Ivoire, 108–109, 111, 347
Council of Europe, 105
Croatia, 105
crude oil. *See* oil and gas
Cruz, Isagani, 463
customary evidence, 556–559
customary land rights, 1–2, 11, 15, 347, 369, 395, 409
  Aceh (Indonesia), 494–495, 538, 549
  Afghanistan, 248, 494–496
  Angola, 178–180, 184
  Bosnia and Herzegovina, 149–152, 168
  Cambodia, 408, 417, 438–439, 442–443, 447–448, 543
  collective land, 110, 476–477, 487–490, 500, 502
  definition, 513
  dispute resolution, 255–256, 347, 494–497, 501, 547–551
  El Salvador, 323–324
  Iraq and Kurdistan, 369, 549
  Islamic law, 491–493

landscape-based evidence, 557–558
leadership, 528–529
legal ambiguity, 537–540
legal pluralism, 108–109, 115n1, 408, 541–545
Mindanao (Philippines), 73–87, 458, 459, 462–469
Ngok Dinka tribe, 36–38, 40–42, 57–58
possessory rights, 108n11, 109–110
regularization of, 526–529
restitution programs, 104, 106, 108–111
Rwanda, 122
Somalia, 493, 494–495
symbolically significant land, 10, 349, 351, 360
Timor-Leste, 511, 518–530, 543, 544, 556–557
  See also Islamic law
customary law (*tara bandu* of Timor-Leste), 409, 511, 519–530, 543, 544, 556–557
  See also customary evidence; customary land rights; legal pluralism
Cyprus, 105, 349

Dahlman, Carl, 162
D'Andrea, Claudia, 527
Danforth, John, 30–31
Darfur, 3, 9–10, 115, 535, 551
Dayton Peace Accords, 96, 148–149, 154, 347n4
Defensor Knack, Paula, 24, 408, 571
defining boundaries (definition), 31n13
deforestation, 430, 515–516, 518, 519
delimiting boundaries (definition), 31n13
Demante, Antoine Marie, 231
Democratic Republic of the Congo (DRC), 115, 136, 349
De Schutter, Olivier, 13
de Soto, Hernando, 301, 311
Deutsch, Robert, 313
developmental Islam, 479–480, 489–490, 491
development-induced displacement, 106

Index   611

Development Workshop Angola, 193, 195, 197, 198–199, 201–202

disarmament, demobilization, and reintegration (DDR), 2–3, 4, 116, 118–119, 544, 561–562
Aceh (Indonesia), 293, 295, 302–309, 313–314, 315, 560
Angola, 193–197
El Salvador, 333, 335, 338, 562
Mindanao (Philippines), 85
Tajikistan, 395

Diskin, Martin, 327n10

displacement and dispossession, xiv, 3, 8–9, 14–15, 95–97, 371–373, 536, 552
Angola, 187, 189–193
Bosnia and Herzegovina, 15, 147–148
choice of destination, 170–171
compensation, 103, 106, 112, 118, 170
ethnic cleansing, 5, 103, 147–148, 155–156, 158–161, 552
forced evictions, 412, 415–417, 421–423, 425–429, 433
integrated approaches, 97, 112, 117–119
internally displaced persons (IDPs), xiv, 3, 8–9, 14–15, 45, 433, 536, 540, 553
international refugee law, 95
Iraq, 3, 15, 97, 209, 213–214, 234–235
Kurdistan (Iraq), 366–367, 369–373
Pinheiro Principles, 95–97, 100, 102–119, 206–211, 216, 345n2, 409, 552
reintegration challenges, 95–96
resettlement, 103
return/repatriation, 101, 103, 107, 116–117
Rwanda, 15, 115
UN Guiding Principles on Internal Displacement, 95, 97, 105, 206–211, 216, 433
See also restitution

Displacement Solutions, 107

dispute resolution, 345–361, 545–551, 562, 564*t*
ad hoc commissions and tribunals, 346–347, 352, 547–549

Communication for Behavioral Impact (COMBI) approach, 376
competing visions of development, 349–350
customary mechanisms, 255–256, 347, 494–497, 501, 547–551
inclusive decision-making processes, 351, 551
local input, 351
multidisciplinary teams, 354
multi-institutional approaches, 347
Pinheiro Principles, 348, 350, 558
political alignment, 355
political assessment tools, 353–354
political engagement, 347–352, 354–356
power of landholders, 348–349, 352
practicability, 356–360, 548–549
process flow maps, 358–360
statutory system, 347, 352, 546–551
structural inequalities, 350
supporting institutions, 357–358, 359*f*
symbolically significant land, 349
See also legal frameworks; restitution

Doyle, Cathy, 87

Drexler, Elizabeth F., 296

Dupuy, Pierre-Marie, 40n29

duress, 230–231

Durham, W. H., 327

East Timor. *See* Timor-Leste

ecosystem services, xiv

El Fadl, Khaled Abou, 217–219, 231

Elhawary, Samir, 95–96, 552–553, 558, 570

El Salvador, 3, 7, 321–340
agrarian-based uprisings, 325–326, 328
Chapultepec Peace Accords of 1992, 7, 242, 321, 332–335, 339, 544
civil war, 331–333
coffee and commercial agriculture, 323–325, 327n11
customary land rights, 323–324
democratic space, 321
Farabundo Martí National Liberation Front (FMLN), 242, 321, 331–336, 338–339, 562
income inequality, 337–338, 339–340

612 Index

land dispossession, 325, 326–328
land redistribution, 242, 321–323, 326,
328–331, 338, 562
Land Transfer Program (PTT), 322,
323, 335–340, 562
map, 15, 323
physical land scarcity, 322
restitution, 101n2, 555
Salvadoran Institute of Agrarian
Transformation (ISTA), 330–331
structural land scarcity, 322–323
subsistence farming, 323, 325–328,
338
tenedores' land occupations, 333–336
UN peacekeeping, 339
urban migration, 337
U.S. aid, 328n, 332, 337
violence, 321–322, 338
Emerging Markets Group, 252, 253
Enders, David, 209
Enemark, Stig, 262
environmental treaties, 398–400
See also Convention on Biological
Diversity; Convention to Combat
Desertification; Framework
Convention on Climate Change;
Framework Convention on
Environment Protection for
Sustainable Development in Central
Asia
epistemic democracy, 216
Eritrea, 101n2
Esmail Kiram, Sultan of Sulu, 461
Estrada, Joseph, 462
Ethiopia, 101n2, 544, 568
ethnic cleansing, 5, 552
Bosnia and Herzegovina, 147–148,
155–156, 158–161, 552
compensation, 103
ethnic identity, 9–10
European Commission, 135
European Convention on Human Rights,
105
European Stability Initiative (ESI), 162
evidentiary documents, 556–559
land records, 379–380
versus landscape-based evidence,
557–558

title and registration documents, xiv,
242, 252–255, 411, 423–425,
432–434, 437–448, 558–559
extractive resources. *See* mineral
resources; oil and gas

Farabundo Martí National Liberation
Front (FMLN), 242, 321, 331–336,
338–339, 562
See also El Salvador
Federation of Bosnia and Herzegovina,
148, 159–161
See also Bosnia and Herzegovina
Foley, Conor, 247, 255–256
Food and Agriculture Organization
(FAO), 122, 132, 170
food insecurity, 14, 550n13
forced eviction and relocation. *See*
displacement and dispossession
Foreign Claims Act (FCA), 223–224,
227
forests. *See* timber
formal land rights (definition), 2n1
forum shopping, 542, 545
Framework Convention on Climate
Change, 399
Framework Convention on Environment
Protection for Sustainable
Development in Central Asia, 400
Free Aceh Movement (GAM),
294–297, 302, 306–307, 309,
312, 313–314
freehold model, xiii
French Civil Code. *See* Continental civil
law tradition

Garang, John, 36
gender considerations, 540
Aceh (Indonesia), 304, 310–311, 316,
499
Afghanistan, 274n8, 499–500, 561
Angola, 196
Cambodia, 430, 561
housing, land, and property (HLP)
rights, 430
Islamic land and property law,
497–500
land access studies, 135

Index   613

landlessness, 103, 430
property rights, 499–500, 561
restitution, 103, 106, 350n, 560–561
Somalia, 499–500
South Sudan, 561
water resources, 373–374
women and female-led households,
430, 497–500, 501
Georgia, 105
geothermal power, 78
Ghai, Yash, 416
Global Environment Facility, 243–244,
392
Global Protection Cluster, 345n3
gold, 78, 79, 80, 88
González-Vega, Claudio, 337–338
Gould, Jeffrey L., 324
governance, 9–12
alternative local regimes, 10
capacity building, 11, 118, 241,
559–560, 562, 565t
corruption, 13n, 81, 85, 88, 297,
412–423, 432–433
land law reform, 11–12, 117–119, 562,
565t
See also customary land rights; land
management; legal frameworks; legal
pluralism
Gration, Scott, 48n42
Great Lakes Pact of 2006, 95, 106,
108–109, 113
Green, Arthur, 242, 538, 556, 570–571
Griffiths, John, 544
Guatemala, 8–9, 101n2, 242
Gutto, Shadrack, 35n21

Habitat Agenda, 198
Hafner, Gerhard, 40n29
Hajabakiga, Patricia, 129
Hamoudi, Haider Ala, 215
Hannam, Ian D., 243–244, 556, 571
Hardin, Garrett, 511
Hare-Hawes-Cutting Act, 458
Hatsukano, Naomi, 408, 543, 571
Heathershaw, John, 387
Hoover, Herbert, 458
Hopkins, Jeffrey, 337
Hotaky, Abdul Rahman, 250

housing, land, and property (HLP) rights,
99, 104–108, 117, 536, 552
Cambodia. *See* Cambodia
evidentiary documents, xiv, 242,
252–255, 379–380, 411, 423–425,
432–434, 437–448, 556–559
forced evictions and relocations, 412,
415–417, 421–423, 425–429, 433
gender considerations, 430
International Covenant on Economic,
Social and Cultural Rights, 415
Islamic law, 409
legal frameworks, 407, 419–432
UN-HABITAT recommendations,
169–170
vulnerable populations, 427–432
See also displacement and
dispossession; land rights; property
rights; restitution; titling
Housing, Land and Property Working
Group, 345n3
Huggins, Chris, 136
humanitarian assessment tools, 353
humanitarian assistance, 4
housing, land, and property (HLP)
rights, 99, 104–108, 117, 169–170
Rwandan projects, 131–135, 139–142
humanitarian law. *See* international law
human rights. *See* housing, land, and
property (HLP) rights; international
law; land rights; property rights
Human Rights Watch, 134, 135
Hun Sen, 413–414, 426
Hussein, Saddam, 364
See also Iraq
Hutu people. *See* Rwanda
hydropower, 78

identity, 9–10, 374
IDPs (internally displaced persons). *See*
internally displaced persons (IDPs)
illegitimate authority, 10, 11
immediate aftermath of conflict
(definition), 4
Inber, Colin, 498
India, 549
Indian Ocean tsunami of 2004, 242, 293,
296, 302–303, 312, 484

614 Index

indigenous peoples
  Cambodia, 411, 420, 423–424,
    431–432, 442–443, 444
  labor for large sacle/commercial
    agriculture, 325
  land rights, 2n1
  Mindanao (Philippines), 462–466, 468,
    538
  Rwanda, 135
  See also customary land rights;
    vulnerable populations
Indonesia
  Aceh. *See* Aceh (Indonesia)
  Basic Agrarian Law of 1960, 298–299,
    300
  community welfare endowments
    (*waqf*), 482–484, 490
  corruption, 297–298
  dispute resolution, 494–497
  Free Aceh Movement (GAM),
    294–297, 302, 306–307, 309, 312,
    313–314
  Helsinki Memorandum of
    Understanding, 296–297, 306,
    307–309
  Indian Ocean tsunami of 2004, 242,
    293, 296, 302–303, 312, 484
  Islamic law, 408–409, 476, 482–484,
    490, 491, 493
  Land Management and Policy
    Development Project, 311
  Law on the Governing of Aceh, 308–309
  map, 15
  mineral prospectivity, 78
  syariah court system, 496–497
  Timor-Leste occupation, 514–518, 566
industrial agriculture. *See* large-scale/
  commercial agriculture
informal land rights, 2n1
  See also customary land rights
Intergovernmental Authority on
  Development (IGAD), 29n8
Interim Security Force for Abyei (ISFA),
  59–61
internally displaced persons (IDPs), xiv,
  3, 8–9, 14–15, 45, 536
  forced evictions, 412, 415–417,
    421–423, 425–429, 433

informal settlements, 540, 553
  See also displacement and
    dispossession; restitution; return; UN
    Guiding Principles on Internal
    Displacement
International Agreements Claims Act
  (IACA), 223, 227
International Court of Justice, 40n28
International Covenant on Economic,
  Social and Cultural Rights, 415
International Criminal Court, Rome
  Statue, 102
International Dialogue on Peacebuilding
  and Statebuilding, 3, 4
international humanitarian organizations.
  See humanitarian assistance
international law
  on autonomy versus secession, 470
  on customary land rights, 543–544
  environmental treaties, 398–400
  on refugees, 95
  on restitution, 101–102
  See also legal frameworks; Pinheiro
    Principles
International Monetary Fund Poverty
  Reduction Strategy, 136
International Organization for Migration,
  306
International Rescue Committee (IRC),
  135, 234
Iraq, 205–235, 364
  Arabization process, 372
  Baath Party, 364
  Coalition Provisional Authority (CPA),
    219n10, 222–227
  Commander's Emergency Response
    Program (CERP), 224–227
  Commission for the Resolution of Real
    Property Disputes (CRRPD), 209,
    211–212
  customary land rights, 369, 549
  displacement crisis, 3, 15, 97, 209,
    213–214, 234–235
  dispute resolution, 549
  ethnic and religious groups, 10, 349,
    351, 366
  general eviction order to squatters, 213
  honor and tradition, 374

Index   615

individual usufruct (*tassaruf*) rights, 485–487, 500, 502
insurgency, 7, 205–206, 226t
Iraqi Civil Code, 97, 206, 209–222, 226t, 228–233, 485, 486–487
Islamic law, 408–409, 476, 485–487, 491
Kurdish conflicts, 364–365
land administration policies, 368–369
Land Registration Law, 228, 229
Lease Law No. 87, 228–229
map, 15, 207, 365, 366
military damage, 222–227
Ottoman Land Code of 1858, 478, 494
Property Claims Commission, 347, 352, 358, 359f, 360
restitution policies, 99, 103, 210–216, 349–350, 555
state (*miri*) land, 485–486
symbolically significant land, 10, 349, 351, 360
tribal identity, 374
UN Oil-for-Food Programme, 370, 377, 555
water rights, 243, 369–371
See also Kurdistan (Iraq)
Iraqi Civil Code
on destroyed property, 219–220
on dispossession, 217–219
interfering legislation, 228–229
on military damage, 226t
on secondary occupants, 220–222
suggested adjustments, 229–233
Islamic law, xv, 15, 408–409, 475–503, 544
Aceh (Indonesia), 298, 299, 482–484, 490, 491
Afghanistan, 408–409, 480–482, 490–493
collective land tenures (Sufi cooperatives), 476–477, 487–490, 500, 502
community leadership, 501, 502–503
community welfare endowments (*waqf*), 476–477, 482–484, 490, 500, 502
dispute resolution, 494–497, 501

housing, land, and property (HLP) rights, 409
individual usufruct (*tassaruf*) rights, 476–477, 485–487, 498, 500, 502
Indonesia, 408–409, 482–484, 490, 491, 493
Iraq, 210, 217–218, 231, 485–487, 491
jurisprudential schools, 492
knowledge gaps, 500
land tenure models, 409, 491–493
natural resource management framework, 477–480
peace message, 479–480
pluralism of, 492–493, 497, 500–501
political risks, 489–491
redistribution of barren (*mawat*) lands, 476–477, 480–482, 490, 498, 500, 502
Somalia, 408–409, 476, 478, 487–491, 496–497
state (*miri*) land, 485–486, 498
terminology, 476, 508–509
womens rights, 497–500
Israel, 8, 557

Jabar, Haji Abdul, 249
Jamaat al-Islamiyah, 76
Jamalul Kiram II, Sultan of Sulu, 457
Japan International Cooperation Agency, 428
Johnson, Douglas, 35n21
Jones, Lisa, 124–125, 126, 128, 129, 131, 142
Judd, Mary, 80
Jwaidch, Zuhair, 210

Kälin, Walter, 207, 208n3
Kalyvas, Stathis N., 9
Kampala Convention, 106–107
Karzai, Hamid, 482
Keats, John, 246
Kenya, 113
Al-Khasawaneh, Awn, 40n29, 45
Khaurin, Hazrat Hussain, 250
Kingsbury, Damien, 305
Kiram-Bates Treaty, 457
Kirkuk (Iraq), 10

616 Index

Kosovo, 146
Housing and Property Claims
Commission, 347
minority flight, 168
official ethnic discrimination, 167
Pinheiro Principles, 105
restitution, 101n2
Kowalchuck, Lisa, 338n
Krznaric, Roman, 8–9
Kurdistan (Iraq), 243, 363–382
Anfal campaign, 372
community-based approaches,
363–364, 374–377, 380–381
conflict with Iraq, 364–365
customary land tenure, 369
independent government, 367
internally displaced persons (IDPs),
366–367, 369–373
international actors, 378
Kurdistan Workers' Party, 366
land administration policies, 368–369
map, 365, 366
UN protection/safe haven, 364–367
village reconstruction program,
363–364, 370–371, 373–377
water rights, 369–371, 373–374
Kyrgyzstan, 393, 397
See also Pamir Alai Mountain (PALM)
project

land administration. See land management
Land Administration Domain Model
(LADM), 241, 246, 248, 259–261,
262
land-based resources. See natural
resources
land conflict, xiv, 1, 5
land dispossession. See displacement and
dispossession
land disputes (definition), 345–346
See also dispute resolution
land grabbing
Afghanistan, 12–13
Cambodia, 418, 419, 421, 424–425
Colombia, 112
Liberia, 7
Mindanao (Philippines), 451, 470–471
See also large-scale land acquisitions

land law. See land reform; legal
frameworks
landlessness, 112, 117, 262, 415, 565t
Afghanistan, 251, 480–482
Angola, 186
Cambodia, 411, 418, 421, 425,
429–431
El Salvador, 325, 327n10, 331, 340
Islamic law, 478, 486, 497
Rwanda, 122
women, 103, 430
See also displacement and
dispossession; internally displaced
persons (IDPs)
land management, 1, 2–6, 9, 15,
241–244, 536–569
Aceh (Indonesia). See Aceh (Indonesia)
ADAMAP process, 242, 281–286
Afghanistan. See Afghanistan
Cambodia. See Cambodia
capacity building, 11, 118, 241,
559–560, 562, 565t
community participation. See
participatory approaches
coordination and sequencing, 562–567
customary law. See customary land
rights
displaced persons claims. See
displacement and dispossession
dispute resolution. See dispute
resolution
El Salvador. See El Salvador
international assistance, 242, 243
Islamic frameworks. See Islamic law
Kurdistan (Iraq). See Kurdistan (Iraq)
land law reforms. See legal frameworks
land redistribution, 242, 321–323,
476–477, 480–482, 490, 498, 500,
502, 568
legal options. See legal frameworks
Mindanao (Philippines). See Mindanao
(Philippines)
natural resource management, 202,
243–244, 476–480
resettlement. See resettlement
restitution. See restitution
sustainability, 243–244
Tajikistan. See Tajikistan

Index   617

tenure security. *See* tenure security
Timor-Leste. *See* Timor-Leste
titling projects. *See* titling
transboundary resource management,
387–388, 391–401
UNECE definition of, 245
See also governance
land markets, 13n
landmines
Angola, 13, 189, 199
Bosnia and Herzegovina, 148, 155, 166
Cambodia, 418
Iraq, 379
LandNet Africa, 135
LandNet Rwanda, 135, 139
land records, 169–170, 201, 379–380
Aceh (Indonesia), 309–312, 482–483
Afghanistan, 268n1, 272, 277–278,
281–284, 288
destruction, xiv, 9, 482, 536, 546–547,
566
evidentiary documents, 379–380
Kurdistan (Iraq), 368
Mindanao (Philippines), 466
reconstruction, 379–380
Tanzania, 281
See also cadastre systems;
Reconstruction of Aceh Land
Administration System (RALAS)
land reform, 1–2, 11–12, 97, 117–119,
131, 137–139
Angola, 11–12, 96–97, 187–188, 197–
198, 200–202
Cambodia, 101n2, 102, 417–419, 559
governance, 11–12, 117–119, 562,
565t
Liberia, 12
Sierra Leone, 542, 544–545
See also legal frameworks
land registration and titling. *See* land
management; land records; titling
land rights, xiii–xv, 1–2, 108n11,
109–110, 536–537
definition, 5n
as tools of belligerence, 5
See also customary land rights;
housing, land, and property (HLP)
rights; restitution; return

landscape-based evidence, 557–558
land scarcity, 357
Burundi, 357
El Salvador, 242, 322–323, 331, 333,
339
physical land scarcity, 322
Rwanda, 122
structural land scarcity, 322–323, 357
Timor-Leste, 529
land tenure, 1–16, 536–537, 568
armed conflict, 2, 7–10
definition, 5n
peacebuilding, 2, 12–14, 16
possessory rights, 108n11, 109–110
See also customary land rights; land
management; tenure security
Land Titling and Economic Restructuring
in Afghanistan (LTERA) program,
252–255
land use
Bosnia and Herzegovina, 150*f*
UN-HABITAT documents on, 113n18
See also land management
large-scale/commercial agriculture, 1,
536
Cambodia, 13
El Salvador, 323–328
indigenous labor, 325
land acquisition, 550–551
power of landholders, 348–349, 352
large-scale land acquisitions, 1, 13, 100,
346, 550–551
Afghanistan, 254
Mindanao (Philippines), 451, 463
Rwanda, 138
Sierra Leone, 550–551
South Sudan, 550
See also land grabbing
Latin America, 7
See also Colombia; El Salvador
Lauria-Santiago, Aldo A., 324
law. *See* legal frameworks
Leckie, Scott, 211
legal frameworks, 15, 407–409,
537–545
adverse and acquisitive possession,
538
autonomy versus secession, 470

618 Index

Cambodian HLP rights, 409, 411,
 415–434
Cambodian land registration systems,
 423–425, 432–434, 437–448
colonial policies, 58, 70, 73, 130,
 180–186, 455–459, 537, 547
Continental civil law tradition, 210,
 217–219, 231–233, 437, 438
customary land tenure, 108–109, 408,
 409, 511, 519–530, 537–538
forum shopping, 542, 545
international assistance, 409
international law, 95, 101–102, 470,
 543–544
international treaty obligations,
 398–400, 414, 415, 426
interpretations, rulings, and decrees,
 539–540
Iraqi Civil Code, 97, 206, 209–235
Islamic law, xv, 15, 210, 217–218, 231,
 298, 299, 408–409, 475–503, 544
legal ambiguity, 537–540, 562, 563*t*
local contexts of, 409
open-border model, 551
open moments, 544
Ottoman Land Code of 1858, 478,
 481–482, 485, 486–487, 494
Pamir Alai Mountain (PALM) project,
 395–397
See also customary land rights; dispute
 resolution; land reform
legal pluralism, 408, 538, 541–545, 562,
 563*t*
Abyei Area, 541
Aceh (Indonesia), 298–301, 302, 312
Afghanistan, 492, 541, 542
cadastral system, 118
Cambodia, 543
challenges, 108–109, 118, 493,
 541–542, 545
Côte d'Ivoire, 108–109
definition, 108, 115n1
disputes, 546
El Salvador, 544
Ethiopia, 544
international law, 543
Islamic law, 475, 478, 492–493,
 500–501, 544

land registration, 558
Mindanao (Philippines), 541
Mozambique, 544
restitution, 108–109, 117
Sierra Leone, 542, 544–545
Somalia, 493
Timor-Leste, 541, 543, 544
legal security of tenure, 6, 15
legitimate authority, 10, 11, 15
Lemmen, Christiaan, 259
lésion, 231–232
Liberia, 2, 7, 8, 539, 540
alternative tenure approaches, 10
capacity building, 560
dispute resolution, 549–550
documentary evidence, 556–557
land law reform, 12
map, 15
NCR ICLA restitution project, 111
pre-conflict land policies, 9
restitution, 101n2
tenure security, 6
urban squatters, 12, 549
Litvinoff, Saul, 230
local regimes. *See* participatory
 approaches
Lumads (as term), 73
 See also Mindanao (Philippines)
Lund, Michael S., 544
Lutheran World Federation, 134–135
Lyman, Princeton, 51n59

Macapagal-Arroyo, Gloria, 462
Maceda, Ernesto, 82
Machakos Protocol, 28–29, 48
Machar, Riek, 54
Magellan, Ferdinand, 456
Malaurie, Phillippe, 215
Maley, William, 275
al-Maliki, Nouri, 213
Marcos, Ferdinand, 73, 76, 460
Martí, Farabundo, 325–326
 See also Farabundo Martí National
 Liberation Front (FMLN)
Mbeki, Thabo, 48n43, 51n59, 59
McCallin, Barbara, 95, 571–572
Meinzen-Dick, Ruth, 542
migration. *See* urban areas

Index   619

Millennium Development Goals, 419
Mindanao (Philippines), 23–24, 69–89,
  451–471
  administration, 74–75
  agricultural resources, 73
  ancestral domain lands, 73–87,
    462–469
  Bangsamoro Juridical Entity (BJE),
    408, 452
  Christian population, 455–457, 458,
    459, 464, 470
  civil society, 83–85, 89
  colonial era, 455–459
  conflict minerals, 88
  corruption, 24, 83, 85, 87, 88
  costs of conflict, 80
  customary land rights, 458, 459
  Dansalan Declaration, 459
  Indigenous Peoples Rights Act (IPRA),
    462–464, 465, 468, 538
  international actors, 83–84, 89
  International Monitoring Team,
    81, 84
  land grabbing, 451, 470–471
  land laws, 452–455, 458
  legal framework, 451–471, 541
  local sharia courts, 75–76, 86
  Lumad population, 73–74, 77, 455,
    459, 464, 466
  map, 71, 453, 454, 468
  Memorandum of Agreement
    (MOA-AD), 72–73, 80–82, 84–85,
    452, 464–469
  mineral resources, 24, 70, 73–75,
    78–83, 87–88, 467–469
  mining industry, 78–83, 85, 87–88,
    463–464, 467–468, 538
  Moro uprisings, 71–76, 451–462
  Muslim (Moro) population, 70–71,
    451n, 455–457, 457–459, 464
  peace negotiations, 14, 24, 71–73,
    80–82, 469–470
  resettlement, 73
  rido (clan disputes), 23–24, 69, 76–78,
    85–86
  rubber resources, 82
  Tripoli Agreement, 71–72, 74–75,
    451–453, 459–462

  See also Autonomous Region in
    Muslim Mindanao (ARMM); legal
    frameworks; Moro Islamic Liberation
    Front (MILF); Moro National
    Liberation Front (MNLF)
mineral prospectivity, 78
mineral resources, 540
  Angola, 171, 200
  Mindanao (Philippines), 24, 70, 73–75,
    78–83, 87–88, 467–469
  See also mining industry
mining industry
  financial or technical assistance
    agreements (FTAA), 79
  foreign concessions, 79, 87–88
  hazardous chemicals, 87
  insurgent attacks and protection money,
    78–79, 82–83, 87–88
  Mindanao (Philippines), 78–83, 85, 87,
    463–464
  open-pit mining, 87
  strip mining, 87
  See also mineral resources
Misseriya tribe, 23, 25–28, 30n12
  Humr attacks, 40
  rejection of PCA tribunal award, 45,
    47–48, 56
  residence criteria, 33–34
  water and grazing rights, 36–38, 42,
    56–58
  See also Abyei territorial dispute
    (Sudan/South Sudan)
Miyazawa, Naori, 409, 572
Mojumdar, Aunohita, 256–257
Molina, Arturo A., 328
Montaigne, Michel de, 235
Montevideo Convention on the Rights
  and Duties of States, 470
Moro Islamic Liberation Front (MILF),
  72–73, 76–78, 85–86, 89, 464
  mining targets, 78–79, 88
  peace negotiations, 80–82, 459–462,
    470, 471
Moro National Liberation Front (MNLF),
  71, 74–77, 80, 83, 85–86, 459–461,
  469
Moros (as term), 70, 451n, 455
mountain law, 396–397

620 Index

Mozambique, 7, 8
  capacity building, 559–560
  customary evidence, 558
  dispute resolution, 547–551
  General Peace Agreement, 544
  internally displaced persons (IDPs), 3
  Land Law of 1997, 1–2, 554n, 558, 568
  map, 15
  open-border model, 551
  restitution, 101n2, 554
Murad, Ebrahim, 81
Muriuki, Godfrey, 35n21
Murtazashvili, Jennifer Brick, 241–242, 572
Musahara, Herman, 136
Muslims. *See* Islamic law; Mindanao (Philippines); Moros (as term)

Naivasha Agreement, 29n7
Nally, Frank, 87
National Union for the Total
  Independence of Angola (UNITA), 189, 194–197
natural gas. *See* oil and gas
natural resources, xiv, 4, 202
  exploitation, 6, 536, 540
  Islamic law, 476–480
  Tajikistan PALM project, 243–244
  See also agriculture; land management; specific resources, e.g. mineral resources
negotiorum gestio, 232–233
neoliberalism, 339–340
Nepal, 242
New People's Army (NPA), 80–81
Ngok Dinka tribe, 23, 25–28, 47
  ABC tribunal award, 45
  citizenship status, 33–34, 48n45
  Humr raids, 40
  traditional rights, 36–38, 40–42, 57–58
  See also Abyei territorial dispute (Sudan/South Sudan)
Nicaragua, 332n, 338, 339, 568
nickel, 78, 79, 87, 88
nongovernmental organizations (NGOs). *See* humanitarian assistance

Norton, Gregory, 488–489, 492, 494
Norton de Matos, José, 182
Norwegian Refugee Council (NRC), 100, 107
  Afghanistan, 255–266
  Information, Counseling and Legal
    Assistance (ICLA) program, 107–108, 111
Nuri, Sayeed Abdullo, 388

occupied Palestinian territories (oPt), 8, 557
Ogata, Sadako, 365n
oil and gas, 78
  Angola, 171
  coalbed methane, 79 80
  Mindanao (Philippines), 79–80
Oki, Yuri, 23–24, 572
open-border model, 551
open moments, 544
open-pit mining, 87
Organisation for Economic and
  Co-operation and Development (OECD), 394
Organization of Islamic Countries, 71–72
Organization of the Islamic Conference, 83–84, 491
Ostrom, Elinor, 511
Ottoman Land Code, 478, 494
  categories of land, 485
  mawat land, 481–482
Ó Tuathail, Gearóid, 162
Oxfam, 131, 135
Ozerdem, Alpaslan, 335, 338

Pact on Security, Stability, and
  Development in the Great Lakes
  Region of 2006. *See* Great Lakes
  Pact of 2006
Paige, Jeffrey M., 326
Palestinian territories. *See* occupied
  Palestinian territories (oPt)
Pamir Alai Mountain (PALM) project, 243–244, 387, 391–401
  components, 393–394
  global environmental benefits, 396–397, 401
  goals, 393

Index 621

governance principles, 394–395
institutional frameworks, 394, 556
Natural Resource Management
  Governance Framework, 395–398,
  400
Pamir-Alai Transboundary Strategy and
  Action Plan (PATSAP), 393–394,
  399, 400
regulatory framework, 395–397
transboundary approach, 393–394, 395,
  397–398
See also Tajikistan
Pantuliano, Sara, 95–96, 558, 572–573
participatory approaches, xv, 2, 10, 567
  Afghanistan, 241–242, 567
  conflict management, 381
  El Salvador, 340
  Islamic land management, 501,
    502–503
  Kurdistan (Iraq) village reconstruction,
    363–364, 374–382
  land management, 241–242, 243, 340,
    363–364, 374–377, 511–530
  local legal frameworks, 409
  long-term objectives, 381–382
  meetings and forums, 380–381
  reconstruction, 377–382
  Timor-Leste, 511–530
peace accords, 5
peacebuilding, 3–6, 535–537
  as accelerated transition, 116
  actors, 4
  agriculture, 3, 14, 535–536
  challenges, 4
  definition, 305–306
  dispute resolution, 345–361, 545–551
  interactions among components, 12–14
  land tenure, 2, 12–14, 16
  objectives, 4
  UN parameters, 389
Peacebuilding Commission, ix–x
peace consolidation period (definition), 4
peacemaking (definition), 4
peace negotiations, 14, 23–24
  Abyei territorial dispute, 23, 25–65
  Dayton Accords on Bosnia, 148–149, 154
  land and property considerations, 118,
    140

Mindanao (Philippines), 14, 24, 69–89,
  469–470
Rwanda, 121
Permanent Court of Arbitration (PCA),
  25, 39–45, 55–56
Petritsch, Wolfgang, 160–161, 163–164
Petterson, Donald, 35nn21–22
Philippine-American War, 457–458
Philippines
  banana exports, 73n
  colonial era, 70, 73, 455–459
  *Cruz v. Secretary of the Environment and
    Natural Resources ruling*, 462–464
  foreign concessions, 79, 87–88
  human rights violations, 463
  independence, 70, 451, 455, 458–459
  Indigenous Peoples Rights Act (IPRA),
    74, 87, 462–464, 465, 468, 538
  map, 15, 453, 468
  Mindanao peace negotiations, 14,
    69–89, 469–470
  Mindanao rido, 23–24, 76–78, 85–86
  mineral prospectivity, 78–79
  Mining Act of 1995, 79, 80, 87
  mining industry, 78–83, 85, 87–88,
    463–464, 538
  Moro uprisings, 71–76, 451–462
  Organic Act (No. 6734), 72, 74, 461,
    466, 467, 469
  *Province of North Cotabato v. GRP
    ruling*, 452, 464–465
  Spanish-American War, 451, 457
  state-owned lands (regalian doctrine),
    456–457, 462, 468–469
  Tripoli Agreement, 71–72, 74–75,
    451–453, 459–462
  See also Mindanao (Philippines)
Phuong, Catherine, 210
Pinheiro, Paulo Sérgio, 100, 207
Pinheiro Principles, 95–97, 100, 102–119,
  206–211, 345n2, 348, 409, 552, 558
  dissemination and training, 105, 107–108
  impact, 104–108
  international acceptance, 208–209
  international responsibility, 104
  Iraq, 216–235
  limitations, 107–112, 115–117
  Rwanda, 140–142

622 Index

political assessment tools, 353–354
political Islam, 479–480, 489–490, 491
political participation, 8–9
Pol Pot, 438
Posner, Richard, 212, 216
post-conflict period (definition), 4
See also peacebuilding
Posterman, Roy L., 327n10
Pottier, Johan, 137–138
Pradhan, Rajendra, 542
Principles on Housing and Property
Restitution for Refuges and
Displaced Persons. See Pinheiro
Principles
process-flow maps, 358–360
property rights
definition, 5n
possessory rights, 108n11, 109–110
restitution. See restitution
tenure security, 6
See also housing, land, and property
(HLP) rights; land rights
prospects for conflict relapse, 2, 7
Puno, Reynato, 462

Quezon, Manuel, 459

Rahmonov, Emomali, 388
Ramos, Fidel, 71–72, 461
reconstruction
community-based approaches, 377–382
first steps, 379–380
Kurdistan (Iraq). See Kurdistan (Iraq)
land records, 379–380
long-term objectives, 381–382
prerequisites, 378
site selection, 379
Reconstruction of Aceh Land
Administration System (RALAS),
242
refugees. See displacement and
dispossession
regalian doctrine, 456–457, 462,
468–469
Reisman, Michael, 40n29
reparation. See compensation
repatriation. See return
repossession. See restitution

Republic of South Sudan. See South
Sudan
Republika Srpska, 148, 159–160, 165
See also Bosnia and Herzegovina
resettlement, 562, 565t
Angola, 193–197, 540
Bosnia and Herzegovina, 149, 153,
155–168, 170–171
former combatants, 561–562
IDP choice of destination, 170–171
public participation, 194, 197, 200
Rwanda, 127–135, 139
See also Pinheiro Principles; return
resources. See natural resources
restitution, xiv–xv, 95, 99–119, 552–562,
564t
ad hoc commissions, 346–347
alternatives, 112
Bosnia and Herzegovina, 3, 99, 101n2,
102, 112–113, 148–149, 153,
155–158, 163, 165, 170, 346–347,
540, 547n12
capacity building, 559–560
community consultation, 553–556
customary tenure, 104, 106, 108–111
enforcement mechanisms, 104
evidentiary considerations, 556–559
former combatants, 561–562
gender-based protections, 103, 106,
350n, 560–561
international law, 101–102
international monitoring, 102
Iraq, 210–216, 347, 349–350, 358,
359f, 360
Kampala Convention, 106–107
Kosovo, 347
legal frameworks, 407
legitimate owners, 104
limitations, 100, 108–112, 115–117
link with return, 101, 107, 115–117
Pinheiro Principles, 95–97, 100,
102–119, 206–211, 216, 345n2,
552, 558
possessory rights, 108n11, 109–110
Rwanda, 121–142
UN Guiding Principles on Internal
Displacement, 210–211, 216
See also return

Index 623

return
  former combatants, 561–562
  legal frameworks, 407
  link with restitution, 101, 103, 107,
    116–117
  Rwanda, 121–142
  See also Pinheiro Principles; restitution
Revolutionary Front for an Independent
  Timor-Leste (FRETILIN), 514
rido (clan disputes), 23–24, 76–78,
  85–86
Riedinger, Jeffrey M., 327n10
Rome Statue of the International Criminal
  Court, 102
rubber, 78, 82, 540
Rubin, Barnett R., 245–246
rule of law. *See* governance
rural land. *See* agriculture
Rwanda, 2, 96, 101n2, 121–142
  Arusha Peace Accords, 96, 124–125,
    128, 132, 140–142
  Batwa land and people, 135n12
  Belgian colonial policies, 130
  civil society organizations (CSOs),
    136
  customary land tenure, 122
  dispossession of land and property, 15,
    115
  ethnic factions, 121, 122–123,
    138–139
  gacaca process, 136, 138
  genocide of 1994, 96, 125, 138
  international actors, 131–136, 139–142
  Land Law of 2005, 131, 137–139
  LandNet program, 135, 139
  land scarcity, 122
  land sharing process, 129, 132, 137
  map, 15, 123
  National Habitat Policy, 130
  new caseload (Hutu) returns, 128–129
  old caseload (Tutsi) returns, 125–128
  ongoing returns, 136–137
  poverty levels, 122
  resettlement village (*imidugudu*)
    program, 127–135, 139
  return and restitution, 121, 123, 124,
    125–129, 554
  sources of conflict, 122–124

  spontaneous resettlement, 126–127
  tenure security, 6
  ten-year rule, 124–125, 126n6, 128,
    140, 141–142
  UN Assistance Mission for Rwanda,
    132
  UNHCR programs, 131–135
  UN Human Rights Field Operation in
    Rwanda, 132
Rwandan Patriotic Front/Army (RPF/A),
  123–128, 140

Safar, M. Y., 241–242, 573
Saikal, Amin, 275
Sait, Siraj, 408–409, 544, 573
Salam, Akram, 241–242, 573–574
Salman, Salman M. A., 23–24, 574
Salvadoran Institute of Agrarian
  Transformation (ISTA), 330–331
Schiavo-Campo, Salvatore, 80
Schneider, Irene, 492
Schwebel, Stephen, 40n29
secession (definition), 470
security of tenure. *See* tenure security
Sekiguchi, Manami, 408, 543, 574
Seligson, Mitchell A., 327n10
sequencing of interventions, 562–567
Shahrani, M. Nazif, 275, 277
Shia Islam, 492
Sierra Leone, 8, 9, 539–540, 549
  capacity building, 559, 560
  food insecurity, 14
  land policy reform, 542
  Lands Commission, 545
  large-scale land acquisitions, 550–551
  legal pluralism, 544–545
  restitution, 101n2, 555
silver, 78
Socialist Federal Republic of Yugoslavia
  (SFRY), 146, 147, 150–151
Social Tenure Domain Model (STDM),
  261
Somalia, 7, 8
  collective land tenure (Sufi
    cooperatives), 477, 487–490, 500,
    502
  customary land rights, 493, 494–495
  dispute resolution, 494–495

624 Index

Islamic law, 408–409, 476, 478, 487–491, 496–497
Land Reform Act of 1975, 487
local sharia courts, 10, 496–497
map, 15
Sufism, 487–489, 492
Unified Civil Code of 1973, 7, 487
womens property rights, 499–500
South Africa, 103
Southern Philippines Council for Peace and Development, 72
Southern Sudan Liberation Movement (SSLM), 28
Southgate, Douglas, 337
South Sudan
  Abyei territorial dispute. See Abyei territorial dispute (Sudan/South Sudan)
  Comprehensive Peace Agreement (CPA), 28–30, 48, 51
  foreign land development projects, 13, 550
  independence, 26n1, 33n18, 51, 54, 58
  Land Act for Southern Sudan, 111
  land disputes, 349
  map, 15, 27
  oil resources, 56n55
  peace negotiations, 14
  People's Liberation Movement/Army. See Sudan People's Liberation Movement/Army (SPLM/A)
  referendum on secession, 33n18, 45–46, 48, 57
  restitution, 107, 111
  Transitional Constitution, 51–52
  womens property rights, 561
  See also Sudan
Soviet Union, 332n, 388–389, 390, 392
Spanish-American War, 451, 457
Sphere Project, 4, 199
SPLM/A. See Sudan People's Liberation Movement/Army (SPLM/A)
squatting, 12, 538, 540
  Bosnia and Herzegovina, 152
  Cambodia, 424n
  Iraq, 213
Stanfield, J. D., 241–242, 251–252, 558–559, 574

Stigall, Dan E., 97, 486, 549, 574–575
structural land scarcity, 322–323, 357
subsistence farming, 1
  Afghan barren (*mawat*) land redistribution, 480–482, 490, 500, 502
  Cambodia, 411, 421, 424–425
  El Salvador, 323, 325–328, 338
  food insecurity, 14, 550n13
  Sierra Leone, 14
Sudan
  Abyei Addis Ababa Agreement, 59–61
  Abyei territorial dispute. See Abyei territorial dispute (Sudan/South Sudan)
  Addis Ababa Agreement, 27–28, 30, 33n18
  Agreement on Wealth Sharing, 29
  agricultural land, 551
  civil war, 28–30, 57
  colonial administration, 58
  Comprehensive Peace Agreement (CPA), 28–30, 48, 51
  Darfur. See Darfur
  dispute resolution, 551
  Interim National Constitution, 30
  internally displaced persons (IDPs), 3
  Kadugli agreements, 48–50, 55
  map, 15, 27
  Mekelle Memorandum of Understanding, 46n40
  National Congress Party (NCP), 36, 52
  oil revenue sharing, 29, 33–34, 39, 42, 56n55
  peace negotiations, 14
  Permanent Court of Arbitration decision, 541
  restitution, 101n2
  Southern Kordofan elections of 2011, 58–59
  South Sudan. See South Sudan
  UN Mission in Sudan (UNMIS), 38, 49, 52–54
Sudan People's Liberation Movement/ Army (SPLM/A), 23, 25, 28–30
  Abyei Addis Ababa Agreement, 59–61
  Abyei Boundaries Commission (ABC) Report, 35–41, 44f, 55–56

Abyei Protocol, 30–35
Abyei territorial dispute. *See* Abyei territorial dispute (Sudan/South Sudan)
Abyei Town battle, 38
Comprehensive Peace Agreement (CPA), 28–30, 48, 51
Kadugli agreements, 48–50, 55
Mekelle Memorandum of Understanding, 46n40
See also South Sudan
Sufism, 487–489, 492
Sunni Islam, 492
swidden farming, 431
Swisspeace, 135, 138

Taha, Ali Osman, 54
Tajikistan, 387–401
Afghan refugees, 395
civil conflict, 387, 388–389, 390
Commission on National Reconciliation, 390–391, 394
Committee on Environment Conservation, 392–393
economic development, 391–392
environmental treaty obligations, 398–400
Establishment of Peace and National Accord, 388, 390, 394
imbalance of power, 390
international actors, 391, 400
map, 15, 389
Pamir Alai Mountain (PALM) project, 243–244, 387, 391–401
peacebuilding process, 389–391
regulatory institutions, 396–397
restitution, 101n2
Taliban, 10
See also Afghanistan
Tanzania, 136–137
tara bandu (Timor-Leste customary law), 409, 511, 519–530, 543, 544, 556–557
tenure security, 2, 6, 15, 537
Aceh (Indonesia), 293–294, 297–305, 307–309
Afghanistan, 250–254, 268
Cambodia, 411–419, 437

El Salvador, 324
International Covenant on Economic, Social and Cultural Rights, 415
legal ambiguity, 537–541
squatting, 12, 213, 424n, 538, 540
See also customary land rights; land tenure; legal pluralism
territory (definition), 5n
timber, 78, 536, 540
Afghanistan, 284
Bosnia and Herzegovina, 148
Cambodia, 430
deforestation, 430, 515–516, 518, 519
Kyrgyzstan, 393
Mindinao (Philippines), 467
Timor-Leste, 515–516, 518, 519, 526
Timor-Leste, 2
agriculture, 518–519
capacity building, 559–560
constitution and statutory law, 526–527, 530
cultural perception of the environment, 521
deforestation, 515–516, 518, 519
dispossession of land and property, 115
dispute resolution, 549, 566–567
documentary evidence, 556, 560
human and financial resource gaps, 517–518, 529
independence, 515
Ita Nia Rai project, 562, 566–567
Land and Property Directorate, 522
land disputes and resolution, 350, 524–525
legal frameworks, 541, 543
map, 15, 513
military conflict, 514–518, 566
Ministry of Agriculture, Forestry and Fisheries (MAFF), 526
restitution, 99, 554–555
Special Regime for the Determination of Ownership of Immovable Property, 524, 526
stakeholders, 512, 514f
tara bandu (customary law), 409, 511, 519–530, 543, 544, 556–557
UN missions, 516–517, 519

626 Index

titling, xiv, 242, 411
Cambodia's land registration and titling programs, 423–425, 432–434, 437–448
Land Titling and Economic Restructuring in Afghanistan (LTERA) program, 252–255
Torrens title system, 301–302
See also housing, land, and property (HLP) rights
Torrens title system, 301–302
traditional land rights (definition), 2n1
See also customary land rights
Transparency International Corruption Perceptions Index, 297
tree planting, 557
Tripoli Agreement, 71–72, 74–75, 451–453, 459–462
Turkey, 105
Tutsi people. *See* Rwanda
Tydings-McDuffie Act, 458

Uganda, 136, 548–550
UK Defense Geographic Centre, 247–248
UK Department for International Development (DFID), 133, 135, 137
UN Assistance Mission for Rwanda, 132
UN Basic Principles and Guidelines on the Right to a Remedy and Reparations for Victims . . . (UNGA), 101–102
UN Charter, 61n57, 420
UN Civilian Capacity Senior Advisory Group, 3
UN Committee on Economic, Social and Cultural Rights (UN CESCR), 415
UN Convention for the Protection and Assistance of Internally Displaced Persons (Kampala Convention), 106–107
UN Convention on Biological Diversity, 398–399
UN Convention to Combat Desertification, 399–400
UN Department of Humanitarian Affairs (DHA), 366
UN Development Programme, 134, 243–244

UN Emergency Relief Coordinator, 104
UN Environment Programme, 3
Afghanistan, 249–250
definition of peacebuilding, 305–306
PALM project, 392
UN Food and Agriculture Organization (FAO), 122
UN Framework Convention on Climate Change, 399
UN Guiding Principles on Internal Displacement, 95, 97, 105, 206–211, 216, 433
UN High Commissioner for Refugees (UNHCR)
Arusha Protocol on Repatriation and Resettlement, 131–135, 139
Bosnia return projects, 155–157
Dar es Salaam Summit, 131
Guiding Principles on Internal Displacement, 95, 97, 105, 206–211, 216, 433
Kurdistan (Iraq) safe haven, 365–366, 370–371
Pinheiro Principles, 102
repatriation programs, 101, 117
Rwanda, 132
See also UN Office of the High Commissioner for Human Rights
UN Human Settlements Programme (UN-HABITAT), 6n, 105
Cambodia, 427
educational materials, 309
housing, land, and property (HLP) recommendations, 169–170, 247
land use documents, 113n18
UN Interim Security Force for Abyei (UNISFA), 61
United Nations University, 392, 393
Universal Declaration of Human Rights, 420
on property rights, 142
UN Mission in Sudan (UNMIS), 38, 49, 52–54
UN Office for the Coordination of Humanitarian Affairs (OCHA), 193–194
UN Office of the High Commissioner for Human Rights, 102, 416n2

Index 627

UN Peacebuilding Commission, ix–x
UN Principles on Housing and Property
  Restitution for Refuges and
  Displaced Persons. *See* Pinheiro
  Principles
UN Research Institute for Social
  Development, 131
Unruh, Jon, 108, 575
UN Secretary-General, 3, 4
UN Security Council, 364–365, 390
UN Sub-commission on the Promotion
  and Protection of Human Rights, 207
UN Transitional Administration in East
  Timor (UNTAET), 516–517, 519
UN Under-Secretary for Humanitarian
  Affairs, 104
urban areas, 2, 12
  Bosnia and Herzegovina, 155, 168–
    169, 171
  migration to, 337, 411, 425, 432
  peri-urban land occupation, 189–193,
    197–198, 200–202
  squatters, 12, 549
U.S. Agency for International
  Development (USAID), 560
  Afghanistan, 252, 253, 255
  Rwanda, 133
  Timor-Leste, 560, 562
U.S. Office of Foreign Disaster
  Assistance, 378

Van der Auweraert, Peter, 243, 548–549,
  575
van der Molen, Paul, 259
Van Notten, Michael, 493
van Oosterom, Peter, 259
Vidales, Roberto, 327n10

Vikor, Knut, 488
village reconstruction, 363–364,
  370–371, 373–382
Villalobo, Joaquin, 338
vulnerable populations, 540
  indigenous groups, 411, 420, 423–424,
    431–432, 442–443, 444
  women and female-led households,
    430, 497–500, 561
  See also gender considerations

Wardak, Ali, 494
Wicks, Clive, 87
Wildlife Conservation Society (WCS),
  257
Williams, Rhodri C., 96, 229–230, 407,
  540, 543, 575–576
Wily, Liz Alden, 494
women. *See* gender considerations
World Bank, x, 3
  Aceh (Indonesia), 306, 309
  Angola, 192n6
  Cambodia, 419, 424, 428, 429–430,
    444–445, 447
  Poverty Reduction Strategy, 136
World Heritage Convention, 257n3

Yugoslavia. *See* Socialist Federal
  Republic of Yugoslavia (SFRY)
Yusufjonova, Zamira, 389

Zahir, Mustafa, 256–257
Zahir Shah of Afghanistan, 271, 276
Zaire, 128
  See also Democratic Republic of the
    Congo (DRC)
Zimbabwe, 10